# Memoirs of an Ex-Minister

## An autobiography

James Howard Harris Malmesbury

**Alpha Editions**

This edition published in 2019

ISBN : 9789353978594

Design and Setting By
**Alpha Editions**
email - alphaedis@gmail.com

# MEMOIRS OF AN EX-MINISTER.

## INTRODUCTION.

I TRUST that the readers of these Memoirs will not expect a continuous narrative, but rather a *macédoine* of memoranda, diary, and correspondence, recalling the social and political events of a busy life of seventy-seven years. The subject-matter contained in my private political letters appeared more than a quarter of a century ago, in the Blue-books and newspapers of the day, in a more official and less familiar style, but is in substance the same as that which was at the time given to the public. My principal object has been to sketch the three Administrations of the late Earl of Derby, whose colleague I was, and also some incidents respecting one of the most remarkable men of this century —namely, the Emperor Louis Napoleon, who, during all Lord Derby's Governments, played so important a part in his policy and the great game of Europe. I will only add that, of men, events, and common things, I wrote as they appeared to me at the time, and have altered nothing since they were noted.

I was born on March 25th, 1807, in Spring Gardens. My mother, Lady Fitzharris, was at that moment at the mercy of Lucina, and my father sitting alone in the next room, anxiously waiting to be informed of the goddess's gift. A knock at the door seemed to bring him the news ; but, instead of the Æsculapius, to his surprise a King's messenger walked in with a letter from Mr. Canning, then Foreign Secretary, announcing my father's appointment as Under Secretary at the Foreign Office. In a few minutes my arrival into the world was proclaimed.

Now, I have often thought that if Guy Mannering had been present in Spring Gardens, as he was at Ellangowan, he would have taken my horoscope, as he did for Lady Bertram's boy, and found that the star of the Foreign Office was hovering over that locality, destining the son, forty years after, to reign over the same desks to which the father was appointed at the very moment of his son's birth. More than this, that under so mysterious a coincidence and concatenation of circumstances, I could not avoid my fate in 1852 and 1858-9, and whatever credit or blame I may have acquired during my management of foreign affairs, it is certain that the stars must be responsible for both. My father did not long remain at his new post, as the insincerity of politics was little suited to his susceptible feelings of morality and honour, and he told me the chief reason of his resignation was the affair in 1807, when we seized the Danish fleet to prevent Napoleon from doing so. When this wise but high-handed measure was determined upon, he had to keep the Danish Minister in London ignorant of his intentions ; but as the poor man suspected them, and was in the most nervous state, calling daily at the Foreign Office, Mr. Canning used to refuse to see him, and handed him over to my father, whose duty it was to conceal, and even to deny, our designs.

This was not a *rôle* suited to his character, although an indispensable policy.

All this time the great war with Napoleon was raging by sea and land. Few are alive, now that I am seventy-seven years of age, to have any idea of the excitement and resolution which pervaded this country. The name of Bonaparte was till 1815 the bugbear of English mothers and nurses to rule their wayward children. His name was in every one's mind, and pronounced with execration. The country resounded with the arms of volunteers, yeomanry, and militia. Every one of our naval successes and Spanish victories saw the Union Jack hoisted on the towers of our churches, and the details, printed in our then scanty newspapers, were read to shouting crowds in our market-places. No wonder that such scenes made deep impression on the minds of even very young boys, as they did on mine and my brother's. At last, in 1814, when we were seven and six years old respectively,

the allied armies entered Paris, and Napoleon was exiled to Elba.
On the 23rd of June of that year a grand naval review took place
at Spithead to celebrate the Peace, at which my father was obliged
to be present as Governor of the Isle of Wight, and to which he
went in his official yacht. Such a sight can never be forgotten,
however young the spectator may have been.

The Solent was literally covered with vessels of all descrip-
tions. Many men-of-war had been recalled from their stations at
the recent Peace, but had not yet been paid off. The allied
sovereigns stood on the quarter-deck of the 'Impregnable,' where
my father went to make his obeisance, taking us with him. The
Emperor Alexander, standing on the quarter-deck, overawed us
with his tall, stiff figure, and his tight leather breeches and jack-
boots, and we were glad to return on board the 'Medina '—our
yacht. A great many naval officers boarded us, and I remember
that I was struck with the arrogant language and demeanour of
many of them—natural, perhaps, after their services, a long
enjoyment of victory, and the despotic atmosphere of the quarter-
deck. These, however, were mostly young men. The uniform at
that time was very becoming—blue, with white facings, epaulets,
and tight white pantaloons, with Hessian boots and gold tassels.
Of course they were all in full dress for this great naval festival.

The conversation of our visitors varied. Civilians and tax-
payers rejoiced at the prospect of a long-desired peace ; soldiers
and sailors grumbled at what they thought was the end of their
career, and of an active life, and loudly expressed themselves to
that effect. But all were in a fool's paradise ; for, six months
after that day, ' the lion was unchained,' and within five days of
the anniversary of this gorgeous function, in the next year, the
two great captains of the age were engaged in their last and most
deadly struggle on the plain of Waterloo.

I remember being called up one morning in 1815 at Richmond
House, where we lived, to see the Life Guards and Blues march
for the war down Parliament Street, as they passed our windows
with laurel on their helmets and horses' heads, their wives and
sweethearts standing on their stirrups for a farewell kiss. It was
a grand and moving sight, and would have been still more so had
we known that not half of them were destined to return.

I mentioned my father's official yacht, the 'Medina,' but she deserves further notice. She was the connecting link between the ships painted by Vandervelde and those which preceded ironclads. She was built in William III.'s reign, and cutter-rigged ; her sides were elaborately gilded. She was highest by the stern, with such a deep waist forward as to endanger her going down head foremost if she shipped a heavy sea. She had very little beam, and her complement consisted of Captain Love, R.N., the master, and twelve men. She measured 80 tons.

Such was the Governor of the Isle of Wight's yacht, in which, as boys, we were taken to cruise in the safe waters of the Solent.

Commander Love seemed to have perpetual leave, and the yacht was relegated to Mr. Butcher, the master, who always looked like a sailor in a play, and was, indeed, little better, being generally in a confused state of mind as to the course we were to take or the direction of the wind. He was, however, well replaced by the boatswain, an 'old salt.' The continual absence of Captain Love was, I believe, caused by his not being a *grata persona* to the ladies, so that Mr. Butcher had all the responsibility of sailing the craft. This suddenly ceased, after the following occurrence, when our father refused to let us sail any more, and the 'Medina ' was abolished.

One day, the butler, who was acting as steward, rushed on deck the picture of terror. 'My lord, the yacht has sprung a leak, and water is flowing into the cabin.' Down the companion plunged Mr. Butcher, and in a moment confirmed the news. 'My lord, it is already over my shoes, and I must run her on shore in Alum Bay, before she goes down.'

'I don't believe it,' said my father. Mr. Butcher, as pale as death, looks over the side and replies, 'Don't your lordship see she is settling fast ?' 'No, I don't,' says my father. At this critical moment the boatswain comes up with a grin, touching his hat and choking with laughter—'Please, my lord, it's only the cistern of the w.-c. that has got adrift.' So the 'Medina' was not run ashore, but she was never sent to sea again, and Mr. Butcher enjoyed his pension and his grog evermore in peace.

My childhood was passed chiefly at Heron Court, an old manor house near Christchurch, which, with a considerable property, was left to my grandfather in 1795 by Mr. Edward Hooper, the last of a very old Dorsetshire family. He had married Lady Dorothy Ashley, whose sister was wife of Mr. Harris, my great-great-grandfather. The house is Elizabethan, and was once the residence of the Priors of Christchurch. The first Lord Malmesbury repaired and added to it. It has all the character of its origin, standing low among very ancient elms, within a mile of three rivers—namely, the Stour, Avon, and Herne, now called the Moors River, from its rising in the wilds of Cranbourne and running through uninterrupted heaths. Their waters converge in Christchurch Bay. All this district belonged, according to Doomsday Book, to Tosti, King Harold's brother, and was bestowed by William the Conqueror on Hugo de Porth, one of his Norman barons. During the long war with France this wild country, which extended in an uncultivated state from Christchurch to Poole, was the resort of smugglers upon a large scale. The last Mr. Hooper was chairman of customs, and the late Lord Shaftesbury, father of the noble philanthropist now living, told me this anecdote, as characteristic of the times. About 1780 Lord Shaftesbury was sitting at dinner in the low hall at Heron Court with his relation, the latter having his back to the window. The road, which has since been turned, passed by the front door of the house. Suddenly an immense clatter of waggons and horses disturbed their meal, and six or seven of these, heavily loaded with kegs, rushed past at full gallop. Lord Shaftesbury jumped up to look at the sight, but the old squire sat still, refusing to turn round, and eating his dinner complacently. Soon after a detachment of cavalry arrived with their horses blown, and asking which way the smugglers had gone. Nobody would tell them, and no doubt they got safely into the New Forest. The smugglers had dashed through two deep fords in the Stour close by, which the soldiers had refused, and so lost their prey. These fords are the same through which Sir Walter Tyrrell rode red-handed for his life on his way to Poole after he had crossed the Avon at a place which bears his name, Tyrrell's Ford. For many years the Manor of Avon paid a fine annually to the Crown for not stopping the regicide at the ford. At the beginning of the present century, and during the war, a great contraband trade was carried on,

I myself, when a small boy, had an adventure with these heroes.
I was bird-nesting in one of the copses in the park by myself
when a rough fellow seized me, and seeing I was frightened
was very civil, promising to let me go in an hour if I did not
resist. He kept his word, and made me swear I would not tell
of the incident. Although rated when I got home for my long
absence, I did not betray the man or his companions, whom I saw
in the wood hiding kegs of brandy, of which they insisted on
giving me a specimen.

In the worst period of the war, when gold was hardly to be
found, a tenant named King, who held a small farm by Cranbourne Heath, and who was in arrear, sent his little daughter
with the entire rent (100*l*.) in guineas and French louis-d'or to
my father. This way of paying in coin spoke for itself as to Mr.
King's habit of not accepting assignats. The following anecdote
I learnt from Dr. Quartley, who had practised for nearly fifty
years as a medical man at Christchurch. He had not long been
in business there when he was awakened one night by a loud
thumping at his door. Opening his window, he could distinguish
two men muffled up in drab horseman's great-coats and with
heavy whips in their hands, with which they were knocking at
his door. On hearing the window opened they exclaimed, ' Come
doctor, be quick! You are wanted!' Though he did not much
like the look of the thing, he thought it better to slip on his
clothes and go down to them. They told him they had a job for
him, and that he must get his horse out of the stable and come
along with them. After a little hesitation he obeyed their call,
and found himself, with a companion on each side, trotting towards
the old bridge. When they reached it, they whistled and were
joined by two other horsemen. All proceeded in silence some
distance over the heath leading to the New Forest by Bransgore.
At last they turned down a lane and came to a lone cottage, such
as are to be seen in these districts. ' There, doctor,' cried one of
his companions, breaking the long silence—' there is some work
for you! Step in.' On entering he found extended on the floor a
fine young man in a sea-faring garb, who appeared to be suffering
severely. On inquiring he found that he had been wounded in
an affray with the custom-house officers. Dr. Quartley succeeded

in extracting a ball from his back, and when he had done this, one of his quondam companions came in and asked him (Dr. Quartley) what he thought of it. He answered that the wound was dangerous, and that the young man must be kept quiet. ' Well, Tom ! ' said the other, ' willst thee stay here and be hanged, or shall we tip thee into the cart ? ' The wounded man preferred the latter alternative to Dr. Quartley's injunction, and two of them took charge of him, and led him through a dark night and in dead silence back to the old bridge, and there bidding him farewell, cantered off. At the conclusion of the same winter he was again awakened by a loud rap at his door, and in the morning his maid brought in a keg of fine French brandy, which she had found on his steps, and on which was written, ' Left there for the doctor's fee.' Fifteen summers afterwards Dr. Quartley dined at Mr. Mills's at Bisterne, and in the evening they went on the Avon. In getting into the boat, Dr. Quartley observed that one of the men who rowed it was particularly attentive to him, so much so that he observed, ' My man, you look as if I ought to know you.' ' Know me ! please your honour ! I be he from whose back you cut out a slug fifteen years ago. Don't you mind on't ? ' He had been carried into the forest, where by the aid of a good constitution he had recovered, and at the time of this second meeting was working in Mr. Mills's garden.

The principal stronghold round which the smugglers operated was the sea-shore and its hollow cliffs that run from Christchurch Head to Poole, then a district of gorse and heath for ten miles, with fir-woods above them. In this wild country black-game were abundant, and in 1826 I shot an old blackcock on the very spot where St. Peter's Church at Bournemouth now (1884) stands. This waste was a favourite resort and breeding-ground of the Hen-harrier, a very destructive species of hawk. They built their nests under the furze-bushes, and from these impenetrable places used to issue forth and plunder the cultivated country outside for many miles. There was only one way of finding their nests, which our keeper adopted in the breeding season. When he saw one crossing the valley to hunt the fields and carry off its prey to the moors, he watched it till out of sight, and on the next day posted himself at that point. The bird was sure to come along the same line, and again the man followed it as far as he could see, and so again day by day for sometimes five miles, until he arrived at the nest and shot the old birds.

The gamekeepers of my youth had much of the Mohican about them, and had not degenerated into poultry-wives by rearing thousands of tame pheasants to be shot by their masters like pigeons at Hurlingham. The well-known sportsman Grantley Berkeley used to declare that when he engaged a gamekeeper the first thing he did was to look at the knees of his breeches to see if he *trapped* vermin, &c., and if they were *clean* he declined taking him, however good his character might be—all questions as to rough readiness being answered by this test.

The wild heath which I describe is no more, and its rapid metamorphosis into Bournemouth is certainly a wonder of civilisation. In 1830 there were not more than half a dozen houses and cottages where now one of our largest and most fashionable seaside places stands, with all the usual accompaniments of clergymen, doctors, lawyers, and the inevitable M.P. of Radical proclivities. It has already eight churches, each congregation dogmatically pitying the theological *lâches* of the other. I must mention that no part of England affords better opportunities of observing natural history than this district of Hampshire. The Avon and Stour salmon are famous; and these rivers contain large pike, perch, trout, grayling, chub, tench, and crawfish. Every variety of British bird—even the rarest—is in the small museum at Heron Court, all having been killed within five miles of my house. The songsters abound in our woods, whilst every sort of wild-fowl, from the Hooper to the Teal, frequents our three rivers and the ponds on the heaths. Several eagles have been shot here within my memory, and a lesser bustard (a very rare bird) was killed by Lord Palmerston.

The moors are famous for exceptional butterflies and other insects, and used to be the favourite hunting grounds of the celebrated entomologist, Curtis, whose book abounds in references to Heron Court.

On these heaths there are many barrows, of which I have opened three. In the first the layers of turf were perfectly preserved in slices, one upon another, and on reaching the level the body was clearly delineated in black bone-dust. In the second the ashes were in a vase of unbaked pottery, and in the third there was only a beautiful twisted bracelet of solid gold.

Many of these mounds have never yet been opened.

It was in this, at that time very wild country, that, as boys, we disported ourselves and imbibed an eternal affection for it and its traditions. My father lived at Heron Court for ten months out of the twelve, inconsolable at the death of our mother, which happened in 1815, at the age of thirty-two, and for twenty-six years during which he survived her he mourned her with the same sorrow. Until his own death in 1841 not a plant in her garden or a trinket in her boudoir was ever moved or changed.

When in the country during the game season he hardly ever missed a day's shooting, and kept a journal of his sport with a column of every shot killed and missed during forty years. This curious book I showed to Lord Beaconsfield, who was extremely struck with it, declaring it to be the most extraordinary example of patience and a sturdy character he ever saw. With all this devotion to sport he read everything, ancient and modern ; and, having lived with clever men and in anxious times, during the early part of this century, his conversation was most amusing and instructive. Although a Tory of the purest school, and of unbending politics, he was in private life most generous and liberal in all his sentiments ; but he had seen his country borne through all its difficulties, and in its darkest hours, by the proud aristocracy which then governed it, and which the repeated successes of Napoleon never discouraged when the heart of all Europe failed, and he dreaded, like many others, to change this Constitution of England for a democracy which, more fickle and less enduring in its nature, after bravely resisting misfortune at first, would sooner yield to disappointment and disaster. When, therefore, fifteen years after the war, the great Reform Bill of 1832 passed, he helped to resist it by his vote to the last. When I used to hear all around me denunciations and prophecies against it, I little thought that, thirty years later, I should be taking the initiative, as a Cabinet Minister, in framing another reform of the franchise, far more democratic than the first, and of which Lord Derby confessed, when he proposed it in 1867, that it was a 'leap in the dark.'

Long, however, before these events took place my brother and
I, being respectively eight and seven years old, were sent to a
private school at Wimborne, under the Rev. Mr. Bowle, one of
the three incumbents who served the ancient minster. There
were sixteen boys, all out of Hants and Dorset ; not one of these
knew a word of French, for that language had been banished
during the long war, and was considered by the squires of the
day as almost treason. The previous generation had spoken it,
but it seemed to have died out in England with them. As it
was the first tongue which we were taught, I believe we had a
decided French accent when we went to school, and this was
visited upon us accordingly in the shape both of verbal and personal
persecution by our school-fellows. Another indictment attended
with punishment was served against us—namely, that our father
killed foxes. We were therefore called 'vulpecides,' without
knowing what the term meant, but which we soon learnt from
the lickings we got from the boys whose parents kept hounds.
It was useless to protest that we lived in a country which never
had been and could not be hunted, owing to its many rivers, and
in which a fox-hound had never been seen. At last we agreed
that the next time the most offensive of our tyrant squires
attacked one of us we would both fall on him at once, and notwithstanding his superior size, do our best.

The event came off as we hoped, and, contrary to our expectation, the others, although they had joined in the bullying, took
our part. Such is the nature of an English school, which, whatever its faults may be, teaches a man to keep his head with his
own hand. We were three years at Wimborne, learning nothing
but Latin and Greek grammar and coming home twice a year for
our holidays. My mother was dead, and my father never came
to see us, as he thought it disturbed our studies—such studies !
Lord Malmesbury, our grandfather, sometimes did so, and when
his visit occurred it caused great sensation in the house, as seventy
years ago an old earl would not on any account have driven to an
important country town without four horses to his carriage and
his star on his coat. I remember that one of these calls saved me
at the very moment of impending execution.

The old clergyman and his wife were kind and popular,

although he administered, in some degree with justice, corporal
punishment, which, as applied to knowledge, always seems to me
imparting it at the wrong end of a boy. Mr. Bowle was an
eccentric man, and a strict observer of saints' days and dates,
which gave us and himself more half holidays than were necessary.
On this principle, being fond of his garden, he never would plant
his tulips except on Good Friday, which, being a movable fast,
made them come up at the most various periods of the spring.
The dates of the deaths of General Wolfe and Nelson claimed an
annual holiday, and we used to search Moore's Almanack for
obituaries of great men. Mr. Bowle quieted his conscience and
condoned his own idleness by saying that these researches taught
us history. We left Wimborne after three years, and when, in
1852, I was made Secretary for Foreign Affairs, I presented the
old minster with a window as a votive offering of thanks for
whatever Mr. Bowle's school might have contributed to this
success.

We then remained at Heron Court under a private tutor till
we were sent to Eton in 1820, the same gentleman accompanying
us. Mr. Cooke had taken a first-class at Oxford, and was a young
man. I owe him a great deal of instruction on many subjects.
He was an excellent classical scholar, but I think his great merit
was to make his pupils love general information and art in all its
branches—namely, painting, architecture, natural history, and
geology. Everything amused and interested him, and he communicated his feelings to his pupils.

I have said that the country round Heron Court opened a
good field for natural history, but for geology it was equally good.
The east cliffs of Christchurch Bay possess in their recesses the
best specimens of the fossils of the blue London clay, both of
shells and of the Saurians' bones, and Mr. Cooke inspired us
with a real enthusiasm for finding and forming a complete collection of these. Since that time the cliffs have crumbled away and
the sea has gained. The stratum of clay has dipped too deeply to
find them, but at that period they could be gathered near the
surface. A Mr. Brander, who lived in the neighbourhood, had in
the last century made a perfect collection from these cliffs, and
presented it to the British Museum, having engraved each speci-

men in such a beautiful volume that it is now one of the rare
prizes of bibliophiles. This collection was extant at the British
Museum thirty years ago, when I saw it there, but I cannot find
it there now.

Christchurch, till the Reform Bill of 1832, was a close
borough, but the fourteen burgesses, who were the electors of two
members, were bought by Sir George Rose, Mr. Pitt's Lord of the
Treasury, he and his son sitting for it till the Reform Bill of 1832
expelled them. Christchurch has produced two distinguished
men—namely, Field-Marshal Lord Strathnairn and Admiral
Lord Lyons. It has never been a thriving town in comparison
with others which have the advantage of a direct railway to
London. These quiet places appear sometimes as if their great
age prevented any further growth, and as if, at Christchurch, its
old castle and grand old church would not permit the invasion of
modern things, or of what is called 'progress.' Bournemouth, only
four miles off, has monopolised these, and allows its placid neighbour to enjoy the *dolce far niente*.

My brother Edward and I went to Eton in 1821, and were
put in the 'Remove.' There were at that time six hundred boys
at the college. Mr. Cooke accompanied us, and we were the only
boys who brought a private tutor, except the Duke of Buccleuch,
Lord John Scott, and the sons of the Duke of Wellington. It is
a bad plan, as these gentlemen always help their pupils, and
thereby give a false measure of their capacity. I was fag to
Trench, brother of the subsequent Archbishop of Dublin, a very
good-natured boy. We boarded at a dame's, Miss Middleton. I
took to boating in preference to cricket, and used to steal out
early in the morning to shoot moor-hens up the river, borrowing
an old flint honey-combed gun from a cad named Hall. On one
of these occasions, in climbing over the spikes of our garden wall,
I slipped and was impaled by the arm till my shouts brought
assistance, and the pain I suffered long afterwards was allowed by
the authorities to be sufficient punishment.

There were several pitched battles in my day, in one of which,
young Ashley,[1] a most gallant boy, was killed. A very desperate

---

[1] A son of Lord Shaftesbury,

one occurred between a big boy of sixteen, named Kemp, and
Yea, much smaller and younger, which the latter won by sheer
pluck, a quality he long afterwards displayed in the Crimean war,
where he commanded the 7th Fusiliers, and fell at the storming
of the Redan. He was head of one of the oldest families in
Somerset, and, I believe, last of his race. The Windsor and
Slough coaches used to stop under the playing-field wall to see
these duels. My college tutor was Ben Drury, a clever man and
great scholar, but wild in his habits and a thorn in the side of the
immortal Dr. Keate. He presided over the ' Remove,' and we
often found we had a holiday on Monday morning, as the head-
ache which he had contracted in London the previous day confined
him to his bed. He made beautiful Latin verses, and drove four-
in-hand better than any whip between Windsor and London.
The trial of Queen Caroline was going on, and the boys all took a
strong part for George IV.—why, I never understood—and, the
townsmen siding for the Queen, there were constant riots and
free fights between the two parties of ' town and gown.' My
grandfather, Lord Malmesbury, died in 1821, aged seventy-five,
and next year I lost the companionship of my brother, who went
to the Naval College of Portsmouth, and afterwards to sea.[1]   In
1852 I appointed him to the Consulship of Copenhagen, and then
as Chargé d'Affaires in Chili. During our winter holidays my
father used to send us to Wilton and Bowood. He was guardian
to Lord Pembroke's children, and we, having no sisters, enjoyed
our visits there greatly with the daughters of the house, who
were charming children. At Bowood we met Mr. Stanley, afterwards Lord Derby, and Prime Minister, then quite young, but
looked up to by the Whigs as full of promise.

Lord Lansdowne,[2] one of their leaders, and a very distinguished
one, was the type of an accomplished gentleman. We always
found Tom Moore, the poet, at Bowood, who used to sing his own
verses with taste and spirit. He was the smallest man I ever
saw. I recollect that Lord Lansdowne and Mr. Stanley then

1 He was afterwards M.P. for Christchurch and H.M. Minister at Berne and
the Hague.
2 The Marquis of Lansdowne died in 1863.

wore the old Whig dress, a blue coat with brass buttons, and a buff waistcoat.

> Buff and blue
> And Mrs. Crewe,

was the *refrain* of the party in the days of Fox.

I left Eton with great regret in 1823, to remain at Heron Court under Mr. Cooke until I went to Oriel College, Oxford, in 1825. Coplestone, afterwards Bishop of Llandaff, was Provost; Tyler Dean, Dornford—who had served in the Peninsular War—and Newman, tutors. Of this last celebrated writer and controversialist, now a cardinal, no one at that time would have predicted the future career. He used to allow his class to torment him; every kind of mischievous trick was, to our shame, played upon him—such as cutting his bell-wire, and at lectures making the table advance gradually till he was jammed into a corner. He remained quite impassive. I once saw him nearly driven from Coplestone's table, when the Provost, who was an epicure, rudely upbraided him for what he called 'mutilating' a fine haunch of venison, and shouting out, 'Mr. Newman, you are unconscious of the mischief you have done.' At Oriel, the undergraduates who in after-life came more or less to the front, and were my contemporaries, were Samuel Wilberforce, as Bishop of Winchester; Sir Edmund Head, as governor of Canada; Welby, M.P. for Grantham; H. Wise, for Warwickshire; Holford, for Gloucestershire; Parker, for Devon. It was, on the whole, a quiet college. Welby, Lord E. Thynne and I kept a scratch pack to run a bagged fox after lectures, as hunting with regular hounds was forbidden. Ours were called the 'Gazington,' and were hunted by a rascal named Butler, who was hanged a few years after for stealing a horse.

I took my degree as early as I could in 1827, and afterwards paid some visits in the country, such as to Newby Park (Lord Grantham's), and Chillingham, Lord Tankerville's castle in Northumberland. The latter is one of the oldest inhabited in England, and famous for its breed of wild cattle, the date of whose location in this part is unknown; but the park itself, which is 1,500 acres, was walled in during the reign of King John, and they were probably enclosed in it at that date. Lady Tankerville

was Mdlle. de Gramont ; was sent over to England to escape the
Reign of Terror, and was received and brought up by the Duchess
of Devonshire. She was a beautiful woman, and ruled the world
of fashion, together with Lady Jersey and Lady Palmerston, for
many years, all three of these remarkable women having lived to
above eighty. Count d'Orsay[1] was the last of the dandies as a
ruler of men—I speak, of course, of *young* men. He was not
only remarkable for his presence, but for his wit and conversation,
which gained salt from his foreign accent, and also for some talent
in painting and modelling. He made two excellent portraits of
the Duke of Wellington and Lord Lyndhurst, both of whom sat
to him. He lived at Lady Blessington's, at Kensington Gore,
which was an agreeable house for men, although not visited by
Englishwomen ; and there I often met the Bulwers, Disraeli,
Dickens, and last, not least, Prince Louis Napoleon, during his
exile, after his escape from Ham, where he was imprisoned for his
unsuccessful attempt at Boulogne.

On June 1, 1828, Montague Parker (who had been with me
at Eton and Oxford) and I left England in a Rotterdam packet,
accompanied by a *soi-disant* courier, an old Swiss servant of my
uncle, the Rev. A. Harris, and who soon reversed our respective
positions, inasmuch as we had to take care of him. We arrived
at Amsterdam, and thence went to the Hague, where Sir Charles
and Lady Bagot represented our King, George IV.

Here I was much impressed by an example of the marvellous
constitution of Dutch women. Being invited to dinner by Sir
Charles on the day following our arrival, it happened that we
found our white evening waistcoats, which were at that period indispensable articles, so much rumpled by our journey as to be useless. The pseudo-courier came, as pale as a sheet, to say that
'un grand malheur lui était arrivé, et que la blanchisseuse qui
avait les gilets venait d'accoucher.' There was nothing for it but
to submit, and to appear at the Ambassador's in dowdy clothes ;
but what was our relief and surprise, when the hour arrived, to
see the young mother herself walk into our room with the gar-

---

[1] Count d'Orsay's sister had married Lady Tankerville's brother, the Duc de
Gramont.

ments, apparently as well as if nothing had happened to her, although her baby was only twelve hours old !

We travelled all through Holland, a country totally unlike any other, and well worth knowing in its *belle laideur*. We then posted up the Rhine, full of Byron, with whose poetry all Europe was then mad, and who was spoken of as the personification of Satan in sin and beauty. We proceeded up the Rhine by steam, through Switzerland to Geneva, which in 1828 wore a very different aspect from its present one. The luxurious hotels of later times were not thought of ; and the best, but a very old-fashioned one, the 'Balances,' received us. It is the same in which Casanova's romance with his Henriette took place, and they showed the pane of glass, which he mentions, on which he had cut her name with his ring. At the *table-d'hôte* there were several of Napoleon's old officers, with their usual swagger. Our gallant Colonel Brotherton was also there. He was known in the Peninsular war as a *sabreur*, and for his personal courage, and he spoke French like a native. One day at dinner the eternal subject of Waterloo was discussed by various officers, and, as usual, with great heat by the French. Brotherton sat silent and took no part. Suddenly a Frenchman, not a soldier, asked him, as he had been at the battle, why he did not give an opinion. Brotherton replied coolly, ' Je suis venu ici, monsieur, pour dîner, et pas pour discuter.' The foreigner proceeded to sneer at Brotherton, who still continued quiet till the Frenchman called him a coward. Then the colonel jumped up, and, breaking up his wooden chair like a stick, shook the leg in his face. I shall never forget the rapid retreat of the aggressor. All the table cheered Brotherton, and chiefly an old General Rouget, well known in the Peninsular war, who weighed twenty stone and yet had never been hit. The disturber of our dinner turned out to be a hell-keeper from Aix.

General Sir William Gallwey had a villa near, at Châtelaine, and his wife, Lady Harriet, *née* Quin, with two pretty and clever daughters, contributed during three months to the delights of a fine summer. The youngest of these married the Comte de Bonneval, the other died unmarried at an advanced age, and for the last years of her life her little house in Belgravia was the resort of many clever men and politicians. She herself was one of the best-read and most sensible women I ever met, an excellent artist, and with a great appreciation of agreeable society.

My enjoyment of Geneva was suddenly arrested by an accident which nearly proved fatal. Parker and I had taken a house at Paquis, a mile out of the town, next to Captain Moseley, who was a great swordsman, and with whom I took lessons in fencing from a M. Marcelin. One day, as the latter stopped me in a rush, his foil broke short off, and ran into my armpit at the 'défaut du plastron,' and through the right lung. My impression was that Moseley, who was standing behind me, had given me a blow in jest ; and, as I turned to remonstrate, the blood flowed from my mouth, and I fell. Marcelin sucked the wound in vain, as I bled internally. Dr. Jenks,[1] ex-surgeon of the 10th Hussars, pronounced the case to be probably fatal, but when M. Major, an old practitioner of Napoleon's army, was called in, he bled me till I fainted, saying, 'Il n'a que 21 ans ; il faut le saigner blanc.' In a few days I was out of danger, but it was reckoned by all the surgeons a miraculous escape, the diaphragm being pierced. The spasms which I suffered were very painful, but I never thought I was dying, although I heard Major, who believed me insensible, say so in the common but unwritable language of the 'Corps de Garde.' Parker had gone on a tour, and I owe my life to Moseley, who hardly ever left me, night or day, until I was safe. One evening he had gone to dine at his uncle's, Sir William Gallwey, and I was left alone, with the family courier and a garde-malade. The weather was hot, their room was next to mine, and the door open ; they were drinking and talking loud, and I heard them counting my clothes and uniforms, and speculating how much they would get for them when I was dead. At last their conversation appeared to me to be getting dangerous as the potations increased, and, being perfectly helpless, I was quite prepared to feel a thumb on my throat, when, to my relief, I heard Moseley come up the stairs. He found these worthies drunk in the midst of my scattered wardrobe. In a moment he had hurled them both downstairs into the street, and tended me all night, and until I got a nurse.

We little know one another, and if, reader, you had asked

[1] I found Dr. Jenks fifty-three years after at Bath, aged ninety-two, with the diagnosis of my case, which he had kept.

anyone in London the character of Captain Moseley, of the Life
Guards, you would have been told that he was the most selfish and
unfeeling of dandies ; and yet, when this man found me deserted
and in danger of death, no mother could have been more attentive
and tender.  Two years later the poor fellow committed suicide
in a fit of brain fever, for the very want of that attendance which
he had given me.

In October we all three went to Italy over the Simplon, by
the then new road, and descended upon Milan.  The Napoleonic
events were then comparatively recent, and in proportion important and interesting.  Thence to Venice, which was in the hands
of Austria, and, like the whole north of Italy, seething with
hatred of the Tedesco and of the Papal power.  The Carbonari
were very active, and among the most so were the brothers
Bonaparte (sons of Louis), Pepoli, General Pepè, Prince Belgiojoso,
and the Princess.  These were the *entourage* of Queen Hortense,
who had an agreeable house at Rome.  Conspiracy was universal,
and the severities of the governments were in proportion.  England
was at that moment under the Duke of Wellington, a Tory
Government, and consequently Englishmen were in great favour
with the despotic rulers of Italy, and could do anything with impunity.  The Catholic question had not been settled, and the
Reform Bill not yet heard of.  The Whigs had been out of office
for nearly twenty years, and at that time the liberation of Italy
from a foreign yoke seemed impossible, those who spoke of it being
looked upon as fanatics.  The French Revolution of 1830 took
place two years after, changing everything, and showing that all
was feasible, although it was only a beginning of the ' letting in of
waters.'  At Florence we found Lord Burghersh as Minister, a
most pleasant and hospitable one.  He was a fanatic for music,
and had composed several operas.  Lord Normanby was there also,
and both being fond of a theatre, Lord Burghersh had one at which
we acted, and to which all the *beau monde* came.  Nothing could
be gayer than Florence at this time ; parties and balls every
night ; many English girls travelling with their parents, and consequently a great deal of match-making.  Lady Burghersh gave
some very agreeable suppers.  She painted with more than
common talent.  Of course I was constantly in the great galleries,

the Uffizzi and Pitti Palaces. The picture I admired the most in all Florence was the portrait of Cardinal Bentivoglio, at the latter, by Vandyke, and that of the Fornarina the least. I cannot believe that this portrait was either Raphael's work or Raphael's mistress. Parker and I went on to Rome, which, by its first appearance, disappointed us. I found there the Cadogans, Kenmares, Lord Wriothesley Russell, Henry Fitzroy, Mrs. and Miss Villiers, a very clever girl ; she afterwards married Mr. Lister, and *en secondes noces,* Sir George Cornewall Lewis. She was sister to Lord Clarendon, our eminent Secretary for Foreign Affairs. There was a great deal of dining out and some balls. Having just come from England, where George IV. made black satin cravats, then called 'waterfalls,' *de rigueur* at his Court, I went to M. de Chateaubriand's (the French Ambassador's) party in one of these, and was desired to change it for a white one. Other Englishmen who had done the same were very angry, and refused, believing that our King was infallible on subjects of dress, and he had declared that a man in a white neckcloth must be a dentist. There was a great deal of gambling at Rome amongst the English and other foreigners, and, as it was principally at *écarté,* a great deal of cheating. One constant player and winner was a Frenchman, who called himself Colonel Voutier, of the 'Liberating Greek Army.' He was the ugliest man I ever saw, perfectly disfigured by the smallpox, and yet with so clever and intellectual a face that he was known to have had more *bonnes fortunes* than anybody. Nor did his expression belie him, for his conversation was remarkable for its ease and variety. He was much patronised by the Reine Hortense and her son Louis. He won a great deal of English money, Fitzroy being a heavy sufferer. The most beautiful Italian at Rome was a Mrs. Dodwell, so famed for her charms, that a stranger, being asked why he came to Rome, answered, 'Sono venuto a Roma per veder tre bellissime cose : San Pietro, il Vaticano, e la Signora Dodwell.'

She afterwards assisted Pope Pius IX. to escape from his enemies at Rome, by disguising him and herself as servants.

At the end of December 1828 there was a hard frost, and, hearing that good shooting was to be had, we made a party consisting of Henry Fitzroy, Lord Albert Conyngham, Montague

Parker, and myself, to go to Tor Tre Ponti, a miserable inn on
the road to Naples. The building was a post-house, with only one
habitable room and one bed for travellers, the rest being occupied
by the Pope's soldiers, half dead with ague. We had brought
plenty of provisions and our couriers, and were soon encouraged
to remain by the thousands of wild fowl, chiefly wild geese, which
flew in and out of the marshes close over the trees of the causeway.
We tossed up for the only bed for the first night, and I won the
toss. After dinner we sat down to *écarté*—Parker and I against
the other two, 1*l.* the game, and odds bet after the first deal. At
twelve o'clock I went to bed, leaving my hand to Parker, and at
dawn I found he had won 250*l.* for me. The geese began coming
over the road in long strings, close to the trees, and we killed a
great many at first ; but it was curious to see how, after two days,
they measured their distance more and more, until they were out
of shot in crossing the road. We bagged above sixty in this way,
and afterwards I got several by stalking them with an old post-
horse. We also killed a great many wild duck, gadwells, and
snipe by walking through the marshes. In the mountains above
the road, which were covered with brushwood, woodcocks were
numerous ; but we had no beaters except the soldiers, who acted
as gillies each on the intermittent day of his fever. One of us
peppered the sergeant, who, though not hurt, was delighted to
report himself in danger, and so was sent away from this pestilential post. Our couriers, who stayed at home in the house, had
a touch of the ague ; but we remained perfectly well for a week,
which I attribute to our having been occupied and amused. We
then returned to Rome. Two years after, Sir Andrew Barnard,
who was discharging Lord Albert's play debts, called on me in
London, and paid me the 250*l.* which I had won during my sleep.
We were all too poor at the post-house to play for ready money.

One night I was at a ball given by the Austrian Ambassador,
and was much struck by a lady quite unlike the Italian women
who were there, as she had a profusion of auburn hair, which she
wore in wavy and massive curls. Her face was handsome, with
a brilliant complexion and blue eyes, and full of animation, showing splendid teeth when she laughed, which she was doing heartily
at the time I remarked her. When she rose from her chair I saw

she was of small stature, although with perfect shoulders, and a
bust made for a much taller woman.  It is generally the defect in
the figures of Italian women to have legs too short in proportion
to their robust frames, thus sacrificing grace to strength.  I was
told that this was the Countess Guiccioli, of Byronic memory,
and that she was very fond of the English, and courted their
acquaintance ; so I was introduced to her, and was very kindly
received.  Byron had been dead only five years, and she was then
twenty-six.  We became great friends, and I found her a charming companion, with a cultivated mind, yet with all the natural
*bonhomie* of her race, and fond of fun.  She had got over her
grief (which I heard was very violent at first) for the loss of her
poet, and she liked to talk of him and his eccentricities, but was
very proud of her conquest.

As a matter of course I went from Rome to Naples in February 1829, and after a few days, hearing that two brigantines were
to sail for Palermo, I took my passage in the one which appeared
the best, and sent my courier (Picconi) [1] and the luggage on board.
Just as we were getting under way, a police-boat boarded us, and
arrested the captain in the King's name.  As it was most probable that under the rule of King Bomba he might be detained for
months or years, I ordered Picconi to take my things to the other
vessel, whilst I followed.  Shortly after the prisoner was released
and returned, when a row, such as only an Italian can make,
took place.  I refused, however, to go back to his ship, and both
vessels sailed that night together.  After a tremendous storm,
which came on next day, we eventually reached Palermo safely,
with the loss of our foremast—our companion never was heard of
again.  Thus did Bomba save my life.  Many years after I gave
him a great deal of trouble in politics.  Such is the kaleidoscope
of our wayward and incomprehensible destinies.

Many vessels perished in this storm, which affected the whole
Mediterranean.  H.M. seventy-four, the 'Revenge,' lying at
Naples, was forced to put to sea.  In our brigantine were people
of all nations—Jews, Armenians, French, Germans, Turks—and
I never can forget the tumult below when we were battened down,

---

[1] Picconi had been Maître-d'armes in Napoleon's Old Guard, and took part in
his nephew's expedition to Boulogne, being a devoted Bonapartist.

and the foremast fell with a crash louder than the gale. The
Genoese captain behaved very well, and never left the helm, to
which he was lashed after he had locked up the spirit-room. The
effect of fear varied in this medley of nations. Some seemed paralysed, some prayed silently and some aloud, but the Turks showed
the most placid courage of all. I was afterwards amused at
Picconi, my courier, who had been in the Imperial Guard, abusing
a poor old woman of eighty, who was distracted, by pointing me
out as likely to be drowned at twenty-two, which was a much
harder fate than hers, as she had had a long life. I shall always
remember my feeling of gratitude and pleasure when we were all
let loose from below hatches, and rushed on deck to see the glorious Bay of Palermo under our lee, and the thunder-clouds rolling
away before the morning sun. We rigged a jury foremast, and
sailed into port.

Mr. Hill was our Minister at Naples when we returned, a *bon
vivant* and very hospitable. I dined there nearly every day, and
remained at Naples in an hotel at Santa Lucia the whole summer.
I never found the heat oppressive, as exactly at 10 A.M. the sea-
breeze entered my room, and the nights were delicious. Parties
were made to sup by moon-light at the *trattorie*, to eat the *frutti
di mare*, which include all shell-fish. The Duchesse d'Eboli,
Countesses Guiccioli and Trecasi, were often my guests, with
Counts Gamba and Spinola, young men.

The police of Naples were even more actively troublesome
than at Milan and Rome. One day Gamba, Madame Guiccioli,
and I made the ascent of Vesuvius on foot, leaving the carriage
at the bottom, and in it a sword-stick of mine. During our
absence it was discovered by one of the guides who descended the
mountain, and who informed the brigadier of the gendarmes of the
fact. On my reaching the town below we were all arrested. We
asked to see the brigadier, but was told he was gone to bed and
that we must be locked up all night. I stormed in vain for some
time, till at last I convinced them I was English, and I was admitted, and found the gallant officer very drunk and in a very dirty
shirt. He told us a long story of conspiracies, &c., but eventually,
on giving him a napoleon, he let us depart. Such were Bomba's
officials of all classes.

The sight of Vesuvius suggests curious speculations. What must have been the appearance of Europe when almost every country was vomiting its lava, many in seven or eight places at once, as in Ireland, Auvergne, the Hebrides, &c. ? These, and others, all now extinct, give us some idea of the incalculable age of our planet. They had ceased to rage before any record of man exists, and probably countless ages before he appeared on earth, for they show no vestiges of man's works having been injured by any of them, as by those still active in Italy, &c.

Accompanied by the same pleasant companions, I revelled in the classical associations of Pozzuoli, the Bay of Baiæ, Pompeii, and Paestum, and thanked the gods that I had been sent to Eton, and there acquired the enjoyment of knowing their legends. On one occasion I tried to swim across the Bay of Baiæ, but did not accomplish it within a quarter of a mile, owing to the impatient appetite of my party, who were waiting at the *trattoria* at Pozzuoli and sent a boat ont to bring me in to dinner. The feat is easy for a good swimmer, but he should wear a linen jacket, or his back will be painfully blistered by the sun in that climate. In August I returned to Rome, and never heard of fever at that time (1829). Now (1884) it would be dangerous for a foreigner to live there at that season. Mr. Hill presented me at Court before I left Naples. A circle was formed, the royal family going round and speaking to each person, which did not last long, as there were not many present. The old King did not look like a tyrant, but rather the type of an English farmer. The Queen, and the young and handsome Princess Christina, afterwards Queen of Spain, were present. The latter was said at the time to be the cause of more than one inflammable victim languishing in prison for having too openly admired this royal coquette, whose manners with men foretold her future life after her marriage to old Ferdinand. When she came up to me in the circle, walking behind her mother, she stopped, and took hold of one of the buttons of my uniform, to see, as she said, the inscription upon it, the Queen indignantly calling to her to come on. From all I heard then, the King and royal family were not personally unpopular, and there was certainly more discontent in the Papal States than in the Neapolitan ; but the revolutionists were working everywhere to upraise Italy, and the hatred of the Austrians, upon whom Bomba and the other princes of Italy were so imprudent as to depend for their power and policy, acted more against them than any local severities. Palmerston, when Foreign Secretary to Lord Grey's Government, openly encouraged the revolutionists of Spain, Portugal, and of the Italian duchies, and this gave the prestige of patriotism to men who had till then been looked upon merely as rebels. They were encouraged by his success in Portugal and in Belgium, where he had created a new kingdom, and had become the champion of all nationalities except that of Poland. The Emperor Nicholas was too ' big a brother ' even for him to defy, although he was no respecter of persons in his dauntless and successful policy. Far more than Aretino was he ' il flagello dei principi,' and was unconsciously preparing the way to Republicanism.

I found Madame Guiccioli in great distress at having received an order from the police not to quit Rome (she was a Roman subject), all her family and she herself being conspirators. She wished to return to her father, Count Gamba, at Ravenna, then in the Pope's dominions. As I had not seen that most interesting old town, I offered to take her there in my carriage. But how were we to get out of the city, as we should be examined at the Porta del Popolo ? This was accomplished by my starting at night, she walking out of the gate by day, and my taking her up a mile out of the town. Few English then ever saw Romagna, but now that the rail has invaded it, it is not the same thing as driving through its splendid oak forests and quaint old towns as I did then, by Loretto, Forli, Faenza, and Cesena. Whatever *lâches* may have existed in the Papal Government, no fault could be found in the posting department, which was the best I saw anywhere. Count Gamba's house at Ravenna was near the Pinetum, a primæval pine forest, which alas ! I am told, is now dying fast from the soil having been drained by the new railway works. The Gambas might have well been called the Osbaldistones of Italy ; they were all sportsmen according to their knowledge, which consisted of hunting a slow pointer, who stood woodcocks and partridges equally well, through the forests and vineyards. They had just begun to hear of copper caps *vice* flints, and when I gave Vincenzo my double-barrelled Purdy, his pleasure surpassed any demonstration I ever saw. They lived in feudal style as far as an abundant table supplied them and their guests, and were as good a type of worthy though self-educated gentlemen as it was possible to find. The house was large, with a long gallery of bedrooms, the doors of which, from the great heat of the weather, were necessarily open all night, and the inmates could converse from their beds one to another with Italian *sans façon*. There was a permanent priest whom they called Don Juan, Don being the usual title of a domestic Levite, no one but Madame Guiccioli seeing the absurdity. In reference to Byron's famous poem of that name she told me that he wrote all the last cantos on play-bills (some of which I saw myself), or on any odd piece of paper at hand, and with repeated glasses of gin-punch by his side. He then used to rush out of his room to read to her what he had written, making many alterations and laughing immoderately. She was very proud and fond of him, but described him as having a very capricious temper, and with nothing of the passion which pervades his poetry, and which he was in the habit of ridiculing —in fact, with a cold temperament. With all his abuse of England, he insisted on keeping up old customs in small things, such as having hot cross buns on Good Friday and roast goose on Michaelmas Day. This last fancy led to a grotesque result. After buying a goose and fearing it might be too lean, he fed it every day for a month previously, so that the poet and the bird became so mutually attached that when September 29 arrived he could not kill it, but bought another, and had the pet goose swung in a cage under his carriage when he travelled, so that after four years he was moving about with four geese. It was surprising to see the number of letters written to him by women offering themselves to him on any terms. Madame Guiccioli had a large box full of these epistles, which he never answered. They were mostly from English ladies, such was the folly and enthusiasm which his verses inspired at the time.

When Byron departed for Greece, Madame Guiccioli went to Ravenna. She described to me her anxiety as terrible, and when his letters no longer came, she accused him of having forgotten her. Poor woman! he was gone to that land 'where all things are forgotten.'

She introduced me at Rome to the Duchesse de St. Leu (Queen Hortense), who invited me to her evening parties and some picnics, and was a most fascinating woman, although past the middle of life. Her house, though very aristocratic, was the resort of all the Intransigeants of both sexes in politics. Princess Belgiojoso led the female conspirators, and they were so little feared that, as long as they remained in the Pope's domains and could be watched, they were not molested.

Here for the first time I met Hortense's son, Louis Napoleon, then just of age. Nor would anybody at that time have predicted his great and romantic career. He was a wild harum-scarum youth, or what the French call *un crâne*, riding at full gallop down the streets to the peril of the public, fencing, and pistol-shooting, and apparently without serious thoughts of any kind, although even then he was possessed with the conviction that he would some day rule over France. We became friends, but at that time he evinced no remarkable talent or any fixed idea but the one I mention. It grew upon him with his growth, and increased daily until it ripened into a certainty. He was a very good horseman and proficient at athletic games, being short, but very active and muscular. His face was grave and dark, but redeemed by a singularly bright smile. Such was his personal appearance in 1829, at twenty-one years of age. He used to have several old officers of his uncle, the Emperor, about him, men who seemed to me to be ready for any adventure. I recollect one, an old cavalry colonel of dragoons who had seen the whole Peninsular war, relating the following anecdote. One day he was reconnoitring with three or four troopers, when they came suddenly upon a young English officer mounted on a superb thoroughbred horse and similarly occupied. Summoned by the colonel to surrender, he quietly cantered away, laughing in the Frenchman's face. The dragoon pursued, at full gallop of his heavy steed, and when the Englishman had allowed him to get quite close he kissed his hand, and, leaving him far behind, shouted, pointing to his horse, 'Cheval Normand, Monsieur!' Again the Frenchmen pursued, threatening to shoot his enemy if he did not surrender, and pointed his pistol at him, but the weapon missed fire. With a roar of laughter the young officer again shouted, 'Fabrique de

Versailles, Monsieur !' and giving the thoroughbred his head, was seen no more.  It was most amusing to hear the old colonel tell this story and describe his rage, adding, however, that he had always felt glad that he had not shot *ce brave farceur.*

It was in August 1829 that I took leave of the Gambas in Romagna and of their sister, Madame Guiccioli.  She came to England a few years afterwards, and was one of the many foreign ladies who were at Lady Blessington's parties.  Subsequently she married le Marquis de Boissy, an eccentric man with a large fortune and a fine house at Paris, where I dined at a magnificent banquet, the contrast being very striking after the frugal existence which in former years she led in Italy.  The change was great between the old quiet lodging with a solitary maidservant and the sumptuous establishment of the Marquis.  I found the *bonhomie* of the Italian altered for the artificial manner of a *grande dame,* and not to its advantage, although she retained the kindly instincts of her nature.  She survived her husband, who was an *Anglophobe,* and died in 1879 at Florence, where she had been living on a large jointure.

I posted to England night and day by a most desolate road, and it took me sixty-eight hours to reach Paris, where I stayed a day to rest, and crossed the Channel on September 7, 1829.

After a short visit to my father at Heron Court, I was invited to Chillingham Castle, and during my stay there engaged myself to the only daughter of the Tankervilles, Lady Emma, whom I married on April 13 the following spring, and who for forty-eight years unceasingly deserved the epitaph which is written on her monument in the Priory Church at Christchurch :—

> From her it never was our fate to find
> A deed ungentle or a word unkind :
> The mildest manners with the bravest mind.—ILIAD.

In 1827, Mr. Canning's death, that of King George IV., and the Duke of Wellington's difficulties after he had emancipated the Roman Catholics, all prepared the country to see the fall of the Tory Government.  The Tories had ruled England almost without interruption for thirty years, and in the most critical time of our history their statesmen, generals, and admirals, had

weathered the hurricane when all Europe had despaired, and in
1815 brought the great ship to a safe anchorage, although shaken
and damaged in all but honour.  It seemed almost natural that
a new set of men should repair the *lâches* of a long war and
attempt to remedy grievances which could not be attended to
during war.  There was a general sentiment that new men, with
new ideas of domestic policy, were required, and that the reform
of the franchise was the most pressing subject.  The old Whig
leaders pitched upon it as their first point of attack, and in the
summer of 1830 their combinations were made.  My father-in-
law, Lord Tankerville, was an old Whig, and a friend of Lord
Grey, and he took me on a visit to Howick, where the old Earl
lived in patriarchal retirement amidst his numerous family.  Two
of the latter, Lord Durham and Mr. Ellice (commonly called
' Bear Ellice '), both clever and ambitious men, had great influence
with Lord Grey, and used it without mercy.  He was one of the
most striking figures I ever saw, the very type of a *grand seigneur*
and of an intellectual man.  Whilst I was at Howick I was
struck with two peculiarities of the family, one of which was
that all the sons and daughters called their parents by their
Christian names, 'Charles' and 'Mary,' which had a strange
effect ; the other was the taste of the whole family for argument.
They were always in a state of discussion, even as to the distance
between Howick and Alnwick, and the shortest road to and from
each, which one would suppose they had verified long ago.  Lady
Georgiana was very agreeable, and played beautifully on the harp,
an instrument then much appreciated.  As I suppose I was looked
upon as a mere boy by the party, politics and future onslaughts
on the Tory Government were freely spoken of without *gêne* in
my presence ; and I remember one day Lord Grey breaking out
and declaring that the three greatest rascals in the world were
Lord Castlereagh (then dead), Brougham, and Talleyrand, and
I recollect this explosion the more, because when he formed
his Government three months later [1] he was obliged to make
Brougham his Chancellor, and to receive Talleyrand as the Ambassador of France.

---

[1] The Duke of Wellington resigned in November 1830, and Lord Grey suc-
him as Premier.

Ellice and Lord Durham were often at Chillingham at this time, and their talk, of course, was chiefly as to the coming change and of the rearrangement of the boroughs and franchise, their great object being to ' cook ' them (as they themselves called it), so as to expel as much as possible all local interests belonging to Tories.

The battle for and against Reform proceeded with the greatest acrimony on both sides, both in and out of Parliament. In the House of Lords I myself heard Lord Carnarvon, a man of great weight in public opinion, and who was a Whig, apostrophise Lord Grey, and declare that ' to propose so revolutionary a measure he must have a fool's head on his shoulders or a traitor's heart in his bosom.' Out of Parliament the following history will speak for itself.

When the Reform Bill was thrown out by the Peers in 1831, Lord Tankerville voted against it. My wife and I accompanied him on his journey to Chillingham, which at that time took four days to accomplish, being three hundred and thirty miles, although posting with four horses. When we got to Darlington, we halted for luncheon, and perceived a large crowd at the door of the hotel examining the crest on the panels and apparently quiet, but we were hardly reseated in the family coach when a storm of stones assailed it and a furious mob tried to stop us. The post-boys behaved well and ran the gauntlet at full gallop till we cleared the town, but in what a condition ! The coach was full of stones of all sizes, the front part of it was smashed and the panels stove in, yet we all escaped with a few scratches. When I saw what was coming, I pulled my wife under the seat, which saved her from a large paving-stone that struck the place where she had been sitting. When some miles from Darlington, we stopped at a village inn till dark, as our battered condition would have invited another pelting, out of mere mischief. This outrage was committed deliberately and with preparation for the first Peer who passed Darlington after having voted against the Reform Bill. The stones stood in heaps ready, piled like ammunition, and the victims were to be thrown into the river. The feelings of these ferocious politicians may be imagined, as the presence of two women, my wife and her maid, in our carriage did not prevent their murderous attempt. This was but one of many similar acts of violence all over England and Scotland connected with the progress of the Reform Bill.

The local authorities in no way interfered to prevent them, and in our case they and the Lord-Lieutenant even refused Lord Tankerville to identify and punish our assailants. During the Parliamentary struggle for this Reform Bill, the most strange delusions as to its results seized the lower classes, who were convinced that it could do no less than alter their whole condition. Servants left their places, feeling sure that somehow they need never serve again. Marriages were put off until the great redemption of the poor from poverty was effected, and orators were not wanting to foster these follies. In short, whilst the contention lasted the country was in a delirium. The years 1830, 1831, and 1832 will be remembered as the most agitated of the century. Discontent and disease pervaded Europe in the shape of revolution and cholera. In France, Charles X. had been exiled, and the throne occupied by his cousin. The Duc de Guiche accompanied the King to Edinburgh, with all his family, he being Lady Tankerville's brother. He brought with him his boy, who became afterwards Duc de Gramont, and in 1870 was Foreign Minister to Louis Napoleon, when he declared his fatal war with Germany.

In Paris the cholera was raging during 1831-2. In London it was less virulent, but numbers died, and I did not escape it, but recovered after being dosed with spirits of wine, which was the only thing that relieved the spasms. It was Dr. Quin's remedy, and his patients used, like myself, to carry a small bottle always with them. The Court physician, Sir Henry Halford, was at first very shy of attending cholera cases, until Brougham launched at him one of his diatribes, which was as terrible as the disease. Twenty-five thousand had died in Paris.

In the winter of 1830 there were serious agrarian riots all over the South and West of England. My two brothers and I were sent for one night from Heron Court by the Ringwood magistrates, urging us to collect what force we could, and to repair there to stop the advance of a large mob marching from Salisbury, and burning the corn-ricks of the farms on their way. Their object was to destroy the thrashing-machines, but they went further and set fire to all kinds of property. They were led by a man on horseback, who called himself Lord Hunt, and had marched through all Sussex. When we were summoned they had attacked the house at West Park, near Fordingbridge, where there was a party of visitors, who, with the gamekeeper, Woodroe, defended themselves, and fired a volley, wounding several of the assailants, some of whom died. The mob then retreated. My brothers and I hastened to Ringwood and joined Mr. Compton and Mr. Mills. The next day our army of mounted farmers, gentlemen, servants, and many tradesmen, met the rioters just beyond Fordingbridge, charged and routed them. Hunt and three others were taken and hanged at Winchester. Some were found dead in West Park Woods, and I never heard that any inquest was held over them. At that time there was no cavalry nearer than Dorchester, forty miles off, and no infantry nearer than Portsmouth, the same distance—no railway to bring either, and no electric telegraphs. The rebellion—for such it was—was put down by the landed proprietors, their tenants, and the respectable shopkeepers at Christchurch, Ringwood, and Lyndhurst. A most medley and grotesque force they were, everyone arming himself with the first weapon he could find. Lord Melbourne was Home Secretary, just appointed with Lord Grey's Government, and he wrote the magistrates a letter of full approbation of their conduct and courage. In Berkshire the rebels were beaten in the same way by Lord Craven and his friends. The Duke of Wellington, who was our Lord-Lieutenant, took great pains in establishing and fitting out a regiment of five troops of yeomanry, recruited from the New Forest and its neighbourhood. I commanded one of these for five years, when, just as they had become trained and available, Lord Howick, then Secretary for War, disbanded them, he and his colleagues disliking the accidental fact that all the officers and most of the men were Tories and voters for the county,

It was in 1834 that I made the acquaintance of Lord Derby, then Lord Stanley, which ripened into a mutual and sincere friendship, lasting till his death in 1869. When the great disruption of the Tory party under Sir Robert Peel took place in 1846, I for the first time took a strong part in politics—not for

any liking of that stormy life, which I had always shunned—
but from a sincere conviction that the abolition of the Corn Laws,
proposed by Peel, would be the ruin of all who depended directly
or indirectly upon land.  The gallant Duke of Richmond,[1] Lord
George Bentinck, and I, were among the first to rally our partisans
in and out of Parliament by all the means which political hostility
allows.  Disraeli then came forward in all his strength, and displayed his genius by some of the most remarkable speeches ever
heard in Parliament.  We succeeded in obtaining the invaluable
support of Lord Stanley's [2] prestige and eloquence, though at first
he naturally hesitated to break with his colleagues.  In February
1852 he became Prime Minister, and appointed me to the Foreign
Office.  I had published in 1844 the ' Diplomatic Journal and Correspondence ' of my grandfather, the first Lord Malmesbury, and
the experience I gained by reading and collating, with great trouble,
the contents of above two thousand letters and despatches from
and to him by all the important personages of the period from
1768 to 1800 stood me in good stead at this trying time.  Without
this accidental education I should have been as great a novice
in political business as were most of my colleagues.  My former
personal relations with Louis Napoleon were also a lucky accident,
and placed us on a footing which saved much trouble and anxiety
to both of us when he proclaimed the Empire in 1852.  At the
end of that year we were turned out of office, to which we were
recalled in 1858, I having again the Foreign Office.  In 1859,
after a tenure of fifteen months and a general election, we were
beaten on a false issue, which is explained in my diary of that
year.

From 1834 to 1869 I used to pay an annual visit to Knowsley,
where the late Lord Derby had brought *battue* shooting to perfection.  We used to go out six or seven guns, each one having a
loader and marker, the latter pricking down each shot killed by
his master ; and it was very remarkable at the end of the day,
when the total killed were counted up, how very accurately each
gun found his calculation verified.  What was extremely striking
was the large and peaceful crowd that accompanied us for beating

---

[1] The late Duke.
[2] Afterwards fourteenth Earl of Derby and Prime Minister.

in line. I have seen two and three hundred of these volunteer beaters, working men and artisans, pour out of the villages near to see the sport, keeping the most perfect line and order ; and the custom was so known and valued by them, that if by chance any individual was not steady and disciplined, his comrades sent him home at once, without any trouble to us.

Such was the respect and goodwill which Lord Derby inspired by his character and genial manner. He himself was the keenest sportsman I ever met ; whilst he was in the field his whole attention was in his present pursuit, and woe to him who attempted to divert him to politics at the time. When over, he could divest his mind completely of the sport and sit down at once to write the longest and most important paper straight off, in a delicate hand and without a single erasure—so completely could he in a few moments arrange his subject in his mind. I have often witnessed this intellectual *tour de force* both in and out of the Cabinet. He died on October 23, 1869, in his seventieth year, completely worn out by constant attacks of acute gout, and, although at my age I inevitably miss nearly all my early friends, I have never so deeply felt the loss of any one of them as that of this noble character. When he became Prime Minister for the third time in 1866, he made me Privy Seal, after offering me again the Foreign Office, which my bad health obliged me to refuse, and I held the Privy Seal under Disraeli again in 1868 and 1874, until 1876, when I resigned my place, being rendered useless from deafness either in Cabinet or House of Lords.

# DIARY.

## 1832

ON February 23, 1832, Lady Fitzharris and I started for a tour abroad, and here I will quote from my journal to show what travelling was fifty years ago for a married couple who wished to visit France and Italy, taking a courier who was bound to ride post and order horses for a *britshka* and a *fourgon*.

*February 23rd.*—Left Dover in a steamer ; only three passengers beside ourselves. Fine when we started, but fog came on with hard, black frost, and Captain Bushill, neglecting to sound, ran us aground five miles west of Calais. We were within a stone's throw of the shore, but not allowed to land on account of quarantine for cholera. Cold intense, twenty degrees, and no possibility of a fire. The Coastguard watched us all night to prevent our landing, as the vessel was high and dry at low water, and also to assist in case of danger.

*February 24th.*—Entered Calais harbour ; *Commission sanitaire* inspected us. On asking a member of it how soon we were to be released, he replied, 'Mêlez-vous de vos affaires ! Ven I come I come.'

*February 26th.*—Hard frost and fog. Released at 8 A.M. Breakfasted at Dessins Hotel. Slept at Montreuil, where the snipe pies and dinner are excellent.

*February 27th.*—Reached Grandvilliers.

*February 28th.*—Arrived at Paris at 7 P.M., after travelling all day.

*February 29th.*—Took best rooms at Hôtel Bristol for only twenty francs a day. Such is the effect of the Revolution and cholera on the first hotel at Paris.

*March 4th.*—Paris. Went to the Opéra and saw ' Robert le Diable.' Singing and dancing far superior to that in our theatres. Nourrit a splendid tenor.

*March 6th.*—Vaudeville Theatre, where ' Le Régent ' was acted. The most barefaced allusions in favour of the Court were received in silence. Trade ruined and much dissatisfaction. Duke of Orleans accused of flirting instead of occupying himself with politics. A very handsome and amiable man. Duc de Nemours not in the army.

*March 7th.*—Dined with the Walewskis. He the son of Napoleon, and very like him. She a daughter of Lord Sandwich. Met the Flahaults and Lord Harry Vane. Gay party. Young Count Candia was there and sang splendidly.[1]

*March 9th.*—Breakfasted with the old Duc de Gramont, my wife's grandfather, who has been a ' Garde du Corps ' of Louis XV., and was on duty at Versailles on the day on which he arrested the Cardinal de Rohan, whose history is well known in connection with Marie Antoinette and the famous diamond necklace. He told us many anecdotes of Louis XV., and gave us a dish which he said the King had every day of his life on his table, and which he seldom omitted to eat. It was of chicken or pheasant *écharpé*, with a *Béchamel* sauce, with truffles or *chicorée* and *gratiné*. I got the receipt from the Duke's cook and have found it very popular. The Duc said that ' La Du Barry était peinte comme mon carrosse.' We afterwards drove with him to Versailles, and I never spent a more interesting day, walking over this famous palace with this old man, who had known it in all its former glories. It was like listening to one from the dead to hear his anecdotes and legends about events in which he had acted a part. Although eighty-two years of age, his memory was perfectly good, and he was as gay as a man in the prime of life. He showed us the room in which he had arrested the Cardinal, and amongst other places the immense flight of stone steps down which, when the palace was invested by the bloodthirsty mob in 1789, he and his guards had to ride to save their lives. Three men were killed when their horses fell and rolled to the bottom, the rest escaping by this desperate feat. The mob had stopped every

[1] Afterwards famous as Mario.

other issue, and thought this one impassable. The old Duke had a Basque servant, who looked upon his master with feudal adoration. He was called Irygoyen, and used to join in the conversation from behind the Duke's chair. His fine castle, Bidache, near Bayonne, was burnt in 1793 by the Bande Noire, and has not been restored. This ancient family were once sovereign princes, coined money on their Basque territory, and supplied Henri Quatre with it and troops through Corisande de Gramont.

At this moment the prices of dress are very moderate in Paris. A velvet gown requiring eight yards costs only 10*l.*, and ladies' silk or satin shoes by the best maker only six francs a pair, the effect of the Revolution.

*March 15th.*—Left Paris, our *fourgon* being well stocked by the old Duke, according to ancient fashion, with various eatables and a proportionate variety of wines.

*March 19th.*—Reached Lyons, after sleeping at Avallon, Châlons, and Mâcon. The mountains of Auvergne covered with snow and weather bitter. Spent twenty-two francs a day in firewood. The Lyonese very Carlist. In 1789 they were the most savage Republicans.

*March 21st.*—We hired a boat for 400 francs to take us and our carriages to Avignon, and stopped at Condrieu. The whole country on both banks of the Rhône is beautiful even at this time of year; with its hills, vineyards, and castles, it is far superior to the Rhine. At Condrieu the wine is celebrated and deserves its reputation. It is a white hermitage, and costs thirty sous a bottle. Fifteen thousand bottles of this wine are made annually from the vineyard on the hill.

*March 22nd.*—This journey by water is the only way to see the valley of the Rhône. We passed Tain and Valence, opposite which is the ruined castle of Crusol, like an eagle's nest, from which the view of the great river is splendid. Here you see the Alps for the first time, looking like an impassable barrier. We slept at Bourg St. Andeol, a wretched tavern for bargemen, where I kept my pistols under my pillow by the advice of my courier, who said it was a notorious den of brigands; but our boatmen refused to go farther. The people stared at us like savages. The whole country and roads were full of refugee Polish soldiers,

escaping after their defeats into France, and wherever they passed
not an orange or a drop of brandy was left.   They appeared to
live entirely on these two articles of food, and to fall on them
like locusts.

*March 23rd.*—Shot through the bridge of St. Esprit, built by
the Romans, and having twenty-two arches.   The current is so
rapid and the arches so narrow that the boatmen dare not go
through them at night.   Arrived at Avignon, at l'Hôtel de
l'Europe, after three days' enjoyment of the grandest scenery,
without the slightest fatigue.   What a difference from the same
journey, cramped in a carriage, and only half seeing one bank of
this glorious river !   The view from the castle, which the Popes
once occupied here, is at sunset one of the finest spectacles it is
possible to behold.

*March 24th.*—We hired a carriage to go to Vaucluse, quite
equal in beauty and curiosity to our expectations, and to its rich
traditions.   The last, however, did not interfere with a luncheon
of trout and crayfish at the inn kept by the infamous Fouché's
famous cook.   Our return to Avignon very disagreeable in an
open carriage, with a furious *mistral*, which had risen suddenly
since the morning.   The dust penetrated even into my writing-
desk.   Bill at the Hôtel de l'Europe at Avignon only 110 francs
for three days.

*March 26th.*—Arrived at Aix, in Provence, an old town
seldom visited by English ; once the capital of King René, the
musical ruler of the land of Troubadours.   The cathedral is built
upon a Temple of Diana, the pillars of which remain, two of
granite, and the rest of Egyptian marble.   The water of the
famous baths is 24° of Réaumur, and yet gold-fish will live in it.

*March 30th.*—Stopped at Toulon.   Had a letter to the general
to admit us into the dockyard.   They were very proud of the
frigate 'Proserpine,' taken from the English.   The number of
convicts at Toulon is 4,000.   They work from sunrise to sunset,
with the exception of two hours in the middle of the day.
Beautiful carvings are made by a man of the name of Miron, who
stole Mademoiselle Mars' jewels, and who is condemned *aux
travaux forcés* for twenty years.

*March 31st.*—Reached Cannes over the Estrelle mountains.

Slept at the Hôtel de la Poste, close to the sea, one of the worst inns I ever was in.

*April 1st.*—Left this miserable hole and arrived at Nice. Detained long at the Douane on the Italian frontier. The Douaniers pay no attention to articles of dress, but are exceedingly strict in the examination of books. The man who searched us, not understanding a word of English, took Lord Byron's poems for a dictionary and confiscated them. This excessive surveillance is since the Revolution in Paris. Excellent hotel at Nice, but a bitter north wind prevails.

*April 4th.*—Reached Genoa by the Corniche Road, newly made and very dangerous in many parts, with sharp turns and no parapets; was a nervous journey, although very beautiful. We had slept at St. Remo, a miserable village.[1]

———

Having written thus much to show what travelling was fifty years ago, and quoted my diary textually so far, I shall now only use it as reminding me of events in which I took part more or less.

From Nice we went to Genoa, and, after visiting all the palaces there, we proceeded to Spezzia by Chiavari; thence to Carrara, where the marble works were wonderfully cheap. I bought a handsome chimney-piece of the whitest marble, with bas-reliefs from the Vaso Borghese, for 20*l.* Proceeding to Lucca, we were told that we required an escort of gendarmes, as travellers had been lately robbed passing the mountain. We took two mounted guards with us, who would have been of little use if the brigands (said to be twenty-seven in number) had attacked us. The country from Lucca to Florence is hideous and the weather was Siberian. We met many people we knew at Florence—among them Mr. and Mrs. Ferdinand St. John. I had known him in 1829 at Naples, a very handsome and clever man. At that time he fought a duel with Count Coteroffiano, who was the best shot and swordsman in the country. When they met it was agreed they should stand at forty yards apart, and, at a signal given by the seconds, they might advance or not as they pleased, and fire when they liked. Both stood still, and St. John fired first, apparently without the least effect. Coteroffiano then advanced, and St. John thought himself lost, when his adversary walked half way and fell stone dead, having received the bullet without wincing, and intending to kill St. John *à bout portant.*

When we came to Florence, St. John had lately married Miss Keating, an heiress, and one of his amusing stories was that his wife being *enceinte,* and he being very poor, he asked his relation, Lord Wenlock, to promise to purchase a commission in the Guards for his son, if she had one. The old peer refusing his request, St. John asked him whether he would do so in the event of her having twin boys, to which Lord Wenlock acceded, when in due time Mrs. St. John won the event.

There was at that time at Florence a Scotch banker of the name of Lawrie, who had a very good gallery of pictures. He had married a most beautiful girl of poor parents in Florence, having taken her as a child and educated her for his wife. We made her acquaintance, and found her a very pleasant and ladylike person.

After spending a month at Florence we went with my brother to Geneva. One evening we took a sailing boat and went upon the lake. The halyard slipped out of the block, and my brother's swarming up the mast capsized the boat. Lady Fitzharris, with the most wonderful coolness, turned to me, both of us being in the water, saying, ' Don't be afraid ; I won't lay hold of you, but tell me what to do.' My brother, who had got entangled under the sail, came up, and by putting her hands on our shoulders we kept her up for a quarter of an hour, till a watchmaker, who was rowing his wife, took her in, whilst we hung on to the stern till we reached the shore, which was a quarter of a mile off. Nothing but my wife's cool courage saved us, as, if she had been frightened, we should have been drowned by her struggles. A week afterwards the watchmaker came to ask for what he called ' damages.' I thought he alluded to damages to his boat or loss of time, but it was to his wife, who, in consequence of her alarm at the accident, had miscarried, and, as he insisted, deprived him of a son and heir. As he could not prove this, or show how he was the worse, or give any items in a bill, and as I had paid him salvage, I resisted this new specimen of Swiss avarice. We returned to London in July, 1833.

This was the first year that the Highlands became the rage, and that deer forests were made and rented, but for prices not exceeding 300*l.* a year. Sir Harry Goodricke, who was a leader among the young hunting men, hired Mar Forest, and Lord Kinnaird, Fealar in Athol. We paid the latter a visit, in August, at Rossie Priory, and I went with him, Mr. Errington, and Count Matuschewitz (the Russian Ambassador), to a bothy at Fealar. The Russian (in reality a Pole) was a very able man, and a great favourite with *la jeunesse dorée* at Melton, where Sir H. Goodricke kept the hounds, followed by Lords Wilton, Gardner, Macdonald, Kinnaird, and Mr. Gilmour, all first-rate riders, who had the best horses in England, and kept open houses, as I know from having enjoyed their hospitality. The hunting was not what it is now that it has become racing. At Rossie Priory, in the Carse of Gowrie, Kinnaird lived in great luxury ; his two handsome sisters did the honours admirably to a mixed party, the eldest of whom was twenty-six. Mrs. Norton was there in the zenith of her beauty, and added much to the *entrain*. I went later to the Isle of Skye and to Harris. I was harboured at the latter by Mr. Stewart, a gentleman farmer and breeder of cattle, and had the run of the island, which belonged then to MacLeod, and the grouse, deer forest, and fishing, all of which are first-rate, were offered to me for 25*l.* a year. It has been purchased since by Lord Dunmore, and the sporting right let for 2,000*l.* a year. At that time (1833), a stranger could fish and shoot over almost any part of the Highlands without interruption, the letting value of the *feræ naturæ* being unknown to their possessors. Chillingham Castle being on the posting road north, a great many visitors stopped there on their way south in the autumn. Landseer was a constant one, and this year painted for me a portrait of Lady Fitzharris [1] in a cloak, standing on the ramparts of the castle ; but such were his dilatory habits about his pictures, that I only received it from his executors forty-four years after. It is at

1 This picture cost 80*l.* In 1884 his 'Monarch of the Glen' fetched 6,000*l.* at Christie's.

Heron Court, and has been engraved. He painted another of
her the following year, lying on a sofa with a deerhound looking
out of window, and a spaniel in her lap. The former is the portrait
of a dog who saved the keeper's life under the following circumstances, as recorded in my diary.

. . . .

## 1833

*November* 9.—A large party at Chillingham ; Mr. Landseer,
Charles Mathews, Lord Macdonald, Lord Ossulston, and Mr.
Gilmour, settled to kill one of the wild bulls the next day. Cole,
the park-keeper, came to the castle early this morning to say
that a bull had been driven out of the herd, and that he was
extremely savage. He advised the gentlemen to be very careful
how they approached him. Nobody, however, seemed inclined to
listen to him, and Mr. Gilmour and Lord Macdonald went to put
on their red coats to irritate him. The bull was near a little oak
wood, where Cole had left his son and Barnes, the under-keeper,
to watch him. After he had received his orders for the *chasse*,
he returned to his post, and the gentlemen began their preparations
in great spirits at the prospect of the fun. All at once we saw
Cole running back to the castle as fast as he could. He rushed
up to the windows pale and breathless, and exclaimed with a
voice of horror, ' Barnes is killed by the bull ! '—and then left us
without further explanation. We were all too much shocked to
be able to utter a word, and remained looking at each other ;
but went out after a time and saw a crowd running across the
park towards a cart which was conveying Barnes to his house.
Ossulston accompanied it to the village, and sent a man on horseback for the doctor. As he could not possibly arrive under an
hour, Cole bled the poor man, who was not dead as was at first
supposed, though severely hurt, several ribs being broken, with a
deep wound in the thigh. The accident happened thus : When
Cole came to the castle for orders, he left his son and Barnes to
watch the bull and prevent his breaking away to join the herd,
which he had several times tried to do. The two men were in
the oak wood, and Barnes seeing the bull approach the fence,

came out to frighten him away. The beast instantly rushed at him ; he turned to run away, but his foot slipped and he fell. In one moment the bull overtook him and tossed him clean over his head. Young Cole could do very little, for, though he had his rifle, he had no means of loading it, and the other spectators were also unarmed, and too much frightened to be of any use. Young Cole, however, did as much as possible under these circumstances, coming out several times towards the bull and trying to entice him to run at him, but in vain. The bull tossed Barnes five times over his head, then lifted him with his horns, placed him across his knees, and threw himself down with his whole weight upon the man, whom he trampled upon and gored for full ten minutes. The bloodhound refused to go in ; but at last Ossulston's deerhound, Bran, fastened upon the bull's hocks and worried him so that he left his victim. The cart arrived fortunately just at that moment, and they succeeded in getting poor Barnes into it. Had it not been for the dog, nothing could have saved his life.

The gentlemen went out to kill the bull, and fired several shots at him before he dropped. He had six balls in his head, and even then was not dead, and made an effort to get up again. Then Cole and several others threw themselves upon him and held him down whilst he was stabbed in the throat. Mr. Landseer made a beautiful sketch of him after his death, and Lord Tankerville ordered a picture to be painted of Ossulston and the animal. It is now at Chillingham Castle. Barnes eventually recovered.

# 1834

*October 24th.*—Chillingham. Lord Durham and Lady Fanny Lambton came to-day on their way to Glasgow. Lord Durham seems very much out of spirits ; he confesses that he is very nervous about the Glasgow dinner, which he regrets now having accepted. All his friends blame him for having done so, as they say it will commit him. He says he intends to make an attack upon Lord Brougham, but is afraid he will not be able to keep his head and command his temper sufficiently to do it with effect.

*November 2nd.*—Left Chillingham, and reached Alnwick by a

new road. Were kindly received by the Duchess. The Duke is
very infirm. After dinner we adjourned to the library, where the
ladies established themselves, according to the rule and custom of
the house, in a row on one side of the room.

*November 16th.*—Left Stocken Hall, Sir Gilbert Heathcote's
place, and arrived in London. We heard at Wandsford that the
Whigs are out of office, the King having dismissed his Government,
and that the Duke of Wellington is sent for. As soon as I
arrived, I sent a message to Norman Macdonald, who confirmed
the news. The Duke having advised the King to send for Sir
Robert Peel, who is in Italy, he cannot get an answer under three
weeks. The Duke of Wellington says he will answer for keeping
the country quiet. He walked into the Foreign Office to-day,
about an hour after he had been appointed, to the great discomfiture of Norman Macdonald and other secretaries of Lord Duncannon.

*November 28th.*—I went to Manor House, Mr. Compton's
place, to accompany him to a Conservative meeting at Southampton. The meeting was ill-attended—not above two hundred
present, and some of these Radicals. The Tories, as usual, mismanaged the business, and never took any pains to assemble
people of rank and influence. They voted Mr. Sloane Stanley in
the chair, and, whilst he slept, made a number of foolish speeches,
which, considering they only met for the purpose of addressing
the King on his prerogative, was a useless thing to do. When
the meeting was over, Lord Normanton, Mr. Andrew Drummond,
and a few more, got Mr. Compton into a private room and succeeded in persuading him to stand for the southern division of the
county. Having a large family, he was at first disinclined to do
so, but Lord Normanton and Mr. Drummond having offered to
guarantee him free of expense, he could no longer refuse, and the
business was settled. Messrs. Compton and Fleming stand
against Lord Palmerston and Sir George Staunton.

*December 10th.*—There is no news yet respecting the new
Ministry, but some reports. It is hoped that if Lord Stanley
does not join Sir Robert Peel he will give his support to his
Government. Lord Ossulston is opposed in Northumberland by
Lord Grey and Mr. Liddell, son of Lord Ravensworth, and, I

much fear, will be defeated in consequence ; but the Duke of
Northumberland has promised him all his interest until he sees
him safe. I have received a strong requisition to stand for the
Isle of Wight, but my father has taken such a decided line
against my coming into Parliament that, although I consented at
first, I found it impossible to risk a serious quarrel, and had to
renounce all hope of being in the House of Commons. I might,
at this time, have walked over for Christchurch.

I paid a visit to Mr. Compton in the New Forest. The party
consisted of Lord Alvanley, Col. Damer, Mr. and Lady Gertrude
Stanley, Sir Henry Fane, and Mr. Irby. Lord Alvanley was as
amusing as usual, and told some good stories. One which he related was of the late Sir Watkin Wynn. He was playing at
whist with Lords Granville, Sefton, and another famous player—
all playing very deep. It was Sir Watkin's turn to deal, and
whilst he did so, Lord Granville turned round to speak to someone
behind him. This deal was to decide the rubber, upon which
several hundreds were staked. The whole party were, therefore,
in anxious expectation of the result. One may, therefore, better
conceive than describe the surprise and dismay of Lord Granville
when, upon his turning to take up his hand, he found none. At
the same time his partner, Sir Watkin, said, ' I think I have
rather too many cards.' He had dealt himself *two* hands, and
had 26 cards instead of 13 ! The confusion was indescribable at
this discovery ; all the best whist-players were consulted, but
they could come to no decision. Hoyle had never thought it
possible.

## 1835

*January 9th.*—Went to shoot at Somerley, where I was
strongly attacked for not standing for the Isle of Wight, and
obliged to explain my reasons for not doing so.

*January 16th.*—Drove to Ringwood, and met Lord Palmerston's mob at the end of the town, and we were, of course, hooted
by them. Norman Macdonald, to our delight, was covered with
mud by his own friends. He went about Ringwood all day with

the Whig attorney in order to retrieve his character, which he considered damaged by having been seen with us.

*January 17th.*—The election was decided in favour of Fleming and Compton.

*February 13th.*—Left Heron Court for Mr. Fleming's place, Stoneham. Dinner had been ordered at six o'clock, but did not take place till eight, when Mr. Fleming returned home, and we did not sit down till half-past. We were equally unpunctual for the ball at Southampton. Lady Dundonald was there, covered with diamonds, which her husband, I conclude, had won in South America during his adventurous career.

*February 18th.*—We left for London.

*February 19th.*—Mrs. Norton and Mrs. Blackwood are looking wonderfully handsome this year. I pointed them out to Madame Sebastiani, who was in great admiration of their beauty.

*February 22nd.*—Dined with the Duke of Devonshire, and met Lady Granville, Lady Burlington, Lord Elphinstone, William Cowper. He has offered Lady Fitzharris his boxes at the Opera and both theatres whenever she likes to ask for them.

*February 23rd.*—Left London for Brighton with Miss Kinnaird. Although it is but fifty-one miles, the stages are long and killing.

*February 24th.*—Brighton. The Effinghams, Gallweys, and Beauclercs are here ; Colonel Lyster and Francis Mills ; so we have a very pleasant knot of acquaintances. We shall stay here for three months, as I do not expect that London will be agreeable this year. Politics absorb everybody's thoughts, and party feeling is stronger than ever. The Government expect to be beaten to-night on the Irish Church, and, if they are, it is impossible to say what may happen. They cannot coalesce with the Tories, and are sure to do so with the Radicals. Lord John Russell has evidently joined O'Connell, for the latter dined at a public dinner to Lord John the other day, and flattered him in the most fulsome manner. It is said Peel does not intend to dissolve if beaten, but resign at once, in which case Lord Grey is to form an Administration. It is said that the King is quite firm, and will not hear of Whig government, but that, if he is forced to it, he will abdicate and go to Hanover. Who could have supposed five years ago that matters would arrive at such a pass, that such an idea could suggest itself to a King of England ?

*March 31st.*—The debate upon the Irish tithes began yesterday, and Lord John Russell proposed a resolution, of which he had given notice, to consider the present state of the Church Establishment in Ireland, with a view of applying any surplus of its revenue not required for the general purposes of the Church to the moral and religious instruction of the people.

*April 2nd.*—Nothing is yet known about the dissolution. Lord Grey says that the present Government would lose 110 votes by it, but that is evidently wrong. Poulett Thomson says thirty. The general opinion, however, is that Government would gain, but not sufficiently to justify the measure. Lord John Russell's speech is thought to be a bad one, and his proposition to send up the Address straight to the King, supposing the House passed it, without consulting the Lords was very coldly received. Peel is harassed and disgusted, as well he may be, and, it is thought, will resign on the first favourable occasion, in which case the King would send for Lord Melbourne, Lord Grey, or Lord Stanley. Poulett Thomson says that all the Opposition would vote against the latter. The debate has been again adjourned. The only good speech last night was Lord Stanley's ; it was very clever, but not at all conciliatory. He attacked the whole Opposition *en masse*, calling them a ' miscellaneous multitude,' and cut them up in the cleverest and bitterest manner. From the whole tenor of his speech, I think he will be obliged to join the Tories, as he has offended his former friends.

*April 3rd.*—Peel made a splendid speech this morning on Lord John Russell's resolution ; but all his eloquence was in vain. The ' miscellaneous multitude' were determined not to listen, and Ministers were beaten by a majority of 113—a larger one than was expected. The numbers that divided were—322 for the motion, 209 against it. I went up to London.

*April 7th.*—Lord John Russell's resolution passed the Commons yesterday by a majority of twenty-five. The Whigs are so certain of turning Peel out that they have already formed their Government, into which Lord Grey would force Lord Howick, though against their will. Lords Brougham, Palmerston, and Auckland are to be left out, but Lord Lansdowne stipulates for the latter, hitherto without success.

*April 8th.*—Lord John Russell moved yesterday in the House of Commons ' that it is the opinion of the House that no measure upon the subject of tithes can be satisfactory to Ireland which does not embody the principle contained in the foregoing resolution.' The House divided on this motion, and carried it by a majority of twenty-seven—285 against 258.   Sir Robert Peel made, as usual, an excellent speech.

*April 9th.*—Peel has resigned, and the King has sent for Lord Grey.   It is not yet known how the new Cabinet will be formed, but the King is said to be staunch against admitting any Radicals. Addresses are coming in from all parts of the country praying the King to continue Peel in his present office, and praying Peel not to resign.

*April 10th.*—Sir Robert Peel made a magnificent speech on Wednesday, the 8th, announcing his resignation and his reasons for it.   He was enthusiastically cheered from all parts of the House.   Even his enemies cannot help admiring him, and confess that he is a great man.   It is not yet known whom the King has chosen as a successor.   Lords Grey and Melbourne have had interviews with him.

*April 12th.*—Addresses are still pouring in from all parts of the country in immense numbers.   Peel's resignation has created a greater sensation and more alarm than any event in politics for many years.

*April 14th.*—If Lord John Russell takes office he must be re-elected for Devonshire, and Mr. Montague Parker is already canvassing against him, with every probability of success.   All sorts of rumours about persons and places, but not sufficiently well authenticated to be worth reporting.

*April 22nd.*—We dined with the Sebastianis.   One of his attachés asked me whether *la chasse au renard* was not *bien dangereuse.*   I answered, ' Mais oui ; on peut se casser le cou ! '   ' Oh, ce n'est pas cela que je veux dire,' answered he, ' car on peut aller doucement.   Mais n'est-ce pas que le renard se défend quelquefois et vous saute à la figure ? '

*April 26th.*—I hear that Lord Alvanley has called out O'Connell

for the language which he used in the House of Commons, calling
Lord Alvanley a *bloated buffoon.* O'Connell had left London for
Dublin only a quarter of an hour before Colonel Damer, who was
charged with the message, reached his house. Lord Alvanley told
Lord Tankerville that he did not mean to let the matter drop, and
that if O'Connell would neither fight nor apologise he would disgrace him in the eyes of the country.

During this month there was a large party at Mr. Compton's
to hunt with the Queen's staghounds, which were sent down to
the New Forest. Among them came Lord Cardigan and Mr.
Assheton Smith, both celebrated riders, and jealous of their reputation as such. I remember both at dinner on the day before
the hunt glaring at one another as if they were mortal enemies
about to fight the next day. Nor did they belie their looks, for
they rode a regular race till both their horses were completely exhausted, Lord Cardigan's going two or three hundred yards farther
than Assheton Smith's, and he thus claiming the victory. There
is a story of that impetuous Earl and of Lord Alvanley—namely,
that at the opening day at Melton, when they met on the field,
the latter, with his hat off, said to Lord Cardigan : ' I beg to
apologise to you not only for any past offences, but for all that I
may commit during the ensuing season.'

*May 4th.*—Lord Alvanley fought a duel to-day with Morgan
O'Connell. Lord Alvanley received three shots and only fired
two. The cause of the duel was an impertinent letter which
Morgan O'Connell sent to Lord Alvanley, in which he said that
he had challenged his father knowing that he would not meet him.
Lord Alvanley immediately sent Colonel Damer to make the
necessary arrangements, and the duel took place that same afternoon in a field near the Barnet Road. Lord Alvanley showed
great *sang froid* throughout, though Morgan O'Connell fired before
the signal was given. Lord Alvanley agreed to consider it as
a mistake, and they each fired two shots afterwards, Morgan
O'Connell jumping back, very much startled. Colonel Hodges
was his second. Mr. O'Connell saying he was satisfied after the
last two shots, Colonel Damer withdrew Lord Alvanley from the
field without his having made any apology or withdrawn what he
had said respecting Mr. Daniel O'Connell. When Lord Alvanley

E

paid the hackney coach which had brought him to the ground, he
gave the coachman a sovereign, saying : ' I give you that, not for
taking me here, but for having brought me back.'

It is said that Disraeli has called out Mr. Morgan O'Connell
this morning, in consequence of an abusive speech of his father
at Dublin, in which he said that Mr. Disraeli is probably a
descendant of the impenitent thief who was crucified with our
Saviour.

*May 6th.*—Mr. Montague Parker has just beaten Lord John
Russell by 674 for the county of Devon, which is the first turn
of fortune for the Tories. Mr. Morgan O'Connell refused to
fight Mr. Disraeli, who thereupon wrote a letter to Mr. Daniel
O'Connell of rather questionable taste and language, although
deserved.

Sir John Byng is to be made a peer (Lord Strafford). His
eldest son is canvassing Poole, and with such managers as Messrs.
Bonham and Ross, the Tory side will probably fail.

*May 16th.*—London is *en émoi* to-day on account of the
elopement of Miss Colquhoun Grant with Mr. Brinsley Sheridan.
The whole thing has been arranged for some time between the
parties, through Mrs. Norton, for Sir Colquhoun Grant would not
allow his daughter to speak to Mr. Sheridan. They could not
find an opportunity till Sir Colquhoun Grant left London to
canvass Poole. Mrs. Norton then called for Miss Grant and took
her to her house, where Mr. Sheridan was waiting, and they
started for Scotland.

*May 17th.*—We dined with the Sebastianis (the French Ambassador). He was employed by Napoleon I., both in the army
and diplomacy, and has a high reputation. He has married Lady
Tankerville's sister. He is extremely pompous and a boaster.
After being beaten by the Duke of Wellington at Talavera, his
mother used to say of him, ' Mon fils ressemble à un de ses
tambours—plus il est battu, plus il fait du bruit.' Sir Colquhoun
has returned to London to consult his lawyer, and to prosecute
the Sheridan family for conspiracy. His first step has been to
shoot Miss Grant's favourite horse.[1]

Mrs. Norton came to Mme. Sebastiani's party, wishing, I

---

[1] Sir C. Grant became completely reconciled to his son-in law.

suppose, to feel the world. She talked in a most extraordinary manner, and kicked Lord Melbourne's hat over her head. The whole *corps diplomatique* were amazed.

*May 19th.*—Mr. Spring Rice and Lord Wellesley have resigned, which must embarrass the Government considerably.

*May 26th.*—Went to the opera to see ' I Puritani,' a new opera by Bellini, which has been the rage at Paris the whole winter.

*June 5th.*—Poulett Thomson called to-day in great spirits. He assured us that Sir Robert Peel did not mean to oppose Municipal Reform, and that the bill would pass both Houses of Parliament without material alterations. I ventured to doubt the fact, and he offered to bet me 2 to 1 on it, which I accepted.

*June 6th.*—Upon reading Peel's speech, I am convinced that he does not intend to let the bill pass without great alteration, as he said he would not oppose its being brought in ; but that he reserved to himself a right of objecting to it in detail.

*June 19th.*—Went to Sion. The Duke of Wellington came up to me whilst I was walking with Lady C. Herbert, and asked me if I had been at Lady Antrobus's concert the night before. I answered that I had not, upon which the Duke turned to Lady C. and said : ' *You* were. Did we not send the French Ambassador to the right about ? ' alluding to the foolish conduct of Sebastiani, which was this:—The 18th of June being the anniversary of the battle of Waterloo, the Duke, as usual, gave a great dinner, at which the King was present. After dinner the Duke came to Lady Antrobus's party, and the moment he entered the room everybody rose, and the singers struck up ' Rule, Britannia,' set to Italian words, and alluding to him and his glorious victory. Marshal Sebastiani very foolishly chose to consider this as a personal affront, took his wife's arm and walked out of the house. It is a pity they should have done this, as they have made themselves ridiculous, and more unpopular than they are already. She is blind, he is dumb, and they give neither dinners nor parties—an unpardonable offence in their position.

*June 20th.*—Lady Tankerville called this morning, and says that Sebastiani is so angry at what he chooses to call an insult

that he declares he never will set foot in Lady Antrobus's house
again.

*June 29th.*—The papers to-day announce the death of the
famous Carlist chief, Zumalacarregui, who was killed before
Bilbao. This is an irreparable loss to the Carlist cause. The
Duke of Wellington expressed a very high opinion of his military
capacity.

*July 30th.*—News arrived yesterday of an attempt having
been made to assassinate Louis Philippe by an infernal machine
on the 28th. Marshal Mortier was killed and many others severely
wounded, but the King was untouched. The machine was placed
at an open window on the first floor of a wine-shop on the Boulevards, and was composed of thirty pistols loaded with slugs and
contrived so as to be all fired off at once. When the National
Guard broke into the house, they found that the assassins were
themselves wounded by the explosion, and arrested them. This
reminds me that poor Marshal Mortier was once the victim of a
clever robbery. He attended some great public dinner in a full
marshal's uniform, which was very handsome, being highly em-
broidered and covered with medals. One of the waiters, apparently
by accident, upset the contents of a whole sauce-boat over him,
upon which another waiter offered, if he retired for a moment and
took off his coat, to remedy the mishap. The Marshal did so,
waited a long time, but never saw his coat again.

*September 1st.*—Yesterday the discussion on the Corporation
Bill came on in the House of Commons. Lord John Russell
made a temperate speech, willing to let the bill pass if the Peers
would give up some of their amendments. The Radicals were,
of course, for throwing it out at once, but the Conservatives
mustered very strong, and the Radicals were not even listened
to. Peel supported Lord John and threw over the House of
Lords. He, however, would not consent to give up the clause
preventing Dissenters from naming to livings in the gift of
corporations.

*September 5th.*—There has been a meeting of Peers at the Duke
of Wellington's, and they were unanimous not to give up a single
point and furious with Peel. I fear they will spoil all by too
much obstinacy.

*September* 10*th.*—The Lords and Commons have had an interview and agreed to pass the Corporation Bill with the amendments of the Lords ; Ministers were so afraid of losing their places if they insisted on the Lords giving up any important clause.

Jules de Polignac told me that he was not half as culpable as we supposed, and that the fatal ordinances were entirely Charles X.'s making, and that, in fact, he is guilty of nothing but of too blind obedience to his King, to whom he is quite devoted. When the Chambers voted the address to the King, praying him to dismiss his Ministers, Charles X., instead of doing so, dissolved the Chambers. When they met again, Polignac, finding that the same members had been re-elected and that he consequently could not hope to carry on a Government, begged the King to accept his resignation. Charles X. refused, upon which Polignac said, ' Vous voulez donc ma tête, Sire ? ' The King answered most brutally, ' Et pourquoi pas ? '

## 1836

*January* 1*st.*—My youngest brother Charles announced to me that he was engaged to be married to the youngest daughter of Sir Edward O'Brien.[1] He has also determined on entering the Church.[2]

*February* 6*th.*—Lady Pembroke[3] and three daughters arrived at Heron Court. All in great beauty—Lady Mary and Lady Catherine as handsome women as can be seen. My father is their guardian, and has a great affection for the family.

*June* 22*nd.*—The trial of Lord Melbourne came on to-day, and in spite of strong evidence against him the jury gave their verdict in his favour. Mrs. Norton must consider herself very fortunate in being let off so easily. All the Whigs are in raptures, which provoked an old Tory to say that ' he really couldn't see why Lord Melbourne should be so triumphant at the verdict given, as it had

---

1 Afterwards Lord Inchiquin. He was father of the rebel.
2 He died in 1874, Bishop of Gibraltar.
3 Afterwards Lady Ailesbury, Lady Dunmore, and Lady Shelburne.

been proved that he had had more opportunities than any man
ever had before, and had made no use of them.

*July 25th.*—The 'appropriation clause' was carried yesterday
in the House of Commons, by a majority of twenty-six only.
Ministers expected a much larger majority, and could not disguise
their annoyance.

Alibaud's execution took place at Paris perfectly quietly, probably owing to the immense quantity of troops under arms. He had
improved upon the infernal machine of Fieschi, but was arrested
before he could use it. The King goes about in a bullet-proof
carriage.

The Constitution of 1812 has been proclaimed at Madrid, and
the Queen forced to acquiesce. Colonel Evans, who commands
the Westminster Legion in Spain, enrolled by Lord Palmerston
in defiance of international law, to assist Christina against Don
Carlos, is in a miserable state—defeated, his men starving and
destitute of clothing.

Lord Tankerville related to me to-day an anecdote respecting
Sir Philip Francis, whom Wraxall conjectures to have been the
author of 'Junius,' and which supposition was very well founded
and corroborated by many facts. It was supposed that he intended his name to be disclosed after his death, and had left
papers establishing his identity with 'Junius,' but they were destroyed by his son-in-law. He determined not to acknowledge
himself as the author of those letters during his life-time, and
disliked to be asked questions on the subject. One evening at
Brooks's, the conversation having fallen on a book just published
which proved Francis to be 'Junius,' Rogers, the poet, went up to
him and said, 'Sir Philip, will you allow me to ask you a question ?'
To which the other one replied very fiercely, 'Yes, sir, at your
peril.' Upon which, Rogers turned round to someone near him
and said, 'If he *is* "Junius," he is Junius Brutus.' Sir Philip
used to say that he had written memoirs which he meant to be
published after his death, which would be the ruin of every lady
in society, and have the effect of destroying all filiation, as he
clearly proved that not a single person was the son of his reputed
father.

*August 18th.*—Hunted with the staghounds at Chillingham ;

at least two hundred horsemen out. After a run of several miles the stag was lost in a large wood. It is a fine country to ride across, but dangerous from the coal-pits.

## 1837

*February 2nd.*—Address upon the King's speech moved in the Lords by the Duke of Wellington, and by Sir Robert Peel in the Commons. They attacked Lord Palmerston's foreign policy with respect to Spain, but neither moved any amendment.

*February 5th.*—French very indignant at no mention of them in King's speech. Their Government paper calls the omission an insult. No doubt the Ministers are angry with Louis Philippe because he will not go the length they do about Spain.

*February 9th.*—Debate on Irish Corporation Bill. O'Connell made a signal failure. His presence of mind seems to have deserted him. Debate adjourned.

*February 10th.*—Debate resumed. Sir Robert Peel made a splendid speech. Bill read first time without a division, our party reserving themselves for second reading. Whig papers threaten to indict Lord Ranelagh for high treason for joining Carlist army, which is absurd, as England has never declared war against Don Carlos, and he has as much right to join him as General Evans has to fight for Christina. Espartero still remains in Bilbao.

*February 23rd.*—Another plot discovered against the life of Louis Philippe. The assassin, called Champion, had constructed a machine after the plan of Fieschi's, but improved, the barrels being arranged in a semicircle and in three rows. The discovery took place by means of a person who lodged in the same house, and who, suspecting, from various circumstances, and also from some things told him by the maid (who was the mistress of Champion), that he was engaged in a plot against the King, wrote to Louis Philippe and to the police, and so the house was searched and the villain arrested, the machine being found nearly completed. He was taken to prison, where he contrived to hang himself with his neck-cloth, thus making it difficult to detect his accomplices.

*February* 24*th.*—I drove to Bournemouth to see the new buildings. It will be a large place some day.

Lord F. Egerton's amendment to the Irish Municipal Bill has been thrown out by a majority of 80, which I suppose puts an end to all idea of a dissolution.

*February* 25*th.*—A good deal of division exists amongst the Tories, who are very careless in their attendance, and who prefer their pleasures to their duties. Not so the Whigs, who are always ready to obey their leader's call, and never dream of thinking for themselves.

The King has declared that he won't dissolve for either party. Mrs. Norton made her *début* at Lady Minto's a few nights ago, and was very well received. Her reception had been made a party question; indeed, the whole business has been so from the beginning.

*March* 7*th.*—News from Spain very favourable to Carlists. Forcadel, a lieutenant of Cabrera's, has defeated near Valencia a corps of 3,000 Christinos. Their Brigadier, Aznar, with forty officers, were taken prisoners and shot after the engagement. Four of Evans's men have been taken prisoners and shot by the Carlists. These poor Englishmen are the more to be pitied as they had been forced to remain in the service against their will. At the expiration of a year, which was the term for which they had enlisted, they applied to General Evans to be sent home, but he refused their request. They belonged to a Scotch regiment, and their fate has produced a great sensation at St. Sebastian. Evans must bitterly reproach himself for his conduct to these poor soldiers, for the only way in which he could have obliged them to remain in Spain was by refusing to give them the pay due for their year's service, which would have enabled them to return to England. General ' Lazy ' Evans, as his soldiers now call him (his name being Lacy), after a great deal of blustering, threatening, and issuing ridiculous proclamations to the Basques, remains at St. Sebastian, as he has done for the last six months, and Espartero is inactive at Bilbao.

*March* 16*th.*—I published my pamphlet on the Basque War, which was an answer to one that came from our Embassy at Madrid.[1]

[1] The late Lord Carnarvon wrote a very interesting work on the Basque War and the *fueros.*

*March* 17*th*.—The attack on the Carlists has at last begun. Evans left St. Sebastian on the 10th with 12,000 men, and after several hours' hard fighting and great loss on both sides, succeeded in taking the heights of Asurzegana, the Carlists retreating to Hernani, where they intend to make a stand.

The Abolition of Church Rates Bill passed first reading, House of Commons, on the 15th, by a majority of only 23, which was considered a defeat.

*March* 19*th*.—Ministers, with the exception of Mr. Spring Rice, all voted for Mr. Clay's motion to abolish the Corn Laws. The motion was negatived in spite of the support of the Government.

*March* 21*st*.—Evans has been totally defeated ; a heavy fall of snow having made the mountain roads impassable, obliged Saarsfeld to retreat towards Pampelona. Don Sebastian immediately marched upon Evans, and after a severe engagement drove him and his whole army into St. Sebastian.

*March* 24*th*.—The heavy loss which Evans suffered would have been still greater if it had not been for the gallant conduct of our Marines, who, though not more than four or five hundred in number, withstood the attack of the whole Carlist army and protected his retreat, or, more properly speaking, his flight. His left flank had been turned, and his men offered hardly any resistance. The employment of our Marines by Lord Palmerston against a people who were fighting for their liberties, and with whom we were not at war, is another example of his contempt for international law.

---

I shall quote nothing more from my diary about the Carlist War, of which there is a great deal. Everyone knows how it ended. After an heroic defence of their *fueros*, the Basques were sold by their general, Marotto, and after a desultory resistance by Cabrera, who actually reached the gates of Madrid, the Northern provinces were subdued. Cabrera came to England, and, under the auspices of the Duchess of Inverness, married Miss Richards, a considerable heiress, which marriage turned out very well till his death. He had been a sacristan in Andalusia,

General Sir de Lacy Evans afterwards commanded a division in the Crimean War, and was esteemed a good officer ; but Marshal Pélissier told me that when a council of war was held after the battle of Inkerman to consider the necessity of abandoning the Crimea, he was the first to recommend it. The Marshal gave a very graphic description of the scene. He described Lord Raglan, as Commander-in-Chief, being the last to speak, in unusual agitation moving the stump of his lost arm convulsively, and when Pélissier voted for remaining, rushing up to him to shake hands, declaring that nothing would make him stir.

---

*April 8th.*—Received a requisition from Portsmouth. Met Count Pozzo di Borgo, Russian Ambassador at the Tuileries, and was struck with a remark he made as rather undiplomatic. I happened to say that I had been present at the opening of the House of Lords after the sudden dissolution of Parliament upon the rejection of the Reform Bill, when the King was nearly coming in a hackney coach to the House of Lords. Upon this he replied, ' Quand il a jeté sa couronne dans la poussière.' He is one of the cleverest of living diplomatists.

*April 19th.*— Lady Fitzharris and I started from London by steamer to Boulogne on our way to Paris.

*April 23rd.*—Reached Paris, and went to the Hôtel de Londres, Place Vendôme. Excellent apartments for forty francs a day.

*April 27th.*—We went with Lady Pembroke and Lady Mary Herbert (who was engaged to Lord Bruce) to the Champ de Mars races. Lord Pembroke famous for his turn-out. I never saw a handsomer equipage. His groom being asked by him whether he had exercised the horses, said : ' Yes, my Lord, I have walked them twenty times round Wyndham Place'—meaning Place Vendôme.

Lord Pembroke lives in great state at Paris, and is as famous for his cook as for his horses. He is a very handsome man.

Dined at Lord Granville's, our Ambassador. Lady Granville has made a rule to present no English at Court, so Lady

Fitzharris will be presented by her aunt, the Duchesse de Gramont.

*May 3rd.*—Madame Sebastiani took us to the Tuileries to present us. We entered by the Pavillon de Flore, which is a private entrance. After passing through several magnificent apartments, the Queen received us. She was sitting at a round table with Madame Adelaide and the Princess de Lieven. We were asked to sit down by the Queen, who talked a great deal to Lady Fitzharris. It was altogether the most formal business. Nothing could be kinder than the manner of the Queen and Madame Adelaide to both of us ; but I thought they behaved very coldly to Madame de Lieven, and appeared much more at their ease when she left. Madame de Lieven, after she had been ambassadress or rather ambassador in London, went to Paris, and her *salon* is one of the most agreeable, not only for fashion, but is one to which all the cleverest statesmen of the time resort. Guizot is never missing, and Molé generally there. Mademoiselle de Mensingen—a very handsome *chanoinesse*—presides at the tea-table, to which those who are young and careless of politics congregate. The other evening a very good-looking and smart gentleman was announced. The Princess stared at him, saying : ' Monsieur, je ne vous connais pas.' The poor man, looking very foolish, exclaimed, ' Comment, Madame ! Ne vous rappelez-vous pas, à Ems ? ' ' Non, Monsieur' —and she bowed him out. I never saw anything so cool ; but it was clear to the company, who could not conceal their smiles, that a gentleman who may be useful at Ems may be *de trop* at Paris.

*May 21st.*—I left Paris. It is high time I should look after Portsmouth. Nothing is talked of but the marriage of the Duke of Orleans. The Duchess is said to be plain. Palmyre, her dressmaker, has been ordered to make her gowns different from any that have ever been worn, and has accordingly invented one.

*May 24th.*—London. The Church-Rate Bill has passed by 287 to 282.

*May 27th.*—Finding it useless to go to Portsmouth till I can canvass the whole borough, I shall wait for the July registration, so returned to Paris, and found on arriving that my butler, named Stephens, whom I had taken from Madame Visconti, had gone off with a considerable quantity of property belonging to Lady

Fitzharris and me, of which he had the care. I sent for the Commissary of Police, who, after listening to the case, very coolly stated that as Stephens had been gone for two days he should probably not catch him, and in consequence of a book of poetry found in his room (I believe 'Byron'), that he was probably of a romantic nature, and had drowned himself in the Seine! The next morning he called to say that the thief was not to be found. I expected this from his former manner— evidently showing that he never meant to take him. The next day Lady Fitzharris's maid received a pathetic note from Stephens, praying her to save his life by bringing him that night his passport, which he had forgotten, to a certain bench in the Champs Elysées. I persuaded the girl with some difficulty to go, and I followed close behind her. It was a dark night, and when she came up to the seat I went round it, collared, and threw him. He made no resistance, and I brought him to our house. I sent again for the Commissary, and, showing him Stephens, I said, ' Je suis obligé, Monsieur, de faire votre besogne.' He was furious, but walked out of the room with his prisoner, who I afterwards ascertained was one of the principal and regular *mouchards* of the police. Hence the attempt to save him.[1]

*June 11th.*—Having been invited to the *fêtes* at Versailles for the Duke of Orleans' marriage, we went to the Gramonts, who have a house there. On presenting my ticket at the *Musée*, I was told that foreigners were not to be admitted. On appealing to Madame de Flahault, she said that a mistake had been made. It was first intended to invite them, but it turned out that there was not sufficient room, as one hundred more people had been asked than could be accommodated at the dinner, and of course they had to give way to the heroes of July.

In the evening we were admitted to the presence of the Royal Family. The Duchess of Orleans is not pretty, but graceful, and looks very young. We then all went to the theatre, where there was plenty of room. A great many more might have been invited, yet the *coup d'œil* was splendid—the theatre being nearly as large as Drury Lane, and every one in full dress—the ladies covered with diamonds, the gentlemen in uniform.

[1] Stephens was tried and condemned to two years' imprisonment.

The company invited to dinner sat on the *balcon.* In the seats behind were ladies, the Chamber of Peers and Deputies, and above were all the foreigners. Half the pit was appropriated to the Royal Family and their suite. The performance began by the 'Misanthrope,' which, though beautifully acted, was a terrible bore. Mademoiselle Mars was perfect. Afterwards two acts of 'Robert le Diable,' in which Dupré, the tenor, sang splendidly. The whole concluded with a ballet, in which one scene represented Versailles as it was in Louis XIV.'s time, giving a most complete idea of the magnificence of those glorious days of France when the King himself danced in a ballet !

*June 12th.*—Returned to Paris and heard a very bad account of our King.

*June 15th.*—No hope of our King's recovery. A horrible accident has happened in the Champ de Mars during the military representation of storming a fort ; and the ball at the Palace is put off in consequence of thirty people having been crushed to death. It made a serious impression on the Duchess of Orleans, who looked on it as a bad omen at her marriage. The Duke is extremely kind and civil to me, and asked me to hunt at Chantilly. The stag broke away from the forest, and took us nearly to Beauvais. His Royal Highness presented me with the foot, which the artist Susse has turned into a pen-rack. The Duke also gave me the buttons of his hunt. The costume is dark blue with a red collar, his crown and initials on silver buttons.

*June 21st.*—Our King died yesterday between two and three o'clock. Everybody regretted him, for he was a good man, though not a great king. He showed much firmness and composure in his last moments, and it is said that, two days before he died, being the anniversary of the battle of Waterloo, the Duke of Wellington had sent him, according to custom, the banner by which he holds his estates. Lord Munster, thinking to please him, brought it to him, when the poor King, though almost expiring, raised himself up, seized the folds of the flag in his hand, and exclaimed, 'Ah, that was a glorious day for England.' These were his last words, and well worthy of an English king.

*June 22nd.*—Left Paris for Portsmouth.

I repaired to Portsmouth, in consequence of a requisition, and stood for the seat in conjunction with the celebrated Admiral Sir George Cockburn ; his nephew, Mr. Cockburn,[1] being our legal agent. We canvassed Portsmouth for three weeks during the hottest July I ever remember, and at the election were deserted and thrown over by many of the very men who had signed the requisition. Almost immediately afterwards I received one from Christchurch, which I declined. A sharp contest took place there between Sir George Rose (Tory) and Colonel Cameron, a Liberal, in which the latter was defeated. Since that time, another Reform Bill has added the new town of Bournemouth to the borough of Christchurch, which has completely swamped it. My brother, Capt. Harris, R.N., sat for it for eight years.

---

*September* 18th.—Arrived at Chillingham, where Lord and Lady Stanley came, and I made his acquaintance for the first time. He is very amusing, and with his high spirits and cleverness kept a large party in roars of laughter.

Poulett Thomson, who was there, was the victim of his jokes, but all made so good-humouredly that it was impossible to be angry.

*September* 21st.—Went out partridge shooting with Lord Stanley, and I think we have taken a decided liking to one another. The Stanleys leave to-morrow, and we are to pay them a visit at Knowsley on our way South.

*October* 19th.—Left Chillingham for Howick. Found Poulett Thomson and Bear Ellice and the family. Lord Grey bitter against the present Government. I asked P. Thomson what the Earl's politics were at present, and his answer was : 'What they always have been—Charles Lord Grey.' The evening was formal, but all the family very kind. Lord Clanricarde was one of the party.

*November* 1st.—Dined with Sebastiani, where we met the Duke and Duchess of Terceira. She is the daughter of the unfortunate Marquis de Loulé, who was murdered by Don Miguel.

---

[1] Afterwards Lord Chief Justice of England.

*November* 17*th*.—Took the Duke and Duchess of Terceira to the House of Lords to hear the Queen's speech—her first one—which Her Majesty delivered in a very clear and distinct voice.

*November* 20*th*.—Parliament is only to be prorogued to January 16, instead of to February 1, in consequence of the bad news that has been received from Canada. The long-expected insurrection has broken out, and the English troops have been defeated at St. Denis. The whole number of troops in that province does not amount to 4,000 men, and the insurgents include nine-tenths of the population. Constant defeat must therefore be expected, for it will be impossible to send reinforcements to Canada for five months to come. Ministers are terribly frightened. They will have great difficulty in finding excuses for their culpable negligence, as they have been repeatedly warned of what was likely to happen if they delayed any longer in taking decided steps for the safety of the Colony.

*November* 27*th*.—The news from Canada is better to-day, although there is no doubt that Colonel Gore's detachment was beaten at St. Denis. The affair was of very little importance, the number of troops engaged not amounting to more than 200, and Col. Wetherell, who commanded another party, in attacking St. Charles gained a complete victory, and made a great slaughter of the rebels.

## 1838

*January* 1*st*.—For the last few days the news from Canada has been very good. The insurrection seems to be nearly suppressed. Papineau has fled, and it is said that Colonel Browne has been murdered by his own party for cowardice. Troops are, however, going out to Canada as soon as possible, and, in order that their arrival should be more certain and speedy, they are to be sent out in frigates instead of transports.

*January* 25*th*.—The news from Canada continues very favourable. Sir John Colborne has been perfectly successful in his attack upon St. Eustache and Grand Bulé; both of which places he has taken and burned with very little loss on his side.

*January* 26*th.*—I killed five white-fronted geese to-day, stalking them with a pony, which is the only way of getting near them.

*January* 29*th.*—Sir Robert Peel having obliged the Government to consent to adopt his amendment to their Canada Bill; they did it with enough ill grace to show that their doing so was compulsory.

*January* 31*st,* *February* 1*st,* 2*nd,* *and* 3*rd.*—The American Radical papers are in a state of the greatest fury with this country, and are doing all they can to incite their countrymen to a war, because a party of Canadians attacked and captured a steamboat, the ' Caroline,' belonging to the rebels at Navy Island, which they had bought for the purpose of transporting men and arms to the island. Even if it had belonged to the Americans, the Royalists had a perfect right to take it, as it was employed against them, by every law of neutrality. The American papers are making themselves very ridiculous, threatening vengeance, and writing the most absurd tirades.

*February* 4*th.*—The news from Canada continues very satisfactory, the American Government being evidently averse to war with England, and anxious to preserve neutrality by all the means in their power. The President even goes so far as to demand additional power to be vested in the executive force in order to compel the population on the frontiers to abstain from any acts of aggression. The news of the capture and burning of the ' Caroline' had reached the Government ; there had been a debate in Congress on the subject, and the almost universal feeling seemed to be that we were justified in our attack upon that vessel, as the Americans had been themselves the first to infringe the neutrality laws. The destruction of the Emperor of Russia's Winter Palace at St. Petersburg by fire has occurred ; then the Italian Opera House in Paris ; and within the next few days the palace of the Duke of Würtemberg, which the Duchess (a daughter of Louis Philippe) was supposed to have caused, as it was in her room the fire originated. The Duchess has lost all her jewels and *trousseau.*

*February* 5*th.*—I killed four wild swans to-day.[1] An immense

---

[1] I shot thirty-two of these splendid birds during this severe winter, some of

flight—I counted sixty—passed over my head, and a beautiful sight it was. They alighted a long way up the river Avon. I followed them, when, after waiting for some time longer, I saw the whole flight get up again and fly backwards and forwards, dividing into several parties, then unite again, some ending by alighting again in the Avon, but further down, and the others in the direction of the Moor's River, screaming like a pack in full cry. The cold was intense. The river was choked with mountains of ice and snow, so the scene was very striking. Hundreds of wildfowl were flying about, seeking for a resting-place where the water was open—some very rare species.

*February 14th, 15th, and 16th.*—News has been received of the evacuation of Navy Island by the rebels, on the evening of January 14 ; and of the returning of the cannon to General Eyre, the American officer in command of the frontier. The American Government seems sincere in its professions of neutrality, but the citizens have behaved infamously.

*February 26th.*—Lord Maidstone brought forward his motion to-day against O'Connell, and carried it by a majority of nine in a House of over five hundred members. He then moved that O'Connell should be reprimanded by the Speaker, upon which Lord John Russell got up in a passion, and said such a course was a most shabby ending to the proceedings of the Conservatives. This greatly disappointed O'Connell and his party, who had made up their minds to be sent to the Tower in a body, and thereby to excite a popular cry in their favour, as in the case of Sir Francis Burdett, who was escorted to the Tower by all the ragamuffins in London. The Conservatives observed a firm front, and the Government, seeing that they would be beaten, moved the adjournment of the House. Two divisions took place, and, although the Government were beaten each time, Sir Robert Peel, seeing that they were determined to continue dividing, agreed to postpone the discussion on Lord Maidstone's resolution until the following day.

*February 27th.*—The Government brought down to-day every man they could muster—sick, halt, and blind—but notwithstand-

which were of a smaller species, called Bewick's Swan, weighing about 10 lbs., whilst the Hoopers reached 25 lbs.

ing all their exertions were beaten by a larger majority than last
night.   In the first division the Conservatives had a majority of
24, and in the second 29, upon which the Ministers, seeing that
they were losing by continuing to divide the House, gave up the
point.

*February* 28*th.*—I went to Mr. Landseer's, to whom Lady
Fitzharris gave a sitting of two hours.   He is very anxious to
finish her picture for the Exhibition.   It has been very much
admired, and Lord Conyngham, amongst others, was so pleased
with it that he mentioned it to the Queen, who desired that we
should send it to her as soon as finished, so that I have no doubt
his vanity will stimulate Mr. Landseer to exert himself to do his
best.

*March* 9*th.*—Left London at 11 A.M., and arrived at Dover at
7.30 in the evening, although coming all the way with four horses.
We went to the York Hotel, which we found very comfortable
and particularly quiet.

*March* 10*th.*—Embarked at 8 A.M. on board the 'Duke of
Wellington' steamer for Boulogne.   There were not more than five
or six passengers besides ourselves.

*March* 18*th.*—The first people I met at Paris were Count
Pahlen, and then the eternal M. de Bonneval, whom I can never
see without thinking of the Duc de Richelieu's observation about
his success at masquerades :—' Bonneval a toujours un succès fou
aux bals masqués, car il est si bête que tout le monde s'adresse à
lui, étant bien sûr de n'être pas reconnu.'   Mme. le Hon, who is
said to be M. de Morny's *belle*, is a handsome fair woman, and at
the head of all the fashion.   Went to a *tableau* given by Mrs.
Locke.   It was not begun when we arrived, but we were not kept
waiting long before being admitted into the room where the stage
was erected.   The first *tableau* represented a scene in 'Les
Brigands,' in which Lady Wallscourt, Mrs. Locke's little girl,
Mademoiselle Dentici, an Italian, and M. Antonin de Noailles
performed.   There were three *tableaux*, all pretty, particularly
the last, which was taken from Lord Byron's 'Parisina.'   Lord
Douglas represented Hugo, looking very handsome ; Miss Raikes
was Parisina, and did it remarkably well.   Count Zichy acted
the part of the husband, and M. Antonin de Noailles that of the

executioner, but all with the exception of Miss Raikes were seized with an unfortunate fit of laughter as soon as the curtain was drawn, occasioned by the Duchesse de Poix exclaiming, ' Ah ! le bel homme !'—a remark which she applied to Count Zichy, who laughed to that degree that he rolled in his chair, which was peculiarly unlucky, as he ought to have looked the stern and unbending tyrant. The curtain was closed for a few minutes to give them time to recover, and when they had regained their composure they went through their parts with great effect. I also saw the famous Madame Martinetti, who was mistress to Napoleon in his first campaign in Italy. She is now sixty-five, but does not appear to be more than forty, her face being still very handsome, and her figure like that of a young woman.

*March 24th.*—We went to Princess Lieven's, where there was rather a pleasant party. I saw M. Guizot for the first time. He is a very remarkable-looking man, ugly, but with a very sharp, clever countenance, though with the expression of the old Puritans.

*April 7th.*—Lady Fitzharris went to see her cousin Adèle, Superior of the Convent of the Sacré Cœur, who made a violent attack upon her Protestant religion. To make up for all the harsh things she said, she proposed to her to go and see the corpse of the Archbishop of Toulouse, who had died in the convent a day before. She assured her he was ' dressed,' and not at all a disagreeable object ; notwithstanding which we made our escape as quick as possible, determined not to return to the convent until he is buried, as Adèle is quite capable of having him brought to us, if we don't go to him. Went to Princess Lieven's in the evening and found M. Guizot there ; M. Berryer, the famous Royalist lawyer, and Lord Brougham, who kept everyone in a roar of laughter by the absurd things he said in his bad French. Amongst others, talking of the Princess Charlotte having run away from her nurse to her mother, he said : ' Dans ce temps-là j'ai passé un nuit avec Madame de Flahault—un nuit très agréable entre elle et la fille du Roi.' Everybody was amazed at this speech : poor Madame de Flahault looked perfectly horrified. Madame de Lieven, with all her good breeding, could not keep from laughing, and of course the rest followed her ex-

ample. It is quite decided that M. de Flahault is not to go to
England as ambassador, and the King has named Marshal Soult,
and Soult thanked him for his appointment. The King said :
' You must not thank me ; it is the young Queen of England who
has asked for you.' Madame Graham came up to Lady Fitzharris
in the evening, when she was sitting by Madame de Lieven, and
said : ' Eh bien, miladi, quel est l'amoureux que vous voulez que
je vous amène—choisissez ? ' Mr. Raikes, who heard this wonderful speech, said, alluding to the report that Madame Graham
was formerly a milliner, ' Cela est plus modiste que modeste.'

*April 27th.*—Dined with the Sebastianis ; the Marshal in a
bad humour, and dinner went off heavily.

*May 1st.*—Nobody at Madame de Lieven's this evening except
the faithful M. Guizot, so we went on to Madame de Ségur. I hear
the Duke de Valenciennes will not go to England with Marshal
Soult, as he does not like that M. Airgues, who is appointed Secretary to the Embassy, should have the *pas* over him. This would not
have been the case under the old *régime*, as gentlemen who accompanied an Ambassador Extraordinary were never designated
as Attachés, but simply as *gentilshommes*, which left them precedence according to their rank. Now the appellation of *gentil-
homme* is prohibited, and all who accompany the Ambassador
must go as Attachés, which of course places them below the
Secretary to the Embassy. We went to the reception at the
Tuileries this evening at eight o'clock with Madame Sebastiani,
but notwithstanding that we started so early, all the seats were
taken, and we had to stand the whole time. It was a very fine
sight, and, though a great fatigue, we are glad we went. The
crowd was very great, but the apartments were so large that we
suffered no inconvenience, except not getting seats, for there was
no pushing and scrambling such as I saw at the Queen's Drawing Rooms in England. The reception also took place in the
evening, and it was very pretty, owing to the effect on both the
complexions and the dresses of the ladies, which look much
better by candlelight. .

*May 9th.*—Dined at home with Lord Douglas. We went at
eight to the Russian Ambassador's to fetch the Sebastianis, and
from thence to the Tuileries, where there were a good many

people. All the chairs were occupied; but the Queen ordered Lady Fitzharris to be placed next to her, and talked to her the greatest part of the time we remained.

*May 12th.*—We dined at the Tuileries, and I was introduced to the Duchess of Orleans. The King came in soon after six, and immediately led the Duchess of Orleans to dinner. The Queen followed with the Duke of Würtemberg, the Duke of Nemours with the Duchess of Würtemberg, the Duke of Orleans with the Princess Clementina, and one of the unknown Bavarians fell to Lady Fitzharris. The dinner was in the Galérie de Diane, and everything of course was very handsome in the way of plate; but the dinner itself was execrable, and the wine the same. The attendance was very perfect, every person at table having a servant behind their chair, whose sole duty it was to wait upon them. The dinner lasted very little more than an hour. We all returned to the room where the Queen received, and everybody remained standing while coffee was served. I was near Mme. Sebastiani, to whom the King was talking, and I overheard her say 'Oui, Monseigneur,' and very foolishly, instead of letting it pass as a slip of the tongue, said : ' Ah, pardon, sire ; c'est sire que je voulais dire.' The King answered : ' Mais, vous n'avez pas d'excuses à me faire ; c'est bien naturel que vous m'appeliez " Monseigneur ; " il y a beaucoup de personnes qui le font, c'est une méprise bien excusable.' She then tried to get out of it by saying that, having sat at dinner next to the Duke of Orleans, she had got into the habit of saying it, and forgot that she was no longer talking to him. The King again repeated : ' C'est très excusable ; vous avez été habituée pendant si longtemps à m'appeler " Monseigneur," que la méprise est bien naturelle.'

*May 16th.*—I went to Chantilly, where the Duke of Orleans entertained a party very handsomely.

*May 21st.*—I returned from Chantilly. The Duke of Orleans was extremely kind and civil, and on the day of the hunt, having arrived before the other foreigners at the taking of the stag, he gave me the foot as a souvenir of himself and of Chantilly. We dined afterwards at the Rothschilds, where we met the Sebastianis, the Apponyis, Lord Granville, Marshal Soult, &c.

*May 22nd.*—Prince Talleyrand's funeral took place this morn-

ing at the Church of the Assumption. There was a great crowd
collected to see the procession, and of course a large military force
to prevent any disturbance. He died on the 17th, having received
the sacraments, although during his life he was supposed to have
been an unbeliever, and in fact did not deny it. His memoirs,
which must be most curious, are not to be published for twenty
years.[1] He received the sacraments from M. Dupanloup.

*June 7th.*—I hear there have been dreadful riots in Kent.
The country people had been persuaded by a madman calling
himself Sir William Courtney that he and they were invulnerable,
and accordingly they fought desperately, and, in spite of their
inferiority in numbers and arms to their opponents, would not give
in until Courtney and eight or nine of their side had been killed.
Lieutenant Bennett was killed by Courtney in the act of rushing
upon him. Courtney was immediately shot by the soldiers, after
which the rioters attacked them with such ferocity that they were
obliged to fire in self-defence. This morning Louis Philippe had
a review of the troops of the Line garrisoned at Paris. He
stationed himself near the Obelisk at the Place Louis Quinze, and
they all passed by *en grande tenue.* Before the attempts were
made to murder the King, the reviews used to take place on the
Boulevards ; now they are always in the Place Louis Quinze,
where he is as safe as in his palace, for not a single carriage or
foot passenger is allowed to approach him, and guards are placed
in all the streets leading to the Place, who stop everybody without
any exception. The Gardens of the Tuileries are closed, so that
the road from the Palace along the Quays is quite safe, the river
being on one side and the empty gardens on the other.

*June 14th.*—We left Paris at twelve, stopped for an hour at
Beauvais to dinner, and reached Grandvilliers at nine.

*June 15th.*—Reached Montreuil at seven ; got along very
slowly, as there was much travelling on the road and a deficiency
of postboys.

*June 16th.*—Reached Calais at four.

*June 17th.*—Embarked on board the ' Ocean,' a large steamer
with bad accommodation. The sea was smooth. Amongst the
passengers there was a man who said he was returning for the

---

[1] They are not published yet, 1884.

coronation, which he was to attend as a page. He talked of nothing but Italy, himself, and his travels, telling many marvellous stories which his audience swallowed with the greatest readiness.

*June 18th.*—Found London occupied by the duel which had just taken place between Lord Castlereagh and M. de Melcy, Grisi's husband, in which the former was wounded in the wrist. It is said M. de Melcy intercepted a letter from Lord Castlereagh to his wife, and immediately called him out.[1]

*June 27th.*—Owing to the Queen's coronation, I never saw anything like the state of the streets to-day. It was nearly impossible to move along them for postboys and strings of carriages going at a foot's pace. They are stopped up at every turn by carts carrying planks for the scaffoldings that are being erected along the line of the Coronation procession.

*June 28th.*—The coronation took place to-day. We called for Poulett Thomson, who accompanied us to the Board of Trade. The Government, or rather Lord John Russell, had given no orders to the police to make carriages keep the line, and there was in consequence a good deal of confusion, coachmen cutting in, &c. But the day was so very fine, and the appearance of the streets so new to us, as we had never been in London during a coronation, that we were in no hurry to arrive. The crowd was in perfect good humour, and behaved very quietly. We reached the Board of Trade at ten, when the firing of cannon announced that the Queen had left the Palace, and at about eleven the procession appeared in sight. It was a magnificent show, though we had to thank the foreign ambassadors for a great part of its splendour, as without them the procession would have been very little more brilliant than when the Queen goes down to the House of Lords to open Parliament. The only people cheered besides the Queen were the Duchess of Kent, the Duke of Sussex, the Duke and Duchess of Cambridge, and Marshal Soult. The latter was quite overcome by his reception, which was entirely unexpected by him, and he said it was a most noble trait in the English character to receive an old enemy so enthusiastically, for the cheering proceeded from all classes.

[1] Lord Castlereagh appeared at the Opera the same night.

*August 4th.*—I started for the Isle of Skye with Mr. Compton, M.P. for South Hants, and arrived at Oban on the 10th. I found the state of the population rather deteriorated than otherwise since my last visit. The crofters seem to have entirely worked out their little plots and have no manure to refresh them. Lord Macdonald has done all he could to improve their position by building new and clean cottages ; but so fond are they of their old state of dirt, that they pulled up the planks of the floor, preferring to lie on the bare ground. What is to be done with these Celts ?

*August 29th.*—I returned to Chillingham Castle.

*October 4th.*—At a great agricultural dinner at Wooler ; from thence I went to Cornhill to fish for salmon in the Tweed. I killed seventeen in one day.

*October 20th.*—The papers to-day announce Lord Durham's resignation of the Governorship of Canada. Mr. Poulett Thomson, who was staying at Chillingham, shot one of the wild bulls in the park, which is considered high treason by Lord Tankerville. Mr. Thomson, thinking it was not known, was thunderstruck at seeing a long account of his performance in the 'Newcastle Journal,' which his host read out at breakfast and covered him with confusion.

*November 8th.*—I left Chillingham for London. This is a journey of four days, with four horses and well-paid postboys. The inns on the road are most of them as comfortable as one's own house, quiet and very well served, with generally good wine, and the landlord attending in person. Horses are changed in four minutes, as the relays stood at the door, with the postboys ready mounted.

*December 3rd.* — Another insurrection has broken out in Canada, and Sir John Colborne has proclaimed martial law—a vigorous measure, which Lord Durham never would have dared to resort to.

*December 5th.*—Good news from Canada. There has been an engagement between the rebels and the volunteer forces commanded by Colonel Taylor, which ended in the total defeat of the former after two hours' hard fighting. Mr. Ellice and some other gentlemen who had been taken prisoners made their escape ;

those who had been left to guard them having run away. Sir John Colborne marched against the rebels, but they did not wait for him. The insurrection is at an end. Lord Durham has arrived in London and looks quite subdued. He must be greatly vexed, now that he hears how easily the rebellion in Canada has been quelled, that he did not remain, for he would have got all the credit Colborne has obtained, and without any risk whatever; Quebec and Montreal having remained perfectly quiet.

*December 23rd.*—We went to Wilton. There is a very large party now staying in the house; among them being the Count and Countess Woronzow. Madame Woronzow is now old. She is clever and agreeable, but evidently very much afraid of Lady Pembroke, before whom she is silent and reserved. Count Woronzow is still a very handsome man, and quite the Russian grandee. The whole party is occupied in rehearsing a play that is to be acted next week.

*December 27th.*—We left Wilton for Savernake; a charming villa belonging to Lord Bruce in the Park at Tottenham, and I should think much preferable as a residence to the great house.

# 1839

*February 5th.*—Parliament opens to-day.

*February 6th.*—The Queen's Speech was a very poor composition as usual. The Ministers dare not make any allusion to the Corn Laws. Nothing is said respecting the dreadful state of Ireland; very little about Canada, and that little evidently framed to avoid giving offence to Lord Durham, attributing the suppression of the disturbance to the valour of the troops and the loyalty of the inhabitants. Not a word in praise of Sir John Colborne.[1]

*February 7th.*—The debate yesterday on the Address was a triumphant one for the Opposition. Peel made a splendid speech in favour of the Corn Laws, turning Mr. Wood, the seconder of

---

[1] Sir J. Colborne commanded the celebrated 52nd Regiment in the Peninsula and at Waterloo.

the Address, into ridicule.   Mr. Heathcote, hitherto a supporter
of the Government, declared in favour of the present system of
the Corn Laws, and none of our side, with the exception of Peel,
said a word.   Tommy Duncombe proposed an amendment to the
effect that the Reform Bill didn't go far enough.   It was opposed
by the Government, and thrown out on a division by a majority
of 426 to 86.   The debate in the House of Lords was equally in
our favour.   The Duke of Wellington made an excellent speech,
and Lord Brougham a very eloquent one, in which he inveighed
against O'Connell in the strongest terms.   A meeting took place
at Sir Robert Peel's two days before, at which he implored the
Conservatives to be united and not to split upon minor differences
*with respect to the Corn Laws, declaring himself in favour of the
present system, against fixed duty or any alteration whatever.*   My
father received to-day a letter from Milan, which makes it
necessary that I should proceed there immediately.   I shall have
a very fatiguing and tiresome journey at this time of year, as the
weather is as bad as possible.

*February 22nd.*—I arrived at Paris with my uncle, Admiral
Dashwood, on the 19th, after a very tedious journey, the roads
being hardly passable and like nothing except a ploughed field.
Lord Ebrington has been appointed to the Lord Lieutenancy of
Ireland.   It is the old story of the mountain and the mouse, for,
judging by the boasting language of Poulett Thomson, that their only
difficulty was *embarras de richesses*, I expected at least the Duke
of Sussex or the Duke of Sutherland.   Lord Ebrington is to be
called up to the House of Lords by the title of Baron Fortescue,
which will make a vacancy in the representation of North
Devon, and there is no doubt that the Opposition will gain the
seat.

*March 11th.*—Reached Milan to-day.   The debate on Mr.
Villiers' motion terminated by a triumph for the Conservatives;
195 voted for the motion and 342 against, giving a majority of
147.

*March 25th.*—I returned to England, having succeeded in the
object of my journey, through deep snow.

*April 7th.*—Lord Ossulston arrived from Paris, and amused us
very much with the accounts of his journey.   He travelled in

company with Lord Brougham and Mr. Leader ; the former going under the name of Mr. Edmunds, and Mr. Leader as the young Edmunds. At every inn they stopped at, if it was only for a few minutes, Lord Brougham got out to write a letter to some lady or other. He is more mad than ever.

*April 15th.*—Lord John Russell brought forward this afternoon his motion in support of the Irish policy of the Government. I went to Lord Clanwilliam's, where there was a large concourse of Herberts and Woronzows assembled to see a conjurer. I sat by the great heiress, the young Countess Potocka, who was rather good-looking—one may say beautiful, considering that she has above forty thousand a year.

*May 7th.*—The division on the Jamaica Bill took place this morning. The Ministers had only a majority of five against Peel's amendment. A Cabinet Council was held a few hours afterwards, at which the Ministers decided to tender their resignations to the Queen. Poulett Thomson wrote me a note at half-past two from the Council announcing the news. Lord Melbourne had announced his resignation in the House of Lords, and added that the Queen had accepted it. Lord John Russell made the same announcement in the Commons, omitting the last important fact. I afterwards met Thomson, who said that the Queen had sent for Lord Spencer, who would of course advise her to send for Peel, as none but a Tory Government could stand.

*May 8th.*—The Duke of Wellington and Sir Robert Peel were sent for to-day by the Queen, who received them most graciously, and gave the latter a *carte blanche* to form an Administration.

*May 9th.*—Sir Robert Peel had an audience with the Queen yesterday, lasting for three hours. She received him very kindly and said she would not conceal from him that she was much grieved at parting with her old Government, but she felt it was necessary, and the good of the country was her first object, superseding every other consideration whatever ; she had perfect confidence in him, and would act fairly towards him, and give him every assistance in her power to carry on the Government. The list of the Cabinet is to be out to-night.

*May 10th.*—Sir Robert Peel has resigned in consequence of the Queen refusing to change her ladies. Went to the Queen's

ball. The Queen danced a quadrille with the Grand Duke of
Russia. He is far from being handsome—has a great deal of the
Calmuck in his features, and, though of a fine height, he stoops,
which gives him an awkward appearance. I talked for some time
to Pozzo di Borgo, who is in a terrible state about Sir Robert Peel's
resignation. The Duke of Wellington came downstairs as we
were waiting for the carriage, and spoke most affectionately to us.
Everybody at the ball seemed anxious and pre-occupied. The
men, instead of making themselves agreeable to the ladies, were
assembled in groups all over the rooms talking earnestly ; and
people disseminated every sort of fabrication—saying that Peel
wanted to turn away the Baroness Lehzen, &c. Lord Normanby
had said openly at the dinner which Lord Palmerston gave the
day Peel accepted office that he was determined his wife should
not be dismissed, and that he would take good care she was not.

*May 13th.*—Sir Robert Peel made his explanation to the
House of Commons, which was perfectly satisfactory to his party,
proving his conduct to have been most honourable, his demands
very moderate, and their rejection by the Queen perfectly inconceivable, except under the supposition, which now amounts almost
to a certainty, that she has been misled by a party, and that she ·
was told to refuse to give up *any of her ladies*, which Lord
Melbourne and his colleagues knew that Peel would not agree to,
and that he would therefore be obliged to resign, as has been the
case. The House was very crowded, and Peel loudly cheered by
the whole of his party when at the termination of his speech he
appealed to them for an approval of his conduct. The Ministers
looked in very good spirits before he began, but as he proceeded,
the clearness of his statement and the strong case he made out in
favour of the extreme moderation of his demands, produced a
sensible change in his opponents' countenances. It turns out that,
far from having required 'the dismissal of the whole of the
household and the friends who had surrounded the Queen from
childhood '—meaning the Baroness Lehzen [1]—Peel only wished to
dismiss the wives and sisters of the Cabinet Ministers, and only
those who were of the rank of ladies of the bedchamber and
above that rank, but none below. The number dismissed would

[1] The Queen's governess,

not therefore have exceeded three or four. The opinion that Lord Melbourne's resignation was a sham gains ground every day. Even Lord John Russell's reply to Peel confirms it, as he admits that a Cabinet Council was held on the Thursday, at which Lord Melbourne and his colleagues agreed that the Queen ought not to give up her ladies, and drew up a paper to that effect. Lord Melbourne also wrote a letter to Peel, informing him of her determination not to do so, in consequence of which he sent her his resignation on Friday. The Ministers are, therefore, proved by their own evidence to have given this advice after they were no longer responsible, or in other words by an intrigue on their part.

*May 27th.*—The House of Commons met to-day for the first time since the holidays, and chose Mr. Shaw-Lefevre as Speaker by a majority of 18 votes against Mr. Goulburn, the Tory candidate.

*May 31st.*—Lord Brougham has made a very clever and bitter speech against the Government. He reproached them with having given the Queen treacherous and unconstitutional advice, and with having circulated lies all over the country, which, though they were contradicted by Lord Melbourne and Lord John Russell, were repeated by their friends. He attacked O'Connell, and said if the Government leaned upon him for support they deserved the contempt of the country, but if they raised him to the Bench they deserved to be impeached. His speech was the most damaging to the Government of any made this session. Lord Melbourne bore it good-humouredly, and made a Conservative declaration which will probably lead to his again resigning, as the Radicals are almost sure to throw him over.

*June 7th.*—We went to the Opera. Heard Mario di Candia, an officer in the Piedmontese army, of noble family, who has taken to the stage. He has a beautiful-toned voice, but not strong enough to fill the theatre, and his style and execution are unfinished ; but as he is still very young he will probably improve both in his acting and singing.

*June 18th.*—Mr. Grote's motion for the ballot was negatived by a majority of 333 votes to 215. Lord John Russell and Lord Howick both voted against the motion.

*July 4th.*—Lady Flora Hastings is dying, and the dinner at the Palace put off in consequence. The Ministers are becoming more unpopular every day ; even the Duke of Wellington is losing all patience, and made a violent speech on the subject of the late riots at Birmingham. He said, alluding to the mob having plundered several houses and burned the property in the streets, 'I have often been present at the sacking of towns, but I have never seen any town treated like Birmingham.' He accused the Government of not having taken proper precautions to prevent these outrages, for they knew the town had been in a state of insurrection for the last ten days. He also said the conduct of the magistrates—most of whom had been appointed by Lord John Russell, and some illegally, not having been submitted for the approbation of the Queen or recommended by the Lord-Lieutenant of the county—was most reprehensible, and ought to be inquired into. This put Lord Melbourne on his mettle, and he made a very angry speech, to which the Duke alluding the following day, I believe, said : ' The noble lord ought not to get into those towering passions.'

*June 27th.*—The Capitan Pasha has revolted against the Turkish Government, and has sailed with the whole of the fleet to join the Egyptians, who, it is believed, will march upon Constantinople, unless the European Powers interpose.

*August 9th.*—The House of Lords have passed the Penny Postage Bill without a division.

*August 14th.*—We sailed for Dundee from Wapping, and arrived there after a very rough passage ; from thence to Lord Kinnaird's country seat—Rossie.

*August 30th.*—Poulett Thomson is going as Governor to Canada.

*September 4th.*—I am just returned from Lord Eglinton's Grand Tournament, given at his castle, in Ayrshire. Nothing equal to it has occurred for many years, and the expense to him must have been enormous. Besides filling his castle with all the rank and fashion of the day, he quartered an immense number of guests at his farm-houses. It may be said all London, if not all England, was there. The actors in the pageant were chosen from the finest young men in society, and the women from the greatest beauties of the day. Lady Seymour [1] was elected Queen of Beauty, and certainly deserved her throne. The horses mounted by the knights and their attendants were all picked animals, and nothing could exceed their gorgeous trappings and the arms of their masters. Two banquets were given in the great hall, and balls afterwards, but the badness of the weather, as it rained two out of the three days, injured the show. The principal knights who performed in the lists were Prince Louis Napoleon, then in exile, and his faithful squire, Persigny, Lord Waterford and his stalwart brothers, Mr. Gilmour, the celebrated horseman, and Lord Eglinton himself, in a cuirass entirely inlaid with gold. I never saw a more general display of gaiety and enjoyment than that which prevailed during the whole of this splendid pageant, given by one of the most generous and popular men in Great Britain.

*November 22nd.*—The Queen's marriage is to be announced to-morrow. The Duke of Wellington has been ill—report says, alarmingly—but I hope it is exaggerated. His illness seems to have been occasioned by over-fatigue.

*November 24th.*—The Queen's Speech announcing her marriage is as follows:—'I have caused you to be summoned at the present time that I may acquaint you with my resolution in a matter which deeply concerns the welfare of my people and the happiness of my future life. It is my intention to ally myself in marriage with Prince Albert of Saxe-Coburg Gotha. I have thought fit to make this resolution known to you at this early period in order that you may be fully apprised of a matter so highly important to me and my kingdom, and which I persuade myself will be most acceptable to my loving subjects.' The announcement was received with great enthusiasm.

## 1840

*January 7th.*—The accounts from Algiers are most unfavourable to the French. Though not positively defeated by Abd-el-Kader, they are completely hemmed in by his army, obliging them to abandon all their camps and outposts, and take refuge within

---

[1] Afterwards Duchess of Somerset. She died December, 1884.

the walls of the town.   Accounts have arrived of an affray at
Macao between the English and the Chinese, which ended in the
former being expelled from China.   We must, of course, go to
war with them ; but for the present there is an end of our trade,
and tea will soon become extremely scarce, if it does not altogether
fail.   In the Queen's Address announcing her marriage, she made
no allusion to Prince Albert being a Protestant.   The Duke of
Wellington proposed an amendment to insert the word 'Protestant' before that of 'Prince,' and, notwithstanding the opposition
of Lord Melbourne, the amendment was carried without a division.   Peel proposed no amendment to the Address in the Commons, but Sir J. Buller gave notice of a motion of want of confidence in the Ministers for the 28th.   A meeting had been held at
Sir Robert Peel's house, where this motion had been decided on,
and the announcement of it by Peel was greatly cheered.

There is a report that the Chartists meant to set fire to London
on the night of the 14th or 15th, in consequence of which troops
are kept under arms all night, and the police and fire brigade ordered to be in readiness to act at a moment's warning.   The riots
at Sheffield have been of an alarming character.   The intention of
the Chartists was to fire and plunder the town, and there is little
doubt they would have succeeded in their plans, as they were well
arranged, and they had a clever leader of the name of Holdbury,
but fortunately their delegate at Rotherham got frightened and
disclosed the whole plot to Lord Howard.   Troops were stationed
at all the entrances to the town, and the rioters, seeing their
plans discovered, ran away after firing a few shots.   Several were
arrested.

*January* 18*th.*—It is curious that no mention has yet been
made of the settlement for the Queen's marriage.   It is the more
extraordinary as Parliament has been assembled a fortnight earlier
than usual for that purpose.   It formed the first paragraph in
the Queen's Speech, and it looks rather as if the Ministers feared
the result of the division on Buller's motion, and foreseeing the
possibility of being forced to resign, intend to leave the trouble to
the Tories of making all the arrangements.   Frost, Williams, and
Jones are sentenced to death for leading the riots in Wales, at
Newport ; and several others to confinement and transportation.

*January 23rd.*—Prince Albert's Naturalisation Bill has passed the House of Lords without discussion. Lord John Russell has given notice that Ministers intend to ask the House of Commons to grant 50,000*l.* per annum, and Hume immediately intimated that he would move an amendment to the effect that 21,000*l.* would be sufficient.

*January 24th.*—Lord Stanley writes to me a few lines at Heron Court, and says that the Ministers expect a majority of nineteen on the 28th, but that must depend upon the elections this week and also how the extreme Radicals mean to vote. Went out shooting with Lord Canning.

*January 25th.*—Mr. Wood, the Ministerial candidate, has been returned by a majority of 524 for Southwark.

*January 26th.*—Mr. Tufnell has been returned for Devonport by a majority of 332 ; and the Solicitor-General by one of 9 for Newark. In the latter town serious riots occurred, and the authorities were obliged to call out the military. Mr. Thesiger was beaten. At Birmingham Mr. Muntz has been returned over Sir Charles Wetherell.

*January 27th.*—Lord John Russell has admitted that the expense of Prince Albert's household would not exceed 7,000*l.* or 8,000*l.* ; such a large sum, therefore, as 50,000*l.* is unnecessary.

*January 28th.*—Left Heron Court this morning for London, where I shall remain till after the division on Sir John Buller's motion ; and if by any chance, which is I fear very unlikely, the Government should have a majority under ten, I shall probably remain a few days longer to see the event, which must be either a dissolution or resignation.

*January 29th.*—On Monday last the House of Commons went into committee in consideration of the proposed settlement on Prince Albert. Mr. Hume made a long speech, and moved that the grant should be reduced from 50,000*l.* to 21,000*l.*, the amount allowed to the Royal Dukes. On a division the motion was negatived by a majority of 267—the numbers being 38 for and 305 against the proposed reduction. Colonel Sibthorp then moved that the allowance should be 30,000*l.*, and Russell, in supporting the original proposition, insinuated that the opposition to it evinced a want of respect for the Queen. Lord Eliot and Sir

G

James Gordon denied this ; Hume advocated the smallest grant
and O'Connell the largest. Sir Robert Peel expressed his astonishment at the insinuation that had been thrown out of the
want of loyalty on his side of the House, and said it was unworthy of Lord John Russell's position as a Minister. He
himself had nothing in view but to support the honour and dignity
of the Crown by guarding it against the unpopularity that would
follow this grant. Peel concluded by saying that he was resolved
not to enter into a party contest of who should go farthest to
please the Court ; that he had no difficulties to reconcile on the
subject of his loyalty ; that he had never made the Sovereign's
political support a condition of his allegiance ; and that he had
never been guilty of disrespect either to the Queen or Royal
Family, and could afford to take his own straightforward course
without needless professions of the loyalty he felt. The House
divided on the resolution, and there was a majority of 104 in
favour of 30,000*l.*—the numbers for the proposal of the Government being 158, and against it 262. In the House of Lords the
Lord Chancellor moved the second reading of the Prince Albert
Naturalisation Bill, observing that one of the objects of the bill
was to give Prince Albert precedence next after the Queen. The
bill was framed on the precedent of Mary and Philip, but the
Duke of Wellington condemned the proposals of the bill, particularly the precedence clause, and after some conversation the
second reading was postponed until Friday next, the 31st.

*February 2nd.*—The division on Sir John Buller's motion took
place yesterday, and the Ministers had a majority of 21—287 for
the motion, 308 against. Sir Robert Peel's speech was very fine,
lasting three hours, but it was not so effective as Lord Stanley's.
In the House of Lords the Lord Chancellor, in answer to a question, said he intended to introduce a clause in the Naturalisation
Bill giving Prince Albert precedence after the heir-apparent to
the throne. After some discussion the bill was read a second
time and ordered to be committed on the 3rd. General Sebastiani is recalled.

*February 5th.*—In the House of Lords yesterday Lord Melbourne said he was so anxious to get the Naturalisation Bill
passed, that, to prevent opposition, he would withdraw the pre-

cedence clause, and added, in answer to Lord Brougham, that it was not intended to withdraw it altogether, but only for the present. Lord Brougham asked whether the Crown intended to make any attempt to give precedence to Prince Albert without an Act of Parliament, but no answer was given. The bill was then read a third time and passed. Colonel Sibthorp in the Commons moved that the annuity granted to Prince Albert should cease in the event of his surviving the Queen and not residing six months in every year in England (this in consequence of Prince Leopold's re-marriage and compensation), or in case he married a Catholic or ceased to profess the Protestant religion as by law established in these realms. Sir Robert Peel opposed the motion, and persuaded him to withdraw it. The French papers give as the reason for Sebastiani's recall that, connected as he had been with the Bonaparte family, he would not keep as active a surveillance over Prince Louis Bonaparte, now in England, as was desired by the French Government.

*February* 10*th.*—The marriage of the Queen with Prince Albert took place to-day. The title of Royal Highness has been conferred upon him. The Duke of Sussex gave her away, and the 'John Bull' says that he is always ready to give away what does not belong to him. There were only two Tories present at the ceremony, the Duke of Wellington and Lord Liverpool. The Queen was very much cheered by the mob on her way to and from the chapel. They left Buckingham Palace for Windsor.

*February* 18*th.*—The Duke of Wellington has been ill, but is much better. A large number of Peers and members of the House of Commons went to Windsor with the Address congratulating the Queen on her marriage.

*February* 23*rd.*—The French Chamber has rejected the Duke de Nemours' Dotation Bill. M. Guizot was to have set out to-morrow for London, but this event may probably delay his departure. Louis Philippe has not yet formed a Ministry. It is not known whether he has accepted the resignation of Soult and his colleagues.

*March* 3*rd* —Prince Louis Bonaparte was to have fought this morning with Count Léon, who has been sent over here by the French police, either to get rid of him or to get him expelled the country by inducing him to infringe the laws. This villanous project was defeated by the interposition of our police, who took all the parties before a magistrate, and they were bound over to keep the peace for a year under a penalty of 500*l.* Count d'Orsay was to have been second to the Prince.

*March 30th.*—We dined at the Palace. The Queen entered the room at eight, shaking hands with all the ladies, and then went into the dining-room with the Prince. After dinner the Queen and the Duchess of Kent went into the gallery, where the rest of the company were assembled. The Queen danced the first dance with the Duke of Devonshire, and valsed afterwards with Prince Albert, but the band played so fast and out of time that she only took one turn and then sat down, looking annoyed. We remained till the Queen retired, which was about 1.30.

*April 2nd.*—The debate upon the Corn Laws was adjourned, and it is supposed will last two nights longer at least, and it is said will be adjourned again, as the Government hope to get rid of the China question, which would come on if it were not.

*April 4th.*—The Corn Laws debate has terminated in the most unexpected and absurd manner. As soon as Sir Robert Peel had sat down, having made a splendid speech, Mr. Warburton, fearing probably the result of an immediate division, rose and moved the adjournment of the debate till Monday next, when there voted for 129, and against 245, giving a majority of 116. Mr. Warburton then moved the adjournment of the House, the Speaker put the question, and the Conservatives, amidst loud laughter, shouted 'Aye,' and the motion was carried. The Corn Law question is therefore at an end for this year.

*April 9th.*—Went to the Drawing Room. Amongst the company was Mrs. Lushington, *veuve* Carnac, who last year married a man young enough to be her grandson. They are now separated, and she was presented this year in her former name of Mrs. Carnac. She was Indian, and very rich. Left London for Cassiobury.

*May 1st.*—There was a tremendous row last night at the Opera to force Laporte to engage Tamburini. He came forward five or six times to explain, but the audience would not listen, and he was obliged to retire amidst the groans of almost everybody present. The occupants of the boxes and stalls were the most active in the disturbance, especially gentlemen in the dandy and stage boxes. The row began immediately after the opera was over, and lasted till one o'clock. The ballet would begin, but would not be allowed to proceed, as every time the orchestra attempted to play, and the dancers came forward, they were assailed with such a chorus of cries that they were obliged to give up the attempt. They, however, enjoyed the treatment which was conferred on their manager, and they were all laughing, and seemed much amused at the treatment he received. The gentlemen in the stage-boxes, who had been the ringleaders throughout the evening, sprang upon the stage and lowered the curtain. They were not, however, quick enough to get beyond it before it fell, and were therefore obliged to cross the stage to gain the scenes, amidst the applause of the rest of the audience.

*May 6th.*—All London is in a state of consternation that I never saw equalled, Lord William Russell, brother to the late Duke of Bedford, and father to Mrs. Bennett, having been found murdered in his bed this morning. It appears that the housemaid went downstairs at half-past seven to her work, and found everything in great confusion—plate, clothes, and furniture scattered about the staircase and hall, doors broken open, &c. She immediately called the valet, who slept in a room adjoining that which she and the cook occupied, and acquainted him with her suspicions, upon which he accompanied her into Lord William Russell's bedroom, whom, on opening the shutters, they saw lying dead in bed with his throat cut in such a dreadful manner that his head was nearly severed from the body. They then came downstairs and gave the alarm, and the police and surgeon were sent for. The latter declared Lord William must have been dead for three or four hours; and, from the nature of the wound and the fact of no instrument being found with which it could have been inflicted, it was clear he had not committed suicide, but had been murdered. The police examined the house, but could not find any appearance of anyone having forced an entrance, as the marks on the back door had evidently been done from the inside, and they thought as a blind. The way also in which the different things were strewn about looked more like design than the confusion that would have prevailed after thieves had been disturbed. A chisel corresponding exactly with the marks on the drawers which had been forced open was found in the valet's box, and though the police say they are sure he is guilty, the evidence is not strong enough to convict him, and the coroner's jury therefore returned a verdict of murder against some person or persons unknown. The police are to keep a strict watch over him, and, if he is guilty, as they suppose, they hope by allowing him to remain at large he may do something to criminate himself. It is supposed from different circumstances that the murder must have been committed at about two in the morning.

*May 8th.*—Lord William Russell's house was searched again this morning. One of the two bank-notes that the valet mentioned as having seen in a box at the head of his master's bed, for 10*l.*, was found behind the skirting-board in the pantry. The valet, whose name is Courvoisier, showed the greatest uneasiness when it was proposed to search the pantry, which of course made the police more particular in their investigation, and when the fact of the note having been found was mentioned to him he became quite ill.

*May 21st.*—The division upon Lord Stanley's bill [1] took place this morning, and the result was a majority of three in favour of the motion 'That the Speaker do leave the chair'—the numbers being 301 for and 298 against. Lord Howick and Mr. Charles Wood voted with Lord Stanley.

*May 22nd.*—Courvoisier was again examined to-day, and a good deal more evidence was brought forward as to the extreme agitation of his manner after the discovery of the murder. The instrument has not been found, but a pair of gloves spotted with blood were discovered in his portmanteau, which must have been placed there by him after the search had been made by the police, for everything in the portmanteau was turned out, and they were not there. But as Courvoisier was allowed to sleep alone two nights after the murder he might have placed them there, thinking that as he had been already searched it was the safest place.

*May 23rd.*—The Cambridge and Ludlow elections have ended in a triumph for the Conservative candidates. The examination

[1] The Irish Registration Bill.

f Courvoisier was resumed to-day, but, with the exception of
wo handkerchiefs stained with blood, both marked with the
nitials of Lord William Russell, nothing of any great importance
ame out.  It is quite evident that no one could have broken
nto the house, and this of course implicates those inside, as they
nust have either done it themselves or permitted others to enter
or that purpose.  The different things that have been found
elonging to Lord William Russell must also have been concealed
y some one constantly in the house ; as they were concealed with
o much care, it is evident the different hiding-places had been
repared beforehand.  The boards of the pantry were taken up,
nd a sovereign was found under one of them which could not
ave slipped in between the crevices, as the boards fitted quite
lose.  It is evident the boards under which it was placed
nust have been lifted and then fastened down again, for it was
ound necessary to have regular workmen to take them up.  A
ocket was also found under the hearthstone in the pantry.  The
risoner is remanded until next Wednesday, the 27th.

*May 26th.*—Mr. Villiers's motion for a Committee on the
orn Laws was defeated by a majority of 300 to 177.

*May 27th.*—Courvoisier was again examined to-day, and
ommitted to take his trial.  No further evidence was pro-
uced, and it is said if no more can be procured he can't be
anged, as, though no doubt can exist of his guilt, there is not
ifficient legal evidence to convict him.

*June 10th.*—Mr. Smythe rode up to me in the Park and
aid the Queen had just been fired at as she was leaving
uckingham Palace to take a drive.  The man who fired did
ot attempt to escape.  The Queen showed great courage, as
ne always does, and went immediately to the Duchess of Kent
o inform her of her safety.

*June 12th.*—The House of Commons divided last night on
ne amendment proposed by Mr. Charles Wood,[1] and the motion
or the Speaker to leave the chair on Lord Stanley's bill—
aving for its object to postpone the Irish Registration Bill of
ord Stanley, and to give precedence to the sham measures
f the Irish Solicitor-General and Lord John Russell—was

---

[1] Afterwards Viscount Halifax.

supported by the whole strength of the Administration, the
numbers being, for the Ministerial amendment, 195, against
206 ; giving a majority of 11 against the Ministers. The
Corn Laws were discussed in the House of Lords, and Lord
Fitzwilliam's motion for an inquiry rejected. The missing
spoons in Lord William Russell's house and two gold and
silver ear-trumpets have been discovered. It appears that
Courvoisier left a parcel a week or a fortnight before the murder
in the care of Charlotte Piolini, who keeps the Hôtel de Dieppe,
in Leicester Square, desiring her to take charge of it for a few
days. He never returned, and the day before yesterday she
sent the parcel to her solicitor, who opened it in her presence
and in that of some other persons, and it was found that it was
the missing property that had been advertised by the police.
She also identified Courvoisier as the person who had left it.
Although under a different name, he had lived in her service
about a month four years ago, and since that she had not seen
him.

*June 20th.*—Courvoisier's trial concluded to-day. He was
found guilty of the murder and sentenced to death. He confessed afterwards having committed the crime because Lord
William Russell found him stealing. He did it with a carving-
knife.

*June 21st.*—Courvoisier was induced to confess his crime
in consequence of the discovery of the plate, for as soon as he
had seen Mrs. Piolini, who identified him as the person who had
left it at her house, he sent for Mr. Phillips, his counsel, and
confessed his guilt. He said Lord William had been taken
suddenly ill after he went to bed, and in going downstairs
caught him packing up the plate. He taxed him with intending
a robbery, and threatened to call in the police, but on begging
his pardon he after some altercation forgave him, and promised
not to prosecute him, but told him to leave his service the
following day. The villain added : ' His Lordship and I then
parted quite comfortably,' and Lord William went to bed un-
suspicious of the fate that awaited him. Courvoisier waited an
hour at his door until he was sure he was asleep ; then he went
gently into the room and cut his throat while he slept. He

says Lord William never awoke, and must have died with little
or no pain, as he did not struggle at all, and there was only a
slight tremulous motion of the right hand, which he raised
almost involuntarily.

*June 25th.*—Lord Stanley has gained another victory over the
Government, Lord Morpeth having proposed an amendment to
the Irish Registration Bill, and when a division took place he
was beaten by a majority of four.

*July 6th.*—Courvoisier was hanged this morning. I went
to see the execution, and was admitted into the condemned cell,
where he was praying with the clergyman, and I followed the
procession to the scaffold, which was erected on the outside of
the prison. He showed great firmness, and though very pale
seemed perfectly composed even to the last moment. Several
of the City authorities were assembled in the room of the prison,
and I was not a little shocked to see punch, or some beverage of
that sort, handed round, as if it was a pleasant festivity. It
seems to be the custom, and the sooner it is abolished the better.

*July 7th.*—Lord Stanley has given up his Irish Registration
Bill, but announced that he will bring it on next year at an
early period of the session, upon which Lord John Russell
withdrew his sham measures for the Irish and English Regis-
trations amidst the laughter of the House.

*August 1st.*—The French are very indignant with this
country, and threaten us with war because Lord Palmerston,
finding that he could not induce them to take any steps towards
a settlement of the Eastern Question, has signed a treaty with
Russia, Prussia, and Austria, leaving out France altogether.

*August 7th.*—News arrived this morning of Louis Napoleon
having landed yesterday morning at Boulogne with fifty
followers. None of the soldiers, however, having joined him,
the attempt totally failed, and he and most of those who
accompanied him were taken. This explains an expression he
used to me two evenings ago. He was standing on the steps
of Lady Blessington's house after a party, wrapped up in a
cloak, with Persigny by him, and I observed to them, 'You
look like two conspirators,' upon which he answered, ' You may
be nearer right than you think.'

*August 8th.*—The mad attempt of Prince Louis Napoleon at Boulogne is confirmed. He had hired a steamer from the Commercial Company, called the 'Edinburgh Castle,' for a fortnight. He embarked at London on the 5th; and on Thursday, the 6th, landed at Vimereux, a mile from Boulogne, with fifty followers. He marched to the barracks, and tried to seduce the soldiers from their allegiance, but having failed in consequence of the accidental absence of the officer on guard, who was in the plot, the soldiers at the barracks remained faithful, and the National Guard being called out, the Prince and his followers were obliged to fly. They had taken possession of the life-boat, which was swamped, and the Prince was picked up by a steamer while clinging to a buoy a short distance from the shore. The Custom-House officers, fortunately for him, had seized the vessel whilst the disturbance was proceeding on shore, and were bringing her into the harbour, by which means his life was preserved. Some of the party made their escape by taking forcible possession of horses belonging to some English gentlemen, but were pursued and most of them taken. Some were killed by the soldiers after they had surrendered. The Prince had issued a proclamation to the French nation appointing Marshal Clausel chief of the troops at Paris, General Pajol and other officers and sub-officers to military appointments, and promising many recompenses. Ever since I knew the Prince he has a fixed notion, which nothing can eradicate, that he will some day govern France; and so strongly is he impressed with this idea that it is the only way to account for his repeated attempts under what appeared to be hopeless circumstances.

*August 21st.*—Received a letter from my father to say that Lady Pembroke has offered the living of Wilton to my younger brother Charles, and that he has accepted it.

*September 2nd.*—Lady Pembroke and her daughters visited us at Heron Court. We went out with Mr. Grantley Berkeley's otter-hounds, which, although we did not kill, was very amusing in that wild country.

*September 7th and 8th.*—News is in that an insurrection has broken out at Madrid, Lisbon, and also at Paris—the latter not serious. The French papers are very warlike in their tone, and if the news from the East be true, it will be very difficult to preserve peace. Commodore Napier has issued a proclamation inciting the Syrians to rebellion, and has also taken twelve or fifteen small vessels belonging to the Pasha of Egypt, old Mehemet Ali. The latter is very firm in his refusal to accede to the Quadruple Treaty, being, it is supposed, supported by France. Orders have been sent to Admiral Hugon, who commands the French fleet, which, if acted upon, a collision must occur, and war then becomes inevitable. News may soon be expected from China, if Mehemet Ali does not stop the mails, which he threatens to do.

*September 11th.*—The French papers continue very warlike, and the English Ministerial papers are the same. I think that peace will be preserved, as Louis Philippe is very much against any wars.

*September 17th.*—The blockade commenced at Alexandria on the 1st, by Admiral Stopford. Several of the Pasha's vessels had been sequestered by the British naval authorities. His fleet, both Egyptian and Turkish, was drawn up in order of battle in the roads of Alexandria, and Admiral Hugon took command of the French fleet on the 26th. It appears that the blockade has been commenced before the expiration of the time allowed by the Treaty of London to the Pasha to refuse or accept the Ultimatum of the Powers. Count Walewski, who had been sent by France on a mission to Mehemet Ali, had left him to return to France. It is reported that he succeeded in persuading the Pasha to accept the terms offered by France.

*September 27th.*—There is no news from the East, and the report which was current on the 22nd that Mehemet Ali had agreed to the terms proposed by France, not being confirmed or alluded to in any way, is probably false. The tone of the French papers is more warlike than ever ; great preparations are being made in all the ports of France, the fortification of Paris is begun, and the different fortresses are being put in a state of defence. The telegraph at the North Foreland says the Russian fleet of eighteen sail was off the Graveline Sands.

*October 2nd.*—Prince Louis Napoleon's trial is begun and

excites no interest whatever. It is thought that the sentence will be confinement for life.

*October 3rd.*—The following important news has arrived from the East through France. The 'Prometheus,' which arrived at Beyrout on the 20th, announced that, after a bombardment of nine days, which reduced the town to ashes, it was evacuated by the Egyptians in the night, and the Allies took possession. The 'Oriental,' which quitted Alexandria on the 24th, makes known that the firman deposing Mehemet Ali had been communicated to him on the 21st, as well as to the Generals of the four Powers, who instantly struck their flags and retired on board their shipping. An attempt has been made to fire Sheerness Dockyard. H.M.S. 'Camperdown,' 120 guns, was set fire to in the basin by some incendiary. It was first discovered in a midshipman's berth, but it was extinguished after burning a locker. On a further search a well-laid train was discovered in the warrant officers' store-rooms, consisting of resin, oakum, and lucifer matches. The inquiry respecting the fire at Plymouth is still going on. The King of Holland has announced his intention of abdicating in favour of his son.

*October 5th.*—Three persons named Wright, Grigg, and Britt have been taken up on suspicion of attempting to fire the 'Camperdown.' The preservation of the ship as well as the dockyard, and probably the town, is entirely owing to an accidental circumstance. The ship had been visited as usual and reported ' all safe,' when, just as the officers were leaving the yard, Mr. Henty, the ship's carpenter, remembered that he had left his umbrella behind. He returned to the ship, and on going down to the lower deck he perceived a thick smoke issuing from the cockpit, and at the same time heard heavy footsteps, although it was too dark for him to see the person. He instantly gave the alarm, and one of the firemen of the yard came immediately, and by his exertions and those of Mr. Henty, the fire was extinguished before it had done any serious damage, the fire casks and buckets being close at hand. It is said the Albanians are deserting fast from the Pasha's army and the Druses are arming. This attack upon Beyrout seems to have been solely for the purpose of keeping up communication with the insurgents in Syria, for the possession of such a miserable place could not have been of any other advantage to the English. A list of the fleet is given, which, including English, Austrian, and Turks, consists of twenty-eight sail, of which twenty-three are English. It is reported that the terms offered by the Sultan to the leaders of Mehemet Ali are as follows :—To Soliman Pasha (Colonel Selves) and his son the island of Cyprus for inheritance as a Pashalik ; to Mahmoud Pasha the Pashalik of Tripoli ; also an hereditary fief ; and, lastly, to Sherif Pasha the remainder of Syria on a similar tenure—but that they have all refused and acquainted Mehemet with the proposals made to them. The French are perfectly frantic at the news of the burning of Beyrout, and threaten immediate war.

*October* 19.—A reinforcement of a thousand Turks has arrived in two Austrian steamers with the newly-appointed Pasha of Syria. The only loss we have sustained is at Ghebal, whence the Marines were driven back by a most unexpected fire, having four men killed and thirteen wounded. When we took possession of the fort next morning the Albanians had evacuated it. It was a very strong fort, bomb-proof, and commands the road to Tripoli.

*October* 8*th.*—The rage of the French at our proceedings has not in the least abated. A schism has broken out in the French Cabinet on the question of war ; four Ministers, with Thiers at their head, are for it, and four are against it. It is said that M. Thiers tendered his resignation to the King, who accepted it. Izzett Mahomet Pasha has been appointed Pasha of Egypt in place of Mehemet Ali.

*October* 11*th.*—The bombardment of Beyrout has been exaggerated. Not a shot was fired into the town, but only at the citadel. Ibrahim Pasha is in the neighbourhood of the camp and reconnoitred it on the 14th. His force amounts to fifteen thousand men ; but the English have fortified their lines with cannon, and are, therefore, a match for him, though inferior in numbers.

*October* 16*th.*—Mehemet Ali has replied with moderation to the action of deposition, but was preparing to oppose an energetic resistance. He received the news with great *sang froid*, observing that such denunciations were nothing new to him ; that this was the fourth, and he hoped to get over it as he had done the

other three, with the help of God and the Prophet. He then
ordered both his fleets to get ready to put out to sea, but the
French Consul dissuaded him from committing such an imprudent
act.

*October 19th.*—The Queen-Regent of Spain abdicated on the
12th. This is the second royal abdication within one month, and
it is probable that this event will add to the difficulties that
already existed towards the settlement of peace between England
and France, as Lord Palmerston and M. Thiers are sure to take
opposite views on this question as well as that of the East. The
general opinion in Paris is that the Ministry will resign at the
beginning of the session, and that M. Thiers will join the ranks
of the *Gauche*, or ultra-Radical party. M. Guizot's arrival is
anxiously expected, and he holds in his hands the fate of the
Cabinet. The deposition of Mehemet Ali having been made
known at Alexandria, the Turkish officers refused to remain in
his service.

*October 25th.*—The cause of quarrel between the King and
Thiers arose from a paragraph that the latter wished to insert in
the King's Speech, and which Louis Philippe objected to on
account of its hostile tone, observing that it would be highly inexpedient to introduce into the discourse expressions calculated
to alter the pacific character that the Eastern Question had within
a few days assumed. Discussion on this point had been going on
for some days, but at twelve last night the difference came to such
a height that the Ministers resigned in a body and the King accepted their resignation. An attack had been made upon Ibrahim
Pasha's advanced position, which was perfectly successful. The
Syrians were coming in, and great desertion was taking place
amongst the Egyptians. Sidon has been taken and the garrison
made prisoners. From all appearances the affairs of Syria will
soon be terminated ; the insurrection makes progress, and fourteen
thousand mountaineers have joined the insurgents. The Turks
behaved nobly. Tyre and Tripoli have been taken. Sidon was
defended by three thousand men, and capitulated after a battle of
ten hours.

*October 30th.*—M. Guizot has accepted the Ministry of Foreign
Affairs.

*November* 1*st.*—The Allies have gained an important victory over Ibrahim Pasha, and are in possession of the greater part of the coast.

*November* 6*th.*—The speech of Louis Philippe on opening the Chambers is extremely pacific, and, therefore, cannot please the French. We dined yesterday with the Tankervilles, and met Lord Lyndhurst, Mr. Smythe, Mr. and Mrs. Disraeli, and Count d'Orsay. Much struck by Mrs. Disraeli, who is a most extraordinary woman both in appearance and in her conversation. She was a widow with a large jointure and twenty years older than him, but he seems much attached to her.

*November* 8*th.*—News has been received from China, and gives an account of the capture of the island of Chusan by General Burrell.

*November* 17*th.*—The Sultan refused to revoke the *déchéance* of Mehemet Ali.

*November* 18*th.*—The ashes of Napoleon having been brought from St. Helena to Paris, their funeral took place on the 15th. It went off quietly. The procession must have been magnificent. The King was present, but made himself as little conspicuous as possible, and hardly anybody saw him, as he took no part in the procession and contented himself with receiving the body at the entrance to the church, after which he hid himself in a corner. The medical and law students followed the procession to the number of two thousand, singing the *Marseillaise* and shouting 'Guizot à la lanterne!' None of the Foreign Ambassadors were present, as Lord Granville refused, and all the others followed his example.

# 1841

*January* 27*th.*—The Queen opened Parliament in person, and was very well received on her way. Syria is spoken of, but not as settled, and the hope only expressed that its affairs will soon be terminated.

*January* 28*th.*—The Address was carried in both Houses without a division. Mr. Hume proposed an amendment cen-

suring the Government for forming an alliance with the four
Powers to the exclusion of France, but was not supported.

*February 18th.*—Lord Cardigan's trial in the House of Lords
for fighting a duel with and wounding Captain Tuckett has ended
in his acquittal, there not being sufficient evidence to prove the
identity of the Captain.

*February 20th.*—It is said that Poulett Thomson has had a
quarrel with Sir John Harvey, Lieutenant-Governor of New
Brunswick, in consequence of which the latter has been recalled.
The difference arose from a dispute respecting the disposal of
some troops along the frontier, and as Poulett Thomson is not a
military man the probability is that he was quite wrong.

*February 24th.*—The debate upon Lord Morpeth's[1] Irish
Registration Bill began the day before yesterday. Lord Stanley
made a splendid speech opposing the second reading, and the
House adjourned.

*February 25th.*—Debate again adjourned.

*February 27th.*—The second reading of Lord Morpeth's bill
was carried.

*March 12th.*—News from America is very warlike. It is
said that ten sail of the line are to be sent there immediately.
The news from the East is also unfavourable, the Sultan being
apparently disposed not to keep faith with Mehemet Ali. Affairs
in China are not more prosperous. Great sickness and mortality
amongst the troops at Chusan. Admiral Elliot has resigned his
command.

*April 10th.*—The news from China is better. Admiral
Elliot has concluded a treaty with the Chinese, after battering
down the forts, which cannot be considered satisfactory, as he
only stipulates for six millions of dollars as an indemnity for the
opium dispute, which is equal only to a million sterling, whereas
our first claim was three millions. He also consents to allow the
Chinese six years for the payment of this sum.

*April 14th.*—Ministers will neither resign nor dissolve, in
which case the Tories must propose a vote of want of confidence.
The Chancellor, Lord Lansdowne, Lord Melbourne, and Lord

---

[1] Lord Morpeth was Secretary for Ireland.

Duncannon wish to resign, the others to dissolve or stay in. There is great excitement.

*April 16th.*—At this moment there is a meeting at Lord Aberdeen's, which is attended by Sir Robert Peel, Lord Stanley, the Duke of Wellington, and Sir Henry Hardinge.

*April 19th.*—The long-expected division on Lord Sandon's [1] amendment took place this morning, and the result has surpassed our expectations ; the Ministers being defeated by a majority of 36. There is very little chance of their resigning, as Lord John Russell, before the House divided, talked of discussing the question of the Corn Laws more fully.

*April 20th.*—Lord John Russell declared this afternoon in the House of Commons that the Government intend to go on as long as they can. The discussion on the Corn Laws is put off to June 3. They think that will carry them on to the middle of the month. They would then probably dissolve ; and as Parliament could not meet before the end of July, they will prorogue it immediately, and thereby keep office till next session. This is supposed to be their plan, but some say that Lord Melbourne will resign, not being prepared to go so far as Lord John Russell, in which case the latter will be Premier. It may be, indeed, that Lord John Russell is intriguing to turn out Lord Melbourne in the same way as Lord Grey was pushed out by his colleagues some years ago.

*April 24th.*—Sir Robert Peel gave notice this evening that on Thursday next he would move : 'That Her Majesty's Ministers do not sufficiently possess the confidence of the House of Commons to enable them to carry through that House the measures which they deem to be of essential importance to the public welfare, and that their continuance in office under such circumstances is at variance with the spirit of the Constitution.' It is said that the Ministers are determined not to resign even if beaten on Peel's motion next Thursday, but to proceed with the Corn Laws and then dissolve.

*April 26th.*—I went to the Derby, and to a party given by Lady Salisbury, to hear Mademoiselle Rachel recite some scenes out of Racine and Corneille, and was much pleased with her. Her style is completely French, and therefore not very natural,

---

[1] The present Earl of Harrowby.

but is the perfection of art. She is not handsome, but is very
pleasing in her appearance and manners.

*June 5th.*—The Ministers have been defeated upon Sir Robert
Peel's motion of want of confidence. The Opposition did not expect such a victory, but their majority is only one. The division
took place at a quarter before three this morning, the numbers
being 312 in favour and 311 against the motion. The announcement of the numbers was received with deafening cheers by the
Conservatives, and the Ministers looked completely overcome.
Lord John Russell grew very pale and nervous. When the division
was over he gave notice that next Monday he would move for
a vote of supplies to meet the present wants of the country,
but said nothing about the Corn Laws, resignation, or dissolution.
The news from China is favourable. Bogue Fort was taken on
February 25, and Canton in March. The Chinese fought better
than could be expected in defence of the town, which was taken
by storm, with 400 Chinese killed or wounded.

*June 6th.*—Went to hear the school children of Mr. Compton
catechised. Some of the answers were very amusing. 'Who was
Adam?'—'The eldest son of Abraham.' 'What countries are
there in Europe besides England?'—'America and Asia.' 'What
difference is there between town and country?'—'None.' 'What
is an island?'—'Plenty of water.' 'Of what religion was St.
Paul before he became a Christian?'—'A Roman Catholic.'

*June 9th.*—Lord John Russell announced the day before
yesterday that the Government intended to dissolve Parliament
immediately, proposing merely to take such estimates as were
essential for the public service. Sir Robert Peel then rose and
said he would oppose the granting of the supplies demanded unless
Lord John Russell would declare that Ministers intended to
advise the convocation of the new Parliament at once. Lord John
Russell replied that the intention of Ministers was to advise the
immediate summoning of the new Parliament, with which Sir
Robert expressed himself satisfied.

*June 16th.*—I received a letter from Sidney Herbert desiring
me to start immediately as a candidate for the borough of Wilton.
He says that he has consulted precedents, but cannot find that in
the memory of man anybody has ever put out an address for that

borough, but that I must canvass it as exactly as if it were Birmingham, and I had Lord John Russell standing against me. Accordingly I shall start for Wilton to-morrow.

*June* 19*th.*—I completed a most tiresome and uninteresting canvass, there being no opposition to me ; but it is an extensive borough, entirely agricultural, and necessitated long drives from one point to another.

*June* 22*nd.*—Parliament is to be prorogued to-day by the Queen.

*June* 23*rd.*—I received alarming accounts of my father's health.

*June* 25*th.*—The Proclamation dissolving Parliament appeared in the 'Gazette.'

*June* 26*th.*—I must attend Christchurch election in support of Sir George Rose ; having previously declined the request of the electors to offer myself as a candidate.

*June* 29*th.*—I went straight to Christchurch, and arrived in time for the election proceedings. Sir George Rose was elected by a large majority. The City of London has returned two Conservatives and two Whigs.

### *Lord Sydenham to Lord Fitzharris.*

Government House, Kingston :
July 13, 1841.

My dear Fitzharris,—I am in your debt for a letter, but it is so long ago that I cannot pretend to pay it. If I remember right, it was written shortly after *your friends* had made so unwise a move last year by the opening of the session, and by the rejection of their want of confidence vote fixed *mine* in the saddle for another year. This time the tables seem to be turned, though I rejoice at the course which the Government have pursued, even if it end, as I hear it will, in their discomfiture. Free Trade and Corn Laws are in my opinion worth fighting for, although I did not think Irish questions and Church reforms were. So though the result may be to place a Tory Government where a Whig one sits, I think it the *dignus vindice nodus* and the ring well established. Of course *you* will get all the counties, *we* all the great towns, and the small boroughs will be anybody's money. Neither party will, I daresay, get so good a Parliament as mine, nor be able to manage them as easily, for my assembly, though composed of

H 2

elements of as little affinity as oil and vinegar, unite a good deal on one point—to do what I wish. So I am not sorry to be out of the turmoil at home. I shall have enough of it, I have no doubt, when your great battle is decided in August or September, and I find upon my return a renewal of it under the business session of 1841 and 1842.

I am delighted, however, to hear that, let what will happen, you are to be returned for Wilton, where the seat is sure and money need not be spent. I have always regretted that you are not in Parliament, where I am sure you will distinguish yourself, and where there is certainly a good opening for your doing so. You must have had enough, too, by this time of shooting and hunting, and want more interesting occupation. If the Tories come in I conclude that you will have some post offered to you. If so, and I may volunteer the advice of an old stager to you, I would strongly advise you to take only such a one as will give you business to do in the House, for your department at least —such as Under Secretary, or India Board, if the President be a Peer. Otherwise, I should, in your situation, feel my way independently in the House, which no man who takes a Lordship of the Treasury or Admiralty can do : his hands and his tongue are both tied.

I am sorry to say I am almost done up, and very like an old foundered horse. The gout has played the deuce with my hands and feet, and I have no strength to walk, or move, or pull a trigger, so I shall dwindle down into a respectable old gouty proser, of which I am giving you a specimen beforehand by offering advice unasked.

· · · · · · · ·

Yours, &c.

SYDENHAM.[1]

*July* 17*th*.—The news of my father's health is worse, and I fear there is little hope of his recovery. He has taken Lord de Grey's villa at Putney.

*July* 25*th*.—Lord Seymour moved the Address in the House of Lords yesterday. An amendment to the Address was moved by Lord Ripon,[2] representing dissatisfaction at the financial state of the country. The Duke of Wellington, Lord Melbourne, the Duke of Richmond, and Lord Lansdowne spoke. After which the House divided, and there appeared for the Address 96, for

---

[1] Poulett Thomson, Lord Sydenham, had just been made a Peer, and soon after the date of this letter died in Canada from a fall in riding. He was a remarkably agreeable man.

[2] Lord Ripon had been Prime Minister as Lord Goderich in 1827.

the amendment 168—majority 72. In the House of Commons
the Address was moved by Mr. M. Phillips, and seconded by Mr.
J. Dundas. The amendment, which was exactly the same as
that proposed in the House of Lords, was moved by Mr. James
Wortley, and seconded by Lord Bruce. A debate followed, which
was adjourned until the following day, and again adjourned on
the 26th and 27th. The division took place on the 28th, and the
Ministers were beaten by 91 votes; the members who voted for
the Address were 269, against it 360. Mr. Sharman Crawford
gave notice that he would move an amendment to the Address,
and the Conservatives were desired to attend again at twelve.
None of the Ministers were present, and Mr. Crawford's amendment was negatived.

*July 29th.* — The Government have resigned and Peel is
Premier.

*September 11th.*—My father, Lord Malmesbury, died yesterday
at Lord de Grey's villa at Putney, aged 63.

*October 7th.*—Canton has been stormed. The Chinese capitulated after losing about three thousand men, and agreed to pay
six millions of dollars. But it appears that Admiral Elliot has
agreed to take a much smaller sum than he ought to have asked
for : which sum he immediately gave to the opium merchants
without thinking of demanding money for the expenses of the
war. This will cause additional expense, for the person who is
sent to supersede him has instructions to insist upon the payment
of sixteen million dollars, besides the whole of the cost incurred
by England and the East India Company.

*October 16th.*—Prince Nicholas Esterhazy, who is engaged to
Lady Sarah Villiers, has not yet returned, so the marriage is
postponed.

*October 18th.*—There is such a tremendous flood in London
that passengers were carried up the steps at Vauxhall on men's
shoulders. From the accounts in the papers it seems that the
insurrection at Madrid is suppressed. The attack upon the Palace
for the purpose of carrying off the young Queen and her sister
was defeated, most fearful fighting being carried on in the
apartments of the Palace itself. The insurgents got so far into
the building that the balls penetrated into the Queen's room, who

was only saved by the gallant defence of a small body of men.
After some time of hard fighting, Generals Concha and Leon
deserted their men, who immediately dispersed and tranquillity
was restored. The citadel of Pampeluna is still in possession of
the rebels.

*October 23rd.*—The Carlist insurrection seems to be going
badly for the Christinos. Don Diego Leon has been taken prisoner
and shot.

*October 30th.*—In Spain the excitement is subsiding, so I hope
there will be no war. The Spanish insurrection seems to be at an
end, most of the troops who had joined the insurgents having
returned to Espartero.

*November 3rd.*—A great fire has taken place at the Tower.
The armoury has been destroyed, as well as a number of our
trophies, nothing apparently having been saved but the Duke of
York's sword and sash.

*November 4th.*—We drove from Tottenham Park to Littlecote,
the scene of a very horrid story which Sir Walter Scott relates in
his notes to ' Rokeby.' The boards in the room where the child
was burned have been taken up and oilcloth nailed down over the
floor. A large cabinet has been placed to conceal the fireplace,
and all the curtains, out of which it is said a piece was cut, are
destroyed. General Popham, a descendant of Judge Popham,
who acquitted the murderer Darrell contrary to all evidence, and
to whom the property was left, it is supposed, in consequence of
an agreement to that effect between them, does not like any
allusion to this story. He has done all in his power to obliterate
the traces of the transaction. The house is a very fine old
building in the Elizabethan style of architecture. The hall is
large, with very handsome painted windows, the walls of carved
oak hung with armour, buff jackets, and arms. It is, however, a
very gloomy-looking residence, and few people would like to live
in it. Prince Nicholas Esterhazy has arrived at Middleton Park,
Lord Jersey's place, bringing letters from his family to Lady
Sarah, so the marriage will take place soon.

*November 16th.*—The Queen Dowager is said to be dying.
Lord Saltoun is appointed to the command of the force sent to
China, so that negotiations will give way to force.

## 1842

*January 1st.*—The town of Amoy, in China, has been taken by our fleet, with only the loss of one man. The fortifications were so strong that our ships' guns made no impression on them, and after four hours' continual firing the town was taken by escalade. If the Chinese had had good artillery, or understood gunnery, we should probably have been defeated, as they would have sunk our ships long before we could have made any breach in their walls, which were of solid granite fifteen feet thick, and covered with a coat of mud and cement, which nothing could penetrate, of the thickness of two feet. Very little money was found in the town, the Chinese having carried it off in split logs of wood.

*February 7th.*—Sir Robert Peel has brought in his bill upon the Corn Laws, which is no less than taking off more than half the present duty. Nobody expected such a sweeping measure, and there is great consternation amongst the Conservatives. It is clear that he has thrown over the landed interest, as my father always said he would.

*February 26th.*—Mr. Villiers's motion for the total repeal of the Corn Laws has been thrown out by an immense majority—393 to 90. Mr. Christopher is to propose an amendment to Peel's bill to increase the duty upon foreign corn, and Lord Worsley intends to propose another for a still further increase of duty. My steward says that the landed proprietors will lose at least 15 per cent. of their rents by Peel's bill.[1]

*February 27th.*—Mr. Christopher's amendment to Sir Robert Peel's bill has been rejected by a majority of 306 to 104. Alarming news has been received from India. It is officially announced that our envoy, Lieutenant-General Macnaghten, and two officers who accompanied him, have been murdered by the son of Dost Mahomed during a conference to which they had been invited by the latter to arrange terms for the evacuation of Cabul. This treacherous act of course puts an end to the treaty; but since then it is reported that our troops, being nearly famished, without the

[1] Experience has shown that this is far under the mark; wheat is now (1884) thirty-two shillings a quarter!

chance of obtaining supplies or relief, all the passes around Cabul
being stopped up with snow, and the town surrounded by a
greatly superior force, attempted to cut their way through the
Khoord Cabul Pass towards Jellalabad, to effect a junction with
Sir Robert Sale; the whole, numbering five or six thousand men,
was destroyed, the 44th Regiment to a man. Sixteen ladies,
wives of the officers, were taken prisoners by the Afghans.
General Elphinstone is said to be dead. Lady Canning called to
confirm the news.

*February* 10*th.*—Letters have arrived from India to-day, and
state that all the troops except about five hundred men, who were
taken prisoners with General Elphinstone, were cut to pieces.
The ladies, it was thought, would come off tolerably well, as Dost
Mahomed's son's wife and children are in the hands of the English,
and for their sake he will not injure them.

*April* 1*st.*—It appears that General Elphinstone, trusting
Akbar Khan's promise of a safe-conduct to Jellalabad, and thinking he could no longer hold Cabul against the Afghans, left it on
January 6. His troops were attacked almost immediately. General Elphinstone seems to have relied upon Akbar Khan's fidelity
and honesty, and, not suspecting him of treachery or want of
power to control his own people, allowed him to settle everything
about the march and encampment of our troops. If he had
pushed on as fast as he could, he might have reached Jellalabad
as Sir Robert Sale did some short time before with an inferior
force, but he seems to have been incapacitated by illness or age,
and quite unequal to the circumstances, which required a man of
unusual energy. He had been unfortunate in his career, as he
was almost the only English officer taken prisoner at Waterloo.
When he was summoned by Napoleon during the battle to give
information as to our forces and resources, which he very honour-
ably refused to do, the Emperor grew furious, and abused him
before all his staff. Sale behaved like a hero, and when the summons to evacuate Jellalabad was brought to him he answered that,
though he had more at stake than any man, having a wife and
daughter (Mrs. Sturt) in the power of the Afghans, he would hold
Jellalabad to the last, and that nothing but an order from the
Council would induce him to give it up. Ghuznee and Kandahar

are saved. Went with Lady Ailesbury to the Duchess of Cambridge's to settle about the quadrille for the Queen's ball.

*April 12th.*—Started at eight for the Palace. The quadrilles were admitted by a private door and taken to separate rooms. The Duchess of Cambridge's set assembled in a large room below stairs. We were marshalled by our respective heralds, and proceeded, with the Duchess of Cambridge at our head, through the hall into the Throne Room, where the Queen received us, sitting on the throne, and surrounded by all her Court, in the dress of the time of Edward III. Most of the costumes were beautiful, and the whole arrangements very well managed. There were a great many people already arrived, but none were allowed to enter the Throne Room, which was perfectly empty with the exception of the Queen and her Court. When the whole of our quadrilles had passed her, they went through the gallery into one of the drawing-rooms, where we had to wait until the other quadrilles and the general company had arrived, after which we returned into the drawing-room, a few couples were selected out of each set, and dancing began. My partner was Lady Craven.

*April 14th.*—Dined at Lord and Lady Stanley's. A very pleasant party. The Clanwilliams, Mahons, St. Aulaires,[1] the Cannings, the American Minister, Mr. Everett, Brünnow, Lord Aberdeen, &c. Mr. Everett, without waiting to be introduced, asked me how much beer-money I gave my servants, and seemed to think it was too much. He was dressed in a green coat, not a common colour for a dinner in London.

*April 24th.*—Went to a *bal costumé* at Stafford House, where almost everybody wore the dresses they had at the Queen's.

*April 30th.*—The Queen was shot at this morning on Constitution Hill, as she was returning to the Palace, by a man called Francis.

*June 6th.*—The news from India is that Ghuznee has fallen, the garrison having been forced to capitulate for want of water. The Afghans promised to take them in safety to Cabul, but, as they have not been heard of since, it is feared that they met with the same fate as the Cabul army, and have been massacred. This bad news is somewhat counterbalanced by the success of Colonel Pollock

---

[1] M. de St. Aulaire was French Ambassador.

in forcing the Khyber Pass, which he did most gallantly, though opposed by a superior force. Sale, hearing that he was marching to relieve Jellalabad, made a sortie with his whole force against the army that was besieging him, and after a brilliant action, that lasted the whole day, totally defeated the Afghans. There is, therefore, but little doubt that Colonel Pollock has succeeded in joining Sir Robert Sale. The conduct of Colonel Palmer in giving up Ghuznee is very much censured, and Lord Ellenborough, the Governor-General, is going to bring him and General Elphinstone before a court-martial.

*June 16th.*—The Duke of Orleans is dead. His horses being restive, he jumped out of his carriage, fell, and was killed on the spot. What will be the result of this sad event ? Probably another rebellion as soon as the King dies, and the restoration of the Duc de Bordeaux. The French never will bear a regency quietly, and certainly not a long one, as this would necessarily be. The present King is sixty-nine, and the Comte de Paris only four years old. It will give the Republicans a chance. The Duke was carried into a shop close by, where the King, Queen, and royal family soon arrived, but he never recovered his senses for a single moment, and died in their arms. His body was carried to Neuilly and placed in the chapel, the whole royal family following the procession on foot. He was only thirty-two years of age, very handsome, clever and amiable, and liked by all who knew him. The army bitterly laments his loss. The poor Duchess of Orleans arrived at Neuilly after the Duke's death. She had heard of it at Plombières by telegraph, and set off for Paris in the middle of the night. At a few posts from Plombières she met the Duke's aide-de-camp, and then guessed the truth. She is reported to have said, 'I was too proud of him, and God has taken him away from me as a punishment.' He was certainly the flower of the flock. A *post-mortem* examination showed that he gave promise of living to a great age. The funeral is to take place at Notre-Dame.

*June 28th.*—Louis Philippe opened the session of the Chambers on the 26th, and after alluding to his calamity, he made a very peaceful speech on foreign affairs, but he broke down several times during his address.

*August 25th.*—There have been great disturbances at Manchester and throughout the whole of the manufacturing districts. The pretence was a strike for an advance of wages, but the real cause is political, and the whole insurrection excited by the Chartists and the Anti-Corn Law people. The troops were called out ; some were brought from India, and a regiment from Ireland.

*November 6th.*—Peace is proclaimed with China. The capture and destruction of Ghuznee, in India, by General Nott took place on September 6 ; the defeat of Akbar Khan, at the head of sixteen thousand men, at Tezeen on the 13th by General Pollock ; and the occupation of Cabul by that General on the 16th. The prisoners left at Cabul have joined the Indian army, and it is expected that the remainder who were taken away by Akbar Khan will be recovered in a fews days. So the campaign in Afghanistan is quite concluded, and the army has returned in safety to India. Lord Ellenborough has issued a proclamation which is much abused by the saints. It is certainly an injudicious one, but I cannot agree as to its being irreligious or un-Christian-like. The gates of the temple of Sumnauth are given to the Hindoos ; they are merely a military trophy taken from one Pagan nation and given to another, and none but those who are determined to cavil and find fault can view it in any other light. The Duke of Wellington, speaking in the House of Lords on the subject, said he looked upon it 'only as a song of triumph.'

# 1843

*June 6th.*—There was a report that Lord Stanley and Sir James Graham had resigned on account of Sir Robert Peel having given up some clauses in the Irish Arms Bill, but no one seemed to believe there was any truth in the rumour ; though there certainly has been a disagreement between some members of the Cabinet and Peel on the subject. Many Conservatives think that Peel truckles to the Radicals and throws over his friends. Carmarthenshire is in a very disturbed state, and has been so for some time. A gang of four or five hundred men, led by a man in woman's clothes, under the name of ' Rebecca and her daughters,' have been pulling down turnpike gates and doing a great amount of mischief. No one can identify them, as they are all disguised and their faces blackened, most of them being armed. Most of the farmers and even some of the gentry, are said to be in league with them. They burned the workhouse and committed other ravages.

*July 2nd.*—News from Spain states that Espartero has raised the siege of Seville, having bombarded and destroyed the greater part of the suburbs and commenced a retreat to Cadiz, where the ' Malabar' is placed at his disposal, and that the English and French are ordered to unite in assisting him to escape, as there is no doubt if he fell into the hands of his opponents—Republicans, Christinos, or Carlists—he would be put to death without mercy.

*July 24th.*—Espartero and his wife and daughter have arrived at Woolwich. He was very well received by the authorities, and expressed himself very grateful for the kindness and attention with which he was treated on board the ' Malabar.'

*August 2nd.*—Marshal Sebastiani has left London and gone to Eu to meet the Queen, so there is no longer any doubt about her intention of visiting Louis Philippe. I believe it will be the first time since Henry VIII. that an English sovereign visits France except as an exile.

*October 12th.*—I drove to Highcliffe and saw Lady Canning, who gave me an account of the expedition to Eu and Brussels with the Queen, with which she was very much pleased. The Queen did not go to the field of Waterloo.

*October 17th.*—I hear that O'Connell and six others have been arrested for sedition. This is a good move of the Government, and will strengthen them, as for some time they have suffered the reproach of want of energy.

*November 6th.*—I arrived at Knowsley from Hooton, and found Lord Derby's keeper had been shot by poachers. Two men have been arrested on suspicion, and the poor man's case is almost hopeless.

*November 17th.*—The Duc de Bordeaux's visit to this country is beginning to assume a political aspect. He acknowledges that he came to see those friends who are still attached to him and his fortunes, and says that, though he will not disturb France, still if a change should take place, and he should be wanted, they will always find him ready.  He said in talking of his visit to England, ' I went to Rome to see the south of France, and I come to England to see the north.'

*November* 19*th.*—The Duc de Guiche[1]. called.  He said that the Duc de Bordeaux is coming to London on the 25th, and he has taken a house for him in Belgrave Square.  He has sent for his cook, and means to give dinners and receive two or three times a week.  Lord Shrewsbury gave him a grand reception at Alton Towers, and had a party of eighty people in the house to meet him.  It was continually changing, each person only staying two days.  The Duc de Guiche, being a personal friend of the Duc de Bordeaux, was invited for the whole time of his visit.  It must have been very tedious, for each time the Duc de Bordeaux [2] went out of the house or returned to it cannon were fired.

*December* 12*th.*—The Government at Madrid has again been thrown into confusion, the young Queen having made a declaration that her Prime Minister, Olozaga, had forced her to sign a proclamation for the dissolution of the Cortes.  She said that he first attempted to persuade her, but when she refused, saying that she would not do such an ungracious thing as dissolve an assembly that had just paid her the compliment of declaring her of age, he used menaces and very violent language to terrify her into compliance.  She then got up and tried to escape by a private door that led into her apartment, but he anticipated her, locked the door, forced her back to her seat, and made her sign the paper by force, holding her hand the whole time.  After his departure she made this statement, which was communicated to the Cortes.  Olozaga denies every word, says it is a falsehood of the Queen's, and that there is not the slightest foundation for any part of the story ; and adds, with great appearance of probability, that had he been guilty of such conduct, it is not likely he could have quietly walked out of the Palace through an ante-room filled with attendants and guards, who would have come to the Queen's assistance had she called out, and would have arrested him at the

[1] Twenty-seven years after this date he was Foreign Minister to the Emperor Napoleon III., as Duc de Gramont, at the declaration of the German war of 1870.

[2] He died in 1882.

least word or sign from her.   In the meantime he is deprived of
his office and seat in the Cortes.

## 1844

*February 28th.*—I went to Christchurch election, and hope
that my brother will come in.  He is opposed by a Mr. Harvey,
who has been sent down with a large sum of money, and I hear
that all the Dissenters, many of whom had promised to vote for
my brother, and some to remain neutral, are going against him.

*February 29th.*—My brother is elected for Christchurch by a
majority of a hundred.

*April 25th.*—I dined with Sir Robert Peel, who gave a great
dinner for the celebration of the Queen's birthday.  None but
Peers were present.

*May 23rd.*—By Lord and Lady Canning's advice I have hired
Cameron of Lochiel's place, Achnacarry, for the ensuing shooting
season.   I hear it is a beautiful place, with an excellent house.
It was hired last year by Lord Douro.

*June 2nd.*—The Emperor Nicholas of Russia arrived yesterday unexpectedly, and went to Count Brünnow's, his Ambassador.
The King of Saxony arrived at Buckingham Palace on the same
day.

*June 8th.*—We went to a breakfast at Chiswick given by the
Duke of Devonshire.  The day was beautiful, and nothing could
be prettier than the whole sight.  The Emperor of Russia was
there, with his circle around him.  He is a magnificent looking
man, and remarkably handsome as to features, but appears older
than his age, as he is stout and bald.  His hair and moustache
are fair, and he has rather a cast in his eye, but with a perfect
profile.  His manners are courteous and dignified, and rather like
those of George IV., but with more dignity, and with nothing of
the fine gentleman about him.  He is supposed to have come
over through some important political motive.  Sir Robert Peel
and Lord Stanley were both there, as well as Lord Palmerston and
all the diplomatic corps.  The Emperor spoke chiefly to the Duke
of Wellington during the breakfast.

*June 15th.*—Went to a party at Lady Palmerston's, where it was said that Peel has tendered his resignation. He is furious with those of his party who voted against him or stayed away. He persuaded the Conservatives to rescind their vote on Mr. Miles's amendment to the sugar duties, and the Ministerial proposal was carried by a majority of 22.

*June 22nd.*—At another party at Lady Palmerston's. There was a new lion, an Indian, called the Nizam of some place I forget. He is immensely tall and fat, and all the ladies were staring at him and pressing round him without the slightest regard to decorum, and I could not help thinking that he could not but have formed a very strange opinion of our English women. With his strict notions of propriety with regard to the conduct of the sex which all Asiatics possess, the manners of ours must appear to him the height of effrontery.

*July 28th.*—Left Chillingham Castle for the Highlands by Edinburgh and Glasgow, and embarked on board the steamer at Greenock. Stayed on deck the whole time, as, in spite of the heavy rain and wind, the heat in the cabin was intense, all the passengers agreeing in keeping the ports shut. We reached the Crinan Canal at midday, where, leaving the track-boat, we walked to the other end of it, about seven miles. The boat was crammed. This gave rise to a very absurd incident, for, as there was not room for each passenger to be seated in this barge, a number of women were obliged to stand between the benches, and the rope by which the boat was being towed having suddenly broken as we were entering a lock, the barge struck the side with great violence, and the whole row of women, a dozen at least, fell as if they had been shot one upon the other, amidst the roars of laughter of the rest. We were two hours passing through the canal, which has nine locks. We then embarked on board another steamer, the sea being quite smooth, and at five o'clock sat down to dinner in the cabin. We reached Oban that evening.

*August 1st.*—We were very glad this morning that we didn't go to Staffa yesterday, as the party who went there in the steamer could not land owing to the heavy sea, and were very ill. We left Oban in the morning, and reached Corpach, a small village on Lochiel, where we landed and took a conveyance to

Achnacarry, ten miles, which we reached at 5 P.M. The house is excellent, and the country around quite magnificent. Loch Lochy is about a mile from the house, and Loch Arkaig less. The latter is fifteen miles long and about two miles wide in its broadest part.* It is surrounded by mountains, the lower range nearly covered with the most picturesque woods of pine, birch, &c., of all sizes and ages. The trees not growing very close allow one to see the heather, fern, and rocks that cover the face of the mountain, which add extremely to the beauty of the scenery. Beyond these hills rise some much higher and more rugged, covered with rocks and heather and broken granite and haunted by ptarmigan. Achnacarry is situated in a deep glen between these two lakes, and with a beautiful clear river rushing over rocks, forming cascades close under the windows. There are a great many woods round the house, and the hills on both sides of the valley are so thickly clad that there is splendid shelter, and I think the storms which later in the year sweep down from the mountains would not be much to be feared in the glen. Lord Ossulston and Mr. Parker went out deer-stalking. The ladies in a boat kept up with them, as they were on the opposite face of the mountain. At about a mile from the end of Loch Arkaig, but now almost covered with trees, is an island which was once the burial-place of the MacFies. A little farther on the river Maly runs into the lake, and a mile beyond that are the primeval forests of Gusach and Gerraran, where the heather is so strong that a walking-stick can be cut out of it, and the jungle so impenetrable that I have known a dead stag lost there as one might a partridge in a turnip-field. At the farthest end of the lake Scournahat rises in the shape of a volcano. The whole scenery is in such admirable proportion in reference to the mountains, forests, and water that it is certainly one of the loveliest combinations that can anywhere be seen. On the bank of the river adjoining the two lakes there is a beautiful glen called 'the Dark Mile,' and a magnificent waterfall. An excellent road runs through it and joins that to Fort William. There is a cave in the rocks in this valley, in which Charles Edward Stuart concealed himself after his defeat at Culloden in 1746. We found the traditions respecting his hair-breadth escapes still fresh in the memories of the Highlanders, it being just a century since the rebellion took place. We got excellent ponies and very intelligent gillies ready to be engaged at five shillings a week and food, but no doubt if the fashion of going to the Highlands increases, they will not be found for that price. The pines in this primeval forest are some of them twenty feet round, and stand like white skeletons that have died in their old age. The natural growth of these forests at one time must have been of oak, as some very large trunks are lying buried in the more recent growth of pine. One I found was sixty feet long, and completely embedded in the stratum of bog. It is what is called a 'hind forest,' stags not coming in till late in the year. We seldom went out without seeing eagles, and Lord Edward Thynne killed one as it was soaring above him with a rifle and a single ball.

*August 31st.*—Some of my party went up Ben Nevis, which took them exactly twelve hours, it being fourteen miles off. The greatest drawback to this beautiful country is the climate, which s so wet on this coast that it is said to rain 220 days in the year, and we found this unfortunately true.

*September 2nd.*—The French having occupied Mogador, Lord Aberdeen insisted on their immediate evacuation of it. Prepara- tions for war are going on in all the dockyards. Lord Canning, Under-Secretary at the Foreign Office, writes to me after the bombardment of Tangier and says that for some days there had been every probability of war with France, but now he thinks the danger passed. The occupation of Mogador is since Lord Canning's letter, and will greatly complicate the business, as it is much worse to retain possession of a place than to knock it down.

*September 12th.*—Letters say that all danger of war is at an end. Prince de Joinville is ordered back to Neuilly, and the King, Louis Philippe, is coming over next month on a visit to the Queen. The latter is to embark for Scotland, and to live at Blair Athol, quite retired, whilst her castle at Balmoral is building.

*September 22nd.*—We accompanied the gentlemen and Lady Seymour to see the woods of Moich driven for deer. We went there in a boat, and then ascended the hill where we were posted.

There we drew a blank. We then descended to the shore and mounted our ponies, when another wood was driven two miles farther on, in which two stags were seen, and in a third a stag was killed. The sun set before we descended the last hill, and I never saw such a glorious sight. The mountains on one side were of the richest purple, while on the opposite shore of the lake the woods were as black as ink. The rays of the sun were reflected in the most dazzling manner on Glen Maly and on the peaks of the mountains, which contrasted exquisitely with the intense darkness of the corries and the woods of Gusach and Gerraran. The scene was so wonderfully beautiful that everything else was forgotten, and during the short time that the vision—for I can call it by no other name—lasted not a word was spoken. We could only gaze in wonderment and admiration. I never saw anything so surprisingly lovely before, and never expect to do so again. We then returned home in the four-oar. The papers have been full of Louis Philippe's visit to Windsor. His reception has been most cordial wherever he went, not only by the Queen but by the people. The officers of the French fleet have met with a most enthusiastic reception at Portsmouth. The English officers gave them a ball and a dinner ; healths were drunk and speeches made, and an immense quantity of humbug exchanged ; but the French like that, so I hope it will put them in a good humour. The Queen has given Louis Philippe the Garter.

*September* 16*th*.—Left Achnacarry by Glencoe and Loch Lomond.

*November* 7*th*.—Dined with the Cannings and met Mr. Gladstone and Mr. Phillimore. We were curious to see the former, as he is a man who is much spoken of as one who will come to the front. We were disappointed at his appearance, which is that of a Roman Catholic ecclesiastic, but he is very agreeable.

*November* 30*th*.—Mrs. Portman and her sister, Lady Sale, and Mrs. Sturt,[1] the widow of an officer killed at Cabul, came to luncheon. The latter is pretty and very interesting-looking. I never saw a countenance that bore such evident traces of past

---

[1] This lady married again and returned to India, and was one of the first people murdered on the outbreak of the Mutiny.

sorrow. She does all she can to appear cheerful, but her gaiety seems forced, and I saw once or twice an expression of agony come over her face. She has a pleasant manner, and is wholly free from affectation ; has a very graceful figure and a fascinating expression of countenance when she talks and smiles, and does not look above eighteen. But suffering of mind and body have deprived her of the freshness of youth, and she is deadly pale. I was agreeably surprised in Lady Sale, whom I imagined to myself to be a tall, masculine, overbearing sort of woman. Far from this, she is not above middle height, with quiet, ladylike manners, very proud of her husband and of the number of enemies he has killed in battle with his own hand. She is very fond of India and delighted to return there, which Mrs. Sturt is not. We made Sir Robert Sale's acquaintance the same day at dinner, who, being ill with an attack of ague, could not come to Heron Court. He did not talk much about events in India, as his daughter was just opposite and would have heard what he said. He is a little man, with blue eyes and very white teeth, which a gentleman at table who was suffering from toothache said he envied him more than his victories.

## 1845

*January 19th.*—Heron Court. Edward Stanley, Lord Derby's grandson, arrived, and a good conversation about politics took place in the evening. He argued with great acuteness and good temper, possessing a remarkable fund of information, seeing that he is only nineteen. I am greatly mistaken if he does not distinguish himself much some day. He is of rather advanced opinions. Some important and ominous changes have taken place in the Government within this week. The first was occasioned by the death of Lord St. Germans, which removes Lord Eliot to the House of Lords and obliges him to resign the Irish Secretaryship. Sir Thomas Fremantle is appointed in his place ; Mr. Sidney Herbert to be Secretary of War with a seat in the Cabinet ; Mr. Corry to take his place at the Admiralty. Mr. Gladstone has resigned office altogether, nobody knows why, but it is supposed to be either upon the Church Act—not being inclined to go as far as Peel intends going upon that subject—or on some question connected with trade and the sugar duties.

*March* 21*st.*—Good Friday. I went to Paris with Lord Ossulston.

*April* 10*th.*—The Queen has lost her keys, which she dropped out of her pocket as she was riding. As they were those of the Government boxes, the offices were in consternation at the idea of having all the locks altered. The day they were missed I was passing up King's Road when I saw Colonel Arbuthnot walking slowly in the middle of it with his eyes fixed on the ground. Behind him was a strong body of police and park-rangers drawn in a line across the road and looking down also. The effect was very absurd, and of course people amused themselves by giving false intelligence about the keys and sending them in all directions after supposed finders of the lost treasure.

*April* 11*th.*—Dined with Brünnow and the Duc de Broglie.

*April, London.*—I am just returned from the Castle of Ham, on the Somme, where I have been to see Prince Louis Napoleon in the prison, in which he has been confined since 1840. Early last January he sent M. Ornano to London to ask me to come and see him on a matter of vital importance to himself, bringing a small almanack for the year, with a vignette of the fortress of Ham painted in miniature on the cover. I was unable to go till now, and having obtained with some difficulty a permission from M. Guizot to see the Prince, I went to Ham on April 20. I found him little changed, although he had been imprisoned five years, and very much pleased to see an old friend fresh from the outer world and that world London. As I had only half a day allowed me for the interview, he confessed that, although his confidence and courage remained unabated, he was weary of his prison, from which he saw no chance of escaping, as he knew that the French Government gave him opportunities of doing so that they might shoot him in the act. He stated that a deputation had arrived from Ecuador offering him the Presidency of that Republic if Louis Philippe would release him, and in that case he would give the King his parole never to return to Europe. He had, therefore, sent for me as a supporter and friend of Sir R. Peel, at that time our Prime Minister, to urge Sir Robert to intercede with Louis Philippe to comply with his wishes, promising every possible guarantee for his good faith. The Prince was full of a plan for a new canal in Nicaragua, that promised every kind of advantage to British commerce. As a precedent for English official interference I was to quote Earl Grey's in favour of Prince Polignac's release in 1830. I assured the Prince that I would do my best ; but added that Lord Aberdeen was our Foreign Secretary, and that there was nothing of romance in his character. At this time Prince Louis was deeply engaged in writing the history of Artillery, and he took an hour in making me explain the meaning of several technical words in English, which he wished translated. He gave me a full account of his failure at Boulogne, which he declared was entirely owing to the sudden illness of the officer of the day whom he had secured, and who was to have given up the barracks at once. The soldiers had mostly been gained, and the prestige of his name in the French army was universal. To prove this he assured me that the cavalry escort of lancers who accompanied him to Ham made him constant gestures of sympathy on the road. He then said, ' You see the sentry under my window ? I do not know whether he is one of *mine* or not ; if he is he will cross his arms, if not, he will do nothing when I make a sign.' He went to the window and stroked his moustache, but there was no response until three were relieved, when the soldier answered by crossing his arms over his musket. The Prince then said, ' You see that my partisans are unknown to me, and so am I to them. My power is in an immortal name, and in that only ; but I have waited long enough, and cannot endure imprisonment any longer.' I understood that Count Montholon and Dr. Conneau, with his valet, Thelin, were his fellow-prisoners at Ham. After a stay of three hours I left the prison, and returned to London deeply impressed with the calm resolution, or rather philosophy, of this man, but putting little faith as to his ever renouncing the throne of France. Very few in a miserable prison like this, isolated and quasi-forgotten, would have kept their intellect braced by constant day studies and original compositions, as Louis Bonaparte did during the last five years in the fortress of Ham.

The day after I arrived in London I saw Sir Robert Peel, and related my interview and message to him. He seemed to be greatly interested, and certainly not averse to apply to the French Government in the Prince's favour on his conditions, but said he must consult Lord Aberdeen, which of course was inevitable. That evening he wrote to me to say that Lord Aberdeen ' would not hear of it.' Who can tell how this decision of the noble lord may influence future history ?

*May* 11*th.*—Dined with the Hamiltons ; nobody was there but the family. The Grand Duchess of Baden cross, as she wished to be godmother to Lady Douglas's child, but, being a Roman Catholic, the Bishop of London objected, and Lady Douglas was so annoyed that she would not attend the ceremony.

*June* 6*th.*—Started for the powder ball at the Palace. My costume, dark blue velvet coat, gilt lace ; gold tissue waistcoat, pink satin shorts, and powdered wig. There was an immense crowd all through St. James's to the Palace. They were in high good-humour and pleased at our letting down the glasses and showing ourselves. The minuet was danced very fairly, no mistakes being made, the Queen being decidedly the best performer. After the minuet a quadrille was danced, after which we passed the Queen.

*August* 8*th.*—Lord and Lady Seymour went with us to Achnacarry. Lady Seymour used to go out stalking, and killed one of the best stags.

*Achnacarry, August* 19*th.*—The newspapers are full of accounts of the failure of the potato crop all over England and Ireland. It will be a sad thing for the poor this winter. Corn is also very high, another misfortune, which will probably be taken advantage of by the enemies of the Corn Laws to urge a further reduction of tariff. The French have sustained two defeats in Algeria. In the first a body of 450 men were cut to pieces by the Arabs under Abd-el-Kader, only ten escaping. In the last 200 men and five officers laid down their arms and surrendered prisoners of war.

*August* 24*th.*—We have had the most awful storm. The wind was so violent that nobody in the house could sleep, and the servants actually got up at three in the morning and came downstairs, fearing the roof would be blown off. This storm continued the whole of the next day, with heavy rain. I went down to the loch and was well repaid for it. It was impossible to see anything finer in its way. It was like a sea—immense waves of deep green tipped with foam breaking against the shore, and dashing the spray to an immense height.

*October 25th.*—We left Achnacarry with the Seymours on a fine bright morning.

*October 30th.*—Parted with the Seymours at York and went to Knowsley. Found that Lord Stanley had been called to London for a Cabinet meeting.

*November 3rd.*—Left Knowsley for Grimsthorpe, Lord Willoughby d'Eresby's place. Nothing is talked of in London to-day but the elopement of Lady Adela Villiers with Captain Ibbotson. Poor Lady Jersey is much distressed. Lord Stuart de Rothesay is dead. He was the Duke of Wellington's right-hand man in the Peninsular War, as Commissioner managing the Spaniards and Portuguese Juntas, which he did with great ability. Afterwards Ambassador at Paris.

*December 11th.*—Heron Court. My brother came down, bringing news of Sir Robert Peel's resignation. It is not yet known what occasioned this extraordinary and unexpected event, but it is supposed to be connected with the Corn Laws.

*December 13th.*—Sir Robert Peel has advised the Queen to send for Lord John Russell, which her Majesty has done. He came in four years ago, professing to be a friend of the agricultural interest, and having six months ago declared positively that he would not vote for the abolition of the Corn Laws, as he thought the advantage which might be gained by the manufacturer would be more than counterbalanced by the mischief it would do to the agriculturist. He has now not only proposed the total abolition of those laws, and resigns office because the majority of the Cabinet is against him, but advises the Queen to entrust the formation of a new Ministry to Lord John Russell, thereby throwing the country into the hands of the Radicals, for no moderate Government under Russell, Grey, and Morpeth is possible.

*December 15th.*—Lord John Russell has been sent for by the Queen, but it is not yet known whether he accepts office ; he is to give a definite answer to-morrow. It is said Peel proposed a total abolition of the Corn Laws, and was opposed by all the Cabinet except Lord Aberdeen, Sir James Graham, and Mr. Sidney Herbert. The Duke of Wellington came over next day, and with him all the rest except Lord Stanley, but the Duke afterwards repented and Peel resigned. He expected that the Queen would have made more difficulty about accepting his resignation than she appears to have done, for when he went down to Osborne House with his colleagues he told Mr. Gunnell, the inspector of the railroad, to keep a special train for him next day, as he did not think he would return with the other Ministers. But he came back with them, and his opinion was not asked as to who should be his successor.

*December* 19*th.*—Lord Canning writes that Lord John Russell is believed to have formed a Government, and that the ports are to be opened directly, wheat being only at 57*s.*

*December* 20*th.*—Nothing decided as yet. Lords Aberdeen and Lincoln, Sir James Graham, and Mr. Sidney Herbert met on Friday at Sir Robert Peel's house.

*December* 21*st.*—Lord John Russell has given up the attempt to form a Cabinet, because Lord Palmerston insists on being Foreign Secretary, to which Lord Grey objects. There is great diversity of opinion amongst the Whigs on the subject of the Corn Laws, many being against total repeal, and others for a fixed duty. In short, this dissension has ended in the Queen sending again for Sir Robert Peel.

*December* 25*th.*—Sir Robert Peel has resumed office with the same Cabinet except Lord Stanley, who remains out.

*December* 30*th.*—I went to a meeting at Christchurch called by the Anti-Corn Law party. There was a good deal of speaking, and the Radical party were defeated by three to one on a resolution which they proposed.

## 1846

*January 12th.*—Heron Court. The Cannings arrived to-day. He evidently expects that Peel's Government will not stand, and, being Under-Secretary for Foreign Affairs, he should know.

*January 22nd.*—The Queen opened Parliament to-day in person. Sir Robert Peel gave his explanation of the events which led to the dissolution of the Ministry and its re-formation in a long speech, half threatening and half apologetic. It was eloquent, but his cause is very weak and his position very pitiful. The statement was listened to in solemn silence by his own party, while it was occasionally cheered by the Opposition, which must have been very mortifying. Disraeli then got up and made a very clever and bitter attack, full of personalities and sarcasms directed against Peel, every one of which was received with laughter and cheers from both sides of the House. The Address was carried in both Houses without opposition. The Duke of Richmond and I spoke in favour of Protection, and were both cheered ; rather an event in the House of Lords.

*January 27th.*—Saw Lady Stanley, who says her husband resigned for no other reason than his objection to Sir Robert Peel's policy on the Corn Laws. Sir Robert Peel has brought in his bill for the repeal of the Corn Laws. He proposes to keep a sliding scale, though reducing the amount of protection for three years, at the end of which time there is to be a total repeal of all duty on corn. He proposes at the same time to diminish the duties upon manufactures, one-half directly ; but whatever amount of protection he leaves them now they are to keep at the end of three years, while the agriculturists are to lose theirs entirely. The compensation he promises them is a mere mockery, and will do more harm than good.

*February 9th.*—The debate on Peel's Corn Bill begins to-day. Mr. Miles made a good speech on our side.

*February 14th.*—The debate on the Corn Bill still continues, and no decision has yet taken place. Almost all the speaking has been on the agricultural side, Lord John Russell, Lord Morpeth, and Mr. Roebuck being the only Whigs of note who have spoken on the other,

*February 15th.*—I heard yesterday that Lady Powerscourt's marriage with Lord Castlereagh is settled. I am going up to London this morning at the Duke of Richmond's request to speak upon his motion for an inquiry into the burthen on land. Lord Beaumont also brings forward a motion to the same effect.

*February 17th.*—News from Algeria gives bad accounts of the state of the French army. Abd-el-Kader harasses them on all sides in a most indefatigable manner, and in a way which makes all their bravery and knowledge of war perfectly useless, for he never waits for their troops. His system is one of alternate attack and retreat, and as all the inhabitants are for him the French are never warned of any intended attack, but he falls upon them unexpectedly when they are least prepared, and then disappears as suddenly as he came, without their having time to do him any injury. In addition to this harassing mode there is a great deal of sickness in their army. It is said that the Duc d'Aumale is going out to take command, and that more troops are to be sent.[1]

*February 18th.*—Lord Stanley declares himself against Peel's Bill, and for a dissolution. Peel is said to be very unwell, and has been cupped three times. He can think and talk of nothing but famine. Lords De la Warr and Forester have resigned their Court places.

*February 19th.*—Returned to Heron Court from London, and saw Lord Stanley there, who is decidedly against Peel's measure, and though disinclined at present to take the lead of the Agricultural party, will certainly do so at some future period. He thinks that any attempt to form a Government at present from amongst our party would be premature, from the want of an experienced leader in the House of Commons, and the only way to rally and unite the party is in opposition. Therefore, the Whigs must first come in. The Duke of Wellington, though he supports the measure, is against it, and told Lord Stanley that his only reason for staying in and supporting Peel was for the sake of the Queen and the peace of the country. He deeply lamented that Peel had brought the measure forward, thought he was quite

---

[1] The Duc d'Aumale defeated Abd-el-Kader, and took his camp. Abd-el-Kader was a prisoner in France until Louis Napoleon released him in 1853.

wrong, that he had broken up a noble party, and that it was for him (Lord Stanley) to rally it again, his own career was nearly ended, and that Stanley must be leader of the party.  Lord Beaumont went to the Duke and asked him to grant him a committee for an inquiry into the burthen on land, and he first tried to persuade him to give it up, but finding him firm, he said, 'Well, my good fellow, you must have it.  I will not oppose it; I am quite of your opinion on the subject; it is a d——d mess, but I must look to the peace of the country and the Queen.'  It is evident from his whole conduct lately this is his sincere opinion, for though he retains office he has never said a word in defence of Peel or his measure.  He sits on the Government bench with his hat drawn over his face, apparently indifferent to all the attacks made on the Government, never saying a word in answer.

*February 22nd.*—Heron Court.  The Cannings arrived.  He supports Peel, so of course politics were not talked.

*February 24th.*—News has arrived from India of our having gained a great victory over the Sikhs, who were the aggressors, crossing the Sutlej and invading our possessions.  Sir Henry Hardinge, Sir H. Gough, and General McCaskell advanced to meet them, and a battle was fought at Moodkee on the 18th, which was decisive, it having continued till the 22nd, when we stormed and took their camp with a hundred pieces of cannon.  Our loss was dreadful.  Sir Robert Sale was killed, also General McCaskell, Major Broadfoot, and Major Somerset, Lord Fitzroy Somerset's son.  In all about 150 officers and about three thousand men were killed and wounded, a thousand of them being English.  Many were killed in the enemy's camp, which was mined, and blew up when we had taken possession of it, and many others whilst engaged in burying the dead, through want of cavalry.  We were only twenty thousand against sixty thousand, and had only fifty guns.  Our troops behaved with the most desperate gallantry.  The battle of the 22nd was fought at Ferozeshah.  Sir Henry Hardinge, who is Viceroy, was present at both that and the engagement at Moodkee, having volunteered to serve under Sir Hugh Gough, to whom he afterwards addressed a despatch describing the battle.  This at first sight seems absurd, but it was due in accordance with the etiquette observed on these

occasions, this kind of despatch being intended as a public document.   The army under the command of Sir H. Gough had
marched 150 miles in six days previous to the battle of Moodkee,
and on the same day had marched thirty miles.   The men were
exhausted with fatigue, and dying of thirst, without time to
refresh themselves, when they were hurried into battle against
fresh troops.   These they repulsed, but with severe loss.   They
then bivouacked on the field of battle, and the next day entrenched
themselves, expecting a fresh attack, but being recruited by two
other regiments they advanced to the relief of Sir John Littler,
who was supposed to be beleaguered in Ferozeshah by the Sikhs.
Having effected a junction with him, they attacked the camp of
the Sikhs, and the fighting continued the greatest part of the
night.   Next day the attack was again renewed and the enemy
driven out.

*February 24th.*—After this the Sikhs advanced again with
30,000 fresh troops and numerous artillery, and though we had
not a single gun to oppose them, and had made up our minds to
be destroyed, they most unaccountably retreated, and since the
date of the last despatch on December 25 they had not been
heard of.   Sir Robert Peel has sent a good report of his health
to 'The Times,' saying that he has not been cupped and was never
better in his life.

*March 9th.*—There was a meeting of Peers at the Duke of
Richmond's, at which Lord Eglinton read a letter from Lord
Stanley advising as to the course to be pursued in opposition to
Peel's bill, and promising his support to the Protection party.   In
consequence of this it was decided to look upon Stanley as the
leader of the party, and to do nothing without consulting him.
Lord Eglinton and I, who have been chosen Whips on this
occasion, informed Lord Stanley of what had passed at the meeting that same afternoon in the House of Lords, and he was
evidently very much pleased and flattered at the confidence reposed in him.

*March 15th.*—We took a box at the opera with Lady Seymour,
and went afterwards to Lady Palmerston's.   Mr. Sidney Herbert
was there, and came up to me in a great state of excitement,
saying that my conduct in leaving Peel was unworthy a gentle-

man, that the whole Protectionist party were a set of fools, and
Lord Stanley the greatest fool among us, and that Peel was
delighted at having got rid of us, &c.  In short, he said every-
that was most obnoxious.  If he had not been in such a frantic
passion I should probably not have been able to keep my temper,
but there was something so absurd in his unprovoked attack that
I retained perfect command over myself.  It was certainly very
extraordinary, as I had not spoken to him that evening, or seen
him since he came to London, and had given him no provocation
whatever.  He is generally careful of what he says; in fact, he
carries caution to that degree that he is famous for it.  We met
again at the tea-table that evening, when Mrs. Norton joined us,
and by that time Mr. Herbert had recovered his good humour.
He called on me this morning, partly to make up for his extra
vagant conduct last night, and partly to find out whether Lord
Stanley meant to accept the leadership of our party.  This shows
the violence of party feeling at present, as Sidney Herbert and I
have always been like brothers.

*March 21st.*—Lord Stanley is now established in the direction
of the Protectionist party.  He presented some petitions yesterday in favour of Protection, and took the opportunity of declaring
himself against Peel's bill for repealing the Corn Laws.  This
will fix many waverers who have been inclined to vote with Peel
though disliking his measure.

*March 26th.*—News has arrived of another great victory over
the Sikhs.  The battle took place at Aliwal, and the troops engaged were commanded by Sir Harry Smith.  The Sikhs were
much stronger in numbers and well provided with artillery, but
we took their batteries at the point of the bayonet.

*April 1st.*—Another great victory over the Sikhs at Sobraon
on February 10.  The whole army, including Sir Harry Smith's
division, which had joined Sir Hugh Gough and Sir Henry
Hardinge on the 8th, was engaged.  They stormed the entrenchments of the Sikhs, taking about sixty cannon, and drove them
over the river with great slaughter.  There is now every probability that the war is ended, this last battle having been a very
decisive one.

*April 18th.*—Louis Philippe has again been shot at when

driving in the forest of Fontainebleau. No one was hurt. The English army entered Lahore on February 20 and occupied the citadel.

*May 13th.*—A great dinner at Lord Stanley's, who observed that it was a curious state of parties when a Liberal like Lord Bessborough whipped up the bishops to support the Duke of Wellington on a Free Trade question.

*May 11th.*—The third reading of the Corn Bill took place, and the numbers were—for the bill, 327; against, 229; majority for the Ministers, 98, being one more than for the second reading Peel's position, however, has not improved, and the general impression is that he must resign before long. The treatment he received is truly humiliating, and I cannot conceive his submitting to it. The Whigs are in high spirits. The plan now seems to be to propose a fixed duty in committee, which, if supported by the Protectionists and Whigs, must be carried. Peel, who goes for the total abolition, will then be obliged to go out or dissolve Parliament, but it is probable that he will not attempt to prolong the struggle and will resign at once.

*Lord George Bentinck to Lord M.*

Harcourt House: May 16, 1846.

My dear Malmesbury,—I have set an engine to work to get Lord Hawke if possible. Lord Galway must be my instrument.

Disraeli made a wonderful speech last night; even O'Connell says it was the greatest speech he ever heard within the walls of Parliament.

Ever yours sincerely,

G. BENTINCK.

*May 18th.*—Colonel Bowles called, and told me he saw Peel yesterday, who said he could no longer bear the treatment he received and had determined to resign. In the last night's debate on the Corn Bill Disraeli made a most violent attack upon him, which was cheered, not only by the Protectionists but by his own friends, who, though they voted for him, are very angry with him for getting himself and them into such a scrape. They now see they have gained nothing by following him. Nothing could be more violent than party feeling at this moment, especially between the Peelites and Protectionists, who seem to have lost all power of commanding their language.

*May 22nd.*—I have refused all pairs in the Protection party until after the second reading of the Corn Bill in the House of Lords.

*May 23rd.*—A great meeting of Whig Peers at Lansdowne House, at which they pledged themselves to support the bill. We shall therefore be completely beaten if they do not vote for the fixed duty. We expected after Lord Normanby had made overtures to us, through me, which were agreed to by Lord Stanley, that they would support our amendment. It is said the majority of the meeting at Lansdowne House were for voting with us, but they were overruled by Lords Clarendon, Minto, and John Russell, and are now pledged to vote for the total repeal. Many of the Whigs are much annoyed at this decision, and expressed themselves so to me.

*May 25th.*—The debate on the second reading of the Corn Bill began to-day, when Lord Stanley made a most splendid speech on the subject—extraordinarily argumentative and eloquent, and free from all personality. It had an immense effect, and was praised by all parties.

*May 27th.*—On returning home from White's Club, a man ran over the street and stopped my horse, and at first I did not recognise him, but to my great surprise I saw Prince Louis Napoleon, whom I had left a year before as a prisoner in the fortress of Ham. He had just landed in England after his escape, and was going into the Brunswick Hotel in Jermyn Street. On the same day we dined with the Duke of Beaufort at Hamilton House, and as the party was sitting down to dinner I saw opposite me Louis de Noailles, who was one of the Attachés at the French Embassy, and said across the table to him, ' Have you seen him ?' ' Who ?' he asked. ' Louis Napoleon,' I replied ; ' he is in London, having just escaped.' De Noailles dropped the lady who was on his arm and made but one jump out of the room, for it seems that the news had not yet reached the French Embassy. I never saw a man look more frightened.

*June 4th.*—The Government has been defeated in the House of Lords on a bill respecting Lord Hardinge's and Lord Gough's pensions. The Duke of Richmond moved that the pension proposed to be paid to their two next heirs should be paid to the present holders of the titles in addition to that given by the East India Company. The Government opposed this, and were beaten by 12. *

*June 15th.*—The Duke of Buckingham moved an amendment to continue the protection to agriculture after a lapse of three years had taken place, but the Government had a majority of 33, and it was rejected.

*June 16th.*—Lord Winchilsea's amendment for a fixed duty was rejected by the same majority.

*June 25th.*—The Corn Law Bill passed to-day without a division. Lord Stanley entered his protest against it, which will probably be signed by all the Protectionist Peers. The second reading of the Coercion Bill came on in the Commons, and the Government were beaten by a majority of 73 ; 106 Protectionists voted with Peel, and 70 against him, and all the Whigs and Radicals. The defeat of the Government was reckoned so complete that neither Whigs nor Protectionists cheered.

*June 26th.*—There was a Cabinet this morning, after which Sir Robert Peel went down to Osborne to acquaint the Queen with the decision of the Cabinet, and, it is supposed, to tender his resignation.

*June 27th.*—Dined with Lord and Lady Lansdowne. Met. the Beauforts, the Clarendons, Lord de Grey, and the Duke of Richmond. It was a dull dinner, everybody occupied with politics, and the party so mixed that the subject could not be mentioned. Sir Robert Peel went down again to Osborne to-day.

*June 29th.*—I hear the dinner at Lansdowne House has made a great sensation from its mixture, and is called the ‘Coalition’ dinner, which is absurd. Sir Robert Peel declared in the House of Commons this afternoon that he had resigned office, and would give his support to Lord John Russell in all Free Trade measures. This will bring back to the Protectionists a great many of the Peelite party, and is a good move for them. Various rumours, as usual, as to the posts given to the members of the new Government. Peel flattered Cobden immensely, saying that there was one name which would go down to posterity, which was neither his nor Lord John's, but that of Richard Cobden.  Peel was escorted to his house by about a hundred people, who cheered as loudly as their limited numbers would permit.

*August 21st.*—News from Spain has been very interesting of late.  The marriage of the Queen with the Duke of Cadiz is settled, in spite of her abhorrence of him ; and that of her sister with the Duc de Montpensier is announced to take place at the same time.  This is a masterpiece of Louis Philippe's cunning, because it is known that the Queen would not have children, even if her own bad health made it possible.  Her sister will then be heir to the throne.  The English Government, especially Lord Palmerston, are much displeased, and Mr. Bulwer and M. de Bresson, their respective Ministers at Madrid, are on the coolest terms since the announcement has been made, it having taken Lord Palmerston completely by surprise.  Mr. Bulwer did not attend the public announcement of the Queen's marriage ; and, to complicate the question, Don Carlos's son, Count Montemolin, Cabrera, and other Carlist generals, have made their escape, and the whole country is in a ferment in consequence of this French alliance, which is generally detested.  If I know Lord Palmerston, he will never forgive Louis Philippe this trick which he has played upon him, and will pay him off some day.

*October 7th.*—We left London for Dover with my brother-in-law, Lord Ossulston ; sailed for Ostend, thence to Liège, where the engine was taken off and we went down the steepest-inclined plane I ever saw on any railway.  If the rope had given way we must all have been smashed.  Thence by Verviers to Cologne, and up the Rhine by steamboat.  The King of Prussia is employing four hundred workmen in finishing the Cathedral at Cologne, which will consume seventeen years before it is completed, if the money and stone do not fail.  The latter is procured from a quarry near Drachenfels.

*October 12th.*—Have reached Godesberg.  We walked up the hill to the castle of Drachenfels.  The ruin, which is very picturesque, is disfigured by hundreds of English names scrawled upon the battlements, a habit that seems peculiar to our nation.

K

*October* 13*th.*—Left Godesberg and reached Coblenz. We walked to the fortress of Ehrenbreitstein, which contains a garrison of twelve hundred men. The magazines are victualled for seven years, but are always renewed every three years.

*October* 14*th.*—We arrived at Mayence and went on to Mannheim.

*October* 15*th.*—Reached Heidelberg. The road runs along the banks of the Neckar and is very beautiful. This magnificent castle was destroyed by fire, but the exterior is uninjured, excepting some parts which were blown up by the French in the Thirty Years' War.

*October* 16*th.*—Left Heidelberg by the railway, with the Cannings, whom we met here, and reached Fribourg. Walked to the cathedral, said to be the finest in Europe after that of Burgos. In size it is not larger than that of Salisbury or even Christchurch, but in the richness of its architecture and decorations it immeasurably surpasses both. The windows of painted glass exceed any.

*October* 17*th.*—Left Fribourg by the road through the Höllenthal, which is very wild. The approach to Stuhlingen is magnificent along the brow of a very steep hill, the declivity of which is so abrupt that you see nothing over the parapet wall from your carriage but the valley at an immense depth under your feet. The sun was just setting as we were descending the hill, and threw the most glorious light over the valley and the woods and mountains in the distance. It was quite dark before we left Stuhlingen, and we, therefore, lost the scenery to Schaffhausen. We went to Wiebur's hotel, which is just opposite the falls of the Rhine.

*October* 18*th.*—Reached Constance, close to the lake, which at this point expands into an immense sheet of water. Lord Ossulston left us to-day for Zurich, on his way to Milan, and will join us at Venice.

*October* 19*th.*—Left Constance for Italy over the Brenner Pass, by Bludenz, Landeck, and the Tyrol.

*October* 21*st.*—Reached Innspruck. I never saw anything so frightful as the women of this country. They all look old, more like old men than women, and as they wear men's hats the resemblance is still more striking. I suppose it is hard labour and bad living which makes them so uncomely. All have the same ugly features, high cheek bones, large mouths, small eyes, with enormous feet and legs. The museum is entirely supported by the contributions of the inhabitants, each paying ten florins per annum. The guardian showed us a miniature of Hofer, the famous patriot, who opposed the French in '96, the only likeness taken of him ; also his sword and accoutrements, all of which are held in great veneration by the Tyrolese. As we were going away he took us into a private room and produced a letter which was written by Lord Bathurst, our Minister, to the Tyrolese during the great war, sending them a subsidy of 30,000l. from the English Government to assist them in opposing the French invasion. In reading the letter I found to my surprise that, though it was signed ' Bathurst,' it was written by my father, who at that time was Under-Secretary at the Foreign Office. We carried away a copy of it, and the superintendent said that most of the English who came here wanted one, so he always kept some ready written. This letter is apparently much valued here as a relic, together with a German copy of it.

*October 23rd.*—We met the funeral of an officer of the Tyrolese corps, an immense number of people following the procession. Those nearest the coffin carried lighted tapers, after them the priests in full canonicals, then the coffin, with a yellow pall and black borders, and two pictures painted or worked upon it. Four men walked beside the coffin carrying lanterns on the top of long poles ; behind, the military band playing the gayest opera music, and afterwards an immense crowd of men, women, and children. The effect was strange, for during the time the band played their opera airs, the great bell of the church, the most tuneful and melodious one I ever heard, every stroke resembling a full chord of the finest wind instrument, tolled slowly ; so the whole was a great mixture of solemnity and frivolity, but still certainly striking to one who, like me, witnessed it for the first time. The ascent of Brenner is very easy, and only took an hour and a half.[1]

---

[1] There is now a splendid railway over this pass down to Venice.

*October* 26*th.*—After leaving Mittenwald reached Niedern-dorf. It snowed a little when we started, and by the time we reached the first post to Landau it lay so thick upon the ground that we thought we should not be able to proceed. It was above the axletrees of the front wheels, and the track was nearly ob-literated. The atmosphere looked nearly as white as the ground, and the snow increased rapidly till it reached the top of the front wheels. At this anxious moment we met a party of men with a snow-plough, dragged by twenty horses, who had got through the drift, and this enabled us to pass and reach Landau. The next stage to Cortina was nearly as bad, the snow reaching over the parapet, which it hid, making the road very unsafe going down the sharp turns in the descent. The horses, however, were so good and well-trained that they go along the worst roads perfectly safely and never jib. We breakfasted at Cortina, which is the first Italian town. There we fell in with Mr. Waghorn's Indian courier. He was making experiments to find the shortest road from India through Italy and France.

*October* 27*th.*—Arrived at Mestre, and embarked in a large gondola for Venice. The town has been lighted by gas since we were here fifteen years ago, and the railway and bridge are no disfigurement to it.

*October* 31*st.*—I went with the Websters to hear mass at Saint Mark's, the Patriarch of Venice officiating. The greatest part of the ceremony appeared to consist in dressing and undressing him. The music good, but nothing remarkable.

*November* 2*nd.*—I went to the Manfrini Palace to admire again Ariosto's portrait by Titian.[1]

*November* 3*rd.*—Went to the Academia, where I was con-firmed in my opinion that 'The Assumption' and 'The Presenta-tion of the Virgin as a Child' are the two finest pictures by Titian in Europe. The latter is the superior one. Titian's last work is also in this collection, painted when he was ninety-nine years old, but shows the effect of years even upon him.

*November* 16*th.*—I have been seriously ill with a quinsy, and till now unable to go out. Left Venice to-day and reached Padua,

---

[1] This collection was sold, and this picture is now in our National Gallery.

thence to Ferrara. Detained an hour and a half crossing the Adige and the Po, being delayed by a carriage that was before us embedded in the mud.

*November* 18*th*.—We reached Bologna, where Lord Ossulston rejoined us.

*November* 20*th*.—Reached Florence.

*November* 25*th*.—Went to Bartolini's and Power's studios. The latter is making a duplicate of his ' Greek Slave ' for Lord Ward. His statue of ' Eve ' is also beautiful in the shape of the head, which is quite lovely both in feature and expression, but the figure is much less modest and graceful than that of his ' Greek Slave,' probably from its being rather larger than life. But the statue which pleased me most was one of a girl of fourteen by Dupré, and which he calls ' Innocenza ; ' the figure being that of a girl just on the verge of womanhood. The papers mention the occupation of Cracow by the Austrians, who, in concert with Russia and Prussia, have declared that the Republic of Cracow no longer exists, and have annexed it to the Austrian Empire, Russia declaring that if Austria did not take it she would. This has been done without the knowledge of either England or France, and is said to be a consequence of the coolness existing between those Powers, for if the *entente cordiale* was still in force they would not have dared to do such a thing.

*November* 27*th*.—Left Florence at ten, and arrived at Arezzo at seven. The roads were very heavy and covered with loose stones.

*November* 28*th*.—The towns we passed through bore marks of great antiquity, and are very curious old places. The whole aspect of the country and the people is so different from what we have lately seen, and they are apparently so far behind in civilisation, that one could easily fancy oneself a thousand miles from Florence. We were shown in the church at Arezzo the skeleton of a man who had been immured. It was still covered with skin-like parchment, and the features were quite preserved. The wretched creature had been walled-up evidently alive, and seems to have struggled either to escape from his prison or died from suffocation.

*November* 29*th*.—Reached Civita Castellana in ten hours.

*November* 30*th.*—We reached Rome at 3 P.M., having received a very bad impression of the climate, as it had poured with rain during the whole journey from Florence.

*December* 10*th.*—The rains have been so heavy that the greatest part of Rome is under water, which is deepest on the Corso, the Piazza del Popolo, and some parts of the Via Babuino. In the Corso the depth is as much as four or five feet ; in fact, a man was nearly drowned there, but was saved by the Prince Borghese, who was going about in a boat carrying bread to the poor people who were prisoners in their houses. In the Via di Ripetta the depth is seventeen feet. This is the highest flood since 1805 ; and as during the last three or four days it had been predicted, the people who inhabit those parts of the town liable to inundation have had time to remove their property, but they have not done so, and do not care, as the Government always indemnifies them for their losses.

*December* 12*th.*—The most violent storm of thunder and hail occurred to-day ; our windows were blown in.

*December* 21*st.*—Went to Cardinal Marini's *ricevimento.* He is extremely unpopular, and it was said those who went to his house would have been pelted, but we went there safely. Lady Lichfield and her daughter, the Cannings, Shelburnes, and a quantity of English and Americans, were there. We were presented to the Princess Lancellotti, who received for the Cardinal. It was not worth seeing, as the Roman ladies were frightened at the rumour I have mentioned, and but few came. Those who did were covered with the most magnificent diamonds, but were not handsome.

*December* 22*nd.*—Lord Ossulston and I went to Cisterna to shoot, but found the Pontine Marshes flooded, and could not approach the wild geese or any sort of wild fowl, so we had to beat some woods for woodcock. One of these was called the ' Wood of the Dead Woman,' why we could not find out. But as the marshes were under water the woodcock could not get their food, and we found very few, so returned on the 25th to Rome.

## 1847

*January 1st.*—We called on Signora Gagiotti, surnamed the 'Corinne' of Rome. She is very handsome, twenty-three years of age, speaks English and three other languages perfectly, has a very fine voice, is a good musician, playing both harp and piano, and writes poetry, for which she was crowned last year at the Capitol. She paints portraits better than a great many artists.

*January 4th.*—We went with Lord Walpole, who understands Etruscan vases very well, to see the great collection of Mr. Campana. Lord Walpole told us there were rules by which to distinguish the different sorts, and the epochs at which they were made. The latter are divided into four. The first is recognised by the rudeness of the drawings, which represent unnatural and fictitious animals painted upon a light-coloured ground. The oldest of all are quite black without any figures. The second period represents figures resembling the style of the Egyptians, very stiff, with few lines, generally black or black and white upon a red ground. At the third period, when the art was brought to its greatest perfection, the figures were beautifully drawn in the Grecian style, representing historical subjects, many taken from the 'Iliad,' and called 'Homeric.' These are generally red on a black ground. The fourth period marked the decadence of the art, and its products were very inferior to the third. I went to see the famous statue of Pompey at the Palazzo Spada, at the foot of which Cæsar fell. I consider this the most interesting association to be found in all Rome.

*January 11th.*—Left Rome for Naples. Slept at Cisterna. All the people looked wretched, as the infection from the Pontine Marshes extends to this place. The greatest part of the population have the fever, and chiefly men who work in the fields and are exposed to the malaria. My courier says that the points of the shoots of walnut trees steeped in water and put out all night is the usual and most certain remedy, and more effectual than quinine.

*January 13th.*—We slept at Mola, and we reached Naples in the evening following.

*January 14th.*—Went to the Museum, where the pictures are not first-rate, but there are curious paintings from Pompeii. We stayed at. Naples till the 18th. Vesuvius was nearly silent during that time. From Naples we went to Salerno, seeing Pompeii on our way.

*January 19th.*—We started with Lord Ossulston at 7 A.M., and reached Pæstum at 10.50 ; remained there until 2 P.M., and got back to Naples at 6 P.M. We had our luncheon in the Temple of Neptune, a magnificent structure, and most interesting, but the swarm of beggars greatly spoiled one's pleasure, and it is impossible to get rid of them.

*January 20th.*—We returned to Naples, and went in the evening to Princess Torella's ball. Pretty and not crowded. All the handsome women were English.

*January 22nd.*—The Duke of Devonshire, who is staying here, hired a steamer, and invited us, the Kenmares, and three painters to make an expedition to Capri. The Duke had prepared luncheon when we reached the island, but just as we were starting, his butler, who was very active in regulating matters, unfortunately fell back from the pier into the sea, creating great alarm and confusion, and delaying us over half-an-hour while he changed his dress. Half way to Capri it began to rain, which forced us to go below, and finally there was too much swell for us to enter the cave safely, and we had to return to Naples, having failed in our projects.

*January 23rd.*—We went to the opera at San Carlo in Mr. Temple's (our Minister's) box. It is the largest theatre in Europe.

*January 24th.*—An eruption of Mount Vesuvius has begun, and has been very fine for the last two nights. Went to the Princess Dentici.

*January 26th.*—We all three left Naples, slept at Castella-mare, where we met Wrottesley and Bridgman, and proceeded to Sorrento. We walked all over the town, saw the fortifications which baffled the French the first time they laid siege to it, though they took it two years afterwards. There is a manufactory of inlaid wood here.

*January 27th.*—I went to Ravello, where I visited the

cathedral, which has some fine old mosaics. A curious discovery has just been made of a manuscript which mentions the exact spot in the church where the bones of St. Andrew the Apostle were buried. Searches were accordingly made, and they have been exhumed, and the skull placed in a gold box, and the ceremony of canonisation takes place to-morrow. A service in honour of the saint was going on in a crypt where we descended. I afterwards walked up the Valley of the Mills, which is very beautiful. Had some excellent maccaroni for luncheon. It is reckoned the best in Italy and very cheap, two hundredweight costing only forty francs.

*January 29th.*—Returned to Castellamare and caught the train for Naples.

*February 3rd.*—We all went this evening to the King's ball ; it was worth seeing, the apartment being fine and beautifully lighted. In the ball-room there were five enormous chandeliers of crystal, but they were hung too low, the room being immensely high.

*February 5th.*—Left Naples, and reached Rome on the 7th. Our party consisted of the Shelburnes, the Cannings, the Herberts of Muckross, the Comtesse and Mdlle. de Flahault, M. Latour-Maubourg, and Ossulston. We hired a balcony on the Corso to see the humours of the Carnival. We had a large box full of *confetti*. I believe about 1,200 lbs.

*February 9th.*—The pelting was slacker to-day. There were numbers of pretty *contadine* in very rich costumes ; they were spared, but everybody else who passed under the balcony we overwhelmed.

*February 11th.*—This was the great day of the Carnival, and we all started at two o'clock for the Corso. We hired a large carriage with two boxes, and high enough to be out of the reach of the pickpockets, who comprise almost the whole Roman population. The day was fine, though very cold, and all the *contadine* appeared in costume ; many were very lovely and their dresses uncommonly rich. We threw and received quantities of *bonbons* and nosegays, but with the exception of those on the balconies and a few from the carriages, English and Americans, nobody pelted us. We returned to the balcony for the race of the *barberi*, as they call their horses.

*February* 12*th.*—The Cannings gave a supper, and some of the party before mentioned went to the masquerade at the Apollo Theatre, which was extremely amusing. We went in and out of the boxes in different disguises, changing our dominoes frequently. A great many people, men and women, came into our box, but all were very civil, and nothing disagreeable was said. We came home at half-past four, very tired.

*February* 15*th.*—Very wet to-day. There were some carriages with Roman women in costume, but all looking very wretched, their rich dresses soaked and dripping with water. Most of them wore nothing on their heads, and their dresses being all made low with short sleeves, they must have suffered dreadfully from the weather, which was extremely cold, besides the rain, which came down in torrents.

*February* 16*th.*—No *confetti* were thrown in our faces to-day, but the usual quantity of nosegays and sweetmeats. We went to the balcony, after which we lit our *moccoletti*, and had a great battle for about half an hour. The crowd, almost all of whom had lighted candles, was immense, and the noise so deafening that we were glad to get away and rest a little before the *festino* which was to take place that evening. This consists of a masquerade at the theatre, to which we repaired at eight o'clock.

*February* 24*th.*—The last few days have been spent at dinners given by several of our party. We have been very fortunate in finding this season at Rome almost all the most agreeable and clever people of our acquaintance. The Shelburnes and the Cannings are remarkable for both qualities, and it is a real pleasure to see the wonders of Rome in such company.

*March* 1*st.*—Went with Lord and Lady Canning to Baron Kessner's, who has a good collection of pictures ; some curious ones by Giotto, and a beautiful portrait by Raphael, supposed to be that of the lady he was engaged to marry a short time before his death. Mr. Augustus Villiers[1] is lying dangerously ill, having broken a blood-vessel in the chest.

*March* 2*nd.*—We left Rome, covered with snow, and reached Civita Castellana that afternoon. It snowed all the way from there to Terni and also to Foligno. I never suffered so much

[1] Lord Jersey's son, who died soon afterwards.

from cold during the severest weather in England as in both those places.

*March 4th.*—Left Foligno and stopped at Spello, where we saw the cathedral of the Franciscan church of San Lorenzo. Here we got into the country of Raphael, Perugino, Pinturicchio, and Spagna ; and some of the finest specimens of those artists' paintings are to be seen here. At the church of San Lorenzo there is a splendid picture by Pinturicchio over the altar, and at the other end of the church is one by Spagna. But the monks discouraged our going to see it, and I found out afterwards the reason they had done so was because there was a dead body in the church, which we must pass, and they thought must be disagreeable to us to see, as it was uncovered. From Spello we went to Assisi, where we saw the church of St. Francis, containing some fine Giottos. The upper church is in the Gothic style, with painted glass windows, and the walls in fresco by Cimabue and his pupils. In the lower church there is a beautiful picture by Spagna of the Virgin and Child ; also a curious portrait of St. Francis painted in A.D. 1230, supposed to be by Giunta di Pisa, who was his friend. From Assisi we went to Perugia. It stands very high, and it was so bitterly cold that we could not leave the house to see it.

*March 5th.*—The weather having improved, we went to Casa Domini, where there are a few good pictures of the Umbrian School. Went to Casa Penna, but could not gain admittance. We heard to-day that the Cavaliere Penna, who is the guardian of the young man to whom the pictures in the house belong, sold one for 750 scudi to a foreigner about three years ago. It was a very beautiful portrait of a woman by Raphael, and on hearing this it struck me from various circumstances that it was the identical picture we had seen at Baron Kessner's the day before we left Rome, and which he told us he bought at Bologna three years ago. The face, he said, was painted over, but judging from the extreme beauty of the rest of the picture, he had the courage to have the paint taken off, and the face of the present lovely picture was discovered. The snow came on again at night, and the cold was so intense that I fear the country must suffer. The principal source of wealth of its inhabitants is the olive, which is very delicate. I saw quantities on the higher ground nearly stripped of their leaves, which were strewed over the fields and roads from the severity of the frosts, looking as if they were burnt.

*March 7th.*—We reached Florence, where we stayed till the 12th, when we went to Lucca. There is a very nice collection of pictures at the Palazzo Manzi ; among them a beautiful Madonna and Child by Francia, one of the most lovely pictures I ever saw ; also a good collection of Dutch pictures, with the names to them most ignorantly misapplied.

*March 13th.*—We reached La Spezzia. Found the torrents that cross the roads quite dry ; the one between Sorzana and Spezzia is a very bad one. Found the prices of the work at Carrara very much increased to what they were sixteen years ago, when I could buy a very handsome chimney-piece for 20*l.*—they now ask 60*l.*

*March 15th.*—We reached Genoa, where I bought from the Marquis de Brignole a very fine circular portrait of Titian by Sebastiano del Piombo, painted on a solid block of cypress wood, and an inscription burned by a hot iron at the back, with the names of those two great men, and the date '1548.' It is now at Heron Court.

*March 22nd.*—After having paraded all the galleries and palaces of Genoa, we left it, returning by the Corniche, stopping at Savona and San Remo.

*March 25th.*—Left San Remo, which is a detestable village, and reached Nice ; the journey from thence to Nice is trying to the nervous traveller, the roads being very narrow and in most places without parapets. The postboys descend the hills at such a pace that any accident happening to the harness must send them down the precipice.

*March 26th.*—In passing Cannes we saw Lord Brougham's villa building. It is a Cockney whitewashed house, close to the high road, which passes between it and the sea, with an apology for a garden round it.

*March 27th.*—We found the little inn, ' La Poste,' at Cannes very comfortable and clean ; fifteen years ago it was scarcely habitable.

*March 29th.*—We reached Avignon and travelled the road to

Lyons, passing an immense quantity of grain carts, there being a famine in the North of France, where bread costs twenty pence English a pound.

*April 4th.*—We reached Paris, where we heard of the death of my wife's uncle, Jules de Polignac. There are quantities of English here.

*April 5th.*—Went to see Marshal Soult's pictures which he looted in Spain. There are many Murillos, all beautiful, but one of them representing the Assumption finer than any I ever saw. Also some very good ones by Zurbaran. M. de Portalis has also a very valuable gallery, including a good Giorgione, Titian, and Sebastiano del Piombo. In his private apartment there are two pictures by Delaroche representing the death of Cardinal Richelieu, and a lovely Greuze.

*April 8th.*—Left Paris, and went as far as Abbeville.

*April 9th.*—Arrived at Boulogne, but the storm too heavy to cross. A very angry sea was running, and it was really alarming to see the steamer pitch as she crossed the bar, the waves washing clean over her. The passengers must have been wet through before they got a quarter of a mile out. The storm increased, and we remained at the Hôtel des Bains.

*April 18th.*—Reached London on the 11th. The Queen of Spain has dismissed her Government and household, and has ceased to quarrel with her husband. She has quite thrown over the French party for the English, which has pleased her subjects, who receive her everywhere with acclamation. She drives out every day without guards and always accompanied by her husband. The French say that her conduct is very bad and that General Serrano is her lover. But all this does not at present prevent her from being very popular, which enrages the French more, as they cannot be blind to the fact that her popularity has been chiefly occasioned by the dismissal of the party that had favoured the French alliance. The Duc de Broglie is appointed to succeed M. de St. Aulaire as Ambassador in London.

*April 24th.*—A great political dinner at Lord Stanley's. They say Lady Normanby, our Ambassadress at Paris, speaks French very imperfectly, and at the time of our quarrel with M. Guizot, intending to explain that it had arisen through a mistake, she said, 'c'étoit par mépris !'

*May 8th.*—Dined with the Eglintons. General Sir Harry. Smith was the great lion of the evening. He is a little old man, very clever looking. She is a Spanish woman, and has been very handsome.

*May 13th.*—The Queen's ball. A debate in the Lords on the Irish Poor Law Bill, the Government being anxious to get the Peers to rescind their votes on the clause making the measure temporary. They had a majority of twelve, eighteen bishops voting with them.

*May 15th.*—We went to the amateur play for the Irish. *Ernani* was acted. Mrs. Butler, *née* Kemble, has grown very old and affected, but acted well in the last scene, the first part being all whining and snorting. The Queen was present, and a very fashionable audience.

*May 19th.*—Lady Malmesbury left London for the German waters, and went to Ems.

*June 18th.*—Lord Stanley's motion condemning the Government for their intervention in Portugal ended very unfortunately, owing to Lords Ellenborough and Brougham not choosing to speak in support of it; the consequence being that the division took place much earlier than was expected, and most of our men were at dinner, Stanley amongst them, so we were beaten by twenty. In the House of Commons the debate came on the same night, but the House was counted out. In the meantime the English fleet has taken the Portuguese ships and made 2,000 prisoners, whom they have conveyed to Lisbon and shut up in the fortress. This *coup de main* appears to have been done without warning, for the Admiral's letter to the Junta cautioning them that if their vessels sailed they would be captured was not delivered till after the capture had actually been made, and nine days after the date of the letter. This will probably put an end to the civil war, but it is very tricky and unworthy of England.

*August 4th.*—We left London for Achnacarry, where the Cannings joined us on the 16th, as well as Mr. Cholmondeley and Mr. Temple, Lord Palmerston's brother.

*August 23rd.*—We were very much shocked to-day by reading

an account in the papers of the murder of the Duchesse de Praslin. It appears her maid was awakened between four and five o'clock in the morning on the 1st by the ringing of the Duchess's bell. She went to her room, and found it was locked on the inside ; but on listening she heard a feeble groan, upon which she alarmed the other servants, who broke open the door, and the Duchess was found lying in a pool of blood on the floor with several deep wounds in her throat and breast. She was unable to speak, and died in a short time without recovering her consciousness. The police were immediately sent for, and it was ascertained that no robbery had been committed, and it is supposed the act was one of vengeance. It is suspected that a governess whom she lately dismissed, and said to be the Duke's mistress, was the instigator of the crime. They had only arrived the night before the murder from the country. Everybody in the house has been arrested, and a telegraphic despatch sent to recall Marshal Sebastiani, father of the Duchess, from Corsica, where he has gone.

*August 24th.*—We received a letter from Lady Tankerville. The Duc de Praslin has been arrested on suspicion of having committed the murder. The police went to the governess's lodgings, but she was absent ; they, however, seized all her papers. The investigation is continued with great activity, and though very little is known, there must have been very strong evidence against the Duke for such a step being taken as that of arresting him, as he would naturally be the last person suspected. But it appears when on the first alarm the doctors were sent for, the servants expressed a suspicion of him, so there must have been circumstances which have not been made public and which warrant those suspicions. The poor woman seems to have struggled hard with her murderer, for her hand was full of his hair, and there was a good deal of hair, some of which was hers, scattered about the carpet. The furniture in the room was very much disturbed, the tables knocked over ; but on the closest examination no traces could be discovered of anyone having broken in or out of the house, and if, as it is said, the room was locked on the inside, the murderer could not have escaped that way. If, therefore, any private communication existed between her room and that of the Duke, suspicion naturally fell upon him. A pistol, it is said, stained with blood was found in his room.

*August 25th.*—There is now no doubt as to the Duke's guilt, which seems to have been suspected almost from the first ; for, on the alarm being given, one of the servants, finding the door locked, ran screaming round the house to the garden, either to try and gain an entrance that way or to stop any person who might attempt to escape. The same servant saw a man whom he thought was the Duke opening the window of the Duchess's apartment, but who retreated precipitately on seeing him. In addition to this, when the servants went to call the Duke they found him dressed, which, as he had been in bed, was a very extraordinary fact, at that early, hour. There are also stains of blood on his dressing-gown; and water tinged with blood was found in the basin in his room. The magistrates, observing that he wore gloves, made him take them off, when several slight wounds were discovered, like scratches or bites ; also a bruise and a large wound on one of his legs. The magistrates then decided on having him kept in sight, not having power to arrest a Peer without an order from the Chamber. The police have also arrested Mdlle. Luzy, the governess, and she has been transferred to prison, where she is kept *au secret*. She loudly asserts her innocence, not only of the murder, but of having been the Duke's mistress. The circumstance most against her is, the Duke having gone to see her, with two of his daughters, the moment he arrived at Paris, and that the Duchess in consequence was very angry, and a quarrel took place between them on his return. They both afterwards retired to their separate apartments, and no disturbance took place till the ringing of the bell alarmed the maid. The struggles of the poor Duchess must have been dreadful, the smallest number of wounds mentioned as being inflicted on her being seven. A pistol was found in the room covered with blood, which the Duke admitted belonged to him, but said he took it in for the purpose of defending the Duchess, hearing her cries. This, however, does not agree with the surprise he affected on being told of the murder.

*August 29th.*—The papers contain full details about the Duchesse de Praslin's murder, and every circumstance confirms the Duke's guilt. He has attempted to poison himself by taking laudanum, and has been removed to the Luxembourg. The Chamber of Peers has been summoned to try him.

*August* 31*st.*—The Duc de Praslin died on the 24th from the
effects of the poison, which turns out to have been arsenic.  He
was attended by three of the cleverest doctors in Paris, who
treated him for poisoning by laudanum, which has naturally given
rise to some suspicion that they did not wish to save him, and
perhaps had orders not to do, so as to avoid the scandal of an
execution, the evidence against him being so strong as not to
leave a doubt of his guilt.  He is said to have confessed to a
priest, but to no one else, and has never apparently expressed
either remorse or sorrow for the murder.  The messengers sent to
Marshal Sebastiani, father of the Duchess, found him at Vevey,
and communicated the news, which had not yet reached him, but
without telling him who the murderer was.  That was to be told
him by his physician, who had set out to meet him.  He was
much afflicted, but no fear is entertained for his health.

*September* 6*th.*—Two men were found this morning on the
moor near Fort William quite dead, having apparently perished
from cold.  One was a fine young man above six feet high and
not more than twenty-two years old ; the other about thirty-five,
and equally strong.  Their money and watches were found upon
them, so that no robbery has been committed.  There were no
marks of violence, and they looked as if they were asleep.  They
were tradesmen from London, and were on a pedestrian tour for
their pleasure.  It appears from the evidence relating to the
murder of the Duchesse de Praslin that she might have been
saved if the maid and valet had shown any quickness or courage.
They heard her screaming for a long time before they got up to
see who it was, and even when they found that her door was not
locked they did not dare to go in, as the room was dark and they
smelt blood.  The Duke had time to return to his room, where
he burned some papers and linen, washed his dressing-gown, hid
the dagger, and went back to her room, of which he himself
unlocked the door leading into the hall at the moment the
servants tried it, and pretended he had come to her assistance on
hearing her screams.  He also at once desired that the doctor
should be sent for.  The servants at first suspected Mdlle. Luzy
of the crime, but very soon after the arrival of the magistrates
suspicion was excited against the Duke, and he, perceiving these

L

suspicions, took an opportunity when the arrival of another magistrate diverted attention for a moment from him to retire to his room and swallow poison. The evidence of the doctors is published, and proves either gross ignorance, unpardonable carelessness, or wilful blindness. The first doctor pretends to think the symptoms are occasioned by distress of mind, then he suspects poison, but neither gives an antidote nor communicates his suspicion to his colleague, who pronounces the case at once to be cholera, and leaves him a whole night without any assistance at all, whilst they go comfortably to bed. No doubt they wished him to die.

*September 14th.*—Lord Ossulston has killed 'the great stag of Gusach,' after a very long and difficult stalk. This fine animal, which weighed twenty stone when clean, had baffled us for several years. There is very little news, but what we have is very unsatisfactory. Several people in society are ruined, amongst others Massey Stanley, who has gone abroad owing 280,000*l.*, and Hooton is for sale. The commercial smashes are also very many, and are due to over-speculation in railways. Peel went a few days ago to Liverpool, dined with the mayor and made a speech, but avoided giving any opinion as to the causes of our commercial failures.

### Lord Canning to Lord Malmesbury.

Madrid : Oct. 21, 1847.

My dear M.,—I promised you a letter, but it has been a long time coming. The fact is that this is a despairing place to write from. It is difficult enough to believe, and much more so to understand one half of what one sees and hears passing about one, but to convey it to one who is fresh from the simplicities of Inverness-shire is impossible.

I arrived in the nick of time for sport—on the very day on which Salamanca was turned out and Narvaez came in, just in time, too, for the birthday drawing-room, the ball at Court, the bull fight, &c. (why didn't you come ?) The journey, too, was nothing. I left Grosvenor Square on a Monday, spent a day at Paris (such a *bisque* at the 'Trois Frères ! ') and a day at Bayonne, and got here on the Monday following.

The hotels are infamous, but Bulwer is very hospitable and wanted to lodge me. But he is only in temporary lodgings himself just now, so I only feed with him. This is very convenient, for he asks two or three notabilities of all colours every day, and one hears what they say of themselves and of each other.

Of all the sudden convulsions and changes that the country has gone through, I believe there never was any more sudden and unexpected than this last one, nevertheless it all passed off quietly enough. The rationale of it is shortly this : Salamanca as a politician was a Liberal, but a stock-jobber from the beginning, and chiefly bent upon making a fortune. He is supposed to be already of enormous wealth, but how much of it is real no one here seems to know. All that I can speak to is that he is at this moment building two immense houses— one, almost as grand as Stafford House, for himself and his wife, the other, about the size of Montagu House, for his mistress. Narvaez, a bold, unscrupulous soldier, of immense energy (the rarest of all qualities and therefore the most telling here), eaten up with ambition, but also anxious for a fortune at the country's expense (this any Minister can make in more or less time according to his scruples). He is just like Lord Combermere in face, figure, and get up, but a little bigger.

Serrano, or the 'Influence' as he was modestly called, was supposed to be honest, but weak, and under the dominion of an avaricious old mother and a homœopathic doctor (Nuñez), who is an apostate priest and Carlist. Serrano is very like Cradock, but darker. These were the principal actors. Serrano had felt for some little time that his power over the Queen was on the wane. His mother and the doctor, bribed by Narvaez *and others,* persuaded him to use a last effort to get the Queen to remove Salamanca and send for Narvaez, and that then, after placing the Queen in the hands of a Minister who has a majority in the Cortes (for the Cortes was elected under N.'s former Government, and packed to a man), he might retire with dignity upon some command or governorship at a distance, and avoid being thrown over in the face of the Court for some more lucky successor. He did as he was bid, and succeeded. Narvaez was sent for, and immediately telegraphed for Queen Christina, who has since arrived. Serrano has received an estate in Estremadura, bought with the Queen's money, and has been named Captain-General of Grauada. (Here, however, there is some hitch, for within a day or two there is news of his having stopped half-way and sent in his resignation. The motive probably is that he has heard of differences in Narvaez's Cabinet, which may break it up as suddenly as it was formed, and that he thinks he may as well be on the spot.) Salamanca is supposed to have got 150,000*l.* by a gigantic job in the funds. And the homœopathic doctor is rewarded with the Grand Cordon of Charles III.

There are all sorts of under-currents which have been going on while this has been worked out, but it would be endless to give them, and impossible to make them intelligible.

As matters stand now, Serrano is without any apparent successor. Narvaez is not on good terms with two or three of his necessary colleagues, nor with the Queen-Mother. The Queen is displeased and frightened at her mother's return, and bored by Narvaez, and, as she has not the smallest sense of responsibility, may at any moment, if things are not made smooth to her, send him about his business and appoint some new man. And this, I am convinced, will be the state of things with every Government that may come into existence here until the 'Minister' and the 'Influence' are united in the same individual (as was the case with Catherine and Elizabeth). And if Serrano had had any head or heart he would have done this, and made himself Minister in name and appearance, even if he did not feel equal to the reality.

I said there was no apparent successor to Serrano as yet, but we shall not have to wait long. The day before yesterday a singer at the Opera came home to his lodgings at six o'clock in the morning and found them occupied by the police, who had a carriage ready to take him off to Valencia, the reason being that his night had been passed at the Palace. To say the truth, this appears to me rather hard, for nothing is deducible from the hour at which he left the Palace, inasmuch as the Queen turns night into day, sees her Ministers after the Opera, sups at four or five, and does not go to bed till morning. However, as this man is not her singing-master, I suppose Narvaez considers that he had no business there. At all events, it is certain that he is packed off. What a fortune Bunn might make of him!

The Queen is infinitely better to look at than I expected, rather tall than short, not too fat, built pretty much upon Lady Walpole's lines, and a face rather like Lady Londonderry. Her manners when she is still, and speaking, are extremely dignified, but her movements, every now and then, hoydenish. The King, I have not seen, although Narvaez has just brought him back to the Palace, for which the French papers, and I daresay the English too, will puff him as a paragon of morality. But it is one thing to take a horse to the water, and another to make him drink, especially if he should happen to have the hydrophobia. Don't believe a word in a reconciliation on either side.

The Court is very royal, the Palace magnificent, finer than any I know, and larger, and the ceremony and attendance is very grand. The Halberdiers of the Palace, who defended it so manfully in 1841, are almost as picturesque as the Pope's Guard—long black gaiters half-way up the thigh, broad skirted blue coats with the red flaps buttoned back, long waistcoats, and three-cornered hats—exactly the French Mousquetaires of the last century. As to the pictures, are they not written in the book of Ford? By-the-bye, I am a little out of conceit with Ford. It is a charming book to be read at leisure in one's room, but his quotations and illustrations (sometimes rather far-fetched) get in the way and provoke one when one is in a hurry for a fact. However, he is very good, generally upon the pictures, which are gloriously magnificent. Seriously, I do not think that Rome and Florence and Heron Court together could make up a gallery that I would take in preference to the Museo. And you would think so too, for, after the Spanish, the great force of the collection is in the Venetian school—Titians, P. Veroneses, Tintorets, Giorgiones, all in their perfection. There are also two or three good private collections, and one (belonging to the President of the Museo) where any of the pictures may be bought; but I saw nothing very covetable except a beautiful Vandyke of a man in armour, for which he asks 1,000l., and a Rubens, which is too large for any space in my gallery. I forgot to say that in the Museo is a portrait of Titian by himself, taken at exactly the same age as yours, with the same dress, gold chain, &c., but in profile. There is no difference in the faces and expression.

I went all over the town in search of curiosities, but could find nothing, except some very fine old crystal chandeliers, which were too large.

The bull fight was not equal to those I have seen in the South. The bulls were not so good, and the matador of the day is not equal to the great Montes, who has retired into private life, while life is left him. However, I did not sit out more than five or six bulls, and I was told afterwards that the last was a really good animal, and had eight horses dead in the ring at once, which certainly is out of the common way.

I have only made one country expedition as yet, to Segovia, about fifty miles off, over the Guadarama mountains, seeing the Escurial and La Granja by the way. There are no post-horses or any other means of moving to be found on the road, so I was obliged to hire a carriage (a small English brougham and a team of four enormous black mules, covered with red and yellow harness and tassels—rather an imposing equipage). All these places are worth seeing (La Granja least so), and part of the road, that over the mountains, is very beautiful; old weather-beaten firs (almost equal to Glen Mealy) growing from amongst large boulders of granite, with high fern at their feet. You would not know it from a bit of Achnacarry. But this is a brilliant exception to the general appearance of the country within many dreary miles of Madrid. For the most part it is a treeless, fenceless, houseless undulating waste, without a blade of grass, of one interminable brown where it is ploughed, and, where it is not, covered with great slabs of granite which give it the appearance of a huge ptarmigan hill rolled flat. Where the people who scratch the ground come from it is impossible to guess, for the Campagna is not more desolate. Nevertheless Spanish farmers pay their rents to the day invariably, bringing the money to Madrid themselves, and are always clamouring for leases. This description of the country, however, applies only to the Castilles. North of Burgos the valleys are as grassy and the hills as well wooded as in England; indeed, the Basque Provinces are very like South Wales, and the streams look very troutish.

I daresay you will want to know something of the morals of the place, and they are soon told. Whenever one asks at the Opera, or at Court, or indeed anywhere who such and such a lady is, the answer is always in the same form : she is the wife of D——, the daughter of C——, and Mr. So-and-so is her lover. It is really no exaggeration to say that this is invariable. I have met with only one exception, and that is the wife of Sotomayor, who was in London, and who has Anglo-Saxon blood in him, and may therefore be considered as not in point, but nobody believes that even in his case such a state of things can last. I am convinced that if a Peerage were published in Madrid, as in London, the name of the happy individual would be put down as much as a matter of course as if it were the motto or country seat of the family. Some few ladies have made themselves notorious for inconstancy and versatility in this branch of their establishment, and then they begin to be a little talked about; but I believe this to be rather the exception than the rule, and certainly the instances in which fidelity continues to be affichéd, long after the ladies have got fat and pursy and the Caballeros grey-headed, are numerous.

I have written a much longer yarn than I, or probably you, intended, but it's your own fault. And now I am not quite sure how it will go, for I have just heard that Bulwer's messenger is not likely to start for some days. Probably I shall be in England myself soon after you get it, for unless the weather (which has been raining for the past week) tempts me to Toledo and Aranjuez, I shall not stay here after Sunday next. Adios! Remember me to Lady M., &c.

Ever yours sincerely,

CANNING.

*September 26th.*—We left Achnacarry, embarked at Corpach, and arrived at Greenock that evening. Had a very bad passage. The scene in the cabin was disgusting, as no preparation had been made on board for people who were ill, and no conveniences whatever provided. Yet nobody could go on deck without being drenched. We reached Chillingham Castle on the 27th.

*November 5th.*—Arrived at Knowsley, and reached London on the 10th.

*November 19th.*—I went to London for the meeting of Parliament. I hear Ministers intend to propose an increase in the income tax. Affairs in the City are very bad. There is to be a meeting at Lord Stanley's on the 23rd of Peers and Commons, when he is to give them an outline of the policy he intends to follow this session.

*December 23rd.*—The papers have been full of the dispute in the Church respecting Doctor Hampden's appointment to the bishopric of Hereford. The opposition evidently comes from the Puseyite party, and would therefore be of little value in the estimation of the true Protestant, had not Hampden laid himself open to censure by some expressions in his writings, which he may perhaps be able to explain. The Bishop of Oxford threatens to put him on his trial for heterodoxy, from which I hope he may be able to clear himself, though if he is tried by a Court composed of Puseyites he will certainly be condemned.

*Christmas Day.*—Heron Court. The rivers here are all flooded.

# 1848

*February 9th.*—I got a letter to-day from my brother, who has attended the meeting held by Lord Stanley, and he gives an account of the proceedings relative to Lord George Bentinck's resignation of the leadership of the Protectionist party in the House of Commons. Lord Stanley made a very eloquent speech praising Lord George Bentinck's abilities and devotion to the party, &c., &c., and expressed great regret at the misunderstanding which led to his resignation, and wished to induce him to recal his determination. Mr. Banks then read to the meeting a letter from Lord George announcing his intention to resign, saying that he would serve the party with as much zeal and devotion as he had hitherto done. Mr. Beresford then got up to explain, and proved himself by his own account to have acted most injudiciously, for he confessed to having written to Lord George stating that his party were dissatisfied with him, but added that he did so without authority.    This, however, was enough for Lord George, who is a very proud man, to give up the leadership at once, and he immediately wrote to Mr. Banks announcing his intention to do so.    After these explanations Lord Granby's [1] name was mentioned as being a fit person to succeed Lord George, but Lord Stanley said they must settle among themselves whom they would elect, and dismissed the party.    An arrangement was made to meet next day at Mr. Banks's to elect a leader.

*February 10th.*—Lord Granby has been chosen leader of the Protectionist party without opposition.    A deputation has been sent to Lord George, thanking him for his services, and expressing regret at his retirement.    My brother adds that there is no doubt Peel has lately declared to his party that he never means to take office again.    If this is really the case, we may expect some of them to come over to us.    It appears strange that in these proceedings Disraeli's name was not put forward, but whoever may in future take the lead in the House of Commons by election he must virtually and practically hold that office.    There can be no doubt that there is a very strong feeling among Conservatives in the House of Commons against him.    They are puzzled and alarmed by his mysterious manner, which has much of the foreigner about it, and are incapable of understanding and appreciating the great abilities which certainly underlie, and, as it were, are concealed by this mask.    In the insurrection in Sicily the King's troops have been beaten.    The insurgents want the Constitution of 1812, which was guaranteed by England, but since revoked by the King, and apparently without opposition from this country.    The King still resists, but has granted the Constitution to Naples, which has been received with acclamation.    There are two English ships of war at Palermo and Messina for the protection of the English residing there, but with the exception of the bombardment having been delayed twenty-four hours through the remonstrances of the Consuls in those towns, there has been no interference on either side.

[1] Afterwards Duke of Rutland,

*February* 13*th.*—The second reading of the Jewish Disabilities Bill was passed by a majority of 73 in the Commons. Lord Granby has refused the leadership, and the whole Protectionist party is in confusion. A rescript from the Pope has appeared, counselling the Roman Catholic clergy to adopt a more moderate course, not to meddle in politics, and condemning denunciations from the altar and all violence. This has produced a great sensation. Of course the Irish priests say the Pope has been deceived, but the English Roman Catholics are inclined to obey.

*February* 16*th.*—The King of Naples has granted the Constitution of 1812 to his Sicilian subjects, which, however, they have only accepted on condition that they are to have a Parliament at Palermo. He has not yet agreed to this, but he has published an amnesty for political offences, has withdrawn his troops from Sicily, and they have arrived at Naples in a wretched state. The cavalry killed all their horses, eight hundred in number, before they left Palermo. The King of Sardinia has also promised a Constitution to his subjects on the model of the French one ; and the Pope and the Duke of Tuscany also promise something of the same sort to their people. Austria, Russia, and Prussia have protested through their Ministers at the Court of Naples against the Constitution granted by the King, as being at variance with the secret article in their treaties with Naples.

*February* 17*th.*—Paris is in a great state of excitement, in consequence of the Government having forbidden the Reform banquet taking place. There was a violent scene in the Chamber of Deputies, and the Opposition persevered in their determination to attend the banquet, which is fixed for the 20th. There has also been a great disturbance at Munich, the people insisting upon Lola Montes being sent away. The King, however, is so infatuated with her, that he actually dismissed his Prime Minister, Prince Wallenstein, who had advised him to expel her, and appointed in his place M. de Mauren, who had signed the decree conferring upon her the title of Countess Landsfeldt.[1]

---

[1] This was a most remarkable woman, and may be said by her conduct at Munich to have set fire to the magazine of revolution which was ready to burst forth all over Europe, and which made the year 1848 memorable. I made her acquaintance by accident as I was going up to London from Heron Court in the

*February* 18*th.*—I went to London to vote on Lord Eglinton's amendment to the Diplomatic Relations with Rome Bill, in which he moved that no ecclesiastic should be sent as Ambassador or Minister to this country, although a layman might be received. It appears that the King of Naples has played false with the Sicilians, having given them, not the Constitution of 1812, but the French one, which they will not accept. The Emperor of Russia supports Austria in her Italian policy, and the latter has forbidden the Grand Duke of Tuscany to grant a Constitution to his subjects, threatening that if the people are clamorous, Austria would march an army into Tuscany at once. Mr. Gladstone has supported the Jewish Disabilities Bill, and Peel has changed his mind and vote upon that subject.

*February* 19*th.*—Lola Montes has been driven out of Munich, the King having at last perceived that further resistance to the will of the people would endanger his crown, as the troops refused to act against the populace. When she left the city the mob broke into her house, which they plundered, and destroyed all her property, including some very fine pictures. The next morning she re-entered Munich, but fortunately for her she was arrested and sent away by force, for if she had been recognised by the people her life would have been sacrificed, their rage

railway. The Consul at Southampton asked me to take charge of a Spanish lady, who had been recommended to his care, and who had just landed. I consented to do this, and was introduced by him to a remarkably handsome person, who was in deep mourning, and who appeared to be in great distress. As we were alone in the carriage, she of her own accord informed me in bad English that she was the widow of Don Diego Leon, who had lately been shot by the Carlists after he was taken prisoner, and that she was going to London to sell some Spanish property that she possessed, and give lessons in singing, as she was very poor. On arriving in London she took some lodgings, and came to my house to a little concert which I gave, and sang some Spanish ballads. Her accent was foreign, and she had all the appearance of being what she pretended to be. She sold different things, such as veils, &c., to the party present, and received a good deal of patronage. Eventually she took an engagement for the ballet at the Opera House, but her dancing was very inferior. At last she was recognised as an impostor, her real name being Mrs. James ; she was Irish by extraction, and had married an officer in India. Her engagement at the Opera was cancelled, she left the country, and retired to Munich. She was a very violent woman, and actually struck one of the Bavarian generals with her riding whip as he was reviewing the troops. The King became perfectly infatuated with her beauty and cleverness, and gave her large sums of money, with a title which she afterwards bore, when she returned to England.

against her being unbounded. It appears she has long indisposed the whole kingdom against her by the unlimited influence she exercised over the King, who was completely governed by her and did nothing without her sanction. She made him change his Ministers three times in one year, because they had in some way offended her, and, in short, she ruled the kingdom despotically. The last event which led to her disgrace was an order given to the King to close the University on account of the offence given her by a majority of the students, who made a practice of insulting a class amongst them protected by her, called 'Alemanen,' and who wore her colours. The remainder of the students slighted them on every occasion and refused them any satisfaction, declaring them unworthy of being treated as men of honour. This led to a disturbance. Lola was insulted, it is said even roughly treated, by the people, and the University was closed. When the students were marching peaceably in procession they were attacked by the troops, a fight ensued, and two or three men were killed and several wounded. The mob then surrounded the Palace, insisted upon Lola Montes being dismissed and the University re-opened, which the King was forced to grant.

*February 22nd.*—Lord John Russell has made his financial statement and announced his intention of increasing the income tax to five per cent., to be levied in the same manner as it is at present. He gives no hope of ever taking off the three per cent., and though he only asked for this increase for two years, it is probable, if granted, it will never be taken off again.

*February 23rd.*—Lord Stanley means to oppose any increase of the income tax, and limit the present one to three years instead of five.

*February 24th.*—Accounts from Paris are very alarming. The King, on the 21st, prohibited the banquet of the Reformers, and issued an order that none of the National Guard were to appear in the streets in uniform except by order of their officers. The Opposition Deputies then countermanded the banquet and begged the people to make no disturbance, declaring that they would impeach the Ministers, and if beaten would all resign their seats. It was feared the people would not submit quietly, and that there would be bloodshed, as thousands were collected in the Champs Elysées. The troops of the line in Paris amount to a hundred thousand men, and are well provided with artillery, as are also the forts, the Government having foreseen the disturbance and taken every precaution to suppress it, but the National Guards are not to be trusted.

*February 25th.*—The disturbances in Paris have assumed a very formidable character. Everything now depends upon the energy of the Government, for the people are determined not to give in. The troops of the line, with the exception of one regiment, the 5th—the same that joined the people in 1830 –have remained faithful, but the National Guards have gone over to the rebels. On Tuesday night, the 22nd, the mob obtained some arms and threw up barricades, from behind which they attacked the Municipal Guards, but were beaten and several ˊprisoners taken. The troops bivouacked in the Boulevards, the markets, and other public places, and the mob burned the depôt of omnibuses and the guardhouse in the Champs Elysées. The Place du Carrousel, the Place de la Concorde, the bridges and other places in the neighbourhood of the Tuileries were crowded with troops, and there were forty pieces of cannon on the Esplanade of the Invalides. The *rappel* was sounded early on Wednesday morning, but not one-tenth of the National Guard answered the summons. The Municipal Guard seems, on the contrary, to have behaved gallantly, though some fraternised with the National Guard, and though they did not actually join the people, they refused to fire upon them ; but the majority did their duty. There is a great want of energy on the part of the Government ; all the Ministers have resigned, and M. Odilon Barrot has impeached M. Guizot.

*February 26th.*—The insurrection gains ground in Paris. There has been a great deal of fighting and many lives lost. The mob have broken up the railroad and stopped all communication with Paris. If Louis Philippe is driven from the throne, nothing remains but a Republic.

*February 27th.*—Louis Philippe abdicated on the 24th in favour of his grandson, the Comte de Paris, and left Paris immediately afterwards with an escort of dragoons for Neuilly. The

Duchess of Orleans went to the Chamber of Deputies with her sons and the Duc de Nemours to ask for protection, which was granted, but they refused to recognise the right of the Comte de Paris or the Regency of the Duc de Nemours. Directly after the royal family had left the Tuileries the mob broke in, gutted the palace, and destroyed everything except the throne, which they paraded about the streets in derision. A Provisional Government has been formed in Paris, of which M. Lamartine is at the head. The Municipal Guard behaved with great courage and fidelity, but were not supported, and have been almost all massacred.

*February 28th.*—Left Heron Court for London. The Duc de Nemours, with one of his children, and the Duke and Duchess of Saxe-Coburg (Princess Clementina), arrived last night at the French Embassy. The Duchesse de Nemours with her children are still in France, and nothing is known of them or of the Queen, except that they reached Dreux in safety, and there agreed to separate. The King had only five francs in his possession, but the Queen had fortunately carried off about fifteen hundred francs, which they divided. None of the fugitives had been able to carry away any of their property. The Duc de Nemours appeared very much dejected, overcome with fatigue and anxiety. From what is at present known of the events of last Thursday, it appears that MM. Thiers and Odilon Barrot are the cause of Louis Philippe's dethronement, for they had pledged themselves, if he would make them Ministers and order the troops to cease firing, quiet would be restored immediately. Till this the majority of the troops had remained faithful, but they were so disgusted at the cowardice which apparently dictated these orders that they joined the insurgents. The nomination of M. Thiers did not in the slightest affect the insurrection. The mob attacked and took the Palais Royal after great sacrifice of life, and the King being informed that they were coming to attack the Tuileries, signed his abdication in favour of his grandson, and left the palace with the Queen and the Duchesse de Nemours. The Duchess of Orleans, with her two sons and the Duc de Nemours, went to the Chamber of Deputies, where they ran the greatest danger, the mob having broken in and pointed their muskets at the Royal Family. The Deputies, however, surrounded them, and they got

out in safety; but the rush was so tremendous that the two
children were separated from the Duchess and recovered afterwards
with great difficulty.  In the House of Commons the Government
have declared their intention not to interfere with the fall of the
King and not to intermeddle in any way with the internal affairs
of France.  They then announced the abandonment by the
Government of the increased income tax.  The Duchesse de
Montpensier arrived at the French Embassy yesterday.  She was
recognised at Abbeville and ran great danger of her life, being
saved by having taken refuge in a private house and escaping
through the back door.  Nothing is known of the rest of the
Royal Family.  The French Provisional Government have pro
claimed a Republic.  A steamer arrived yesterday morning at
Southampton crowded with passengers from Havre, who say the
town is full of English waiting to embark.  The Government
have, therefore, despatched several steamers to the different ports
on the French coast to take them off.

*March 1st.*—No news of Louis Philippe or the rest of the
Royal Family.  A steamer under the command of Captain Smithet
has been sent to cruise off Dieppe and Tréport in hopes of finding
them, but returned yesterday and telegraphed 'No passengers.'
It is reported to-day that the Duchess of Orleans and her two
children, accompanied by General Lefèvre and M. Guizot, have
landed at Jersey from a cutter.  Order is now restored in Paris
though not, indeed, in the provincial towns, and travelling
is attended with danger.  Neuilly has been burned, and one
hundred and twenty of the mob who were lying dead drunk in
the cellars were roasted alive unknown to their companions.  There
is a detailed account in to-day's papers of the departure of the
King from Paris.  He left the Tuileries on foot, leaning on the
arm of the Queen, preceded and followed by a party of the
National Guard on horseback, who escorted him to the Place Louis
Quinze, where he and the Queen got into a small carriage with
one horse which was waiting for them, and drove away at full
gallop.  It is said they arrived at Dreux the same night, slept
there, and started next morning for Vernon in a hired carriage.

*March 2nd.*—It is said that the Count de Flahault, who is
Ambassador at Vienna, will lose his Embass  in consequence of

a letter to M. Guizot, which has been found since the formation
of the rebel Government, in which he begs him to unite with M.
de Metternich to persuade the Pope to allow an Austrian army
to pass through his dominions and assist the King of Naples.
The French Government have offered the Embassy of London to
M. de Jarnac, who is at present Secretary to the Embassy, if he
will serve them with sincerity. He has very nobly refused, saying that he could not engage to do so, and therefore begged they
would replace him directly. The Duchesse de Nemours and
the Duc de Montpensier arrived yesterday morning at Southampton, and sent a messenger to London to announce the fact.
The Duc de Nemours was too lazy to go down to meet them,
and made the excuse that he could not leave the Duchesse de
Montpensier, though in reality she was under the care of Madame
Van de Weyer at the Belgian Embassy. It is now known where
Louis Philippe and the Queen are. Lady Carrington called this
morning and told us she met Captain Smithett in the street, and
he told her he had been at Dieppe, having a most awful passage,
starting in the very height of the storm, and in fact spoke as if
he had run very great danger. He had been summoned before
the authorities at Dieppe, who seemed to suspect what he had
come for, and cross-questioned him very closely. In the meantime
he sent a boat to Tréport for information, and having received
a despatch from some one unknown who said he was going to
Belgium, and supposing it to be from the King, he rejoined his
ship and returned to England. The Duc de Montebello had a
narrow escape at Havre, being saved by the courage of the captain
of the steamer, who refused to allow the French police to search
his ship, and told them that he would not do so unless they killed
him first. They began to bluster, when he added, ' I'll tell you
what it is, if you don't leave my ship by the time I say "Jack
Robinson," I'll take you all over to England ! ' and called upon
his men to get up steam and set sail, upon which they tumbled
into their boat as quickly as they could. When the Duc de
Nemours was crossing to Dover the Duke and Duchess of Saxe-
Coburg were in the same ship, but remained below in utter
ignorance of his being on board. The Duchess had just been
saying that if she knew he was safe she would be happy, for it

appears he was the one she loved best of all her family, when
some one who had recognised him informed her that he was on
deck.  She immediately rushed up to him, but he was so disguised
that she made a mistake, and threw herself into the arms of the
gentleman who accompanied him, who, not knowing her and
being taken by surprise, pushed her away.  This must have
annoyed the Duc, who, knowing her to be on board, had kept
out of the way to avoid a scene.  It will always be a question
whether the Duc de Nemours and the Duc de Montpensier ought
to have fought for the Crown in defiance of the old King's orders
to the contrary.  The troops had been kept inert from Tuesday
morning to Wednesday night in the streets, and without food,
and the mob finding this supplied them with all they wanted,
and of course fraternised with them.

*March 3rd.*—Prince Louis Bonaparte is already returned
from Paris.  I met him to-day, and he said that M. Lamartine,
who is at the head of the Government of the Republic at Paris,
had received him very civilly, said that his great name might at
this moment produce a commotion which it was desirable to avoid,
and therefore, if he wished well to France, begged him to leave
it directly.  This Prince Louis did, and seems rather flattered
than otherwise at being sent away.  It is rumoured that Louis
Philippe has arrived in England, but no one knows where the
Duchess of Orleans is, and it is still a matter of doubt whether
the Duchesse de Nemours has yet come.

*March 4th.*—Louis Philippe arrived yesterday at Newhaven,
but, owing to the state of the tide, could not land before twelve
at night, when he and the Queen drove to the Bridge Inn, which
is little better than a public-house.  The landlady did her best to
give them a reception befitting their rank, and it appears the
King and Queen were so pleased with her hospitality and the kind
way in which they were treated, that they refused all offers, of
which many were made, to remove to a more comfortable house,
and determined to remain there until they received an answer to
the letter written by them to our Queen, which was sent off by
express.  The account given of the King's departure from Paris
was quite correct, except that it was only the Queen who accompanied him on Thursday night to Dreux, where they stayed the

night at a farmer's on whose fidelity they could rely, and who procured them disguises. The King shaved off his whiskers and discarded his wig, wearing a cap and cloak, which disguised him completely. They arrived at Dreux before daylight on Friday, and reached Honfleur at five on Saturday morning. There they remained a short time at the house of a gentleman the King knew, then crossed to Trouville, intending to embark there, but, owing to the boisterous state of the weather, they were obliged to remain there two days, when, finding they could not get away, they returned to Honfleur with the intention of embarking from that place, but, the weather still continuing rough, they remained there till Thursday. In the meantime information was secretly conveyed to the 'Express,' the Southampton steamer, that it would be required to take a party from Havre to England, so it and some other vessels cruised off the French coast. On Thursday afternoon the King and Queen, with Generals Dumas and Rumigny, embarked in a fishing-boat, found the 'Express' waiting at Havre with her steam up, and at nine they set sail for England, where they arrived the next morning. The moment the King set his foot on shore he exclaimed, 'Thank God, I am on British ground!' They arrived in London on the 4th, and went immediately to Claremont. Great respect was shown to them, everybody taking off their hats as they passed.

*March 6th.*—There was a great mob in Trafalgar Square, called together by Mr. Cochrane to petition against the income tax ; they plundered a baker's shop and broke the lamps at Buckingham Palace. They also attempted to win over the sentries there, saying, 'Shake hands, my fine fellows, and let us fraternise as the French have done ;' to which they replied in the English shibboleth and turned out the guard. The crowd then scampered off.

*March 15th.*—M. Ledru Rollin has addressed a revolutionary circular to the Departments. He tells them that their power both over the civil and over the military force is unlimited, and that they must exercise it in getting the most violent Republicans elected. M. Carnot has also addressed a circular to the schoolmasters, desiring them to tell their pupils that education and property were

M

not the least requisite for Deputies, who made better statesmen when least learned and experienced.

*March* 16*th.*—Madame de Bonneval, who has just arrived from Paris, called. She says it is completely ruined, and that the distress is dreadful; no enthusiasm is felt with the Republic, and in the Departments the feeling is strong against it.

*March* 17*th.*—The Bank of France has suspended cash payments. This measure has been recommended by M. Emile de Girardin in the 'Presse.' However deplorable, it could not be avoided, as the rush upon the Bank during the whole of the 15th was tremendous. The applicants were so numerous that they were obliged to place themselves *en queue*, as at the entrances of theatres. We gave a dinner, and Prince Louis Bonaparte was one of the guests.

*March* 18*th.*—Lady Malmesbury got a letter from her uncle, the Duc de Gramont, expressing great apprehension for their lives, fearing that the brigands who filled the streets might at any moment attack and plunder their house. Their only defence was the National Guard, the Government not having the power, even if they had the will, to protect anybody. M. Lamartine, the only one in whom the Moderate party could feel confidence, was in a minority and could do nothing. The workpeople had got up a counter demonstration to that of the National Guard, and from thirty to fifty thousand men had marched to the Hôtel de Ville. It is said that two hundred thousand men of the Paris mob are provided with arms, and, except for the want of cannon, perfectly able to resist the National Guard and very likely defeat them. The troops of the line have been sent out of Paris by the Government, who thus show that they mean to rely upon the support of the rabble. There was a great dispute between the members of the Government on the subject of a decree proposed by Ledru Rollin and not approved by the rest. Finding himself overruled, he threatened to call in the mob, as he did on February 24, when the Duchess of Orleans and the Duc de Nemours went to the Chamber of Deputies. At this infamous threat Garnier Pagès got up, pulled a pistol from his pocket, and told him if he moved a step towards the door he would blow his brains out. Up to this time, however, there is no disposition among the people to shed blood, and the man who exhibited a model of a new sort of *guillotine* which he had invented, and which he said could cut off a thousand heads in half an hour, was nearly stoned to death. Lady Alice Peel came to see my wife, her object being to sound her on the subject of a reconciliation between the Protectionists and the Peelites, who said that Lord Stanley would be glad to unite the party again, but could say nothing about Sir Robert Peel. Lady Alice said that her husband the General was quite on our side and anxious for a Protectionist Government with Lord Stanley at the head, but that we must throw over Lord George Bentinck and Disraeli. This Lady Malmesbury told her was out of the question, adding that at this moment we had no wish to turn out the Whigs.

*March 20th.*—There have been great disturbances at Berlin. The troops fired on the people, who were led by the students, killing ten and wounding about a hundred of them. They then dispersed, but the town remains in a very unquiet state. Princess Esterhazy writes that there has been a very alarming insurrection at Vienna, and the town was in the hands of the mob, who pillaged and got the better of the troops, who only amounted to eight thousand men. Prince Metternich had fled, which had in some degree pacified the people. They have burned his villa and destroyed his beautiful collection of pictures and statues. Hungary has declared itself an independent kingdom, and chosen one of the Archdukes for its King.

*March 21st.*—Accounts from Germany are very alarming. Fresh disturbances at Berlin ; the troops charged the mob and were repulsed, and the King had fled to Potsdam. It is said that a Republic is proclaimed at Vienna, but the rumour is doubted.

*March 22nd.*—There has been a second outbreak at Berlin. The troops charged the people, and it is said ten cannon shots were fired, but the tumult soon subsided. At Vienna things are quiet since the first insurrection, and the people seem satisfied with the Emperor's concessions. At Berlin the King grants entire liberty of the press, and convokes the Diet for April 2, and he also publishes a manifesto declaring his intention to put himself at the head of the national movement in Germany. The King of Naples has also agreed to all the demands of the Sicilians through

Lord Minto. He gives them a separate Parliament, to be elected by universal suffrage, everybody to be eligible as a Deputy who possesses ten pounds a year. Paris continues quiet, but the panic increases. All the rich people have turned off their servants, and nobody buys anything but strict necessaries. Imprisonment for debt is abolished, so debts are not paid, and there is hardly any silver in circulation. The Marquis of Hertford, who is anxious to come back to England, has not been able to do so from the impossibility of getting any money to pay his journey, and has sent to England for some. The Government have laid an embargo upon his plate and furniture, and have forbidden him and everybody to carry off any heavy luggage from Paris. The same has happened to Lord Pembroke. The mob burned the carts in which he was carrying off his property, and destroyed everything in them. M. Guizot says he expects a famine in Paris, as the country people are beginning to be afraid of bringing their corn or cattle into the city, thinking they are not likely to be paid for them.

*March 28th.*—Paris is quiet, but the scarcity of money increases ; the dividends are paid in paper, with the exception of a very small proportion of silver, and tradesmen prefer giving credit to taking paper in payment of their bills. Sebastiani has had a thousand pounds of silver plate melted down into five-franc pieces.

*March 29th.*—Went to a party at Devonshire House. The Prince of Prussia [1] was there. He is a very soldierlike-looking man, with a determined but very harsh countenance. He is middle aged. The Comte de Montemolin was also there, a little insignificant-looking man.

*March 30th.*—The King of Sardinia has issued a proclamation to the people of Lombardy and Venice, promising to assist them in regaining their liberties. It was dated 23rd, and on the same day the Austrians evacuated the town of Milan and retreated upon Mantua. Masrhal Radetsky held out for three or four days to give time to the Emperor of Austria's troops to arrive from the frontier, and then formed a junction with them behind the Mincio, guarding Mantua. The Piedmontese troops then entered

1 Afterwards Emperor of Germany in 1871.

the Milanais.  Parma and Modena have revolted, and also the district of Como.  The Austrian garrisons have been taken prisoners and disarmed.  An insurrection at Venice, Trieste, and throughout the whole Austrian dominions in Italy.  Paris is quiet, the population passing their time in processions.  There was one of wet-nurses, and another of laundresses, to whom Lamartine said, ' Repassez, mesdames ! '

*March* 31*st.*—Venice has proclaimed a Republic, and all the towns in the Austrian dominions in Italy are in open revolt. The Sicilians have refused the Constitution offered them by the King of Naples and guaranteed by England, and want a Republic.

*April* 5*th.*—The alarm about the Chartists increases.  Everybody expects that the attack will be serious.  Every precaution is taken, and all the troops within reach have been ordered to London, even those at Windsor, whose duty is to be performed by the Buckinghamshire Yeomanry.  The bridges in London are to be defended with cannon, and all, therefore, depends upon the fidelity of the troops.  Doubts are expressed as to some amongst them, and also about the police, but I cannot believe a word against either.  General Lord De Ros says the troops are to be concealed as early as four o'clock on the morning of the 10th, in the neighbourhood of Kennington Common.  Their officers are to be present at the meeting in plain clothes.  The whole force, with its artillery, is to march out and fire upon the mob.  The soldiers are all perfectly loyal, and furious with this mischievous attempt to disturb the peace.

*April* 8*th.*—Lady Jersey says that the Duke of Wellington has told her there is not the slightest danger to be apprehended, and he advised the ladies to drive about as usual.

*April* 9*th.*—The alarm to-day is very general all over the town.  The Government have made great preparations, though the extreme precautions that are known to have been taken have, of course, increased the people's fears.  The Duke of Wellington is to command the troops, and the orders he has given are that the police are to go first to disperse the meeting ; if resistance is offered and they are likely to be beaten, then the troops are instantly to appear, and the cannon to open with shell and grenades, infantry and cavalry are to charge—in short, they are to be made an example of. The Admiralty is strongly garrisoned and filled with arms, as also are the Horse Guards and the Treasury. There are eight hundred men in Buckingham Palace with cannon ; and steamers and gunboats on the river. The Ministers are to assemble in Downing Street to be ready for any emergency, but both Houses of Parliament will sit as usual.

*April* 10*th.*—My five keepers have arrived at my house this morning, each armed with a double-barrelled gun, and determined to use it if necessary. A great many have done the same, and filled their houses with trusty men. A battalion of Grenadier Guards is at the Horse Guards, besides the usual force of Life Guards. The mob was not very considerable, and the best behaved I ever saw, and though there were very few police or special constables to keep order, there seemed to be no excite-ment—nothing but curiosity. Everybody walked about as safely and as quietly as on any other day. We went to Lord Carring-ton's house to see what would happen. I was much amused by seeing an old gentleman, who rode up in front of the Horse Guards, stop his horse, let the reins fall on his neck, and quietly wind up and set his watch by the clock, an operation which lasted fully three or four minutes. The mob took no notice whatever of him, although I expected they would have laughed at him. Among the special constables stationed round Trafalgar Square, Prince Louis Napoleon was on duty. The way the Chartist meeting ended was certainly very absurd and has covered them with ridicule. A little before one o'clock, Mr. Mayne, the chief officer of police, rode up to Kennington Common, where there were from fifteen to twenty thousand Chartists assembled, accompanied by Lord Duncan. Not a soldier was to be seen, and only two policemen. Mr. Mayne sent to beg Feargus O'Connor to come and speak to him. He did so, as pale as ashes, trembling from head to foot, and said to Mr. Mayne, 'What do you wish me to do ? I am ready to do anything you advise me.' Mr. Mayne answered, ' What do you intend to do ? Do you intend to persevere in your plan of marching in procession ? for if you do we must prevent you ; though at the same time we have orders to facilitate the presen-

tation of your petition, if it is presented in a proper manner.'
This seemed greatly to relieve Feargus O'Connor, who apparently
expected to have been arrested, for he exclaimed in a delighted
tone, 'Thank you, Mr. Mayne; you are my best friend. Shake
hands, I'll do anything you like.' He then turned to the people
and said, ' Fools! I always said you were fools; this is not the
way you ought to act. You are a parcel of fools. Mr. Mayne is
the best friend I have in the world. Disperse directly and go
home.' Thus ended this ridiculous exhibition, which had created
universal alarm, and from which, but for the extraordinary
precautions taken by the Duke and the Government, and the
loyalty and courage shown by all classes in uniting for the preservation of order, serious consequences would have ensued. Mr.
Smith O'Brien made his appearance in the House and denied
having gone to Paris to ask for assistance, saying he only went
to sympathise with the French; but Sir George Grey read his
own letter to Duffy, in which he said the French were ready to
send fifty thousand men to Ireland. O'Brien had not a word to
answer. I hear everybody means to cut him, and when he said,
in his speech in the House, 'I have been called a traitor,' the
yells and shouts were terrific, and lasted so long that the newspapers say it was dreadful even for an indifferent spectator to
witness such a scene.

*April 12th.*—The news from Lombardy is better. General
Radetsky has concentrated his forces and entered Verona, and
General Walmoden, Mantua. The Chartist petition, which
Feargus O'Connor had stated to be signed by six million persons,
had less than two million signatures, or what purported to be
signatures, appended to it. Whole pages were written by one
hand, and many of the names gross forgeries, such as 'Victoria
Rex,' 'Duke of Wellington,' and a great many such words as
'Pugnose,' 'Flatnose,' &c.

*April 15th.*—Lady Tankerville, Lady Malmesbury, and I
went to Claremont to pay our respects to the exiled sovereigns.
On our arrival we were ushered into the drawing-room by a
person out of livery; it was difficult to say whether he was a
servant or a general. Madame de Montjoie came in immediately
and said the King and Queen were busy writing. However, in

a few minutes the King entered the room, and was soon after
followed by the Queen.  They were both looking well in health,
but in wretchedly low spirits ; the King in particular could
hardly hold up his head.   He appeared anxious about the
elections, from which he evidently anticipated favourable results,
and it was clear he still entertains some faint hopes, which are
probably kept up by his friends in their desire to please him
rather than tell him the honest truth.   He told us that Lord
Brougham had not been naturalised in France, as all acts of
naturalisation were signed by him, and were not valid without
his signature.   M. Guizot then came in, and told the King that
he had heard that morning from Count Dietrichstein that Prince
Metternich was not coming to England.   Mr. Monckton-Milnes[1]
then arrived and sat by the King, while Lady Tankerville and I
were talking to the Queen.   We saw the King suddenly start up
and exclaim, ' Ah ! c'est le dernier coup !'   The Queen jumped
up and inquired, ' Qu'est-ce que c'est, mon ami ? Calmez-vous !' to
which he replied by repeating, ' C'est le dernier coup !'   It then
appeared that Mr. Monckton-Milnes had informed him public
opinion thought his son the Duc de Nemours had not shown the
courage the occasion required.   Why he did so I cannot under
stand.   In the evening I told Lord Palmerston of our visit to
Claremont, which seemed to interest him.   He hoped it was true
that  Prince  Metternich  was  not  coming  to  England, as this
*réunion* of foreign statesmen would look too much like a congress.
He suspected the King of Sardinia's illness was feigned ; that all
countries wanted us to take their part, and thought it very ill-
natured our refusing to do so, but that our best policy was to
keep aloof and let them settle their own quarrels.

*April* 17th.—The report of the defeat of the Austrians is true.
The Piedmontese attacked them at the bridge of Goritz on the
8th.   The Austrians retreated after blowing up the bridge, but,
not having done it effectually, the Piedmontese crossed over, took
four pieces of cannon and two thousand prisoners, driving the
Austrians upon Mantua.   But this is the Sardinian account, and
certainly exaggerated.

*April* 30th.—Heron  Court.   Mr. Stanley left us.   Lords

[1] Now Lord Houghton.

Canning, Castlereagh, and Salisbury have been fishing here, but with no luck. Yesterday Lords Canning, Granville, Douglas, and Rivers came from Highcliffe, where they had been staying for the hunting in the New Forest. They were all so disgusted with the danger of the ground that they declared they never would hunt there again. One man, a groom, was killed, three gentlemen very much hurt, and Lord Granville had his face cut by the boughs of a tree against which his horse carried him. In Paris everything is quiet, and the elections have gone off peaceably. Lamartine is at the head of every list, and Ledru Rollin and Louis Blanc at the bottom. There is, therefore, every reason to hope that the Moderates will have a majority in the Assembly. Yet the language at the clubs is of the most violent description. There is no doubt if these men get the upper hand the horrors of 1793 will be repeated.

*May 8th.*—It is feared if the Austrians continue to be successful the French will interfere, as a large sum has been decreed for the expenses of the army. M. Dietrichstein [1] appears to expect this, and is very much out of spirits at the state and prospects of his country. The Danes and Prussians have accepted our mediation. The former had blockaded Hamburg, Lübeck, and Bremen.

*May 12th.*—There have been serious disturbances at Rome to force the Pope to declare war against Austria, which he was unwilling to do, as Austria threatens in that case to withdraw her spiritual allegiance to Rome. The whole National Guard joined the people, surrounded the houses of the cardinals to prevent their leaving, took possession of the gates of the town, and threatened to depose the Pope if he persisted in refusing to accede to their desire. He at once gave the promise and declared war against Austria, whose Ambassador immediately left Rome, and he consented also to form a new Government, of which no one in Holy Orders would be a member. Count Nugent has not yet effected a junction with Radetsky.

*May 15th.*—The telegraph from Dover announces that the National Assembly at Paris was again taken possession of by the mob yesterday. After a scene of great confusion, one of the

---

[1] Austrian Ambassador in London.

leaders, a man named Hubert, proclaimed the dissolution of
the Assembly.   Afterwards Barbès, Raspail, and others, followed
by an immense mob, went to the Hôtel de Ville, where they
established a Terrorist Provisional Government ; but a strong
body of the National Guard having assembled by this time,
arrested them, cleared the National Assembly of the mob, and
order was once more restored.   The attack upon the National
Assembly was not a *coup de main*, as was at first supposed, but
the result of a deep-laid conspiracy, in which General Courtois,
the Commandant of the National Guard, was chief.   He has
been superseded.

*May 24th.* —' La Presse' announces the defeat of Generals
Zucchi and Durando, who have been annihilated by Count
Nugent, who has taken Palmanova and Tréviso.   Sir Henry
Bulwer has been ordered to leave Madrid by the Spanish
Government.   The Emperor and Empress of Austria have left
Vienna in consequence of a fresh disturbance, and have gone to
Innsprück for refuge.   Barbès nearly made his escape from
Vincennes, having corrupted two of his gaolers, but a third
recognised and stopped him.   The intention of the conspirators
was to set fire to the theatres and murder all the Deputies they
met with.   Madame Lamartine [1] gives herself such ridiculous
airs that she actually refused to receive Lady Louisa Tennison
unless she was presented by Lady Normanby, the Ambassadress.

*May 25th.* —The Jew Bill was thrown out in the Lords by
a majority of 35.   Mr. Lionel de Rothschild and his brother
Anthony were present.   I never saw the House so full.   The
Rothschilds stood like elder sons of Peers on the steps of the
throne, and would not even retire when the division took place.

*June 3rd.* —There has been another insurrection at Vienna.
On the 26th the Government attempted a reactionary *coup d'état*
by ordering the Academical Legion, which was guaranteed by the
Constitution, to disband.   This they refused to do, and the whole
population joined them, barricades were erected, and at last the
troops were forced to retire.   The people then demanded the
continuance of the Academical Legion, and that the Emperor
should return in eight days, or appoint one of the Princes to

[1] The temporary President's wife.

represent him. Both demands were granted. Lord Palmerston has refused to receive Count Miresol, saying that he will only transact business with an accredited agent of the Spanish Government, so that any explanation they have to give must come from the Spanish Ministry.

*June 26th.*—Fighting in Paris for the last two days. Loss of life dreadful—greater than in most battles. Ten thousand are said to be killed or wounded on the two sides. Lamoricière had two horses killed under him. Horrible cruelties were committed on the wounded soldiers. To prevent them from firing at the windows the mob placed their women and children before them, and fired from behind, thinking themselves safe. But after some time the soldiers returned the fire, killing several women and children, whose bodies were thrown into the streets by their own friends, and perhaps their own relations.

*June 30th.*—London has been very gay for the last fortnight. We have had the Spitalfields ball, which was exceedingly brilliant, and realised 1,000*l.* for the charity, after 1,800*l.* had been deducted for expenses. Lady Londonderry had a quadrille of forty kings and queens, very splendid ; but they were received with shouts of laughter mingled with applause as they entered.

*July 25th.*—Radetsky totally defeated the Piedmontese after four or five days' hard fighting, in which he retook all the positions which it had cost Charles Albert two months to gain. He retired towards Cremona, and the Austrians bombarded Peschiera. The King, being completely beaten, has appealed to the French Republic to send sixty thousand men to his assistance, which they have refused to do, proposing to settle the question by negotiations in concert with us. The long-talked-of rebellion in Ireland has at last broken out and been suppressed by fifty policemen ! W. S. O'Brien headed the attack upon the police— or rather sent three thousand men to attack them whilst he concealed himself in a garden close by. O'Brien is proclaimed a traitor, and a reward of five hundred pounds offered for his apprehension, and all who harbour or assist him are proclaimed guilty of high treason. Our army in Ireland is now about forty thousand men, and Lord Hardinge has gone over to take the command. O'Brien has been arrested. Radetsky has driven the

Piedmontese out of Cremona, and they are now in full retreat upon Pavia or Milan. The Lombards have behaved infamously towards them, and deserted them in their utmost need, never supplying them with food or wine. They fought most gallantly, and were defeated much more by hunger and fatigue than by the Austrians. The King showed great courage, but no military skill.

*August 8th.*—Lord Palmerston yesterday announced that England and France were to mediate between Austria and Italy, which was received with loud cheers. We dined with the Palmerstons, where the French Minister told us he was recalled for speaking to M. Guizot in the street. I can't say I believed him.

*August 9th.*—We left London for Achnacarry by our usual route through Glasgow, and afterwards by steamer to Corpach.

---

We passed the autumn at Achnacarry as usual until October 22, during which time we were visited by the Charteris, Wrottesleys, Sidney Herberts, Lord and Lady Bruce, Lord and Lady Jocelyn, the Duke and Duchess of Montrose, &c. On September 25, we heard of the death of Lord George Bentinck, which took place suddenly on the 21st. He was staying at Welbeck, and being engaged to dine with Lord Manvers, he sent his servant with his clothes in a gig, saying he would walk himself, the distance being only about five miles. However, he never arrived, and the servant becoming alarmed drove back to Welbeck and inquired if anybody had seen him. A search was made, and he was found in a field, about a mile from Welbeck, quite dead. He will be a dreadful loss to our party, for he was not only a very clever, but a most honest, courageous, and high-minded man. The inquest was held on the 25th, and it appears from the medical testimony he died from a spasm of the heart, brought on, it is supposed, by excitement and the hard work he has gone through for the last two or three years. There was no disease in the heart or in any other part of his frame, which the surgeon said promised a long life. It must therefore have been quite an accidental attack, and one that anyone might have if they overworked themselves. The sensation his death has caused throughout the country is extraordinary, and is likely to bring about very important changes in our party. No one but Disraeli can fill his place. Although of perfectly different natures, they pulled together without any difficulty. It will leave Disraeli without a rival, and enable him to show the great genius he undoubtedly possesses without any comparisons.

*October 11th.*—Mrs. Norton arrived at Achnacarry and stayed with us three or four days. We found her very agreeable and amusing, but her beauty, her manners, and her conversation are all of the most masculine character—and the latter is often coarser than even a man should use. Sidney Herbert told us a funny story about the origin of the name of Trollope. A son of Mrs. Trollope, the authoress, who was with him at Harrow, first told it of his own accord, but used to be made to repeat it by sufficient punchings on the head, as follows:—'Tallyhosier the Norman came over to England with William the Conqueror, and being out hunting one day with his Majesty in the New Forest, happened to kill three wolves, and "*trois*" being French for "three," "*loup*," French for "wolves," he was called "*troisloup*," which with many changes and corruptions during countless centuries became "Trollope"'!

*October 14th.*—We rode to Glenquoich, belonging to 'Bear' Ellice, crossing the Garry, where the water came up above our saddle-girths. The house at Glenquoich is a wooden construction, small but well furnished. There was a party of the Abercorns and Jocelyns staying there. On Sunday 'Bear' Ellice read prayers of his own composition, and we afterwards drove to Loch Hourn. The path leading to it is the finest I have yet seen in Scotland, not excepting even Glencoe. The 'Bear' is a regular showman and has got his lesson by heart, and when he is interrupted forgets where he left off.

*October 16th.*—Returned to Achnacarry and found that a good deal of snow had fallen since yesterday. It is not yet known what the Government mean to do with Smith O'Brien. The jury found him 'Guilty,' but with a recommendation to mercy. A fresh rebellion broke out at Vienna on the 6th, and Count Latour, Minister of War, was murdered. The Emperor fled, and after some severe fighting all through the 6th and 7th, the arsenal was taken and the town remained in the hands of the insurgents.

*October 19th.*—Matters at Vienna remain the same. The

garrison has taken up a position on a hill commanding the town, and the troops are loyal. Jellachich, who is Ban of Croatia, has arrived before Vienna, with the intention of commencing a bombardment. Cholera has broken out again in London.

*October 27th.*—Left Achnacarry by Loch Laggan, Dunkeld, &c. Stayed at Chillingham Castle.

*November 10th.*—Went to Knowsley. Heard that Vienna was taken by Windischgrätz on the 31st, on which day the Viennese agreed to capitulate. But after the terms of surrender had been agreed upon, hearing that the Hungarians were advancing to their assistance, they resumed hostilities, and, contrary to good faith, fired upon the Austrians, who were entering to take possession. Windischgrätz thereupon immediately ordered the cannonade and bombardment to begin, by which much damage was done. At the same time Jellachich advanced to meet the Hungarians, whom he totally defeated, and next day, November 1st, Vienna was in possession of the Austrians. We met at Knowsley General Talbot, nearly eighty years of age, a remarkable character. He was one of the early settlers in Canada, where he cleared several acres of land with his own hand in a part of the country which was then quite unpeopled and has now a population of two hundred thousand. He is very rich, and is a sort of king there.

*November 24th.*—Heron Court. Lord Canning and Adolphus FitzClarence arrived for dinner. The latter commands the Queen's yacht. Count Rossi, whom we used to know at Rome two years ago, and who was then French Ambassador, and since Louis Philippe's abdication Prime Minister of the Pope, has been assassinated on the staircase of the Chamber of Deputies. No attempt was made to arrest the murderer. His son nearly shared the same fate in trying to assist his father.

*December 2nd.*—News from Italy very bad. After Rossi's murder the mob and soldiers attacked the Quirinal, fired into the windows and killed Cardinal Palma. The Swiss Guards behaved very gallantly, but were too few to oppose any effectual resistance, and the Pope was obliged to accede to the demands of the rabble and appointed Mamiani Prime Minister. For about a week the Pope remained in his palace closely watched, when he succeeded in making his escape on the 24th to Gaeta, where a steamer was waiting to take him to France. The Pope was assisted in his escape by Mrs. Dodwell, an Italian lady, who provided disguises.

*December 5th.*—Went to Tottenham, Lord Ailesbury's place, where there was a large party. It appears that the Pope made his escape from the Quirinal disguised as the Bavarian Minister's servant. Having by this means got downstairs, he mounted the box by the coachman and reached the Bavarian Minister's house; he changed his dress, and, post-horses having already been procured, he started directly for the Neapolitan States. His escape was not discovered for some time, as his attendants had been told he was at prayers and must not be disturbed.

*December 11th.*—The Emperor of Austria has abdicated in favour of his nephew, the Archduke Franz Josef.

*December 20th.*—Prince Louis Bonaparte has been proclaimed President of the French Republic by a *plébiscite.* He had an immense majority over General Cavaignac. This, no doubt, is the first step to the Empire. His name has acted like magic on the nation.

## 1849

*January 22nd.*—The Herberts, Shelburnes, Cannings, and [1] Lord Eddisbury arrived. There has been some hard fighting in India on the banks of the Chenab, which has ended in the retreat of the Sikh army. But this slight advantage, if it can be called one, where we have not taken a single prisoner, gun, or standard, has been dearly bought by the loss of General Cureton and General Havelock, who were killed at the head of their regiments. The former greatly distinguished himself in the late war under Lord Hardinge, and was considered the first cavalry officer in the service.

*February 1st.*—Parliament opens to-day. All mention of the grievances of the agricultural interest having been omitted from the Queen's Speech, Lord Stanley brings forward an amendment to the Address in these words:—'We regret being compelled humbly to represent to your Majesty that neither your Majesty's

[1] Afterwards Lord Stanley of Alderley.

relations with foreign Powers, nor the state of the revenue, nor the condition of the commercial and manufacturing interest, are such as in our opinion justify us in addressing your Majesty in language of congratulation, and that a large portion of the agricultural and colonial interests of the Empire is labouring under a state of progressive depression calculated to excite the most serious apprehension and anxiety.' This amendment was received with loud cheers, and was lost only by two, the numbers being 52 to 50. The Ministers complained of having been taken by surprise. It was settled at a dinner the evening before, when Lord Stanley read the Queen's Speech to his guests; and when they were all gone, with the exception of the Duke of Richmond, Lord Redesdale, and myself, he drew up this amendment with us. The Duke of Wellington supported the Government, but he has lost his influence in the House of Lords from constantly taking their part, and I do not believe he can now command more than three or four votes, but this number made the difference on this occasion. The same amendment was proposed by Disraeli in the Commons, but not pressed to a division. The triumvirate (Mr. Disraeli, Lord Granby, and Mr. Herries) appointed to be our leaders in that House is an evident failure, the latter two being in the way of the first.

*February* 19th.—The deposition of the Pope was passed in the Roman Chamber by a majority of 136 out of 144 votes, and the proclamation of the Republic of Rome by 120. His spiritual power is, however, guaranteed, which seems an absurdity. A Republic has also been proclaimed at Florence, and the Grand Duke of Tuscany is at San Stefano, where two English ships of war await his orders.

*February* 20th.—My audit dinner took place, and was very ill attended, with a great deficit of rents. I made a speech to the farmers to prove to them that the repeal of the malt tax would do them more harm than good, which I feel certain is the case.[1] Prince Louis Napoleon is gaining great popularity. Trade in France is reviving and strangers beginning to flock to Paris. It will soon be as gay and agreeable as ever. The Austrians have entered Ferrara, and are said to be on their way to Rome. There

---

[1] This proved true, as it cheapened barley when it was repealed in 1880.

is a very important piece of news, the advance of the Russians against the Hungarians in consequence of the demands for assistance from Austria, which will enable the latter to send a larger force into Italy. Lord Palmerston has made a speech in the House of Commons, charging the King of Naples with every sort of crime and tyranny. Much of it may be true, but a great deal is certainly false, and a great deal exaggerated. Our Ambassador, his brother (Mr. Temple), believes every absurd story that is told against King Bomba, and repeats it to his chief.

*February 22nd.*—Letters from Vienna announce the complete destruction of the corps of Hungarians commanded by General Bem.

*March 3rd.*—The Austrians entered Ferrara on February 18, and found that an officer of the garrison and three soldiers had been killed by the townspeople; and that the Austrian Consul had had his house plundered without any effort on the part of the authorities being made to prevent it. Marshal Radetsky determined to punish the people of Ferrara and ensure the safety of the garrison there. A deputation waited on Field-Marshal Haynau, who insisted on the following conditions :—(1) To deliver up the murderers of the soldiers; (2) That six hostages should be given for the fulfilment of the conditions now made; (3) The army of the Pope, their liege lord, to be reinstated; and (4) That a fine of twenty thousand dollars should be paid.

*March 5th.*—Bad news from India. Lord Gough has again attacked the Sikhs in a very strong position, with an inferior force, and exhausted by a long march. Notwithstanding this the troops took their positions, but being unsupported at night they were obliged to abandon them after a tremendous loss of life; nearly one hundred officers and two thousand men being killed or wounded. Some of the cavalry, both native and English, behaved badly. Lord Gough himself fought in the thickest of the *mêlée*, and was not to be found when it was necessary to give orders, and in fact the battle was won in great confusion.

*March 7th.*—Lord Stanley asked the Government whether it was true that arms had been furnished to the Sicilian insurgents by our Government, to which Lord Lansdowne replied that it was so, but threw the whole blame on Lord Palmerston, saying that it

N

was done by his orders, and that when the rest of the Government were informed of it they were highly displeased at the measure, and sent an apology to the King of Naples, promising that it would not occur again. Lord Lansdowne in his speech attacked the Sicilian Government, and Lord Brougham when replying said : ' The noble Lord said, " the Sicilian Government," I conclude he means "the insurgents ; " ' to which Lord Lansdowne answered, 'I mean the Government *de facto*.' ' Yes,' said Lord Brougham, ' that is the Government of the insurgents, and is no more the Government of the Kingdom of all the Sicilies than Smith O'Brien's Committee was the Government of England.'

*March* 11*th.*—Sir Charles Napier says that in the position Lord Gough is he must either destroy the Sikhs or be destroyed himself, as there is no middle course.

*March* 13*th.*—The second reading of the bill repealing the Navigation Laws passed the Commons last night by a majority of 56. The Peelites voted different ways, some for and some against the bill.

*March* 14*th.*—We dined with the Colchesters, and were introduced to Sir Charles Napier. He is a little man with grey hair brushed back from his face, with an immense hooked and pointed nose, small eyes, and wears spectacles, very like the conventional face of a Jew. He is appointed to retrieve our affairs in India, and when the Duke of Wellington named him to the post he at first hesitated, until the Duke told him if he didn't go he would go himself. Great notice was taken of Sir Charles, and it was a curious scene altogether, for the Duke of Wellington arrived at the party, and for a few minutes those two great men were engaged in close conversation in the centre of the room, and the company formed a circle round them, though at a respectful distance.

*March* 17*th.*—Disraeli's motion for an inquiry into the burthens on land was thrown out by a majority of 91. It gave the Peelites a fair opportunity for a reconciliation with us, as it had nothing to do with Free Trade ; they, however, voted in a body with the Whigs.

*March* 22*nd.*—The papers contain a proclamation by Radetsky to his soldiers announcing the recommencement of hostilities on

the 21st, and stating his intention of marching on Turin. The
troops are perfectly well disposed and in high spirits, and there is
little doubt that Charles Albert will be made to regret his rash
and treacherous conduct. The armistice which was granted by
the Austrians six months ago, at a time when they could have
conquered the whole of Piedmont, was effected for the purpose of
settling the preliminaries of peace, but it has been employed by
Charles Albert in making preparations for war. This last time he
has been urged on by the Revolutionary party against his own
will, preferring to fight the Austrians to losing his crown. It is
conjectured that he does not mean to defend Turin, but will throw
himself back on Alessandria and Genoa. The invading army is
said to be in high spirits and confident of success. The Piedmontese have the disadvantage of being commanded by a foreigner,
Chrzanowski, a Pole.

*March 29th.*—Was at the Drawing Room. Great complaints
made by the ladies that the wives and daughters of the Queen's
servants and the ladies' maids of many of themselves obstructed
the gallery and had comfortable seats, whilst they themselves were
obliged to stand till their carriages came up ; this, after standing
so long upstairs, was rather hard. A despatch from the French
Minister at Turin states that the army of Charles Albert has been
forced back on to the mountains of Biela, and that the Austrians
have occupied Novara, Vercelli, and Trino. The King has abdicated and fled, and the Government has requested Mr. Aber-
cromby, our Minister, and himself to apply for an armistice to
cover Turin. Charles Albert, after his abdication in favour of
the Duke of Savoy, passed through Nice on his way to France.
The Piedmontese army has been totally beaten at Novara, but has
saved its honour. Lord Mahon told me a story of Mrs. Disraeli,
who was paying a visit somewhere in the country, where she met
Lord and Lady Hardinge. It happened that Lord Hardinge's
room was next to the Disraelis', and the next morning Mrs.
Disraeli said to Lord Hardinge at breakfast, 'Oh, Lord Hardinge,
I consider myself the most fortunate of women. I said to myself
when I woke this morning, "What a lucky woman I am ! here I
have been sleeping between the greatest orator and the greatest

N 2

warrior of the day ! " ' Lady Hardinge did not appear pleased at
the statement.   I left for Paris.

*Saturday, March* 30.—I arrived at Paris this morning, and
having informed the Prince President, Louis Napoleon, of my
being here, he immediately gave me an audience. Lord Stanley
being at the head of the Opposition, the Prince seemed anxious to
know what he might expect from him if he succeeded the present
Government.   He himself was only just in the saddle, in a position of great difficulty, and very anxious about the future.   He
said the danger to Europe lay in the absolute necessity of modify-
ing the treaties of 1815, which should be done before a war broke
out.   What would England do if Austria and Prussia went to
war ?   What would England do if such a modification was proposed by a Congress ?   France, he said, would not now be jealous
of our gaining more power in Egypt, and France and England together could remodel everything.   This seems to me to hint at an
idea that France would take part with Prussia, and if that Power
gained territory in Germany, France would advance her frontier
and allow England compensations in the Levant.   The Prince
said that Russia was, unfortunately, popular with the upper classes
in Paris.   He regretted the Roman business having turned out so
ill, but it had been badly managed.   Of France he said the Legi-
timists were really the most unpatriotic and *bêtes*, and turned the
elections here.   They hated England the most of any of the different parties.   If he (the President) chose to write an article
as long as his finger against them in the ' Moniteur,' he could
rally the *Rouges* and Republicans round him, but this he would
not do.   The Royalists wanted him to play the part of Monk,
without seeing the difference of the situation of public opinion as
well as his own personally.   He would in that case betray the
7,000,000 who had elected him, even if he had the power, which
he had not.   He considered the army staunch.   The worst of the
situation was that he had not one friend on whom he could depend ;
he was quite alone, and his only friends were those he did not
know.   He seemed to me very thin-skinned about the English
newspapers and the reports regarding himself.   He dislikes Lord
Aberdeen.   He has only 200 votes in the Chamber in his favour.

This conversation I afterwards repeated to Lord Stanley, who agreed with me in thinking that the mind of the President was full of schemes for the revision of the map of Europe, that he was the principal author of those which had been lately published in that sense, that no positive policy was fixed in his mind as long as he considered himself fettered by the Chamber and had not overcome his national enemies by some decided act, but that, although his position was precarious, it was not at all hopeless.

*April 1st.*—News has been received of a great victory over the Sikhs near Goojerat on February 21. They left their camp on the 11th, and having failed in their endeavour to draw Lord Gough out of his entrenchments, they retired, when it was ascertained that they had gone in the direction of Goojerat, which they took, having surprised the Afghan garrison. They then attempted to cross the Chenab at Sodra, but were met by a detachment of General Whish's army from Mooltan, which had advanced by forced marches to the relief of Lord Gough, where they were attacked by the combined armies of Lord Gough and General Whish, and were completely defeated, losing most of their cannon and all their ammunition and tents.

*April 13th.*—The Austrians have taken Brescia, and Genoa has surrendered. Jellachich has beaten the Hungarians, who latterly had been very successful, having defeated the Austrians and Russians in several encounters.

*April 14th.*—I returned from Paris. The President, who received me in the most friendly manner, was under the impression that if the Whigs were turned out Peel himself would come in, and that if in that event Lord Aberdeen is our Foreign Minister, he would intrigue for the restoration of the Bourbons, both of which suppositions are erroneous, as we shall certainly never again interfere in the domestic arrangements of France. There is a story now very much talked of in London which, if true, must tell against Lord Palmerston, as to his attention to public affairs. It is this :—The armistice between Denmark and Germany had already been far advanced, and was to expire on April 2, when a courier from Copenhagen arrived in London on March 26, who was the bearer of the final proposals of the Danish Government in answer to the conditions offered by the German Plenipotentiary. This communication was immediately forwarded to Lord Palmerston as the mediating Power, and it was all the more important not only from the nature of its contents, but because the Danish courier was strictly ordered to leave London, with or without an answer, so as to reach Copenhagen again before the conclusion of the armistice. This period of time, short in itself, and decisive as to the settlement of the question of peace or war, accordingly passed away ; the courier left London without any notice having been taken of the communication, and his return to Copenhagen was the signal for the precipitate departure of that expedition which has cost the lives of many seamen and the Danish fleet two of its finest ships. At length, on March 29, the Queen happened to hold a Drawing Room, at which some sort of a personal explanation took place between the Ministers and the members of the Diplomatic Corps. It was then ascertained that the all-important despatch upon which the question of peace or war turned had not been opened or read by Lord Palmerston during the interval of two or three days allowed for an answer. No answer at all was therefore given. The German Plenipotentiary remained in total ignorance of the fact that any such proposals had been made, as, on the other hand, the Danish Plenipotentiary does not appear to have been clearly apprised of the extent of concessions made in favour of his Government. Thus the messenger of actual war was allowed to leave this country because an English Minister did not read a letter.

*April 15th.*—Lord Seymour called and said that the story about Lord Palmerston and the Danish despatch was quite true.

*April 16th.*—A suspension of hostilities has been agreed upon at Genoa, and it does not expire until the 9th. Lord Hardwicke, who commands the ' Vengeance,' is in the harbour ; he has taken all the English residents on board, and is doing all he can to arrange matters. The leader of the Republican party sent a message to say he would order the batteries to fire upon the ship and sink her, but Lord Hardwicke despised the threat and remained. He landed at the peril of his life, a large mob being on the shore, apparently ready to attack him and his boat's crew. But on getting out of his boat he went straight up to them, and seeing a woman advance, evidently in a great fury, to attack him, he caught and embraced her before all the mob, who cheered him violently.

*April 25th.*—The Navigation Bill passed the Commons by a majority of 61.

*May 2nd.*—News has arrived from India of the termination of the war, the Sikhs, to the number of sixteen thousand men, having laid down their arms without fighting to General Gilbert. Forty-one pieces of cannon have been given up, making in all one hundred and sixty taken in this campaign. The state of Europe continues unsatisfactory so far as Austria and Denmark are concerned. The Russians have entered Transylvania, and the Hungarians will probably be defeated. The King of Prussia has refused the title of Emperor of Germany. There was a meeting of Peers yesterday at Lord Stanley's, and I remained with him afterwards to arrange the course of speakers on the Navigation Bill. Lord Stanley wished Lord Brougham to speak just before Lord Grey, intending to speak last himself. He said, ' Brougham must poke him up, and I will knock him down.'

*May 8th.*—The debate took place on the Navigation Bill in the House of Lords. It was perfectly crammed in every corner, many of the Peers finding it difficult to get seats.

*May 9th.*—The Ministers have only a majority of ten, and we had one of fourteen present, so they won it by proxies. They looked very downcast and dispirited when the numbers were announced, as it is the first time such an important question has been decided by proxies. Not one of Lord Stanley's party was absent, and he had sent them a message of thanks for their support.

*May 10th.*—The French expedition left Civita Vecchia on the 28th, and reached Rome on the 30th ult., expecting to be received with open arms ; but instead of that it seems they got a good beating, after several unsuccessful attempts to take the barricades, which were defended by Poles ; the Romans contenting themselves with looking on and applauding. The French were obliged to retreat, and are in waiting for reinforcements.

*May 15th.*—An insurrection has broken out in Canada. It appears that the sanction of the Governor-General was given at Montreal on the 25th to the Rebellion Losses Indemnity Bill.

Directly it became known the rage of the populace knew no
bounds, immense mobs collected, drove the members out of the
House of Parliament, and set fire to the building, which with the
library, containing a large collection of valuable books, was
destroyed. Lord Elgin was pelted with eggs, and his immediate
recall insisted upon.

*May* 18*th.*—Nothing could be worse than the foreign news.
Germany is in the most dreadful state ; the Austrians are being
beaten on all sides by Bem and Dembinski ; there has been an
insurrection at Dresden, which was not put down until after
three days' hard fighting and great loss of life ; the Grand Duke
of Baden has been driven from his dominions ; and the Red
Republicans are triumphant at Rome. General Oudinot, who
commands the French army there, has made no further attempt
on the city since his defeat. It is quite true that the Romans
took five hundred prisoners from the French.

*June* 5*th.*—Lady Blessington died yesterday in Paris, of
apoplexy. The French army remains stationary before Rome,
though it amounts to twenty-five thousand men. The malarial
fever has begun to attack them. M. de Lesseps has left Rome,
fearing assassination.

*June* 14*th.*—News has arrived that the French made an
attack upon Rome on June 3, took possession of the Villa
Pamphili Doria, but have not entered the town. Oudinot was
attacking the Porta del Popolo with his artillery.

*June* 18*th.*—The French army has not gained an inch of
ground. General Oudinot is anxious to spare the town, which
must be destroyed if he uses his heavy artillery against it, but he
will probably find himself compelled to do so in the end, as the
honour of France is now involved. Macdonald, the sculptor, has
arrived in England. He used to be a violent Radical, but the
scenes he has witnessed have effected a great change in his
opinions. He says a grape-shot entered a window of the Vatican
and lodged in the wall within two or three feet of the Apollo
Belvidere. Some of the palaces have also been struck, but
without doing much mischief.

*June* 29*th.*—The French have taken possession of a portion
of the outer walls of Rome, but have not yet entered the city.

They have simply effected a lodgment in the breach. The Austrians took Ancona on June 18, but Venice has not yet surrendered.

*July 4th.*—The French are probably by this time in possession of Rome, which offered to capitulate on the 30th, after two days' hard fighting. It is said that Mazzini and his colleagues have been forced to this by the people, who when the moment approached that they must risk their lives shrank from the danger. The Princess Belgiojoso tried to encourage them to resistance, but in vain. On the receipt of this intelligence in Paris, General Bedeau, who had been sent to supersede General Oudinot, was recalled.

*July 6th.*—Went to Lady Wilde's.[1] There was a French play acted by the famous Doche. It was so improper that many of the ladies slipped away.

*July 7th.*—Lord Ward gave us his box to see Madame Sontag's *début* in ' Linda di Chamouni.' It was most successful ; her face is still lovely and her voice and execution perfect. Lablache was present in a stage-box, and his expression of rapture was indescribable. I never saw a face convey such admiration and delight. He certainly is the best judge of singing in the present day.

*July 9th.*—Met Mario. I asked his opinion about ' Le Prophète,' and he said it was not so fine as the ' Huguenots,' but he could not yet quite judge, as they did not know their parts ; but that there was not a single piece in it to be compared to the grand duet in the fourth act of the ' Huguenots,' which he thought the finest that had ever been written. We went in the evening to a ball at Cambridge House, where of course we found the *élite* of society. I see that the Opera has been very nearly closed : the orchestra, not having been paid, refused to play, but Mario generously paid them out of his own pocket.

*July 12th.*—The French entered Rome on July 3, and on the same day Garibaldi left the city with his corps unmolested. It is supposed he intends to throw himself into Calabria and excite an insurrection there.

*July 17th.*—The Government were beaten yesterday on the Irish Poor Law Bill in two divisions.

[1] *Née* Mademoiselle d'Esté.

*August 1st.*—We left on our annual journey to Achnacarry, *viâ* Carlisle, Greenock, and Corpach.

*August 26th.*—The war in Hungary is ended. Görgey, to whom Kossuth made over the dictatorship, made his submission to the Russians on the 13th inst. The latter were under Paskiewitch. Görgey's conduct must until further news excite suspicion of treachery ; but he may have acted wisely for his country, as the forces against him were overwhelming, and if, as is said, there were differences amongst his own people, no other course was open to him.

*September 1st.*—We went to Ardverikie, a beautiful place on Loch Laggan, hired by the Abercorns.

*September 4th.*—We went with Lady Abercorn, Lady Granville, and Lady Jocelyn to Cluny Castle, nearly fifteen miles off, starting, with a fat coachman to drive us, about four in the afternoon. Of course the horse knocked up before we arrived at our destination, and we were obliged to get out and walk up the hill from the lodge to the house. The woman in charge took us for ladies' maids and valets, and when she found out who we were, as she insisted upon knowing our names, I thought she would have fainted. After seeing the castle we procured a horse with some difficulty to take us home, but did not arrive till near midnight. I believe Macpherson's ground at Cluny is supposed to be the best for grouse in Scotland.

*September 6th.*—Returned to Achnacarry. At Mulcomer Bridge we very nearly backed over the precipice, as the horse jibbed.

*September 10th.*—Venice is surrounded, and the Austrians entered it on the 28th ult.

*September 22nd.*—I had been out deer-stalking, and as I was returning home alone, and by bright moonlight, I saw a hind on the hill a little above the road and shot her, but just as I was stooping over her with a knife, she sprang up and struck at me with one of her fore feet, hitting me in the forehead just between the eyes. The blow was so violent that it knocked me down and stunned me for a short time, and on recovering my senses I found I was quite blind, but this was only from the blood. Her hoof had cut a deep gash in my forehead and along my nose. The animal was lying quite dead by my side. I walked to the house, which was not far off, and the maid who opened the door was so frightened at my appearance that she fainted forthwith. This laid me up for a week, but with no further consequences.

*October 24th.*—We left Achnacarry. Our party had been composed of the Jocelyns, Calcrafts, Charteris, Herberts, Lord Cardigan, &c.

*November 8th.*—We went to Chillingham Castle, where Mr. Burrell, a clergyman, told us the story of a little girl at his school who was asked what the outward visible sign in baptism was, to which she replied, 'The baby.' Also Lady Goodricke's little daughter, who, seeing her mother was very uncomfortable before the birth of her children, said she was 'determined to have all her children before she married, and enjoy herself afterwards.'

*November 14th.*—The Mannings have been executed for the murder of O'Connor. She kept up her character to the last, and showed the most extraordinary nerve ever possessed by a woman. He confessed having assisted, though he affirmed that she fired the shot, and had originated and planned the whole crime. She, on the other hand, persisted in affirming her innocence, and died with perfect composure, thinking apparently of nothing but of exhibiting her beautiful figure to the best advantage. Her dress was very handsome, being of black satin, with a lace *canezou*, and a black veil over her head. The attendants wished her to put on a cloak, but the proposal annoyed her so much that they did not press it. She had been lady's maid to the Duchess of Sutherland. After having murdered O'Connor, they buried him under the hearthstone, and ate their supper upon the spot for several days after.

*Mr. Disraeli to Lord M.*

Grosvenor Gate : November 21, 1849.

My dear Lord,—It is most vexatious that we should have missed each other, as there was no one with whom I wished more to confer than yourself, having every confidence in your intelligence and firmness, and should long ago have written to you on many affairs had I not found it impossible to write on subjects so complicated.

I probably leave town to-morrow, and have no prospect of being here again oh December 2, as on the 5th I have a Bucks meeting which in the present awkward condition of affairs I must attend.

The state of our Press is deplorable. I approve of your suggestion respecting the 'Post,' but it would be as well, I think, previously to communicate with Knox, with whom I only some months ago had a casual conversation on the subject in the hall of the Carlton.

Ever yours sincerely,<br>B. DISRAELI.

*December* 11*th.*—We went to Savernake, where there was a large party.

*December* 13*th.*—A sad accident happened this afternoon to one of Lord Bruce's keepers, who blew off two fingers of his right hand in loading Lord Jocelyn's gun. Fortunately, the day's sport being nearly over, we were not more than a hundred yards from the house, and by a most lucky chance the family doctor was there, having come to see one of the servants, and had his surgical instruments, so that the poor man had immediate assistance, and his fingers were amputated in a few minutes. All the gentlemen stood round to witness the operation and encourage the man, who showed great pluck. A curious incident occurred, proving how uncertain the action of such sights is upon our nerves. Every one of us bore the sight pretty calmly but Lord Raglan, who had seen a hundred battles, and who nearly fainted away, and was obliged to retire. Yet in action he was known to be remarkable for his unmoved calmness and *san froid.*[1]

---

[1] Marshal St. Arnaud said : ' C'est toujours le même calme qui ne le quitt jamais.'

## 1850

*Mr. Disraeli to Lord M.*

Hughenden Manor : Jan. 1, 1850.

My dear Lord,—My absence at Quarter Sessions prevented my receiving your very kind letter until to-day. I am very sorry indeed that it is not in my power to have the pleasure of becoming your guest, as you propose, but I have engagements at home from which I cannot extricate myself.

Sir Robert's letter is pompous and trite. There is really nothing proposed in it which might not have been done with equal propriety if the Corn Laws had not been repealed ; but he has succeeded in conveying an impression that his estate is in bad condition, and that he is conscious he has led his friends into a hopeless scrape.

I think Sidney Herbert is in a pretty scrape ; 85,000 needlewomen to be deported at 15*l*. a-piece (his own estimate) would take upwards of 600,000*l*. He should have subscribed at least one year's income as an example, and if he succeeds in his object, which is impossible, he will do no good.

I am sure you will make a capital speech at Salisbury, but I wish the movement was not merely agricultural. There are the other great interests (in buckram) that your friend G. F. Young talked so much of. Why does not Limehouse at least stir ?

Ever yours faithfully,

D.

P.S.—Let nothing prevent you looking at the last article in ‘ Blackwood ’ on high farming in Scotland.

*Lord Stanley to Lord M.*

Knowsley : Jan. 2, 1850.

My dear Malmesbury,—I omitted some time ago to thank you for your list of Peers. I have noted down a few to whom I think for various reasons it would be unnecessary for me to write, and we never, I believe, send circulars to the Bishops. I have also put down three names which appear to me to be omissions from your list. Is Dunsany yet elected ? If he is, he should be written to. Take care to have it as generally known as possible that Redesdale is to be our candidate [1] whenever old Shaftesbury retires, which I think he will

[1] As Chairman of Committees.

do this session, though probably not at the very commencement; still we ought to be prepared for anything that may happen.

Love to my lady. I am very glad to hear you are all pleased with what you see and hear of Ossulston's choice.

Yours very sincerely,<br>STANLEY.

*January 4th.*—Heron Court. I went to-day to a Protectionist meeting at Salisbury, where I had to propose a resolution and make a speech.

*Mr. Sidney Herbert to Lord M.*

Wilton: Jan. 6, 1850.

My dear Fitzharris,—I have been long enough in public life to know how often public duty impels a course which is very painful to private friendship, and I confess I am far more grieved on public than on private grounds at the line taken during the last months by yourself and your friends. Farmers and landlords were beginning to settle down and adjust themselves to the new state of things when that unfortunate delusion that Protection can be restored has come to disturb and unsettle everything. In the face of the thriving and daily improving state of all classes, except the one which has to go through the process, never very pleasant, of giving up a pecuniary advantage which they enjoyed at the expense of the rest, it is hopeless to attempt the re-imposition of the Corn Laws. If it were possible by any combination of circumstances to do so, even for a time, I believe such success would be fatal to the order to which you and I, in our different degrees, belong.

However, there is little use in our discussing the point. I know enough of you and those with whom you are acting to do you the justice to believe (what others will not) that you are acting upon a strong conviction, that the course you advocate would benefit all classes of the community as well as your own, and that you would not move a finger for it if you did not think so.

I wish I could foresee with any confidence the time when this fiscal question shall be no bar to our co-operation on social and political matters which are far more important to the vitality of this country.

Believe me, my dear Fitzharris,<br>Most affectionately yours,<br>SIDNEY HERBERT.

*January* 14*th to February* 19*th.*—I was laid up and in considerable danger from an attack of rheumatic fever. Lord Cantelupe and Mr. Pelham were seized at the same time with the same complaint, and both died. The London doctors had treated them with acids, principally lemon juice, whilst my country practitioner had given me calomel and strong alkalis—two diametrically opposite systems of treatment.

*February* 22*nd.*—The division upon Disraeli's motion upon taxation took place this morning, and the Government had only a majority of 21. The Ministers looked rather annoyed, for though it was not for a return to Protection, it was a move in that direction, and is considered so by all parties. Sir Robert Peel and Sir James Graham both spoke and voted against us. When the former got up and expressed great sympathy for the sufferings of the agriculturists, Colonel Sibthorp lifted up both his hands in a mock-tragic manner, exclaiming, 'Oh dear! oh dear!' which set the whole House into a roar of laughter. Peel, instead of paying no attention to the interruption, turned to Colonel Sibthorp and gave him some explanation, adding, he hoped he believed him, to which Sibthorp replied, 'I can't say I do.' A good many Peelites voted for us. There was a great row at a Protectionist meeting at Dorchester. The mob attacked the farmers, pelting them with stones; they bore it for some time, and then made a charge upon the mob with their hunting-whips and dispersed them.

*March* 3*rd.*—The Government have introduced a bill for lowering the franchise in Ireland, which is of course only a prelude to a similar measure in England.

*April* 16*th.*—In Paris. On arriving I wrote to the President, who asked me to breakfast the next morning at the Elysée. He was more than cordial, and began by reminding me that he had always told me in his darkest days he would some day govern France. 'I told you so,' said he, ' when you came to visit me in my prison at Ham, and you and every one thought I was mad. But although I am here I know nobody; the friends I have I don't know, and they don't know me, even by sight. Although a Frenchman, not fifty of them had ever seen me when I came over from England. I have tried to consolidate all political parties,

but I can conciliate none; there is now a conspiracy to seize me
and send me to Vincennes, and General Changarnier and Thiers
are at its head.   The Chamber is unmanageable.   I stand perfectly alone, but the army and the people are with me, and I
don't despair.   Yet every day may see me a prisoner.   Your
Ambassador, Lord Normanby, is intriguing against me, although
his chief, Lord Palmerston, and some of your Cabinet Ministers are
in my favour.   I believe Lord Normanby carries on a private correspondence with Prince Albert to my detriment.'   After this he
invited me to drive with him at St. Cloud and see the *haras*,
which I did.   Among the horses was a splendid dark chestnut,
which the stud groom, an Englishman, led out to show me.   The
President, after admiring him much, ordered the man to send him
to his stables at Paris.   'I can't do that, Sir,' he replied, 'the
horse belongs to the Republic.'   As we were sitting in the phaeton
Louis Napoleon jogged my arm and observed, 'You see my position; it is time to put an end to it.'   Driving home, he made no
secret of his intention of being beforehand with his enemies, and
there was no mistaking the means he would take to be so.

*April 21st.*—I gave a dinner to Lord Normanby and a few
friends at Philippe's café.   I found his lordship knew of my
breakfast with the President, and could not conceal his curiosity
and displeasure, which was foolish and unwarrantable, as I had
never taken part in foreign politics, nor even held any office.   He
showed his personal antipathy to the Prince President in a very
undiplomatic way, foretelling his impending fall.   He said his first
speech was a failure, and was made with a strong German accent,
but long as I have known him I never perceived he had one.   It
is evident Lord Normanby and his chief, Lord Palmerston, are at
variance in their policy, and the former is with Lord Aberdeen,
whose *bête noire* is Louis Napoleon.   After this the President
invited me to dinner, and after it was over took me into an inner
room where we had a long conversation.   The rest of the com
pany, which consisted of Lord Normanby, Lord Ailesbury, Lord
Clanricarde, and Lord Brougham, came to take leave of the
President, as it was getting late.   I also got up to go, but he
stopped me, asking me to remain to finish our conversation.   It
was chiefly relating to the difficulties he was in.   This annoyed

Lord Normanby exceedingly, and was considered important enough for some one to write home that Lord Normanby was much chagrined at not knowing what the subject of our conversation had been. He must have guessed that it related to his treacherous hostility. Left Paris.

*April 26th.*—Dined with the Eglintons, where I met General Cabrera, to whom I was introduced. He is very much what I expected, a little dark man, with a very intelligent countenance, and a lively, energetic manner. He is not handsome, but his eyes are so bright and expressive, and his whole appearance so indicative of energy, cleverness, and courage, it is impossible to think him ugly. He speaks horrid French, and I had great difficulty in understanding him. We sent him a ticket for our box at the Opera next day, and he came to it. I was much amused at hearing Lady Suffield, who did not know him, but found out he was a Spaniard, ask him whether there was any truth in the report that Cabrera was to marry Miss Richards, the great heiress. He laughed and answered, ' Yo soy Cabrera,' but did not deny the fact, which I believe to be correct. Another lady asked Cabrera, not knowing him, whether the report of his marriage with Miss Richards was true, and after giving him a long dissertation on the lady's fortune, she added she thought it a great pity that Miss Richards should marry a man like Cabrera, who had not a farthing in his pocket and nothing but bullets in his head. Cabrera laughed and said, ' I whom you are speaking to am that unfortunate individual.' Then he revenged himself by asking her if she was not a relation of Parodi, who was singing at the time.

*April 17th.*—The French Ambassador has been recalled in consequence of Lord Palmerston's conduct on the Greek question. It had been agreed upon in London in the event of the conditions approved by M. Gros being rejected by Mr. Wyse, our Minister at Athens, that the blockade should not be resumed without special orders from England. Lord Palmerston neglected to send instructions to that effect, and Mr. Wyse having received no orders, and not agreeing to M. Gros' proposals, acted upon his former instructions and resumed the blockade. Upon which the King consented to the terms proposed by us. This has very much offended the French, who talk of going to war with us.

*June 7th.*—Went to Lady Grey's party.  Mr. Bernal Osborne
was there, and gave a very amusing account of the Nepaulese
Ambassador, whom he knew in India, having come to Calcutta to
explain his reasons for having shot the Prime Minister of the King
of Nepaul.  Mr. Bernal Osborne says he had committed a great
number of murders, though he looks very young and gentle.

*Lord Stanley to Lord M.*

St. James's Square: June 16, 1850.

Dear Malmesbury,—I have just seen Aberdeen, and we have gone
over your lists [*re* Redesdale's election] together.  He thinks you have
taken by no means a sanguine view, as far as the names we looked over
are concerned.  Of the ten Peelites whom you give to the Government,
he expects Ellesmere and Wharncliffe to vote with us, De Grey to stay
away, Ashburton, Bristol, and Cowley to be with them, and Athole,
Churchill, Denbigh, and the Bishop of Winchester he knows nothing
about.  Of the twelve doubtful Peelites, he expects we shall have
Bathurst, Clare, and Howe ; Seaton and Shaftesbury are against us ;
Gough, Hardinge, Wellington, and Ripon will stay away ; he knows
nothing of Hertford, Northumberland, and Winchester.  You may add
to the Whigs who will not vote, Lord Lovat.  He thinks Manners will
follow him (Aberdeen).  He asked me, and I could not tell him how
you had reckoned Cawdor.

Yours ever,

STANLEY.

*June 17th.*—Lord Stanley made a great speech on the affairs of
Greece in the House of Lords.  He moved a resolution condemning Lord Palmerston, which was carried by a majority of 37 in a
very full House.  The Peeresses' Gallery was quite full, several
ladies sitting on the floor, and many were obliged to return home
for want of room.  The evening began by an attack on the
Prussian Minister, Count Bunsen, who was seated in the Ladies'
Gallery, and not in the part appointed for Ambassadors.  Lord
Brougham had previously gone into the gallery with Lady
Melbourne and Lady Newport, and told Bunsen he had no right
to be there.  Bunsen refused to give up his place, upon which
Lord Brougham descended to the House and called attention to
' a stranger being in the Peeresses' Gallery,' saying, ' If he does

not come down I shall move your lordships to enforce the order
of the House. . It is the more intolerable as he has a place assigned
to him in another part, and he is now keeping the room of *two* [1]
peeresses.' This was received with shouts of laughter and cheers ;
but Bunsen refused to move till Lord Brougham sent Sir Augustus
Clifford, Usher of the Black Rod, to him, when he got into a fury
and left the House, taking his wife and daughter with him.  Lord
Stanley then got up and made a magnificent and extremely amusing speech, which lasted from five till nearly eight.  I went after
wards to Lady Waldegrave's, and there saw Madame Van
Weyer, who had already heard of Lord Brougham's attack on
Bunsen, and was perfectly wild at the insult offered to a Minister.
I told her I did not approve of the way Lord Brougham had
behaved, but that Bunsen had no right to sit in the Peeresses'
Gallery.  She would not agree to this, but if she tried herself she
would find I am right.

*June 20th.*—Went to the Drawing Room, which was more
crowded than anything I had ever seen, and a disgraceful scene—
the ladies screaming and fainting, their gowns torn into shreds
by the spurs, and their arms scratched by the epaulettes of the
men.

*June 27th.*—The Queen was attacked this evening as she was
coming out of Cambridge House, by a man, who struck her on
the head with a cane.  Her Majesty showed her usual courage,
amd went in the evening to the Opera.  When she arrived, in
the middle of the skating scene in the 'Prophète,' the audience rose
and cheered her for full five minutes, after which 'God Save the
Queen' was sung by the Italian artists.

*June 29th.*—I heard this afternoon that Sir Robert Peel had
been thrown from his horse on Constitution Hill, and was very
much hurt.

*June 30th.*—Several people called on their way from Sir
Robert Peel's.  The accounts of him are bad.

*July 1st.*—Sir Robert Peel is worse to-day.  He suffers
great pain, and the doctors say he is in a very precarious state.

*July 2nd.*—The doctors give hardly any hope of Sir Robert
Peel's recovery.  He suffers dreadful pain, but is conscious,

---

[1] Bunsen was a very stout man.

Lady Peel is so distracted that the doctors will not allow her to go into his room. She came in once, but when Sir Robert saw the state she was in he went into convulsions, and since then she has not been permitted to go near him.

*July 3rd.*—Sir Robert Peel died this morning. His wife saw him before his death, having been allowed to go to his bedside as soon as the case was quite hopeless. He took the Sacrament, which was administered to him by the Bishop of Gibraltar, all his family being present. The post-mortem examination in the case of Sir Robert Peel proved that the fifth rib on the left side had been fractured and pressed upon the lungs, which must have produced intolerable agony. The accounts of the accident differ very much. Some say he was seen reeling in his saddle for a moment before he fell, and that it was through dropping the reins that the horse swerved. The general opinion is that his horse, which was a young one, started at being passed by Miss Ellice's groom, who was riding a very spirited animal. The accident was seen by several people, but all give different accounts; the majority think he was simply thrown by the horse starting; and that is the most probable story. We went to the French play with the Ossulstons to hear Rachel in *Bajazet.* She acts very finely, but her voice has grown like that of a man, and she has lost all pretensions to good looks. Her countenance has become so diabolical and unfeminine that it is quite disagreeable to look at her.

*July 9th.*—The Duke of Cambridge died last night. The Duchess of Gloucester arrived a short time before he expired, and a messenger was sent to Prince Albert to come immediately to the Duchess of Cambridge. It is a singular accident and coincidence that the Duke, Sir Robert Peel, and Lord Cantelupe were all invited and engaged to dine yesterday with the Duke and Duchess of Norfolk. But considering the length of time that invitations are sent before the day appointed for dinners, there must be many cases of the kind.

*August 12th.*—Left London for Achnacarry, *viâ* Carlisle and Corpach. After remaining there till October 27, we took a steamer for Glasgow, whence to Chillingham Castle.

*November 15th.*—Heron Court. Lord Clanwilliam and Lord

Stanley arrived. The two being the quickest men I know, amused us much by chaffing one another, and I think on the whole Lord Clanwilliam had the best of it. They both of them enjoyed the wild-fowl shooting very much, and were as eager as two boys.

*Lord Eglinton to Lord M.*

Eglinton Castle : November 24, 1850.

My dear M.,—

.        .        .        .        .        .        .

We had a reviving meeting of Protectionists here this week, and, as we were all of one way of thinking, the arguments used were most convincing. There is the best possible feeling among all the gentlemen of our party, and no desire to rush to extremities, or drive us to a certain defeat; but in many parts of Scotland, as in England, the farmers think us too lukewarm, and accuse the landlords of deserting them. I think we must fight about something next session, and we shall have plenty of scope for it if we oppose the income tax, and stand out for equalisation of local taxes. As to the Papal Aggression, the country seems to be very like my late Protectionist party.

Very sincerely yours,

EGLINTON AND WINTON.

*November 26th.*—I hear Mrs. Norton and Sir Edwin Landseer have quarrelled. They have been great friends for the last two years, and she encouraged his admiration to get his drawings and instructions in painting. He is very angry and spiteful about her.

*December 1st.*—Sir William Stanley, whom I saw at Paris, is now hopelessly deranged. It is supposed it was occasioned by a fall he had in the riding school at Paris.

*Lord Stanley to Lord M.*

Lathom House : December 2, 1850.

Dear Malmesbury,—. . . . Disraeli writes me word that he has a great financial scheme which he is concocting with Herries, and which he wishes to talk over with me. I shall probably go up to town for a day or two early next month to discuss it with him; but until I have done so I hardly know what line it would be best to hold, and am not fond of opening our game too soon through the medium of the papers, even if we were quite resolved upon it. My own impression is that we must resist the income tax, and probably fight for a relaxation of the monetary laws and an amendment of the poor law. I am myself very much inclined in favour of your crotchet, if you can work it out.[1] On the Popery question I quite agree with you that we should rather follow the stream, which is running quite strong enough, than attempt to take a lead of our own. I think the Government are in a most awkward dilemma, from which they will find it very difficult to escape; and the more rope you give them the more chance there is of their hanging themselves at one end or the other. . . .

We had a good day while Clanwilliam was with us in Bickerstaffe Wood—five guns, 560 head; and another after he left us, in the Trap —four guns, 471. My scores were 126 and 153. We expect a great rabbit day on Friday, for which Jocelyn will come in, but it is the worst year for woodcocks that I ever remember.

Ever yours sincerely,

STANLEY.

## 1851

*January 1st.*—Lady Tankerville informed me that Lady Olivia Ossulston was confined of a son, an event long wished for in our family.

*January 12th.*—The Prince President has dismissed Changarnier from the command of the army in Paris, and all the Ministers have resigned. All the principal men have been summoned to the Elysée, and all join in disapproving of the step, but the President remains firm. It is supposed it will end in some compromise, but up to this moment no fresh Government has been formed. The President declares he has a right to dismiss any officer from his command, and will preserve his privileges inviolate. Regarding his dotation, the President says the Assembly can do as they please, as he can shut himself up in one room in the Elysée and turn off his servants, but he will not submit to be deprived of the privileges of his office. I admire his firmness, and trust he will not allow himself to be persuaded to give in, for if he does he will lose greatly in the public estima-

---

[1] To make personal property pay its share of the Poor Rate like the Income Tax as a principle.

tion.  At present the country is with him, and it is evident the
hostility of the Chamber is solely occasioned by the ambition of
the different *parties* in it, each of whom expected him to play
into their hands, and finding him honest and determined to do
what he thinks right towards his country, have now coalesced to
overthrow him.  The Moderates had better take care what they
do or they will drive him into the arms of the ultra-Republican
party.  As to Changarnier,[1] he is decidedly hostile to the President and the Republican party, and aims at being Dictator.  He
is a fine old soldier, and distinguished himself greatly in Africa,
but his appearance is against him.  He dresses like an old dandy,
with a wig and very tight stays, and indulges in a great affectation of youth and physical activity which he does not possess.

*January 17th.*—I hear that Mr. Roebuck wrote a letter to
Lord Brougham on the subject of the paragraph respecting Lady
Hastings, which some injudicious friends of hers had put in the
newspapers, and Lord Brougham's answer was very characteristic.
He told Lady Hastings she had better touch thirty Italians than
one newspaper.

*January 21st.*—The new French Government have been
defeated on a vote of confidence by a majority of 415 votes to
286.  They immediately tendered their resignations, which the
President refused to accept.  M. Thiers sent to him to say that
the vote was not directed against his Government, but against his
Ministers, and that if he composed a new Cabinet, even taken
from among the members of the minority, Thiers would support
him, and, subject to this, his dotation would be voted without the
least difficulty.  The President thanked them, but, seeing no
reason to change his Ministers, could not avail himself of their
suggestions and offers.

*January 22nd.*—The President has accepted the resignation
of his Ministers, and it is said a new Cabinet will be constructed
out of the minority.  Many members threaten to send Louis
Napoleon to Vincennes.

*February 2nd.*—Dined with Lord Stanley, Lord Redesdale,

---

[1] Changarnier continued to oppose the Emperor during his prosperity, but after
his defeats in 1870 he joined his army, offering him the aid of his sword, and he
was taken prisoner at the capitulation of Metz.

Mr. Disraeli, and Mr. Herries, and sat talking politics till one in the morning.

*February 3rd.*—Went to the christening of my little nephew,[1] Charley Bennet, for whom I was one of the godfathers.

*February 4th.* — Parliament opened, and Lord Effingham moved the Address in the House of Lords. Lord Stanley spoke well, as usual, and raised a great laugh by saying, in allusion to the restoration of tranquillity in Europe, 'that the increased tranquillity in Europe was to be attributed to the increased inactivity of the Foreign Secretary.' Lord Lansdowne answered him, and after him Lord Roden got up, which was the signal for a general clearance of the galleries by the ladies. Lord Stanley proposed Lord Redesdale for the office of Chairman of Committees, in the room of Lord Shaftesbury, deceased, and he was elected unanimously, as there was no other Peer who came within any distance of him for that office. One of the ladies praised Lord Stanley for having made an eloquent, and at the same time a very temperate, speech. He started, and exclaimed, 'Good God! temperate! I hope I didn't make a milk-and-water one.' Considerable fears were entertained about the solidity of the Crystal Palace, and some M.P. proposed to march a regiment of soldiers through the galleries to test it, a singular idea under the circumstances. Lord Willoughby has taken a house in London during three months of the Exhibition for his tenants, without telling Lady Willoughby, who learned it first from the newspapers, and consoled herself for the outlay by saying, 'Well, it will neither improve their taste nor their morals.' Grisi was at Brighton, where she has lately been staying, walking on the cliff and escorted by two black fiddlers and two nurses, one carrying the last baby and the other the one before. When she arrived first she was so weak that the fiddlers had to support her, one on each side ; but now she stumps away on her heels and looks as well as ever. Mario is at St. Petersburg. There never was such an adoration as she has for him.

*February 9th.*—The Government is supposed to be in a mess about their bill against Popery, and also anxious about the continuance of the low prices, which affect their pockets as well as

[1] He died in India in 1880,

ours. They don't, however, dare to do anything for the relief of agriculture, though they would probably be glad that we should do so, and many people think they would willingly go out for a time and leave us the odium and trouble of arranging these two matters.

Lord Stanley to Lord M.

St. James's Square: Feb. 15, 1851.

My dear Malmesbury,—You might have been very sure that I would not have given any notice on your behalf without your authority; and you rightly conjecture that the notice I actually did give was for the presentation of Hardwicke's petition. It was merely an error of the newspapers. I have told Nelson to have a London Whip, and to send word to Exeter, Richmond, Winchilsea, &c., that such a debate is coming on, but without *urging* their attendance. I think we had better not interfere by any specific resolution with the battle now raging in the Commons. Next week they will have the Income Tax, on which, I think, we may contrive to take a division (on Friday), and perhaps beat them, without pledging ourselves to its absolute and immediate repeal, against which there might be valid objections raised from the state of the Revenue. Disraeli's speech—or indeed speeches —were most masterly. Graham was very bitter, but very *telling*. It is clear we have nothing to hope for from the leading Peelites but opposition. Our division was very good, but not as good as it looked, for we had several with us on whose general support we certainly could not count.

Ever yours sincerely,

STANLEY.

*February* 16th.—The House of Lords has done nothing lately; in the Commons the adjourned debate on the Ecclesiastical Titles Bill was resumed on Monday. On Tuesday Disraeli moved 'That the severe distress existing in the United Kingdom among that important class of her Majesty's subjects, the owners and occupiers of land, and which is justly lamented in her Majesty's Speech from the Throne, renders it the duty of the Government to introduce without delay such measures as may be most effectual for the relief thereof.' On Wednesday the Ecclesiastical Titles Bill was again discussed and the debate adjourned. On Thursday the debate on Disraeli's motion was resumed, and the House divided upon it, when the numbers were—267 for the motion, and 281 against, giving the Ministry only a majority of fourteen. The Ecclesiastical Titles Bill was divided upon, when 395 voted for, and 63 against, its introduction.

*February 17th.*—Went to London for the Agricultural debate to-morrow, and spoke on the subject. Lord Stanley was much pleased and amused. Returned to Heron Court on the 20th. At Christchurch Petty Sessions a boy was brought up to give evidence in a poaching case. As there were great doubts whether he understood the nature of an oath, my brother undertook to cross-examine him. He inquired, 'Are you aware of the meaning of an oath?' The boy scratched his head with a puzzled look and then said, 'Ees.' 'And you know in whose presence you stand?' continued my brother. The boy looked up and caught sight of Colonel Cameron, who was seated wrapped up in a cloak, with his hair standing on end, and looked quite the most awful person in the room. After a moment's consideration the boy again answered 'Ees.' 'You are then aware of the solemnity of the act you are going to perform, and the danger of swearing falsely?' 'Ees,' he answered. The oath was then administered, and the boy began to tell the most awful lies, which was pointed out to Mr. Berkeley, with the remark that he was committing perjury. 'No,' replied Mr. Berkeley, 'fortunately he did not do so, for he swore by Colonel Cameron.'

*February 21st.*—Mr. Berkeley amused us very much this morning by telling us that Lady Stuart de Rothesay, when at Highcliffe, passed her time in throwing stones and handfuls of gravel over the cliff to try and stop it up and preserve it from the encroachments of the sea. When he was walking about there one day he saw the gardeners very busy collecting the sweepings of the walks, consisting of gravel and dead leaves. He asked them what they were going to do with them, and they answered that they were going to throw them over the cliff by Lady Stuart's orders for the above-mentioned purpose. Highcliffe is a most beautiful house, built by the late Lord Stuart de Rothesay, a part of it consisting of an old abbey brought from Caen ; but it stands so near the edge of the cliff, which is falling daily, that if the destruction is not stopped it cannot last above twenty years.[1]

*February 22nd.*—Lord John Russell moved yesterday that the Committee of Ways and Means should be postponed until next Monday, when he would state his reasons for the request, and also the course he intended to take. There was a Cabinet Council yesterday morning, after which Lord John went to the Queen. It is not yet known what passed, but the postponement of the Budget is a tolerably clear indication.

*February 23rd.*—Heard from Lady Tankerville, who said the Government was out. There were many unhappy faces and some happy ones at Lady Granville's party. My brother writes that the Queen has sent for Lord Aberdeen. Lord and Lady Stanley dined at the Palace on Friday, having been asked some days before. It must have been rather awkward both for them and the Queen.

*February 24th.*—Lord John Russell and Lord Lansdowne had inteviews on Saturday morning with the Queen. Immediately after their departure she sent for Lord Stanley, who arrived at the Palace at one o'clock and remained in close conference with her for an hour. When he reached his house in St. James's Square he found a second letter awaiting him from the Queen, who had written to him again after he left the Palace. At five o'clock Prince Albert wrote to Lord Aberdeen, who, being absent from town, only went to the Palace at nine o'clock and remained till twelve in consultation with the Queen. At six o'clock Lord John Russell had a second interview with the Queen, and remained more than two hours. Sir James Graham visited Lord Aberdeen yesterday, and Graham and Aberdeen visited Lord John Russell in the morning, having an interview at a later period of the day with Mr. Disraeli and Lord Stanley.

*Lord Canning to Lord M.*

Grosvenor Square : Feb. 24, 1851.

My dear M.,—I did not know until Lord Tankerville told it me last night that you were out of civilized society, or I would have written on Saturday.

[1] Lady Waterford has saved it by some extensive and expensive works on the cliff.

To begin at the beginning, Lord John's announcement on Friday was at first misinterpreted by most of those who were not in the secret. We thought that, as usual, we were to be treated to many budgets, and that the respite till Monday was asked for the purpose of preparing the second edition. But the truth was known in the course of the evening; and it is a fact that Lord John decided on resignation in the morning before he summoned the Cabinet; from which, when it did meet, Lords Lansdowne and Carlisle were absent—the one with gout at Bowood, the other in the City on business; and before either of them knew they were out, Lord John had been to the Queen. Minto, too, who is sick in bed, was kept in the dark.

There was some division amongst them as to the necessity, or even propriety, of going out. Carlisle does not disguise from his friends that he saw no need of doing so; and others share his opinion. Lord Lansdowne, I believe, is glad to be quit of office on any terms.

As to the cause, we shall hear Lord John's motives this evening. I suppose the minority on Locke King's motion will be the ostensible reason; but of course the bad reception of the Budget was a more cogent one. I have reason to think, however, that what nettled Lord John most was the cold reception given to his promise of dealing with the Franchise next session, which did not prevent some even of his own people from voting against him.

On Saturday afternoon Stanley was sent for. What passed you will know, sooner or later, better than I can tell you; but I believe his refusal to form a Government was not absolute—*i.e.* that he desired to reserve the reconsideration of the matter if any other party should fail.

I hear that Disraeli's language is that ' unconstitutional conditions ' were proposed. If he really says so, it probably refers to some limitation as to dissolving; but I know nothing authentic.

In the afternoon Lord John was with the Queen again; and in the even she saw him, Lord Aberdeen, and Graham together for more than two hours. All yesterday negotiations were going on; but, so far as I know, without any result up to the present moment.

Every kind of speculation is afloat—a reconstruction of the Government, with only an infusion of new Whig blood; a coalition between the Peelites and the Government; a junction of Graham simply with the Government; or a Government under Stanley. I should be sorry to have to bet upon the issue; but what I wish is, that Stanley should form a Government, receiving from the present Ministers and from us the promise of support in getting his money, and against Radical attacks, upon the condition that he should not dissolve Parliament until after the harvest, and that meanwhile he should not attempt to disturb Free Trade ; he being at liberty to take any course he pleased as soon as this Session is over, and we being then released from the promise of supporting him any longer. I see nothing impracticable in this. I have little hope of a wholesome state of politics or parties until you have been in power, and have tried your own cause after your own fashion ; and, under some such limitations as I have mentioned, I think that the risk which is to be apprehended from a Protectionist Government attempting, or being suspected of attempting, a reversal of commercial policy would be avoided, and certainly it would be no bad bargain for Stanley.

### Mr. F. Mills to Lord M.

1 The Terrace, Whitehall Gardens : 4.30 P.M., Feb. 24, 1851.

My dear Malmesbury,—To give you the news, I have ordered a seven o'clock newspaper to be put into the post at 7.25 to go to you to-night.

Lonsdale kept sending to your house yesterday, thinking it were impossible you should not be up. At half-past six yesterday Stanley had made no communication of any sort to him. This is at least strange. He was the first man Peel used to consult.

I think the counties would stand at 5s. duty with the income and property tax taken off.

Bright told Roebuck yesterday, ' We will never stand Lord John as Prime Minister again.'

I go to Lowestoft on Friday, and on the following Friday to Brussels.

They talk of Labouchere, Francis Baring, and Sir C. Wood being made Peers.[1]

Lord Harrington is all but dead. He is at Brighton, and by the last accounts there was not the least spark of hope. There is, then, another loss, as Leicester, his brother, is worse than Cobden.

Ever yours, &c.

F. MILLS.

*February 25th.*—Lord Stanley has declined to form a Government at present, though it is understood he has expressed his willingness to do so should Lord John Russell fail in reconstructing his Ministry, which he declared last night in the House of Commons he had undertaken to do at the Queen's request. He

---

[1] They were created Taunton, Northbrook, and Halifax.

has asked till Friday to make the necessary arrangements, and in the meantime all public business is suspended. Mr. Disraeli accused Lord John Russell of not being quite correct in his statements ; and Lord Stanley in the House of Lords refused at present to say one word of what passed between him and the Queen, though he promised a full statement later. It is supposed that Lord John will try to form a coalition with the leading Peelites, but Sir James Graham asks for Lord Clarendon and six Cabinet places, which are hard terms. Nobody knows what part Lord Aberdeen will take. I came up to town to-day, and Sidney Herbert told me that Lord John Russell had failed in his endeavours to reconstruct his Government.

*Lord Stanley to Lord M.*

St. James's Square: Feb. 25, 1851.

Dear Malmesbury,—I must see you without a moment's delay. John Russell's attempted reconstruction has failed, the Peelites cannot form a Government, and I shall have to try my hand. Let me see you, if possible, in the course of to-morrow.

Yours ever,

STANLEY.

*February 26th.*—Lord John Russell has failed, and the Queen has again sent for Lord Stanley.

*February 27th.*—All the Peelites have refused to join Lord Stanley, although he offered Gladstone and Canning Cabinet places—the former Foreign Affairs. I think Lord Stanley will be unable to form a Government, but a few others and myself are to meet at his house at one o'clock, when it will probably be decided whether he gives up the attempt or not. My impression is that he will do so. Lord Aberdeen refused to attempt the task of forming a Cabinet, and yet the Peelites decline to join either the Whigs or us. I can't imagine what they want, for, being the weakest party in the country, they can't hope to govern by themselves.

*February 28th.*—We met at Lord Stanley's in St. James's Square, and have failed in forming a Government. He had previously requested me to take the Colonial Office, which I consider a great compliment, as it is one of the hardest worked of places. Those assembled were—Mr. Disraeli, Sir John Pakington, Mr. Walpole, Lord Hardwicke, Mr. Henley, Mr. Herries, Lord John Manners, and Lord Eglinton. Everything went smoothly, each willingly accepting the respective post to which Lord Stanley appointed him, excepting Mr. Henley, who made such difficulties about himself and submitted so many upon various subjects, that Lord Stanley threw up the game, to the great disappointment and disgust of most of the others present. Mr. Henley seemed quite overpowered by the responsibility he was asked to undertake as President of the Board of Trade, and is evidently a most nervous man. Mr. Disraeli did not conceal his anger at his want of courage and interest in the matter. Lord Stanley had written to Sir Stratford Canning, who was at Constantinople, asking him to take the management of Foreign Affairs, which he at once consented to do. In the House of Lords, Lord Stanley announced his failure, and did not conceal it as being caused by the want of experience in public business which he found existed in his party. This is probably the case, but what really caused the break-up of the conference was the timid conduct of Mr. Henley and Mr. Herries.

*March 1st.*—Lord Stanley's speech was a fine one, manly and straightforward, but I fear it will discourage his party. He says, alluding to them : 'A party, numerous no doubt, but still undoubtedly in a minority in the House of Commons on several occasions, and which unfortunately, though it no doubt numbers in its ranks men of talent and intellect, contains, I will not say no single individual, but hardly one individual of political experience and versed in official business. I feel that is a great disadvantage for any party to labour under ; but there is a third party in the House of Commons, not indeed very extensive numerically, but most important as regards official experience and the talents of the great portion of its members. I mean that small party, in point of numbers, which has adhered to the policy of the late Sir Robert Peel.' This will appear to many as rather praising his opponents at the expense of his friends, and it will have the effect of making the former more difficult to deal with, and at the same time give discouragement, if not offence, to his own party. He then states the financial measures he would have proposed if he had come into office. His plan was to put on five shillings fixed duty on corn, and take threepence off the income tax preparatory to its total repeal, whenever the revenue of the country admitted it. Lord Stanley told me afterwards that 'the total want of decision in Mr. Herries and Mr. Henley made him see at once that they would be of no use. The latter seemed frightened rather than pleased at being in the Cabinet, and appeared paralysed.' This was quite true. As to Herries, he looked like an old doctor who had just killed a patient, and Henley like the undertaker who was to bury him. The difficulties Lord Stanley would have had to contend with were also very great—a majority against him in both Houses, the Mutiny Bill not passed, supplies not voted, and the time not favourable for a dissolution of Parliament—all confirmed him in his determination to give up the attempt; and he accordingly went to the Queen at five o'clock and announced his failure. The Queen had authorised him to say that if he had asked for a dissolution she would not have refused. The Duke of Northumberland would have had the Admiralty. The Queen has sent for the Duke of Wellington to ask his advice. I expect that Lord John will reconstruct his Ministry *tant bien que mal*, and that even the Peelites will join it. I called upon Lady Stanley, who seems in great spirits at her husband not being in office.

*March 2nd.*—Norman Macdonald is appointed Comptroller of the Lord Chamberlain's Department, a place for life worth twelve hundred a year. He called upon me to announce it as an old colleague at Oriel College. After Lord Stanley's speech Lady Jocelyn asked him whom he had meant by the person he alluded to who refused to join him on account of the pressure of his domestic duties. He answered 'Not Jocelyn,' at which she looked put out, for she evidently thought she had a good joke against him, the phrase having created a laugh. A few days ago, as I was returning home, I saw the Duke of Newcastle, Mr. Sidney Herbert, and Mr. Bonham Carter standing together near the gate of Sir Robert Peel's house in close consultation, looking as if they were invoking his ghost to inspire them.

*March 6th.*—Saw Ben Stanley, who was very much out of

spirits, and confirms the report that the Government is in great difficulties. Nothing has occurred since they resumed office to strengthen them.

. *March 11th.*—The Government were beaten last night on Lord Duncan's motion for paying the money derived from the revenues of the Crown into the Exchequer. They so little expected this that Ben Stanley, their Whip, prevented Lord Douro's voting for them, as he was ready to do, telling him there was no occasion for his staying, as they were sure of a majority. Lord Stanley seems confident of soon going into office, and has asked me to take his son Edward for my under-secretary, which is an additional compliment, and desires me to make out a list of those that I thought ought to have places. Nothing could be kinder or more flattering. Ben Stanley was walking a few days ago with Lord Bessborough and Lord Granville, the former of whom is Master of the Buckhounds, while the latter at one time held the place, talking of Lord Stanley's appointments. One of them asked what Lord Stradbroke was likely to have. ' Oh, answered Ben, ' the Buckhounds, of course ; that is the only place for a fellow like that.' The other two looked rather foolish at the *lapsus linguæ* of their companion. The motion upon Ceylon, accusing Lord Torrington of tyranny when Governor there, is put off. He seems confident of making out a good case for himself. The present Sir Robert Peel spoke in the House of Commons, and Disraeli says his speech was very clever, and so straightforward and honest that if his father had been there he would have disowned him.

*March 26th.*—The second reading of the Papal Aggression Bill passed this morning by a majority of 438 to 95.

*March 28th.*—Talking to Mr. Fortescue, he told me that Mrs. Lawrence, the American Minister's wife, said to him, speaking of her husband, ' A wonderful man, a very heavy man (meaning clever) ; when he goes to the east he tilts over the west.'

*April 1st.*—I hear that Lord Torrington made a very good speech this evening in defence of his conduct in Ceylon, and was cheered on all sides when he sat down.

*April 2nd.*—Sir Gilbert Heathcote has left all his landed property to his eldest son, who is also residuary legatee, with the

P

exeeption of the Durdans, which he has left, with 5,000*l.* a year,
to his youngest. Lady Olivia Ossulston and Lady Malmesbury
went to a banquet at Merchant Taylors' Hall. Mr. Disraeli spoke
well, but there was nothing particularly interesting in his speech.
The most eloquent part of Lord Stanley's was that in which he
alluded to Lord George Bentinck, which he did in the most feeling
manner. The enthusiasm of the Conservative audience was unbounded, and the cheering when his health was drunk must have
lasted five minutes.

*April 5th.*—Lady Lansdowne died the day before yesterday at
Bowood, the immediate cause of her death being a paralytic stroke.

*April 6th.*—Edward Stanley called and told me we had no
chance of turning out the Government this session, as they had
evidently made friends again with the Radical party by promising
to introduce a new Reform Bill this year.

*April 8th.*—The division on Mr. Herries' motion on the
income tax took place yesterday, and the Government had a
majority of 48.

*April 12th.*—The debate on Mr. Disraeli's amendment to the
Assessed Taxes Act took place last night, and Ministers had a
majority of 13. The amendment was that if any relief was
given by the remission of taxes, the owners and occupiers of
land should be the first to profit by it.

*May 1st.*—London Exhibition was opened to-day by the
Queen. Went off quietly.

*May 2nd.*—Jew Bill passed second reading House of Commons
by 25 ; 202 to 177. This will encourage the Peers.

*May 6th.*—Lord J. Russell refers income tax to Select Committee, and saves Government from another defeat. The Queen
is going to give a fancy ball in June. Period, Charles II. Not
becoming for ladies ; handsome for gentlemen.

*May 7th.*—Ministers again defeated on Lord Naas's motion
on spirits duty. Numbers equal. Roebuck made an insolent
speech advising resignation. Lord John declined.

*May 10th.*—Mr. Urquhart moved resolution that the recent
act of the Pope in appointing bishops in England was encouraged
by her Majesty's Government. Beaten by 79. This will enable
Ministers to go on to end of session.

*May 17th.*— Lady Londonderry appeared at Duke of Devonshire's play in a gown trimmed with green birds, small ones
round the body and down the sides, and large ones down the
centre. The beak of one of the birds caught in the Queen's dress
and was some time before it could be disentangled. Lady L. very
proud of the episode.

*May 21st.*—I think we shall not beat Government on the
cruelties at Ceylon by Lord Torrington. But I hope to succeed
in effecting a reconciliation between our party and forty-five
members of the National Club who went against us on Mr.
Urquhart's motion from their foolish dislike of Disraeli and Mr.
Beresford. I have had an interview with Mr. Bellamy, their
leader, and think I shall succeed.

*May 30th.*—Adjourned debate on Ceylon resumed; majority
for Government, 80. We dined with the Disraelis. Met M.
Thiers, Mr. McCulloch, and Mr. Denison. I sat by Thiers, who,
knowing that I was intimately acquainted with Prince Louis
Napoleon, asked me a number of questions about him, and ended
by saying, 'Je l'ai beaucoup étudié de près et de loin, et c'est un
homme absolument *nul.*' To me, Thiers seemed the incarnation
of vanity.

*June 12th.*—We went to the Queen's ball. It is said that
her Majesty received 600 excuses out of 1,400 invitations, and
that she did not fill up their places. I thought it very inferior
to the first two. Most of the fancy dresses shabby, as if they
had been got up cheap. At the others everybody went to great
expense, and they were magnificent. The period chosen was also
more becoming. The dresses of most of the ladies resembled
much the present fashion, differing only in the sleeves and the
little curls. The gaunt figure of Sir Charles Knightley appeared
in a pair of white satin shorts, which looked as if they had been
put on hind part before, for they bulged out much in front and
were tight behind, and he had neither coat nor cloak.

*June 21st.*—Went to Lady Palmerston's party, where I saw
Narvaez and the Spanish beauty, Mademoiselle Montijo. Narvaez,[1]

[1] Narvaez, after being Prime Minister and heading several *pronunciamientos,*
when asked on his deathbed whether he forgave his enemies, replied: 'I have none,
as I always got rid of them.'

an ugly little fat man, with a vile expression of countenance ; Mademoiselle Montijo [1] very handsome, auburn hair, beautiful skin and figure.  Her grandmother was Scotch, a Miss Kirkpatrick, which may account for her lovely complexion.

*June 28th.*—Lord Stanley sent for me early this morning, having received alarming accounts of Lord Derby, his father.[2]

*June 30th.*—Ben Stanley told me the Government were determined not to go out, and would rather submit to any humiliation. He was the eldest son of Lord Stanley of Alderley, and a member of the Government.  He was nicknamed Sir Benjamin Backbite when at Oxford, from his satirical powers.  He was a very amusing man, and clever.

*July 4th.*—My brother, member for Christchurch, came up for third reading of Ecclesiastical Titles Bill, which was passed, with Sir Frederick Thesiger's amendments, before eight o'clock.  Numbers on first division—208 for amendment ; 129 against.  Lord J. Russell moved omission of words giving power to common informers to institute proceedings.  Lost by 124 to 175.  House then divided on question that 'Bill do pass.'  Carried by 263 to 46 ; majority 217.  Irish members left House in a body before divisions.

I went to a great *fête* at Fulham, given by Mr. Lumley, manager of the Opera.  All the Corps Diplomatique there.

*July 7th.*—We dined at Lord Cardigan's ; thence to concert at Buckingham Palace.

*July 10th.*—Went in the evening to Madame Van de Weyer's. I hear the ball to the Queen at the Guildhall was extremely amusing.  People very ridiculous.  The ladies passed her at a run, never curtseying, and then returning to stare at her.  Some of the gentlemen passed with their arms round the ladies' waists, others holding them by the hand at arm's length, as if they were going to dance a minuet.  One man kissed his hand to the Queen as he went by, which set her Majesty off in a fit of laughter.

*August 7th.*—Left London for Achnacarry, Lochiel's place, which I hired, and remained there till November 5.

[1] Afterwards Empress of the French.
[2] He died a few days after.

*Lord Derby to Lord M.*

Knowsley : Sept. 5, 1851.

Dear Malmesbury,—I quite approve of your answer to Mr. Knox,[1] whose letter I enclose. It is not very easy to write civilly to a man that his paper is conducted with very little talent; and I admire the way in which you have managed to compliment the Editor, and smooth down any possible soreness he might feel.

.     .     .     .     .

I send you one of the first impressions of the Menagerie[2] catalogue. You will, at all events, like to look at it, and perhaps some of the water birds may tempt you to become a purchaser. They are all to be sold by auction without any reserve, beginning on the 6th of October; and from the great number I think it probable they may go for very little. If you are inclined to give me a commission to buy for you, you shall be treated very honestly.

Ever, &c.

DERBY.

*November 9th.*—Chillingham Castle. Mr. Collingwood, a Northumbrian squire, told us that the people at Tynemouth will not have their daughters christened before their sons, as they say when that is done the sons never have any whiskers. I asked whether in that case the daughters had them instead ?

*November 10th.*—Arrived at Knowsley. Lord Stanley (now Lord Derby) looks very ill. Great *battue* shooting for next three days.

*November 19th.*—Lord Palmerston made a very Radical speech two days ago in reply to an address to him by the Finsbury Committee in favour of Kossuth,[3] the Hungarian patriot. Almost all London is talking of it, and almost all blaming it.

*November 23rd.*—It is reported that Lord Palmerston is to go out in consequence of his Radical speech to the Finsbury deputation. His colleagues are all furious with him.

[1] Editor of the *Morning Herald.*

[2] The late Lord Derby had left the finest menagerie in England and probably in Europe, to supply which he used to send agents to all parts of the world.

[3] Lord Palmerston was always tampering with Kossuth and the Hungarian insurgents, and so was Louis Napoleon ; but neither ever took a practical course in their favour, their object being to bully and frighten Austria and help Italy. Kossuth published a very curious conversation which he had with the Emperor.

*November 24th.*—No truth in Lord Palmerston's resignation. Rain has fallen, after a very long drought.

*November 25th.*—Called on Madame and Mdlle. Gaggiotti. The latter a very remarkable person, and at Rome is surnamed Corinne, in consequence of her various talents. She is extremely handsome—of the Roman type—a great musician, speaks four languages, and paints very much above the average of professional artists. She has created a great sensation in London, and is making a good many portraits. She goes by her maiden name, but is married to, and separated from, a Mr. Richards, who is connected with the press.

I spoke the previous day at an agricultural dinner at Christchurch. It was difficult to satisfy the farming interest without compromising Lord Derby, whose name, however, I never mentioned ; but I had to keep up their spirits without raising them too high by expectations that the old Protective duties could ever return even if we came into office. Lord Derby complimented me on it, and sent me a message to say that he was ready to father every sentiment in it. Lady Augusta Lennox's marriage with Prince Edward of Saxe-Weimar went off very well, to the great edification of an immense congregation. The church was so full that several ladies got into the pulpit.

*November 28th.*—Lord Derby praised my speech to the Duke of Richmond, and says he wishes its tone to be followed at the meeting on December 12.

*November 29th.*—Dined with the Palmerstons. Met Sir H. and Lady Bulwer, Count and Countess de Flahault, and several foreign Ministers.

---

*December 2nd.*—Great news from Paris. Generals Changarnier, Cavaignac, Lamoricière, and Charras and M. Thiers have been arrested and taken to Vincennes, the President having discovered that they meant to anticipate him, as he told me when I saw him in April last. He has been well received by the people and with enthusiasm by the soldiers. A great many Deputies have been arrested. Changarnier is said to have resisted and Charras to have killed one of the police. The first proclamation is as follows :—

1. National Assembly dissolved.

2. Universal suffrage re-established and Law of May 31 abolished.

3. French people convoked in its electoral colleges from December 14 to 21.

4. State of siege decreed.

5. Council of State dissolved.

A second proclamation declares that the President's good intentions towards the people have been frustrated by the Assembly, and having proclaimed its dissolution he proposes to establish the following Government :—

1. A Chief Magistrate elected for ten years by universal suffrage.

2. A Ministry depending upon the Executive alone.

3. A Council of State.

4. A Legislative Assembly elected by universal suffrage without scrutiny of the electoral list.

5. A Senate.

---

This *coup d'état* seems to have been determined upon and executed by Louis Napoleon unknown even to his Ministers, whom he dismissed the evening before, though no doubt Morny,[1] Persigny, Colonel Fleury, and Maupas were concerned in the plan. The movements of the troops on the two preceding days were supposed by all parties to be intended as a precaution against any insurrection in consequence of the Paris election then going on. About 200 representatives met on the morning of Tuesday at Count Daru's, one of the Vice-Presidents, but receiving a message

---

[1] Morny was a recognised natural son of Count Flahault by Queen Hortense, and therefore the Emperor's half-brother. He was his right-hand man and generally gave him good advice, as he possessed great intelligence and tact, and was a man of the world. Morny told me that at the first period of Louis Napoleon's Presidency he was eager to fight for the Rhine, but that he had told him roughly that, if he did, 'les Allemands le flanqueraient dans le Rhin,' an opinion verified in 1870. Morny was made a duke, and being in a favourable position for speculating acquired a large fortune, married a Russian princess, and died before the fall of the Empire, being thus spared seeing a painful close to an eventful and prosperous life. I first knew him in Paris in 1834, when he was a man of fashion, and appreciated for his wit, and when he rode a steeplechase against an Englishman at La Croix de St. Berny, which he lost.

from Colonel Lauriston, commanding the 10th legion, saying that he placed the Mairie of the 10th Arrondissement at their disposal, and that his legion would defend them, they repaired there and proceeded to deliberate, Daru in the chair.    After a debate conducted in due form, and at which the shorthand writers of the 'Moniteur' were present, the conduct of Louis Napoleon . was declared to be illegal.   In consequence they affirmed him to have forfeited all claims to the high dignity of President of the Republic, in conformity with Article 68 of the Constitution.   Another decree frees the officers of the army and navy and the public functionaries from their oath of obedience to Louis Napoleon ; the High Court of Justice is convoked to judge the President and his Ministers.

These decrees were signed by the members present, with Daru's name at the head.   After they were passed, a body of the Chasseurs of Vincennes surrounded the building.   M. Berryer addressed the people out of window, telling them they had pronounced the *déchéance* of the President.   This was received very coldly.

The officer commanding the troops insisted upon entering, and in a few minutes the chamber was cleared.   MM. Daru, Odilon Barrot, De Broglie, and Molé remained in the apartment.   Daru was arrested, but the others were allowed to depart.   The officer refused M. O. Barrot's request to be taken, saying he had no orders to do so.   The President, with a numerous staff, rode along the Quays at eleven o'clock, and reviewed the troops in the Place de la Concorde and in the Square of the Tuileries.

*December 4th.*—Attempt at insurrection yesterday at Paris, M. Baudin, a representative of the people, having harangued the workmen in the Rue St. Antoine and summoned them to take up arms for the delivery of the members arrested.   Two barricades were erected, but were immediately taken by the soldiers and Baudin was killed.   This put an end to the *émeute*, the insurgents having fled in all directions.   The news from the Departments is good, so I trust Louis Napoleon is safe.

Sir Robert Peel has advertised his stud of hunters for sale in the following terms : 'To be sold at Messrs.Tattersalls', the entire stud of Sir Robert Peel, Bart., who is declining hunting with the Atherstone hounds in consequence of the unsportsmanlike conduct and political animosity, even in the hunting field, of certain Protectionist farmers.' They had insulted him and warned him off their land.

*December 5th.*—The French Minister of War has addressed a circular to the generals of the army : ' The soldiers are to vote for the election of a President within forty-eight hours from the receipt of the circular. " Yes" or "No " is simply to be replied to the proposition.'

### Lord Derby to Lord M.

Knowsley : Dec. 5, 1851.

Dear Malmesbury,—I ought sooner to have returned you the two letters which were enclosed in yours on the 14th, for which many thanks. That from Paris is very interesting, and the parallel between 1851 and 1797, to which I referred, very curious. Your friend (the President) has it all his own way, thanks to his own cleverness and boldness and the folly of his opponents. What use he may make of his power remains to be seen. I hope he will not verify the anticipations of your Paris correspondent; but for good or evil he has a great game before him. I hear Aberdeen is violent against him. I suspected the language in the ' Times ' was of his inspiration. Palmerston, on the other hand, has taken him up warmly. Has that anything to do with his sudden ostracism ? for it is quite clear he has not resigned, but that his colleagues have combined to turn him out. He will be a thorn in their side; but his ardent support of the *strong* measures taken by the Prince (President or Emperor ?) will have lost him some of his popularity with the extreme Radicals. Tell me what you hear ; I know nothing but from the newspapers.

.    .    .    .    .

Yours very sincerely,

DERBY.

*December 6th.*—Serious *émeute* at Paris on 4th. Barricades erected and much fighting. Fifty thousand troops marched along Boulevards at 1.30, and were fired upon from some of the houses. All quiet again by 6 o'clock P.M., and placards announced the restoration of order. News from Lyons and provinces satisfactory.

*December 7th.*—Paris quiet. Funds risen two per cent. Only

thirty-one representatives have been arrested. Election of the
President takes place 20th or 21st. Some new regiments entered
Paris, shouting 'Vive l'Empereur ! ' and all ' Vive Napoléon ! '
Changarnier, Cavaignac, Lamoricière, Leflô, Bedeau, Charras,
Roger du Nord, are prisoners at Ham. What an irony of fate
for these men, who had sent the Prince to the same prison a few
years ago !

*Christmas Day, Heron Court.*—Sir George Bowles writes that
Lord Palmerston is out of office, and that either Lord Granville
or Lord Clarendon is to succeed him. There has been a quarrel
between him and the Queen and Lord John, and various reports
respecting the cause, which we shall soon know.

*December 26th.*—Article in the 'Times,' apparently official,
giving clearly to understand that it was Lord Palmerston's
approval of the President's *coup d'état* of December 2 which was
the cause of his dismissal from office. It is, however, evident there
has been some intrigue besides. Lord Palmerston is not a man
to sit quiet under this mortification, and his secession will probably
lead to a break up. Lord Granville is made Foreign Secretary.

*M. de Persigny to Lord M.*

Paris : Dec. 26, 1851.

My dear Lord,—Des préoccupations extraordinaires qui tiennent
aux événements derniers m'ont empêché de répondre, aussi promptement
que je l'aurais désiré, à votre dernière lettre. Je m'empresse
aujourd'hui de profiter d'un moment plus tranquille pour vous dire
d'abord que j'ai remis votre lettre au Prince, et qu'il est entièrement
de votre avis sur ce qu'il y a à faire pour attirer les capitaux anglais
dans notre pays et cimenter de plus en plus l'alliance qui doit exister
entre les deux grands peuples,

Nous voyons ici avec beaucoup de regret l'ardeur de certains
journaux anglais à dénaturer les événements qui viennent de s'accomplir ;
nous craignons que la persistance de cette hostilité n'égare les
sentiments du peuple anglais et ne crée pour l'avenir des difficultés.

Je comprends en effet qu'il est difficile à l'esprit anglais de comprendre
notre caractère national, habitué à un régime de gouvernement
qui est admirable avec les éléments qu'il possède. L'Angleterre se
rend difficilement compte des faiblesses de notre système parlementaire.
En Angleterre la liberté et votre système parlementaire sont au profit

de l'influence aristocratique. C'est le gouvernement des classes élevées, et ces classes élevées sont faites au gouvernement et admirablement intelligentes des intérêts publics. En France, au contraire, les classes élevées sont complètement impropres au maniement des affaires. Elles sont, à l'exemple de notre ancienne noblesse, brillantes, légères, chevaleresques, frivoles, et guerrières ; mais sans aucune des vertus nécessaires en un état libre, de sorte que le système parlementaire ne fonctionne qu'au profit du désordre, de l'anarchie, et aux dépens de l'autorité.

La France, en un mot, n'est qu'une grande démocratie qui a besoin d'être disciplinée, et nul élément n'est plus propre à la personnifier que l'élément Napoléonien. C'est là le secret de cette immense ovation populaire. On peut chercher à dénaturer le caractère des événements et dire, comme le ' Times,' que c'est la violence, la compression militaire qui forcent la population à donner leurs voix à Louis-Napoléon, mais cela ne peut se dire qu'en Angleterre, où l'on ne connaît pas le génie national de notre pays. Pour tout homme non prévenu il y a une réflexion bien simple. Comment une armée qui n'a pas fait la guerre et qui n'est composée que de jeunes soldats, aurait-elle l'esprit du despotisme militaire ? Comment pourrait-elle se séparer des sentiments des masses et violenter le pays, quand elle sort chaque année des entrailles du pays et qu'elle y rentre chaque année ? La vérité c'est que l'armée est pleine du sentiment national. C'est le secret de tout ce qui vient de se passer. Quand le sentiment national était contraire au gouvernement, comme en 1830 et 1848, l'armée n'a été d'aucun secours au pouvoir. Aujourd'hui, au contraire, qu'elle a exprimé le sentiment public, elle a pu tout faire, sans aucune résistance sérieuse. Quant aux grandes masses, elles sont ivres de joie et d'enthousiasme, et jamais révolution ne fut si facile ni si populaire. Je sais bien qu'on peut se demander si après le rôle qu'elle a joué dans les derniers événements l'armée ne sera pas avide de se produire et de se jeter dans les aventures.

Ce danger n'est pas sérieux. L'armée n'a pas le sentiment d'avoir violenté la nation, mais d'avoir, au contraire, servi à l'expression de son opinion. Il n'y a pas dans les têtes militaires la moindre trace d'ambition guerrière ; personne ne songe à recommencer les aventures, et le Prince Président moins que personne.

La plupart des officiers supérieurs sont mariés et âgés, et ils ne demandent qu'à vivre en paix ; ils redoutaient la division des parties parlementaires, puisqu'à leurs yeux c'était le triomphe certain des éléments révolutionnaires, et qu'avec le triomphe de la démagogie leur position, leur grade, leur retraite—tout cela était perdu, et ils se sont

sauvés en sauvant la nation.  Voilà tout.  Et ils sont satisfaits maintenant, ne demandant que la paix et le repos.  Ce serait donc une folie
inconcevable que d'ameuter les esprits en Angleterre contre un péril
qui n'existe pas, car ce serait le moyen de le créer.

Si les efforts que l'on fait en Angleterre pour dénaturer les événements réussissaient, ce n'est pas du côté de l'armée française que vien-
drait le danger, mais du côté du peuple, dont on ranimerait les anciennes
haines nationales, quand elles ne demandent qu'a s'éteindre complètement.  J'espère donc que les hommes d'état d'Angleterre s'efforceront
de maintenir la bonne amitié qui existe, heureusement, entre les deux
pays.  Plus l'on cherche en ce moment à égarer le peuple anglais, plus
il importe que les deux gouvernements se donnent des témoignages
d'estime et de confiance, et plus il est nécessaire, comme vous le com-
prenez si bien, de lier les deux peuples par les intérêts matériels.  Le
Président est tout-à-fait dans ces sentiments ; il fera tout pour favoriser
les idées que vous lui soumettez.  Rien ne lui serait plus odieux que
d'être amené par des mouvements d'opinion publique en Angleterre à
reprendre cet héritage de haine et de jalousie qu'il a le premier répudié.
Du reste, je ne crois pas que l'on parviendra en Angleterre à agacer
l'opinion publique ; tout ce qui se fait et se prépare ici éclairera les
esprits et la vérité se fera jour, et bien loin d'amener le refroidissement
entre les deux peuples, j'ai la conviction profonde que le grand acte du
deux décembre aura, au contraire, pour résultat de cimenter plus que
jamais la bonne harmonie entre les deux nations.

Pardonnez-moi ces réflexions, faites à la hâte.  Soyez assez bon pour
me faire connaître de temps en temps ce que vous savez de l'opinion en
Angleterre et tâchons tous les deux de contribuer à l'œuvre commune.

Votre bien dévoué,<br>
F. DE PERSIGNY

*December 30th.*—Lord Palmerston never went to Windsor t
give up the seals, and after waiting for him some time Lord John
delivered them to the Queen, who gave them to Lord Granville.

# 1852

*Mr. Disraeli to Lord M.*

Hughenden : Jan. 2, 1852.

My dear Lord,—I have arrived at the same conclusion with respect
to Lord John's *coup d'état*, and am gratified that my view is sanctioned

by one of your acumen and knowledge of circumstances and persons. The fact is, the Government have entirely changed their foreign policy; under ordinary circumstances, instead of making a victim of the Secretary of State, they should have resigned. I assume, therefore, from Lord John's conduct, that, after our self-confessed incapacity of last February, he and the Court no longer recognise us as a practical power in the State.

I return you Lonsdale's letter. When he objects to the prominence given by my motions in the House of Commons to the subject of local taxation, he forgets those motions last year gave us the government of the country. Whether abstract Protection will be as successful is a problem not yet solved.

Yours very truly,

D.

*January 3rd.*—Louis Napoleon has been elected President for ten years by 7,600,000 votes. Ceremony at Notre Dame on January 1 seems to have been splendid. He was received with immense enthusiasm, and a great many cries of ' Vive l'Empereur ! ' He has restored the eagle on the standard and the Legion of Honour. Receptions to be at the Tuileries. It is said that the Queen received Lady Palmerston very coldly some time ago, before Lord Palmerston's dismissal, when she went to present the Portuguese Minister's wife and other ladies. The Queen asked them all to stay, but did not invite her, so she had to return alone to London. Lord Palmerston's speech about Kossuth has done him great harm at Court and everywhere.

*January 4th.*—Our Ambassador at Paris, Lord Normanby, insinuated to M. Turgot, French Foreign Minister, that our Government did not approve of the *coup d'état.* Turgot replied, he could hardly believe that, as Count Walewski,[1] the French Ambassador in London, had written to say that Lord Palmerston

---

[1] I first knew Count Walewski during the Polish Rebellion of 1831, when he came to London, sent by the Revolutionary Committee, to negotiate with our Government for assistance. He was then only twenty-one, and a very handsome and pleasing young man, being a softened likeness of his father, the Emperor Napoleon. He was very well received in society, and elected at our fashionable clubs. He soon afterwards married Lord Sandwich's daughter, who died. His second wife was a Florentine, a beautiful woman, who did the honours of their embassy to perfection. He died quite suddenly, and comparatively young, at an hotel at Strasburg at 1869.

told him he cordially approved of it. Lord Normanby then wrote, it is supposed, to Lord John Russell, informing him of this ; and this I believe is the real cause, or rather pretence, for Lord Palmerston's dismissal. Count de Flahault gave me the official return of the killed and wounded in Paris on December 4, from which it appears that, beside the soldiers, 215 persons were killed ; of these, 137 fell at the barricades, and 88 have since died of their wounds ; 115 were wounded as well. Some were hidden from fear of prosecution. Only ten *curieux* were killed.

### Lord Derby to Lord M.

Knowsley : Jan. 7, 1852.

Dear Malmesbury,—I only write a line (for I have had much to write, and my wrist is not so long-enduring as it used to be), to thank you for your letter of the 5th, and the current reports of the day. I have had accounts from many quarters of the cause and mode of Palmerston's 'resignation,' and they all agree so nearly, with some variation in the minor details, that it is not difficult to make out a complete history of the transaction, nor, consequently, to estimate the frame of mind in which it has left the ex-Foreign Secretary. I think Wodehouse's appointment not unlikely, and, as far as it goes, not an unfit one ; but it would give them no strength in the Commons, where they want it. I do not think they will apply to Graham, nor that he will join them if they do. On the whole, their prospects are gloomy enough ; but whether any Government can be formed, and stand, out of the heterogeneous materials to be dealt with, is a very different question. The same post which brought me your letter brought me one also from Disraeli ; but so far from being 'mopy,' I never knew him write or speak in a more sanguine tone. I expect to find him quite up to the mark when I go up to town, which I propose to do on the 29th, leaving this place on the 27th, and taking Burghley and Hatfield on my way. I have probably got your letter about Louis Napoleon, and, if so, can put my hand on it at once when I go to town. It will be at least curious, and may be useful to look back to it.

Ever yours sincerely,
DERBY.

*January 11th.*—Papers announce arrival of a boat at Brest with twenty-five people from the 'Amazon,' burnt at sea. This dreadful disaster will confirm the superstition of seamen as to ill-luck of starting on a Friday, the 'Amazon' having started on her first voyage, Friday, January 2. Cause of burning yet a mystery.

### Lord Derby to Lord M.

Knowsley : January 18, 1852.

My dear Malmesbury,—I received your letter at the railway station yesterday, as I passed through London on my way home from Windsor. You are perfectly right in the instructions you have given to Knox. Mr. Phillips has no authority whatever to speak or write in my name, nor have I in any degree made him acquainted with my views. I continue to think that a recurrence to duties on imports, including corn, is desirable both on financial and on political grounds; and I can neither abandon this belief, nor a line of policy founded on it, until a general election has convinced me that that which I think the best thing for the country is an unattainable good. Should the country prove not to be with us, I should feel absolved from the duty of protracting a hopeless struggle, which, while it continues, must cause serious injury by the uncertainty it creates as to the final result; but to take office as a Protectionist, and then spontaneously abandon the principle of Protection, would involve a degree of baseness, from the imputation of which I should have hoped that my 'antecedents' (to borrow a French expression) might have relieved me. I return you the correspondence between Messrs. Knox and Phillips.[1] A few days will give me an opportunity of stating to the party my views in a way not to be open to any misapprehension.

Your friend in Paris is going an alarming pace. He must have an utter contempt for his countrymen, and, if he finally succeeds, they most richly deserve it.

Ever yours sincerely,

DERBY.

*January 22nd.*—Letter in 'Morning Herald,' very absurd one, written by Mr. Blood, the clergyman who was saved from the 'Amazon,' who in the most canting and ridiculous language says he was warned by a mysterious voice, when he lay down in his cabin, not to undress. The voice said : 'Blood, don't take off your coat ; Blood, don't take off your spectacles ;' and he ends his letter by saying that 'his health has greatly benefited by tossing on the billows.'

[1] Journalists.

*January 25th.*—A decree of President issued, confiscating whole property of Orleans family—i.e. obliging them to sell, which is nearly the same thing. M. de Morny and M. Fould refuse to sign the decrees, and after two days' discussion, President insisting, they resigned. M. de Persigny [1] replaces M. de Morny as Minister of the Interior. These tyrannical measures will do harm to Louis Napoleon. This last one, so evidently of revenge, is sure to be much abused.

*January 31st.*—Called on Lord Derby. He thought a 20*l.* franchise for the counties quite as good for us as the 50*l.* ; but 10*l.* would be destruction. If Lord John did not resign and had a dissolution it would make all government impossible. He is himself determined to accept office if it should be offered him.

*February 1st.*—Dined at Lord Derby's. Too many to discuss politics satisfactorily. We are not to oppose introduction of the Reform Bill.

*February 3rd.*—Parliament met to-day. No amendment proposed to the Queen's Speech. Lord Derby made a magnificent one, which will I hope satisfy farmers. Lord John in the Commons stated his reasons for dismissing Lord Palmerston from office. His speech was a good one—very eloquent—but his case against Lord Palmerston very insufficient. Lord Palmerston's defence feeble. He could not deny any facts brought against him of official disobedience, but they were not serious enough to warrant his dismissal. It is pretty evident that the Queen and Prince Albert insisted upon it, and Lord John seized the oppor-

---

[1] Persigny, whose real name was Fialin, was one of those adventurers who looked forward with confidence to the success of Louis Napoleon's fatalism and dreams of ambition, and proved it by the most absolute devotion, and, I must add, personal affection for his master, whom he always accompanied bravely through his failures and imprisonments. Faithful to the Emperor, the Emperor was faithful to him, and loaded him with honours. He was a courageous and impetuous man, and his hot temper was against his success as an ambassador, but he was intelligent and, I believe, did not, like most others of the Napoleonic category, prepare his pockets for a stormy day, for he died poor, soon after the fall of the Empire, expressing on his death-bed his devotion for his master, and his regret at having, in the irritation of defeat, reproached him for his misfortunes. This message was delivered to the Emperor, who mentioned it to me. I first made Persigny's acquaintance at the Eglinton Tournament, at which he rode as squire to the Prince.

tunity to quarrel with him and turn him out. The whole dispute
turned upon Lord Palmerston having in the first instance, in conformity with the decision of the Cabinet in consequence of the
*coup d'état* of December 2, written an official despatch to Lord
Normanby, saying he was to continue his relations with the
French Government as usual, and that it was the Queen's desire
that nothing should be done by her Ambassador at Paris which
could bear the appearance of interference of any kind in the
internal affairs of France.

Then, in a conversation with Count Walewski, Lord Palmerston
told him he approved of the *coup d'état*. Lord Normanby wrote
to Lord John complaining of the embarrassing situation he was
placed in by this declaration of Lord Palmerston not agreeing
with his official instructions. Lord John thereupon wrote to Lord
Palmerston for an explanation, but got no answer. Several days
elapsed, and on December 13 he received a messenger from the
Queen, at Woburn, asking for an explanation of Lord Normanby's
letter. Again he wrote to Lord Palmerston, who never sent any
answer till the 17th, when he sent him copies of two despatches,
one to and one from Lord Normanby, which, not being satisfactory,
and the whole conduct of Lord Palmerston in the matter being
considered by Lord John contrary to the principle laid down—
namely, 'that no important steps were to be taken on foreign
affairs without the concurrence of the Prime Minister'—and also
that he had shown disrespect to the Queen, he, without consulting
his colleagues, intimated to Lord Palmerston that he was to retire
from office. Lord John wrote on Saturday, December 20, to the
Queen, advising her to require Lord Palmerston's resignation ;
and on the 22nd, at the Cabinet, he read the whole correspondence to the other members, who (he says) approved of the course
he had taken. Lord Palmerston denies none of these statements,
but rests his defence upon the principle that a private conversation is very different from an official communication, and that no
business could be done if there were any restraint upon the intercourse between the Foreign Secretary and Foreign Ministers. He
asked in his speech, 'Is her Majesty's Minister to sit like a dolt,
when a Foreign Ambassador converses on some great event,

Q

without giving him any answer or making any observation ?' Here
the matter rests for the present.[1]

*February 11th.*—Dined with the Montroses—a Tory party of
twenty-four. Lord Colville is to be our whip in the House of
Lords, *vice* Lord Nelson. I was almost all the afternoon with
Lord Derby, discussing the Reform Bill, but without much effect,
as we are not strong enough either to amend or throw it out
unless the Peelites join us.

*February 13th.*—Lord Derby seems quite knocked down by
this Reform Bill, for which, strange to say, he seems to have
been unprepared. I found him to-day without his usual energy.
I am very anxious he should meet it by a counter bill or resolution,
but he will not hear of it, and treated Disraeli coldly when he
proposed it. A mutual dislike between them might have serious
consequences, but the two men are so different in character that
it can hardly be otherwise ; yet they cannot do without one
another at present. I have great confidence in Disraeli's good
temper and ambition to see that such is the case.

*February 15th.*—Went to Heron Court with Mr. Bentinck
and Lord Anson. Lady Adelaide Vane's elopement with her
brother's tutor, Mr. Law, engages the attention of all society, to
the exclusion even of the Reform Bill.

*February 16th.*—My brother, M.P. for Christchurch, arrived
for Lord Derby's meeting at Lord Eglinton's house. Only
House of Commons.

*February 19th.*—Lady Derby asked Lady Malmesbury whether
I should not prefer the Foreign Office to the Colonial, which he
had offered me last year at the crisis, as she thought it might be
arranged if I wished it.

*February 20th.*—Lord Naas brought forward his motion of
censure with respect to the Irish Government. Lord John
Russell and Lord Palmerston defended Lord Clarendon, who
was Viceroy, and the Government had a majority of 92. Lord

---

[1] Old diplomatists must know the difference between an *officious* and an *official*
conversation. The first is the free interchange of opinions between the two Ministers,
and compromises neither ; the latter would do so, and bind their Governments. I
always, when at the Foreign Office, prefaced a conversation by saying on which
footing it was to be understood.

Clarendon had committed himself with a disreputable journalist. Very imprudent ! The division pleased our party, though beaten. My brother came in the evening announcing defeat of Government on Lord Palmerston's amendment to the Militia Bill by majority of 11, upon which Lord John said he would resign. This event was so unexpected that Lord Derby went this morning to Badminton on a visit.

*February 21st.*—Went to Disraeli's after breakfast, and found him in a state of delight at the idea of coming into office. He said he 'felt just like a young girl going to her first ball,' constantly repeating, 'Now we have got a *status.*' With all his apparent apathy when attacked in the House of Commons, he is always, when out of it, in the highest state of elation or lowest depth of despair, according to the fortune of the day. People are talking of a combination between Lord Palmerston, Lord Clarendon, and the Peelites. Dined with the Cannings. Have seen Lord Derby, who wants me to take the Foreign Office, which I am very unwilling to do, as it will keep me in London the whole year. Nothing, however, can be settled until Lord Derby has seen the Queen, which he is to do to-morrow at 2.30.

*February 22nd.*—Lord Derby had an audience of the Queen, and accepted the Government. He proposed me as Foreign Secretary. H.M. also agreed to Lord Palmerston taking office again, but not to lead the House of Commons. Lord Palmerston had written to Lord Derby yesterday, offering to open communications with him ; so, on his return from the Palace, Lord Derby wrote to ask him to call. I was with him when the answer came saying that Lord Palmerston would come immediately. I then went to the Carlton Club, whence I saw Lord Palmerston passing our window, with his jaunty air, towards St. James's Square. I returned to Lord Derby's at 9 P.M., and have arranged many of the appointments with him, Disraeli recommending the names of the members of the house of Commons.

Paris : ce 23 février 1852.

Mon cher Lord Malmesbury,—Si l'éloquente vengeance de Lord Palmerston aboutit à vous faire monter à une place que j'ai toujours pensé devoir tôt ou tard être réservée aux nobles qualités qui vous distinguent, je ne veux pas être la dernière à venir vous en faire mes compliments. Vous savez s'ils sont sincères, car vous n'avez jamais douté de mon amitié bien dévouée.

Et si le Ministère doit se composer en dehors de vous (ce dont je ne saurais vous plaindre, car les honneurs de nos jours plus que jamais sont chèrement achetés), venez alors nous faire une petite visite à Paris pendant vos vacances. Ce n'est pas sans profit pour un homme comme vous de venir voir de près la physionomie étrange de cette France dans une époque s'. incroyablement extraordinaire !

A mon retour en France dans le mois d'août je suis partie pour l'Italie, où j'ai passé quatre mois dans la terre que j'ai près de Florence. Là j'ai pu souvent parler de vous avec mon frère, qui m'a chargé de vous dire mille choses.

Lorsque j'ai quitté Florence le ciel politique de la France était seulement très-orageux, mais la nue n'avait pas éclaté. J'ai employé six jours à parcourir la belle route de la Corniche le long de la Méditerranée, et les parfums des orangers et la douce végétation tropicale que protège le vivifiant soleil de ce pays enchanteur m'ont fait oublier tellement la politique que je n'ai pas demandé un journal jusqu'à Nice. Là j'ai appris les étranges événements de Paris. Mon mari est parti de suite pour Paris, en traversant avec son intrépidité ordinaire les départements en feu. Moi, je suis restée à Nice quelques jours, et puis je me suis hasardée, moi aussi, au milieu du feu. J'ai vu le spectacle de toutes ces malheureuses populations égarées en lutte avec la force armée— moitié en fuite, se cachant dans les bois le jour, et moitié enchaînée—de tout âge, de tout sexe, n'ayant plus d'humain que les noms.[1]

Mais, malgré mon équipage, peu du goût des socialistes, je n'ai souffert aucun affront, et je suis arrivée saine et sauve à Paris.

Et vous, mon cher Lord Malmesbury, vous aussi, vous avez passé vos jours d'automne au mileu de massacres ! que de victimes vous devez avoir fait dans vos belles chasses d'Ecosse !

Si vous avez un instant, veuillez me donner de vos nouvelles, et me dire si votre santé est bonne, et si nous avons quelque chance de vous revoir cette année.

Croyez à mon amitié bien sincère.

MARQUISE DE BOISSY.

P.S.—La Duchesse de Grammont devait diner chez moi hier. Elle ne l'a pu, parce que le Duc est tellement malade qu'on ne le quitte plus un instant.

---

[1] The horrors committed by the French mobs were too unnaturally dreadful to be described, especially at Clamecy.

*February 23rd.*—Lord Palmerston refuses to join Lord Derby on account of Protection. Lord Derby has made his list, and there is to be a general meeting of the new Cabinet at his house this morning. I got a letter from Louis Napoleon the day before yesterday, renewing his assurances of amity towards England, but complaining of our armaments, which he said showed suspicion. Got a message from Lord Derby at 8 P.M., desiring me to go to him directly to help him to settle the Court appointments. The Queen wants the Duchess of Northumberland to be Mistress of the Robes. I hear M. Brünnow, Russian Ambassador, was very much alarmed at Madame Walewska's party at being told Sir Stratford Canning was to be Foreign Secretary. He said, ' Allons, donc ! c'est une mauvaise plaisanterie ! ' Lord Derby had sounded Sir Stratford last year about taking the Foreign Office, when he jumped at the appointment, but on reflection, after the long antagonism between him and the Emperor of Russia, it would have been looked on as an insult by Nicholas. Sir Stratford will never forgive me for being the innocent cause of this apparent slight. His talents are beyond dispute, but his temper is so despotic and irritable, that he can only display them in a peculiar kind of diplomacy. He managed the Turks in their own way, and it was Sultan *versus* Sultan. With him at the Foreign Office there could have been no peace with Russia or in the Cabinet. I went to the Carlton Club, the state of which I can only compare to the Bourse at Paris, or a fair in England, such was the excitement.

*From Louis Napoleon, Prince President, to Lord M.*

Elysée : 24 février 1852.

Mon cher Lord Malmesbury,—Je ne veux pas tarder à vous féliciter du poste élevé où la confiance de la Reine vous a appelé, mais je m'en félicite surtout pour les bons rapports qui doivent en résulter pour les deux pays. Nous avons reçu ici avec grand plaisir Lord et Lady Cowley, et nous serions très-heureux si le changement de Ministère ne les entraînait pas à sa suite. Croyez, mon cher Lord Malmesbury, que vous trouverez toujours mon gouvernement franc, loyal, animé des sentiments les plus amicaux, et prêt à s'entendre avec le vôtre pour tout ce qui peut assurer la paix et les progrès de la civilisation.

  Je vous renouvelle l'assurance de ma sincère amitié.

LOUIS-NAPOLÉON,

*Lord Palmerston to Lord M.*

C. G.: February 24, 1852.

My dear Malmesbury,—I shall be happy both on personal and public grounds to give you any information which I can give, and which you may think useful to you, with reference to the state of our foreign relations, and I will either receive you here or call upon you, as best may suit you, at any time most convenient to you to-morrow. Your time is not entirely at your disposal, mine is at my own command; I shall, therefore, await your appointment.

Yours sincerely,

PALMERSTON.

*February 25th.*—I called on Lady Palmerston and Lady Jersey—both at home ; Lady Jersey in greatest delight at Lord J. being Master of the Horse. Lady Clementina *rayonnante.* Lord Brougham called, and in his mad manner fell on his knees before Lady Malmesbury, kissed her hand, and then asked me whether Louis Napoleon was not my son. I answered I did not know, but there was one reason against it—namely, that he was nearly, if not as old as myself. Lord Brougham laughed, and said, ' It would have been still more curious if he had been older.'

*February 26th.*—Duchess of Northumberland has refused to be Mistress of the Robes, on the plea that she would have to manage the Duke's private business, now that he is First Lord of the Admiralty.

*Lord M. to President Louis Napoleon.*

London : February 26, 1852.

Sir,—I have to express to your Royal Highness my sincere thanks for the honour you have done me by the kind letter I received from your Royal Highness yesterday.

To the high gratification I feel at the mark of Her Majesty's confidence by which I have been just distinguished is added that of knowing that your Royal Highness is personally pleased with my appointment, and also with that of Lord Cowley at Paris.

Lord Derby entertains the highest opinion of his abilities and honourable character, and it is a satisfaction to him to know that your Royal Highness has already appreciated them.

Your Royal Highness may feel assured that I shall enter upon my duties with the most complete conviction that amity between France and England is not only necessary to the prosperity of both these countries, but also to the general interests of civilisation ; and it was with the liveliest pleasure that I read this sentiment so-frankly and loyally expressed in the letter of your Royal Highness.

I have known your Royal Highness too long to fear that, with your great power for good or for evil, you will hesitate between them.

With every assurance of personal friendship, I have the honour to be, &c.,

                                  MALMESBURY.

*February 27th.*—I went to the Queen this morning at Windsor, to kiss hands, and to receive the seals of office. The joke on Dizzy's appointment is, that ' Benjamin's mess will be five times as great as the others ! ' I began my work this morning, I have settled to do the writing at my house, and to see the Foreign Ministers at the office. The whole of the Corps Diplomatique have received me most kindly, with the exception of the Van de Weyers. I believe it is because they are strong Orleanist partisans and think I am a Bonapartist. He is a clever, agreeable man, and was formerly a librarian in Belgium. He married a rich American, Miss Bates, who always gave herself great airs.

         *Lord M. to Lord Cowley, Ambassador at Paris,*
                   *on Neufchâtel, &c.*

                        Foreign Office : March 2, 1852.

Dear Lord Cowley,—The reply to your last despatch, giving officially the views of Lord Derby's Government on the Swiss question, will follow in a few days.[1] Suffice it to say, that at present we cannot sanction or approve in any way the conduct of the French Government in this matter, and still less the reasons on which they found their course towards Switzerland. At the same time, as Austria supports the President, and Russia is neuter, we cannot effectively prevent his intentions, and must urge on the Swiss the expediency of acting with moderation as long as they do not sacrifice their independence for the future. The last despatch of Mr. Magenis (English Minister at Berne) is reassuring on this point, and I send it to you.

I believe you are aware of my having formerly had an intimate

---

[1] The French wished the Swiss Government to expel the refugees.

acquaintance with the President—an accident that he has had the *maladresse* to put forward ostentatiously in his newspapers. When I was appointed, and before I kissed hands, I received from him a letter of congratulation, expressing in the strongest terms his peaceable intentions and desire of promoting civilisation. I enclose a copy. I answered it in my *private* capacity. There is no reason you should not allude to this letter (which the *Queen* has seen), and tell him how satisfactory its receipt is to this Government. Before the last Government resigned, and about a month since, I wrote to him a strong remonstrance on the subject of the Orleans property decrees. He replied, with continued and repeated assurances of friendship to England, but declared the confiscation necessary, as even some of his own new Senators had been tampered with by Orleanist agents and money. This is quite a *marotte* with him, and Walewski is strongly against him on this point. You may depend upon his being a man of action and counsel, relying on no other agent but his own inspirations, but with great self-command and power of self-denial if his passions are at variance with his interests. He is very superstitious, and was formerly very accessible to romantic and chivalrous impressions, and in private transactions most jealous of his *word* and his *honour*. I give you these hints (*experto crede*), because you will at once see their value where future events must depend on the single will of one man.

.       .       .       .       .       .       .

My belief is that, on the Swiss question, if anything can be done, and the President is not seeking a quarrel, you cannot do better than communicate with him personally. He will, if it suits him, throw over Turgot.[1]

I must add that in his note he expressed a wish that you should remain at Paris, of which, of course, there never was a doubt.

Yours truly,<br>
MALMESBURY.

*Lord Westmoreland, Ambassador at Vienna, to Lord M.*

March 4, 1852.

My dear Malmesbury,—I write you these few words to say that Prince Schwarzenberg has, I know, transmitted this day by messenger to Count Buol a despatch, in accordance with his promise to me as reported in my letter of the day before yesterday; and from the report I have received of this despatch, I believe you will be satisfied with the sentiments it expresses. The speech of Lord Derby, and the language

---

[1] Turgot was French Minister for Foreign Affairs.

he holds as to foreign Governments, has had the best effect here both with the Government and the public. As a proof of it I enclose the articles from two of the semi-official newspapers of this town.

Very sincerely yours,<br>Westmoreland.

*Marquess of Lansdowne to Lord M., on his Accession to the Foreign Office.*

March 1852.

My dear Lord Malmesbury,—Having been prevented from going to the *levée* yesterday, where I might probably have met you, I have had no opportunity of thanking you since the last sitting of the House of Lords for the very kind and cordial expressions of kindness you used in alluding to what I had said on that occasion.[1]

I assure you that they were doubly gratifying to me as coming from you, awakening some of the most agreeable recollections of my early life and of former friendships.

Apart from all political considerations, I sincerely wish you success in the discharge of the new duties you have undertaken, and remain,

Very truly yours,<br>Lansdowne.

*Lord Derby to Lord M.*

St. James's Square : March 1852.

Dear Malmesbury,—If I am late for dinner you will have made me so. The despatches [the Austrian Notes] you have sent me are very satisfactory, and I am glad we have got them just at this moment. I must have them again if they are left with you, as of course they must be, to be answered. Our tone should be as cordial as possible, but we must take care what we say, for there is rather *too* great a desire to exhibit us as following exactly the same line as Austria, and I have no idea of committing the Government to another Holy Alliance. The despatch about France is as singular as it is satisfactory. Austria would seem to say, 'How happy could I be with either!' but just at this moment she thinks us the *safest* ally.

Ever yours,<br>Derby.

*March 6th.*—Met Lord Grey, who told me they meant to oppose us in both Houses, and expected to turn us out in three weeks.

[1] His intended retirement from public life. He died in 1865.

Dined at Northumberland House ; met a large party, including almost all the Cabinet. Lord Derby said to my wife, ' I have been driving a team of young horses this morning ; not one had ever been in harness before, and they went beautifully ; not one kicked amóngst them.' All kinds of jokes were made in respect of our being such novices in office ; and Lady Clanricarde, intending to quiz Lord Derby about the appointment of Sir John Pakington to the Colonies, said, across a large dinner table, 'Are you sure, Lord Derby, that he is a *real* man ? ' To which he replied, ' Well, I think so—he has been married three times.'

*Lord M. to Lord Westmoreland, H.M. Ambassador at Vienna,
on his first interview with Count Buol.*

London : March 8, 1852.
My dear Lord Westmoreland,—

.  .  .  .  .  .  .

I grieve at the contents of your last despatch, received yesterday, which describes the animus of Prince Schwarzenberg towards this country. Your private letter to Granville I have not opened, and it has been sent to the country after him. When we came into office I hoped to find at once a positive disposition to reconciliation on the part of Buol. Having had my *levée* on Monday, the 1st inst., he asked for an appointment the next day. When he arrived he began, certainly, by hoping that the new Government would establish better relations between our Courts ; but immediately proceeded to ask for a condemnation of Granville's last despatch to him on the subject of the Modena and Papal Notes, and of his refusing to read those Notes. He took a very high tone, describing it as a positive affront to him, unsupported by any precedents in the forms of diplomacy. He hinted at being bound to retire altogether from communicating with us till he heard from Vienna. He foresaw great anger from the Emperor, who was so young; and, in short, spoke of the fact of the despatch, and of the circulating that despatch among our Ministers at other Courts, as an *ensemble* requiring reparation to him personally and to his Court, a reparation which we ought to grant in the form of a written condemnation of my predecessor's conduct in this matter.

I contented myself by asserting the *right* we had to refuse Notes of this important nature when presented by *unaccredited* persons. So far I approved of Granville's *act*, but of course would not be responsible if in his *manner* he had committed any solecism.

.  .  .  .  .  .  .

I must say Buol's manner was anything but agreeable, and he alternately tried to bully and to mystify me as to diplomatic usages in a way which can only be accounted for from his supposing (and justly so) that he was dealing with an inexperienced hand.  I must leave it to you to assure Prince Schwarzenberg of our anxious desire to resume our old relations of cordial amity with Austria.  Surely the best way is to drop any further correspondence whatever on these Notes and the Refugee Question.  The latter we cannot entertain for a moment, even if Lord Derby did not feel as strongly as he does the injustice and impossibility of yielding to any demand for the expulsion of refugees from this country as long as they conform to its laws and do not give their conspiracies a practical form.  You must be aware that no Government which complied with such demands could exist a month in England.  I trust you will be able to have orders sent here to let bygones be bygones, and to avoid all reference to the past.

The President (Louis Napoleon) is full of peaceful and friendly pro-fessions, and the last despatch from Magenis states the Swiss to be in-clined to yield to reasonable demands.  Walewski says that Austria first proposed the occupation of Switzerland, and that it is to prevent it that France has taken up the question.

.        .        .        .        .        .        .        .

Yours truly,

MALMESBURY.

*Lord M. to Sir Stratford Canning, H.M. Ambassador at Constantinople, on the Tanzimat Law.*

London : March 8, 1852.

My dear Sir Stratford,—

.        .        .        .        .        .        .

I should like to have your opinion as to the expediency of inviting Russia, France, and Austria to join us in urging the Sultan to exempt Egypt from the new law respecting capital punishment, and to reduce our demand to five years, which would cover the construction of the Suez railway.

.        .        .        .        .        .        .        .

MALMESBURY.

*March 10th.*—Duke of Wellington, Jerseys, Brünnows, Van de Weyers, Buols, Derbys, and Lord Bath, dined with us.  The Duke is nearly stone deaf.

Lord Hardwicke confiscated the latchkey of forty housemaids

at the General Post Office in London, at the risk of a revolution in his Department.

*Lord M. to Lord Cowley, H.M. Ambassador at Paris,*
*on Neufchâtel.*

Foreign Office: March 11, 1852.
Dear Lord Cowley,—

．　．　．　．　．

I have now to inform you that Bunsen has come forward with a proposition (I enclose it) respecting a recognition by the four Powers of Prussia's rights over Neufchâtel. Now, however we may and do acknowledge these rights, which are confirmed by the Treaty of Vienna, there would be no advantage in repeating such an undisputed fact by a new protocol, unless collateral objects recommended it. One of these, it is thought, would be worth having in the repeated recognition of Swiss independence and neutrality. Assuming the project to be desirable, it appears to me doubtful whether France would consent to it as well as the other Powers, and if she refused she would then be on another line. I would therefore request you to discover privately whether, in the event of such a proposal as this of Bunsen's being made, France would consent to join the other four Powers.

My own opinion (even supposing we are convinced of the policy of strengthening the liens of the Treaty of 1815 respecting Switzerland) is that this is not the time to do it—that we ought at this moment to appear to the Swiss as the independent and real friend, offering honourable and reasonable advice in their present difficulties. I think that if, simultaneously with our present representations in this sense, we urged the acknowledgment of the King of Prussia's claims in conjunction with two nations who are in the act of bullying them, the Swiss would no longer follow our advice with the same confidence which they have apparently shown.

．　．　．　．　．　．　．

I have just received your two letters and despatches. I have known Persigny long and well. He is a most fearless fellow, but the essence of vanity and a great *pérorateur*. Formerly, by flattery and piquing his vanity in assuming his ignorance, anything could be extracted. He his now, perhaps, more catious by experience, but only a year ago, by applying the above medicine, I relieved him of every word of his famous conversation with Changarnier an hour after it had taken place, and all he had done and not done at Berlin. The President knows he is faithful but does not think more of his steadiness than I do.—Yours truly, MALMESBURY.

*March* 11*th.*---Our Cabinet is now formed, and consists of the following :---

| | |
|---|---|
| Premier . . . . | Lord Derby. |
| Lord Chancellor . . . | Lord St. Leonards. |
| Lord President of the Council | Lord Lonsdale. |
| Lord Privy Seal . . . | Lord Salisbury. |
| Foreign Secretary . . . | Lord Malmesbury. |
| Home Secretary . . . | Mr. Walpole. |
| Colonial Secretary . . | Sir J. Pakington. |
| War Office . . . . | Colonel Beresford. |
| Navy . . . . . | Duke of Northumberland. |
| Woods and Forests . . | Lord John Manners. |
| Post Office . . . . | Lord Hardwicke. |
| Board of Control . . . | Mr. Herries. |
| Chancellor of the Exchequer and leader of the House of Commons . . . . | Mr. Disraeli. |

The only men who have ever held office before are Lord Derby and Lord Lonsdale and Mr. Herries ; and the country is to a certain degree anxious as to a Government composed of men so inexperienced in public business. The Opposition papers are loud in their abuse of us personally, to an amount of scurrility that does them no honour. With regard to myself, I get a good share of their epigrams and insults, but I thought all this natural enough under the peculiar circumstances, and have cared little for it, until I found out that the most bitter and disparaging articles were written by Sidney Herbert and Lord Lincoln, both of whom have been for years my most intimate and ' familiar friends,' [1] and I confess their anonymous and treacherous warfare gives me great pain ; but such are politics, destructive of all the gentler sentiments between man and man, Lord Palmerston, who had been the ward of the first Lord Malmesbury, and had always maintained the most constant friendship with my family, knowing that I was inexperienced in official life, and that I must have considerable difficulty in managing so high and important a charge as that of the Foreign Office, kindly offered to call on me and give me some advice upon the main principles of our English policy with foreign

---

[1] These two had set up a paper of their own, the *Morning Chronicle,* by which they eventually lost a great deal of money.

countries. Of course, I gratefully accepted his offer, and he came
to my house in Whitehall Gardens, giving me a masterly sketch
of the *status quo* in Europe, and some general hints as to my
procedure. The pith of them was ' to keep well with France ; '
but adding, ' that she was ambitious to have the principal influence
in the East, and that in this respect we were " like two men in
love with the same woman." ' He said, ' You have no idea till
you know more of your office what a power of *prestige* England
possesses abroad, and it will be your first duty to see that it does
not wane. All the Foreign Ministers will try at first to get objects which they have been refused by successive Governments ;
so take care you yield nothing until you have well looked into
every side of the question. When the *diplomates* call, do not be
too reserved, but preface your observations by stating that what
you say is *officious.*' He said, that of course being unaccustomed
to this sort of work—namely, reading a number of papers and
answering or taking note of them—they must cost me more time
and labour than they did him, but that the advantage I had was
in having young eyes, as he suffered much from his sight. He
recommended me to insist on all official correspondence being
written in a plain hand with proper intervals between the lines,
and he mentioned some Ministers who were quite illegible. On
the subject of appointments abroad he said, satirically, ' You will
be struck with a very curious circumstance—namely, that " no
climate agrees with an English diplomatist excepting that of
Paris, Florence, or Naples ! " ' He said that the advent of Louis
Napoleon to power was a good thing for France, and, from the
extraordinary figures of the *plébiscite,* proved she was weary both
of Bourbons and lawyers ; but that, as it was quite possible that
his tendencies might be to avenge his uncle's fate, we must turn
all our attention to strengthening our national defences both
by forts and an increase of armaments. This is also the ruling
feeling at Court and throughout the country, as the long rule of
the Whigs has let down all the defensive powers of Great Britain.
If in 1840 Thiers had had his way, and France had gone to war
with us, we should have been totally unprepared, even in our
navy.

After this interview, I called by appointment on the Duke of

Wellington, whom, being Lord-Lieutenant of my county, and having often seen him respecting the yeomanry, &c., I knew very well. His advice was much the same as Lord Palmerston's. He had a bad opinion of the Emperor Nicholas's character for sincerity, and said there was much in him of 'the Greek of the Lower Empire.' He wound up as I was going out, 'Mind you keep well with France, as that is a most important object for us ; but be careful as to this new change of dynasty. I don't believe Louis Napoleon will ever go to war with us if he can help it, but he must keep up his popularity, and then God knows what he may do.' He urged me to press on Lord Derby the increase of our armaments by sea and land. We talked as above in a small room, sitting in the middle of it, on two board chairs (the only ones) just opposite each other. He was very deaf, and therefore spoke louder than he used to do.

Lord Derby had appointed his son, Edward Stanley, as my Under Secretary, but as he was in India for his pleasure, I was without anyone whom I knew, and this made my position more difficult. I received, however, the most cordial assistance from the Permanent Under-Secretary, Mr. Addington (who was a Tory and had been our Minister at Washington), from the moment I entered the Foreign Office. The chief of the clerks was Mr. Hammond,[1] a very strong partisan on the other side. All the staff were kindly disposed, but I could see that they expected me to give them much trouble, and to ask their advice. They were surprised to see how I knew the routine work, and all the *verbiage* of the profession, as I did thoroughly, from having in 1844 published the Memoirs, State Papers, and Correspondence of my grandfather, the first Earl. For two years I was employed in reading not only his public despatches to Ministers at home, but also to his brother diplomatists abroad. I went through above 2,000 of these, embracing the period between 1768 and 1809, as if I had been an Under-Secretary at the Foreign Office for forty years, arranging and collating them, and investigating their contemporary history.

I shall have, therefore, no difficulty in expounding our policy to our diplomatists abroad, and to foreign ones in London, as

[1] Now Lord Hammond.

soon as our Cabinet has fixed it. I owe much to the Queen and
the Prince, who, in the kindest and most gracious manner, give
me a great deal of private information of which I could know
nothing as to foreign, especially German, Courts. Lord Granville and I had been friends, as my grandfather and his father
were before us, the latter having served with Lord Malmesbury
in his missions. He called on me, as is usual, to explain the
*status quo* of foreign affairs. The pressing questions are—treatment of political refugees and French demands on Switzerland
to expel them; the claims of Prussia on Neufchâtel; the claim
of Abbas in Egypt, of power of life and death refused by the
Sultan : the treaty settling the Greek and Danish Crowns; but,
above all, the great uncertainty of Louis Napoleon's intentions as
to his policy, and making himself Emperor. Rome and Modena
had sent notes, suggested by Austria, through Count Buol,
demanding the extradition of their refugees, which Lord Granville met by throwing them after him when he went out of the
room ; and this was my first diplomatic interview with Buol,
who was raving against England and Granville. He behaved in
the most coarse and insolent manner when I refused to receive
the notes which he presented, and to such a degree, that I at last
asked him if he was accustomed to speak to English Ministers in
that style ; because I must tell him at once that I would not
bear it, and should inform his Court of his violence. He then
left the room.[1]

Soon after, Prince Schwarzenberg came into power, recalled
Buol and repudiated his demands respecting refugees, expressing
as strongly as possible his pleasure at our party coming into office,
and his wishes for our good understanding. Turgot is Minister
for Foreign Affairs for France, Walewski Ambassador to England.

*Lord M. to Lord Cowley, H.M. Ambassador at Paris, on
opening the River Plate.*

Foreign Office : March 16, 1852.

Dear Lord Cowley,—I have only time to request you to discover
how far the French Government would be prepared to go hand in hand

---

[1] Lord Granville denies having been in any way discourteous to Count Buol,
whose conduct and manner to me, and his account of Lord Granville's to himself,
was a *comédie diplomatique* played on my inexperience of official forms.

with us in trying to persuade the South American States to open the
rivers Parana and Uruguay to us on free-trade principles. We must
try to get America to join with us in this great plan, which (now that
Rosas is defeated and an exile) may, I hope, be accomplished. We
should probably send a special mission to negotiate this, and arrange,
if possible, the Brazilian loan.

 .       .       .       .       .       .

Yours truly,<br>
MALMESBURY.

*March 17th.*—Our immemorial Cabinet dinner was at Lord
Lonsdale's. Each of us gives one on a Wednesday.[1] Lord Ossulston beat Sir George Grey for Northumberland, and came in with
Lord Lovaine. Saw Lady Derby, who wishes Lady Malmesbury
to present Princess Edward of Saxe-Weimar at the Drawing-
room as Countess of Dornberg. The Prince and the Richmond
family hope she will be allowed the title of Princess by courtesy
in society. Lady Derby begged Lady Malmesbury to send them
an invitation to her party next Saturday, giving her the title of
Princess, which she did.

*Lord M. to Lord Bloomfield, H.M. Ambassador at Berlin, on the
Danish Succession and the Treaty of London of* 1852.

Foreign Office: March 18, 1852.

Dear Lord Bloomfield,—Referring to your conversation with M.
Manteuffel upon the contingencies dependent upon a French invasion
of Belgium, I have only to say that your language was exactly what
her Majesty's Government wishes to be held on that subject. You
must take care that there is no such *secret understanding* as to fetter
our discretion as to the extent or even character of our interference in
a supposed case, which at present appears very improbable. We are
not disposed to enter into any offensive and defensive alliances,
although we shall readily acknowledge our responsibility as laid down
by treaties.

If the President ever contemplated an invasion of Belgium, he has,
I think, relinquished the idea for the present, being made aware that

---

[1] Until the next Administration, the Cabinet always had dinners once a week,
giving them by turns, and it was at one of these, always held on Wednesday, that
Thistlewood and his gang meant to murder the Ministers.

from no quarter will he receive encouragement, but probably resistance
from every Power of consequence in Europe.

You will be glad to hear that all our wrangles with Austria are
terminated, and that we have received a most friendly note from Prince
Schwarzenberg. •

The Swiss question is softening down, and the only really very
important point now is the speedy signature of the agreement for the
Danish Succession.  You will, I hope, use all your influence at Berlin
to show the King that the Duke of Augustenberg only delays his assent
to the indemnity from a foolish hope that a row may take place somewhere and somehow amongst the Five Powers, and that in the scuffle
he may get something more.  It would be very desirable for the King
of Prussia to make him understand that the only chance he runs is
that of losing the terms now offered him by further delays.

I also wish you to induce M. Manteuffel to write to M. Bunsen
instructions to join us in signing the agreement on the Danish Succession.  M. Brünnow has full powers to do so, and is anxious to terminate
this business at so favourable a moment; so is France; and I conclude
that Austria would follow Prussia in the move.

Yours turly,<br>
MALMESBURY.

*Lord M. to Mr. Crampton, H.M. Minister at Washington.*

Foreign Office:  March 26, 1852.]

My dear Sir,—I send you the copy of a despatch I have written to
Lord Cowley, which will inform you of the intention of her Majesty's
Government to send a special mission to Buenos Ayres with the object
of obtaining as free a use as possible of the great tributaries to the
Plata.  It is the wish of her Majesty's Government that you should
mention this fact to the Government of the United States, stating at
the same time that we desire no commercial advantages for ourselves
in particular, but are only anxious that the whole world should profit
by any liberal policy which the Argentine Confederation may be induced
to adopt.  Lord Derby has already spoken on the subject to Mr.
Lawrence here, who, I believe, has informed his Government of that
conversation.  We have reason to believe that the Government of the
United States will receive the information with favour; but if you
should find any dissatisfaction expressed at our not having invited it to
join with us and France in this mission, you will account for the fact
by representing that our success depends upon the most rapid movements, and that no time was left to put ourselves in communication

with the United States, and to receive a reply.  Should any questions
be asked you respecting our primary proposals, you will not fail to state
that we can only demand the opening of the Parana as a privilege to
be obtained by negotiation and not as a right.

You will at once see how this point touches our rights to the
navigation of the St. Lawrence, and the importance of our not appearing to hold different principles on different sides of the Equator.

.        .        .        .        .        .        .        .

Your obedient servant,
MALMESBURY.

### Lord M. to Lord Cowley, H.M. Ambassador at Paris.

Foreign Office : March 26, 1852.

Dear Lord Cowley,—

.        .        .        .        .        .        .

I have always held to Walewski the same language, that we would
give that 'advice to the Swiss Government which was consonant with
their interests without compromising their independence.'  Walewski
after having described to me the ultimatum of France, *asked me* to
communicate it privately to Magenis, and to instruct him to let the
Federal Government know how they could settle the matter.  He repeatedly said the demands upon future refugees would not be pressed,
and *never had been* intended, and made use of the expression,
'L'avenir appartient à tout le monde.'

Your language to M. de Turgot should still be in the words I have
quoted above as used by me.  If the Executive of the Federal Government has, by its own laws, the power of expelling foreigners deemed
dangerous to the State, their doing so at the request of France is a
question of opinion and justice on the part of the Executive, and not a
breach of constitutional law and liberty.  Thus Dr. Fürrer may, if not
afraid of the Opposition party, *exiler et interner* whom he pleases
without sacrificing Swiss rights.

.        .        .        .        .        .        .

Yours truly,
MALMESBURY.

### Lord M. to Sir Hamilton Seymour, H.M. Ambassador at St. Petersburg.

Foreign Office : March 29, 1852.

My dear Sir Hamilton,—Notwithstanding the impression which you
appear to have that the Prince President has relinquished his anxiety

to possess the title of Emperor, I confess I do not feel the least convinced that any change has taken place in his ambitious intentions. I have known him personally for many years, and I can answer for the most remarkable feature in his character being an obstinacy of intention, which, as it is maintained on all subjects with an unruffled temper, is held to the last against all opposition. All projects once formed and matured in his head remain there perfectly uncommunicated in detail, but their practical attempts of fulfilment will be a mere question of time. To be Emperor has been his *marotte* since he was twenty years old, when I recollect his mother used to laugh at him for indulging such a dream. Walewski tells me (on his return from Paris) that the whole army is most eager to crown him. He is universally called ' Altesse Impériale,' and there is good reason for supposing that his mantle is in the hands of the *brodeuses*. I do not, myself, see that any title he may please to assume can seriously influence European or monarchical interests. France has so long desecrated royalty and its prestige upon its own ground, from the time it decapitated Louis XVI. until it elected and banished Louis Philippe, that any of its acts relating to *personal dignities* must be looked upon as a masquerade of mummers. The impression made by these successive actors of royalty upon legal and hereditary titles can only induce a comparison in favour of the latter. As to political consequences, I think the assumption by Louis Napoleon of the Imperial purple would be null, and if not null rather likely to put an end to his *velléités*, as it has been his primary object—it *may* be his last—and having obtained all he can obtain, except by force of arms, and being himself no soldier, and jealous of generals, I do not think it unlikely that he will rest quietly at the Tuileries. One object of making himself Emperor is undoubtedly to obtain a royal bride.

These are my ideas, founded on my personal knowledge of the man ; but if I am mistaken as to the results of his elevation to the throne, I am not so as to his general character. He certainly entertained formerly the idea of a territorial redistribution of the arrangements of 1815, and you may depend upon it the idea still remains in his brain.

It is, therefore, most necessary that he should be made to feel (of course as civilly as possible) that the great Powers look upon the settlement of 1815 as final. He is much pleased at our invitation to join us in renewing negotiations to open the Plate and its tributaries to the world, and is to send M. St. George in a man-of-war, in company with our envoy, Sir C. Hotham.

Yours very truly, MALMESBURY.

*April 1st.*—Drawing Room. Lady Malmesbury had to present all the wives of the Foreign Ministers.

*April 5th.*—We dined at the Palace. Queen very gracious to both of us ; so was the Prince, by whom Lady Malmesbury sat at dinner. Party : Comte d'Aquila, Duke of Cambridge, Prince Leopold of Saxe-Coburg, Carinis, and Brünnow. I was attacked in the House of Lords by Lord Beaumont on the old question of refugees, whom he pretended to suppose I would give up. Prince Schwarzenberg, Prime Minister of Austria, died yesterday, and Count Buol is appointed in his stead. News has been received of the loss of the ' Birkenhead,' large steamer, carrying out troops to the Cape. She was wrecked on a reef not above two or three miles from the shore in Simon's Bay. Above 400 men perished. The courage they showed was wonderful. Not a word was uttered or a cry heard till the vessel sunk. All the women and children saved.

*Lord M. to Hon. Charles Murray, H.M. Consul in Egypt.*

Foreign Office : April 8, 1852.

My dear Murray,—Many thanks for your congratulations and your ' digest ' (as Brougham calls it) of the affairs of Egypt. I have seen Layard, Larking,[1] and others of equal experience in travel and business over the East, and I find them all differing as much as your officials do respecting the real practical results likely to occur should the Tanzimat be enforced in Egypt.

I can't form any opinion beyond this, that the two Turks do not look upon it so much as to its effect on their respective populations as on the symbolical importance which the power of life and death gives to a turban.

However this may be, you must consider the Tanzimat as a question of time only, and as passed. Successive Secretaries of State have acknowledged the Sultan's right, nor do I see how it can be denied. Vide the Treaty. This being the case, we must make the best of it now that he seems determined not even to postpone the law, and you must look farther than 1852. The next heir to Egypt is a Frenchman. If Egypt by any act of ours be helped to more independence and power, those advantages *now*, it is true, used *for* England, will then be used *against* her, and if they have been gained at the expense of

[1] Formerly Consul in Egypt.

the Porte's goodwill and political power, we shall have made a seedy bargain. We must look at the Sultan as the most lasting and secure force of the two, and so shape our policy that we shall preserve the use of Egypt for the present, without creating a ready-made dependency of it to France hereafter. You must, therefore, take care not to appear in any degree a partisan of either side, but supply the Pasha with proper arguments, which must be urged without asperity. I consider (and so does Larking) the Commissioners to be so many irritators, and they should go home again. If Canning can't shake the Sultan at Stamboul, nor I his Minister here, I am sure that your Commissioners are more likely to drive him mad than to soothe him and his viziers.

I am grieved to hear from your brother that feuds are not confined to the Turks, but that you, Canning, and Rose are all in hot water. This is most fatal to the interests of your country, which ought to be the first object in the minds of each and all of you, and it is a source of great regret to the Government. Pray, therefore, bury them in oblivion—at least, till you leave the East.

Yours truly,<br>MALMESBURY.

Lord M. to Hon. P. C. Scarlett, H.M. Chargé d'Affaires at Florence.

Foreign Office : April 9, 1852.

Dear Mr. Scarlett,—You must if possible get 500*l*. for Mather, or he should have such a sum as would bring him a small annuity. That is what he would have got in England. As a last resource, you might ask for arbitration.

I send you Prince Schwarzenberg's letter, which is satisfactory in a national sense, but is not enough as regards the Tuscans, who close their courts of justice to us.

Of course you must not talk of an apology from the officer, as it would be *bathos* after we have got Schwarzenberg's note. Two days before his death he told Lord Westmoreland that Tuscany ought to have allowed Mather to plead in a civil court.[1]

I hope you will have the credit of doing this before Bulwer arrives.

Yours truly,<br>MALMESBURY.

---

[1] Mr. Mather refused to make way for an Austrian detachment at Florence, pushing his way into the band, upon which an officer wounded him by a sabre cut. *Hinc illæ lacrymæ.*

*Lord M. to Lord Westmoreland.*

Heron Court : April 10, 1852.

Dear Lord Westmoreland,—We first heard of Prince Schwarzenberg's death on Tuesday at three o'clock, by the submarine telegraph. He must have died at the very moment we were debating on his correspondence in the House of Lords. We are of course anxious to know who will be his successor, and are now under the impression (given by himself) that Buol will be the man. When he left me at the Palace, where I took him to make his parting bow, he was very civil, which has not always been the case. He took a strong view against Mather's case, and argued that the Austrian army was one of occupation. It is not so, but an auxiliary army. But were it even an army of occupation, that is no reason Tuscany should close her civil courts. The Duke of Wellington says the Portuguese courts were open the whole time of his occupation and whilst the war was raging, and that his soldiers were amenable to them.

Bulwer goes to Florence about the 20th, by which time I hope Scarlett will have got 500*l.* for Mather, which is about what an English jury would have given. Buol almost promised to use his influence with Austria to induce Tuscany to do this. If she refuses, we shall withdraw our mission. We have nothing but worry from this trumpery little Court, and I am sorry to say till now the only other that has followed this same course is your Imperial one. In Rome, where there are ten times as many English, and a French army, nothing of the sort happens. In France, where John Bull is everywhere seen in all his varieties, not a dispute ever occurs ; and although I know some of my countrymen abroad are eccentric fellows, I think you may in proper place and season observe on this monopoly of vexations which Austria and its dependencies have upon them.

. . . . . . . .

Yours truly,

MALMESBURY.

*Lord M. to Lord Cowley, H.M. Ambassador in Paris.*

Heron Court : April 11, 1852.

Dear Lord Cowley,— . . . Sir H. Seymour's private letters speak of the Emperor Nicholas's fixed purpose to stand by the treaties, and to look upon any march into Belgium as a *casus belli.* I quite agree with every word you said to Addington about Buol, who, however, was extremely civil to me before he went away. I presented him on his

departure, and he spoke to me a long time at the Palace on the subject
of Louis Napoleon's possible aggression, stating that there could be but
one policy for Russia, Austria, and Prussia—viz. to oppose a wall to
him which would be impenetrable ; but he never will get over Granville's
shying the 'note' after him as he went out.

The Swiss note you sent me last bored me quite as much as it did
Turgot. No wonder they were so longer transcribing it for Magenis.
I look upon that cloud [1] as nearly dissipated, and I am sincerely obliged
to you for the handy way you have managed the question with Barman
and Turgot. Magenis did well as soon as he got to Berne.

I can't help thinking the peril of exercising the Tanzimat in Egypt
has been exaggerated. However that may be, the Sultan, who looks
upon it as a symbol of dominion, refuses to give way. But I have
written to Sir Stratford Canning to try a middle course, and to get the
power of life and death continued to the Pasha for murder, or for murder and robbery, till the rail is finished to Alexandria. Nesselrode
proposed the same thing to Seymour, o I have pressed it there, and I
wish you would tell Kisseleff that if the Court of Russia wishes to
please us, it would recommend a delay of the Tanzimat, or a partial
adaptation of it, until the work is complete.

Yours truly,<br>MALMESBURY.

*Lord M. to Lord Westmoreland, H.M. Ambassador at Vienna.*

Foreign Office : April 20, 1852.

Dear Lord Westmoreland,—I shall be much obliged to you to convey (at the proper time and place) to the Emperor the sympathy which
her Majesty's Government feel for him personally in the loss of a
servant to whom he was so attached as to Prince Schwarzenberg.

We trust that the return of friendly feelings which he had evinced
towards England before his death will be continued to us by his successor, and we hope that he has passed sufficient time in England to
understand the somewhat anomalous co-existence of great license and
great order which is incomprehensible to foreigners who have not resided
here.

You will have got my despatch on the Turkish affair, and I depend
upon you to prevail on Austria to join us in recommending a *terme
moyen* to the Porte respecting the law of capital punishment, and to
oppose any attempts to change the Viceroy of Egypt. The next heir
is French by habits and education, and although we entirely admit the

---

[1] The French claims against the refugees in Switzerland,

right of the Sultan to exercise the Tanzimat in Egypt, we could not, as one of the Powers who signed the settlement of 1841, agree to his changing the succession to the Viceroyalty for no better reason than the remonstrance of his vassal against altering a law which he thinks would render life and property unsafe in his province.

Another question I trust you will urge to a termination is the Danish succession. Russia wishes some alteration in the *projet de convention* as it was presented by Denmark, to which we see no objection, but we must resist all question of its being referred to the Diet. Austria and Prussia can answer for Germany as far as they go, and if we go to other States the affair will never be ended.

Yours truly,

MALMESBURY.

*Lord M. to Lieut.-Col. Rose,[1] H.M. Chargé d'Affaires at Constantinople.*

Foreign Office : April 21, 1852.

My dear Rose,—I write you a line in answer to your letter to say that, although we receive the most contradictory accounts of the practical effect of the Tanzimat as a question of police, we are disposed to concur with you and Murray, that its exercise in Egypt would endanger our commerce and countrymen. Be that as it may, you must abstract your mind from local prejudices and look *ahead.* It is not our policy to make Egypt independent, even if we cared, against all principle, to break through the settlement of 1841. It is there distinctly stated that the Sultan can exercise the laws he pleases, and the last article declares that, if the Pasha does not adhere to the terms of the treaty, he forfeits his Pashalic. But I repeat, it is not our policy to make him independent of the Sultan, because he may die any day and a French Pasha succeed, when our want of faith and selfishness would turn against us. It is our interest to maintain the solidarity of the Turkish Empire, but to use the Pasha as an instrument more capable and calculated to keep the road to India safe than his distant master. You must not run one against the other, nor give an excuse to the Sultan to degrade his vassal. If the Sultan is obstinate about the Tanzimat, Abbas must obey, but the Sultan will have to stand the consequences if English property is not protected.

.    .    .    .    .    .    .    .    .

Ever yours truly,

MALMESBURY.

1 Afterwards Field-Marshal Lord Strathnairn.

*April 21st.*—I went to the Levée. French insist on Switzer land giving up Socialist refugees, and King of Prussia on having Neufchâtel, as under the treaties of 1815. This cannot now be done without a war.

*April 27th.*—Our Militia Bill carried by majority of 150. Many Peelites and Whigs voted with us.

*April 28th.*—Government had a majority of 53 last night against 10*l.* franchise for counties.

*Lord M. to Hon. P. C. Scarlett, H.M. Chargé d'Affaires at Florence.*

Foreign Office : April 27, 1852.

Dear Mr. Scarlett,—Sir Henry Bulwer will start to-morrow for Florence, notwithstanding the crisis you describe as going on in the Tuscan Court. I am still in hopes that you will settle the Mather compensation, by arbitration or otherwise, before he arrives, and I see no reason why you should not push it on before the present Government is turned out. It appears to me that the next, being utterly bigoted, would be still more intractable, and not care if our mission at Florence were to be closed—nay, might rather desire it.

Lord Westmoreland has sent me an offer from Count Buol, to refer the case of compensation to Mr. Mather to the Emperor if we fail in Tuscany, where he states that Austria has given a voice in favour of our claim. I am, however, unwilling to accept Count Buol's proposal further than to ask him to give his good offices privately to us, and recommend such payment as Mr. Mather would be allowed by an English court of justice. He and the Tuscan Government must settle the question of who is to be the loser between them ; but we who have never treated the matter officially with Austria, but insisted on the responsibility of Tuscany as an independent State, cannot accept the money from Austria for Tuscany.

* * * * * * * *

Yours truly,
MALMESBURY.

*May 1st.*—Dined at the Royal Academy. Disraeli's speech on introducing his Budget has produced a bad effect in the country, for the farmers, though reconciled to giving up Protection, expected some relief in other ways, and he does not give a hint at any measure for their advantage. I fear this will tell at the next election. Lord Derby is much annoyed. I expect we shall be turned out before December.

*May 5th.*—Crowded ball at the Palace. Persigny, at Paris, has been blustering to Madame de Lieven about war and empire, which will all go to Nicholas.

*Lord M. to Lord Bloomfield, H.M. Ambassador at Berlin.*

Foreign Office: May 10, 1852.

My dear Lord Bloomfield,—You will have been as glad as any one to hear that the Danish Convention was signed on Saturday by *all* the plenipos. Bunsen refused to do so the day before (which would have been a matter of convenience to the Ministers invited to the Chiswick *fête* on Saturday) ' because his seal was at the engraver's.'

This act and puerile excuse have rendered him still more unpopular than he was with his colleagues. I should like to know whether he expected some further instructions by the telegraph on Saturday morning. As it was, he made no mention of reference to the Diet at the Conference, but only suggested to me privately that the Convention when signed should be so referred; but I replied, I should object to *that* until *after* .the ratifications, when according to one of its articles it would be submitted to the other Powers for adhesion. You will see that I instruct you in a despatch sent by this messenger to ascertain whether Bunsen really has had recent orders to catechise me respecting an absurd incendiary proclamation printed in London seven months ago. A week before Granville went out of office he put the same questions to him regarding this document, which he did not condescend to answer.

Yours truly,
MALMESBURY.

*May 11th.*—Disraeli moved to bring in a bill to appropriate the four seats vacant by a disfranchisement of Sudbury and St. Albans, and proposed to give two additional members to the West Riding and two to South Lancashire. Mr. Gladstone moved the order of the day as an amendment: I think this will do us more good than harm with the country. I hear that the review at Paris on the 10th went off very well. I had an audience of the Queen yesterday. She asked me whether Lady Tankerville had gone to Paris for the review, expressing wonder that any one should do so.  I told her Majesty that she had gone to see the Gramonts.  At the opera of 'Il Flauto Magico,' the hero of the piece was Ronconi as Papagallo, dressed all in feathers.  He has added to his costume a crest of red ones, which by some contrivance he occasionally raised upright, as cockatoos do when pleased or surprised.  He tried this piece of buffoonery whenever he was applauded, and made the whole house roar with laughter.

*May* 12*th.*—My turn to give the Cabinet dinner.

*May* 14*th.*—Lord and Lady Ossulston just returned from Paris. They were invited to the *fêtes* at the Tuileries, but the string was so long that they returned home.  No cheering from the mob, only from the soldiers.  Lord Cowley was hissed for using his privilege of cutting into the string, and Lord Alfred Paget, who was with him, shared his treatment.  A great many arrests made in Paris.

*May* 20*th.*—We went this evening to the Walewskis, who had a French play, 'Brutus lâche César,' acted to perfection by Rose Chéri, Lafont, and Léon.

*May* 21*st.*—My Under-Secretary, Lord Stanley, arrived this morning from India.  Dined with the Castlereaghs.

*Lord M. to Lord Bloomfield, H.M. Ambassador at Berlin.*

Foreign Office : May 22, 1852.

My dear Lord Bloomfield,—Bunsen has called upon me to beg you will explain to the King that Manteuffel was quite right in not pressing a reference of the Danish Convention to the Diet upon the six Powers at the time of their signing it.  Bunsen informs me that Manteuffel was ordered by the King to instruct him to make the demand, and put it in the shape of a note ; and I recollect that you also gave me notice that such was the case before Bunsen received his full powers.  He furthermore declared that Manteuffel never gave him the order.  Be this as it may, it is certain that none of the Powers would have recognised the right of the Diet to interfere, and I told Bunsen that I was ready to argue this point, and that if he persisted, we would sign without him.

I should be glad, if it is necessary, that you should set Manteuffel right with the King, who, had he brought the question of the 'right of the Diet' before the six Powers on this occasion, would have obliged them on a public and solemn occasion to vote against his opinion,

His Minister, therefore, served him well in not acting so indiscreetly as to do so.

Yours truly,

MALMESBURY.

*May 24th.*—Kept until past ten in the House of Lords. Government beaten in the Commons on Mr. Duncombe's amendment on the Bribery Bill, proposing to extend its provisions to counties. My brother voted against the Government.

The French Senate refuse to part with the Crown jewels until the President marries. He says : ' Je ne suis pas pressé.'

Lady Malmesbury gave a party at the Foreign Office. The Opposition had spread a report that the staircase was not safe, which they might have said with more truth of the rest of the house, as a few days after my appointment the ceiling came down upon the table at which I wrote, and would have killed me if I had been there.

*May 28th.*—I fear this business of Mr. Mather at Florence will give me a great deal of trouble, as Mather *père* is furious at only obtaining 250*l.* for the injury done to his son's head, his first demand being 5,000*l.* The latter gentleman chose to stand in the way of a body of Austrian soldiers marching through the street with their band, and refused to move, on which the officer commanding struck him with his sword, and cut his head open, though not dangerously. I took up the affair, and claimed compensation from the Tuscan Government, as it was very important in a political sense that we should establish the fact of the independence of Tuscany, although occupied by Austrian troops. Mr. Scarlett, who was Chargé d'Affaires in Bulwer's absence, was ordered not to accept less than 500*l.*, and disobeyed his instructions. The Opposition, in view of the coming elections, are making capital of this and other freaks of travelling Englishmen who get themselves into scrapes abroad, and, being often deservedly punished or arrested, call upon their Government for protection. This conduct on their part is very much due to a blustering speech made some time ago by Lord Palmerston, declaring that John Bull, wherever he was, or whatever he did, was to be as sacred as the ancient ' civis Romanus.'

*May 29th.*—Mr. Scarlett, besides accepting half the *minimum*, did so as a generous act of charity on the part of the Grand Duke, instead of a compensation due to the injured Englishman. I have written a strong remonstrance to Sir Henry Bulwer against Mr. Scarlett's acceptance of the money, and his still worse abandonment of the important point of responsibility of Tuscany as an independent State, declaring that unless they admit that *it is for the injury inflicted,* we shall withdraw our Minister from Florence. I suspect Mr. Scarlett did so from anxiety to have the credit of concluding the business anyhow before the return of Sir Henry Bulwer.

*June 1st.*—The Tribunal de Première Instance has decided against the President 'on the Orleans decrees. He was asked about that, but is not at all annoyed, and among other subjects told my informant, 'Tenez ! en cherchant dans un journal que j'ai écrit en Suisse j'ai trouvé ce passage : "Je suis né pour rendre le bonheur à la France et les Aigles à l'armée : le reste sont des bagatelles." ' His journey to that wretched district La Sologne has made him very popular, and induced people to hope that he will abandon the sword for the plough and the trowel. He is much perplexed, as he is averse to marriage, and yet feels that none of the Bonaparte family are fit to succeed him, and could not maintain an imperial dynasty. Jerome and his son lose no opportunity of annoying and crossing the President's views. He despises but fears them. Persigny marries Marshal Ney's granddaughter.

*June 2nd.*—Dined with the Walewskis, and thence to the Duchess of Gloucester, then back again to the Walewskis. Turgot is very unmanageable on the Tanzimat, and unwilling to give the Pasha of Egypt the power of life and death over criminals, thereby supporting the Sultan.

*Lord M. to Lord Cowley, H.M. Ambassador at Paris.*

Foreign Office : June 3, 1852.
Dear Lord Cowley,—

Walewski spoke to me about the affair of the 'Charlemagne.' Look at the Treaty, July 18, 1841, arts. I. and XI. The latter gives permis-

sion to the Sultan to let 'light vessels' up the Dardanelles, which
certainly does not apply to the 'Charlemagne.' You will see by Lord
Stratford's despatch that he gave no advice, but I have no objection to
your saying that the Treaty is so clear that the French Admiral exposed his Government to awkward remonstrances by either asking for
the Firman or accepting a promise of it, and that I conclude he did
not know how stringent the Treaty is. The eyes of Europe are so
attentively fixed on the President to observe how he respects conventions
that he should avoid all appearance of encroachment.[1]

> Yours truly,
> MALMESBURY.

*June 3rd.*—Drawing Room. Dined with Lady Ailesbury.
Heard an amusing account of a dinner given by the Douglases at
Paris, to introduce the President to Madame de Lieven. It was
diamond cut diamond, and she admitted that she could make
nothing of him.

*June 4th.*—Queen's concert. Lord Cowley at Paris considers
the Empire as settled in the mind of the President. He has dismissed his mistress, Mrs. Howard, after giving her the title of
Comtesse de Beauregard

*Lord M. to Lord Westmoreland, H.M. Ambassador at Vienna.*

Foreign Office : June 8, 1852.

Dear Lord Westmoreland,—

The Mather case has reached a very disagreeable crisis.[2] I send
you the papers, and you will see by my last two despatches to Bulwer
how the matter stands.

Pray tell Buol that it was impossible for us to accept such a note as
Casigliano's of the 10th ult.—not a word of regret or good feeling, but
an insulting assertion that he paid the money from charity, and that
Mather had no right either to protection as an English subject or to
reparation for the assault. If the Austrians are not liable to be tried by
the Tuscan Civil Courts, we must have an admission from the Tuscan
Government that the Executive in Tuscany will protect and adjudicate

---

[1] The Treaties with the Porte forbade ships of war like the 'Charlemagne'
which carried M. de Lavalette to go up the Bosphorus.

[2] Mr. Scarlett had accepted 200*l.* only, and that as a charitable gift. His
instructions were to insist on 500*l.* as the minimum.

for English plaintiffs and afterwards settle with Vienna. We have otherwise no place of appeal, but are bandied from one to the other, each refusing responsibility, or Austria asserting jurisdiction in Tuscany and suppressing entirely her character of independence.

I attribute Scarlett's spontaneous offer to abandon the spirit and letter of his instructions to illness.

The Queen received Coloredo immediately and just before she went to Windsor. Make the most of this, which really was very gracious and well-judged of her Majesty.      Yours very truly,

MALMESBURY.

*Lord M. to James Hudson, Esq., H.M. Minister at Turin.*

Foreign Office: June 8, 1852.

My dear Mr. Hudson,—M. d'Azeglio's conduct respecting the Editor of the 'Opinione' is only one of a thousand proofs that the ablest foreigner can never perfectly apprehend the principles of constitutional liberty. To banish a man for abusing the Austrians would deservedly have forfeited his position. You should, if possible, make him understand that as for their own interests the proprietors of journals must take different sides, he should have sufficient authority established in whatever newspaper supports the Government to reply to or denounce therein any attack upon his colleagues or foreign allies. When Buol spoke to Lord Westmoreland on the subject and referred to me, that is what I stated to be the total of what Buol could expect to get, and he told Lord Westmoreland that he was satisfied with my opinion.

In my speech to which you and M. d'Azeglio refer I did not at all exaggerate my admiration of the conduct and results of the King and his Ministers since 1849. From all you say I fear these fair promises will not bring permanent liberty to Sardinia or any part of Italy, but it is our interest and duty to give at least all the moral force we possess to assist this constitutional monarchy in its development. You do not say who is to be ' Le Roi du Royaume d'Italie.'

Yours truly,

MALMESBURY.

*June 9th.*—We went to Windsor. Party consists of Cambridges, &c. A ball in the evening. The Queen danced a great deal, and ended with ' La Tempête,' a sort of English country dance.

*June 10th.*—Ascot Races. Dined again in St. George's Hall. Ball till one o'clock.

> Lord M. to Hon. P. C. Scarlett, H.M. Chargé d'Affaires
> at Florence.

> Foreign Office: June 12, 1852.

My dear Mr. Scarlett,—I have just received your letter explaining all the difficulties you had to contend with in the Mather case, and your reasons for making the arrangements the Government felt it their painful duty to disavow. We are convinced that it was from no relaxation of the activity which you have uniformly shown during this harassing business that you brought it to a close so unsatisfactory to them, but that you considered the re-establishment of friendly relations with Tuscany and the liberation of the Stratfords as objects superior to a literal compliance with your instructions. It was, however, quite impossible for her Majesty's Government to forego the important, nay, paramount principle of Tuscan responsibility either through her Courts or Executive, and equally impossible to accept the note of M. de Casigliano, which treated the payment as an eleemosynary gift instead of a just reparation, whilst not a single expression of amity or regret was added. It was, I assure you, a source of sincere regret to me that I should be obliged to disapprove publicly of your act, but I stated as publicly that it could only be attributed to an error of judgment.

> Yours truly,
> MALMESBURY.

*June 15th.*—Lord John Russell brought forward the Mather case, and made a very violent speech. Disraeli's answer good. Opposition papers abused me, and take the unexpected line that redress ought to have been demanded from Austria. If I had done so, I should have been accused of sacrificing the liberties of Italian States to the despotism of Austria. But the whole thing is got up for the coming elections.

*June 16th.*—Our Militia Bill passed second reading last night in the House of Lords. The President wants Napoleon's will sent to Paris.

*June 18th.*—Lord Derby showed me his list for the elections, giving us a majority, but I don't believe it.

*June 21st.*—Lady Malmesbury embarked for Ems. Debate on

Mather's case went off well in Commons. Parliament is to be dissolved on July 2.

*Lord M. to A. Buchanan, Esq., H.M. Minister at Berne.*

Foreign Office : June 28, 1852.

Dear Mr. Buchanan,—I have had some conversations with Count Walewski on the Neufchâtel question. Our object is to put aside the subject, and to prevent the King of Prussia making an imprudent demonstration. You will see that the Protocol states we are to consider the best *time* for a Conference. We have not done that yet, and we shall not take this primary step at present. If, however, the Swiss could devise some method of settling the business it would be desirable. I have repeated assurances that France would never suffer armed intervention, and I need not tell you her Majesty's Government would be equally averse to it. The Swiss must know this from all I did this year to settle their dispute with Louis Napoleon.

Yours truly,

MALMESBURY.

*Lord M. to Sir H. Bulwer, H.M. Minister at Florence.*

Foreign Office : July 2, 1852.

My dear Bulwer,—I send you an official despatch, which I wrote some time ago to Freeborn,[1] as being the only instructions the Government could give then and repeat now with respect to Mr. Murray's case. If he has been tried by the laws of the country in which he was living and actually serving, we cannot interfere by menace, but we must appeal to the friendly feelings of Rome and make the most of his long imprisonment to save his life. I showed your note, asking what language you should hold, to Lord Derby, who agreed with me that a conciliatory tone was most likely to prevail in Murray's favour, but that, as you had better means of judging than we have, we must leave it to your discretion.

Murray's case can never be one authorising us to use force, which is another reason for adopting the language of argument. Pray send Mr. Barron to Berlin immediately.

The House of Commons cheered you handsomely *re* Mather.

Yours truly,

MALMESBURY.

[1] British Consul at Rome.

*July 17th.*—Lords Stratford, Howden, and Palmerston, &c., dined with me.

*Lord M. to Sir H. Bulwer, H.M. Minister at Florence.*

Foreign Office: July 19, 1852.

My dear Bulwer,—Your correspondence with the Duke of Casigliano was sent by him to Vienna, and has brought a note here which shows that the Austrian Government does not at all relish the principle of Tuscan responsibility which you obliged the Duke to admit. The note which Coloredo was instructed to read to me was written in a spirit which I do not at all like, not only because the interpretation given to it by Coloredo was that treaties overrode international law, but I see in every word an intention to hold Tuscany and reduce it to the state of Modena and Parma. Against such a consummation it will be your duty and your glory to struggle.

I believe the Tuscans always have been wise enough to resist all financial incorporation with Austria. Keep them hard to that resolution.

Your first despatches gave reason to hope that Tuscany was anxious to get rid of its incubus, and to hire foreign troops. Is it still so? I do not think an Irish Legion would do, as it would create jealousy, but a Foreign Legion of Irish, Swiss, &c., might. I admit that the Austrian and French are necessary in the Papal States to prevent anarchy, but that is not the case in Tuscany. Cannot you make the Grand Duke see this?

Since I wrote the above I have heard from Hudson. In case he should have omitted giving you any information from his agent at Rome (I have begged him to do so), I advise you that the Pope is supposed to be rather friendly than otherwise to our Government, but that Irish influence and Jesuitism are strongly working at him against us, and that (as formerly) Lord Shrewsbury is the tool. It would not, however, appear difficult to persuade his Holiness that the peace of Europe, and consequently of Italy, depends not a little on a Conservative policy. Hudson's account so far tallies with yours and confirms its correctness.

I am very glad to hear you are getting better. The elections are nearly over, and we have got 310 Derbyites in. *Reste à voir* whether with 40 doubtful we can drive on.

Yours truly,

MALMESBURY.

s 2

*July 26th.*—Lord Ossulston has won his election for Northumberland, beating Sir George Grey by 35.

*July 27th.*—Elections look bad. I don't think we shall muster above 300 Derbyites. Went to Osborne to present Duke of Oldenburg. Hope the Queen will send a steamer, so that we may not have to swim and run as we did the other day when I went with Lords Stratford and Howden. We arrived in the royal presence as if we had been snipe shooting.

*August 11th.*—Our dispute with America about the fisheries will be settled very well if there is no fighting amongst the fishermen.

*Mr. Disraeli, Chancellor of the Exchequer, to Lord M.*

Hughenden : August 13, 1852.

My dear M.,—I return you Lord Cowley's confidential despatch. I am not disposed to reduce our duties on French brandies to obtain a reduction of their duties on our coals. We had better leave our mutual tariffs as they stand, unless the French are willing to treat these matters on a much more extensive scale. If they would reduce their duties on linen, yarn, cottons, or iron, I should recommend our meeting them with reductions on their brandies and silks. The latter would be a great card for France. We ought now to be for as complete free trade as we can obtain, and let the English farmer, and the English landlord too, buy the best and the cheapest silks for their wives and daughters.

In case anything is to be done in this respect, it should be done with as little knowledge by the Board of Trade as practicable. That office is filled with our enemies. Lord Cowley, therefore, should conduct the business entirely; or we should send some confidential and circumspect agent of our own.

It is useless now to vex ourselves about the Protectionist rock ahead. If this section exist, it can do nothing until the financial statement is made. Every expression of opinion on their side will be suspended until they have heard our financial measures. I confess I have no great fear of them, and I think they and their constituents will be satisfied.

The Fisheries affair is a bad business. Pakington's circular is not written with a thorough knowledge of the circumstances. He is out of his depth, more than three marine miles from shore.

These wretched colonies will all be independent too in a few years, and are a millstone round our necks. If I were you, I would *push matters* with Filmore, who has no interest to pander to the populace like Webster, and make an honourable and speedy settlement.

Yours ever,

D.

*Lord Bloomfield, H.M. Ambassador at Berlin, to Lord M.*

Berlin : August 16, 1852.

My dear Lord Malmesbury,—I have just addressed to your lordship a despatch respecting a dinner party at which I assisted yesterday, given by the French Minister in honour of the President's *fête*.

The Governments of Austria, Prussia, and Russia have acted closely together on this question, as they will do on every one concerning their general foreign policy; and in the present instance it is evident that my Russian colleague has been the *cheville ouvrière* in spoiling the French projects at Berlin, and he has done so most successfully; but his game was easy, for he acted before a willing audience.

I trust that I did right in attending the dinner party; and, indeed, I do not know how I could have declined the invitation under the circumstances which your lordship will find related in the despatch. I felt, unimportant as my presence might be, my refusal to attend the invitation would have been extremely uncourteous, and unnecessarily so, towards the Chief of the French Republic; nevertheless, I am anxious to learn the judgment your lordship may pass on my conduct, and I trust at all events on your indulgence in case I should not have acted in exact conformity with your wishes.

All we can say of the French demonstration here is that it was a complete failure, and has only served to draw out the real feeling of this Government, and of its immediate allies, towards Louis Napoleon.

Believe me, &c.,

BLOOMFIELD.

*August 18th.*—Lady Malmesbury returned from Ems without any benefit. I was at a Privy Council at Osborne. Turgot has been superseded as Foreign Minister by Drouyn de l'Huys.

*September 1st.*—The Queen reached Holyrood. I had attended her from Basingstoke. The journey was very prosperous, but we had to post the last forty miles to Balmoral up the Spittal of Glenshee. Nothing can exceed the good nature with which I am treated both by her Majesty and the Prince. Balmoral is an old

country house in bad repair, and totally unfit for royal personages.
It was occupied as a shooting lodge by Sir Robert Gordon.   The
Queen intends building a castle on or near the site.   The royal
party consists of the Duchess of Kent, the ladies-in-waiting,
Colonel Phipps, and Sir Arthur Gordon.   The rooms are so
small that I was obliged to write my despatches on my bed and
to keep the window constantly open to admit the necessary
quantity of air, and my private secretary, George Harris, lodged
somewhere three miles off.   We played at billiards every evening,
the Queen and the Duchess being constantly obliged to get up
from their chairs to be out of the way of the cues.   Nothing
could be more cheerful and evidently perfectly happy than the
Queen and Prince, or more kind to everybody around them.   I
never met any man so remarkable for the variety of information
on all subjects as the latter, with a great fund of humour *quand
il se déboutonne*.   They evidently enjoyed to the utmost the
beauty and tonic climate of the Highlands.   The river Dee, running close to the house, gives excellent salmon fishing, but the
deer forest is as yet very small.

*G. Harris, P.S. to Lord M., on his Mission to Prince Louis
Napoleon.*

20 Jermyn Street: September 2, 1852.

My dear Fitz,—I had my audience of the President on Tuesday
evening, the 31st ult., at St. Cloud, and I assure you that in order to
obtain it I was obliged to have recourse *aux grands moyens*.   Saturday,
Sunday, and Monday morning passed away without my receiving any
order from his Highness; so on Monday evening I got Stuart, of the
Embassy, to give me a private letter of introduction to the aide-de-camp
in waiting, and I drove to St. Cloud and had my name put down, the
suite—such as General Canrobert, Tascher, and Roquet—giving me
hopes that in a *week's* time I might be appointed to an audience;
whereupon I returned to Paris and called on Mrs. Howard, toadied and
flattered her, stating that I was in a great hurry to get back to London,
and only wanted to see his Highness the President for two minutes.
She sent off an orderly at once, and before night I received an invitation from Louis Napoleon to accompany him out shooting, to say my
say at 5.30, and dine afterwards (the next day, the 31st August).

I got off the shooting and dinner, being too ill for either; but in my interview I told him exactly what you desired me to tell him, viz., the *menées* of the refugees at Jersey, their threats of assassination, their general project, and expectations of help from Mazzini and Kossuth, and, in fact, all the pith of Mr. Sanders's reports and General Love's [1] apprehensions, not omitting certain details from reports of the A Division about money and arms ; and, finally, letting his Highness know that the Jersey authorities knew what to think of Stoffell and other agents of the French Government.

The President desired me to thank you most cordially for the intelligence, part of which (viz. the refugees' intention of landing and rendezvous in the South, not far from Bayonne and the frontier), he said was quite new to him. He mentioned that that very morning Manteuffel had sent him a warning about the *exilés des Isles Normandes*, that amongst their *projets insensés* they meditated a descent upon the coast of Algeria, where they counted on being able to 'corrupt' two regiments of the line, with which, under Mazzini's orders and inspiration, they were to return to Italy and revolutionize the whole of that country.

In fact he laughed, or affected to laugh, at their plans ; and said with more seriousness that assassination was the only project in which they had a chance of success.

He seemed to dread the frightful *tournée* in store for him, making the whole circuit of France.

He asked very much about you.

GEORGE HARRIS.

*September 4th.*—The Prince had a wood driven not far from the house. After we had been posted in line two fine stags passed me which I missed ; Colonel Phipps fired next, and lastly the Prince, without any effect. The Queen had come out to see the sport, lying down in the heather by the Prince, and witnessed all these *fiascos*, to our humiliation.

*September 10th.*—Left Balmoral for Achnacarry, riding across country part of the way. Whilst I was at Balmoral Colonel Phipps received a telegram from a clergyman, whose name I forget, and who was executor to a Mr. Neale, to say that the latter had left 200,000*l.* to the Queen. Neither her Majesty nor Phipps would believe that it was not a joke ; but I thought otherwise, and on requiring further information it proved to be correct.

[1] Lieutenant-Governor of Jersey.

The Queen immediately declared that if he had any relations she would not accept it, but it finally appeared that he had none.

### Lord Derby to Lord M. on the American Fisheries.

Balmoral : September 15, 1852.

My dear Malmesbury,—I send you an interesting letter received this morning from Sir G. Seymour[1] to the Duke of Northumberland, to whom, when you have read it, I will thank you to return it. The Queen has seen it. Crampton's private letter, which you left for me here, was not altogether satisfactory; but I do not see anything to be uneasy about in his public despatches, and this letter from Seymour appears to negative all probability of any collision. We must hold very temperate, but very firm, language; and assuredly, though God forbid it should come to that, I am prepared to fight for our undoubted rights, rather than yield to a spirit of democratic encroachment, which, if not steadily resisted, will have no limits to its demands. But on this account it is doubly important that we should come to an early understanding on this same Fishery Question with our French neighbours. I took the liberty of slightly altering your amended draft, in which, I think, you had asserted the right under the Law of Nations rather too broadly, without confining it to the three-mile limit from the coast. I also transposed two of the paragraphs. The Queen has seen and approved the amended draft, and the Prince told me they thought it an excellent paper.

.     .     .     .     .     .     .     .     .

DERBY.

*September* 16th.—George Harris arrived at Achnacarry with the news of the Duke of Wellington's death.

### Lord Malmesbury to Lord Derby on the Lord-Lieutenancy of Hants.

Achnacarry : September 17, 1852.

My dear Derby,—The news of the great Duke's death has just reached us, and a long life of prosperity and honour appears to have been providentially closed without suffering.

The event gives you an unusual burden of patronage, which will doubtless be squabbled for handsomely, and I write to remind you of our

[1] British Admiral on the Station.

conversation upon one appointment now in your gift—namely, the
Lord-Lieutenancy of Hampshire. You were kind enough to allude to
me as the Duke's successor, but, as I told you then, you have done for
me more than I deserve, or can repay you for in services, and I should
prefer much your strengthening the party by giving the post to Winchester. He is the oldest peer by family and title in the county.
Should he refuse it, mine would come after Lords Carnarvon and
Portsmouth, who are not in a situation to act; but if you thought it
well in the event of Winchester refusing to offer it to Palmerston, I
should not consider it unfair or unwise.

Yours sincerely,

MALMESBURY.

### Lord Brougham to Lord M.

Brougham : September 20, 1852.

My dear M.,—Many thanks for your letter, but after your former
one of August 14 I am a little let down. However, resignation and
patience must be the lot of the unfortunate, how great soever their
merits.

I was going to write you when your letter came, to tell you that I
had yesterday a letter from a very trustworthy man at Paris, who,
though not himself in public station, has long had access to those who
are, and whom I have always found to be very accurate in his information, and to have a very sound judgment. Were I at liberty to name
him (which I am not), you would agree with me in considering his
statement worthy of attention.

He says that within two months the President's marriage will take
place (the hitch having apparently been removed, though he don't say
so), that in less than three months there will be the Empire, but that
Louis Napoleon will have himself ' solicited.' Meanwhile the tour has
really, and not merely by the official accounts (sent to the ' Moniteur '
—all other reporters prohibited it should seem), been very triumphant.
But the guards are doubled at the offices of the Ministers, and part of
the men in each regiment in Paris are *consignés*. Yet for all this there
is not believed to be any occasion whatever, only it is to be so during
Louis Napoleon's absence, and the kind of panic the Ministers are
habitually in seems to descend from one Ministry to another pretty
regularly.

Yours sincerely,

H. BROUGHAM.

P.S.—My own belief is that Louis Napoleon's difficulties will begin
when the Empire is proclaimed. He *may* foresee this, and be content
with the Presidentship for life.

*Lord Brougham to Lord M.*

Brougham : September 30, 1852.

My dear M.,—I received another letter from the *knowing person* of whom I spoke when I last wrote to you; but not knowing where you were, I wrote to young Stanley in Downing Street. It was to the effect that this Belgian dispute is pretty certain to be a German quarrel, got up by Louis Napoleon in the intention of paying court to the coal, iron, cotton, &c., interests, as he is canvassing in all directions for support. But it seems Leopold is in great indignation, and expects the general opinion in Europe to go along with him when the case is known. My informant added that Leopold would not make any speech at the opening of his Chambers, but leave the whole matter to them. I supposed he (Leopold) had changed his intentions, but I believe now he had not. My man added that these Belgian proceedings of Louis Napoleon's have been very reluctantly acquiesced in by his (Louis Napoleon's) Ministers.

I feel somewhat uneasy with this Louis Napoleon, and fear he will, when he has nothing else to occupy the French with, turn his mind to worse things than *fêtes* and mummery.

In the South the flocking has been much exaggerated by his account, but there has been quite enough to let him take the title if he chooses.　　　　　　　　　　　　　　　　　　Yours very sincerely,

H. B.

*Lord Brougham to Lord M. on his Apprehensions of War.*

Brougham : October 1, 1852.

My dear M.,—I assure you that, independent of the circumstances mentioned in my last letter, and from quarters wholly different, I have received accounts which are anything rather than calculated to relieve me from my anxiety as to what is now passing in France, and I fear preparing for Europe, and for England more than all the rest. There is everywhere, and in these proceedings in the tour of Louis Napoleon, a most unpleasant military feeling breaking out on every occasion. You may rely upon it he is appealing to the vile national feeling more or less openly, and to the feeling of the army especially. You may also be assured of one thing—that the Cavaignacs regard war as inevitable, and don't believe that he could control the army on that subject.

I quite feel the force of the remark that persons in Cavaignac's position are to be listened to with very great caution, and that their disposition always is swayed by their situation. There is one of Machiavel's chapters of which the title preaches this distrust.

Nevertheless, in this case all the probabilities are with Cavaignac, and that such is his strong impression you may rest assured. I know it in detail. *Assuredly we cannot be too well prepared.*

Yours,

H. B.

*Sir Charles Phipps, P.S. to H.M., to Lord M.*

Balmoral: October 1, 1852.

My dear Lord Malmesbury,—

.   .   .    .    .    .    .

I was very sorry that you could not give a better account of Lady Malmesbury, for I had before heard that she had not been well.

The Queen felt severely the death of the Duke of Wellington; it had been long imminent, but I do not think that this circumstance even makes the loss, when it occurs, less painful. She felt his loss as an ornament to his country, as a devoted servant, and a safe counsellor, and as an old and intimate friend for whom she had a very deep and sincere regard. But such a life as his could not have been better ended.

Our life here varies little in its routine. Your successor, Sir John Pakington, was very successful in his first day's deer-stalking, killing two stags. Yesterday the Prince killed two very fine ones, and upon the famous stormy Monday he was fortunate enough to get *five* stalking.

Yours, &c.,

C. B. Phipps.

*Lord Derby to Lord M. on the Greek Succession.*

Goodwood : Thursday.

My dear Malmesbury,—I received your box this morning, and have taken an early opportunity of questioning the Duke of Parma upon the subject on which you wrote to me. He seemed very much surprised at the reports of his resignation which I named to him, and assured me, and desired me to assure you most solemnly that there was not a syllable of truth in them. *Je ne suis pas si fin, ni si bête.* He added that he had the greatest confidence in Mr. Ward, and was quite sure that he would not deceive him, or take any step adverse to his interests. His manner had every appearance of entire sincerity ; and if there is any project afloat for his abdication I am pretty confident that he is himself no party to it.

I have also had a conversation with Brünnow on Greek affairs; and have arranged with him that you should write to Petersburg and Paris, sending a *résumé* of the case, suggesting the necessity for a revision of the Greek treaty, so as to bring it into harmony with the Constitution, and proposing to call jointly on the King of Bavaria to state the intentions of his sons with regard to the acceptance of the Greek religion or the renunciation of the rights of succession. I did not say anything to Brünnow about your having had any communication with Paris on the subject; and he evidently desires that the invitation to reconsider the question should proceed from you, and be addressed simultaneously to the two other Powers. On the propriety of adhering to the Constitution, if it should clash with the treaty, he entirely agrees with us. The King of Greece should be a party to the new treaty. He was not to the original one, which in point of fact has never been made public, at least, so it would appear.       Yours,

DERBY.

*From S.E. Count Walewski, French Ambassador, to Lord M.*

Londres : 5 Octobre 1852.

Mon cher Malmesbury,—On nous avait annoncé ces jours-ci que le parlement serait réuni le 25 courant. Cette nouvelle m'avait fait espérer votre retour avant le 16, mais on m'assure que rien n'est changé aux arrangements primitifs. Je vais passer quelques jours à Broadlands. Si vous deviez être à Londres avant le 15, veuillez me l'écrire et je reviendrai en ville sans délai, ayant besoin de vous voir aussitôt votre arrivée. J'ai à vous entretenir de mille choses, et entre autres du règlement de la succession grecque. Votre ami Brünnow, avec lequel j'ai longuement causé, presse vivement une solution, et d'un autre côté, on laisse gratter l'oreille d'un Oldenburg. Dans tout cela, je désire que vous et moi nous marchions unis comme les doigts de la main. Il faut, donc, que nous nous entendions bien avant de nous prononcer l'un ou l'autre. J'apprends à l'instant que le pacte de famille est signé à Munich et à Athènes et qu'il est satisfaisant.

Mille et mille amitiés.

A. WALEWSKI.

P.S.—Le Prince marche de triomphes en triomphes. À son départ de Paris on criait : 'Vive Napoléon !' et un peu 'Vive l'Empereur !' à son retour il y aura un chorus unanime de 'Vive l'Empereur !' et 'Vive Napoléon III !'

*Lord Derby to Lord M.*

My dear Malmesbury,—I have received several notes from you which I have not answered, but I have attended to all the subjects to which they related, and have passed all your boxes. Stanley, who is here for three or four days, and returns on Tuesday, has brought me this morning the copy of your letter to the Prince on the subject of the Madiai[1] affair, in which I entirely concur. The Queen and Prince both spoke to me on the subject just before I left Balmoral. I had not then seen the papers, but I ventured to express my opinion that though undoubtedly it was a case which would justify an unofficial representation, it was not one in which we were entitled to interfere officially, or as of right; and I am fully of opinion that if there is any chance of obtaining a mitigation of the sentence, and a milder system for the future, private, rather than public, remonstrance and representation afford the best chance.

I am afraid, however, that chance is not a good one. The Grand Duke seems to have thrown himself body and soul into the hands of the *parti prêtre*; and John Russell hardly used too strong an expression when he said, two years ago, that there was in that body an organised conspiracy against the liberties of Europe. It is clear that Bulwer will do nothing at Rome; and the last declaration of Antonelli, that in the business of the Irish priests they could not take the initiative, inasmuch as it would be an interference with the affairs of another country, is a declaration which it must have been difficult even for an Italian cardinal to make with a grave face. It is the same party which is at work in Naples; but *there* we have got an irresistible case, and we must not only hold firm language and insist upon our rights, but, if need be, enforce them by the significant hint of the presence of our Mediterranean fleet in the Bay of Naples. I wish we had there a more energetic representative. I do not half like the attitude which France has assumed towards Belgium; and I fear that country being thrown into confusion by the recent defeat of the Government, again under the *parti prêtre* influence, backed up by France in secret—and, indeed, hardly in secret. If France invade Belgium on any quarrel arising out of the liberty of the Press, it is quite clear that we shall have no co-operation from Austria; and I do not like the tone, upon this subject, of the very last despatches, even from Russia. The *Empire* is fast approaching, but I conclude Louis Napoleon will give the assurances

---

[1] Imprisoned at Florence for proselytism.

required by the Northern Powers, that they will recognise him personally, and that he will be content, for the present, to drop the question
of *hérédité*.   Certainly in his case that question is not as pressing as in
the case of Greece, where I certainly think that Adalbert ought at once
to declare his acceptance of the succession on the condition of his
immediate adoption of the Greek faith, for himself, and not only for
his unborn children.   France, I am afraid, is playing an underhand
game in this matter, and intriguing with Bavaria ; though what she
has to gain by it is not so apparent. 'Her language and her actions
towards us, so far, have been perfectly friendly; but I cannot help
mistrusting Louis Napoleon's *patte de velours*, and we must continue to
make all ' snug ' at home, in case of a sudden outbreak.   On this subject I think it worth while sending you an extract from a letter I
received some days ago from Emerson Tennant, who has been at Paris,
and has necessarily been brought much into contact with Lord Hertford, on account of the borough of Lisburn.   He says : ' I have been
startled in my conversations with Lord Hertford to find the deep conviction on his mind of an intention on the part of Louis Napoleon to
attempt, ere long, some hostile movement against England.   Were it
any other Englishman speaking of French politics, I should attach less
importance to his repetition of mere *obiter dicta* ; but Lord Hertford
is himself more than half a Frenchman, and his intercourse with the
Court here most intimate.   He speaks to me, not naming Louis
Napoleon himself as his authority, but leaving me to infer that it can
be no other ; and he looks to such a movement against England, not
only as something longed for by the President, but as a thing that his
position is rendering every day more and more inevitable ; and that,
once the Empire is constructed, its excitement passed, and the fireworks burnt out, a landing on the shore of England will be forced
upon him by the aspirations of the French, the eagerness of the army,
and his own emergency.'   I should, of course, wish you to keep this
opinion of Tennant's secret.   The period to which he refers, when ' the
fireworks are burnt out,' will certainly have to be looked to with great
anxiety, for he will then want another *coup de théâtre* ; but if he
meditates any such project at present, I must give him credit for the
*most consummate* hypocrisy.

    I think our American affairs look well; but we have evidently got
the Yankees in hand, and the three-mile limit, which is what they
really want, is so clearly and absolutely ours, that negotiate they must,
sooner or later ; and in the meantime I have no doubt that the part
we have taken will do us good in our most important colonies, and will
have widened the breach between them and Jonathan, so as to afford

little apprehension on the annexation question. *If* we did go to war with them, however, which God forbid, I cannot say that I should look without uneasiness on the state of Canada. We have a large and undefended frontier, and I cannot but fear that recent events have greatly shaken the loyalty, more especially of the West Canadians, the first to be invaded and the most distant to be succoured. On the other hand, I have no doubt whatever of our immense maritime superiority; and I hope and believe that a large portion of British seamen, now in the United States service, would return to ours if a war were to break out between the two countries. Meanwhile, Crampton should certainly, without showing too great anxiety to effect a treaty which will be fully as beneficial to the United States as to us, manifest every readiness to come to terms which shall be mutually fair; and though I certainly should have preferred that the negotiations should have been conducted in London, I think you are right in not objecting to Washington, and even in giving Congress a *quasi veto* upon the terms agreed on.

I had not had occasion for your reminder on the subject of the Hants Lord-Lieutenancy, but immediately recommended Lord Winchester to the Queen, who approved of him; but having written for his direction, I learnt that he had gone to Germany, no one knowing where, and had left orders that all his letters were to be kept till his return, at his lodgings! I have, therefore, had no opportunity or means of communicating with him. If, however, he does not accept, you must take it; it would not do to offer it to Palmerston. The Queen had expected me to name you. I go to town the 12th or 13th, and we shall probably have a Council on Saturday, 16th. I cannot, therefore, let you remain much longer at Achnacarry, where, I am glad to hear, Lady M. is improving, though not, I fear, rapidly.

Ever yours sincerely,

DERBY.

### Lord M. to Lord Derby.

Achnacarry : October 8, 1852.

My dear Derby,—I was very glad to hear by your letter of the 3rd that you approved of what I had done respecting any interference in the Madiai case, and with regard to the pending negotiation with the United States. In the former matter Prince Albert's letter has already done some good, and moved the Grand Duke of Tuscany to a promise of future mercy.

I send you to-day a very satisfactory letter from Crampton. We have asserted our rights firmly and moderately, and placed ourselves in a much more advantageous position with the United States than we stood in before.

All you say about the French President's views has been for a long time on my mind. *Everybody* agrees with you, and the feeling of apprehension is universal. I hear it from various quarters—from Brougham and his French correspondents, from my private secretary Harris and his French relations, and, in short, from what must be considered the best authority for *prophecy*. This general terror of what is coming is a *presentiment*, for none can give any reasons founded on facts to show the sinister feelings and intentions of Louis Napoleon. I believe I stand alone, therefore, in disbelieving them ; and these are my arguments :—He has no natural dislike to the English. Ever since I knew him, he courted their society and imitated their habits. Twenty years ago, when he could not have been playing a part with me—who had even less chance of being Foreign Secretary than he of being Emperor—he always said that his uncle's great mistake was not being friends with England. I never knew him to hint at revenge for his degradation at St. Helena, but it is possible that that sentiment may rankle in his breast. Assuming that it does, and that eventually he intends if possible to indulge it, why should he go such a roundabout way to make war with us as through the Belgian Guarantee ? We are unfortunately bound by treaty and interest to protect Belgium and the Scheldt, and *must* do it. Russia, Austria, and Prussia are equally bound with us, and may, or may not, do it. Louis Napoleon knows all this, and that he runs the risk of bringing two, three, or four Powers upon him if he invades Belgium for the sake of quarrelling with England ; whereas, if he picked an independent quarrel with us— which he might easily do at Newfoundland, in Egypt, or about *our Press*—no Power is obliged by treaty, or likely by affection, to support us against him. It would be a single-handed fight, in which the spectators (with the exception of Russia and Belgium) would applaud him and pray for his success. Now, since Louis Napoleon has been in power, he has lost no opportunity of showing friendly feeling. If a Consul has been disagreeable, he has had him trounced ; if we wanted his help, as in Egypt and Cuba, he gave it at once. He has avoided pointedly every subject of dispute, and has with this feeling just expressed a wish again to negotiate for the exchange of the territories of Albreda and Portendie. So with regard to our tariff. If Disraeli was ready, we might now get a quasi free-trade treaty with France. The belief after all this that the President is concocting a great scheme against England can, therefore, only be called a *pressentiment* ; but it nevertheless does exist throughout his own country and ours. Material circumstances also militate against it. If our informers are correct, the French dockyards never were more sluggish. I write all this to you, not of course to recommend supineness, for I would not reduce a single ship or seaman, and I trust Disraeli's scheme will not require *that*, but only to give you my opinion of the man's nature, feelings, and intentions at present. I believe that he is convinced that war with England lost his uncle the throne, and that he *means* to try *peace* with us. He wants to marry and have heirs, and I do not at present see that the 7,000,000 who have twice elected him, and will do so again, require the 'fireworks.' The first time he was elected he did not know twenty people in all France by sight. The second, he had just committed a gross act of public violence. Neither his obscurity nor notoriety made any difference, and I believe his *name* to be enough to sustain him among the masses for *his* life, and I do not foresee the circumstances that are to force him out of his course. Enough, however, of that.

On Greece. I think the safest way will be to content ourselves with placing the 40th Act of the Constitution and the Treaty in unison, and leaving the rest to death. The Bavarian family then will not commit suicide when the present King dies. Walewski, speaking for his Government, only wants a Russian kept out. Russia may *know* that Adalbert will not now renounce his religion, and if so would press the question. My plan would prevent this.

Yours ever,<br>MALMESBURY.

*October* 14*th.*—Arrived in London from Achnacarry.

*October* 15*th.*—Saw Walewski on Greek Succession.

*October* 16*th.*—Cabinet. Settled Duke of Wellington's funeral for November 18. Parliament to meet November 4. I hear the enthusiasm shown for the President during his progress in the South of France surpasses that given to him at Strasburg. I heard a characteristic anecdote of him. When at one of the places through which he passed the bishop met and told him that he was adored, and that whereas there were many Socialists in the town who had Louis Blanc's picture in their houses, they now had Louis Napoleon's. 'Croyez-vous, Monseigneur,' replied the President, 'que tous ceux qui ont le portrait de la Vierge suspendu dans leurs maisons sont de bons Catholiques ?'

T

*October* 17*th.*—Saw Brünnow on Greek Succession. He was startled at my plan, which he said was new. Would give no answer. Tricoupi of course in favour. Cetto wanted the signatures of the Bavarian family compact to be introduced into the new treaty. My *projet* was intended to avoid this, as it would be self-acting.

*October* 18*th.*—Conference on Greek Succession. Brünnow and Walewski both adhered to my *projet*. After a discussion as to allowing the Bavarian to attend as an equal, Brünnow and I refused, as we are the three protecting Powers, and we knew Cetto would try to oppose my *projet*.

*October* 19*th.*—Macedo, Brazilian Minister, called. I told him the Government was not prepared to accept his proposed slave treaty yet, but when Brazil had proved a little longer her sincerity to suppress the slave trade we would do so, as I considered Lord Palmerston, in his zeal to destroy slavery, had taken a highhanded line by forcing Brazil to submit to a right of search within her own waters, and that nothing but necessity excused it.

Van de Weyer and Lavradio came to frighten me as to a French invasion and the annexation of Belgium, whose safety we have guaranteed.

Bunsen has told his Government an untruth by saying that their condolence for the Duke of Wellington's death was uncivilly received by us. I gave him my mind on this ill-natured fable.

I refused to join officially with Prussia in a remonstrance to Tuscany about the Madiai, who were imprisoned for proselytising, but we are using our unofficial influence as far as we can, and with success.

*October* 20*th.*—Cabinet. Disraeli's financial scheme.

*October* 21*st.*—Lord Derby inaugurated as Chancellor of Oxford. He made an excellent Latin speech.

*October* 22*nd.*—Cabinet. Discussed Highway Bill and transportation. Lundy Island suggested for the latter.

*October* 23*rd.*—Cetto refuses to adhere to Greek protocol without reference to Munich.

*October* 24*th.*—Went to St. Leonard's, near Windsor, which Lord Derby has hired. The Queen writes anxiously about the national defences. Universal apprehension of war if the French

Empire is proclaimed.   This panic is spread far and wide by King
Leopold, who has spoken to me repeatedly on the subject, and will
not believe that Louis Napoleon's policy at this time is to gain and
secure the alliance with England and consolidate his position with
the Great Powers by a pacific policy.   An attack on Belgium would
have the contrary effect, and I consider it out of the question.

*October 25th.*—Cabinet from 1 till 5.   Subject : national defences.   Duke of Northumberland asked for 4,000 more seamen.
Disraeli's Budget.   Nothing settled but the abolition of half the
malt tax.

*October 27th.*—Shooting with the Prince at Bagshot.   Queen
anxious about the Madiai, and her mind much occupied with
Louis Napoleon and the Empire.

*October 28th and 29th.*—Cabinets.   Local taxes discussed.
Disraeli wishes to abolish law of Poor Law Settlement, and make
county rates managed by a more popular board.

*October 30th.*—Bulwer writes to say Murray's life is saved.
He was condemned to death for murder by the Roman Court,
and his guilt as an accessory at least is undoubted.   Butenval,
French Minister at Turin, and Massimo d'Azeglio, Prime Minister,
quarrel.   Latter resigns.   Cavour succeeds.   Lavalette overbearing in Turkey.   I had to complain of him, and he is recalled.

French agents everywhere assume an arrogant tone.   Louis
Napoleon to us is all civility.   Statements are sent me of a plan
to invade England[1] (which Lord Raglan had received), and carry
off the Queen from Osborne by a *coup de main.*   Lord Hardinge
very anxious about the want of artillery, *the gun-carriages being
the same as those used at Waterloo, nearly forty years ago.*   Lord
Hardinge is made Commander-in-Chief by the Queen.   Saw
Mr. Newton, the victim of Verona, who was imprisoned for a
short time for sketching the fortifications.   An absurd young man
with a beard and a fancy hat, which are now the symbols of the
Communists.   He seemed to have no idea what compensation or
apology he ought to ask for.

*October 31st.*—Brünnow called to talk over 'the Empire' and

---

[1] I received several of these pseudo-plans, which were no doubt suggested, but
hardly seriously.   It is, however, true that Cavaignac believed it feasible in case
of a war with England.

Napoleon III. How are we to recognise his title ? I replied that
we should accept the President as Emperor *de facto in presente*,
and would not allude to hereditary chances, retrospective or future,
but leave those to the French people ; that I considered it absurd
at the moment we broke the treaties of our ancestors of 1815
respecting the Bonaparte family, thereby proving the short-sight-
edness of mortal prevision, we should again attempt to decide
for unborn generations, As to calling him Napoleon III. when
we had never recognised Napoleon II., it seemed absurd, inasmuch
as we accepted Charles X. and Louis Philippe during the life of
the Duc de Reichstadt. Russia will not recognise the Empire if
Louis Napoleon assumes the title of 'Protector of Eastern
Catholics.'

*November 1st.*—Cabinet upon title of Napoleon III. Massimo
d'Azeglio, who had resigned the Premiership of Sardinia, is reinstated. A. Fitzclarence, from Paris, says the army is peaceably
inclined, and that Mrs. Howard, the President's mistress, declares
he has no wish for war.

*November 2nd.*—Brünnow and Coloredo on the title of
Napoleon III. Dined at Walewski's. I tried to persuade him
what a mistake it was to assume a numeral that would make
difficulties. In six months his money, portraits, &c., would bear
the style of Napoleon III., and everybody would call him so ; but
to force us and the Great Powers to give the lie to history and
stultify ourselves as to everything we had done and recognised for
thirty-seven years seemed absurd. At first he flared up, said it
would be war to refuse it, but ended by admitting ' que j'avais
raison et qu'il donnerait mes conseils au Prince.'

*November 3rd.*—Austria declines sending officers to the Duke
of Wellington's funeral, so furious are they still at the attack made
upon Marshal Haynau in the streets of London.[1] Called on
Disraeli, just returned from Windsor. He had had a discussion
of two and a half hours with the Prince upon the national defences.
Disraeli, in very low spirits, said it would destroy his Budget, and
ridiculed the panic.

---

[1] He was accused of having had women flogged during the rebellion of 1848,
which, true or false, the mob in London believed, and when he went to see a brewery
he was attacked and insulted.

*November 4th.*—An article in the 'Morning Post' from its correspondent in Paris on the title of Napoleon III., retailing nearly every word of my last conversation with Walewski.

*November 5th.*—Sent for Walewski. He confessed that the French Government paid the 'Morning Post,' and that he saw Borthwick, the editor, every day.

I proposed that when Louis Napoleon announced the title we should recognise it with a 'protest' against his retrospective right to the throne.

*November 8th.*—Cabinet. Irish affairs. Tenant Right Bill appears to me to discourage any investment in Ireland. Agree to give back Napoleon's will to the French Government. Lord Derby writes an elaborate Memorandum upon the new titles of Louis Napoleon. One of the best papers I ever read. Addington and Mellish, the oldest and ablest *rédacteurs* at the Foreign Office, said that neither Canning nor Palmerston could have done the like, being written straight off without a single erasure in copper-plate hand.

*November 9th.*—The Queen sent for Lord Derby and me to Windsor, to talk over the Memorandum. Satisfied with it. I persuaded Lord Derby that my plan of the 'protest' was the best and safest way out of the difficulty now that Napoleon III. was a *fait accompli*, and that the Senate had declared that he had an hereditary claim to the crown.

Mr. Newton, the Verona victim, called. He admitted that when he arrived at his own home his hat and his beard had so changed him that his own mother did not know him. No wonder that with these revolutionary appendages the Croatian sentry arrested him.

*November 11th.*—Parliament opened. The Russian Generals Gortschakoff and Benckendorf present. No amendment to the Speech moved in either House. Lord Derby declared his compulsory adherence to Free Trade, as did Disraeli in the Commons. Gladstone and the Peelites very bitter.

*November 12th.*—Heard from Lord Cowley that Louis Napoleon had sent for him, and stated that he did not consider his empire hereditary retrospectively for the following reasons :—

First, If he did, he would have called himself Napoleon V.,

because both his elder uncle Joseph and his father Louis outlived the Duc de Reichstadt.

Secondly.  Because, if he had considered himself hereditary, he would not have required an election.

Thirdly.  That, if hereditary, he would have dated his reign from his cousin's or father's death.

Walewski repeated this argument to me.  Disraeli in very low spirits at the demand for additional expenses for army and navy.

Palmerston supposed to have joined the Peelites.  I went to see the Duke of Wellington lie in state at Chelsea.

*November* 13*th*.—Cabinet.  Colonial affairs.  Several persons killed in the crowd at Chelsea.  Sent for to Windsor.  Lodged in the Round Tower, next door to Brünnow and Prince Gortschakoff, who was an inveterate smoker, and was thus kept at a distance.  He was dressed, I believe for the first time in his life, *en bourgeois*, in an evening suit, in which he felt miserable.  But Brünnow insisted on it.  Not having his jack-boots on, but pumps, he slipped up on his way to dinner, and rolled some way down the Tower staircase, but without any damage to his gaunt and iron frame.  The Duke of Brabant dined ; very uneasy at Louis Napoleon's elevation.  Long conversation with the Prince on national defences.  Agreed with him we should want 2,000 artillerymen, 1,000 horses, and 5,000 seamen, which would be a permanent additional expense of 230,000*l.* a year.

*November* 15*th*.—Saw Disraeli and Lord Derby on national defences.

A great number of ladies and gentlemen had tickets to view the preparations at St. Paul's for the funeral.  Among them were Lady Jersey, Lady Clementina Villiers, Lady V. Talbot, Lady Chesterfield, Mrs. Anson, Lady Derby, Lady E. Stanley, Lady Ailesbury, &c.  It was like an evening party.  All in black, except Lady ——, who was in pink, and Lady —— in a *grenat* velvet and blue bonnet.

*November* 16*th*.—Twenty-seven foreign officers are arrived as deputations from all the European Courts.  Walewski was coquetting about attending the funeral, and asked Brünnow whether he thought that, as a Frenchman, he ought to do so, to which Brünnow

replied : ' Mon cher, si nous allions *ressusciter* ce pauvre duc, je
comprends que vous pourriez vous dispenser d'assister à cette
cérémonie ; mais, puisque nous sommes invités pour l'*enterrer*, il
me semble que vous pouvez, vous, en faire votre deuil.' Walewski
had positive orders to attend the funeral from Louis Napoleon,
who spoke with great respect of the Duke.

*November 17th.*—Nesselrode wrote to Brünnow, proposing
exactly what I did to the Cabinet—namely, that a protest should
be made against the numeral inferring any hereditary right.

*November 18th.*—Duke's funeral. I started for the place of
rendezvous, St. James's Park, at 8 A.M. A dreary morning, and
raining. The signal-gun fired at a quarter to nine, and at the
same moment the sun broke out for the first time since last month.
The weather had been awful, and the whole country is deluged.
All the Corps Diplomatique present at St. Paul's except Brünnow,
who shammed ill for fear of a row.

The *cortège* proceeded up the Mall and Constitution Hill
through a countless mass of silent people, almost all in deep
black, passing Buckingham Palace, where the Queen and Prince
stood on the balcony in deep mourning, then turned down
Piccadilly, straight to St. Paul's. The Ministers in their carriages followed. The streets were lined with troops, and no one
can forget the solemn silence and unbroken order that prevailed
throughout this long route. On arriving at St. Paul's, which was
completely full from the pavement to the roof, the same order
prevailed. Round the entrance of the vault sat the Corps
Diplomatique, the deputations of foreign officers, the Duke's old
generals, Lords Anglesea, Hardinge, Napier, and his other
companions in arms, also the distinguished officers of the navy,
like Sir George Cockburn, and members of Parliament of both
Houses and both parties. Anthems by Handel were played, the
words of one of which were, ' His body is buried in peace, his
soul liveth for evermore,' accompanied, it is said, by 2,000 voices.
When they turned over the leaves of their music-books, which
they did simultaneously, it sounded like a sudden blast of wind.
Lord Douro, as chief mourner, stood at the entrance of the vault,
while the guns, fired from different parts of London, saluted the
descent of the coffin. The emotion produced upon all was the

same, and unchecked tears rolled down the cheeks of the oldest veteran.

> Such honours Ilion to her hero paid,
> And peaceful slept the mighty Hector's shade,

*November* 20*th.*—We signed, at my house in Whitehall Gardens, the treaty of the Greek Succession after a tiresome wrangle with Cetto. He signed *sub spe rata*, and put in a foolish declaration, which Tricoupi answered. Both were added to the documents, and are valueless paper. Brünnow said to me afterwards, ' Cetto is so toff,' meaning 'tough.' I received twenty-seven foreign officers at dinner, together with Lord Anglesea, Sir H. Smith, Lord Hardinge, Lord Gough, Lords Derby, Cowley, and Westmoreland, &c. Three hundred cannon were planted at Cherbourg and thirty at Granville last week.

*November* 21*st.*—Our party alarmed, and, to the amount of seventy, they refused to vote for Disraeli's amendment on Mr. Villiers' [1] motion (Free Trade). Disraeli's amendment renounces Protection ; but as the first division will be against Villiers' words, and they will stand by us on that, it signifies nothing, provided they do not absent themselves.

> *Lord M. to Sir Hamilton Seymour, H.M. Minister at*
> *St. Petersburg.*
>
> Foreign Office: November 21, 1852.

My dear Sir Hamilton,—I take this chance opportunity of sending you a line.

Cowley is come over and considers Louis Napoleon's conversation to him respecting the meaning of the numeral III. as perfectly *official.* Louis Napoleon twice stated two most important principles—1st. That he acknowledged all the acts which had taken place since 1815, such as the reigns of the elder Bourbons and of Louis Philippe ; 2nd. That he laid no claim to *hereditary* right to the throne of France, but only to that by election.

I understand that there will be no special ambassador, but that the notification will be made at the respective Courts.

---

[1] If any one deserves the credit of ably defending Free Trade in Parliament and of being the first to agitate for it, it is the Hon. C. Villiers, although Cobden has been somewhat unfairly held up as its first champion.

Brünnow does not like our (nearly) fixed intention of recognising Napoleon III. under this officially declared interpretation of the numeral. Of course it must be more solemnly and officially declared than it has yet been. Our William III. is a case in point; the *third* of that name acknowledged by the English, but no descendant of William Rufus.

Brünnow had a cold in his head on the day of the funeral, and did not attend it. The truth is, he thought there might be a crush, during which some refugee Pole might insult his person.

.     .     .     .     .     .     .     .     .

We signed the Greek Treaty yesterday. Cetto's nose was brought to the grindstone, and he was two hours under the operation, *la peine forte et dure*, before he released us from a torture worse than his own.

Yours truly,

MALMESBURY.

*November 22nd.*—Went to Windsor. Dined sixty-eight in Waterloo Gallery. All the foreign officers and the principal English generals. Lord John Russell has sent to Lord Hardinge to say he would support the Government on the subject of national defences.

*November 24th.*—Wrote to Lord Derby on national defences. We went to Windsor. Conversation on state of affairs and reforming Lord Derby's Cabinet. He was of opinion that he could not do without Palmerston, Gladstone, and Sidney Herbert. Lonsdale and Hardwicke were ready to resign and make room.

*November 25th.*—Lord Derby had full power from the Queen to arrange a Government and fusion on two conditions—namely, that Palmerston was not to lead the Commons. He had been last night with Disraeli and said he had nothing to do with the Peelites. They declare through Lord Jocelyn that they will go with Palmerston if he is leader of the House of Commons. No one to negotiate with.

*November 27th.*—Privy Council at Windsor. The Queen pleased at our vote of 5,000 seamen, 1,500 marines, 2,000 artillery. Great dinner and party at Lord Derby's for foreign officers. Russian despatches arrive of 20th. They accept the Empire, but reject the numeral.

*November 28th.*—Saw Lord Derby. He averse to letting

Palmerston into Cabinet alone. I think him wrong. If he, Gladstone, and Herbert came into it, he would be overwhelmed in the Commons by this portion of the Cabinet. Nor would I object to Palmerston and Herbert. I cannot make out Gladstone, who seems to me a dark horse.

*November* 29*th.*—I told Walewski what instructions I had given Cowley about the title of Napoleon III. He said, with much excitement, that the French Government never would give the assurances in *writing.* Walewski spoke of condescension in their replying. I said we had a right to ask questions, and if they were not answered we should take the same line as the other Powers. He ended by suggesting that either Drouyn de l'Huys could read my despatch and declare to Lord Cowley that he recognised the verbal assurances there described verbally, or make his (Walewski's) *note verbale officielle.* I said the first would not do, but the latter might.

The Russian despatches show that the Emperor Nicholas is very much caught by Louis Napoleon's character, and that Brünnow and Nesselrode have prevented him from recognising him at once.

A great dinner to the foreign officers given at the United Service Club. Gortschakoff made a racy military speech, which, after a panegyric on the Duke of Wellington, ended thus : ' Vive cette armée qui a combattu avec lui ! Vive cette belle marine qui a nettoyé son chemin, et aidé ses efforts ! Mais, avant tout, vive la vieille et glorieuse Angleterre ! '

This last sentiment, which he declaimed in a voice of thunder, was electrical.[1]

*Lord M. to Lord Cowley, H.M. Ambassador at Paris.*

Foreign Office : November 29, 1852.

My dear Lord Cowley,—I have received your note, and, to be as explicit as possible, I again write to you to say that we *must* have the explanations in *writing.* If you find Drouyn de l'Huys will not give an amplified statement similar to the *note verbale,* we may, I think, be satisfied by his mere adhesion to the statements made by the President

---

[1] Just two years after, we were at war with Russia, and that same Gortschakoff was holding Sebastopol against us with the most obstinate courage and skill.

and Walewski, which are recapitulated, or alluded to, in my despatch of this day. These statements you will repeat *at length* in the note which you will send in to him—namely, the three reasons given to you and me, and the words, *original* and *additional*, which I quote from the *note verbale*.

To your note Drouyn de l'Huys must reply. He has only to say that he officially confirms the language used to us verbally and cited in your note, and he need make no observation on ours respecting Napoleon III.

If you tell him this privately before you send the note in, I think they cannot but be satisfied at being let down so easily.

Yours truly,

MALMESBURY.

*Lord M. to Lord Cowley, H.M. Ambassador at Paris.*

Foreign Office : November 29, 1852.

My dear Lord Cowley,—Walewski, after an unsuccessful attempt to see me, at last waylaid me on my way to the House, so I was obliged to have a conversation with him. It has not been satisfactory, and will be sent to Drouyn de l'Huys before you see him. Walewski began by saying that Kisseleff had seen Drouyn de l'Huys, and had agreed to everything, although he said he had no instructions respecting the title. Yet, according to Walewski, he did not object to that. This brought on the subject of Napoleon III., and Walewski said we should have the notification here on Thursday morning, that it would be made to you Wednesday evening, and to him by that night's mail. He then urged me to send you instructions accordingly, and asked me what I should say. I stated to him the tenour of my despatch, upon which he declared that he did not believe that Drouyn de l'Huys would exchange notes formally or even *write* you an answer to a despatch inquiring of him whether he confirmed officially the substance of the *note verbale* and the assurances of the Ambassador. He spoke of the explanation as a condescension, and I was obliged to tell him that we had a right to ask the meaning of the cypher, and that we considered it more important than any assurance of peace and order which he might make ; and that, if they meant to be 'loyal,' I could not understand their objection to *write* what they were ready to *say*. He suggested that you should lay my version of our conversation before Drouyn de l'Huys, and that he should verbally assure you that it was correct and recognised by him, and that your account to me of this transaction would be a voucher sufficient for Parliament. As he found

I was not satisfied, he ended by stating that he thought Drouyn de l'Huys *would consent to making the* note verbale *an official document* (as annexed to this letter).   It appears to me that this would be sufficient if done in the proper diplomatic form.   Walewski evidently seemed to think a formal note almost impossible, because he states we have no right to ask a question which relates to the *internal* arrangements of France—as he pretends the title does !

> .        .        .        .        .        .

   If Drouyn de l'Huys refuses either to *write* an acknowledgment of the substance of the *note verbale*, or to endow it bodily with an official character, you will tell him that you must refer to your Court for further instructions; but that, if he does one of these two things, her Majesty's Government will receive the notification without further remarks than those of cordial amity.        Yours truly,
                                        MALMESBURY.

   *December 1st.*—Cowley has failed to get a written assurance upon the cypher III.   If he does not do so, I shall state the conversations of the President and Walewski to Parliament.

   Disraeli much annoyed at the panic.   Walewski came at one o'clock to notify the Empire.

   *December 2nd.*—Cabinet.   Budget settled.   Malt duty reduced one-half.   Tea duties 4*d.* per pound.   Light dues and salvage taken off.   Income tax extended and modified.   House tax doubled and extended.   600,000*l.* to be the supplementary estimate for national defences.   French Government gives *a written assurance of their interpretation of Napoleon III.   Emperor repeats it in his speech to the Senate.*

   *December 3rd.*—Disraeli moves his Budget.   Well received He spoke five hours and a quarter, and brilliantly.

### Lord M. to the Queen.

Foreign Office : December 3, 1852.

   Lord Malmesbury presents his humble duty to the Queen.   Your Majesty will have learnt with satisfaction that Lord Cowley has obtained a formal and written acknowledgment from the French Secretary of State of the explanations given verbally by him and the French Ambassador to your Majesty's servants.   This demand on the part of your Majesty's Government having been complied with, they determined, at a Cabinet Council which they held yesterday, to advise your Majesty to recognise the new Empire and Emperor without further reserve. Count Walewski has brought to Lord Malmesbury the notification of these facts, and Lord Malmesbury respectfully submits to your Majesty two drafts, one being a reply to this notification, and the other for Lord Cowley's credentials. Should they meet with your Majesty's approbation, both will be forwarded immediately.

*December 4th.*—Official recognition of French Empire.

*Lord M. to Lord Cowley, H.M. Ambassador at Paris.*

Foreign Office : December 4, 1852.

My dear Lord Cowley,—We are much obliged to you for the manner in which you have brought the thorny question of the numeral to a successful issue. Your conversation with the Emperor was very curious respecting his naval armaments. If we keep 10,000 good seamen always in the Channel I do not care what he does in that line. . . . You may assure the Emperor that we hail with sincere satisfaction the language which he and his Ministers have held to us, both as regards the title he has assumed and his future policy, and the Queen expressed herself much pleased at his speech to the legislative bodies.

The Great Powers seem determined to refuse him the numeral. It is with them, especially with Russia and Austria, a personal question.    Yours truly,

MALMESBURY.

*December 6th.*—Debate on Free Trade, and resolutions in House of Lords. Budget in the Commons. I announced the recognition of the Empire, and was attacked by Lord Canning for commenting upon it favourably. Like all Peelites, he is most bitter against me. They have got it into their heads, most absurdly and erroneously, that I was the principal in causing Lord Derby's secession from them in 1846. Nor do they forgive my sudden elevation to Cabinet office without having ever previously laboured as they have done through preparatory grades.

*December 9th.*—Went to Osborne to present the Walewskis and *his* new credentials. Prince still very eager on army and navy.

*December 11th.*—Lord Derby and Disraeli agreed to resign if beaten on house tax.

*December 12th.*—Saw Disraeli. Our opinion is that he must give up doubling the house tax, and halving the malt tax.

*December 13th.*—Walewski came to ask the hand of the Princess Adelaide of Hohenlohe in marriage for the Emperor. I had foreseen this, and told the Queen. Walewski said the Emperor's marriage with the Princess Wasa was off. He blamed the disputes of France with Russia about the *Lieux Saints* in Palestine.

*December 14th.*—Debate on Budget still raging in the Commons. Lord Derby announces in the House of Lords that he shall resign if beaten.

Conversation with Walewski about Cuba and American disclosures thereon. In 1849 they offered 100,000,000 dollars for it to Spain. We and France have offered to renounce our possession of Cuba for ever if the United States will agree to do likewise. As yet they refuse.

*December 16th.*—Carini, Neapolitan Minister, called about the schoolmaster Hamilton's case, whose school was closed by the Neapolitan Government. He told me to name a sum of compensation, and agreed to 100*l.*, which satisfied Mr. Hamilton. Great excitement about the division of to-night, which settles the fate of our Ministry.

*December 17th.*—We are beaten on the Budget by a majority of 19—305 to 286. Disraeli made a magnificent speech. The Peelites number forty-six only in the Commons. Lord Derby went to Osborne to the Queen. I adjourned the House of Lords till Monday. The general conviction is that the Peelites and Whigs have coalesced.

*December 18th.*—Lord Derby came back from Osborne. The Queen had told him to send Lord Aberdeen as well as Lord Lansdowne, and they went down; the Prince observing that, constitutionally speaking, it was not necessary he should recommend any one. The Queen asked who was likely to form a Government, and Lord Derby told her Lord Aberdeen had, he believed, coalesced with the Whigs and was ready to be Prime Minister. The Queen objected to the idea of Lord Canning being Foreign Secretary, no doubt partly in consequence of his anti-Bonapartist speech when I announced the Empire, which at this moment would be an awkward introduction.    The House of Commons is now composed thus :—

| | |
|---|---|
| Derbyites . . . . . . . | 292 |
| Peelites . . . . . . . | 30 |
| Whigs . . . . . . . | 130 |
| Radicals . . . . . . . | 160 |
| Irish Brigade . . . . . . | 50 |
| In round numbers . . . | 662 |

*December 19th.*—Brünnow called.    Disturbed about the question of the Holy Places in Palestine between the Russians and French.    Turks in despair between the two combatants.    He paid his farewell compliments and observed, with apparent pleasure, that we had never had a disagreeable discussion.    He is undoubtedly the most able of the Diplomatic Corps and a first-rate *rédacteur.*

Coloredo, who afterwards came, spoke in a similar sense, and I value his remarks, as he is a gentleman in every sense of the word.

Lord Aberdeen went down alone to the Queen to-day, as Lord Lansdowne was too ill.    The coalition is said to be complete.

*Lord M. to Lord Cowley, H.M. Ambassador at Paris.*

Foreign Office, December 20, 1852.

My dear Cowley,—The new Government are so much involved in difficulty that I am likely to be Foreign Secretary for a week longer, at least, and under these circumstances I must beg of you to do all you can to show Drouyn de l'Huys that the Holy Places question, if roughly handled, is one that may bring on trouble and war.    It is one of those points upon which the moral power of the Emperor of Russia rests, and I can as much believe that he would give up the despotic principle by having a Russian House of Commons as surrender his prestige over the populations of the Greek faith by any appearance of cession on this claim.    It is giving Russia an opportunity of bullying and degrading the Porte, and when she thinks she is losing ground at Jerusalem, she tries *de se rattraper* in some other place like Montenegro. The Emperor has done quite enough to satisfy the *parti prêtre* without taking up the cause of a minority like the Latins in the East. Perhaps at Compiègne you might have an opportunity of giving him my opinion, which is in his interest.        Yours truly,

MALMESBURY.

*December 20th.*—A meeting of the party at Lord Derby's—about 150 Lords and Commons. He addressed them with great effect, promising to continue to lead them, deprecating faction, recommending union. Lord Aberdeen has asked for a week to form his Government.

*December 21st.*—Great difficulties in forming a Government. Palmerston refused Aberdeen, who went to him. Lord John Russell is to give his conditions to-night. Clarendon to be Foreign Secretary if the coalition succeeds.

*December 22nd.*—They are much disconcerted at Palmerston's refusal. Walewski, whom I saw at his house, told me the Emperor meant to ask for the Princess Adelaide's hand from her father.

Everyone must appreciate the pleasure—*laudari a laudato viro*—which is my excuse for quoting Lord Derby's speech in my praise in the House of Lords on the 20th :—' My Lords, I have no hesitation in saying with respect to the foreign affairs of the country that we leave them in a much more satisfactory condition than when we acceded to office—that our foreign relations are far more friendly and satisfactory than when my noble friend the Foreign Secretary received the charge of his department. I rejoice in having this opportunity of bearing my testimony in reference to one man than whom no person has been more unsparingly, and, I will venture to say, more unjustly maligned, and of stating that from the first to the last I have had no cause for anything but self-congratulation in having obtained in the Foreign Department the services of one who, without previous political experience, has brought to bear a diligence, ability, and good judgment on the affairs of that great department which reflect the highest credit on himself, and which, I may venture to say without fear of contradiction, have extorted the applause and admiration of old and experienced diplomatists, whose views on more than one occasion he has combated, and successfully combated.' This generous compliment, so publicly made, more than compensates me for the excessive abuse which I have from first to last received from a 'ribald press.' The expression is not mine, but that of Lord John Russell.

*December 24th.*—Cabinet formed as follows :—

| | |
|---|---|
| Lord Chancellor . . . . | Lord Cranworth. |
| Prime Minister . . . . | Lord Aberdeen. |
| President of the Council . . | Lord Granville. |
| Privy Seal . . . . . | Duke of Argyll. |
| Foreign Secretary . . . | Lord John Russell. |
| Home Secretary . . . | Lord Palmerston. |
| Colonial Secretary . . . | Duke of Newcastle. |
| Admiralty . . . . . | Sir James Graham. |
| War Secretary . . . . | Mr. Sidney Herbert |
| Chancellor of the Exchequer . | Mr. Gladstone. |
| Without office . . . . | Lord Lansdowne. |
| Woods and Forests . . . | Sir W. Molesworth. |

*December 26th.*—It is said that Lord Palmerston joined Lord Aberdeen's Government in consequence of a letter from the Queen asking him to do so. The general opinion is that, without him, the Peelites could not have formed one.

*December 27th.*—Lord John Russell called on me, as is the custom, in the morning, to know the *status quo* of our foreign affairs.

*December 28th.*—I went to Windsor with the rest ·of my colleagues (except Lord Derby, who took leave of the Queen last Sunday) to give up the seals. Her Majesty gave me an audience of half an hour, and was very gracious. Lord John had said to Walewski about Lord Derby : 'C'est une gloire pour Lord Derby d'avoir gouverné le pays comme il l'a fait ces derniers dix mois. Nous avons trouvé tout en meilleur état que quand nous l'avons laissé.' The Queen told the Chancellor she was sorry to lose his services. When I went into the room her Majesty began on the subject of the proposed marriage of her niece.

The Prince read a letter from Prince Hohenlohe on the subject, which amounted to this, that he was not sure of the settlement being satisfactory, and that there were objections of religion and morals. The Queen and Prince talked of the marriage

U

reasonably, and weighed the *pros* and *cons*. Afraid the Princess should be dazzled if she heard of the offer. I said I knew an offer would be made to the father. Walewski would go himself. The Queen alluded to the fate of all the wives of the rulers of France since 1789,[1] but did not positively object to the marriage.

*December 29th.*—We went to Heron Court. Whole country under water. Lord Cowley relates a curious anecdote as to the origin of the numeral III. in the Emperor's title. The Prefect of Bourges, where he slept the first night of his progress, had given instructions that the people were to shout ' Vive Napoléon ! ' but he wrote ' Vive Napoléon ! ! ! ' The people took the three notes of interjection as a numeral. The President, on hearing it, sent the Duc de Mortemart to the Prefect to know what the cry meant. When the whole thing was explained the President, tapping the Duke on the shoulder, said : 'Je ne savais pas que j'avais un Préfet Machiavelliste.' I hear the new Emperor's civil list is to be 25,000,000 francs (1,000,000*l*.), and all the palaces, which he is to keep up. He now talks of making Jerome Governor of Algeria, but this is opposed by St. Arnaud and the Ministers.

Some one said to Berryer : 'Louis Napoléon veut faire le lit de Henri IV.' 'Au moins,' replied Berryer, 'il ne lui manquera pas de paillasses.'

*From S.E. Baron Brünnow, Russian Ambassador, to Lord M.*

Chesham Place : 30 décembre, 1852.

Cher Lord Malmesbury,—Je vous ai manqué hier matin de cinq minutes en passant chez vous pour vous remercier de votre aimable billet qu'on venait de me remettre de votre part. Il a été pour moi une nouvelle preuve d'amitié dont je vous suis bien reconnaissant. Permettez-moi de saisir encore cette occasion pour vous dire de nouveau combien j'ai eu à me féliciter de nos bons rapports durant votre ministère, dont je garderai le souvenir le plus agréable et le plus reconnaissant.                    Votre très-dévoué,

BRÜNNOW.

[1] A prophetic presentiment.

# 1853

*Count Nesselrode to Sir H. Seymour after Lord Derby's
Resignation.*

St.-Pétersbourg : 1 janvier, 1853.

Voici, mon cher Sir Hamilton, une lettre que je me permets de
recommander à vos soins obligeants.   C'est une réponse et un adieu
que je fais à Lord Derby.   Ne m'étant pas trouvé dans des relations
personnelles semblables avec Lord Malmesbury, j'éprouve néanmoins
le besoin de lui dire combien j'ai su apprécier les dispositions obligeantes,
ainsi que les facilités que nous avons trouvées en lui dans toutes les
affaires que nous avons eu à traiter avec votre gouvernement sous son
ministère.   Veuillez vous charger, mon cher Sir Hamilton, d'être
l'interprète de ces sentiments auprès de Lord Malmesbury.

Mille amitiés et hommages,

NESSELRODE.

*Sir G. H. Seymour, H.M. Ambassador at St. Petersburg,
to Lord M.*

St. Petersburg : January 13, 1853.

My dear Lord Malmesbury,—The enclosed letters will show you
exactly on what terms you part with Count Nesselrode—as he writes,
so he always speaks of you.

If you collect autographs, you may perhaps like to keep the writing
of a man who belongs to a class of Ministers becoming, alas! very
scarce.   He is about the last of his class.

Believe me, &c.,

G. H. SEYMOUR.

*January 3rd, Heron Court.*—Lords Anson, Tankerville, and
Stanley, and Colonel Blair [1] came.   Gladstone standing for
Oxford.

*Sir G. H. Seymour to Lord M.*

St. Petersburg : January 7, 1853.

My dear Lord Malmesbury,—I feel very much obliged to you for
your letter of December 26, and for the kind assurance you give me of

[1] Killed at Inkerman.

my having been one of the number of 'our correspondents' whose reports were of some use during the time that you directed our Foreign Affairs.

On my side I can assure you that I am pretty sensible of the attention and kindness which I have met with at your hands, and that I can well understand your being satisfied with the success of your diplomatic existence.

Of others I cannot speak—of myself I can, and with full *connaissance de cause*. Now this much I know, that I have passed thirty-six years in diplomatic exercise, that I am not troubled with weak nerves, and that, notwithstanding these two advantages, I would not undertake the office which you have been conducting—no, not for ten days—and not for any consideration that could be offered. The reason why, I, perhaps, should do well to withhold, but I like being frank, and here it is. I would not attempt to do what you have been doing, because before the ten days were over other people would discover that of which I am already aware.

Be you in or be you out of Downing Street, believe me, &c.

G. H. SEYMOUR.

*January 8th.*—Gladstone has a majority of 56 at Oxford.

*January 18th.*—My brother, Captain Harris, has exchanged ...... Lima, to which I had appointed him, for Chili.

*January 19th.*—I left for London, Hatfield, and Knowsley. Duchess of Sutherland made Mistress of the Robes.

*January 22nd.*—The Emperor's marriage with Mdlle. de Montijo is quite settled, and is to take place at Notre Dame on the 29th.

*Mr. Disraeli to Lord M.*

G. Gate: January 24, 1853.

My dear M.,—It is said that everything depends on a great muster at the Captain's on the morning of the 31st. A great muster will be better for us at this moment than a great division.

To ensure this, all his men ought to be asked to dine with him. He has offered only three dinners; the cards are out, they will only include ninety of his followers. There wanted nine dinners. The cards should all be out; if the dinners took place a month hence it would not matter. What they want is to be asked to their leader's, and to have their cards meeting them on their arrival in town.

You must remember this is a new Parliament, full of *new men who have never entered his house,* for last year *he gave no dinners at all,* from domestic circumstances.

Those who understand these things have all been to me to say, how critical this is; every man who is not asked is offended. I cannot mention these matters to him; you are the only person who can.

Lord Salisbury[1] also should be asked to invite the men. His dinners last year did great good, when our fortunes were darkest.

I have given the 'Press' another 500*l.*, which will keep them till the end of March; during the interval, we must consult as to the course we ought to pursue. The sale increases greatly, and its influence: but the expenses do not much diminish. You had better keep the subscriptions you have received till we meet and consult over this.

The enclosed will show you that the *actual sale* has increased six hundred per week since I left Hughenden in November.

Yours,<br>D.

*January 29th.*—Returned to Heron Court. We have had great shooting at Knowsley.

*January 31st.*—Lord Anson and Mr. Bentinck arrived; we three went out duck-shooting on the Moor's river, and killed 166 teal. I record this feat because I believe it to be unequalled with three ordinary guns. They were in thousands after a long flood throughout November and December.

From the Emperor Napoleon to Lord Malmesbury.

Aux Tuileries : le 7 février 1853.

Mon cher Lord Malmesbury,—Je ne veux pas laisser partir le Comte Walewski, sans le charger pour vous d'un petit mot pour vous exprimer ma reconnaissance pour tous les bons procédés que vous avez eus pour moi pendant votre passage aux affaires; combien je vous ai regretté, ainsi que vos collègues. Néanmoins, je pense que tous les hommes de bon sens comprendront comme vous (et les nouveaux ministres m'en ont déjà donné des preuves) que mon désir le plus fervent est de maintenir avec votre pays, que j'ai toujours tant aimé, les relations les plus amicales et les plus intimes.

Recevez, mon cher Lord Malmesbury, l'assurance de ma sincère amitié.

NAPOLÉON.

---

[1] This Marquis of Salisbury died 1868.

*February 7th.*—Austria sends Count de Leiningen to the Sultan to force him to evacuate Montenegro, which he does with great loss. Other humiliating demands are made. The Emperor Nicholas follows in his wake, and sends Prince Menschikoff to claim full authority over the Holy Places, over which Lavalette, the French Ambassador, had assumed partial privileges and protectorship for the Latin Church.

*February 10th.*—I went up for the meeting of Parliament.

*February 11th.*—Parliament met. Lord Aberdeen made a weak speech in the House of Lords, refusing to give any information as to his future measures. Lord John, in the Commons, announced that Reform was given up for this session, and the income tax would be continued for a year as it is at present. Disraeli gave notice that next Monday he would ask Sir Charles Wood whether the report of his speech at Halifax, so abusive of Louis Napoleon, is correct.

*February 12th.*—Very heavy fall of snow. Returned to Heron Court.

*Lord M. to Louis Napoleon.*

Heron Court : February 15, 1853.

Sir,—I hasten to acknowledge to your Majesty the sincere pleasure with which I received the honour of your Majesty's kind letter. When I left office, the experience I had there gained of foreign affairs had impressed me with the deepest conviction that the respective interests of England and France, and the general happiness of the European populations, depend mainly on the friendly alliance of our two countries, and that as long as such an alliance exists they are both all-powerful.

It therefore gave me the greatest satisfaction to learn from Lord John Russell's own lips, that he was most anxious to maintain, as regards your Majesty, the same policy which I had considered it my duty and a pleasure to follow.

I have the honour, &c., &c.

MALMESBURY.

*February 23rd.*—Lord Anson arrived. He had scarcely entered the house when an extraordinary tornado suddenly took place, lasting only about five minutes, but its violence was such that I expected the roof to be blown off. The thermometer went

down ten degrees in that time. The weather had been perfectly
calm and mild all day up to the moment when this gust arose.
It did great damage, cutting, as it were, a narrow lane through
the woods of about fifty yards wide, and destroying everything
before it.

*February and March.*—An attempt has been made on the
Emperor of Austria's life by a refugee, and the Austrians' hatred
to us has increased to such a degree that Count Buol has been
obliged to send a police force to Lord Westmoreland's, our
Ambassador's, house to protect him from the mob.

*March 7th.*—I went to London. An outbreak has taken place
at Milan, repressed with great rigour and cruelty. The Ticinese
Swiss, to the number of some thousands, are expelled from
Lombardy. Mazzini not to be found. His always escaping the
foreign police is very suspicious. He left England on January 2,
four days after Lord Derby's Government resigned. He is said
to be very clever at disguises ; but I can hardly understand it, as
I met him at Madame Parodi's, and he is more terribly marked
with the smallpox than any one I ever saw, with piercing black
eyes, and much resembling Ugolino Foscolo.

*G. Harris to Lord M.*

Vienna: March 14, 1853.

My dear Fitz,—Perhaps you may not dislike to hear a *can-can* or
two from the Chancellerie of H.M. Legation here.

It appears that Manteuffel made a most insolent demand (insolent
*au fond*, not *quant à la forme*)—viz. that our Foreign Office passports
should give the personal description of the bearers. Lord Clarendon,
in reply, refuses most peremptorily, amongst many obvious reasons for
this one, that we are not to be dictated to by foreign Powers as to the
form of our passports or anything else ; the reply in question is evidently Mellish's, and is a stinger.

Lord Westmoreland told me this morning, and I hear the same
from everyone else, that the irritation against England is now *au
comble*. The Austrians impute everything outrageous and absurd to
us ; and the revolutionary partisans profess to expect everything from
England. His lordship said he had received this very day a despatch

from Lord Clarendon, authorising him to make use of the *very strongest language* to express the indignation of her Majesty's Government that the refugees should abuse the hospitality of England, and should direct from London their manifestoes, conspiracies, &c., that (the old, old story) our laws were such and such, and our hands as a Government were tied within those laws ; lastly, and not least, 'that the Imperial Government must not suppose that the sensible and honest portion of the people of England felt anything else but abhorrence and disgust at the conduct of these conspirators and their agents.'

Several Englishmen have assured me they have been treated lately in travelling in Hungary and Bohemia with *marked civility*. I can say the same for myself, from the moment I crossed the frontier the other side of Prague. The *employés* of the rail and Custom House never opened a portmanteau or anything else, and to the natives and other travellers I observed that they *did*.

I have not yet obtained my *exequatur*. Lord Westmoreland says it will be three weeks before it follows me to Venice ; and yet, if he chose to press the matter on Buol, the thing would be done in an instant. Lord Westmoreland is too *bon* for Buol and Co. I go on to-morrow to Trieste, and shall make myself comfortable at Venice *en attendant*.

The Emperor's illness threw all the public business on its beam ends. His Majesty is the War Minister, going through all that frightful routine himself; the accumulation of papers was such at the end of a week that they invented the *alter ego*, the Archduke Francis William. On the 12th his Imperial Majesty went in very simple state to the Cathedral. The whole population turned out in holiday clothes, and the line was kept by the burghers ; not a soldier *on duty* was to be seen, except at the church door, three battalions as a guard of honour. The multitude uttered but one mighty cry of ' *Vivat* ! ' The day was lovely. After the Duke's funeral it was one of the grandest spectacles I ever beheld. The Emperor was much *ému*, and his father, who was with him in their little open barouche, roared like a calf. The *attentat* was no joking one. Never man had a narrower escape than his Majesty ; if the assassin had not weakened the point of his knife by having the back of it sharpened, and changed it into the lancet form, he must have smashed the Emperor's skull ; as it was, the point of the blade bent up two inches. His mother, the Archduchess Sophia, got a setting down by asking him never to *walk* again in Vienna, and to take pre-cautions (as of police and military following his carriage and his horse). The Emperor, said Lady Westmoreland, was seriously angry with her ; insisted that the subject should never again be mentioned to him.

'Was he to distrust his good, honest Viennese?' This was hi
Majesty's first quarrel with his mother.

.　　.　　.　　.　　.　　.　　.　　.　　.

Yours affectionately,

G. HARRIS.

*March* 18*th*.—Started for Paris with Frank Mills, in a gale
from N.E. and snow.

*March* 19*th*.—Arrived at Paris at 11 P.M. Found an invitation from the Emperor to dine that day.

*March* 20*th*.—Went with Lord Cowley to the Tuileries, he
having told me that the Emperor wished to see me immediately.
Review in the Place du Carrousel. We met in the great room
under the clock tower. The Emperor came in soon after with
the Empress. Saw me and received me very heartily. He presented me to the Empress, who said she had often heard him
speak of me as an old friend. He then went down to mount his
horse, and reviewed his troops, who received him very well. The
Ministers—Fould, Ducos, and Persigny—came up, and began
immediately talking on the subject of Rose's summons to our
fleet to the Bosphorus. They seemed to think that England had
not acted loyally in the matter, as it ought to have been a simultaneous movement. All I could reply was, that it was the act of
Colonel Rose alone, who was a man of great energy; and that
although I owed the Government nothing, I must do Lords J.
Russell and Clarendon the justice to say that I believed they
were as anxious as I had been for a French alliance, and that
they had approved both in Parliament and privately to me of all
my French policy. The Emperor had sent off his fleet at once
without choosing to wait for an explanation from England and
an answer to Admiral Dundas's request for orders. This act,
though notified immediately to Lord Cowley and by him to our
Government, was not communicated to Walewski in London, and
occasioned great confusion. A Cabinet was called, and Walewski
was so positive that the French fleet had not sailed that our
Government thought Lord Cowley misinformed. This was a
trick of the French Foreign Minister, Drouyn de l'Huys, to spite
Walewski, who had, he thought, been intriguing to get his place.

I dined at the Tuileries this evening, and found a great
military banquet of all the marshals, generals, and colonels, who
had commanded at the review of this morning.  The Emperor
again thanked me before everybody ' pour ce que j'avais fait pour
lui,' alluding to the recognition of the Empire by England, and
with a very frank courage, at such a time and place, mentioned
my having visited him in his prison at Ham.

I sat by the Empress at dinner.  She is still very handsome,
with a beautiful bust and shoulders, and small hands and feet.
Hair auburn.  She spoke English easily, and talked to the
Emperor in that language when they wished not to be understood.
They did this two or three times, forgetting my presence, and
laughed heartily at the mistake.

After dinner the etiquette was very stiff, and we stood for
two hours.  During one of these the Emperor took me to a corner,
and spoke on several subjects.  He seemed to avoid the details of
the Turkish question, which occupied the public mind this day,
but did not conceal his ill-humour with our Government, and his
suspicions that Rose had been ordered to send for the fleet.  I
begged him to wait for further information, and at all events not
to send his fleet beyond Naples, as ours remained at Malta, but
he was silent, as he always is when he disagrees.  He then asked
very anxiously whether the Queen's feelings had changed towards
him, being influenced by Lord Aberdeen.  I replied that it was
very natural that at first she should feel strongly for her Orleanist
relations, but that beyond that her Majesty had no sentiments
of enmity against him, and that I had always found her Majesty
alive to the importance of friendly relations with France.  He
said that that was his earnest wish, that he had even risked his
own popularity by enduring the abuse of the English press for a
year ; that this press infuriated the officers of the army, numbers
of whom knew English perfectly ; and that it required the whole
power he possessed among the provincial masses to enable him to
exercise his own judgment and not to be obliged to kick the
newspaper correspondents out of Paris.

He said he was most anxious to go *bras à bras* with England
on every question, not *pour les beaux yeux* of one another, but for
our solid interest ; that two great subjects were now paramount—

namely, the maintenance of the Turkish Empire and the new International Code broached by America called the 'Monroe Doctrine ;' and that these two points comprehended the whole policy of the world, the maintenance of peace, and the advance of human civilisation and improvement. Russia was a barbarous Monarchy, and America a barbarous Republic, but both young, vigorous, *et pleines de sève.*

As to Europe, the safety of the West depended on the alliance of France and England ; that he had been urged to join in a quadruple alliance against us as a focus of revolutionary doctrines, but he refused, because he knew that if England were to sink, France must be sacrificed to the Northern Powers ; and that if his uncle's prophecy respecting the Cossacks were not physically realised, it would be so morally ; that even now Austria was the Czar's valet, since he had saved her in Hungary ; that, although wearing different forms of government, as different nations wear a different cut of coat—England, France, Sardinia, Spain, and Portugal, all had the same foundation for their governments— namely, public opinion and the will of the people, more or less developed ; whilst the other great European States and Italy had no law but the fancy of the divine autocrat who ruled them.

As to himself, his whole power came from the people, and if he lost their confidence he could not exist an hour. The difference of government, therefore, was not so great between France and England as our newspapers said it was. We did not make sufficient allowance for the Revolution of 1848, which prostrated the country and was felt by all France to be only the forerunner of the Reign of Terror prepared for 1852 by Mazzini, Louis Blanc, &c. ; that it was natural for John Bull, who had never seen a drop of blood shed, and read of 1688 as a romance, to enjoy the diatribes of the 'Times' over his breakfast, and calling him a tyrant, not to perceive that whatever he (Napoleon) was, he was the *consequence of the events of* 1848.

He went on to repeat his desire to be inseparable from England, but added : 'The great difficulty is your form of Government, which changes the Queen's Ministers so often and so suddenly. It is such a risk to adopt a line of policy with you, as one may be left in the lurch by a new Administration.'

I replied that I saw no danger in this, as far as France was concerned, because he knew what Lord Derby's had been, that no more Conservative or Tory Administration could ever be in power again, and that the animus of the Radical party was almost hostile to Russia and Austria ; that there was no possibility of any English Ministry joining in a coalition against France, unless he played his uncle's game again. He said ' Bah ! you know my opinion long ago on that subject ! ' He lamented the conduct of Austria in Italy, and said it was impossible it could go on, and that it would be a great advantage if we could agree upon granting her an equivalent somewhere else—but where ? There seemed none but some Turkish province. He said Italy gave him great anxiety, and especially Austria's insolence to Sardinia. The Emperor of Austria was a very energetic and clever man, and would make a figure. I remarked that I believed him to be ambitious, and that Buol did not attempt to control him. He agreed, and abused Buol's character, adding that he had that day received from him a letter full of flattery. I said I thought the Emperor Nicholas loyal and trustworthy. Upon which he observed : ' Plus prudent que loyal.'

The Emperor then suddenly broke into the question of refugees in England, stating his opinion that sooner or later it would bring us into a quarrel with other States. I answered, that as we knew that half of them were rascals we should be very glad to be rid of them. Every country had its subject on which no cession could be made. The Holy Places in the East was that of Russia, the Refugees was ours, and it was useless to torment us about an impossibility, for no English Minister could alter the law at present. He said, ' I do not care about their meetings, speeches, and proclamations, but they are a nest of assassins. You know I am neither fanciful nor timid, but I give you my word of honour that three men have been successively arrested within fifty yards of me armed with daggers and pistols. The last fired at the gendarme and wounded him. I have taken great pains to have these attempts hushed up. These men all came straight from England, and had not been twelve hours in France. Your police should have known it and given me notice.' I reminded him that I had done so, ' Oui, mais pas vos successeurs.' And then he added, ' Can I believe their protestations, when Graham and Wood spoke as they did of me at Halifax and Carlisle ? [1] Their excuses are nonsense. One of three things : either they are fools, which is not the case, or they really felt what they said, which, being Cabinet Ministers, is very serious for me, or they abused me to please their audience, which is still worse, as it would imply that the English people are hostile to me. However, I shall act in public, as I have always done in private life, treating Governments as they treat me, and I believe what you say of Lord John Russell ; but what of Lord Aberdeen ?'

I replied I would only answer for the two I had mentioned, not having had any relations with the others.

He then spoke of old times and of his mother with great affection, saying the thing he regretted most was her not living to see him where he was. He alluded to the offer he had made to the Princess of Hohenlohe, and asked me what I thought of the Empress. He said he had no time to lose, if he was to leave an heir grown up. The revenue had increased sixty millions of francs in 1852, and this quarter was already ten millions above the corresponding one of last year. He had greatly improved Paris, and in two years his system of railways would be completed if he could preserve peace. He desired me to thank Lord Derby for his policy, and concluded by saying, ' The English are manly enemies and manly friends, and that is more than I can say for others.' I put the above conversation on paper as soon as I returned to my hotel, so I can answer for its being almost textually correct.

The Empress asked me a great many questions about the Emperor's former health, whether ' he was subject to headaches.' I suggested that these hot rooms were enough to give headaches to anybody who worked hard, and she said they both suffered from them, but that nothing could cool the Tuileries. She spoke of his assassination as a thing talked of, but to her conviction impossible ; that she had not the least fear about it, and that they walked about alone at St. Cloud, and meant to do so.

[1] Their speeches, whether from a moral or political point of view, were perfectly unpardonable, being suggestive of any crime which an ignorant man might mistake for patriotism.

In a conversation with Marshal Vaillant, who commanded at the siege of Rome, and Marshal Magnan, who carried out the *coup d'état* of the 2nd December, they stated that the army would dislike going to war with Russia for the question of the Holy Places.

Marshal Vaillant showed an evident jealousy and dislike of England. Some of the colonels expressed a contrary feeling, but all are imbued with the idea that any alliance with us must be unstable, in consequence of our constant change of Ministry, and they viewed the organisation of our militia as dangerous to ourselves, misjudging it from their experience of their National Guard.

Although the banquet and establishment of courtiers and servants was as splendid as possible, there was a feeling in the air which impressed me with the idea that the whole pageant must be ephemeral. I cannot explain this sentiment, unless it was that I observed that the members of the household appeared not to have perfectly learnt their parts, and also that, having seen and known the Emperor for so many years in such a totally different position, his present one looked like a dream or a play ; but when each actor becomes acclimatised by time, it will be a magnificent Court, with a Sovereign who will command the attention of all Europe.

*March 21st.*—Dined with Frank Mills at the Trois Frères,[1] the famous *café* in the Palais Royal, established during the Reign of Terror by three brothers who came from Provence. I had spent the day in leaving cards on the officials.

*March 22nd.*—Dined with the Cowleys.

*March 23rd.*—Dined with Nat. Rothschild. Kisseleff there.[2] Said to be in great favour with his master, Nicholas. Saw the Duc de Guiche,[3] going as Minister to Turin. Has orders to support Sardinia.

*March 26th.*—Dined at Cowley's. Had a long conversation with Kisseleff. He said that the men in the secret of the *coup d'état* were Morny, Magnan, Maupas, Persigny, and a Captain

---

[1] Closed by the Commune in 1871.

[2] Russian Ambassador at Paris.

[3] Afterwards Duc de Gramont and Foreign Minister in 1870.

Fleury.[1] Count Flahault (the father of Morny) knew nothing about it, and this Drouyn de l'Huys assured me was the case. He certainly denied it himself. Morny and the Emperor had secured to themselves a refuge in the event of a failure with a woman devoted to them.[2] At the Prince de Lieven's I met Molé, Duchâtel, and other Orleanists.

*March 28th.*—Dined with Persigny, Cowleys, Fould, &c. Long conversation with Persigny on French affairs. He is strong for an English alliance. He opposed the marriage with the Empress, and still says it was a great mistake. This reminds me of a circumstance when the Emperor was an exile in London five years ago. He one day walked me twice round Berkeley Square, inquiring if I thought he should have any chance of being accepted by Lady Clementina Villiers if he proposed to her. I could not give him any encouragement, as I knew Lady Jersey had a particular dislike to him, and avoided showing him any civility.[3]

*March 29th.*—Dined with Drouyn de l'Huys. Fifty-two covers. Deputation from the City recommending peaceful policy were present, with Gurney the Quaker and Sir John Duke. French Ministers and Emperor very much pleased at it. It was got up by De l'Huys and Mr. Powles, and signed by 4,000 names. The object was to neutralise the effect of Sir Charles Wood's abominable speech at Halifax and the articles in the 'Times' against the Emperor. That journal has received such representations from its commercial customers at Manchester that it has abated its tone. I sat by Madame de Bourqueney. He is gone as Ambassador to Vienna. Ducos, Minister of Marine, spoke anxiously in favour of an English alliance, but I know him to be naturally hostile, and he and Changarnier concocted a plan in 1851 for a piratical descent on England, and for seizing the Queen's person at Osborne, they said, for their amusement only.

[1] Captain, afterwards General, Fleury was a very clever and useful servant to the Emperor, during his reign, and was Ambassador at Petersburg at the time of the fall of the Empire. He died in 1884.

[2] This was Madame Favart de l'Anglade, a creole, who lived some time at Kensington Gate, and used to give excellent dinners and whist parties.

[3] A strong trait in the Emperor's character was that he always returned kindness and civilities, and *vice versâ* When Lady Jersey went to Paris he would not invite her to the Tuileries.

Lavalette is just recalled from the Embassy at Constantinople, where his zeal involved France in the question of the Holy Places. He intimated to me that he had been ' thrown over.' He is anti-English ; abused Lord Stratford's temper. The fact is that the Emperor Louis Napoleon does not realise that upon the subject of the Holy Shrines, Nicholas (who is Pope and Head of the Greek Church) cannot possibly give way, and encouraged Lavalette in preposterous demands and language to the Sultan, and is now obliged to draw back and recall him. M. de la Tour, a conciliatory man, succeeds him.

*March 30th.*—Dined at the Tuileries with the Eglintons and Clanricarde. The ladies seemed to me very *provincial,* and not at their ease. The Emperor in good spirits and as gay as etiquette permits.

*March 31st.*—Breakfasted with Drouyn de l'Huys.

*April 1st.*—I returned to London in a gale of wind.

### Lord Derby to Lord M.

St. Leonards : April 5, 1853.

My dear Malmesbury,—I have no wish whatever that the Canterbury Election debate should be put off on account of my absence. I assume that the evidence taken before the Commons has been communicated to us, and that it is of such a character as to form a sufficient *primâ facie* ground for further inquiry. It cannot be our interest to screen cases of notorious corruption, or even to prevent the disfranchisement of boroughs notorious for their venality. Whether the case of Canterbury is strong enough for this, I know not. I should rather doubt it.

Ever yours sincerely,

DERBY.

### Lord Derby to Lord M.

St. Leonards : April 7, 1853.

My dear Malmesbury,—I shall most probably be in the House on this day week, but I shall only just get there, coming from Knowsley that morning, and arriving at Euston Square at four o'clock ; therefore I should not have wished any great debate to stand for that day. I have no wish that the discussion on the Canterbury case, as I wrote you word yesterday, should be put off in consequence of my absence.

I was aware of the technical difficulty which will be raised, but hope it may be got over. It cannot, as I apprehend, be any obstacle to our joining in an Address with the House of Commons, praying that a Commission may be instituted ; but it may raise awkward difficulties with respect to the powers legally vested in that Commission, if not strictly in fulfilment of the Act of last year. I have not the Act before me, and cannot, therefore, exactly say how far the deviation is fatal. But I should think, if there is any doubt, that our best plan would be to join in the Address, and at the same time to introduce a bill giving the same powers to the Commissioners as would have been given had the Act of last year been strictly followed, reciting the informality which rendered such a course necessary. Perhaps you would suggest this from me to Lords Lyndhurst and St. Leonards for their considera-tion. Whatever is done, do not let the House of Lords, and especially our friends in it, have the appearance of raising technical objections for the purpose of stifling searching inquiry.

Yours sincerely,<br>DERBY.

*April* 15*th.*—Government beaten last night on motion for taking tax off advertisements. Disraeli supported it, saying the late Government had intended to take it off. Gladstone opposed it, and they were beaten by 31. There were two other divisions to take off the duty on papers and newspapers which our party opposed and supported the Government in defeating the Radicals.

*April* 16*th.*—Lord Derby in great spirits, and quite approving of all that Disraeli had done. We gave a party this evening, which was much more crowded than the last.

*April* 17*th.*—Government have Cabinet Councils almost every day and are in difficulties.

*April* 21*st.*—Budget will probably pass. The extension of legacy duty to real property secures the support of the Radicals.

*April* 29*th.*—Jew Bill thrown out by 49 in House of Lords, in spite of Lord Aberdeen changing.

*April* 30*th.*—Lord Seymour is made chairman of the Com-mittee to inquire into the navy appointments under the Duke of Northumberland, and he says it is a bad business for Mr. Stafford, who was our Secretary for the Admiralty, and the whole of the late Government ; Mr. Stafford having told Sir Baldwin Walker that the appointments complained of had been forced upon him

X

by Lord Derby and Disraeli. Mr. Stafford has behaved foolishly, for he got very well out of the scrape before the House of Commons ; Lord John Russell and others having admitted that he had quite vindicated his character. Instead of being satisfied, he must needs make an attack upon Sir B. Walker, who, having some friends in the House, they asked for a committee, and the result is that Mr. Stafford and Lord Derby's colleagues will be much damaged.

*May 2nd.*—I attended at the Navy Board Committee. Heard Mr. Stafford's evidence. Weak and unsatisfactory. Lord Derby has written to offer to be examined before the Committee, if they are not satisfied that he had nothing to do with the appointments of the Admiralty.

*May 3rd.*—Government had a majority of 71 upon the income tax, and of course they will carry the whole Budget.

*May 4th.*—Mr. Stafford's evidence tends very much to criminate him and exculpate the Government. It is evident that the Duke of Northumberland gave up to him the whole patronage of the dockyard, and there was a jealous squabble between him, Sir B. Walker, and Admiral Hyde Parker on the subject. Disraeli has written to ask to be examined.

*May 20th.*—Government were beaten yesterday in the House of Commons, on the motion of Mr. Spooner to refuse 1,235*l.* for the repairs of Maynooth College. Lord John Russell supported the grant, and was beaten by 74 to 54.

I hear that Mrs. Sidney Herbert has had herself and two children painted as a Holy Family.

*Lord Derby to Lord M.*

St. Leonards : May 22, 1853.

My dear Malmesbury,—I *do* dine at Pembroke College on Thursday, the 9th, and hope you will be able to meet me there. By all means execute your purpose of taking Lady Malmesbury over to Germany on the 11th. We shall miss you in the House of Lords, but that is a secondary consideration, and it would neither do for her to give up her journey nor to undertake so long a one without an escort. I suppose you will be back before the end of the session. I shall be in town tonight, as I have to attend at the Trinity House at ten to-morrow morning. I shall, however, be in the House, as the usual dinner is postponed. I think you should ask a question as to the affairs of Turkey, but without entering on any discussion, or making more of a speech than to refer to the reports prevalent and ask what foundation there is for them and what line the Government have adopted. I think matters look very threatening. I congratulate you on the Paraguay treaty, for to you belongs the merit of it, though I suppose the present men will claim it.

Ever yours sincerely,<br>DERBY.

*May 23rd.*—Went to Lady Breadalbane's ball ; 1,500 people there. Lord Breadalbane bought a house in Grosvenor Street, through which an entrance was made expressly for the cloaks and hats, and built two rooms of zinc for the dancing and supper.

There is no longer any doubt that Lords Aberdeen and Clarendon have been completely deceived by Brünnow. The news from the East is very alarming, and still they will not believe that the Emperor has played them false.

Prince Menschikoff only gives the Sultan to the 16th proximo to decide whether he accepts or refuses his ultimatum. Lord Stratford having no instructions, has referred to the Government at home.

*May 27th.*—Telegraphic despatch says that relations have ceased between the Turkish Government and Prince Menschikoff. This ought to open Lord Aberdeen's eyes.

*May 28th.*—I spoke yesterday on the Turkish difficulty. Lord Clarendon's reply was feeble, and he evidently spoke against the grain when he assured the House that the Government meant to support Turkey, and that our Ambassador at Constantinople was acting cordially with that of France.

*May 29th.*—Prince Menschikoff, it is said, has left Constantinople. Lord Clarendon is very uneasy, but Lord Aberdeen, with childish obstinacy, refuses to believe that Russia intends any aggression, and will not send our fleet to Constantinople.

I met Lord Palmerston in Pall Mall this afternoon ; he stopped me to speak to him, and began at once upon the departure of Prince Menschikoff. He walked his horse by me till we got to Waterloo Place, where we stopped and talked for a quarter of an

hour.    Lord Palmerston spoke very openly on the subject, on
which his policy quite agrees with ours.    He is for decided
measures against Russia, so that between him and Lord Aberdeen
there is a complete difference of opinion.

*May* 30*th.*—Lord Hardwicke asked whether any orders had
been sent to the English fleet to move.    Lord Clarendon refused
to give any answer.    Disraeli put same question in Commons, and
Lord John Russell angrily refused all information.    The question
is to be decided to-morrow at the Cabinet.    It is well known they
are divided on the subject.

*June* 2*nd.*—It is reported that the English fleet is sent to
Constantinople.    Lord Hardwicke, who knows Prince Menschikoff,
says that he was in the navy, and that in some engagement a
cannon ball passed between his legs without injuring him.

*June* 3*rd.*—Walewski and Brünnow are naturally in a state
of great anxiety as to whether the Government will go to war.
The former, who constantly sees Palmerston, hopes and believes
they will, but Brünnow is sanguine that Aberdeen will not do so,
and they respectively are constantly applying to me for an opinion.
I always give them the same answer—namely, that 'the strongest
character of the two, which, undoubtedly is Palmerston's, will prevail.'

There is a circumstance which I think must strongly influence
Lord Aberdeen at this moment ; which is, that when the Emperor
Nicholas came to England in 1844, he, Sir Robert Peel (then
Prime Minister), the Duke of Wellington, and Lord Aberdeen
(then Foreign Secretary), drew up and signed a memorandum, the
spirit and scope of which was to support Russia in her legitimate
protectorship of the Greek religion and the Holy Shrines, and to
do so without consulting France.

When Lord Derby's Government came in, at first I was unable
to understand the mysterious allusions which Brünnow made now
and then, and which he retracted when he saw that either I knew
nothing of this paper or that I desired to ignore it.    Since it was
composed and written, the position of affairs in Europe has totally
changed, and is even reversed.    In 1840 the events in the East
had then totally estranged England and France from one another,
and Louis Napoleon did not exist as a factor in European policy;

Now he is Emperor of the French, and the Duke and Peel are dead, yet it is not unnatural to believe that Nicholas, finding Lord Aberdeen Prime Minister, and the sole survivor of the three English statesmen, should feel that the moment had arrived, so long wished for by Russia, to fall upon Turkey. His menacing conversations with Sir Hamilton Seymour began the moment Lord Derby resigned and not before, and at the same time Menschikoff's arrogant demands were made.[1] He believes that Lord Aberdeen never will join France against him, and probably thinks Palmerston stultified by the drudgery of the Home Office to which he is relegated. It is now quite certain that the Government cannot make up their minds what to do about Turkey, and that when Lord Aberdeen affirmed in the House that the only question between Russia and Turkey was that of the Holy Shrines, he was quite aware that a note had been presented by Menschikoff on March 2, making much more exorbitant demands.

It was refused at once by the Porte, and from the length of time that elapsed before any new proposal, it is clear that Menschikoff sent to his Court for instructions. Lord Clarendon's speech expressing 'perfect confidence' in the Emperor of Russia was made on April 25, so neither he nor Lord Aberdeen could be ignorant of the note of March 22.

*June 8th.*—Saw Clarendon and Brünnow ; both very low.

*June 9th.*—I returned from Oxford, where I attended Lord Derby's installation as Chancellor. Nothing could exceed the enthusiasm. He spoke magnificently, and did the whole thing with great dignity and grace, looking very *distingué* in his Chancellor's robes. He delivered his Latin oration without notes, and the learned critics agreed that they could only find two trifling faults in it. The two Ministers who were best received by the undergraduates were Lord Eglinton and Disraeli.

*June 13th.*—Lady M. and I started for Germany, and reached Ghent that day.

*June 15th.*—Left Lady M. at Cologne on her way to Carlsbad, and returned to London.

---

[1] All the actors are now (1884) dead, and as all the events connected with them have passed away for ever, I see no reason against publishing the above facts from my journal.

*June 25th.*—Found things looking very warlike, Government quarrelling among themselves ; but, as we are doing the same, the India Bill will pass.  Our party are angry with Disraeli, which is constantly the case ; and they are also displeased with Lord Stanley, suspecting him to be coquetting with the Manchester party.

*June 30th.*—Lord Clanricarde brought forward the whole Turkish question.  Dinner at Lady Jersey's, and a party at the Palace for the young Prince's christening.

*August 2nd.*—Queen returns to London to give a ball to the Grand Duchess Olga, who has arrived in England and has been recommended to her Majesty's protection by an autograph letter from her father the Emperor—an odd proceeding at this moment, unless he has sent her Imperial Highness on a sort of mission, which is possible and quite in accordance with Russian policy ; but, to use Lord Clarendon's phrase, 'We are drifting into a war.'

*August 16th.*—Left London; and reached Achnacarry the following day.

*August 20th.*—It is announced by Lord J. Russell to the House of Commons that the note agreed upon at Vienna by the four Powers had been agreed to by Russia, but it was still unknown what answer the Porte will give.  It is a most disgraceful business for this country, for it appears by his own showing that the note above mentioned is a French one, altered by Austria, and submitted to the Emperor of Russia without Turkey having been consulted ; and not only is there no mention made of the evacuation of the Danubian Provinces, but there is every reason to believe that the note is, with a slight modification, virtually the same as that which England and France advised Turkey to reject a short time ago.

*September 11th.*—Still at Achnacarry, with a party deer-stalking and fishing.  Government in great difficulties, as they are divided into a peace and war party ; but from what I know of Palmerston, and from the conversation I had with him in London, I feel certain that the latter will prevail.  The 'Times' writes . very gloomily.  It publishes Reschid Pasha's note to the four Powers, by which it appears that, though in the note agreed upon at Vienna nothing was said about the evacuation by Russia of

the Danubian Provinces, the Porte makes that the first condition
of accepting the note, and insists on a guarantee against any
future invasion of these provinces, so the question seems as far
from being settled as ever.

*September 23rd.*—A very warlike article in the 'Morning Post,'
evidently written by order of Walewski, saying that the Emperor of Russia does not interpret the Vienna note in the sense
of the four Powers, but as granting him all that Menschikoff's
ultimatum demanded. The hesitations and equivocations of our
Government lower England in the eyes of Europe.

*October 8th.*—The papers say that the Turks have declared
war against the Russians, and that Lord Westmoreland told the
Emperor at Olmütz that England would not support Turkey, if
he would not consider the entrance of the combined fleets into
the Dardanelles a *casus belli*. This is incredible, for Lord Aberdeen would never have sent instructions to that effect. The
feeling for the Turks is increasing in England, and several meetings have been held, at which addresses have been agreed upon
urging the Government to interfere more vigorously in their
behalf.

*October 12th.*—I believe it has been decided at the last Cabinet
to support the Turks by force of arms in case of a war between
them and Russia, and to withdraw the note agreed upon at the
Vienna Conference.

The return of Captain Inglefield is announced from the Arctic
regions with the intelligence of the safety of Captain McClure,
who started four years ago to look for Franklin. His ship, the
'Investigator,' had been frozen up nine months, and he was just
preparing to desert her and attempt the journey south on foot,
when his party met one from Captain Kellett's ship, which was
sent in search of him. They came by Baffin's Bay, Captain
McClure by Behring's Straits. So the North-West Passage has
been discovered at last, and Captain McClure has the credit of it.
His despatches are very interesting, and show him to be a man of
indomitable courage and energy.

*October 20th.*—Grantley Berkeley arrived (at Achnacarry),
and was as agreeable as he always is ; but considering his great
reputation as a sportsman, he did nothing in deer-stalking, being

past the age for walking over Lochiel's mountains. The Emperor Nicholas, when he heard that the Turks had declared war against him, swore it should be one of extermination.

*October 24th.*—The only news to-day is the recall of the French Minister from Naples, in consequence of an offence given him by the King. The Emperor had sent three French officers to assist at the review as a compliment to the King, but one of them being suspected of having written a pamphlet which displeased him, he had them all put under quarantine to prevent their attending the review. They returned immediately to France in a fury, and the Emperor recalled his Ambassador at once. The Princess Esterhazy, Lady Jersey's daughter, is said to be dying ; she is gone to Torquay.

*October 28th.*—I killed a good stag, at 168 yards—a running shot through the head (luck, of course)—yet he recovered by the time the dogs and men got up to him and made a good fight, shaking off the hounds several times, charging one of the gillies, and tearing his clothes with his antlers. Berkeley killed a *salmo ferox* weighing 18 lbs. in Loch Arkaig. No news, but the Government is trying to persuade Prussia to be ' *bonâ fide* neutral,' as she is sending arms to Russia.

*November 4th.*—A large detachment of the Turkish army has crossed the Danube, and it was expected that they would attack the Russians the following day, 28th ult. There has been a battle between the latter and the Circassians, in which the Russians were at first beaten, but were reinforced, and the Circassians retreated with the loss of two thousand men.

*November 5th.*—Went to the forest of Gerraran (a primæval wood, stretching along the shores of Loch Arkaig) and killed a magnificent stag with twelve points, a cup on each horn, and double brow antlers. This wood and that of Gusach, lining the shore of Loch Arkaig, are certainly primæval. The hill is clothed with immense pines, and with almost impenetrable heather. Among the *débris* of centuries and in an older stratum lie many gigantic oaks ; one I measured was sixty feet long and perfectly sound. They were evidently the ancient possessors of the mountain, before the younger generation of the red pine usurped their place.

*November 9th.*—Left Achnacarry by Spean Bridge and Loch Laggan. Slept at Perth. Reached Chillingham next day.

*November 11th.*—It is evident from Vienna news that the Turks have gained a victory near Giurgevo.

### Sir Charles Hotham to Lord M.

St. James's Hotel : November 11, 1853.

Dear Lord Malmesbury,—I scarcely had returned to England when the Duke of Newcastle proposed that I should accept the Government of Victoria. My previous habits in no way qualified me for such employment, and I endeavoured to convince both his Grace and the Prime Minister that a better selection might without any difficulty be made. Failing in those quarters, I sought assistance from Lord Clarendon, and prayed to be sent back to the River Plate, in the same rank I before held, assigning as my reason that the French had already a Minister Plenipotentiary there. Here also I failed, and notwithstanding my entire conviction that the Government were mistaken, I had either to decline serving the public or comply with their wishes. Thus placed, I accepted the latter alternative, and with a sorrowful heart go to Victoria.

For whatever little reputation I may have recently gained I am indebted to your lordship, and, anxious that you should understand my sudden change of profession, I have ventured to communicate these particulars to your lordship.

I have the honour to be, &c. &c.

CHAS. HOTHAM.[1]

*November 12th.*—I killed a wild bull in Chillingham Park. He staggered a few paces and then fell, stone dead, shot through the heart. Lady Olivia Ossulston made a very good sketch of him.

The 'Times' says that the Russians lost fourteen superior officers, killed. This last battle was fought between Omar Pasha and General Dannenberg.

---

[1] In 1852 I had sent Captain Sir Charles Hotham to carry out negotiations for opening up the River Plate, in which he was entirely successful. He was a most intelligent man, devoted to his profession, in which he bore a very high character as an officer and a seaman, and it is impossible to understand why the Duke of Newcastle should have thus acted against his inclinations and have forced him to leave it. He did not long survive his colonial appointment.

*November* 15*th.*—I went to London on my way to Paris. There is no doubt that the Russians were repulsed again at Oltenitza.

*November* 22*nd.*—The Duke of Beaufort is dead, and also Princess Sarah Esterhazy, and also the young and beautiful Queen of Portugal, on the 16th, in her confinement. I went to Paris.

*November* 23*rd.*—Paris. Dinner at Persigny's, who is married to Marshal Ney's grand-daughter. She is handsome and lively ; he, very uxorious. He is uneasy about Aberdeen, whom all the Bonapartists know to be hostile to Louis Napoleon. They are all very anxious that Palmerston should counteract this feeling. I reassured them as well as I could by a comparison with respect to the character of the two men. I am going to Fontainebleau to-morrow, where I am invited till the 30th.

*November* 24*th.*—Suffered so severely with toothache all night that I thought I could not go, and, not knowing any dentist at Paris, and my train starting at 10 A.M., I went to the Palais Royal and found the *charlatan* as usual carrying on his trade of tooth-drawer, dressed in his scarlet coat. He operated on me most successfully, and, on my giving him five francs, called me ' Mon prince.' Went to Fontainebleau in the same compartment as Marshal St. Arnaud and General Niel. The former was one of the conspirators for the *coup d'état.* He was said to be a brave but unscrupulous soldier, and one of Louis Napoleon's most useful partisans. He distinguished himself in the African wars, and was in the armies of the First Empire. He is an active and good-looking man, with a strong *ton de garnison* and a good deal of ready wit. It is said he will command the French army in the coming war. He amused me with several stories of the camp, the following among others. An old general, a friend of his, came to him after the battle of Bautzen, saying that his soldier servant was killed, and commanding him to get him another—' Pas de ces vieux grognards, mais un gentil petit conscrit, bien compris.' St. Arnaud found him a raw recruit. The general had lost an arm and a leg, which he had replaced artificially, and when he undressed he told his new valet to pull off his coat. The lad obeyed, and pulled at the stuffed arm, and the general unhooking the apparatus, the young soldier went reeling into the corner. But though much frightened, he said nothing. ' A présent, mon pantalon, mon ami,' when the same thing occurred ; the stuffed leg coming off in the boy's hand, sending him flat on his back at the end of the apartment. Still he said nothing, but when the general told him, ' Maintenant, ma perruque,' he could stand it no longer, exclaiming, ' Le plus souvent, mon général, pour que votre sacrée tête me reste dans les mains.' General Niel, a distinguished engineer officer, was quite of another stamp, and appeared to me superior to his comrade, though very stiff and pompous. They neither of them seemed to have much heart in the work that was before them, openly expressing their opinions that France could gain nothing by a war with Russia, and that the Turks would be very disagreeable allies. They were very complimentary to me as to our army ; the principal fault of their own, they said, was a want of good non-commissioned officers.

The Court at Fontainebleau is magnificent. A servant in the royal livery sat all day outside my door. And the palace is so immense that it is quite a journey from one part to another. The dinner was on the same scale. After it was finished, I had a long conversation with the Emperor, and I was rather surprised to hear him repeatedly calling the Turks ' Bêtes—des amis si bêtes que cela ! ' He expressed again his wish for Palmerston at the head of our Government.

*November 25th.*—Rode in the forest with Madame de Pierre, an American, Lady in-waiting to the Empress, Lord Cowley, and M. de Toulangeon. Disappointed in the forest, excepting in that part called ' Le Bosquet du Roi,' where the trees and rocks are very fine.

Lord Henry Lennox arrived, said by the French to have come on a mission to propose a marriage between young Jerôme and Princess Mary of Cambridge. I hope this is not true for the sake of her Royal Highness, for whom I have great respect and admiration.

*November 26th.*—A grand shooting party in an enclosed space of ground. A squadron of Hussars marched up when we arrived and dismounted to act as beaters. Sky-blue uniform and red trousers. As they wore spurs they were constantly tripping up.

There were a great number of pheasants and some roe-deer ; the latter unable to escape, being fenced in.  The guns were the Emperor, Chaumont, Toulangeon, Edgar Ney, Colonel Fleury, Prince Napoleon, Marshal Magnan, Lord Cowley, and myself. We bagged 210 head.   More than one Hussar was peppered, upon which his comrades cried out, 'Tiens, tu as de la chance, toi !  tu seras décoré.'  The Emperor shot very well, and was most civil, to Lord Cowley and me.

Conversations in the evenings with Drouyn, Persigny, and the Emperor.  Speaking of our Government and their delays, he said, 'Why does this drag on so long ?  why is it not settled ?  Your Government first would not go to Besika, then would not go to the Dardanelles.  When you were at Malta you should have been at Besika ; at Besika when you should have been at Constantinople; and at the latter when you should have been in the Black Sea. The Turkish fleet is bad, and incapable of fighting alone.  Your Admiral Dundas threatened to retire if they attempted to fight alone in the Black Sea.  The Russians have fourteen sail of the line, and have sent their Baltic sailors right through Russia to Sebastopol.'

I combated his idea of the weakness of naval operations, and instanced our war in Spain when we were masters of the sea. Magnan was of the same opinion.

*November 27th.*—Returned to Paris with Jerôme.  No one could be more friendly and kind to me than the Emperor during this visit ; but he is evidently very nervous as to the heartiness of Lord Aberdeen's Government, as he has good reason for knowing his personal and political dislike of him.  But what makes the most impression on me is the undisguised indifference, if not distaste, of the French people and army to the impending war.

The officers were constantly ridiculing the Turks, and would hardly give them credit for their victories at Citate and Oltenitza ; but this is very French.

The Empress looked handsomer than ever, and her manner of receiving her guests and visitors was perfection.  She spoke to me a great deal about the Pope at Rome, and the state of the Roman Catholics there and in Ireland.  On the question of the excesses of the English Press and its, to her, apparent indifference to assassination, I found it hopeless to explain this abuse of our liberty, although I did not tell her the publications in Switzerland against the Emperor are far worse than anything that could be written or tolerated in England, being full of lies and obscenity with regard to him.

*December 3rd.*—I returned to London. Went with Lady Malmesbury to Knowsley; found Lord Derby laid up with the gout. He amused himself during his confinement by translating the 'Iliad' and fugitive pieces from foreign languages.[1] The last are beautiful, especially Manzoni's 'Ode to Napoleon.'

*December 9th.*—Disraeli arrived, at which our host seems much bored, because he is obliged to discuss politics with him. Disraeli came into our room and had a conversation before dinner.

*December 10th.*—Very cold. We went out shooting, and on our return a Cabinet Council was held in Lady Malmesbury's room, which she gave up to us, between Lord Hardwicke, Lord Derby, Mr. Disraeli, and myself. We played at race-horses after dinner, and Lord Derby is as much amused and as eager to win the few shillings of which the pool consists as if it was a real race and heavy stake.

*December 12th.*—Lady Malmesbury left Knowsley, and Disraeli accompanied her to London. He told her that Lord Derby was extremely anxious to come in again, and full of fight. There is a report of an engagement in the Black Sea between the Russians and Turks, in which the latter have had their fleet utterly destroyed in the harbour of Sinope, and Osman Pasha, their admiral, taken prisoner, to Sebastopol.

*December 13th.*—The French papers seem to doubt the truth of the destruction of the Turkish fleet, as it was safe in the Bosphorus on November 28, and the battle is said to have been fought on the 30th; and it is also suggested that, as a convoy of 5,000 troops had left for Asia on the 26th, this may be the fleet the Russians boast of having destroyed.

*December 14th.*—Disraeli called on Lady Malmesbury, and told her the new Reform Bill was to be a slashing one—fifty-three boroughs disfranchised and members divided between the great towns and counties, the latter being swamped by a ten-pound

---

[1] These were only printed for Lord Derby's friends, and he gave me a copy.

franchise. Dizzy added in his satirical way that he believed that every town in which there was a statue of Peel was to have a member. He also said that it was entirely a Peelite bill, and had been opposed by all the Whig portion of the Cabinet, that private orders had been given by the Emperor of Russia to Brünnow and Kisseleff to leave London and Paris the moment the allied fleets entered the Black Sea. He seemed to think that this disaster of the Turks would complicate matters very much. Lord Clanricarde has returned from Paris. He declares that Lord Aberdeen has written to the Princess de Lieven, saying that nothing will persuade him to make war against the Emperor of Russia. At all events she says so.

*December 15th.*—Palmerston has resigned[1]—an event of the utmost importance at this moment, for though the motive assigned for his retirement is his disapproval of the Reform Bill, the public will of course suspect the Eastern Question has more to do with it, and will lose all confidence with regard to the way our foreign relations are likely to be conducted.

*December 16th.*—Lord Aberdeen went to Osborne yesterday to announce the resignation of his colleague to the Queen. Heavy fall of snow.

### Lord Derby to Lord M.

Knowsley : December 18, 1853.

My dear Malmesbury,—Your intelligence turned out quite correct as far as Palmerston was concerned, but not so, as it appears, as to Lansdowne, who ' objects to the bill, but will not break up the Government at this moment '—at least so says Jocelyn, who, I presume, was your informant, but who also wrote to me by the same post. His letter, however, did not reach me till the following morning, and yours arrived only a few minutes before I read in the ' Times,' not only the announcement, but two elaborate articles upon the event, one evidently official, and at which Jocelyn further tells me that Palmerston is much, and justly, annoyed. As *his* lips are sealed, Aberdeen has no business to speak through his newspapers. Palmerston will be, individually, a loss to the Government; but as Lansdowne holds on, I doubt if he will have any following ; and on the ground on which his resignation

---

[1] He returned in ten days, when the Cabinet had sent the fleet into the Black Sea.

is placed, I am not so sure that it will not give them more numerical support than it will lose them.   Jocelyn has proposed to come here about the 28th, and I have charged him to bring me down any details he can, without a breach of confidence.   On my part I have had no hesitation in telling Jocelyn in confidence, that my strongest objection is to the assimilation of the county and borough franchise by swamping the former with ten pounders, and that a different arrangement might at the same time give votes to these last if desirable, and supersede the necessity, on the plea for the disfranchisement by wholesale of the small boroughs.

Foreign affairs look worse and worse.   Can you find out what Palmerston says to them ?

I am mending and well in myself, but my ankle is still very weak and I am hardly allowed to use it.   I have not been out of the house since you left it.

Ever yours sincerely,

DERBY.

*December 21st.*—It appears that the Turkish ships destroyed at Sinope were men-of-war, not transports.   They were detained in the harbour by a strong N.E. wind, and were at anchor ; the Russian fleet, having been informed of this by an Austrian vessel, approached under cover of a thick fog, and when it cleared off the unfortunate Turks saw an overpowering Russian force at the entrance of the bay.   They would not, however, surrender, but fought with such bravery and desperation that every one of their ships was destroyed, and the Russians had not a single prize to carry into Sebastopol.   The Government is much exercised at the loss of Palmerston.   Lord Aberdeen is said to have offered his place (the Home Office) to Sir George Grey or Sir James Graham.   Sir George Bowles arrived at Heron Court, and said Lord Palmerston will resume office if his alterations in the Reform Bill are agreed to, and that Lord Aberdeen never returned any answer to Lord Palmerston's letter announcing his resignation.

Mr. Disraeli to Lord M.

Coventry : December 24, 1853.

My dear M.,—I have waited to the last moment to give you the best information I could gather.   So far as I can learn or judge, P. has

not yet surrendered, notwithstanding the rumours to that effect—
yesterday terribly rife.

If he be obdurate, the Cabinet, I still think, will break up.

Yours sincerely,

D.

*December 25th, Heron Court.*—I got a letter this morning
from Disraeli, saying that Palmerston had resumed office without
conditions and that the Peelites were triumphant, saying he had
'done for himself.' Several Cabinet Councils lately lasted above
five hours, and it is supposed that Lord Lansdowne is only waiting
for the Reform Bill to be laid before the Cabinet to resign, as he
did not attend any of them.

*December 26th.*—Mr. and Mrs. Disraeli, Mr. and Lady Augusta
Sturt, and Lord Anson arrived at Heron Court. Disraeli very
low at Palmerston's resuming office, as he thinks the Government
are now safe. He is very much occupied and pleased with my
library, which was compiled by three generations of men of totally
different literary tastes. The first, my great-grandfather, usually
called 'Hermes,' was a great Grecian and classical scholar, and
collected all the most perfect editions of the ancient writers.
The second, my grandfather, a diplomatist and politician, added
all the best specimens of European authors of the last two centuries, and my father all the most modern literature of his time.
What seemed, however, to strike Disraeli more than anything
was an autograph journal by my father, recording his sporting
pursuits daily for forty years, in which is noted every shot he
fired, killed or missed, with a careful memorandum of the weather
day by day. Disraeli did not show to advantage, as he is not in
spirits, and, the party not being all of one mind upon politics,
which is the subject which now absorbs him, he never alluded to
them except in quiet conversation with Lady Malmesbury or
myself.

*December 28th.*—It is affirmed that Aberdeen and Gladstone
have implored Lord Palmerston to return to them ; the other
Peelites declare that he begged to be let in again.

## 1854

*January 1st.*—I went to Broadlands after luncheon    Nobody there except Lady Shaftesbury, Mr. Milnes, Lord Harry Vane,[1] and Count Bethmann. Lady Palmerston is much aged—falling asleep at dinner and sitting the whole evening wrapped in a shawl. She had a long conversation with me about Turkey, and we agreed very well on that subject.

*Lord Lonsdale to Lord M.*

January 2, 1854.

Dear Malmesbury,—I hear all the Government think war inevitable except Aberdeen. Brünnow wound up his Government's account with the Bank three weeks since. I told you of it at the time. Brünnow had some Consols of his own, £6,000 (?), and an account at the Bank of England. He settled this on Saturday last, which, I believe, was the cause of the funds going down on that day.    There is a man, a shipbuilder at Rotherhithe, who is building the screw frigate steamers for the Emperor of Russia; he received a letter from Palmerston, last Saturday, of warning, upon which the builder went to Brünnow, who saw him, and said he would be prepared to give him an answer to-day. I know a man who has a nephew just come from St. Petersburg; he says there is the greatest enthusiasm amongst all classes for war, which, from my knowledge of the place, I can easily conceive, and that they press all the fine-looking fellows in the country into the army, having no regard for the ladies' coachmen and fine-looking footmen.

I have seen also the uncle of the officer who brought over the despatches a few days since from Admiral Dundas. He fears the Turks will very soon be short of money: that at present the war is supported by the Church and private subscription. This must end soon. The Turks are willing and good soldiers, and individually better than the Russians, but the Russians will outnumber them. It is not thought at Constantinople that Sebastopol can be attacked with success. The French great ship, the 'Napoléon,' of which so much was expected, proved not to be seaworthy, and she is gone home. They would not let a single Englishman on board of her. The Russians have an annoying fort at

<hr>

[1] Afterwards Duke of Cleveland.

the entrance of the Danube. I hope our fleet will destroy this. I believe the French will have to send at last an army to defend Constantinople. The opportunity of catching the Russian fleet is lost —no such opportunity *can* ever occur again. The ships at Sinope had on board 45,000 stand of arms and a great quantity of ammunition, destined for Circassia and Asia Minor.

A Whig, who sometimes speaks confidentially, and whom I generally find about the mark, tells me that the quarrel with Palmerston was this : He (Palmerston) differed from Graham and J. Russell upon some portions of the Reform, and he wrote and spoke to Aberdeen, who spoke to Russell and Graham, who adhered to their scheme. Aberdeen then wrote to Palmerston a *snubbing* letter, saying he had spoken to Graham and Russell, and he agreed with them, upon which Palmerston writes a long letter giving all his reasons against this part of the measure, and concluded by resigning. This created consternation, and Clarendon, Granville, and Gladstone, aided by Charles Greville, and Ned Ellice—in fact, the steam was put on in every way to recover the lost sheep. At first Palmerston was obdurate, but kept mollifying, and I believe Sir George Grey was never offered the Home Secretaryship, except on the condition Palmerston would not come back, and Sir George Grey professed great patriotism, that he would not think of it as long as there was any hope of Palmerston.

This Whig told me that the only consolation was, of the present aspect of affairs, that the Eastern Question would shelve the Reform Bill for the present session ; that no one wanted it, and, with the exception of one or two in the Cabinet, they wished to get rid of it. He thinks the Government will go to war in earnest and raise a large force.

Faithfully yours,

LONSDALE.

*January 3rd.*—Returned to Heron Court. Lord Clanwilliam arrived from Wilton very much changed in his feelings towards the Government, as he was a strong Peelite, and now he says there is no doubt that Lord Aberdeen's timid policy is the cause of the war with which we are threatened, and that a little determination at first would have stopped the Czar. All the newspapers except the Government organs are making furious attacks upon Prince Albert for interfering in the Government of the country, especially in foreign affairs. I believe he wrote a very elaborate paper respecting our position with Turkey, and leaning rather to

Lord Aberdeen's view of our policy than to Palmerston's. This must have somehow come out.

*January 6th.*—I stalked a flock of wild geese behind my pony and got within thirty yards of them, killing five. Very severe weather, with a gale from S.W. and snow.

*January 11th.*—The combined fleets entered the Black Sea, on the 3rd it is said.

*January 14th.*—Rumours of a Russian defeat at Citate fully confirmed. It appears that 15,000 Turks attacked a Russian intrenched position in front of Kalifat and took it by storm. The Russians tried to retake it, and were beaten off, losing 3,000 men.

*January 15th.*—The most absurd reports are rife concerning Prince Albert, and are believed by the public, even to that of his being sent to the Tower for unconstitutional practices. He is accused of writing letters to turn out Lord Hardinge and take his place as Commander-in-Chief, or at least to share his power and patronage ; of giving audiences to the Ministers privately, and thus substituting himself for the Queen. Time will soon do him justice, and convince the world that no sovereign could have at his side a better counsellor, removed as he is from all personal disputes of parties.

My own experience would testify to the fact that on no single occasion did I have any audience upon matters of State except with the Queen in person, the Prince standing on her right hand ; and if he wrote to me, it was in her Majesty's name that the opinions or criticisms were given. His information on the wheels within wheels which revolved in the Northern Courts of Europe was invaluable, as being out of the reach of our diplomatists.

His heart is naturally German.

The 'Morning Herald' has an article on the inconsistency of the late Sir Robert Peel, who, while he constantly in public recommended to the capitalists of England to employ their money in Ireland, where they would find the safest security and very profitable investment, had forbidden in his will any portion of his own great wealth to be invested in Irish securities.

*January 21st.*—Public indignation has been so universally aroused by the manner in which the Russians behaved at Sinope that war has become inevitable, and I have no doubt that the country

will carry it on nobly.   Nothing can exceed the spirit and patriotism shown by all classes.   None seem to have a shadow of fear
as to the result.   Austria has refused positively to listen to Count
Orloff's proposals, and the tone of Prussia is so decided that he
will probably not go to Berlin as was at first intended.   Omar
Pasha is so ill that the Sultan has sent the physician of the French
Embassy to him.

*January 24th.*—Went to London to see Lord Derby before he
goes to Windsor.   The Czar has instructed his Ambassadors to
demand whether by the entry of the combined fleets into the
Black Sea it is intended to take part with Turkey or remain
neutral.   In the former case the Russian Ambassadors in London
and Paris must demand their passports.

*January 25th.*—Invited to Windsor.

*January 26th.*—Had a very pleasant day's shooting in Windsor Park and an amusing play in the evening.   The Queen very
gracious, speaking to me for some time on the coming war.   The
Argylls, Bruces, and Palmerstons were there.

*January 29th.*—Went up to London for the meeting of Parliament, which takes place the 31st.

*February 1st.*—Parliament met yesterday.   Lord Aberdeen
made an angry speech on the war, ending by a vindication of
Prince Albert, and trying to throw the blame of the attacks
(which originated with the Radical Press) upon the Conservative
party.   Lord Derby made a fine speech upon Turkey, and also
exonerated the Prince most completely as well as his own party.

*February 8th.*—The conditions on which Count Orloff offered  . . . .
to treat were four in number :—

1st.   That a Turkish Plenipotentiary should proceed to the
head-quarters of the army, or to St. Petersburg, to open direct
negotiations with Russia, with liberty to refer to the Four
Powers.

2nd.   That the former treaties between Russia and the Porte
should be renewed.

3rd.   That Turkey should enter into an engagement not to
give an asylum to political refugees ; and

4th.   That the Porte should recognise by a declaration the
Russian protectorate of the Greek Christians, which was the

origin of the quarrel. Of course, Lord Clarendon might well say that these proposals are inadmissible, as they amount, in fact, to a considerable increase of Prince Menschikoff's formal demands. Baron Brünnow left London yesterday, so the die is cast.

Kisseleff is also gone from Paris. General Schilder, who has been sent to the Danubian Provinces by the Czar, reports that the Russian army is in a pitiable condition.

*February 9th.*—Government beaten in the House of Commons on a motion of Mr. Chambers to investigate the claims of an English company at Madeira against the Portuguese Government. I fear Disraeli voted against the Government, as it is his policy to join with anybody in order to defeat them. Sailors are coming in very fast. The rapidity with which our ships are equipped excites the astonishment of the French, and now that we fight with them they are quite enthusiastic about us.

*February 13th.*—Three battalions of the Guards and other troops to the number of 10,000 go immediately to the East. The Duke of Cambridge, Lord Cardigan, and General Brotherton are all mentioned as having commands, and Lord Raglan is to be Commander-in-Chief. London is very sad. The papers bluster a good deal for war, but it is still very doubtful whether Lord Aberdeen is in earnest.

The Reform Bill is considered a revolutionary measure, and has created great alarm. Louis Napoleon has written to the Czar without any previous communication with the English Government. When a battalion of the Guards left London yesterday amidst the acclamations of the people, they bought up all the oranges at the stalls along their line of march to give to the soldiers.

*February 21st.*—Disraeli made a beautiful speech yesterday on the Eastern Question. I hear that at a dinner at the Palmerstons, Lord Aberdeen, the Duke of Newcastle, Molesworth, &c., were pictures of woe, and neither ate, talked, nor smiled. There was a party in the evening, and Disraeli came in radiant.

*February 22nd.*—The Czar's answer to the French Emperor is said to be very uncourteous. This passage amongst others is quoted : ' I have the firm confidence that my troops will reply in the same manner as in 1812.'

*February* 25*th.*—Lord Bath has come back from Constantinople, and says that Lord Stratford openly boasts having got his personal revenge against the Czar [1] by fomenting the war. He told Lord Bath so.

*February* 26*th.*—Lord Harry Vane will bring forward a motion to postpone the Reform Bill.

*Mr. Disraeli to Lord M.*

House of Commons: February 28, 1854.

My dear M.,—They say that the Sunday Council was positively on Reform; Palmerston on the Saturday previous having declared that the withdrawal of the Reform Bill was indispensable; Russell, Aberdeen, Graham, and Newcastle thereon threatening resignation. They say that Palmerston is 'firm,' but that the break-up will not occur till the estimates are past.

One apparent proof of this latter theory is that Lord John has proposed to continue the estimates to-morrow (Wednesday)—very unusual—and has given notice of the Budget for next Monday—only a week's notice, and a very sudden and precipitate financial exposition.

My conclusion is that the Cabinet is in convulsions; whether it may be soothed by any Daffy's Elixir remains to be proved, but, at the best, it's a poisonous remedy.

D.

*March* 10*th.*—The Queen reviewed the fleet at Spithead, previous to their departure for the Baltic. The French fleet is not ready, neither are their transports for the troops. Sir Charles Hotham, who is appointed Governor of Victoria, told me that he had asked the Duke of Newcastle to allow him to exchange his appointment for a ship. The Duke answered that 'if he did not take what had been given him he should have nothing,' that the Government hung together in every respect, so there was no use in his applying to Sir James Graham. He did, however, do so, and met with a flat refusal. Nothing can exceed their jealousy of Sir Charles Hotham's success in negotiating the treaty with South America, where I sent him. They have packed him off to Australia, evidently to get him out of the way.

---

[1] For refusing to receive him as Ambassador at St. Petersburg.

*March* 14*th.*—Lord Aberdeen and I have had a quarrel on the subject of an alleged breach of confidence on the part of a clerk appointed by me in the Foreign Office, and whom Lord Aberdeen publicly in the House of Lords accused of having 'scandalously betrayed his trust by divulging some matter connected with a secret correspondence on Russian affairs.' I asked him to name the person, and he said he did not know who it was, as if it was likely that he should not have asked, or taken pains to find out the name. I was taken by surprise and hampered by my utter ignorance of who was the accused and the evidence against him, but I soon ascertained that it was a Mr. Astley, whom I appointed and who left the office some time ago to marry a lady of fortune. The accusation is, that since he left the office he spoke of a secret correspondence at a dinner at Lord Ashburton's, that Lord Stanley of Alderley gave Lord Aberdeen the information upon which he so rashly acted last night.

The discussion was renewed this afternoon, and I completely set down Lord Aberdeen amidst the cheers of my party.

The Government were silent, and not a soul said a word for their chief.

Lords Fitzwilliam and Grey spoke against him. Lord Clarendon, who was present, never said a word, so Lord Aberdeen was quite deserted, and must have seen what a strong feeling he had roused against himself by his unjustifiable accusation, made without any proof to sustain it.

The 'Morning Herald' and 'Morning Post,' in their report of the first night's discussion, mentioned Mr. Byng [1] as the person suspected, though no name whatever had been mentioned. This produced a great commotion among the whole Byng family, and old 'Poodle' Byng came up to me at White's, saying he heard his name had been mentioned as being suspected of giving information to the 'Times,' &c. I replied that that was quite absurd, as it was well known that he had resigned his post at the Foreign Office immediately after the battle of Waterloo.

*March* 17*th.*—I got a letter from Mr. Astley indignantly denying the charge against him, and which I read to the House.

---

[1] A gentleman formerly a clerk in the F. O., and very well known in society as 'Poodle Byng,' a nickname given him by Mr. Canning owing to his curly hair.

Lord Aberdeen of course had nothing to do but to apologise, which he did in the fullest and handsomest manner, expressing his belief in Mr. Astley's innocence.   He afterwards told me privately who his authority was, which enabled me to remind him of Sancho Panza's proverb, 'That the cask as often leaks from the top as from the bottom.'

*March* 18*th.*—Lord Lichfield died to-day, and Lady John Manners is dying of scarlet fever.

*March* 20*th.*—Returned from Farnham, Lord Manners's place. Read the secret correspondence published in the morning papers, which quite confirms what we have always suspected—namely, that the Czar was convinced the English Government under Lord Aberdeen would not object to his demands upon Turkey, telling them honestly what his intentions were, and offering them Egypt and Candia as a bribe.

*March* 23*rd.*—Colonel Rose [1] called.   He tells me that we have lost the alliance of Prussia, chiefly through Bunsen, who frightened his master out of his wits by sending him a plan for the partition of Prussia, which he gave him to understand had been arranged between France and England.   The first step the King took was to recall Bunsen, who, not liking to leave his comfortable house and good income in London, set about thinking how he should retrieve his character as a zealous Prussian.   The expedient he fixed on was to make a violent scene with Lord Clarendon.   He accordingly went to the Foreign Office, and complained bitterly of the articles against Prussia in the English newspapers, and worked himself up into such a passion, using such intemperate language, that Lord Clarendon, not seeing through his real motive for picking a quarrel, lost his temper, and told him never to set his foot again in his house.   This was just what Bunsen wanted.   He immediately wrote off to the King, giving a flaming account of the gallant way in which he had taken the part of his country, and the order for his recall was cancelled.

It is now known through the telegraph that the ultimatum is refused, but the formal declaration of war cannot take place till the despatch has been received.   Lady Palmerston told me that Prussia is quite on the side of the Czar.

[1] Now Field-Marshal Lord Strathnairn.

*March 26th.*—The messenger returned last night from St. Petersburg. The Emperor was absent, but Count Nesselrode kept him for six days and then sent him away, saying the Emperor would not send any answer.

*March 27th.*—Both Houses of Parliament were crammed to-day to hear the Queen's Message read by the Chancellor and Lord John Russell, stating that her Majesty feels bound to afford active assistance to her ally the Sultan against unprovoked aggression.

*April 1st.*—The Duke of Parma's assassination is supposed to have been from revenge and jealousy. He had gone to see some woman at a disreputable house. Her husband or lover concealed himself near the door, and when he came out stabbed him and made his escape. He was found dead by the police in the morning, the body already cold. It is, however, possible that the murder may have been political, and that the murderer knew his habits. The dismissal of Baron Ward from his Government and his exile from the country rather countenance this last supposition.

*April 3rd.*—News from Vienna of yesterday says the fortresses of Hirsova, Metchin, and Baberdagh were taken by the Russians on the 28th. They have now possession of a large tract of marshy country called the Dobrudscha; but the French think this a bad move, as the Russians are without resources or communications, with the Turkish army behind them.

*April 4th.*—Lord Mahon tells me there is bad news; the Turkish and Greek Ministers have been mutually withdrawn from Constantinople and Athens, so the two countries are at war. Until our troops arrive at Constantinople, with the French, the fleets cannot leave the Bosphorus; and, in the meantime, it is feared the Russians will take Varna. This comes of the delays of our Government, who detained our troops for no purpose whatever at Malta. The fleets could have left the Bosphorus long ago, and Varna have been safe.

It appears that the King of Greece favours the insurrection against the Turks; and Lord Clarendon told Baron Cetto the other day that if the King did not behave better we should dethrone him.

*April 8th.*—Left London for Paris.

*April 10th.*—I hear that 200,000 Austrians, under Archduke Albert, have been ordered to enter Servia with the consent of the Porte. It is further stated that the representatives of the four Powers signed a Protocol on the 9th containing a recapitulation of the principle of the integrity of the Ottoman Empire, and comprising the evacuation of the Principalities. The Turks have gained a victory in the Dobrudscha, on the road to Silistria. The combined fleets are stationed, partly at Varna and partly opposite Sebastopol.

*April 12th.*—I hear Lord John Russell announced last night that the Reform Bill is given up for the present ; and that he was so annoyed that he sent in his resignation, but has since been persuaded to resume his seat in the Cabinet. His secession would have broken up the Government, which all parties would regret at the present moment. There is no precedent for a Prime Minister resigning when the country is engaged in war. Bunsen is recalled.

*April 14th.*—The Porte has ordered the expulsion of the Greeks from Constantinople within fifteen days. The Duke of Cambridge has been well received at Paris, but I think the Emperor was rather hurt at his not going to the Tuileries.

*April 15th.*—Sir Charles Napier has left Kioje Bay for the eastward, towards the Gulf of Finland, with his whole fleet. The insurgents in Greece have been defeated in spite of all the exertions made by the King and Queen of Greece to encourage the movement. They deserve to lose their throne. I dined to-day at the English Embassy to meet the Duke of Cambridge. To the great amusement of the company the party got so jumbled up at dinner that Jem Macdonald, Aide-de-Camp to his Royal Highness, sat on the right hand of Lady Cowley, the place of honour, though, besides his chief, there were two Dukes and other Peers. Everything in Paris is enormously dear, especially ladies' dresses. I called on Madame de Bonneval, who, I fear, is dangerously ill.

*April 16th.*—No news from the Danube in confirmation of the fall of Odessa. It would be most important, as General Lüders' army in the Dobrudscha receives its supplies from there. It is, however, blockaded.

*April* 21*st.*—The war is decidedly unpopular here in Paris, as the French think they have no direct interest in it, and care little for being our allies.  A war against Prussia would be popular, as they have still a great hankering after the frontier of the Rhine. The splendour and extravagance of the style of living in Paris far surpasses anything in London.  I only saw the Emperor at his ball at the Elysée.

*April* 22*nd.*—The Duke of Cambridge is gone to Vienna on his way to Constantinople.  I arrived in London from Paris with a total *extinction de voix.*

*April* 23*rd.*—Went to Heron Court.

*April* 25*th.*—The Convention between England and France was signed in London on the 10th inst.  It disclaims all idea of conquest, and leaves it open for every other Power to join.  The ' Fury ' was fired upon by the Russians at Odessa, in spite of her flag of truce.  She captured a Russian schooner ; but, being chased by five men-of-war from Sebastopol, was obliged to leave her prize, which she had cut out under the guns of Sebastopol ; but she escaped with her prisoners, although she did not sink her prize from motives of humanity, one man having been left on board by mistake.

*May* 1*st.*—Odessa was bombarded for an hour on the 18th, and for the whole day on the 22nd.  Four gun batteries were destroyed, one Austrian and eight Russian ships burnt.  This is our revenge for the cowardly attack of the Russians on the boat we sent for the Consuls.

*May* 3*rd.*—I had a long and confidential conversation yesterday with Palmerston, whom I met at dinner at the Walewskis, and we agreed perfectly on all points of foreign policy.  He said the Government had information that the fleets had left Odessa on the 26th, so they had done all they intended.  The Greeks have been defeated in two engagements by the Turks, but the King is obstinate in spite of our remonstrances.

*May* 11*th.*—In the House of Lords I asked the Government whether the attack on Odessa was in violation of the flag of truce, or whether Admiral Dundas's orders justified him in bombarding the town the moment war was declared.  The Duke of Newcastle refused to answer the question.

*May* 12*th.*—Admiral Hamelin's report of the bombardment of Odessa quite agrees with what we have heard already.

The Russian magazines were burnt, but he does not mention any ships of war being destroyed. The conflagration lasted twenty-four hours after the cannonade ceased. All accounts agree in saying that the ' Terrible ' had the honours of the day; she had twelve shots in her hull, and ten men killed and wounded. Government were beaten last night on a clause of the University Bill; this is the second important defeat they have sustained; they have failed in every bill they have brought forward this session—the Scotch Education Bill, their Reform Bill, the Oaths Bill, and the Poor Law Settlement Bill—yet they call themselves a strong Government!

The ' Gazette ' of last night publishes the despatches of Admiral Dundas on the bombardment of Odessa. They are abominably written, give no details, and have not even the merit of being concise. The French Admiral's report is very superior. Madame Walewska's fancy ball last night was very pretty. I saw Lord Derby to-day; he looks very weak and low, and is annoyed at my going abroad for so long as three weeks, which I am obliged to do in order to take Lady Malmesbury to Carlsbad, which her doctors say is indispensable, as she has been very ill. The life Lord Derby leads in London must be very unwholesome; he never walks or rides, but sits all day in a back room, without taking any exercise, until he goes to the House of Lords from St. James's Square. I call on him very often, and he seems always pleased to see me. Disraeli is furious with the war, which he thinks keeps Government in.

*May* 19*th.*—There is a report, I fear too true, that the English war steamer, the ' Tiger,' has gone ashore near Odessa, her captain wounded and her crew taken prisoners.

*May* 23*rd.*—Lord Durham and Lady Beatrix Hamilton were married this morning, and are to spend the honeymoon at Woburn, which place the Duke of Bedford lent, adding that he hoped they would not stay very long. His son, Lord Cosmo Russell, observed that they were better off than a couple he knew, who, not having any place whatever where they could go for their honeymoon, were reduced to call a hack cab, and desire the driver to drive them three times very slowly round the Regent's Park.

*May 24th.*—The news of the capture of the 'Tiger' is confirmed. She was chasing a Russian ship when she grounded.

*May 26th.*—Left London with Lady Malmesbury for Carlsbad. Left Calais at three and reached Ghent at eight.

*May 27th.*—Left Ghent at ten and reached Cologne at six P.M.

*May 28th.*—Sleep has been impossible, from the noise that lasted all night at the hotel.

*May 29th.*—Reached Magdeburg.

*May 30th.*—Here we parted. I went to Dresden and Lady Malmesbury to Zwickau on her road to Carlsbad.

---

I went to Augsburg and returned to London, reaching it on June 10. It is said the Duke of Newcastle is to be War Secretary, at which Lord Palmerston is furious, because he wanted it, and certainly would have been the fittest person. The King of Greece has given in and sent for the English and French Ministers, promising to observe strict neutrality, but he is not to be trusted. The following changes have taken place in our Government : Duke of Newcastle, Secretary for War ; Sir George Grey, Colonies ; Lord John Russell, President of the Council ; Lord Granville, Chancellor of the Duchy of Lancaster, in the place of Mr. Strutt who resigns.

---

*June 18th.*—The Russians have been attacking Silistria for three days, and have been repulsed each time. Captain Gifford, of the 'Tiger,' is dead of his wounds, and the first lieutenant has been sent for by the Emperor to St. Petersburg ; the rest of the crew are sent to Moscow.

*June 19th.*—Dreadful to say, the 'Europa,' a transport carrying seventy men and horses of the Inniskilling Dragoons, has been burnt at sea. The captain of the 'Europa' publishes an account of the burning of his ship. Colonel Moore of the Inniskillings, the surgeon, and twelve privates, were burnt. The colonel might have saved himself, and was repeatedly pressed by his men to do so, but finding he could not save all his soldiers, he chose to

die with them—a magnificent example of heroic devotion. The
rest of the crew and soldiers escaped in boats. The 'Tribune'
came up too late to be of any use, and found the 'Europa' burnt
to the water's edge, and not a living human being to be seen.

We had a great debate on the war to-day. Lords Derby and
Lyndhurst made splendid speeches.

Lord Aberdeen deprecated anger against Russia, &c.

A desperate battle took place on the 14th under Silistria. Generals Schilder and Gortschakoff both wounded; Orloff badly so.

*June 25th.*—A telegraphic despatch from Copenhagen gives
an account of our disaster at Gumba Kusleby. The 'Odin' and
'Vulture' landed 150 men. These were attacked by sharpshooters
in ambuscade and by a masked battery of five guns. Lieutenant
Barrington and five men were killed and sixteen wounded, the
rest being taken prisoners. The Convention between Austria and
the Porte was signed at Constantinople on the 14th; it assures
the occupation by Austria of the Danubian Principalities. The
siege of Silistria has been raised, and the Russians have re-crossed
the Danube.

*July 6th.*—News has arrived that Nicholas has refused all
negotiation, and will make war to the last man and rouble. Six
more regiments of infantry and two of cavalry are to sail this
week for the Black Sea, which will give us altogether 33,000 men.
The 10th Hussars are to go from India. This decision of Nicholas
removes all possibility of disputes about places in the Cabinet.
The House of Commons has become quite unmanageable—showing,
utter want of confidence in the Government and a determination
to support nothing but the war.

*July 18th.*—Lady Malmesbury arrived in London from Carlsbad. She describes politics as running very high there. When
she first arrived, Madame Coloredo, whom she had known as
Ambassadress in London, was very friendly, and constantly with
her, the Duchess of Grafton, Mr. Hope, and other English; but
as transactions of a doubtful nature took place with Austria, and
it appeared uncertain what line that Government would take with
respect to the war, Madame Coloredo and many other Germans
gradually cooled towards the English category at Carlsbad, and
finally cut them.

The progress or failure of a national dispute may easily be judged of by the spectators from the manner and behaviour of diplomatic personages, who think it right to make a personal demonstration of what is going on.

*July 20th.*—Admiral Napier, after making a great demonstration before Cronstadt, has retired without firing a shot, to the disgust of the whole fleet. The English have driven the Russians out of the forts at the Sulina mouth of the Danube. The 'Furious' has gone to Odessa with Russian prisoners, to exchange them against the crew of the 'Tiger.' The Circassian hero, Schamyl, refuses the assistance of English officers; all he requires is ammunition.

*July 30th.*—'The Press' says that Admiral Stopford is gone or going to the Black Sea, as it is said that Admiral Dundas does nothing but pray. It is singular that, of the two admirals in command of the Black Sea and the Baltic fleets, one is always praying and the other always swearing; but they, however, seem to agree on one point—namely, in not fighting.

*August 3rd.*—The cholera has broken out among the French troops at Varna. There is a report that the allied fleets have taken Bomarsund. Admiral Corry, second in command, has come home invalided. It is generally supposed that he has quarrelled with Napier in consequence of his inactivity, and come back to England in disgust. Affairs at home are not more flourishing, as the Government gets beaten almost every night in the House of Commons.

*August 4th.*—We went to Chillingham.

*August 7th.*—Left Chillingham for Achnacarry.

*September 21st, Achnacarry.*—A private letter says that the French force does not exceed 23,000 men, which is a thousand less than the English. However, we shall, I trust, be strong enough not to be beaten in the field, even if we cannot take Sebastopol, for which there is hardly time at this advanced season.

*September 23rd.*—I went out fishing on Loch Arkaig and caught a bull trout of 18 lb., and Lord Edward Thynne a *salmo ferox* of 13 lb.

*September 27th.*—A telegram from Lord Raglan, dated September 16, announces the disembarkation of the allied armies near the Old Fort. The swell had impeded the operations, and the exertions of the fleet under Rear-Admiral Lyons excited the admiration of the whole army, which, with artillery and baggage, has now begun its march upon Sebastopol.

### Lord Derby to Lord M.

Knowsley : October 2, 1854.

My dear Malmesbury,—Urgently as Disraeli pressed it, I will not allow myself to contemplate the possibility of anything so horrible as a November session, and consequently put no faith in Lady ——'s *facts*. If such a fatality should occur, I should probably have a meeting to discuss our course of policy ; but that must be in a great measure guided by the success or reverses of the war. In the Baltic we have made a failure, though Russia has proved herself a far less formidable enemy than was expected. I am looking with anxiety for to-day's papers, as I received yesterday a telegraphic notice of a Gazette Extraordinary having been published late on Saturday night, giving an account of a very severe action, fought on the 20th, in which the Russian entrenched camp was carried at the point of the bayonet after three hours' hard fighting, and with heavy loss to the Allies. If this be true, the affair of Sebastopol may take up less time than was expected ; and the capture of that fortress will make amends for much previous remissness ; but if we should fail there, the country would be greatly and justly dissatisfied at the disproportion between our pre- parations and our performances.

I am sorry to hear that you have had such bad weather and sport. Our weather has been magnificent. I hardly ever remember so fine a month of September, and we have in most places plenty of birds. I had not been shooting well till the last day, but am improving in that and in walking ; and, thanks to Dr. Ferguson and Providence, I am considerably a better man than I was this time last year.

Ever yours sincerely,

DERBY.

*October 3rd.*—News has arrived of a battle fought on Sep- tember 20 between the Allies and the Russians. The latter had entrenched themselves on the heights above the Alma, where they had a force of 50,000 men with numerous cavalry and artillery. The attack began at one o'clock, and by half-past four the Allies had possession of the enemy's camp, which they took at the point of the bayonet. The English lost 1,400 men killed and wounded, and the French about the same. Lord Raglan has written to say that no words can give any idea of the admirable behaviour of the fleet under Lyons, both officers and men having exerted themselves most nobly, and been of the greatest use to the army, sparing themselves neither trouble nor fatigue.

*October* 10*th.*—Lord Burghersh has arrived with despatches announcing the death of Marshal St. Arnaud, Commander-in-Chief of the French army. His body has been sent to Constantinople. The French, who were on the right of the allied army, were close to the sea and protected by the fire of the steamers, which kept close along shore. The sailors behaved with their usual humanity and kindness, carrying the wounded to the ships with the greatest care.

*October* 13*th.*—The English army began its march upon Sebastopol the 23rd, bivouacked two nights on the Katchka and on the Baalbec, both strong positions, which would have given us great trouble had the Russians defended them ; but they were so demoralised by their defeat on the Alma that they never stopped till they got to Sebastopol. We did not pursue them, for as it was important to reach the Tchernaya, where the army was to encamp, this was effected by an easy march the following day, the 26th, and brought the army in safety to Balaclava. Captain Maxse, who had come up with the army, volunteered to return alone to the coast, with a message to Lyons, asking him to come on to Balaclava. This perilous undertaking was so happily accomplished by Captain Maxse, that when the English arrived at Balaclava they found the 'Agamemnon' already there, and Lyons came immediately to meet Lord Raglan.

*October* 25*th.*—No news from the Crimea, except in private letters. All these speak of the dreadful mortality amongst our troops from cholera, arising from the want of tents ; all our men having slept on the bare ground since they landed, whilst the French and Turks have had tents the whole time.

News has at last been received through Dr. Rae of the fate of poor Franklin and his companions ; it is even worse than was anticipated. They all perished from hunger in the spring of

z

1850.   Dr. Rae heard it from a tribe of Esquimaux, who saw forty white men four years ago, who told them that their ships had been crushed by the ice, and they were trying to find their way back to North America.   Some time after, the Esquimaux found the bodies of thirty men lying dead, about a day's journey from Bach's river, and five more on an island.   They had tents, guns, and ammunition, and from the mutilated state of some of the bodies, and the contents of the kettles, it is supposed that they had been driven to eat each other.

*October 26th.*—Mrs. Anson, whose husband has been appointed Commander-in-Chief in India, has sailed.   She embarked at Southampton, and the whole of her friends went to take leave of her.

*October 30th.*—A letter from Louis Napoleon to Madame St. Arnaud is published, in which is the following passage : 'Your husband has united his name to the military glories of France from the time when, deciding on landing in the Crimea, in spite of timid counsels, he gained with Lord Raglan the battle of the Alma, and opened to our army the road to Sebastopol.'

*October 31st.*—The bombardment of Sebastopol began on the 17th by sea and land.   The fleet attacked Fort Constantine and sustained great loss—90 killed and 300 wounded.   The 'Agamemnon' suffered most.   Not much damage was done to the fortifications, and the fleet had not renewed the attack.

*November 2nd.*—A despatch says that a sortie against the French batteries had been completely successful, and that eleven guns and eight mortars had been spiked.   It adds that Lord Dunkellin has been taken prisoner.

*November 6th.*—A despatch from Lord Stratford from Constantinople, dated October 28th, confirms Menschikoff's announcement of a successful attack being made by a force of 30,000 men upon Balaclava.   The Turks fled, but the Highlanders stood their ground, and gave time for reinforcements to arrive.   The light cavalry regiments suffered dreadfully.

*November 8th.*—Left Achnacarry at 7.30 A.M., and reached Dunkeld at 10.30 P.M. ; the whole country is under snow, and has been so for a fortnight.   It looks as if we were to have a very severe winter, and I fear that our army in the Crimea will

suffer dreadfully, the Duke of Newcastle having shown hitherto
no power of organisation.

*November* 14*th, Chillingham.*—The account of the affair of
October 25th at Balaclava is very sad, although most glorious to
our arms, rivalling the most heroic deeds of antiquity. Six hundred cavalry charged the whole Russian army down a valley of a
mile long, defended by artillery and infantry along the heights on
both sides, and a battery of nine cannon in front supported by
numerous cavalry. Our small force cut its way through all these
obstacles, and then cut its way back, but with the loss of two-
thirds of their men.

Nothing could be done to save them. The French did their
best by taking a battery, but the whole army and the Light
Division itself when it started knew they were going to certain
destruction. It is not known who gave the fatal order, for
Captain Nolan, who delivered the message to Lord Lucan, was
one of the first to fall, killed by a shell ; but it is supposed that
Lord Raglan sent an order for the light cavalry to charge to get
back' the captured guns if practicable, and that Lord Lucan
understood it as a positive order, leaving him no discretion. He
therefore ordered the charge, which was led by Lord Cardigan
with the greatest gallantry. There is a telegraphic despatch of
November 6 from General Canrobert, saying that on the 5th the
English positions were attacked by the whole Russian army in
the presence of the Grand Dukes Nicholas and Michael, and
sorties made at the same time on the English and French lines,
all of which were repulsed. Canrobert speaks of the solidity of
the English, who, as usual, bore the brunt of the battle, which
lasted all day. The French supported us gallantly with the division of General Bosquet. Our loss is said to be severe, especially
in the Guards, who fought desperately ; five generals wounded,
amongst whom were two of our best, Bentinck and Brown. It
is, however, a glorious victory, and the more satisfactory as it was
gained in the presence of the Grand Dukes, who will, of course
tell the truth to the Emperor.[1]

Captain and Mrs. Burrell are here. The former related an
amusing adventure which happened to him at Newcastle, where

---

[1] This was the famous battle of Inkerman.

he was quartered.   He had a severe attack of small-pox, and was confined to his bed at the hotel.   During his illness a young lady with her carriage and servants, of fashionable appearance, arrived there, intending to stay for one night only ; but on hearing that a young officer was dangerously ill in the same house, she expressed great interest, and instead of leaving next morning she announced her intention of remaining a few days, constantly repeating her inquiries as to the state of the sick man. Captain Burrell was extremely touched at her romantic conduct, which he took as a personal compliment, but when recovering, the doctors announcing that he was safe, and the lady being informed of the fact, she ordered her carriage, after telling the waiter that she was ' much disappointed, as her object in stopping was to see a military funeral.'

### Lord Raglan to Lord M.

Before Sebastopol : November 14, 1854.

My dear Lord Malmesbury,—I have had the pleasure of perusing your letter of October 15 from the Highlands, and am very much flattered and obliged by your sincere and hearty congratulations on the victory of the Alma.   Let me take this opportunity of saying that I shall ever retain a grateful sense of your kindness and confidence when you were at the Foreign Office.

Poor St. Arnaud !   He went off very suddenly.   He was ill in several instances at Varna, and worse on the transit from thence to the Crimea, but he rallied afterwards, and it was only on the 25th, the day before he resigned the command, that I saw he was very ill.   We have had some very rough work since we sacked Balaclava on September 26, and now we have the most violent gale of wind, which impedes operations for the moment.[1]

Yours very sincerely,

RAGLAN.

*November 17th.*—I hear that Jem Macdonald, the Duke of Cambridge's aide-de-camp, has had two horses shot under him and his cocked hat knocked off.[2]   He is the life and soul of the army

---

[1] The gale here alluded to became a perfect hurricane, and destroyed a great number of our ships and many hundred lives.

[2] When his second horse was killed under him he only laughed and said : ' This sort of thing only happens to younger brothers ! '

and invaluable to the Duke.  Lady Durham is here, quite charming, very pretty, and so unaffected, never apparently thinking of
her beauty or dress, and full of spirits and gaiety.

*November 23rd, Knowsley.*—I arrived with Lord Derby at
Knowsley.  The state of affairs in the Crimea is very alarming,
but nothing remains to us but to take Sebastopol or perish.  I
hear that Prince Edward of Saxe-Weimar writes that all the
officers and men are in tatters like so many beggars, and all from
the highest to the lowest covered with vermin.  They have neither
clothes to change nor water to wash with, having barely sufficient
to drink.

*November 24th.*—There has been a violent hurricane in the
Black Sea on the 14th, and four transports were wrecked.

*November 29th.*—Left Knowsley for London.  The storm on
the 14th in the Black Sea was terrific ; above thirty transports
were wrecked.  The ' Prince,' a large Government screw steamer,
was lost with all on board.  The 'Agamemnon' went on shore, but
was got off without damage.  The French lost a ship of 100 guns
and a war steamer, the ' Henri IV.,' but the crews were saved.

*December 5th.*—Our losses in the Black Sea are confirmed.
The ' Prince,' screw steamer, had landed the 46th Regiment, but
none of their stores.  The storm came on so suddenly that none
of the ships except Admiral Dundas's, off the Katchka, had time
to get an offing.  Fortunately their anchors and cables held, and
they rode out the gale, but all the transports were driven on
shore.  The Russians came down to the beach, and one gentleman
in a carriage drawn by four horses addressed our sailors in very
good English, assuring them that they would be well treated if
they came on shore ; but they refused, and they proved to be
right, for the next day the gale abated and the boats from our
men-of-war took them off in safety.  The French were less fortunate ; their transports, being smaller, were thrown on the beach
and all the crews taken prisoners, among them the crew of the
' Henri IV.,' a 100-gun ship.

The ' Prince' was lost owing to the carelessness of the crew in
not clinching the cables, which ran out with the two largest
anchors.  There was only one small one, therefore, to hold that
immense ship, which was dashed upon the rocks near Balaclava,

and reduced to splinters in ten minutes. Only six men out of 150 saved, and the whole cargo, consisting of the warm clothing for the troops, the medical stores, and a large quantity of ammunition, was lost. Their value is estimated at 500,000*l*.

*December 6th, Heron Court.*—The Duc de Richelieu and General Sir George Bowles arrived. The latter says that the 'Prince' steamer was left seven days outside the harbour of Balaclava, although the authorities there must have known the importance of her freight to the army.

*December 7th.*—We have made a treaty with Austria. I asked Lord Granville if it was satisfactory, but he said it was only a step in the right direction. He also said that Lord Raglan had written to the Government that he had ascertained the Russian loss at Inkerman was 25,000 men. The destruction at the passage of the bridge was tremendous. Our guns had got the exact range and swept away masses at every discharge, the Russians having only one bridge across the river. It was there the two Grand Dukes were seen trampling over their own men in their haste to escape. They left the army that very evening. Menschikoff sent a messenger to the Emperor to announce his defeat, but had not time to write a despatch. The plan of the attack had been arranged by the Emperor himself, who thought success was certain ; and, when the messenger arrived he said, ' Well, we have gained the victory ?' The messenger replied that, on the contrary, the Russians were defeated, upon which the Emperor in a fury cried, ' Vous mentez ! Sortez !' He sent again for him and insisted upon particulars, which only redoubled his rage, and he again dismissed him in the same insulting way, refusing positively to believe in the defeat of his army. This he did three times. The officer is said to have told the exact truth—namely, that there were 60,000 Russians against 15,000 English and French. The intention of this great attack upon the Allies was well known among the Russians at home, as Brünnow told Madame de Lieven three days before that he knew that within that time they would be driven into the sea.

*December 9th.*—The 'Standard' of this morning gives the treaty with Austria. It is so far satisfactory that, although it contains no declaration against Russia, it shows such a decided adhesion to our policy, and wish to give the Allies every passive assistance to make war against Russia, that it is pretty evident that, if a durable peace cannot be made soon, Austria will join us openly. The treaty now published must be so offensive to Russia, that Austria must be aware she has forfeited all claim to her friendship. (Query, Is there any secret article as to our guaranteeing the integrity of the Austrian dominions, in case of her joining us in making war against Russia ?)

*December 11th.*—Left Heron Court. The deplorable state of our troops in the Crimea is described and repeated in all the private letters that arrive. It is impossible for this country to bear these accounts with patience, for every kind of negligence is attributed to the management of those responsible.

*December 12th, London.*—Parliament was opened by the Queen. There was a large attendance of Peers, and the ladies' gallery was quite filled. Lord Derby spoke first and made a very fine speech, though not quite so fluent as usual. The Duke of Newcastle answered, and defended himself in a prosy speech of three hours, delivered in a most monotonous, melancholy, hesitating tone. The House went to sleep after the first half-hour ; at least I suppose the Government bench did so, as they none of them cheered him at all. He spoke like a man who knows he is in a scrape and cannot get out of it, but hopes to make the matter better by the length of his explanations.

*December 13th.*—I hear that the Duke of Cambridge is deeply affected at the losses which his brigade (the Guards) suffered at the last battle, and especially at the death of Colonel Blair, whom he went to see after the action, before he died of his wounds.

His Royal Highness was on board the ' Retribution ' on the 14th, during the great storm, when she was all but lost, as she held on by a single anchor only, her engines going at full speed to east the strain.

Dined with the Cannings, where we met Lord Dunkellin, who seems to have seen nothing during his passage as a prisoner through Russia, at least he can give no account of it. Perhaps he thought he was not justified in doing so.

*December 15th.*—Thanks to the army and navy voted, the Foreign Enlistment Bill came on. Lord Ellenborough made a splendid speech, most damaging to the Government. They carried the bill by a majority of 12 in the Lords, which is considered almost a defeat. I trust, however, they will not go out.

*December* 19*th.*—Lord Hardinge, who is Commander-in-Chief, told me there âre very bad accounts from the Crimea. The weather is horrid, the troops cannot keep dry in their tents, and they have not the ingenuity of the French in making huts. Their officers employ the Zouaves to build them huts, and pay them very highly for it. The soldiers are on half-rations, as provisions are failing. The horses had been eighteen hours without any food, and numbers are dead. Sir John Burgoyne writes to his daughter, Mrs. Wrottesley, that the state of the ground is such that, wishing to send a message to another part of the camp by a mounted orderly, the man could not get there. Quantities of hay floated in the sea after the wrecks, and could have been fished out with perfect ease, and enough wood to build huts for the whole army ; but all was left to rot. It is probable all they can do is to get food. The distance from Balaclava is seven miles, uphill the whole way.

*December* 23*rd, Heron Court.*—The Foreign Enlistment Bill has passed the third reading in the Commons by 38.

# 1855

*Mr. Disraeli to Lord M.*

Carlton : January 6, 1855.

My dear M.,—I found your note on our arrival in town to-day from Hughenden *en route* for Wynyard. I do not think, however, that I shall be able to depart for that latter place before Wednesday morning ; so if you have anything to say, I shall have a London post Monday and Tuesday ; after that, Wynyard, Stockton-on-Tees.

Notwithstanding all that has happened, and the no longer mistakable disgust and indignation of the country with the present Ministry, I think it will last. The House of Commons is determined not to turn them out until their successors are indicated. Waiting for a strong Government, the weak one will proceed.

I fear that Seymour will be going to the House of Lords, which I regret, as I always looked to the possibility of his taking a leading part in the reconstruction of parties.

The Duke of Bucks has just told me that Glengall is dying at Bretby. This is sad; and that poor, dear Lord Ponsonby is in a hopeless state.

The Court will not break up the Government in order that a pure Whig Ministry may be formed.—Yours ever,

D.

*January 9th.*—Lord Hardinge tells me that the Duke of Newcastle had never consulted him on any subject connected with the war; and that he had never seen a single despatch except those that had been published in the newspapers. As he is Commander-in-Chief and a great soldier, this appears incredible; but no one can doubt his word for a moment, and his uncontrolled anger confirms his account.

Lord Derby to Lord M.

St. James's Square : January 23, 1855.

My dear Malmesbury,

.      .      .      .      .      .      .

Great rumours of the Government breaking up, great indignation at their conduct, and great and reasonable alarm for the fate of our army. Disraeli agrees with me as to the patience policy—indeed, he wishes to carry it even further than I do. Our people, however, will be very hard to hold.

.      .      .      .      .      .      .      .

Ever yours sincerely,     DERBY.

*January 26th.*—A letter this morning from Lord Lonsdale,[1] telling me that Lord John Russell had resigned, as he would not oppose Mr. Roebuck's motion for an inquiry into the way in which the war had been conducted. Lord Aberdeen went to Windsor immediately after the Cabinet Council, and yesterday Lord John's resignation was announced in both Houses.

*January 27th.*—Lord Lonsdale again writes that Lord John

---

[1] Lord Lonsdale had held the office of Postmaster-General under Sir R. Peel. He had a very large fortune and great Parliamentary influence in Cumberland and Westmoreland, returning five members in these districts, and he owed it as much to his natural shrewdness and sagacity as to his wealth. He died in 1874, aged eighty-four.

has resigned on account of the mismanagement of the war. He gave this explanation himself last night in the Commons, and Lord Aberdeen read a letter to the same effect in the Lords and seemed very angry, but announced that the Government would await the result of Mr. Roebuck's motion before deciding what course they would pursue. Damaging as Lord John's speech explaining his conduct is to the Government, it is much more so to himself, for his reasons appear quite insufficient to justify his deserting his colleagues and risking to throw the whole country into confusion at such a crisis as this. He says that on November 17 he suggested to Lord Aberdeen that it would be advisable that the office of Secretary for the War Department and that of Secretary at War should be held by the same person, and that it should be given to Palmerston. Lord Aberdeen objected, on the ground of its being unfair and unjust to the Duke of Newcastle to remove him from his post without strong grounds for doing so. Lord John, upon this refusal of Lord Aberdeen, threatened to resign. Being, however, urged by Lord Palmerston and others of his friends not to press the matter further, he consented to give it up, and the subject was not again named by him till Saturday, January 20, when, a proposal being made in the Cabinet which he thought incomplete and insufficient, he gave Lord Aberdeen a paper containing his own views on the subject.

To this it appears he received no answer, and thinking it unlikely that his views would be adopted, he determined on Tuesday night, January 23, to read his resignation to Lord Aberdeen, to whom he wrote the following letter :

Chesham Place: January 23, 1855.

My dear Lord Aberdeen,—Mr. Roebuck has given notice of a motion to inquire into the conduct of the War. I do not see how this motion is to be resisted, as it involves a censure upon the War Department, with which some of my colleagues are connected. My only course is to tender my resignation. I therefore have to request you will lay my humble resignation of the office which I have the honour to hold, before the Queen, with the expression of my gratitude for her Majesty's kindness for many years.

I remain, &c. &c.    JOHN RUSSELL.

Lord John at the beginning of his speech explained the reason he could not resist. Mr. Roebuck's motion was such as could only be opposed on two grounds :—

1st. That no evils existed of sufficient magnitude to call for inquiry.

2nd. That if such did exist they would be best cured by other means, and that, being unable to say 'It is true evils do exist, but such arrangements have been made that all deficiencies and abuses will be immediately remedied,' he could only come to one conclusion, that as he was unable to give the only answer that would stop inquiry, it was his duty not to remain a member of the Government.

Lord Palmerston, in reply to this speech, said 'he admitted Lord John might have a difficulty in meeting Mr. Roebuck's motion, but it was evident he thought that there were in his mind sufficient constitutional objections to that motion, and if he was decidedly of opinion that a different person ought to be at the head of the War Department, he should have given the Government an opportunity before Parliament met of saying whether the proposal should be adopted. The course he had taken was not in accordance with the usual practice of public men, and was calculated to place the Government in a position of embarrassment.'

After these explanations, Mr. Roebuck brought on his motion for a Select Committee 'to inquire into the condition of our army before Sebastopol, and into the conduct of those departments of the Government whose duty it has been to minister to the wants of that army.'

Mr. Sidney Herbert, Sir George Grey, Mr. Monckton Milnes, and Mr. Vernon Smith spoke against the motion, Mr. Layard, Mr. Walpole, &c., for it. Lord Palmerston agreed to the adjournment, upon the distinct understanding that there should be no further one upon this question.

*January* 30*th*.—It is expected that Government will go out whether they are beaten on Mr. Roebuck's motion or not, and that they will reform under Lord Palmerston, Gladstone and Sidney Herbert to stay in. The general opinion about Lord John is that he resigned in the hopes of being called upon to

form a new Government, but he has lost himself by this move.
The accounts from the Crimea are dreadful. Only 18,000
effective men ; 14,000 are dead and 22,000 sick. The same
neglect which has hitherto prevailed continues, and is shown
in everything. No precaution is taken at Balaclava about the
ammunition, of which there are three or four thousand tons.
Officers and soldiers are allowed to smoke pipes and cigars in
the midst of these stores.

*February 2nd, Heron Court.*—Lord Aberdeen has resigned.
I came down here yesterday, but before I left London Lord
Derby sent for me, to tell me that he had been summoned by
the Queen, and entrusted with the formation of a new Government, the present one having resigned. He added that her
Majesty, of her own accord, has expressed a wish that I should
return to the Foreign Office, to which I agreed. He then
stated he had afterwards seen Lord Palmerston, who seemed
inclined to join us, and that Lord Ellenborough would be War
Minister. Lord Derby appeared in high spirits and confident
of success, and when I told him I should like to go to Heron
Court for forty-eight hours to settle my private affairs, he
consented, saying, 'Make haste back, you will find everything
settled by that time.'

Mr. George Bentinck aroused us at four in the morning,
arriving from London, to say that Lord Derby had failed in
forming a Government, Lord Palmerston having thrown him
over, and giving as a reason the immense majority against him
and his colleagues ; that Lord Derby went immediately to
Windsor and told the Queen he was unable under present circumstances to undertake the Government, and that he advised
her Majesty to form one in the best way she could. If it failed,
he would then try with his own friends. Nothing could be
more marked than her Majesty's cordiality. Disraeli told all
this to Mr. Bentinck, in order that he should repeat it to me.

*February 4th.*—Lord John Russell is trying to form a
Government, but the Peelites [1] will not join him, and no
wonder, after his conduct to his late colleagues. His own
party is too weak to stand alone, so that if her Majesty will

---

[1] Gladstone, Graham, and Sidney Herbert,

not have Lord Palmerston, it is probable that she will send again for Lord Derby, who has promised then to undertake the task. I put no faith in this speculation, as, however much she may dislike a Minister, she will always do what she believes to be her duty to the country, and sacrifice her private feelings to her patriotism.

I returned to London with Mr. Bentinck.

*February 5th.*—Lord John having failed, Lord Palmerston is entrusted by the Queen to form a Government.

*February 6th.*—Lord Derby tells me that he had hopes of Lord Palmerston at one time, and if he had joined, Lord Clarendon would have taken the Foreign Office, in which case he would have asked me to give it up to him ; to which I replied with perfect truth, that I should have been delighted to do so, as my health had suffered the last time I was at the Foreign Office from the anxiety and fatigue of such a laborious place.

Palmerston has succeeded, and his Government will be composed of all the ' old lot,' except Lord Aberdeen, the Duke of Newcastle, and Lord John Russell.

Lord Derby's refusal to undertake the Government has been a great disappointment and great offence to his party. When I left him on the 1st, I never saw him more determined, and I do not know what suddenly discouraged him and made him throw up the game. The declaration of the new Government and Lord Derby's explanation come on to-morrow, so I cannot leave London.

*February 8th.*—Lord Panmure is War Minister. Snow continues, with a north-east wind and hard frost.

*February 9th.*—Lord Derby in his explanation last night repeated what he said four years ago as an excuse for refusing to take the Government—namely, 'that he could not govern with his own party without extraneous aid.' He praised the Peelites, talked disparagingly of his own friends, and of course his speech this time is much more damaging to them than the former one in 1852, for then they were untried, and the worst that could be said was that they were inexperienced ; but now he says (at least his words may be so interpreted) that they have been tried and have failed. Disraeli went the morning of his explanation, and begged of him to say nothing against his party. In spite of this warning he makes a long speech praising his opponents and disparaging his friends.  There is no doubt in my mind that his bad health during the last two years, and his physical sufferings from gout, which have been excessive, have shaken his nerve and robbed him of much of his former courage and energy.  Disraeli is in a state of disgust beyond all control ; he told me he had spoken his mind to Lord Derby, and told him some very disagreeable truths.  He charges me, most absurdly, with being to blame for this *fiasco* by leaving Lord Derby at the critical moment when he required support and encouragement.  There can be no doubt, if the Russian War ends successfully and we take Sebastopol, that Lord Derby will have missed a great opportunity, and lost the glory and prestige of the Minister (whoever he may be) who brings the war to a successful end.

That is what I would certainly have told him, had I been present, and no more.

It seems that Lord Ellenborough was quite ready to join us, and would have been a great addition as a colleague.  When Lord Aberdeen resigned Lord Ellenborough came up to Lord Derby in the House of Lords and said the Queen was sure to send for him.  Lord Derby replied, ' Well, if so, I hope you will help me.'  ' Help you !' said Lord Ellenborough, ' I will carry a musket for you !' and then added, ' But mind one thing.  When you go to the Queen, do not leave the room without kissing hands.'  His master-mind saw the necessity for firmness.  I think it was more error of judgment than timidity in Lord Derby, for he thought that no one but himself could form a Government after Lord John and Lord Palmerston had failed, and that he would come in on his own terms.  He said to me, 'I shall then be a most powerful Minister.'

*February 11th, Heron Court.*—The thermometer went down to 12° last night, twenty degrees of frost.  We cannot help thinking of our poor soldiers in the Crimea in this desperate weather.

*February 12th.*—Lord Derby and Mr. Bentinck arrived from London.  The former said that if the Conservatives would only be patient, we should certainly be in office before long.  I forgot to mention that he had invited Gladstone to join him, who had refused.

*February* 13*th.*—Lord Derby, Mr. Bentinck, and I went out shooting wild-fowl. No boy of sixteen could have enjoyed it more than Lord Derby. Eager as everybody is for this peculiar sport, I never saw any one so keen. We killed · six or seven varieties, among which were three white-fronted geese.

*February* 18*th.*—It appears, from Lord Palmerston's speech on the 16th, that when Lord Derby asked him to join in forming a Government and proposed to admit Messrs. Gladstone and Herbert into his Cabinet, he also insisted upon having Lord Clarendon as Foreign Secretary. If he had agreed to this, Lord Palmerston, with these three men and the leadership in the House of Commons, would have been the real Premier and omnipotent in the Cabinet. Last Friday, when Palmerston tried to persuade the House to allow the inquiry into the state of the army to be conducted by the Government instead of a committee of the Commons, it laughed in his face, and men of all parties, some his own friends, declared they would vote for the committee. The navvies have arrived at Balaclava and have begun the railroad.

*February* 21*st.*—Lord Derby had a meeting of his party, which, after passing a vote of confidence in him, went away quite satisfied.

*February* 22*nd.*—Another heavy fall of snow. When is this terrible winter coming to an end ? The papers to-day announce the resignation of Sir James Graham, Gladstone, and Herbert. The motives are supposed to be their unwillingness to face the committee of inquiry into the state of the army. This conduct will, I should think, lower them in the opinion of the country. They first refused to join Lord Derby, and stopped Lord Palmerston, who was ready to do so, by promising to take office under him. They thus prevented a strong Government from being formed, and, having induced Lord Palmerston to accept the Premiership, on the understanding that he would have their assistance, they now leave him in the lurch at a moment of great danger and difficulty.[1]

---

[1] Since the issue of my third edition, I received from Mr. Gladstone a courteous letter denying the justice of this statement, as not borne out by the facts, which, he says, were that he had no *written* or *oral* communication from Lord Derby, but only a message from Lord Palmerston, expressing a desire that if Lord Palmerston joined Lord Derby's Government, he (Mr. Gladstone) should do the same, and, with Lord

*February 25th.*—The three Peelite ex-Ministers—Gladstone, Graham, and Herbert—have made their explanation in the House of Commons.[1] Lord Palmerston slept through Gladstone's speech, and nearly broke down in his own. He appears to be failing under the fatigue and difficulty of his position.

There is no doubt that Louis Napoleon is going to the Crimea, in spite of the entreaties of all his Ministers and of Lord John Russell, who is passing through Paris on his way to Berlin and Vienna. The Russians have attacked Eupatoria, and been repulsed by Omar Pasha and his Turks. The Russians, commanded by Liprandi, lost 500 killed and wounded.

*February 27th.*—Lord Palmerston has patched up his Cabinet, by admitting Lord John to the Colonies and Sir Charles Wood to the Admiralty.

*March 3rd.*—The Emperor Nicholas died yesterday between twelve and one o'clock, at St. Petersburg, of pulmonary apoplexy —(query, a broken heart?); it was announced in both Houses, and received with solemn silence. This event may be of immense advantage to us, if our rulers have the talent to profit by it, otherwise it may only serve for a dishonourable peace.

Lord Stanley writes that Louis Napoleon objects strongly to the committee of inquiry into the war; and says, if it takes place, though his army will still act on the same side as ours, it can no longer do so along with it. He is evidently alarmed at the *lâches* of his own Ministers and Generals being shown up to Europe, and endangering his position. Palmerston is much perplexed, and will probably dissolve Parliament as the only means of getting himself out of the scrape of the committee of inquiry, to which he has been forced to consent.

Palmerston's refusal, this conditional offer fell to the ground. Mr. Gladstone had no share in bringing about that refusal. He further says that he, Sir J. Graham, and Mr. Herbert, joined in the full belief that Lord Palmerston would resist the Committee on the war as they had all done under Lord Aberdeen, and that his submission to it drove them out. Such is, no doubt, the truth of a transaction which the public could not understand. The 'Quarterly Review' of the year believes that both Lord Derby and the trio who left Lord Palmerston in ten days, were all out-manœuvred by the latter, and it is not impossible that Lord Derby foresaw this, and suddenly threw up the cards.

[1] *Vide* 'Hansard,' vol. cxxxvi. p. 1822.

*March 11th.*—I saw Walewski yesterday, who had received a letter from General Canrobert, saying that the English had 20,000 effective bayonets in the Crimea, and that they were men whose equals did not exist on the face of the earth ; men whose iron frames had resisted every fatigue and privation, and whose courage was such that they were invincible. He added that if those 20,000 men were his, he would not exchange them for double the number of any troops of any nation, not even excepting his own. He also said that our newspapers did a great deal of harm by all the accounts given of the misery of our troops, which are translated and read to the Russian army, and, of course, encourage them to persevere in resisting us. Prince Albert told me yesterday that it was quite true that, when the French came to our assistance at Inkerman, they were staggered by the Russian fire, and their officers asked to have the remnant of the Guards brought up for them to form upon, as they could not otherwise get their men to advance. The Prince praised our officers in the most enthusiastic manner.

The Queen most kindly sent Lady Canning this morning to inquire after Lady Malmesbury, who had been taken ill during dinner at the Palace yesterday.

*March 23rd.*—I have positive proof that the French Ambassador, Walewski, throughout the late events, has been most active in the intrigue which placed and kept Lord Palmerston in office, both as against Lord John and Lord Derby.

The Emperor has a great admiration for him, and told me once, 'Avec Palmerston, on peut faire de grandes choses.'

*March 25th.*—We went to Lady Palmerston's party ; there was a great crowd. The Walewskis were there ; both very reserved and awkward in their manner, which makes me think that they are aware we know of their intrigues against us.

*March 31st.*—Left London. The English and French Governments have prevailed upon Louis Napoleon to pay a visit to England, the main object being to prevent his going to the Crimea, which he was bent upon. The Queen has in consequence given them an invitation, which has been accepted. Lady Tankerville called and told me she asked Lady Palmerston yesterday whether it was true that M. Drouyn de l'Huys's mission here was to get

Lord John recalled from Vienna. She denied it positively, saying he had come to discuss the third point of the treaty with
Austria with the English Government, about which there are
some difficulties.

Lady Palmerston complains of Count Walewski's pomposity;
she says that the airs he gives himself are quite ridiculous, and
that he was much displeased at the arrival of M. Drouyn de
l'Huys,[1] being also extremely hurt when Prince Albert went to
Boulogne to meet the Emperor.

*April 13th, London.*—I arrived from Paris, where I had been
for a week with Lord Hardwicke. Lord Lansdowne called and
told me that the members of the Conference at Vienna smoked a
good deal, and one day M. de Bourqueney, the French Minister, proposed to adjourn for an hour for that purpose, upon which the
Turkish Ambassador, who had not yet opened his mouth, jumped
up and supported M. de Bourqueney's proposal. Everybody was
extremely civil to me at Paris. The Emperor as friendly as ever.
Madame Walewska called on Lady Malmesbury, and said she
should not have a moment's peace till the Emperor left England,
as she fears some attempt on his life from the 'Rouges;' but she
told her that the Government had sent word to the principal
leaders that, in the event of any attempt being made, they would
all be expelled from England. This has frightened them so much
that Ledru Rollin and others have left London for Edinburgh, to
be out of the way.

When at Paris, I dined with Persigny, and had a long conversation with him to the following effect :—

He said : 'The Emperor consults no one; that he is incapable
of seeing different sides of a question; that his judgment is good
when he does hear them. The war began without any plan;
everything done by himself. His Cabinet was astonished at his
first announcement of an army going to Gallipoli.'

Persigny pressed a *coup de main*, but the Emperor went to
Varna and Adrianople instead.

'The Emperor is surrounded by flatterers. Fould, &c., rogues,
and robbers. Present negotiations ill-conducted. Second point

---

[1] Drouyn de l'Huys was recalled by the Emperor, who was dissatisfied with the
result of his mission to Vienna.

(Danube) should have been discussed the last, to keep Austria favourable. Persigny strongly for peace, and says France is all for it. Proposes we should return to first objects, the safety of the Provinces and Turkey, and fortify Constantinople. He says that, according to his suggestion, Kamiesh is to be fortified and a garrison left there; the army withdrawn either to Eupatoria or Constantinople. Orders have been sent for this. He says that if the Emperor is to go to the Crimea, there must be peace at any price to prevent it. If not, the war might go on, but if the French army is lost, then there will be a revolution.'

'Canrobert a very undecided man.'

'Refused to act on December 2, but obeyed orders. Could not make up his mind which party to join.'

Persigny said that they should threaten Austria and Prussia on the west, to push them on in a crusade against Russia. Raise Poland and Hungary; nothing but a crusade could stop the destiny of Russia. If we cannot have one, we must patch it up as he proposes for the present.

'The Empress objects to vulgar people, and prevents access to the Emperor.'

At the Council last year, announced attack on the Baltic. Persigny asked if he meant Cronstadt. 'No, of course not; it would require 100,000 men, cavalry included.' 'But Cronstadt is an island.' 'No, it is not,' &c., and the Emperor sent for a map. Everything done with same ignorance and carelessness. The Emperor does not work two hours a day, and yet will order everything. Occupied with such things as his journey to England and his Exhibition.

This conversation is characteristic of the reckless way in which Persigny formed his opinions, and the blunt honesty with which he expresses them.

Madame Walewska especially dreads the Emperor's visits to the City, the Crystal Palace, and the Opera. The Emperor and Empress arrive at Windsor next Monday.

*Lord Malmesbury to Lord Derby.*

London : April 14, 1855.

My dear Derby,—I returned yesterday from Paris, where I saw the *three*[1] persons most interested and most actively employed in the events of the day. I had long conversations with them; their information was spontaneous; and as I heard them separately and they did not differ, I believe it to be correct and worth relating.

First, then, for *Vienna.*

The Allies signed a note last year pledging themselves to the permanent dismantling of Sebastopol.

The campaign has not been such as to justify this demand.

Other alternatives, with the same objects, were to be found.

Lord John Russell was sent to Vienna to discover what these might be.

On the 12th inst. he wrote to her Majesty's Government, stating that the Allies must make great modifications in their demands if they desired to meet the 'prejudices of *Austria*' ('preconcerted opinions'). *Russia* positively refused to pledge herself even to limit the number of her ships in the Euxine, stating that Turkey might build ships and fortresses on her coast *ad libitum*, both claiming the right of independent nations. She admitted the general Protectorate of the Five Powers and the freedom of the Danube. She denied that we had gained any advantages for the redemption of which she should make any sacrifice of power or dignity.

*Austria* so far supported this statement that she advised the Allies to make a peace, provided Russia would agree to limit her fleet to its present number, Turkey doing the same in the Black Sea; Turkey to fortify Constantinople or other places, Russia to admit Consuls at Sebastopol and elsewhere.

Lord John heard all this without at once replying that to allow Turkey to fortify her own coast was no favour, seeing she had a natural right to do so, and that, although we had failed to take Sebastopol, the Black Sea was *de facto* absolutely in the power of the Allies so long as they chose to keep it, and that this was practically the total annihilation of Russian Supremacy in that Sea. We had, therefore, a material advantage, which must be paid for.

The Allied Governments were much dissatisfied with Lord John's silence, and Drouyn de l'Huys was sent to England to settle an ultimatum. All this time the French Ministers, alarmed at the failures of the siege, were completely panic-struck by the idea of the Emperor's

_____
[1] The Emperor, Persigny, and Fould,

journey to the Crimea. They openly stated, and now state, that the great Russian Question is a trifle to this catastrophe, and that *anything* is preferable to it. To prevent it any peace must be made. When Drouyn came over, Palmerston remained firm, and was, I have no doubt, supported by the Emperor.

What the exact ultimatum is, I do not know, but it is certainly one which Russia will not accept, and which Austria will not *openly* support.

I believe another campaign is inevitable. The Emperor's argument is that, even should it be unsuccessful, we can retire upon a plan of warfare which would have been, perhaps, the best at first—namely, to withdraw our armies, have an allied force of 20,000 or 30,000 men at Constantinople, and close the Baltic and the Euxine hermetically with our fleets. The cost would be comparatively small, the pressure, physical and moral, upon Russia immense, and we could hold on at this for any time.

I told the Emperor that while we were negotiating at Vienna our Admirals ought to be shelling Odessa; but he said the war must be carried on according to the 'civilised ideas of 1855.' I observed that if that system was to be followed, at least we ought to resort most implacably to real and universal blockade, for we had now followed neither principle. He means to urge the establishment of a Council of War at Paris, without which no *ensemble* can be obtained in any plans which the Allies are to carry out. Hence, he said, our misfortunes.

Now as to the *theatre of war* in the East. The impression is that Sebastopol is stronger than ever on the south side, and that our bombardment will be like the first; but we *must fire off* the *material* we have brought up, as it cannot be left there or carried off. Canrobert has been ready to begin for some time, but Raglan refuses, and will *give no reason*, at which both Governments are much incensed. They suppose that he wishes to avoid a great slaughter until he sees that the Vienna negotiations are fruitless.

Preparations are made to withdraw the army and re-embark it, so as to throw it upon another point, either of Asia or Europe, if desirable. To effect this it has been found feasible to so entrench Kamiesh as to render it impregnable. Through it the armies may defile to the ships, and re-embark safely, and leave 10,000 men to hold it as a key to Sebastopol. This may or may not be done under the thunder of the general bombardment.

The Emperor told me he should certainly go out to see with his own eyes. He will have 45,000 men and the Sardinians there in May.

The Sebastopol armies are now 20,000 effective English and 70,000 French. The latter have lost 50,000 since the war.

The Emperor stays till this day week, and is very anxious that he may be seen as much as possible in public. He is very angry at Walewski's fright about attempts on his person.

Your reply to his paper and Ellenborough's plan have never reached him, and he begged me to obtain a duplicate for him. Will you ask Ellenborough to draw up another? As I don't know what you sent, and how it went, I cannot act.

Pray keep this letter confidentially to yourself, *Stanley excepted.*

Yours, &c.<br>MALMESBURY.

*April 16th.*—Lady Ossulston, Lady Manners, my wife and I, went to Lord Carrington's house in Whitehall to see the Emperor of the French pass. The weather was beautiful and bright; the streets were choked with people. The *cortège* made its appearance at 6.15 P.M. ; there were six open carriages, four of them escorted by a squadron of Life Guards, and a good many outriders in scarlet liveries. They passed very slowly at a walk, and were enthusiastically cheered the whole way from the South-Eastern to the Great Western terminus. They went along Parliament Street, Pall Mall, St. James's Street, Piccadilly, into Hyde Park, round by the Serpentine and out by the Bayswater Gate, thousands of people lining the road for the whole distance. On going up St. James's Street, the Emperor was seen to point out to the Empress the house where he formerly lived in King Street. This was at once understood by the crowd, who cheered louder than ever. On passing the Horse Guards, which were exactly opposite our window, the Emperor stood up in his carriage and saluted the colours, and was of course immensely cheered. His reception was certainly a triumphant one.

*April 17th.*—The Emperor's passage across the Channel yesterday, though very smooth, was not a safe one, owing to the dense fog, and they were near running on shore on the South Foreland. Captain Smithett fortunately piloted the 'Pelican,' which conveyed them, and got her safe alongside the new pier ; but the French man-of-war, the 'Austerlitz,' went ashore three miles east of Dover.

It is reported that Russia refuses our propositions.

*April 18th.*—We are invited to Windsor, and, after dining at my brother's, started for the Castle at nine. The special train with the London party had not yet arrived. We all waited in the Waterloo Chamber, which was prepared for music. The Queen, Emperor, and Empress, with the royal family, their suites, and those invited to the banquet, entered soon after ten, and seated themselves without speaking to anyone. As soon as the music was over, the company passed before the Queen and Emperor. Lady Malmesbury was afterwards presented by Madame Walewska to the Empress, who spoke to her very kindly. The fatigue of the journey, and all she had gone through since, made her look very delicate, and yesterday she was unable to appear at dinner in St. George's Hall.

We left at twelve ; found the special train ready at the station, and reached home at half-past one. The Queen had arranged everything herself—made out the lists of invitations for both parties at Windsor and the concert for to-morrow at Buckingham Palace. Very few, except Cabinet Ministers, are asked twice. Even Lady Breadalbane, who is one of the Court, was invited only for the evening party last night, and had to sleep at a pastrycook's, there being no room at the Castle.

*April 19th.*—We went at five o'clock to the French Embassy, where Lady Malmesbury was presented to the Emperor ; the whole Corps Diplomatique were there, and in the state of fuss they always exhibit whenever any function is going on, each one being apparently afraid of his precedence being usurped. The Emperor and Empress received us very cordially. Both looked tired with their day's work, having come in the morning from Windsor, gone to the Mansion House, then to this reception and to-night a great dinner at the Palace, and the Opera to go through.

*April 21st.*—We gave a dinner to Lady Ailesbury, Lady Glengall, Lord and Lady Lyndhurst, the Ossulstons, Lord Bath, Lord Somerton, Lord A. FitzClarence, and Colonel Macdonald. I suppose they were amused, as they stayed till twelve o'clock. Lord Adolphus told me that the leave-taking this morning, when the Emperor and Empress left, was most touching. Everybody cried, even the *suite*.  The Queen's children began, as the Empress had been very kind to them and they were sorry to lose her, and this set off the Empress and maids of honour.

*April 24th.*—The Conferences at Vienna are broken off, and Lord John Russell and M. Drouyn de l'Huys have left on their return home.  It is surprising that the Russians should have refused the last proposition, which was to exclude all ships of war from the Black Sea ; as they might have built any number of ships and collected a force there without anyone knowing it.

*April 25th.*—Lord Palmerston announced last night that Lord John had left Vienna, and that M. Drouyn de l'Huys remained there only for another day.  I spoke in the House of Lords, disapproving the terms offered to Russia, and saying that I could not believe the first alternative offered, that the ' Russian naval force in the Black Sea should henceforth be limited by treaty,' had proceeded from Lord Clarendon or Palmerston, but that I imagined it to be an Austrian proposition.  Lord Clarendon did not deny this in his reply, or attempt in any way to vindicate the proposals, but declined a discussion, as the only information the Government possessed had come by telegraph ; but he added that negotiations were adjourned *sine die*, which sounds like a complete failure.

*April 27th.*—Lord Derby returned to-day from Newmarket, so full of his racing that he could think and talk of nothing else, and knew nothing of the last week's events ; and when I alluded to our propositions at the Vienna Conference having been rejected by Russia, asked, ' What propositions ? '—evidently not having looked at a newspaper for the whole week.  Such is the character of this remarkable man, who has the habit and power of concentrating his whole mind upon the subject which occupies him at the moment, and dismissing it totally, with equal facility.  He is very fond of using the expression ' One thing at a time.'

*April 29th.*—The Emperor Louis Napoleon has been shot at whilst riding in the Champs Elysées.  The assassin approached quite close to him, but missed, and was immediately arrested.

*May 1st.*—I never recollect such a bitter 1st of May ; even the sweeps could not stand it,

*May 6th.*—Lord Seymour, who is on the Sebastopol Committee, says it will last another fortnight. They are to examine Lord Hardinge and Mr. Sidney Herbert, and the Duke of Newcastle is going to the Crimea. I should have thought it the last place he would have chosen for a tour of pleasure, considering the obloquy with which his name is mentioned there. I went this morning to Lord Derby's to meet Lord Ellenborough, and we settled to make an attack upon the Government to-morrow week, in the form of an Address to the Queen, praying her Majesty to dismiss her Ministers in consequence of our want of confidence in their policy.

I did not myself approve of it, for I think Lord Derby ought either to have taken the Government last February, or, having refused to do so, he ought not to try to turn out the present one, which, under great difficulties, has not held office long enough to justify a judgment being passed upon their conduct of the war.

*May 8th.*—Count Walewski is made Minister for Foreign Affairs, and M. de Persigny comes to England as Ambassador.

*May 11th.*—It has been decided to give Madame Walewska a bracelet, and the four following ladies are to choose it : Shelburne, Mandeville, Sydney, and Malmesbury. Norman Macdonald is to manage the whole thing. He was rather offended at my saying that he was to be ' foreman of a jury of matrons.'

*May 12th.*—Lord Palmerston has tried to parry Lord Ellenborough's motion in the House of Lords by promising reforms in the Ordnance, Commissariat, and Medical departments of the army. A sham attack on the Government by Major Reed was made, to enable him to do so ; but Disraeli's clever reply showed them both up. At the same time, I think that the result of his speech will be to induce all connected with the army to vote against Lord Ellenborough, as they will be pleased at Lord Palmerston's statement, that for the patronage of the army to be dispensed by a member of the Government of the day would be an arrangement open to serious objections.

A subscription to Madame Walewska's bracelet has raised a sum of 130*l.*, which is sufficient to get a tolerably handsome one ; and the committee meets to-morrow at Lansdowne House to choose one from Emanuel's,

I went to the House of Lords. The Peeresses' Gallery was quite full. Before the debate began every seat was taken by ladies. Lord Ellenborough's speech was below the expectation, and fell flat. Lord Panmure spoke well, but did not answer a single point of Lord Ellenborough's speech. Lord Granville's contained little worthy of notice, except the assertion that the Howards had such wonderful faculties of increase that they were as numerous as the Smiths. Lord Elgin's was remarkable for its spitefulness, and Lord Winchilsea's for its injudiciousness. Lord Derby's was excellent. But throughout the whole debate it struck me that we had no case, and that the attack was not on the present Government but on the last. We were beaten by a majority of 110. The Government had 115 present and 66 proxies; we 71 present and no proxies, our men not having understood that the Government meant to call them. The number of ladies who attended the debate created great displeasure among the Peers. Lord Ellenborough said it had made him nervous; and Lord Lyndhurst positively refused to speak, saying that the House looked like a casino and not like a place where business is transacted. Lord Redesdale was also very angry, as the ladies overflowed from the gallery into the House; this invasion will, I fear, lead to more stringent and less agreeable arrangements in future. We went to Madame Walewska's farewell party.

*May 18th.*—We went to see the presentation of the medals to the officers and men who have served in the Crimea and are invalided or wounded. Lord Panmure sent us tickets for the Ministers' stand. The weather was beautiful. It was really a most glorious and touching sight. The Queen arrived exactly at eleven, and took her place on a platform raised three steps, in the centre of the Parade; and the officers and soldiers, headed by the Duke of Cambridge, Lords Lucan and Cardigan, passed in single file, each receiving a medal from her own hands as he went by. I never saw finer looking men, which was the more remarkable as they were not picked men. Many had lost an arm, and some were still lame from their wounds. I now understand how seven or eight thousand of these men could resist the whole Russian army at Inkerman. Sir Thomas Troubridge was drawn past the

Queen in a Bath-chair, having lost both his feet ; and I hear that she appointed him her aide-de-camp herself, as she gave him the medal.

After the ceremony, Lady Seymour, whom I met, told me that Mrs. Norton, talking about it to Lord Panmure, asked 'Was the Queen touched ?' 'Bless my soul, no !' was the reply. 'She had a brass railing before her, and no one could touch her.' Mrs. Norton then said, 'I mean, was she moved ?' 'Moved !' answered Lord Panmure, 'she had no occasion to move !' Mrs. Norton then gave it up in despair.

*May 26th.*—The Emperor Napoleon has superseded General Canrobert, and appointed General Pélissier as Commander-in-Chief. He has begun well by storming the entrenched Russian camp near the Quarantine Bastion.

*May 27th.*—Went to Heron Court, Parliament having adjourned to June 4.

*May 29th, Heron Court.*—Kertch was taken on May 24, by General Sir George Brown. The Russians destroyed three steamers, thirty transports, and 620,000 sacks of grain. We took thirty transports with their cargoes, and the whole loss of the Russians is calculated at a million sacks of corn, which is almost irreparable to them, as we possess the undisputed command of the Sea of Azof and of the mouths of the Don, down which the greatest part of the produce of the interior is carried.

*June 6th.*—Lords Clarendon and Palmerston have announced that the Conferences at Vienna are closed.

*June 8th.*—I went to the annual Eton dinner, being chairman.

*June 9th.*—Sir Francis Baring's motion, assuring the Queen of the support of Parliament during the war, was carried unanimously. In the debate, Lord Palmerston did not spare Gladstone, Sidney Herbert, and Sir James Graham, and said that when in the Cabinet they had approved of the very conditions of peace which they now denounced—namely, the 'limitation of the Russian fleet in the Black Sea.' To this they made no answer.

*June 12th.*—The London bank of Paul and Co. has failed, and many people in society have lost large sums.

*June 13th.*—Our losses in the attack upon the Gravel Pits at

Sebastopol, June 7, are very severe—eleven officers killed and forty wounded, 730 men killed and wounded.

*June 15th.*—We dined with the Elys. Young Lady Ely was sent for unexpectedly by the Queen, so the Dowager did the honours. The party consisted of the Derbys, Clarendons, Londesboroughs, Lyndhursts, Persigny, and Colonel Forester. Lord Clarendon and Lord Derby chaffed each other all through dinner, which made it very lively for everybody except poor Persigny, who does not understand English.

*June 16th.*—A most atrocious act has been committed by the Russians at Hango, in the Baltic. A boat from her Majesty's ship 'Cossack,' with three officers and twelve men, landed under a flag of truce with some Russian prisoners. The Russians fired upon them, killing all except one man, their own countrymen included. This is of a piece with their shooting their wounded enemies, which many did at Inkerman.

*June 19th.*—Mr. Layard's motion on administrative reform was rejected last night by a majority of 313. Lord Palmerston adopted Sir Edward Lytton's amendment, by which he probably saved the Government from defeat. Sir Charles Wood gave an account in the House of Commons of the massacre of the 'Cossack's' boat's crew by the Russians. Two officers and fourteen men landed at Hango with seven Finnish prisoners ; the flag of truce was hoisted and must have been visible long before the boat reached shore, but the Russians allowed her to approach without any warning, and the officers landed with the flag and the prisoners. The Russians, who were concealed behind rocks, suddenly came out, to the number of three or four hundred, and surrounded our men. The officer who commanded them spoke in English, and in reply to Lieutenant Geneste, said he did not care for the flag of truce, and immediately gave orders for his men to fire, which they did, killing with the first volley our two officers and the seven prisoners. They then fired into the boat, killing everybody except two men, one of whom shammed dead and by that means escaped to tell the tale. The other, who was slightly wounded, they dragged out and bayonetted on the pier. The commander of the 'Cossack,' finding the cutter did not return, sent the gig in search of her, and found her moored close to the jetty with some dead bodies in her, and some people on shore making signs to them to land. Had they done so they would have shared the same fate as their comrades.

*June 20th.*—The report of the Sebastopol Committee was brought up and read in the House of Commons. It is in some respects very fair, though evidently making the best of the case for the late Government. Severe censure is passed upon Lord Raglan for continuing Mr. Ward in his office of purveyor for the hospitals at Scutari after he had been pronounced unfit for his post. This is very unfair, when many others in responsible situations have been left in the exercise of their duties without any such censure being passed upon those who ought to have dismissed them and did not do so.

*June 22nd.*—Very bad news from the Crimea. The French and English attacked the Malakoff Tower and the Redan on the 18th, and were repulsed with great loss. No particulars are yet known. The Russian account of the Hango massacre confirms ours in some degree, saying that the officers are alive, though wounded and prisoners.

*June 25th.*—A list is published of the officers killed on June 18, or who died of their wounds. It amounts to nineteen names. The principal officers killed are—General Sir John Campbell ; Colonel Yea, 7th Regiment ; Colonel Shadforth, 57th. Among the captains is Lord Somerton's brother, Captain Agar. It appears that Strahan and Paul's bank has been insolvent for the last six years, that they have been trading upon the capital of their customers, and kept up appearances so well that no suspicion was entertained of the state of their affairs, and when the crash came it took everybody by surprise and has ruined hundreds. I hear that Mrs. Gore has lost 20,000*l.*, but I hope the rumour is untrue, for she is a very generous woman.

*June 26th.*—It was almost decided at a meeting last Saturday at Disraeli's to support Mr. Roebuck's motion censuring the late Government. Disraeli, of course, takes this view ; and Sir John Pakington, though not for it himself, says that the great majority of the party are so. It was decided to consult Lord Derby.

*June 29th.*—Sickness in the army is increasing. Generals

Pennefather, Codrington, and Brown are all ill ; and Lord Raglan himself has been attacked by cholera.

*June* 30*th.*—The evening papers announce the sad news of the death of Lord Raglan, which took place on the 28th ; the failure of the attack on the Malakoff had such an effect upon him that it increased his malady, and certainly contributed to its fatal issue. He was unconscious for the last four hours. I knew him well, and cannot recollect a finer character. He was the Duke's right-hand man through the Peninsular war, and was greatly esteemed by him. Handsome and high-bred in person, and charming in society, he was one of the most popular of its members. He was remarkable for his coolness under fire, and St. Arnaud, in his famous despatch after the battle of the Alma, says of him : ' Il avait toujours ce même calme qui ne le quitte jamais.' I never saw anything like the grief and consternation amongst military men.

*July* 1*st.*—General Simpson is appointed in Lord Raglan's place. He served in the Peninsula and in India ; but he inspires no confidence, as he is old and broken.

*July 7th, Heron Court.*—Lord John Russell made a curious statement in the House of Commons, saying plainly that his opinions were quite at variance with those of the rest of the Cabinet respecting the war, and yet he keeps his place. He seems to be conducting himself in the same manner he did last Christmas ; for now that he has returned from Vienna, and found the Government would not support his views, he evidently gave way, as he said nothing in Parliament to induce anyone to believe that his opinions respecting the war were not in accordance with theirs, and apparently acted in perfect harmony with his colleagues. At that time our prospects in the Crimea were favourable, and the Government and the war popular. Now, we have had a reverse ; the Government is in some degree shaken by it, and he chooses this moment to make an explanation respecting the Vienna Conference, and the part he took in favour of peace—a statement which must damage the Government in public opinion, by showing that upon such an important question as peace or war the Cabinet is not united. His object is of course perfectly clear—namely, to turn them out and come in himself as a peace Minister. All parties are abusing him at the clubs for his speech, the object of which is evident to everybody.

*July* 12*th.*—Lord Derby, before he left London, settled with Disraeli, without any communication with the rest of his party, to turn out the Government. Many of them would have disapproved of it under present circumstances. Sir Edward Lytton's motion is to be against Lord John Russell, and is fixed for next Monday.

After the way in which he has shown himself up, declaring first for war, then for peace, then again for war, our party is forced to bring forward a motion of censure on him and want of confidence in him, or else they must abdicate their position. If the Government chooses to sacrifice Lord John, they may retain office, but if they take the high line and support him, and Sir Edward Lytton carries his motion, they must of course resign; and then there is no one left but Lord Derby for Prime Minister. There is, however, little doubt that Lord Palmerston has secured the Irish Brigade by promising to vote for the fourteenth clause of the Tenants' Rights Bill (which was rejected by the House of Commons) if anyone proposes its reinsertion. A deputation waited upon him to ask him to do so. Mr. Malins introduced the subject on Friday in the House. Lord Palmerston could not deny the fact of a deputation having waited upon him, and of his having promised them his vote, but he of course denied having received any promise from them in return, and refused even to mention their names. The feeling of the House was strongly against his explanation. Lord Hardinge told me that Lord Panmure, soon after he took office as War Minister, wrote the most rude and abusive letter to Lord Raglan. He showed a copy of it to the Cabinet and to Lord Hardinge, who told him he had never seen such a letter written to an officer of Lord Raglan's rank; indeed, that it was quite unfit to be sent to any officer in her Majesty's service. Lord Panmure wanted him to keep a copy at the Horse Guards, but Lord Hardinge refused, and added, that he would not even have it said that he had ever put such a letter in his pocket. Lord Raglan never sent any reply. The Duke of Newcastle had also written him a very sharp reprimand; and when the Duke left office and was preparing to go to the Crimea, he wrote Lord Raglan an apology, saying he hoped he would forgive the letter which he had previously written, as it had not been dictated by any hostile feeling, but entirely from a sense of the duties of his position. Lord Raglan returned no answer, but it is well known that he felt deeply the way in which he was treated by the Government and the Press, and nothing but the highest possible sense of duty could have induced him to submit to all these insults and injuries, remain in command of the army, share their sufferings, and finally die at his post without a word of complaint or a murmur ever having escaped his lips.

*July* 14*th*.—Lord John Russell sent his resignation to the Queen yesterday, several members of the Government (though not in the Cabinet) having announced that they could not vote against Sir Edward Lytton's motion. Lord Palmerston probably got them to make this declaration to force Lord John to resign, and also to show how determined the Government is on the war question.

*July* 17*th*.—Sir E. Lytton, after making a long and clever speech, withdrew his motion in consequence of Lord John's resignation. Lord Palmerston was weaker than usual. Disraeli spoke well, and cut him up unmercifully, but in a gentlemanlike manner. Roebuck made a violent speech against the Government, but, of course, as the motion was withdrawn, all this is mere talk without any result for the present. It will probably have one in the future and upset the Government, unless they have the good fortune to obtain some great military success. This debate has shown the country that some members of the Government were ready to accept the Austrian proposition for peace, brought back from Vienna by Lord John Russell, had not the French Emperor objected. And this opposition of Louis Napoleon's is the 'unforeseen circumstance' so often alluded to in the course of the debate. Disraeli taxed them openly with the intention of making peace, and asserted that their not doing so was in consequence of the Emperor's disagreement, which was clearly proved by his recall of his Ambassador, M. Drouyn de l'Huys, from Vienna. Neither Lord Palmerston nor any of his colleagues said one word in contradiction of this statement.

*July* 20*th.*—Mr. Roebuck's motion of censure has been negatived by 289 to 182.

*July* 22*nd.*—Government have only carried the Turkish loan by a majority of three, and six Derbyites voted with them. It appears to me a great mistake to entrust five millions to the disposal of a Pasha for the payment of the Turkish troops, as it is pretty certain that the soldiers will see little of it.

*August* 9*th.*—Left London, *viâ* Glasgow, for Achnacarry. From Glasgow we took the 'Iona' steamer, the largest I have yet seen on this line, to Corpac. It was such a dark night that the servant was obliged to hold up the lantern the whole way before the horses. Just after we had passed Gierlochy, we were stopped by my keeper, who made us all get out, as a bridge had fallen in ; without him we should infallibly have gone over into a very deep burn. My servants, too, had a very dangerous journey by sea, their steamer having run aground between Aberdeen and Inverness ; they saved their lives, but lost all their luggage and some of ours.

*August* 21*st, Achnacarry.*—News has arrived of a battle having been fought on the 16th, on the Tchernaya, between the Russians and the French and Sardinians, which ended in the total defeat of the former. The party here consists of Lord Hardwicke and his daughters, Mr. Barrington,[1] Lord Ranelagh, and Colonel Knox.

Lady Mary Yorke is in the height of her beauty.

*September* 14*th.*—News has arrived, with a list of the officers killed and wounded in the assault on Sebastopol on September 8, amounting to near 150, but without any particulars.

*September* 17*th.*—We had an extraordinary day's sport at Achnacarry, by driving Gerraran Wood, killing six stags. Mr. Barrington shot three, I two, and Colonel Knox one. Two of them took to the loch, and were chased by the boat. A most exciting day's sport, which the ladies witnessed.

*September* 24*th.*—General Simpson's despatch of the 9th is published, and though he evidently does his best to soften the

---

[1] Now Viscount Barrington.

truth, there is no concealing the fact that our troops made a
signal failure in storming the Redan on the 8th. It is evident
that our bombardment was very weak, whilst that of the French
was tremendous. Our arrangements were defective, and great
confusion prevailed. Pélissier's and Niel's despatches do full
justice to the bravery of our troops, who kept the Redan for
nearly two hours, and were only forced to retreat from its being
quite open at the back, which enabled the Russians to bring
large bodies of men up in succession. A long list of our killed
and wounded, which exceeds that of Inkerman, shows that they
behaved most gallantly. The French themselves admit that
our task was the most difficult one, as we had 200 yards of
open ground to cross before we could reach the Redan. The
Malakoff, which Pélissier took, was within twenty yards of the
assaulting party, composed of 10,000 men with 8,000 in reserve,
whilst ours were less than half that number.

*October* 17th.—The Russians have had a severe defeat at
Kars. They attempted to storm the town, but were repulsed,
with the loss of 4,000 men, by General Williams and the Hungarian Klapka and Captain Teesdale.

*Lord Malmesbury to Lord Stanley.*

Achnacarry : October 21, 1855.

My dear Stanley,—As the question of making peace or going on
with the war is agitating the public mind, I venture to give you mine
on the subject.

Having all my life been told and felt that Russia intended to conquer
Turkey and the Baltic kingdoms some day or other, I was not surprised
at Menschikoff's mission and the subsequent invasion of Turkey on a
frivolous pretext. Having the help of France, I thought the time come
when we could successfully save Turkey from this invasion, and perhaps
prevent Russia from attempting, for many years to come, these attacks,
which she has made periodically, and invariably to her benefit, four or
five times during this century. We have of course succeeded in my
*first* object, but not yet in my second. This latter security cannot, I
think, be really obtained, unless you divest Russia of the Crimea and
Bessarabia, and make the Black Sea a peaceful lake like our North
American ones. I don't think the Sardinian idea ' absurd.' Whoever
has the Crimea must be assisted in holding it by a guarantee of the
other Powers, just as Belgium is now protected from France and

Holland; and there is this advantage, that the Sardinians would more than any people civilise and make the Crimea a commercial land. They would excite less hatred in Russia than the Turks, and less jealousy among us than Austria, which, by the way, I consider out of the question. The Genoese once held a good part of the Crimea. The objection I see to this is that the Straits might be closed to Sardinia by the Turk himself. On the whole, therefore, it might be better to give it to the Sultan under guarantee, and when he had this Tartar province proclaim the independence of the Principalities. It is, however, rather absurd disposing of the Crimea, which we have not yet conquered; and it is for this reason that I cannot think of a peace at this moment. With half Sebastopol in our hands, but which we dare neither leave nor live in, with a large army in our front undefeated, I do not understand how a country like England (leave alone France) could be the *first* to propose a peace to Russia.

I give you my worthless opinion as if I were the independent Minister of an absolute sovereign, untrammelled by Parliaments or parties ; and this makes a great difference, because in England there is always a party ready to get into office upon the inevitable unpopularity which war, however just and right, must bring at last. This unavoidable weariness will come some day. I doubt, however, if it be arrived yet. Doubtless, Disraeli and Walpole, both men averse by their physical bias to aught like war, are against proceeding with this one. Then you have pseudo-Russians, like Granby and Claud Hamilton—but I can't see any *reaction*. The Conservative party in the country are for it, and all the press, except 'The Press.' But 'The Press' only carps and asks questions, and proposes no solution. Nor do I think you can have one such as I have described, ensuring us from Russo-Turkish expeditions, until you have taken from her the Crimea and Bessarabia.

Depend upon it Napoleon had projects about Poland, but I think they have faded away. What I fear is that, the war over, he cannot withdraw his armies without having something material to show his countrymen. Whether he might take Candia or Cyprus, as a reward for having restored the Crimea to the Turk and set him on his legs, I don't know, but I can't see who would or could prevent him. Perhaps it would not much signify to us, as we hold our own at sea. When the time arrives at which we may reasonably think that Russia's lower limbs are completely crippled, it may require a great deal of courage to persuade Napoleon that enough has been done; but my belief is that he would not like to reduce Russia too low.

If we had had a really wise Minister at the beginning of the war, he would have gladly taken advantage of Napoleon's wish to take all the *land* work himself and give us all the *water* work. We should then have strengthened our fleets, and employed thousands of sailors, who must always be our military counterpoise to the system of Continental conscript hosts. Russia's navy would have been half destroyed as now, and France's not so materially increased and improved; and whilst we were following an effective policy against Russian aggression, we should have been establishing for future days our maritime supremacy over *every one*. As it is, we have shown the world that what Napier says is true—'We are a warlike, but not a military people.'

I do not think the time come for peace, or that we could obtain a solid one.

I do not think that this country *believes* that the time has arrived. I am convinced that our party would make a most false and unpopular move if, in a November Parliament, they followed Gladstone's line.

Yours, &c.,<br>MALMESBURY.

*October* 24th.—Left Achnacarry for Chillingham.

*November* 10th.—The Duke of Newcastle has been telegraphed for from the Crimea, to offer him the Colonial Department, Lord Stanley having refused it. This has placed the Government in difficulties, as they did not expect it.

*November* 13th.—I went to Paris with George Harris. I find the French are getting heartily sick of the war; their finances are in a very bad state. Madame Walewska is *enceinte*.

*November* 23rd, *Paris.*—I dined at the Tuileries. The Emperor was very friendly, and talked to me full an hour; the Empress looking very handsome, and all appearances concealed by the large dresses now worn.

*November* 29th.—The King of Sardinia, who is here, is as vulgar and coarse as possible. He said to the Empress : 'On me dit que les danseuses françaises ne portent pas de caleçons. Si c'est comme cela, ce sera pour moi le paradis terrestre.'

*Mr. Disraeli to Lord M.*

Hughenden: November 30, 1855.

My dear M.,—It is very provoking to have missed you, and only by an hour!

It seems to me that a party that has shrunk from the responsibility of conducting a war would never be able to carry on an opposition against a Minister for having concluded an unsatisfactory peace, however bad the terms.

We are off the rail of politics, and must continue so as long as the war lasts; and the only thing that can ever give us a chance is that the war should finish, and on the terms which may be now practicable. Then we shall, at least, revert to the position we occupied before the fatal refusal to take the reins last February, which lost us the heart and respect of all classes.

As a general rule, silence and inactivity should be our tactics; but anything which indicates a desire to conclude the war on honourable terms in this country assists the Emperor and distracts and enfeebles Palmerston, who cares for nothing but his immediate career.

I should like very much to know, *whether the opinion you have formed as to the probable result of the negotiations is shared by Walewski and Co.* Send me a line if you can.          Yours ever,

D.

*December 5th.*—I returned to London. I was presented to the King of Sardinia by Prince Albert, who told him that I was an 'ancien Ministre des Affaires Etrangères.' 'A quelle époque ?' answered the King. I said, 'In 1852, under Lord Derby's Government.'

The King replied : 'Que faites-vous à présent ?' To which the Prince said : 'Il fait de l'Opposition, car il faut toujours faire quelque chose dans ce pays.' 'Ah,' replied the King, 'donc, vous êtes opposé à mon voyage en Angleterre, et à mon alliance ?' To Lord Clarendon, whom the Prince presented as the present Minister for Foreign Affairs, his Majesty said, 'J'ai entendu parler de vous ;' adding, 'C'est fini'—which, in plain English, means 'Be off, I've nothing more to say.'

*Mr. Sidney Herbert to Lord M.*

Wilton : December 8, 1855.

My dear Fitz,—A thousand thanks for your letter. I have no doubt you are right as to the facts of the case of the French line-of-battle ships passing the Castles ; indeed you are sure to be so as having been cognisant of them, which I was not. I alluded to it only as, if true (which you show it is not), being one of the many evidences of the disposition of France to make political capital in the East by establishing French influence, and possibly acquiring rights if not territory. What with the campaigns of Napoleon in Egypt, the capitulations of Francis I., and even old St. Louis and Tunis, the French have a traditional field for ambition in the East.

But they have not the same *interests* in the East that Russia has, and we have, therefore, far less to apprehend in that quarter from her than from Russia.

Every country situated as Russia is will encroach on its neighbours *if not prevented.* Her relations with Circassia, Georgia, Persia, are the same as ours with Rangoon, Scinde, the Sikhs, and Oude. The stronger and more civilised necessarily absorb the weaker and more barbarous; but Russia, as compared with us, has this to her disadvantage, that one of those provinces, though barbarous and Asiatic in religion and habits, is partly European in geography, and we in Europe won't allow the process of absorption to go on. The public here are right in thinking of Russian aggression, but wrong in attributing it to a wonderful foresight, skill, and design. The Russians are just as great fools as other people; but they encroach as we encroach in India, Africa, and everywhere—because we can't help it. We, however, have an interest in preventing her, and by a combination of circumstances we have the power. We have rightly and justly availed ourselves of it, and we may flatter ourselves that we have, for a generation at least, put a check upon it; more than that we can't say.

Now, as you say, we must not form our opinions from an incorrect view of facts. So I must correct one opinion of yours—namely, that I hold that a Russian is better for us than a French alliance; and that it arises from my having a natural bias in favour of Russia. Now I have no bias in favour of Russia, but the contrary, arising from the natural bias of my mind in favour of a liberal policy. I don't mean I am in favour of intervention to set up Brummagem constitutions, such as Palmerston and John Russell talk about but are too wise to act upon; but I mean that the Russian system and politics are the opposite of ours, and do by their intervention arrest the progress of good government in Europe. Russia is not in these days a possible ally for us, in the sense in which you use the word when talking of a French alliance.

I, from my Russian connection, have heard and known more of their interior and exterior policy than the generality of people here. I recollect your grandfather's letters well, and I believe the old Duke and Aberdeen were right in 1827-8 (I am not sure of the date), when they would have resisted the march on Adrianople, but Palmerston and the Whigs, who were then still full of Phil-Hellenism, and were intriguing with the Princess Lieven to turn the Duke out, succeeded in preventing any move in that direction. Palmerston, I think, called it Austro-Turco barbarism.

Had I held their views I could not have been a member of Lord Aberdeen's Government, nor advocated in the Cabinet the cementing in every way the French Alliance and striking the blow at Russia.

I felt that it must come sooner or later, and that no such opportunity would probably ever again recur.

France is the obvious ally for England, for many reasons. I do not know that I can select a better one from among them than that she is the only country who, if on bad terms, can injure us. There is no other nation we need fear. But there are other and less selfish reasons, which I need not enumerate to you.

My only fear is lest the too long continuance of a state of things bringing us into daily communication, and requiring necessarily great mutual forbearance and much give-and-take, should end in jealousy or coolness. I think it of paramount importance to England, with a view to the future, to end the war before any one of the Allies is tired of it, and before France begins to ask whether she is making sacrifices for her own honour or at our instance. I want to secure all that we have got, and all we have gained, and to lose none of the ulterior advantages if possible.

Now, with this full explanation, I do not think there is much difference between us. I feel some remorse at the length of the letter, but console myself by reflecting that you brought it on your own head.

Believe me, &c.

SIDNEY HERBERT.

*December 17th.*—The news of the fall of Kars is confirmed. General Williams, his staff, nine pashas, and the whole garrison are prisoners of war. They were obliged to surrender from starvation, but not until they had eaten their horses and even the cats and dogs in the town.

*December 28th.*—A triumphal reception was given at Christchurch to Admiral Sir Edmund Lyons, who, it appears, was born there.

## 1856

*January* 18*th*, 1856.—The Russians have accepted the Austrian ultimatum without reservation, which Lord Palmerston announced at Lady E. Hay's wedding.

*From Lord Derby to Lord M. (on the Life Peerages Question).*

Knowsley : January 19, 1856.

The Peerage is a very grave constitutional question ; and I am not at all surprised to learn from what quarter the *coup* has proceeded. I am engaged in examining the case. In spite of Lord Coke's dictum, the legality is very doubtful ; and the exercise of a prerogative which has been dormant for 300 years, and that without the slightest necessity, cannot be passed over without notice. My present idea is that, even *before* the Speech is read, we should give notice of moving for the Letters Patent ; that in moving for them we should challenge the Government to justify their excuse, and then be guided by their tone and the feeling of the House as to a subsequent address to the Crown. We must discuss this matter when we meet ; and I propose to have a small meeting of members of both Houses at my house at 2 P.M. on the Wednesday, which I hope you will be able to attend.

Ever yours sincerely,

DERBY.

The Earl of Malmesbury

*From Lord St. Leonards to Lord M. (on the Life Peerages Question).*

Carlton Club : January 21, 1856.

My dear Lord,—I was unluckily obliged to come to town this wet day.

You might be sure that the Government have a good deal to say upon the question of legality, and Parke himself is no doubt satisfied on that head. But I agree with you, the policy of this step, if legal, is one that must be discussed—in what shape Lord Derby will, I suppose, decide. Probably a committee might be appointed, in the first instance, although we all know pretty well what they are.

I hope to be at Lord Derby's dinner.

Our friends the French will get into a scrape if this finessing should lead to any real difficulty, I always thought that they would look to indemnity [1] in some shape.        Ever yours sincerely,

ST. LEONARDS.

[1] Savoy.

*February* 12*th.*—The Government have not given way on the question of the Life Peerage, and Lord Lyndhurst has announced that he will move to-day, ' That the House resolve itself into a Committee of Privilege.'

*February* 16*th.*—Lord and Lady Clarendon leave London to-day for the Paris Conference. Brünnow affects the greatest ignorance of the Czar's intentions, saying that Orloff [1] is the only man who knows what they are.

*February* 19*th.*—The further consideration of the Wensleydale Life Peerage is put off until the 22nd, to give Lords Lyndhurst, Brougham, and Campbell time for further investigations as to precedents ; but the result at present is that Lord Wensleydale has no right to his seat in the House of Lords.

*February* 23*rd.*—Yesterday, in the House of Lords, Lord Glenelg moved, ' That the following questions be referred to the Judges :—" Is it in the power of the Crown to create by patent the dignity of a Baron of the United Kingdom for life ? and what privileges does such a grant confer ? " ' The House divided. Majority against the motion, 31. The House then resolved itself into a Committee of Privileges, and Lord Lyndhurst moved his resolution embodying the report of the Committee, which denies the validity of the patent of Lord Wensleydale, so far as it gives him the right to sit and vote in Parliament.

*February* 24*th.*—The Comtesse de la Force has been murdered in her house in the Champs Elysées by her groom, a German.

*February* 27*th.*—Lord Derby dined with the Queen on Saturday, and both her Majesty and the Prince told him they had no idea the Peerage question would have been taken up as it has been, or they would not have granted it.

*March* 5*th.*—The Conference is proceeding at Paris. Louis Napoleon's speech in opening the Legislative Assembly was most cordial towards England, and does not leave the slightest hope to Austria and Russia of their succeeding in sowing dissension between us and France. He only professed himself quite ready to continue the war if the negotiations failed.

*March* 7*th.*—Sir William Clay's bill for the abolition of Church rates passed the House of Commons by a majority of 44, Lord Palmerston and the whole Government voting for it.

[1] The Russian plenipotentiary at the Conference.

*March* 8*th.*—The Opera House at Covent Garden has been burnt down by the chandelier being over-heated during the monster benefit of the conjurer Anderson, to whom the theatre had been let for two months. This imitation of American vulgarity ended by a masked ball of the lowest kind, tickets being one shilling. Mr. Gye, the manager, who was at Paris, had refused to allow the masquerade. The loss will not be covered by 300,000*l.*

*March* 10*th.*—I got a letter from M. de Persigny, announcing that the Empress of the French was safely confined of a son. The Emperor, who never left the room, was worked up into such a nervous state that for fifteen hours he cried and sobbed without ceasing ; and when the child was born he was so overpowered with joy that he rushed into the next room and embraced the five first persons he met. Then recollecting that his behaviour was not dignified, he said, ' Je ne peux pas vous embrasser tous.'

*March* 29*th.*—Madame de Persigny called to wish us good-bye, and told us the following riddle : ' Pourquoi l'Empereur est-il changé pour le mieux depuis la naissance de son fils ? ' —' Parce qu'il a un nouveau-né (nez).'

*March* 30*th.*—The signing of the Treaty of Peace with Russia was announced by the firing of cannon from the Tower and the Horse Guards. Numbers collected in the streets, but no enthusiasm was shown.

*April* 5*th.*—Dined with the Palmerstons. He says the French call the medal we have given them 'La médaille de sauvetage.' They want another lesson from us.

There is a new play come out in Paris, the principal characters being Adam, Eve, and the serpent. It is quite a new version— the serpent succeeds in making himself agreeable to Eve, and poor Adam is made to look very foolish.

*April* 10*th.*—I got a letter from Lord Clarendon, saying that he could not be present 'for my amiable invitation to Kars' (I had given notice of a motion with respect to the fate of that fortress), but went on to say that he would be back by the end of next week, and that the Treaty would give our party weapons against him, but that he was, on the whole, satisfied, as things looked very bad two months ago ; and the difficulties he had had to contend with were very great and would probably never be known, by which I conclude the French threw us over and are now toadying the Russians.

*April 11th.*—I spoke in the House of Lords on the subject of the sale of the cavalry horses in the Crimea to the Russians, and this morning I got a letter from the Duke of Cambridge, praising my speech and thanking me for it. Also another from General Lord de Ros to the same effect.

*April 20th.*—Cavour and the Chevalier Massimo d'Azeglio called on me. The former spoke very openly on Italian politics, and I, not being in office, had no reason for not being equally frank.

*April 26th.*—I saw Lord Derby to-day ; he wants to get out of the discussion on the fall of Kars, and is much disgusted with his party for not being willing to support Mr. Whiteside's motion upon it. I can see that many believe Disraeli would like to place himself at the head of the Conservative party, to the exclusion of Lord Derby. These suspicions are strengthened by the tone of his paper, 'The Press,' which avoids ever mentioning the name of Lord Derby, or of anyone except Disraeli himself, whom it praises in the most fulsome manner. I have also myself been sounded upon the subject of making Disraeli or Lord Stanley our leader, but I do not think that the person to whom I allude will ever do so again.

*April 28th.*—I went to the House of Commons to hear Mr. Whiteside's speech upon Kars. It was a very fine one, and I think Mr. Whiteside decidedly a greater orator than Disraeli, although his Irish accent, which is very strong, when he gets animated, spoils the effect to English ears. He was immensely cheered. Lord Derby's meeting this morning was not a very full one ; Lord Granby was present, and, as usual, made difficulties, as did also Mr. Bentinck, without anything leading to it.

*April 30th.*—The Treaty of Paris is to be discussed next Monday, and is open to great objections. I shall withdraw my motion upon Kars.

*May 1st.*—I saw Lord Derby to-day ; he wishes me to begin the debate upon the Treaty next Monday. We shall be beaten to-night in the House of Commons by more than a hundred, fifty of our men voting against us or staying away. Lord Derby has certainly lost a great deal of his influence by refusing office last year.

*May 2nd.*—The Government had a majority of 399 against Mr. Whiteside upon Kars.

*May 3rd.*—I went with some of my colleagues to Lord Derby this morning, when he and Disraeli decided that I am to begin the debate on Monday in condemnation of the Treaty.

*May 5th.*—I spoke for an hour against the Treaty of Paris, and received many compliments upon it both from my friends and the cross benches. Lord Clarendon spoke in answer, and Lord Derby followed, winding up with these words : 'So much for the *capitulation* of Paris.'

*May 7th.*—There was a dinner at the Palace for Baron Brünnow—a dinner of reconciliation, consisting entirely of Ministers and ex-Ministers. Lord John Russell was there, and very civil to me, as, when I arrived, he crossed the room to come and speak to me—a thing he never did before. He began the conversation by saying : 'You gave it them well last night,' and seemed quite delighted at the Government being bullied. He added that the debate in the Lords was very superior to that in the Commons. I had to take Lady Clarendon to dinner. She was at first very cross, but I ended by laughing her out of her bad humour.

*May 23rd.*—A discussion on the Maritime Law was brought on last night by Lord Colchester. Lords Derby and Carnarvon spoke beautifully, but the Government had a majority of 54.

*May 28th.*—I went to the Derby with the Persignys.

*June 5th.*—The American Government have dismissed Mr. Crampton, United States Minister, who is gone to Toronto, which is rather alarming. I dined with the Clarendons.

*June 24th.*—The Alteration of Oaths Bill was rejected by the Lords by a majority of 32.

*June 26th.*—We dined with the Hardwickes to meet the celebrated tragic actress Ristori. She arrived very late, just as we were sitting down to dinner, and made an *entrée* quite in the theatrical style—violent exclamations, gesticulations, and grimaces, giving a long history of how her coachman had lost his way, and her feelings on the subject, all in the loudest tone of voice. She calls herself thirty, but looks fifty. I went to Lady Westminster's ball to meet the Queen. Everybody is talking of a scene that occurred yesterday at the Levée. A vulgar American having gone in a frock coat with a yellow waistcoat and a black neckcloth, Sir E. Cust told him he could not pass the Queen in that costume. He insisted, and Mr. Dallas, the American Minister, took his part, and finding, after an angry altercation, that Sir E. Cust would not give way, he left the Palace with all his suite.

*June 28th.*—We gave a dinner to a large party, among whom were the Clarendons. He told me that he had gone to Lady Westminster's ball in full dress by mistake, and was the only man not in frock dress. Some one observed in the hearing of Mrs. Dallas, ' Why is Lord Clarendon in full dress ?' ' Oh,' answered the person addressed, ' I suppose he has been dining with Mr. Dallas.'

*June 30th.*—I hear that Mrs. Anson has written home a very bad account of Lady Canning, whose health seems to be seriously affected by the climate of India.

*July 8th.*—The Queen reviewed the troops at Aldershot, and made them a speech. Lord Hardinge was seized with a fit at Aldershot in her presence. He was talking to her at the time, and was brought to London very ill.[1] We went to Lord Carrington's house to see the entry of the Guards into London. There were three battalions of above a thousand men each. They marched past in fours, preceded by their colonels on horseback and their bands, in heavy marching order. Certainly they looked as if they had done work; their uniforms were shabby, many having almost lost all colour, their bearskins quite brown, and they themselves, poor fellows, though they seemed happy, and were laughing as they marched along, were very thin and worn.

*August 10th.*—The Russians are at their old tricks again, and have seized the Isle of Serpents, at the mouth of the Danube, which by some oversight has not been mentioned in the treaty, and, as they possessed it before the war, they naturally concluded it belonged to them, no stipulations to the contrary having been made ; but it turns out to be of great importance, as it commands the mouths of the river, and admits of being fortified. This, coupled with their delay in restoring Kars and their blowing up Ismaïl and Reni, is contrary to the spirit of the treaty. The English fleet has received orders to re-enter the Black Sea, and to remain there until the Island of Serpents and Kars are given up.

[1] Lord Hardinge died the following September.

*August 19th.*—I travelled from London to Southampton in the same carriage with Lord and Lady Palmerston. Lord Palmerston talked the whole way in the most open manner of foreign affairs He says nothing can be worse than the way the Russians have behaved in carrying out the treaty. They have tried to evade almost every point, and taken advantage of every loophole and oversight. They have blown up the old castle of Kars, though it never could be of any use, and was merely a curious remnant of antiquity. They are making great difficulties about the settlement of the boundary in Bessarabia, saying that Bolgrad, an old village of that name, is not the one they meant, but another village of the same name, quite out of the intended line. Chreptovitch, the new Russian Ambassador, took a high tone, and talked of leaving England if these complaints were pressed, to which Lord Palmerston replied that the sooner he did so the better, if he did not give way upon them.

*Lord Derby to Lord M.*

Knowsley : August 28, 1856.

My dear Malmesbury,—I found your letter of the 25th on my return from York, whither I had ventured upon going to see my horse run ; but my rashness was punished by a slight return of my enemy, which compelled me to return, *re infecta.* I hope, however, that I may now report myself all right again, though my hand and wrist still continue rather weak, and I have not ventured, or indeed been able to hold a gun. There is plenty of employment for one. We have a good deal of oats cut, but no wheat in this neighbourhood yet. The corn crops look very well, but the extent of disease in the potatoes is fearful. It has not been so bad for years. I hear from Ossulston that you are to be with him at Chillingham towards the middle or end of October ; so I suppose we may look forward to seeing you here on your way back, early in November. Palmerston seems to have been in a very communicative mood with you the other day ; and his report fully confirms what I had suspected to be the case, not only that Russia is playing us false as far as she dares, but that 'our august ally' is less to be depended upon than might be desirable. It is quite evident to me that there is a great desire on both sides for a *rapprochement* between the two Emperors, at our expense. Morny is evidently playing first fiddle at St. Petersburg, and Granville's position will not be made the more agreeable by the coldness of Chreptovitch's reception here. Peace *may* be maintained, but even of this I do not feel confident ; but of this I am very sure, that it will not be long before our Government will have cause to be heartily ashamed of the terms and results of the peace they have 'patched up.' The election of Fremont I should look upon as satisfactory, and as affording the best prospect of a solution of our difficulties in *that* quarter. What is Palmerston doing with all the Church patronage which is pouring in upon him ?

Ever yours sincerely,<br>DERBY.

*September* 6*th.*—Civil war has broken out in the United States between the Abolitionists and the Pro-Slavery Party, and a great deal of blood has been already shed. The Government refused to take part with either side, upon which the Slave party in Congress would not vote the supplies for the army, which accordingly must be disbanded.

*September* 17*th.*—Left Heron Court for Paris, where I expect to meet George Harris. I hear that Lady Stafford and Lady Emily Peel are much admired at Petersburg, where they are gone for the coronation of the Emperor, and that M. de Morny's *fêtes* are quite surpassed by those of Lord Granville ; but the person who has had the most success is Lord Stafford's piper, who, whenever he shows himself in the streets, is followed by crowds, who fancy he is the Ambassador.

*October* 15*th.*—I left Venice after a pleasant visit with George Harris. Made acquaintance with Countess Persico, who has a palazzo at Castelfranco, near Treviso, and received much hospitality from her.

*October* 20*th.*—Arrived at Turin. Dined with our Minister, Sir James Hudson. He says the French do not go with us on the Bolgrad question. There is to be a Congress at Paris to decide that, and that of Serpent Island, which the Russians wish to swindle out of the treaty. Palmerston says he would prefer Petersburg, as being less Russian than Walewski's house.

*October* 22*nd.*—Called on my cousin, the Duc de Gramont, who is French Minister here.

*October* 24*th.*—Started for London. Yesterday I dined with Cavour. The dinner was very agreeable, there being no other guests than Hudson and myself. We talked openly on politics, and in the evening General La Marmora came on purpose to be introduced to me. Nothing could be more amiable than Gramont during my stay at Turin ; but he is evidently little thought of, whilst our Minister, Hudson, is lord of the place and has the most unbounded influence over the King and his Ministers; but he lives openly with the Revolutionary party, and does not disguise his Italian proclivities. The French seem to me completely at variance with us as to the dishonest frauds of the Russians respecting the meaning of our treaty, and, if Palmerston is not firm, they will get what they want.

*November 12th.*—Louis Napoleon is said to have given up his intended parties at Fontainebleau in consequence of the discontent expressed at the extravagance of the Court whilst the people are suffering great distress from the high prices. The English and French Ministers have left Naples, and the English and French fleets are blustering in the bay, pretending to be ready to bombard the town. Everyone feels that such an atrocity could not be committed, and that a gentleman might as well strike a woman as fire upon Naples. At the Lord Mayor's dinner on the 9th, given as usual to the Prime Minister and his colleages, the Corps Diplomatique was represented by the Mexican Minister and the one from the Republic of Hayti, a black man. Such is the result, for the second time, of Palmerston's aggressive policy and offensive communication with foreign Powers. There is no man so pleasant in his manner in private life, and it is extraordinary that he should not be able to exercise the same courtesy in public affairs.

*November 21st.*—Persigny told me Walewski is in disgrace. The difficulty about Bolgrad and the Isle of Serpents arises from the Emperor having been entrapped into a promise by the Russians ; but Presigny has suggested a solution, which has been accepted by the Emperor and our Government—viz. a Congress which is to assemble, into which Sardinia is to be admitted, on condition of voting against Russia. Austria goes with England, and Prussia is of course excluded. This gives England a majority, and the Emperor an excuse for giving way.

*From Lord Derby to Lord M. (on the causes of the Disorganisation of the Conservative Party, &c.)*

Knowsley: December 15, 1856.

My dear Malmesbury,—I return you Jolliffe's letters, enclosed in your desponding one of the 7th. I ought to have done so earlier, but I have had Lichfield with me all the week, alone; and we have been so busy shooting, that I have had no time to give to politics. Yesterday I was threatened with a fit of gout, but it has, I hope, quite passed off; and I expect to go to Hatfield to-morrow, and look forward to being with you on Friday afternoon. I shall be very glad to meet Jolliffe [1] there, and to talk over quietly with him and you the position and prospects of the Conservative party. That it is in a certain state of disorganisation is not to be denied, nor, I think, to be wondered at; indeed, I am disposed to be rather surprised to find how mere fidelity to party ties, and some personal feeling, has for so long a time kept together so large a body of men, under most adverse circumstances, and in the absence of any cry or leading question, to serve as a broad line of demarcation between the two sides of the House. The breach which was made in the Conservative body by Peel, in 1845-6, and which might have been healed to a great degree if his followers had only given us a fair support, or even stood neutral in the session of 1852-3, was widened by the formation of the Coalition Government, on the avowed principle (or no principle) of discarding all previous party ties. Public attention has since that time been mainly fixed upon the war: and since Palmerston came into office he has adroitly played his cards, so as to avoid, with one or two exceptions, making any attacks upon our institutions, or affording much ground for censure from a Conservative Opposition. In short, he has been a Conservative Minister working with Radical tools, and keeping up a show of Liberalism in his foreign policy, which nine in ten of the House of Commons care nothing about. That a Conservative party should have held together at all under such circumstances is rather to be wondered at, than that there should be apathy and indifference when there is nothing to be fought for by the bulk of the party. As to Disraeli's unpopularity, I see it and regret it; and especially regret that he does not see more of the party in private; but they could not do without him, even if there were anyone ready and able to take his place. For myself, I *never* was *ambitious* of office, and am not likely to become more so as I grow older; but I am now, as I have been, ready to accept the responsi-

[1] Whip of the Conservative party, afterwards created Lord Hylton.

bility of it if I see a chance not only of taking but of keeping it.  Of
that I see no chance with the present House of Commons, unless the
Government commit some very gross blunder, and make their continuance impossible.  But I agree with you that, if there is to be for many
years a chance of power for a Conservative Ministry, it must be secured
by active exertions at the general election, which must shortly take
place.

Yours very sincerely,<br>DERBY.

## 1857

*January 1st.*—The conference opened yesterday on the questions of Bolgrad and the Isle of Serpents, which the Russians
falsely claim as being included in the treaty of peace.  The Swiss
are making energetic preparations for resisting the threatened
invasion of Neufchâtel by Prussia, whilst England and France
are using their utmost exertions to prevent a war.  England has
declared war against Persia, and Admiral Seymour has bombarded
Canton to avenge an insult offered to our flag.  As far as I can
understand the cause of dispute, it does not appear to justify
such a severe punishment.  The men arrested were Chinese, and
the ship, though bearing English colours, was not English.  The
Chinese Government has been, however, so troublesome and insolent lately, that probably Lord Palmerston wishes to seize the
first pretext for giving them a lesson.

*January 9th.*—Madame de Bonneval writes that M. de Morny
is engaged to Mademoiselle Troubetskoi, a natural daughter of
the Emperor Nicholas and a maid-of-honour of the Empress.
She is handsome and has black eyes and auburn hair.

*January 25th.*—The news last received from China is unsatisfactory, for though we are in possession of all the forts, the
Chinese have succeeded in setting fire to our factories and banks,
and it has been decided, in consequence, to bombard Canton.

*January 29th.*—Princess Lieven has died at Paris.  When I
came out in the London world in 1826, she was then Russian
Ambassadress, and one of the most fashionable ladies in society.
She was very clever and agreeable, but the greatest *intrigante*

possible, having been all her life employed by the Russian Government as a spy, or rather, I should say, by the reigning Emperor, with whom she always corresponded directly. She was a great plague to our Secretaries for Foreign Affairs. Guizot, towards the end of her life, kept up political and intimate relations with her. Her son, Paul, was a charming dandy.

*January 31st.*—Despatches have been received from Admiral Sir Henry Leeke, giving an account of the operations of the English fleet and troops in the Persian Gulf. On December 4th, 1856, the island of Karrak was occupied; on the 7th the troops disembarked, and advanced upon Bushire under General Storkes, protected by the fire of the ships. The position of the enemy was strong, but was carried at the point of the bayonet, with the loss of Colonels Stopford and Malet, who were leading their men to the assault.

*February 3rd.*—I do not expect any amendment will be moved to the Address, but foreign affairs will be discussed, and I understand that Disraeli will make some terrific revelations in his speech, as Walewski has told him all he knows against Lord Palmerston, and if half only is true, it will damage him extremely. Gladstone and Sidney Herbert appear anxious to join Lord Derby. We reserve our whole strength for the income tax, and support Gladstone's measure—namely, to pay fivepence now, and nothing in 1860. If the latter joined our party, he would only benefit us by his talents, for on the other hand we should lose many of our supporters. The Duke of Beaufort, one of our staunchest adherents, told me at Longleat that if we coalesced with the Peelites he would leave the party, and I remember in 1855, when Lord Derby attempted to form a Government, and offered places to Gladstone and Herbert, that no less than eighty members of the House of Commons threatened to leave him.

This being the first night of the session, Disraeli made a long and eloquent speech, in which he brought forward the following accusation against the Government :—' Will it be believed that at the very time when Lord Clarendon was listening to the passionate representations of Count Cavour, in which he impeaches the very existence of Austrian rule, a secret treaty was in existence, guaranteeing to Austria the whole of her Italian

dominions—a guarantee from France to Austria of her Italian
possessions, given, not merely with the sanction and approval of
the noble lord (Palmerston), but by the advice and at the special
instance of his Government ?' Lord Palmerston denied the existence of such a treaty, saying that Disraeli must have been imposed
upon by the *gobemouches* of Paris ; and went on to assert that it
was the first time he had ever heard of such a treaty, and that,
if he had, he would have given his advice in an opposite direction.
The treaty was an entire romance, without the slighest foundation,
except that in the early part of the war with Russia communications passed between the Austrian and French Governments,
to the effect that the latter would take no part hostile to Austria.
On the 10th Disraeli repeated his accusation, maintaining that
the above agreement between Austria and France had assumed
the shape of a treaty, and that it was executed on December 22,
1854. He reasserted that the English Government had known
and approved of this.

Lord Palmerston then again rose and repeated that, to the
best of his belief, there was no treaty between Austria and France
guaranteeing the former's possessions in Italy ; but he confessed
that, in the latter part of 1854, it was hoped that Austria would
join England and France against Russia, and that an agreement
was made, that if she did so, and Russia instigated insurrections
in Italy for the purpose of distracting Austria, then France would
behave as an honourable ally ought, but that she would not
encourage any such risings, should the Austrian armies join
England and France ; and during the war, should disturbances
break out in Italy, then France would act in concert with whatever force the Austrians might have to defend their possessions.
All this, he said, was known to the British Government. Thus,
although Disraeli may be accused of finding a mare's nest, the facts
which he stated were correct, but do not bear the same intentions
and consequences which he had put upon them. His speech
altogether was inferior to his usual power, and was delivered very
nervously.

*February 4th.*—The Queen's Speech told us nothing. It
was all about foreign affairs. No reform, excepting in the law.
Disraeli's revelations, I think, fell rather flat. Lord Palmerston

denied the existence of a secret treaty with Austria, which he was accused of having made. The country may probably believe him rather than Disraeli, but diplomatists will not be so credulous, for what is the use of a secret treaty if you must confess it to the first person who asks the question ?

*February 6th.*—Lord Derby arrived at Heron Court for the wild-fowl shooting. He seems to think that Lord Palmerston's Government is becoming very unpopular. Lord Aberdeen voted for Lord Grey's amendment to the Address with ten of our men. This is such an invidious thing for an ex-Prime Minister to do, that his intention must have been to show his disapprobation of the Government ; and Gladstone's speech in the House of Commons, which one cannot disconnect from Lord Aberdeen's vote, looks as if the Peelites wished to make up their differences with our party ; but Lord Derby says that he does not mean to make any advances to them, as they would certainly lose us many of our people. He seems very sanguine about turning out the Government in the course of the session ; if we could do it on the income tax, that would be the best, as they would not dissolve Parliament on that question. I made a speech yesterday on moving for returns of the New Forest Commissioners, the number of days they have sat, and the list of claims adjusted, &c. I read my correspondence to the House and was much cheered ; all sides agreed that the Commissioners' letter to me was unjustifiable, and the Chancellor blamed it strongly. I hear that Lord Palmerston took my part, and said that if anything on the subject had been said in the House of Commons he would have got up and defended me.

*February 8th.*—Left for London to attend Lord Derby's meeting.

*February 11th.*—Meeting at Lord Derby's postponed to Saturday next, as Disraeli has sent to say that he was so occupied with the Secret Treaty accusation that he could not attend to any other business.

*February 13th.*—Another discussion last night on the Secret Treaty somewhat alters the complexion of the case. Lord Palmerston got up and acknowledged he had been mistaken with regard to what he calls the 'military convention' between France and Austria not being signed. He now admits it was signed.

Disraeli repeated again and again that there was a secret treaty between France and Austria, that it had been extensively acted upon, and that on its surface there was no limitation to the period of its operation.　Lord Palmerston, upon this, completely lost his temper—a rare occurrence with him, and which makes one believe that he felt himself in a scrape—but he again said, with the strongest asseverations, that it was only a temporary arrangement during the war with Russia, in case Austria joined against her ; that it was not signed at our instigation, but only communicated to us as an arrangement already settled between France and Austria.　If this be believed, it, of course, exculpates him and his Government, but it proves that when he made his first speech he was either ignorant of, or had forgotten, the circumstance.

*February 14th.*—The Chancellor of the Exchequer brought on his Budget last night.　The 9*d.* war tax is taken off, which makes a reduction of nine millions in the year's income.　In spite of this boon, there is much discontent on account of these two new wars, the Chinese and Persian, but the Budget is to be cut up by both Disraeli and Gladstone.

*February 16th.*—I went to Middleton.　Disraeli assured me that the Secret Treaty is a permanent one.　He throws cold water on the China question, which Lord Derby is to bring forward. Gladstone says this Budget is even worse than the famous Budgets of Sir Charles Wood, which were altered half a dozen times.

*February 21st.*—Disraeli made a long and clever speech against the Budget.　The Chancellor of the Exchequer replied, and made, I believe, a better speech than Disraeli's, and still longer.

*February 24th.*—The Government have carried their Budget by a majority of 80.　Many of our men voted with the Government, or rather with Big Ben,[1] the member for Norfolk, who amuses himself with opposing everything on both sides.

*February 27th.*—Lord Ellesmere is dead, and has left his wife 5,000*l.* a year and his yacht.　They married without settlements.

The division in the House of Lords on the China question took place last night, and the Government had a majority of 36.

---

[1] Mr. George Bentinck, member for Norfolk.

Lord Ellenborough and the Bishop of Oxford[1] spoke on our side, both of them very eloquently.

*February 28th.*—If Lord Palmerston had divided upon the China question last night in the House of Commons, he would have been beaten, and he is so nervous about it that he has a meeting this morning to threaten a dissolution in case he is not supported. It seems to me an unpopular question for a general election to turn upon. Nobody knows whether Disraeli will speak. I met him at the Levée, and he answered very sulkily, even pretending not to understand what I meant by asking him if he intended to speak. 'Speak! upon what?' he said. He has always discouraged a debate on the China question, for some reason best known to himself.

Lord Derby had a meeting of his party in the House of Commons. One hundred and sixty attended. He began by alluding to the defection of a few of the members of the Opposition on the Budget, which he understood had been occasioned by a report of his having coalesced with Mr. Gladstone. He denied such being the case, but declared in the most emphatic manner that should any member of the Conservative connection attempt to dictate to him the course he should pursue with regard to any political personages whatever, he would regard it as an insult, and no longer recognise that member as attached to his party. This declaration was received with long-continued cheering, and the greatest enthusiasm and the most complete confidence in Lord Derby were expressed.

*March 4th.*—On the question of the China War, moved by Mr. Cobden, the Government were beaten by a majority of sixteen. The principal speakers were Gladstone, Palmerston, and Disraeli. The latter was very bitter and personal. Gladstone statesmanlike, but dry and heavy. Big Ben tried to say a few words in support of Ministers, but the House would not listen to him. Lord Derby, in the House of Lords, denied the correctness of a paragraph in 'The Press,' giving an account of the meeting of his party on the 27th, saying it was a gross misrepresentation—that words were put into his mouth which he had never used, and that

---

[1] Samuel Wilberforce, afterwards Bishop of Winchester.

he was even made to say the exact contrary to what he really said.   Disraeli will not like this, for 'The Press' is conducted by him, and is his organ, always putting him forward and ignoring Lord Derby.

*March 5th.*—Lord Granville in the Lords, and Lord Palmerston in the Commons, announced the intention of Government to dissolve Parliament in consequence of their defeat on the China War.

*March 6th.*—Dr. Ferguson called.   He says the China question is an unfavourable one for our party, and we shall get a worse Parliament ; also that a coalition with the Peelites is denounced. I fear he is right, for nobody is a better judge of public feeling than a doctor who is constantly seeing all kinds of people.   I went to Lord Derby by appointment, and he sent me to Sidney Herbert to make some arrangements with him in concert with our party for the coming elections—namely, that we should not take a hostile part towards each other's candidates, so that, no personal enmities being made, there should be less difficulty in the two parties acting together, should circumstances make it advisable.   Sidney Herbert rejected this proposal, saying he thought it better that we should be quite independent of each other, and that he would not pledge himself not to support Lord Palmerston.   He was evidently taken by surprise, and did not know what to say, receiving me in a very unfriendly and even uncivil manner.   After a very short interview, Mrs. Herbert coming in with her bonnet and shawl on, he got up and said he must go out with her, almost turning me out of his house.   I said, as he seemed in a hurry, he had better write when he had considered Lord Derby's proposal, as he was so confused that I hardly knew what to report to him.   This he agreed to, so he must in some measure commit himself.

*March 7th.*—I got a letter from Sidney Herbert this morning respecting what I said yesterday about the electioneering arrangements, evidently fancying I meant more than I said, for he added that the Peelite party were much divided, there being hardly a subject on which they agreed, and that of course their influence was now much weakened ; that he himself was anxious to disperse them and to keep aloof from all parties, as he wished to be independent, and that he would only answer for himself, as there were many others with whom I could communicate.

*March 8th.*—I met Gladstone last night at the Carlton Club and had a long conversation with him. He had seen Sidney Herbert, who told him of our interview, and Gladstone said he quite disagreed in his views and had told him so. He was evidently displeased at Sidney Herbert's representing the Peelite party as so weak and divided. His leanings are apparently towards us, but he was quite of my opinion that no sort of agreement should be made beyond the one I had proposed, and that we should remain perfectly free and independent of each other.

*March 16th.*—I have had very unsatisfactory letters about the elections. The report of the coalition with the Peelites has done us irreparable mischief, but Palmerston's personal popularity is the real cause of his successes.

*March 25th.*—I wrote a letter to Lord Palmerston in answer to his address to the electors of Tiverton, which has had considerable success. Lord Derby has a terrible fit of gout, which has attacked both ankles, both knees, and both elbows. It is impossible his constitution can support these repeated trials.

*April 1st.*—I went to Heron Court to attend the sitting of the New Forest Commissioners at Christchurch. I received many compliments on my letter to Lord Palmerston, amongst others from Lords Clarendon and Grey, which are worth having.

*April 2nd.*—News has been received from China, and it turns out that the reported peace was an invention for electioneering purposes, and that the war continues the same as ever. Allum, the baker, and nine others who were tried on the accusation of poisoning bread, are all acquitted, so there is an end of Lord Palmerston's assertion and the ridiculous tirade which he made in the House of Commons about ' poisoning respectable English merchants.'

*April 4th.*—Most of my claims in the New Forest have been allowed by the Commissioners. The elections are going against us. We have lost fifteen seats in the counties.

*April 10th.*—Dined with Lord Lonsdale, and went with him to Paris.

One of the guests at this dinner was a doctor who practised as a vegetarian, and during dinner consistently confined himself to green meat and grapes.  He was the most singular and repulsive looking man I ever saw, over seventy years of age, about five feet high, and completely shrivelled in body and face, the last being like parchment and of an orange colour.  He held a medical commission in the army, and had been through the whole Peninsular war.  Being very quarrelsome, he fought more than one duel with his brother officers.[1]

*April 14th.*—The Queen was confined—a princess.

Lord Ossulston says that our tactics are quite unpopular with the country gentlemen, and that they consider the China vote factious.

*April 19th.*—Returned from Paris.  I dined at the Tuileries yesterday.  The Emperor had invited me for to-day, but hearing I wished to leave Paris, he very kindly ordered his chamberlain to send me an invitation for yesterday instead.  It was quite a small dinner, and I had the place of honour next the Empress, who looked lovely.  The Emperor talked to me in the most friendly and confidential manner.  His opinion of Disraeli was that he ' has not the head of a statesman, but that he is, like all literary men, as he has found them, from Chateaubriand to Guizot, ignorant of the world, talking well, but nervous when the moment of action arises.'  The Emperor is evidently only sensible of Disraeli's peculiarities without doing justice to his genius.

*April 21st.*—Dashwood, who was my secretary, called this morning and says that the Government has already paid Pisani the 13,000*l.* he asks for his picture of the 'Tent of Darius,' by Paul Veronese, at Venice ; but the Austrian Government not only refuses to allow the picture to leave Venice, but have fined Pisani for selling it, and it is expected the English Government will be obliged to pay the fine for him.

*April 28th.*—Lady Ely called, and talked to us of the dinner at the Palace last year, where Lords Palmerston, Clarendon, John Russell, Derby, and Malmesbury met, and which Lord Derby characterised to Prince Albert as an illustration of a happy family,

---

[1] When his death occurred, a few years ago, he was discovered to be a woman! What a story of shame and misery is buried with her in her grave !

a joke which amused him and the Queen very much. It looks as if her Majesty made up the dinner of these discordant materials for fun, and, from the same *malice*, made me take Lady Clarendon to dinner, as it was only two days after I had attacked Lord Clarendon in the House of Lords, and Lady Clarendon would not speak to me at first, but I ended by making her laugh. The Queen, who was opposite, was highly amused, and could hardly help laughing when Lady Clarendon at first would not answer me.

*April* 30*th.*—The Duchess of Gloucester died this morning. She was the last of the children of George III. The new Parliament met at two o'clock, and Mr. Evelyn Denison was chosen Speaker without opposition. Lady Palmerston is very anxious about her husband's health, as he suffers so much from gout and is so weak that he can no longer take either riding or walking exercise. She dreads the meeting of Parliament, as she fears the fatigue and anxiety will be too much for his strength.

*Lord Derby to Lord M.*

Knowsley : April 30, 1857.

My dear Malmesbury,—I am sorry to say that I am again, very *mal à propos*, confined to my bed by a severe and painful attack of gout. I have it at present in *both* elbows and one knee, with every prospect of its running the round of my limbs before it takes its departure. I will, if possible, be in town for the opening of Parliament, but I am afraid it is very doubtful whether I shall be able. At all events, if there is to be any chance of my presiding at the dinner to be given to Jolliffe, it must not be earlier than the 16th. Should I not be in my place, you must manage the House for me, and pray impress upon all our friends in both Houses the necessity, in my mind, of being very guarded in their language on the subject of Reform, and of not committing the party hastily to the adoption of any course. If it is not mentioned in the Speech, it will be better not to allude to it. If it is, our language ought to be that of regret that the Government should have thought it necessary to disturb the existing settlement ; but that, as they propose to introduce a bill on a subject which requires the most careful calculation of its probable consequences, we shall be prepared to give to it a respectful and dispassionate consideration, and shall hope to find it based upon principles which will enable us conscientiously to support it. You know what are the points to which I would

mainly object, but I doubt the prudence of adverting to them until
John Russell, Locke King, or some other, have shown their game, and
perhaps compelled the Government to some extent to disclose theirs.
You may read this letter to Disraeli, in case I should not see him.  I
wish you also to give notice for me that I am entrusted with a petition,
which I will present as soon as the state of my health allows me, from
the colony of Newfoundland against the recent Fishery Convention;
and, as it will require the assent of Parliament, you may as well find
out whether Clarendon will object to refer the petition to a Select
Committee, without which the House will legislate quite in the dark as
to the merits of the case.

Ever yours sincerely,

DERBY.

*May 1st.*—I got a letter to-day from Lady Derby, written at
her husband's dictation, saying that he is again laid up with gout
in both his elbows and wrists, and expected every joint would
have its turn.  It was, therefore, unlikely that he could be in his
place on the 7th, and I must, therefore, replace him and lead the
party during his absence.  The duty of answering the Queen's
Speech will, for this reason, devolve upon me.

*May 2nd.*—Disraeli, who called on me yesterday, would not
agree to my proposal to have a meeting of the leaders of the party
to discuss the Queen's Speech.  He said we might call on each
other and talk it over, but, for some reason, he objected to the
presence of any other member of the party.  I, however, insisted
upon summoning the other leaders and discussing the question
openly with them.

*May 4th.*—I saw Disraeli last night at the Carlton, sitting at a
table with ——.  The latter got up in a few minutes and went away,
when Disraeli came up to me and said, 'I am the most unlucky
man !  I came here to meet Colonel Taylor, and the waiter told
me he was in this room ; but Providence has cursed me with
blindness ; so, seeing a very big man, whom I took for Colonel
Taylor, I rushed to him and fell into the arms of Robert
Macaire, who insisted upon my dining with him, made me drink
a bottle of champagne, which poisons me, and ended by borrowing fifty pounds from me.'  Disraeli, in spite of all these
misfortunes, was in very good humour, and agreed at once to my

proposal to meet some of his late colleagues next Thursday at Lord Eglinton's. I had a letter from Lady Derby saying that Lord D. cannot possibly come up to London, and begging me to send him some news to amuse him, as they are very *triste*.

*May 6th.*—Lord Palmerston sent me the Queen's Speech this afternoon, as is the custom from the Prime Minister to the leader of the Opposition. It does not contain any allusion to Reform, and is the tamest production, even for a Queen's Speech, I ever read.

*From Lord Derby to Lord M. (on the Chinese War).*

Knowsley: May 6, 1857.

My dear Malmesbury,—I hardly think that the Government will call upon Parliament to pronounce its opinion in favour of the justice of the Chinese War, though I think it probable, or indeed certain, that they will ask for our support in it. Even if they should apply to it, though on the part of the Crown, any laudatory epithet, without asking us to concur in the commendation, it must not be allowed to pass without a frank declaration of our opinions. We have never denied that we had grounds of complaint against China for the incomplete fulfilment of the terms of the treaty, although we thought, and think the more from what has occurred since, that the alleged causes were not sufficient to justify the violent measures taken by the local authorities, that such steps should not have been taken without express direction from the Home Government, and that that Government, as a matter of policy, ought not to have permitted such steps to be taken without the previous provision of an overwhelming naval and military force to compel submission to demands which they might think fit to make. Remember, this must not be said as apologetically for our vote, but as repeating the doctrine which we then held, the soundness of which has been amply proved by the horrors which have been the consequence, and not, as Palmerston would fain make them appear, the provocation to our acts. But as matters now stand we are engaged, whether we will or no, in a struggle for our very existence in the Eastern Seas; and it is no time now to consider by whose fault we have been brought into a position in which we have no alternative but to maintain to the utmost the safety and the rights of our countrymen. Such a course of proceeding is entirely consistent with a deep sense of the reckless impolicy which has led to this state of affairs, and involved us in a war the more formidable because it is not with a Government, but with a nation, and that a nation unchecked by those habits of civilisation which in most cases mitigate the horrors of modern warfare. Such a course on our part would be the most dignified answer to the absurd charges which the Prime Minister of the country, with a view to electioneering clap-trap, did not think it beneath himself to bring against his political opponents. If the Government should hint at any project for capital-ising the Maynooth grant on fair and reasonable terms, I think they ought not to be discouraged. . . . I am glad your letter did not come yesterday, as I should have been unable to dictate an answer, having totally lost my voice. It is better, however, to-day, and I am so far on the way to recovery that I hope in an hour or two to be able to get up to have my bed made, which has not been done for above a week.

Ever yours very sincerely,<br>DERBY.

*May 7th.*—We had a meeting of ex-Ministers at Lord Eglin-ton's. Disraeli was not quite satisfied with the result, and he wished the leaders in both Houses to observe perfect silence, neither to blame nor approve the Speech. He and some others wanted me not to get up immediately after the seconder, as is the custom for the leader of the Opposition in the Lords to do, but to let Lord Grey, who is sure to speak, and Lord Ellenborough, if inclined, make their speeches first. I do not know what their motive could be for giving this advice, but the effect would have been that I should have abdicated the position which Lord Derby had assigned to me. So I refused to follow it, and insisted on conforming to Lord Derby's directions. I therefore got up im-mediately after the seconder, and all my friends complimented me when I sat down. Lord Campbell came across the House and said he hoped he was not taking too great a liberty in praising my speech. The Duke of Somerset and other supporters of the Government paid me the same compliments.

*May 16th.*—Lord Derby, having recovered, appeared in the House. Several of the Whigs came across to ask him how he was, and to express their pleasure at seeing him once more in his place, and I was surprised at the rather cold manner in which he received them; but Lord Colville explained it by telling me that he had called upon Lord Derby and accompanied him to the House, and that he had rather tried to dissuade him from going,

thinking he was looking weak and ill, but Lord D. insisted, saying, 'Palmerston says I am dying, but I'll show him I'm alive.'

*May* 18*th*.—The betrothal of the Princess Royal to the Prince
of Prussia was announced to-day in Parliament.

*May* 20*th*.—In the Lords the Divorce Bill passed by a majority of 29—47 to 18 !

*June* 25*th*.—We are suffering under an extraordinary heat.
People are really getting alarmed, for if it is occasioned by the
comet, which is not yet visible, what must we expect when it
approaches our globe ! Lord Alvanley died yesterday—perhaps
the wittiest man of his day. He was remarkable for the manner
in which he could tell a story ; and it amused him sometimes to
relate them at dinner with such fun that he drove the servants
out of the room, who could not remain for laughing.

On one occasion a friend of his came for his advice under the
following circumstances :—'Mr. —— has threatened to kick me
whenever he sees me in society ; what am I to do if he comes
into the room ?' 'Sit down,' replied Lord Alvanley. He was
extremely well-read and full of information, which he imparted
in the most delightful manner, and it is a pity that an account he
wrote of a journey through Russia, and which he showed me,
should not be published.

*June* 27*th*.—Very alarming news from India. The mutiny
amongst the Sepoys in the Bengal army has spread from Meerut.
Three regiments are in open revolt. After some bloodshed they
had been dispersed by European troops and fled to Delhi, where
they were joined by other native regiments. Delhi was in possession of the mutineers, who had massacred almost all the
Europeans, without regard to age or sex, plundered the Bank, and
proclaimed the son of the late Mogul emperor to be king.

*June* 29*th*.—Went directly after breakfast to Lord Derby, to
consult him on what we should say to Mr. Hamilton, who has the
management of the ' Morning Herald,' and had written to me
yesterday to arrange as to the line which was to be taken. The
paper appeared for the first time this morning under the new
management. It seems well arranged, with plenty of fashionable
news to amuse ladies. I found Lord Derby very careless and indifferent on the subject, and unable to suggest anything. The only

thing which seemed to interest him was the subject of the Jew
Bill, and for that he had taken the very unnecessary trouble to
make out lists, a bore that is generally left to the Whips. Lord
Derby has never been able to realise the sudden growth and power
of the Political Press, for which he has no partiality, which feeling is reciprocated by its members. In these days this is a fatal
error in men who wish to obtain public power and distinction.
Lord Derby is too proud a man to flatter anybody, even his greatest friends and equals, much less those of whom he knows
nothing. His son, with greater wisdom (for the day), has taken
the opposite line, and with benefit to his popularity and advancement.

*July 6th.*—Lord Clarendon told me a good story of Corry
Conellan, Lord Carlisle's secretary at Dublin. The Viceroy, who
has taken up the ticket-of-leave men very warmly, told him the
other day that he had engaged two in his house as servants.
Conellan replied, ' Then you'll be the only spoon left in it.'

The news from India continues bad ; General Anson, Commander-in-Chief, is ill. Mr. Roebuck moved a resolution last
night that the office of Lord-Lieutenant of Ireland should be
abolished, which was negatived by 151.

*July 8th.*—I dined with the Brazilian Minister, M. Moreira.
His wife is very pretty and agreeable, but the party was eccentric.
It consisted of Don Juan of Spain, Cardinal Wiseman, the Duchess
of Inverness, Lady Essex, Sir Gore Ouseley, Mr., Mrs., and Miss
Roebuck, and a number of Portuguese. We sat down at a
quarter past eight, and the dinner was not over till a quarter past
twelve.

*July 11th.*—Went to the Queen's ball. Madame Castiglione
was there ; as she is supposed to be Louis Napoleon's mistress,
she was very much stared at and admired. The House of Lords
rejected the Oaths Bill by a majority of thirty-four. In the
House of Commons, in reply to some question from Sir John
Pakington, Sir C. Wood said ' that the latest accounts from China
were from Admiral Seymour, dated May 10, and up to that period
no operations had taken place, the Admiral waiting for reinforcements. No instructions had been transmitted to the Indian
Government directing that the troops embarked for China should

be ⌐employed in India, and the Governor-General had sent his orders to Ceylon to direct the forces, on their arrival there, to proceed to India. He had sent a requisition to Lord Elgin to despatch troops, but Lord Elgin had no instructions to comply. Whether he would deem the case so pressing as to induce him to do so on his own responsibility remains to be seen.' [1]

The news of General Anson's death from cholera on the march from Umballa to Delhi has arrived. He is succeeded by General Barnard. The whole of the Northern Provinces of India are in open insurrection.

*July* 12*th.*—Lady Carrington tells me that Mrs. Anson is in a dreadful state of grief. Lord Panmure sent for Lady Newport, her sister, and she and Lady Forester broke it to her. Her grief seems to have been very great, and her having left him is an aggravation to her sorrow. 'The Observer,' a Government paper, says '*that with vigour and energy we may still keep India.*' As Lady Carrington remarked, 'A fortnight ago, we should as soon have thought of losing Manchester as India.' Sir Colin Campbell is appointed Commander-in-Chief, and started this morning at twenty-four hours' notice. In the Crimea he proved himself a first-rate soldier. Lord Ellenborough made a very eloquent speech, asking the Government what they meant to do, but they refused to give any information.

*July* 16*th.*—Gave a dinner to the Persignys, Jerseys, Lady Glengall and daughter, Lord and Lady Raglan, Comte de Jaucourt, Barrington, and Norman Macdonald. Madame de Persigny was late, as usual, and M. de Persigny came without her in a hack cab, which is the way he generally goes out to dinner, as he is almost always obliged to leave the carriage for his wife. He was much put out, and begged us not to wait, so we went to dinner and the only place left for her was near the door, between Norman Macdonald and Lady Raglan. Poor M. de Persigny looked miserable, could hardly answer, and kept continually looking towards the door. Madame de Persigny arrived in the middle of the first course in a great flurry, her eyes evidently showing signs of tears. They exchanged a furious look of defiance,

---

[1] Lord Elgin, to his eternal honour, complied with Lord Canning's request, and this accidental reinforcement probably saved India.

she eating her bread very fast as if to keep down her rage. At last Lord Loughborough made her laugh by his usual jokes, and by the time we went upstairs she had recovered her good humour, though not so poor M. de Persigny; I could get nothing out of him.   When the party broke up Count de Jaucourt handed Madame de Persigny to her carriage, and returned to us to say, 'Vous serez bien aises d'apprendre que l'Ambassadeur et Madame de Persigny se sont embrassés sur l'escalier.'

Mr. Curzon, General Anson's aide-de-camp, has written an account of his death, which vindicates him from the charge, which the Government followers tried to fix upon him, of slowness and want of energy.   It seems he was perfectly well at Umballa when the insurrection broke out, and he then exerted himself so much, and so incessantly, allowing himself no rest by day or night, that he was quite exhausted when the cholera seized him.   He sank under it, and died at Kurnaul, on the march to Delhi; but he preserved his calmness to the last, gave all the necessary orders, sent for General Barnard, to whom he gave up the command, sent his love to Mrs. Anson, and a message, saying it was a great comfort to him to know she was safe in England.   Mr. Roebuck's motion to censure Government for proceeding with the Persian war without the sanction of Parliament was negatived by 352 to 38.

*July 21st.*—I went to the Duchesse d'Aumale's breakfast at Twickenham.   The Duc de Richelieu called.   I never saw him in such good humour; he is delighted with his life in London, and with the reception that all society has given him.   It is said that the mutiny, up to the present moment, has cost the country seven millions.

*August 5th.*—Lord Ellenborough attacked the Government of India, and was answered very sharply by Lords Granville and Clanricarde, to whom I replied.

*August 6th.*—The Persians, knowing of our difficulties in India, have refused to evacuate Herat, so that the war in which our Ministers embarked so rashly, and to prosecute which they denuded India of its defenders, furnishing the rebels with the very opportunity which they desired, turns out to be a mere waste of human life and treasure, without producing the objects for which it was waged.   I dined yesterday with the Jerseys.   Lady Stuart de Rothesay read an extract from Lady Canning's letters, giving an account of the horrible barbarities practised by the rebels in India, who roast the children, ill-use and murder the women.

*August 7th.*—Left London for Achnacarry. The heat was quite overpowering.

*August 10th, Achnacarry.*—The Emperor and Empress of the French, accompanied by the Walewskis, arrived at Osborne on the 6th at 9 A.M. They were received by the Queen at the pier. The object of their visit is kept very secret, but I have no doubt it is to discuss the question of the Principalities,[1] upon which the English and French Governments are at variance. Their disagreement is so serious that M. Thouvenel has struck his flag at Constantinople. The Emperor has long been very much dissatisfied with Lord Palmerston, and I suppose that, finding Persigny has failed in obtaining any concessions, he has come to try and settle matters himself with the Queen ; and certainly his bringing his Foreign Secretary, together with the fact that Lords Palmerston and Clarendon are summoned to meet him, looks very like a conference.

*August 12th.*—Delhi is not taken, as reported, and the horrors committed there by the mutineers will not bear description. The heat even here continues to be tropical.

*August 13th.*—Extraordinary precautions were taken during the Emperor's visit to Osborne. Eighty detectives were sent down from London, besides French police. The strictest guard was kept round the Palace and over the island. Besides this, a number of men-of-war's boats guarded the shore, and did not allow a single boat to approach.

*August 14th.*—The troops destined for China are arriving daily at Calcutta. Lord Palmerston has given way on the question of the Principalities, so the Emperor has gained his point by his visit to Osborne. The dispute arose on a question of the union of the Principalities, which France, Russia, Prussia, and Sardinia supported. England, Austria, and Turkey opposed the union, and, the elections in Moldavia having been in favour of England, the French, Russians, &c., accused the English Government

---

[1] This was the case, and the Emperor prevailed. The French wished to place them under one Hospodar. We and the Porte insisted on there being two.

of having influenced them unfairly, and demanded that they should be annulled.   The Porte refused this, upon which the Ambassadors of France, Russia, Prussia, and Sardinia struck their flags.   The Emperor Napoleon then, instead of wasting time in useless correspondence, came over himself, and the question was settled at once.   I do not pretend to judge whether Palmerston was right or wrong, but his defeat must have cost him a bitter pang.   Louis Napoleon's Ministers have been completely won over by the Russians, especially Walewski.

*August 31st.*—Count Chreptovitch, who has been here some days, left us this morning to the joy of everybody.   All felt that he hated us, which the Duc de Richelieu says is the case, and we therefore took care never to talk politics or mention India before him.   He has not been able to get on at all with Lord Palmerston. Indian news is very bad, and confirms the account of the massacre at Cawnpore of all the garrison, and 240 women and children General Havelock has defeated the mutineers wherever he could reach them, but his forces are very inferior to his task, and his position at times would appear desperate.

*September 9th.*—Lord Derby arrived, and appears to me to be in very low spirits—quiet without his usual *entrain*.

*September 16th.*—Better news from India.   General Havelock has defeated Nana Sahib in two more engagements, taking all his guns ; but his army has been attacked by cholera, which has obliged him to return to Cawnpore without relieving Lucknow.

*September 29th.*—A tremendous gale and rain.   The whole party sat together in the drawing-room, each obliged to tell a story.   Mine was as follows, and was founded on the fact that Richelieu had refused to shoot with Loughborough in consequence of his always hunting his pointers down wind :—

There was once a young Highland shepherd, who was drinking at a burn, and being in the humour of desiring for all sorts of things that he had never seen or possessed, he wished that one of the fairies he had heard of, who haunted the place, would appear, and give him whatever he wanted.   At that moment his dog howled and a pixie stood before him.   'I have heard you,' she said, 'as I sat under that pebble in the burn, and I will give you whatever you wish for, but it must be one thing only and for ever.'

'Thank you,' said the lad, not at all alarmed, 'I have only one
desire in the world, and that is to go to sea and become a rich
merchant.' This happened before steamers were invented, and
the fairy answered most graciously, 'Mr. MacGuffog, I will give
you what is the most essential thing for a prosperous voyage and
successful trading—namely, wherever you go you shall have a
fair wind whichever way you turn yourself or your ship.' The
young MacGuffog fell on his knees with gratitude, and having
given the fairy a pull at his whisky-flask, went forthwith to Fort
William, and enlisted as a cabin-boy on board a merchantman.
It was not very long before the fact became known that whatever ship he was on board always had the wind astern; all the
trading captains hired him at any price, but he soon gained enough
to sail on his own account, and by the time he was thirty, the
rapid voyages he invariably made cut out everybody else, and gave
him such advantages that he realised a large fortune. He then
remembered his native hills, and determined to buy an estate upon
them. This he did, but he felt that he was not really a Highland gentleman without a deer-forest, and therefore he extended
his domain, took off the sheep, and hired the best stalker in Scotland. All this being prepared for his happiness and amusement,
he started with him to stalk in his own forest, but day after day
he was disappointed by the perverseness of the weather, the
wind constantly changing the moment he went out. Whatever
circuits he took he found himself always going down wind, so that,
whether as single deer or herds, no animal allowed him to approach
within a quarter of a mile. He looked upon this merely as a piece
of bad luck, till by chance, crossing the burn on which he had
seen the pixie fifteen years before, he heard a tiny giggle and
then a long low laugh. Turning round, he saw the little woman,
and then the terrible truth broke upon him that if he lived to
a thousand years he never could possibly kill a stag.

This was my story, and as to that of Lord Loughborough and the
Duc de Richelieu, which suggested it to me, it was as follows :
That Lord Loughborough, being obliged to shoot in spectacles,
could not face the rain and wind on a wet day, which was the case
when the Duke went out with him.

*October 1st.*—General Havelock's force made a second advance

upon Lucknow on August 22, but was again obliged to fall back.
The 5th and 90th Regiments are on their way up the river to rein-
force him.   Three Bombay regiments have mutinied since the
last mail arrived.   It is said that Lucknow has only provisions till
the 21st, and is now upon famine rations.   Letters from Calcutta
bring several very serious accusations against Lord Canning, the
most important being that Lord Elphinstone having telegraphed
to him at the beginning of the insurrection to offer to send a fast
steamer from Bombay, which could easily be done, and by which
a fortnight would have been saved, Lord Canning sent a peremptory refusal.   When General Anson died, Lord Canning named
Sir Patrick Grant Commander-in-Chief, but the Government at
home superseded this appointment by naming Sir Colin Campbell.
Lord Canning is an intimate friend of mine, and was Under-
Secretary at the Foreign Office under Lord Aberdeen.   He is
clever, and deservedly popular, and when he was offered the
Government of India he came to me to ask my advice as to his
accepting it.   Without any hesitation, knowing his character as I
did, I advised him to refuse, and, had he followed my advice, it is
probable that he would have saved his life and distinguished himself in Parliament and held the highest offices in the Cabinet, as
our political leaders had a good opinion of him and he had a great
name.   The offer, however, was tempting, and he accepted it, little
expecting the terrible difficulties he would encounter almost before
his foot was in the stirrup.

*October 3rd.*—This morning my stalker and his boy gave me
an account of a mysterious creature, which they say exists in Loch
Arkaig, and which they call the Lake-horse.   It is the same
animal of which one has occasionally read accounts in the newspapers as having been seen in the Highland lochs, and on the
existence of which in Loch Assynt the late Lord Ellesmere wrote
an interesting article, but hitherto the story has always been looked
upon as fabulous.   I am now, however, nearly persuaded of its
truth.   My stalker, John Stuart, at Achnacarry, has seen it twice,
and both times at sunrise in summer on a bright sunny day, when
there was not a ripple on the water.   The creature was basking
on the surface ; he only saw the head and hind quarters, proving
that its back was hollow, which is not the shape of any fish or of

a seal. Its head resembled that of a horse. It was also seen once by his three little children, who were all walking together along the beach. It was then motionless, about thirty yards from the shore, and apparently asleep, and they first took it for a rock, but when they got near it moved its head, and they were so frightened that they ran home, arriving in a state of the greatest terror. There was no mistaking their manner when they related this story, and they offered to make an affidavit before a magistrate. The Highlanders are very superstitious about this creature. They are convinced that there is never more than one in existence at the same time, and I believe they think it has something diabolical in its nature, for when I said I wished I could get within shot of it my stalker observed very gravely: 'Perhaps your Lordship's gun would miss fire.' It would be quite possible, though difficult, for a seal to work up the river Lochy into Loch Arkaig.

*October 18th.*—General Outram has behaved very generously to Havelock, and has told him he would not deprive him of the glory he so well deserved of relieving Lucknow, but would leave him in command of the expedition and would serve under him. The 'Daily News' gives the Order in Council issued by Lord Canning on July 31, the object of which is noble in its nature— namely, to transfer the power of punishing the mutineers from the military to the civil authorities; but it is the act of a *doctrinaire.* Nothing could be more ill-timed and injudicious. The time to show mercy will be when we have completely regained our autho- rity and restored peace, and when our power will be so undoubted that we may pardon the guilty without our mercy being attributed to fear. Then, again, if the military authorities, instead of judg- ing criminals on the spot, have to send them to Allahabad, which Lord Canning orders, or keep them in prison, a great part of our army will be employed in escorting prisoners and guarding gaols. The only excuse for this proclamation is the impossibility of obey- ing it, though it may serve to show that its author is a Christian and an amiable man.

*October 23rd.*—Left Achnacarry.

*October 24th, Chillingham.*—The Ossulstons are going to Compiègne for the *fête* there. News has arrived of the fall of

Delhi, which was stormed on September 20. The resistance was obstinate, and our loss severe, amounting to 50 English officers and 600 men killed and wounded.

———

In my diary there was of course a great deal about the Indian mutiny, but I have quoted only enough of it to save myself from any accusation of indifference to events which stirred England, and, indeed, the whole civilised world, at the time, with all the emotions to which the human mind is liable. The atrocities of the rebels, who spared neither age nor sex, were only equalled by the courage of the victims. Who can measure the heroic resignation of those English ladies first besieged and then murdered at Cawnpore and Lucknow? Who can measure the difficulties and personal labour of Havelock, that great Christian soldier, who died in the cause? That terrible Sepoy war (admirably described by Kaye) is the moral as well as military glory of our race. The generous Outram resigned his command to Havelock rather than pluck a leaf from his laurels; the veteran hero Clyde, as strong as ever in battle, then the fiery avengers, Neill and Rose—the former forcing the assassins of Cawnpore to lick up the blood of their murdered victims; the latter traversing Central India with his army, and dealing retribution with an unsparing sword. I have passed over the details of these things as they happened at the time, and as I then noted them, and also the emotions which they created in our quiet social circle during my autumn visit to the Highlands. May our Indian rulers profit hereafter by this terrible lesson!

———

*November 11th.*—I was much grieved at receiving news this morning of the death of my cousin, George Harris, who had been my private secretary, and was now consul at Venice. He was a remarkably clever man, and had, by his social qualities and natural ability, obtained great influence in the place, and made it almost a legation. Mr. Conyngham has sent me the telegrams just received from India. Lucknow was relieved on September 25. The enemy's entrenchments were stormed on the 26th, and on the 29th a large part of the city was taken ; but General Neill is killed and 450 men. The death of the former is irreparable. He had commanded the Madras Fusiliers. Our losses at Delhi are 61 officers and 1,178 men. General Nicholson has died of his wounds ; so we have paid dearly for our victories. The old King of Delhi was taken by Captain Hodson, fifteen miles out of Delhi, accompanied by his chief wife, and their lives were spared, but two of his sons and a grandson were shot on the spot, and their bodies brought into the city and exposed in the police office.

*November 12th.*—The Duchesse de Nemours died suddenly at Claremont yesterday. She had been confined a fortnight ago, and was going on so well that she got up. Whilst her maid was dressing her, she exclaimed, 'Je me meurs,' and fell back in a fainting fit, from which she never recovered. The Duke had gone out riding, thinking her quite well, and on his return found her dead.

*November 13th.*—The 'Times' of to-day announces two very important facts. One, that the Government have suspended the Bank Charter Act ; the other that Parliament is to be called together immediately. I have been reading the last two volumes of Raikes's memoirs, which are very interesting, almost entirely political, and some parts well written, though not grammatical in places, the word 'who' not always referring to the antecedent, which produces a ludicrous effect. I knew Raikes well, and read the original in manuscript, which was much more amusing than the publication. Almost all the most racy anecdotes have been omitted, and the few that are left, being given without the names, have no interest. A great deal has been left out in consequence of its not agreeing with the political opinions of the editor, Mr. Charles Greville, who, being a Peelite, would not allow anything against Sir Robert Peel to be published, so that the events of 1846 are suppressed or garbled, though the journal comes down to 1847. That year was not forgotten by Mr. Raikes, who was an uncompromising old Tory and Protectionist, and who let everybody know it.

*November 14th.*—Mrs. Augustus Villiers called and told me the cause of the Duchesse de Nemours' death was ascertained to proceed from a simple drop of coagulated blood in one of the arteries. In all other respects she was perfectly healthy.

The claims that are to be made upon England by the merchants of various countries for compensation in consequence of the bombardment of Canton will, it is said, amount to several millions.

*November* 15*th.*—Havelock has written to Sir Colin Compbell, asking for reinforcements, as he was hemmed in at Lucknow and could not return to Cawnpore. Sir Colin answered that he had not a man to send, and if he had there were no means of transport to send them up the country. Lord Canning is much blamed for not having organised a transport corps since the beginning of the war. Havelock's position is thought to be one of imminent danger. He is now in the same position as the garrison he marched to relieve. He has lost 500 men and his best officer, General Neill.

The English ladies who went to Compiègne for the *fêtes* have just returned, and seem to have been greatly amused. The Emperor as much occupied with Madame Walewska as ever. They were struck with the freedom in conversation and manners of the Court, which is most remarkable in Princess Mathilde. Their forgetfulness of all *convenances* is quite incredible, and in more than one instance excited the disgust of the Empress as well as that of her guests.

*November* 18*th.*—A friend of Lord Canning's told me he supposed I should speak against him. I said I had no such intention; was deeply sorry to hear him abused, and that I had written to him three months ago, urging him to adopt a vigorous line against the rebels, as the feeling in England was very strong, and no other policy would be approved. I had always considered Lord Canning one of my most intimate friends.

*November* 19*th.*—Poor Augustus Stafford has evidently been killed by his doctors, judging by the evidence at the inquest. He had first a tremendous dose of laudanum for spasms, then was bled to the extent of thirty ounces; the bandage afterwards coming off, he lost a good deal more blood, and in this state of exhaustion the doctor and his servant were obliged to keep him walking about to prevent his dying from the laudanum,

When this failed to keep him awake, they beat the soles of his feet for several hours with such violence that they broke the pieces of wood and took off all the skin from his feet. This saved him for the moment, and he went to Dublin for further advice, but died in a few days from utter exhaustion. He told Mr. H. Herbert that he had been horribly treated, and was dying from the effects of that treatment. Mr. Herbert very properly urged an inquiry, and his father also expressing a wish to that effect, an inquest was held, but the jury acquitted the doctor, whose colleagues gave evidence in his favour. I hear that Lord Strangford married Miss Lennox ten days ago. The marriage took place at Lord Stamford's place in the country. Lord Strangford was dying when the ceremony was performed.

*November 25th.*—Good news has arrived from India ; the 53rd and 93rd Queen's Regiments have joined Havelock at Lucknow. Colonel Greathed's flying column will also join him there from Delhi, when he will have 7,000 men, which will enable him to remove the garrison. Colonel Greathed has gained two victories over the fugitives between Delhi and Agra, took forty-three guns and five lakhs of rupees. Miss Anson's marriage with Mr. Curzon[1] is announced.

*November 27th.*—Received a letter from Lord Derby, who comes to London on the 30th to have a conference with the leaders of the party. He says he has heard from Disraeli, who is very pugnacious. Lord Ellenborough also means to speak his mind openly upon India, but, as usual, does not seem willing to work with anybody else. People talk of our victories in India as being proofs of Lord Palmerston's glorious administration. I cannot myself see that anybody deserves any credit for them, excepting our splendid soldiers ; for these successes have been gained by a handful of troops who were there at the time the mutiny broke out and before a single man had arrived from England. Moreover, if he had listened to Lord Ellenborough and our party, who urged his Government to send out more troops two months sooner, the massacre at Cawnpore and a great many other atrocities would have been prevented.

*November 30th.*—Mr. Bentinck called and announced the death

1 Now Earl Howe, 1883.

of Lord Fitzhardinge, whose last words were : ' The angel of
death is hovering over Berkeley Castle, and if you don't feed
those ducks in the lower pond, I'll be d——d if you don't lose
them all.'   Old habit strong in death !

*December 1st.*—Lord Canning is again much blamed for his
conduct to the talookdars, the great native landowners.  The
chief of these is Maun Singh, who is one of the largest holders of
property in Oude, but had been deprived by the late King of a
considerable portion of his estates.  He promised to support us if
we reinstated him.  Our Government was pressed to accede to
this by some of our ablest men, but they temporised, and Maun
Singh decided to act against us, and roused all the other talookdars, and our countrymen had scarcely obtained possession of
Lucknow when they found themselves besieged there.  Saw Lord
Derby this afternoon in high spirits and evidently determined to
make a slashing speech, but nothing can be arranged till he has
read the Queen's Speech.

*December 2nd.*—I was greatly shocked on my return home to
hear of the death of Norman Macdonald from apoplexy.  We
had been great friends since we were at Oriel.  He was Comptroller of the Lord Chamberlain's Department.  He was calling
on Lady Ely at the moment of his seizure, and died the same
day.  He was a very obliging and friendly man, and much liked
in society.

*December 3rd.*—The Queen opened Parliament to-day.  The
Duchess of Manchester was in the House.  She was full of Compiègne.  When Lord Derby got up, people ceased talking.  His
speech was very good, some parts extremely eloquent.  He
attacked Lord Canning and the Government in England and
quizzed Mr. Vernon Smith unmercifully.  Lord Granville made
no defence either for the Government or for his friend Lord
Canning, simply saying that they must stand or fall by their own
acts.  Lord Ellenborough then made a very good, short, and
energetic speech, but in rather too loud and overbearing a tone.
The Duke of Argyll followed ; Lord Panmure speaking as usual
with his terrible fluency.  Lady Stuart de Rothesay is now a sort
of authority upon India, and if she gave her information in a less
voluble manner would be a great acquisition at this moment.

One amusing anecdote she related was about a court-martial which assembled to try a prisoner. When it was over, one of the officers, happening to go into the verandah, knocked against something which proved to be the body of the accused, whom the soldiers placed to guard him had hanged during the deliberations, fearing that he might be let off.

*December* 12*th.*—The news from India continues good Our forces, under the splendid leadership of Grant, Outram, Sir Colin Campbell, and Havelock, are holding their own against Nana Sahib with 50,000 men.

The Chancellor of the Exchequer moved last night for the reappointment of the select committee to inquire into the operation of all the Bank Acts. Disraeli moved an amendment, which was rejected by a majority of 178.

*December* 24*th.*—Great news from India. Lucknow taken on November 17. Sir Colin Campbell reached Alumbagh on November 12, began fighting the next day, and took several positions. He crossed the canal on the 16th, and after an obstinate struggle, took Secunderabad. Early on the 17th communication was opened up with the barracks. A long cannonade was commenced, and the place was carried by assault. The troops pushed on and occupied Motee Mahal before dark. Generals Outram and Havelock then met Sir Colin Campbell, and a most affecting scene took place. At Delhi twenty-four inferior members of the royal family were executed by sentence of a military commission.

# 1858

*January* 1*st.*—A summer's day.

*January* 7*th.*—News has arrived of Havelock's death from dysentery, produced by anxiety and exposure. He has left an immortal name. General Wyndham has been defeated at Cawnpore by the Gwalior insurgents. One regiment, the 64th, suffered greatly, and its tents and baggage were taken. Sir Colin Campbell hearing of this disaster, marched upon Cawnpore, attacked the Gwalior army, and totally defeated it.

*January* 16*th.*—An infamous attempt was made on the 14th

to assassinate the Emperor Napoleon. Three grenades were thrown at his carriage as it stopped at the door of the Opera-house, and all exploded, shattering the carriage, killing the horses, and wounding a great number of persons, but the Emperor and Empress were unhurt. The Emperor's hat was torn and his fore-head slightly scratched, as also was the Empress's cheek. Their reception by the audience at the Opera was most enthusiastic, and their return to the Tuileries a perfect ovation. The number of wounded is 102. Twenty-seven persons are arrested, all of them Italians. Orsini, the chief, was himself severely wounded, which prevented his escaping, and led to his apprehension. His servant foolishly went about inquiring after his master, and when asked his name, fainted. On his recovery he was threatened with arrest if he did not give his address. He did so, and the gendarme went to his house and found Orsini in bed with a severe wound in the head. On seeing them he exclaimed 'Je suis perdu,' and then attempted to pass himself off as an Englishman, but his accent betrayed him.

*From Lord M. to Lord Cowley.*

Heron Court : January 17, 1858.

My dear Cowley,—If you have an opportunity, pray be so kind as to express to the Emperor my congratulations at his wonderful escape. In common with all Europe I rejoice at it for public reasons, but do so also from personal feelings for him. The French must admire the defence of Lucknow, say what they will. They may have generals who would have done as well as Inglis in defending the place, but they have no one who could have written his simple though eloquent despatch.

Yours truly,

MALMESBURY.

*January 20th.*—We are asked to the Princess Royal's wedding.
*January 21st.*—The Queen was exceedingly gracious to me at the ball yesterday, expressing her regret that Lady Malmesbury could not attend. I was much amused at overhearing a con-versation between Persigny and Sir George Lewis on the subject of the attempt on Louis Napoleon. Sir George affirmed that the cause of the attempt was the occupation of Rome by the

French. Persigny replied, 'If we were not there, the Austrians would be.' The other answered : 'In that case, the Emperor of Austria would have been assassinated.' Persigny, at this, got into a towering passion, and said that the cases were quite different. The Emperor of Austria had two hundred heirs to the Crown, and the Emperor of France only one. I tried to appease him, for he was in a perfect fury, and accompanied him into one of the outer rooms, where we sat talking for half an hour.

*January 25th.*—The marriage of the Princess Royal with Prince Frederick William of Prussia takes place to-day. Immense crowds assembled to see the carriage go to the Chapel Royal. The 'Morning Post' says Lord Palmerston carried the sword of State 'with an easy grace and dignity ;' the 'Times' says 'with a ponderous solemnity.' The Princess Royal was quite composed.

*February 1st.*—Persigny is much alarmed at the state of public feeling with respect to the refugees, and says that if England does not make some concession we must have war. The Emperor will do all he can to keep peace, but fears he will be unable to do so should we remain obstinate. This will oblige us to make some alteration in our laws respecting refugees,[1] for at this moment, when our resources are taxed to the utmost to reconquer India, we are not in a position to have war with anyone.

*February 9th.*—Lord Palmerston introduced his bill for an amendment of the law respecting refugees yesterday evening. It was very ill received, and the debate adjourned. The only alteration proposed, however, is to make conspiracy to murder felony instead of a misdemeanour, which it has hitherto been ; but the Emperor has given such offence by countenancing the insults offered to England by the French colonels, that John Bull has got his back up, and though the Emperor declares that he did not know of these addresses of the colonels in the 'Moniteur,' and regrets them, England is greatly offended, and not disposed to please France. A vote of thanks to the Government and army

---

[1] England is now paying for her long-continued reception and protection of well-known assassins who have fled from justice to our shores to teach our criminals the mysteries of dynamite and other deadly compounds. The first inventor of these, and of the clockwork apparatus for exploding them, was a German, who had prepared the destruction of a ship during its passage to America.

of India was also proposed yesterday. Palmerston had given notice that a vote of thanks to the army and navy of India would be moved on February 8. He then, without any notice, added Lord Canning, Lord Harris, and Lord Elphinstone. This of course, gave rise to great discussion, and many things were said which must be very painful to Lord Canning. Lord Palmerston was obliged to declare that if the vote passed it would not prevent any future discussion on Lord Canning's conduct. Lord Elphinstone's name was loudly cheered by all parties, who agreed that he had thoroughly deserved the thanks of Parliament.

*February 10th.*—The discussion on the Refugee Bill was resumed yesterday. Lord John Russell spoke against it. Disraeli supported the Government, and the House divided in favour of the bill by a majority of 299 against 99.

*February 12th.*—Lord Grey in the House of Lords presented a petition of the East India Company, protesting against its abolition, and made a very fine speech.

*February 13th.*—Lord Palmerston introduced his bill for the abolition of the East India Company, bringing no accusation against it, or giving any intelligible reason for this act of spoliation.

*February 17th, Heron Court.*—Lord and Lady Derby arrived with Lord Ossulston. The former talked very openly upon politics, and evidently will not refuse office if it is offered him.

*February 19th.*—Hard black frost. We went out wild-fowl shooting. The Bill for the Abolition of Church-rates passed in the House of Commons by a majority of 53. Mr. Tom Baring's amendment to the India Bill defeated by 145.

*February 20th.*—Ossulston, who left yesterday, arrived again at four o'clock, bringing the news of the defeat of the Government upon Mr. Milner Gibson's amendment to the Refugee Bill, which was to the following effect : ' That this House hears with much concern that it is alleged that recent attempts upon the life of the Emperor of the French have been devised in England, and expresses its detestation of such guilty enterprises. That this House is ready at all times to assist in remedying any defects in the Criminal Law, which, after due investigation, are proved to exist, yet it cannot but regret that her Majesty's Government,

previously to inviting the House to amend the law of conspiracy,
at the present time has not felt it to be their duty to make some
reply to the important despatch received from the French Government, dated Paris, Jan. 20.'  The majority of our party voted for
the amendment, which was carried by a majority of nineteen—
234 against 215.  Lord Palmerston made a very intemperate
speech, and actually shook his fist at the Manchester clique.
Disraeli's face was worth anything—a mixture of triumph and
sarcasm that he could not repress.  Ossulston voted with the
Government.

*February 21st.*—I got a letter this morning saying that Lord
Palmerston has resigned, and that Lord Derby would be sent for.
I telegraphed to Lord Lonsdale, ' What news ?  Ought I to
come ? ' and the answer arrived at two o'clock, simply saying,
' Come up directly.'  So it is evident Lord Derby is sent for.

I go up to London to-morrow.

*February 22nd.*—Went to London, and found that Lord
Derby had accepted office.  He has requested me to take the
department of the Foreign Office.  Lord Ellenborough has the
India Board ;  Bulwer joins in the Colonial Office ;  Gladstone
and Lord Grey refuse to join, and Lord St. Leonards is succeeded by Sir Frederick Thesiger as Lord Chancellor.  The
War Office and Admiralty are not yet filled up.

*February 24th.*—The Cabinet is made up as follows : Premier,
Lord Derby ;  Lord Chancellor, Lord Chelmsford ;  President
of the Council, Lord Salisbury ;[1]  Privy Seal, Lord Hardwicke ;[2]
Foreign Office, Lord Malmesbury ;  Home Office, Mr. Walpole ;
Colonies, Sir E. Bulwer-Lytton ;[3]  Admiralty, Sir John Paking-
ton ;  War Office, General Peel ;  Board of Trade, Mr. Henley ;
First Commissioner of Works, Lord John Manners ;  Board of
Control, Lord Ellenborough ;[4]  Chancellor of the Exchequer,
Mr. Disraeli.  In giving me the Foreign Office, Lord Derby
has imposed a very great responsibility upon me.  At this
moment our relations with France are in a state of more than

---

[1] The Marquis of Salisbury died April 1868.
[2] The Earl of Hardwicke died September 1873.
[3] Lord Lytton died in January 1873.
[4] The Earl of Ellenborough died September 1871.

tension, and it will require the utmost temper both in this country and there to clear away the clouds that threaten a storm. I have great confidence, not only in the good sense of the Emperor, but also in what I consider to be the undoubted disposition he entertains to do all he can to keep well with England. In the numberless conversations I have had with him, I have always observed this feeling to be uppermost, and that he is quite aware that his uncle owed his great misfortunes principally to his constant enmity to this country. I do not feel so much confidence in his Ministers, Walewski and Persigny, but I hope and believe that he holds them firmly in hand, and that he will not allow their prejudices or passions to act upon his policy.

*February 25th.*—All the arrangements are completed, and the new Ministers kiss hands to-morrow. Lord Derby is to make his statement on Monday. Mr. Seymour Fitzgerald is Under-Secretary to the Foreign Office, and I have appointed Mr. Bidwell and Mr. Wolff[1] as my private secretaries.

*February 26th.*—The hard frost continues. Lord Derby's Government has several times been on the point of breaking down. The worst hitch happened yesterday. Lytton was forced to resign the Colonies, finding that he could not be re-elected for Hertfordshire. I persuaded Lord Stanley to take the office to serve his father's Government, so all is right again.

*From Lord M. to Lord Cowley.[2]*

London: February 27, 1858.

My dear Cowley,—I have only a moment to say that I am glad to find an old friend and one so eminently useful as yourself still at Paris. I hope you will give me your assistance as willingly as you did in 1852. Persigny declares, *sur la tête de ses enfants*, that the animus is good at the Tuileries.        Yours sincerely,

MALMESBURY.

---

[1] Now Sir Henry Wolff, M.P. for Portsmouth.

[2] Earl Cowley died in 1884, after a most distinguished career in diplomacy. I never knew a man of business so naturally gifted for that profession. Straightforward himself, he easily discovered guile in others who sought to deceive him, and this was well known to such. He remained Ambassador at Paris till 1867, and was not a little assisted by the remarkable intelligence of his wife, née de Ros, and by her knowledge of the world, of society, and of courts.

*March 1st.*—Lord Derby made his statement this afternoon to an immensely full House, and spoke well. Lady Malmesbury has come up, which is a great comfort to me, as I have been here without servants or carriage, obliged to dine at my club, where I am surrounded by discontented faces, and worried by those who want places. Lord Stanley is Secretary for the Colonies in the place of Sir E. Lytton.

*From Lord M. to Lord Cowley.*

Foreign Office : March 1, 1858.

My dear Cowley,—There can be no doubt that you will be rendering a public service at this moment in assisting me to calm the wayward spirits on both sides the Channel. That is the first and most important point. Then again no one is, or can be, *saturated* (this is Clarendon's word) like you with the questions emanating from the Treaty of Paris and impending in the approaching Conferences. After all this is settled, and if I am still in office, it will be time to talk over your personal wishes respecting yours. I therefore, with much pleasure, consider you to have complied with every request. I will write again to-night if I have anything to tell you after Lord Derby's statement. Pray mention that we think of sending some respectable gentleman to Naples to watch the trial of the Engineers, and give a fair and complete report of their state. He will merely take a letter to Caraffa, and not stay a day after the business is settled. The French appear to have acted *loyalement* in this business at Naples, and they need not think that we have any *arrière-pensée*. There is now only a Deputy Vice-Consul to report, of whom *I* personally know nothing.    Yours sincerely,

MALMESBURY.

*March 2nd.*—Lord Grey said to Lady Tankerville that he would have joined Lord Derby's Government if it had not been for Mr. Disraeli, and that Mr. Gladstone would also have joined him had he been offered the leadership of the Commons. The Duchess of Manchester is made Mistress of the Robes, *vice* the Duchess of Wellington. The Duke of Wellington has given his adherence to Lord Derby, although he accepted the Garter from Lord Palmerston, and Lord Derby had given away his place at Court to the Duke of Beaufort.

*From Lord M. to Lord Cowley.*

London : March 2, 1858.

My dear Cowley,—We find it utterly impossible to proceed with Palmerston's Bill. Lord John Russell has thrown himself into the arms of the Radicals, by whom he has been gladly taken, and he and Gladstone have pledged themselves, with 140 men, to interrupt *any* bill, in *any* way, and for *any* time. If we are beaten now, Lord John must be the next man. Clarendon agreed with me that all moderate men must deprecate such an advent accompanied by a Reform Bill, which would make the House of Commons a revolutionary and unmanageable body. • • •

Yours sincerely,

MALMESBURY.

*From Lord M. to Lord Cowley.*

London : March 2, 1858.

My dear Cowley,—I must now inform you *où nous en sommes* with M. de Persigny upon the Refugee question. I had two interviews yesterday with him, and Lord Derby had another, in which we laid before him (according to previous agreement) the model of such a despatch as might satisfy the House of Commons. It was a suitable protest against the insinuations contained in Count Walewski's despatch of January 28, and would at the same time allow the French Government to find a dignified *échappatoire* from the present position, so painful to all parties. To the general tone Persigny made no objection, but he pressed earnestly that we should not enter into any argument in defence of our law, but confine ourselves to vindicating the honour and character of the English people. • • •

Prepare, therefore, the way for this course and consummation; it is difficult and almost impossible to do so here satisfactorily. With the best animus, Persigny is so *emporté*, that we cannot reason with him; his vehemence and excitability make interviews anything but agreeable. I wish particularly to avoid any sort of complaint being made of him to his enemy, Walewski, or even to the Emperor upon *this score;* but there is one point which *you must* press upon the Emperor, and which *he must* in his turn press upon Persigny— namely, that it is utterly fatal to the carrying out of delicate operations, or even of routine business, if he repeats and relates to the Opposition all that passes between him and her Majesty's Ministers. After my first conversation on the 20th, in which we proposed a course somewhat similar to the present, he went and related the whole to Lord Palmerston, and, that you may not doubt the fact, he himself told me that he had done so, together with Palmerston's observations. You know well enough that, whatever the Government and whatever the Opposition, it is impossible to carry on political matters unless the Foreign Ambassadors are tongue-tied with the Opposition. It always was looked upon as a point of honour, just as it is with our own, many of whom must be always opposed to the *de facto* Government in opinions. Pray, then, let him be warned by his *master*, but not by his *fellow-servant*, whom he hates with all the bitterness imaginable.    Yours sincerely,

MALMESBURY.

*March 4th.*—Sent my despatch in answer to Walewski's to-day. Sir E. Lytton is offended with Lord Derby, whom he accuses of having acted with unjustifiable haste in filling up the Secretaryship of the Colonies. It appears there was some misunderstanding between the two—that Lytton only said he was not sure of his re-election, which Lord Derby understood to be a positive statement that he could not re-obtain his seat.

### *From Lord M. to Lord Cowley.*

Foreign Office : March 4, 1858.

My dear Cowley,—I send you a despatch which is intended by us to be the reply to Walewski's unfortunate production, and which you will present at once, *unless you see good reason for the contrary*, which you will announce by telegraph. The Cabinet find that to pass Lord Palmerston's bill is *impossible*. Even were it not so, it would be so opposed by J. Russell, Gladstone, and the Radicals, that with 140 followers they could keep the question open, and becoming daily a sorer wound, for a month. Do not pledge us to any reform of the law whatever. The law is itself on its trial in trying Truelove and Bernard. Three others, including Pyat, are to be prosecuted for an infamous libel recommending the murder of the Emperor. You will easily understand that the sentence in the despatch alluding to the law having been unused by our Government from reasons of discretion means a want of evidence, or a fear of giving too much notoriety and false importance to the refugee conspirators. But really you ought to remind the Emperor of his view of the case of these scoundrels in 1852, when I came into office.

Austria, Russia, &c., had addressed the strongest remonstrance to us against the refugees, and invited France to join them. He treated them with contempt, and no one expressed it more strongly from him than Walewski, then Ambassador in London. I think he may be reminded of this. If we fail in our prosecutions our hands will be strengthened, and the popular feeling may abate; but it is now passion and not reason, and our Parliamentary opponents are making capital of it. If the Emperor, then, possesses any of his former sagacity, he will see that he had better *drop so hot a coal.* 'I have been utterly misunderstood; I meant to demand nothing; but, after showing to England, whom I believe to be a friend and ally, the danger I have been in, and suggesting by what means she might assist in preventing a repetition of such a tragedy, I am met with misconstruction, and even hostile language. Trusting, therefore, to God, &c., France, &c., I shall say no more about it.' If done in a dignified manner, I think it would have a good effect on all here, except those whose profit it is to work up a row, and he might put in language which, whilst it made his people angry with us, would consign the quarrel to the tomb of Pritchard.

Yours sincerely,<br>MALMESBURY.

*March 6th.*—M. de Persigny is furious at our party coming into office, as he is devoted to Lord Palmerston, and instead of assisting me to restore the friendly feeling lately subsisting between England and France, has done all he can to prevent my attaining that object; not only by relating to Lord Palmerston all that passes between us, but by writing letters to the Emperor to increase his irritation. My impression is that the Emperor is pretending to be more angry than he really is to please the French; but that, if we are firm, he will give way, and intends to do so. I believe, however, that the late attempt on his life has greatly shaken his nerves, that he is spoilt by a life of ease and pleasure, and does not stand being shot at as well as he used to do. Lord Brougham says that Bernard, the assassin, would be bailed, as there were people ready to put down money to any amount, and if he were, he would leave the country. This would greatly complicate our difficulties with France.[1] There was a great party last night at Lord Palmer-

---

[1] Dr. Bernard was concerned in the attempt on the Emperor's life.

ston's, and the language of the Opposition was very bitter. They
look upon office as their birthright, and upon those who
deprive them of it as brigands who have robbed them of their
property.

*March 9th.*—Sir Watkin Wynn's place in Wales has been
burned down. The visitors who were in the house had only
time to escape in their night-clothes. They rushed out by
the back door, the ground being covered with snow, and a
tremendous gale blowing, and the poor women stood long in it
without any other covering. The fright and excitement probably
saved their lives. After the confusion had somewhat subsided,
some coats were found, and they were taken to a house in the
neighbourhood. Lady Wynn's jewels and plate were saved,
and also the title-deeds of the estate ; but Lady Vane lost
everything, clothes and jewels, to the value of 5,000*l.* A few
pictures were saved, and fortunately the most valuable ones
by the old masters had been sent to the Manchester Exhibition.
The damage is estimated at 100,000*l.*

*March 12th.*—Walewski's answer to my despatch arrived
this afternoon. Persigny, who is very unwell, got out of bed
on purpose to bring it to me. He thinks all the annoyance
this business has occasioned him is the cause of his illness.
The tone of Walewski's despatch is very friendly, and must be
considered as giving full satisfaction to England. It is even
better than I expected from Lord Cowley's letters. Persigny,
when he presented it, announced that he had resigned his post
of Ambassador. As soon as he left I went to Lord Derby at
the Treasury, and he was much pleased, the more so as he
feared it would not have arrived in time to enable Disraeli
to announce its receipt to-day to the House of Commons, which
meets for the first time since the adjournment. He had been
with Lord Derby a short time before I arrived, and was much
annoyed at the delay in the arrival of the despatch, so that
when Lord Derby sent a message to him asking him to come to
him, as Lord Malmesbury was there, he rushed up in such a
desperate hurry that he nearly knocked over the messenger,
and entered the room in a great state of excitement. When
the despatch was produced, his delight was indescribable and

amazingly demonstrative, considering the usually phlegmatic
manner in which he receives news of all kinds.

*March* 13*th.*—The House of Commons showed a hostile
feeling yesterday. Not a word of satisfaction was expressed
by the Opposition at the settlement of the quarrel with France,
whilst a violent attack was made upon the Government for not
taking immediate steps for procuring the release of the English
engineers who were imprisoned at Naples, having been captured
in the ' Cagliari.' This was a Sardinian ship, freighted and
manned by the Carbonari, and intended to land a party in
Calabria to stir up that part of Italy. No doubt this object
was known to the Sardinian Government, and was to provoke
a war, either through the seizure of the ship or from the attack
thus intended. The two English engineers, Watt and Park,
were made prisoners in her, and confined at Naples. A bitter
contention has been going on for some time between that
Government and ours as to their release, and also as to the
legality of the seizure of the 'Cagliari,' the Government of
Naples positively refusing to give way on either subject. The
Cabinet to-day lasted four hours. I shall lay the correspondence
with France on the table of the House of Lords next Monday.
Walewski's explanation is more satisfactory than we could
expect, considering that we did not give the slightest hope
of any concession; but, of course, it is far from cordial, and if
unfortunately any more attempts are made on the Emperor's
life by refugees from England, war will inevitably ensue.

*March* 14*th.*—Lady Tankerville dined at Lady Palmerston's,
where she met the Persignys—Madame in dreadfully low spirits
at having to return to Paris. Count Kielmansegge, the Hanoverian Minister, told her it was perfectly ridiculous in Persigny
to make such scenes because Lord Palmerston was turned out
and Lord Derby come in; that a foreign ambassador ought to
have no politics except those of his own country, and it ought to
make no difference to him which party was in office, it being his
duty to be friends with all. I hope Persigny is really going over,
as I am sure it would be both difficult and disagreeable for me to
have anything to do with him. He is perfectly untrustworthy,
repeats everything to Lord Palmerston, and even appears to act

according to his instructions. The first time I met him at the Foreign Office he literally raved, laying his hand on the hilt of his sword (he was in Court dress), and shouting, 'C'est la guerre! c'est la guerre!' during which scene I sat perfectly silent and unmoved, till he was blown, which is the best way of meeting such explosions from foreigners.

From Lord M. to Lord Cowley.

Foreign Office: March 14, 1858.

My dear Cowley,—Your letter of the 13th is very important, and must give rise to the most serious apprehensions, because it foresees the possibility—nay, the likelihood—of our being, by a mere change of a Minister here, the victims of one man's views, and that man not the Emperor. Now I should like to have from *you* (for no one else can tell me) what are Walewski's views? What is his *but*? With regard to Persigny, *we* are old personal friends, and I congratulated myself on finding him Ambassador at this time, but he has behaved in so extraordinary a manner, not only by repeating the confidential conversations which Lord Derby and I had with him to Palmerston, but by going about in the *salons* and abusing his successors with the language and manner of an electioneering agent—in short, with such a total want of dignity and common discretion, that the whole Corps Diplomatique are in amazement. I shall consider such to be bygones if his importance here is what you describe; but it is absolutely indispensable for the furtherance of friendly communications between him and me that he should play his *rôle* in the humdrum way—namely, keeping his ears and eyes open, and his mouth shut, and, above all, not meddling as a partisan in domestic politics. If it ever were known to the public that a foreigner did this, the Press and their readers would be utterly unmanageable on the subject. Pray, then, give me your opinion of Walewski's political views, and why he wants to quarrel with a country the hostility of which was the cause of the first Emperor's fall? His character is not grand enough to think of *revenge*! We shall lay the 'Cagliari' papers before Parliament, and probably refer the question again to our Crown lawyers. It was a great indiscretion —if not worse—of Azeglio to publish Phillimore's opinion. Bernstorff is trying to obtain the freedom of the engineers, and if you have a chance, pray observe to the Neapolitan Envoy at Paris that their liberty must be the first and indispensable step to a reconciliation with his Government,
Yours sincerely,
MALMESBURY.

*March* 15*th.*—I offered the embassy at Vienna to Lord Stanhope,[1] who refused, saying that he was too old.

*March* 16*th.*—The remarks of all the papers on the correspondence with the French Government are favourable, except those of the 'Post,' which obeys the orders of the Emperor to write me down. The 'Times' is most complimentary. Disraeli, encouraged by a good attendance of our party, spoke extremely well on the 'Cagliari' question.

*March* 19*th.*—The Neapolitan Government have released the engineer Watt, on the representation of Mr. Lyons, who reached Naples on the 11th. Park is still in confinement at Palermo, where Mr. Lyons is going to see him. Our Government has hitherto been fortunate. In the short space of three weeks we have arranged the misunderstanding with France, with the exception of the feeling of irritation, which time only can appease, and which is inevitable, as we have refused all concessions on the Refugee question and the claims of the French Government for their extradition. We have obtained the release of the engineer Watt, and a promise of the immediate trial of Park.

*March* 20*th.*—Dined at Lady Molesworth's last night, where we met the Palmerstons and Madame de Persigny, who was crying at her husband's having given up the Embassy. She still seemed to hope they might stay. At that moment Persigny arrived, walked straight up to her, without noticing anybody else, and whispered in her ear. She got up, and went into another room, he following; and they walked about the rooms, out of one into another, in a state of great agitation. Persigny ending by rushing out of the house, to the amazement of the company, to none of whom had he said a word! I had an audience of the Queen this afternoon at six. Her Majesty kept me for an hour, and made me sit down—an honour seldom granted. I dined with the Montroses.

*March* 22*nd.*—I presented Baron Brünnow as Minister Plenipotentiary of Russia. The Queen received him well. She gave me an audience first, so Brünnow was obliged to wait, which must have annoyed him, as he said to me yesterday: 'Ne me faites pas attendre au Palais. Lord Palmerston me faisait attendre

---

[1] The late Lord Stanhope, the historian.

une ou deux heures, et quelquefois ne venait pas du tout.' This unpunctuality of Lord Palmerston's was the grievance and terror of the whole Corps Diplomatique, and Van de Weyer assured me that during his mission he had read through the eight volumes of 'Clarissa Harlowe' in the ante-room, waiting for audiences of Lord Palmerston. A Levée and Cabinet afterwards. Dined at the Palace. Lord Brougham is trying to bring about a reconciliation between Lord Palmerston and Lord John Russell, and is very spiteful in his manner towards our party in the House of Lords. I believe the Duke of Bedford opposes it.

*From Lord M. to Lord Cowley.*

Foreign Office: March 23, 1858.

My dear Cowley,—As soon as your telegram arrived I went to the Queen and informed her Majesty of the intentions of the Emperor in respect of his new Ambassador at her Court. I never saw the Queen more pleased, not only at the choice of so distinguished a person as the Duc de Malakoff, but also at the remarkable delicacy which prompted his Imperial Majesty to select one whose name is so familiar and so popular in this country. The Queen begged me not to lose a moment in replying to you by telegraph how much she felt the compliment thus paid her. I need not tell you that personally I am rejoiced at the choice.

Yours sincerely,

MALMESBURY.

*March 24th.*—I hear the Emperor was unwilling to accept Persigny's resignation, and kept it some days in his pocket without telling Walewski, who, hearing of it, went to the Emperor and insisted on his accepting it, under a threat of resigning himself. The Emperor, who is supposed to be still influenced by Madame Walewska, gave in, and Walewski at once sent a courier to Persigny announcing the fact. The bag contained only one despatch, and that was in these words: 'Votre démission est acceptée.' Poor Persigny was furious at this insult, and I have no doubt on his return to Paris he will succeed in regaining the Emperor's ear, for Walewski in his heart is no friend to the English alliance, and is all for Russia. It is now settled and announced that Marshal Pélissier is to succeed Persigny. Baron

Brünnow is much annoyed, as he expected and wished his friend the Marquis de Moustier to get the place. De Moustier is very Russian in his policy.

*March 25th.*—The Jew Bill has passed the House of Commons by a majority of 153. Mr. Roebuck's motion for the abolition of the Irish Lord-Lieutenancy was rejected by a majority of 127. I have nominated Mr. Elliot [1] as Minister to Copenhagen, Lord Augustus Loftus to Vienna, and Sir John Crampton to St. Petersburg. They are all promotions in the line and by seniority. A subscription is being raised to give Madame de Persigny a bracelet from the ladies.

*From Lord M. to Lord Cowley.*

Foreign Office : March 25, 1858.

My dear Cowley,—Society was at first startled by a Marshal's arrival, and the diplomatists, particularly, looked glum, but I think more at what they knew was a compliment and earnest of the Emperor's goodwill than because they thought it hostile. Almost all hate our close alliance with France, and could not conceal their joy during the late squabble between us. Brünnow is utterly disgusted. The Queen and Prince have again expressed their satisfaction at the Marshal's appointment. I have submitted to the law officers your question as to Bernard's surrender. He will be tried almost immediately on the felonious indictment ; but we fear that at that we may fail, for in neither country could a man be prosecuted for being an accessory to a murder committed abroad by one *foreigner* upon *another.* If Orsini had been English, or any Englishman had been concerned in the actual murder, there would have been no difficulty in bringing Bernard under the English statute. If that fails the other indictment will stand. Allsopp does not come under our Extradition Treaty with the United States, but we hear he has bolted, and will most likely be brought over by some kidnappers from the Havanas or Panama for the 200*l*. I think it quite as well that Pélissier should not come till the 12th.

Yours sincerely,

MALMESBURY.

*From the same to the same.*

Foreign Office : March 27, 1858.

My dear Cowley,—I think it as well to inform you that I have taken the opinion of the law officers on the question whether the French

[1] Son of Lord Minto.

Government can demand the extradition of Simon Bernard, and whether her Majesty's Government would be empowered to surrender him if such demand were made, and I have been informed by them in reply that Simon Bernard, not having been accused of the crime of murder committed ' within the jurisdiction of the requiring party' (the Emperor of the French), the foreign Government cannot, under the Convention of 1843, demand his extradition, and that her Majesty's Government would not be empowered or authorised to surrender Simon Bernard if such demand were made. You will inform Count Walewski of this, and that Bernard will be tried by a Special Commission next month.

Yours sincerely,<br>MALMESBURY.

*March* 30*th*.—I dined with the Persignys. Lady Shaftesbury called to show us three bracelets, on which she wished to have our opinion. We selected two, and proposed giving Madame de Persigny the choice, to which she assented.

*April* 5*th*.—A hurricane from the north-east. M. d'Azeglio arrived, and I appointed to meet him at the Foreign Office. I think he is disposed to give us trouble about the 'Cagliari' question. I believe it to be quite true that Lord John has refused to join Palmerston, who tried to persuade him to coalesce with him to turn us out; but Lord John remembers the way he was treated by Palmerston, and will not hear of a coalition with him or his party.

*April* 6*th*.—Went to Windsor.

*April* 7*th*.—Lady Palmerston has done everything to persuade Lord John Russell to coalesce with her husband and turn us out, but Lord John will not hear of a coalition. Lucknow was stormed on March 9, and completely in our possession on the 15th.

*From Lord M. to Lord Cowley.*

Foreign Office : April 10, 1858.

My dear Cowley,—As I shall see you so soon, it is hardly worth while troubling you with a letter, but I wish you to ascertain before you come over whether the French are prepared soon to renew with us our diplomatic relations with Naples. I cannot do so till the 'Cagliari' case is settled, and I can't settle it till I have our Crown lawyers' opinion, which I shall receive on Monday. I have little doubt as to what it will be in respect of the long detention of Watt and Park—

namely, against the Neapolitan Government; and if so, we shall have
to ask for compensation.  I hear that the Neapolitan Government are
very anxious to renew their relations, and this would make my demand
go down more easily.  What would the French ask as to their conditions?  I am in a singular position on this question.  I am made
Minister on purpose to resist interference on the part of France with
our laws, and I am also expected to keep up a quarrel with Naples in
support of interference with their institutions.  What a set we are!

Your sincerely,<br>
MALMESBURY.

From the same to the same.

Foreign Office : April 13, 1858.

My dear Cowley,—I shall be very glad to see you, as I want to
consult you on a great many subjects.  The law officers have *unanimously* declared the detention of Watt and Park illegal, and that they
have a right to redress for this, and compensation for loss of reason
and health, which in men of that class amounts to starvation.  The
Government will therefore demand it.  If we had had a Minister at
Naples, these men would have been out in a week.  Pray tell all this to
Walewski frankly, and that I am ready to march with him at the proper
time.  If you can get any good advice from any quarter given to the
King on the subject of acceding to our demand, pray do so.  How
would you settle the ' Cagliari' affair if (as it will be) there are four
great lawyers in favour of the seizure and three against it?  Is there
any precedent for such a doubtful but important case being submitted
to a committee of governments, or to a mediator, if he can be so called?
How is maritime law to be settled for all of us?  I wish we had half
our China fleet here at home.  I fear nothing will be done.

Yours sincerely,<br>
MALMESBURY.

*April 14th.*—I got a letter this morning from Colonel Phipps,
saying that the Queen wished us to put off our proposed dinner to
the Duc de Malakoff, as he is only to arrive to-morrow, and it is
etiquette that he should dine first at the Palace.  I therefore
wrote to all our guests to appoint another day.  Two hours after
another letter arrived from her Majesty saying that we could
appoint any other day we liked, and that if we acquainted the
Queen with the date fixed upon she would not give a dinner on
that day, so as not to interfere with us.  We therefore fixed the

24th, and of course asked the same set as I had invited for the
17th. What could be more gracious and good-natured than this
on the part of her Majesty ?

*From Lord M. to Lord Cowley.*

Foreign Office: April 15, 1858.

My dear Cowley,—. . . . This acquittal of Bernard is a very painful affair. There was cheering and every sort of rascally demonstration disgraceful to our country. Pélissier was very well received; and
the Queen and he mutually pleased with each other. He dines at the
Palace to-night, where I am to meet him. The Queen is much disappointed at your not being over here, as she thought you might be, to
join the party.

Yours sincerely,

MALMESBURY.

*From the same to the same.*

Foreign Office: April 15, 1858.

My dear Cowley,— I think you may as well announce to Walewski,
*officieusement*, that our lawyers, being *unanimous* on the question of
detaining our engineers—that they were so detained *unlawfully* and
are entitled to *compensation*—I have demanded the same from Caraffa
in a civil letter; this is an *English* case. The other, the capture of
the ship, interests all maritime Powers, and, therefore, Great Britain
the first. But here, out of seven English lawyers consulted, three say
the capture was legal, four illegal. We cannot, therefore, in this
position take a strong line, although Sardinia is trying, with a somewhat unfriendly zeal, to put the pressure of popular feeling upon us.
It would be very desirable to induce the King to play the part of a
*Grand Roi*, to give our men a competent sum, and to liberate the Sardinian ship and crew. We can't ask him to own himself in the wrong
when the majority of our lawyers are for him; but this plan would
save his *amour-propre*, and put an end to a question which, in the
temper of Sardinia *de se faire mousser*, might bring on an Italian
conflagration—which God forbid! Would the French give good advice
to their two Italian Courts?        Yours sincerely,

MALMESBURY.

*April 16th.*—The Duc de Malakoff called upon me, but did not
touch upon business. He talked of the Crimea the whole time.
I presented him to the Queen at three o'clock. He had never

seen Prince Albert, and, as the Queen did not present him, he
evidently took him for some lord-in-waiting, for he turned his
back upon him whilst talking to the Queen. Suddenly it seemed
to occur to him who the Prince was, for he turned towards him
and exclaimed, "Comment! c'est vous!' and made a low bow.
The Queen and Prince were much amused. I have sent a despatch
to Naples asking for compensation for the imprisonment of the
engineers. Disraeli announced it this afternoon in the House of
Commons, and it was received with cheers from all parts of the
House.

  *April 17th.*—Dined at the Palace. The Duchess of Manchester, the Breadalbanes, the Duke and Duchess of Cambridge,
the Duc de Malakoff, General Sir James Simpson, Sir William
Codrington, &c. Lady Churchill, who was in waiting, looked
charming—such a pretty face and lovely expression. Went afterwards to Lady Palmerston's party.

  *April 19th.*—To the disgust of everybody, Dr. Bernard is acquitted. There is but one sentiment—that of abhorrence at the
disgraceful verdict of the jury. I told Madame Malaret that it
was almost always the same on political questions.

  *April 22nd.*—I went to the Drawing Room, where the Duc de
Malakoff also attended. He was immensely pleased at having
been cheered all the way from his house in Hyde Park by a very
respectable mob. It made a great impression on him, and he said
to me, 'After such a voluntary demonstration from the English
people, how can I obey my orders, which are that I am to behave
with the strictest reserve to everybody in this country? It is impossible for me to do so, and after this compliment I shall certainly
meet the English with the same cordiality as they have received
me, and this will apply to your Government as well as to private
individuals.' He evidently had been prepared for a cold reception,
but the people had taken their own line, which was that of grateful
recognition of the hero of the Crimean war. M. de Jaucourt,
attached to the French Embassy, told me that M. de Persigny
resigned from rage at Walewski's settling the quarrel between
the two Governments without him, and hoped that the Emperor
would not accept it. When the answer came, accepting his resignation, he was completely knocked down.

*April 24th.*—The Duke of Cambridge, the Duc de Malakoff, the Manchesters, the Northumberlands, the Staffords, the Derbys, the Rokebys, Sir R. and Lady Airey, Sir James Simpson, and Jem MacDonald dined with us to-day.

*April 28th.*—The ex-Ministers actually voted the night before last against a Minute they had themselves prepared just before they were turned out on the subject of competitive examinations; and last night they supported Mr. Locke King's bill on the county franchise, though they voted against it last year, and were saved by us from defeat. Our party, I am sorry to say, are, or pretend to be, offended with Disraeli. They, of course, ought to know that we are in a minority and can neither help it nor disguise the fact.

*April 29th.*—I spoke on the 'Cagliari' question, and stated my opinion that it had arisen from a determination of the Sardinian Government and their supporters in this country to provoke an Italian war; but our Government were thwarting this in every way we possibly could, as, when once a catastrophe of that kind had begun, it would probably become European. I was supported in this view by Lord Grey, and I was complimented by Lord Granville, Lord Clanricarde, Lord Clarendon, and Lord John Russell as I left the House. I don't think the Opposition will give us any further trouble on this subject at present. Mr. Kinglake, who was to bring forward a motion on the 'Cagliari' question, expressed himself perfectly satisfied.

*May 7th.*—We dined at the Palace—a party of 85—in honour of the Queen of Portugal. Duchess of Kent and the Royal Family, Prince Hohenzollern and his son, father and brother of the Queen, Terceiras, Manchesters, Exeters, Abercorns, Beauforts, Derbys, Hardwickes, Chelmsfords, Clarendons, Lady Palmerston, and Lady John Russell; the dinner magnificent; all served on gold plate, and did not last long, but the standing afterwards was dreadful. The Queen of Portugal is certainly pretty, with an innocent expression, tall, and graceful in her manner. No one could sit down till eleven o'clock, when the Queen and her guests retired to one of the drawing-rooms, where the round table was placed. The rest of the ladies sat on sofas round the room.

*May 8th.*—Lord Ellenborough has got us into a scrape by pro-

F F

ducing his answer to Lord Canning's proclamation. He gave only extracts to the House of Lords, but by some blunder the despatch in full was laid on the table of the House of Commons, and must be productive of mischief both in India and at home ; and what makes it worse is, that it was given by Mr. Baillie, the Under-Secretary of the Board of Control, to Mr. Bright.[1] Nothing can be worse, and it may lead to the resignation of the Government, or, at all events, to a dissolution.

*May* 10*th.*—I think the Government must go out, unless Lord Ellenborough resigns. The Whigs and Radicals have united, and a vote of censure is to be brought forward in both Houses.

*From Lord M. to Lord Canning.*

London : May 10, 1858.

My dear Canning,—I am sure you will believe that, as perhaps your oldest friend, I am much annoyed at the events of the last few days. I must, by the laws of *solidarité*, take my share of blame in acts which, though marked with inexcusable indiscretion, had no motive of personal hostility to yourself. *I* never saw the Proclamation nor Lord Ellenborough's despatch until I read both in the 'Times' of the 8th inst., for neither came before the Cabinet. I consider that I am justified, although a Minister of the Government that has committed towards you and the country the blunder of publishing Lord E.'s secret despatch, in advising you strongly, as a private friend, not to follow the bent which your mind may probably take *at first*, if it be that of resigning your post. Neither Lord Derby nor any of our party wish it, and the whole country is ready to give you all the credit you merit for having so well encountered the extraordinary difficulties of your position. To resign on a point of party and political honour at the moment when you have all but consummated your work, would be sacrificing your future fame to a *temporary* provocation, which ought not to weigh an ounce in the balance. The Opposition are to bring on the subject this week in the most hostile form, and may very likely turn us out; but if we remain in office, I repeat that Lord Derby and the Cabinet are friendly towards you. I told the Queen last night that I should write to you in this sense, and she seemed very anxious that I should do so. You will, of course, consider this advice as strictly confidential.          Ever yours sincerely,

MALMESBURY.

[1] This has been contradicted by Mr. Baillie, who says he left it on his table when he went to the House of Commons.

*May* 11*th.*—I have appointed Sir Henry Bulwer Ambassador to Constantinople. It has always been the object of his ambition. Lord Ellenborough has resigned, and has written a very handsome letter to Lord Derby, promising to give him every support in his power out of office. I never heard a more noble and affecting speech than Lord Ellenborough's, announcing his resignation in the House. It took everybody by surprise, and the consternation on the front Opposition bench was great, as it defeated their intentions, and made us safe.

*May* 12*th.*—It is expected that the Opposition will move the vote of censure on Friday, as before arranged, but perhaps the exact terms of it will be changed in consequence of Lord Ellenborough's resignation.

*May* 13*th.*—The motion of censure is to be brought forward in both Houses on Friday, and I think it will be carried in the Commons.

*May* 14*th.*—Went to the House of Lords, where there were only two seats left in the gallery when I arrived, all filled with ladies. The steps of the Throne, the Peers' and Strangers' galleries crammed, and all so attentive to the debate that every word was heard. Lord Ellenborough's speech was very fine. The division took place about twelve, and the Government had a majority of nine. For the resolution—93 present and 65 proxies, total 158 ; against—118 present and 49 proxies, total 167.

*From Lord M. to Lord Cowley.*

Foreign Office : May 14, 1858.

My dear Cowley,—Since writing this morning, we have received news from Churchill at Ragusa and from Vienna, to the effect that the Montenegrins, on the night of the 12th, treacherously attacked the Turks during their voluntary and settled evacuation of Grahova, and cut them up, killing the Pasha and Delarue, the negotiator. These are the brigands the French are supporting. It will add to our complications, inasmuch as the Porte will naturally be more unwilling to allow things to be settled quietly, and to sit down quietly under such a defeat. On the other hand, you should induce the French to understand that it can do them no credit to be *partisans* of such fellows, although they are justified in joining with us and the three other Powers to put a stop to a war which may spread throughout Turkey. If her other provinces

should rise against her, her Majesty's Government could not interfere
at all, and if it is a case of Christian sympathy, such a civil war would
fall on our co-religionists most awfully.  The first thing Walewski has
to do is to stop his cursed hero Danilo, who is now evidently the
aggressor.                               Yours sincerely,

                                              MALMESBURY.

*May 16th.*—A reconciliation has at last been effected between
Lord Palmerston and Lord John Russell.  Mr. Ellice arranged a
meeting at his house, where they shook hands.  This was followed
by Lord John Russell's speech on Friday night on Mr. Cardwell's
motion of censure on the Government.  Even without this we
should be beaten in the Commons, but of course now the majority
will be larger.  The longer the debate is protracted the better it
will be for us, and the news from India, if unfavourable, would
influence the division.  Lord Derby has seen the Queen, and
though he is not at liberty to make use of her name, still he may
announce a dissolution of Parliament on his own responsibility.
After I got home I received a despatch from Lyons, announcing
that the Sardinian Government would accept my proposals.
D'Azeglio was to have called, but never came, and I suppose he
must have got the same news, and did not think it necessary to do
so.  Besides this, he is certainly annoyed at my having settled
matters with the Sardinian Government, and defeated their plan
for a war, and didn't like to be the bearer of the good news.

*May 17th.*—Lady Tankerville says that at Lady Palmerston's
party last Saturday she was seated next to Lady William Russell,
who, talking of the reconciliation between Lord John and Lord
Palmerston, said, 'They have shaken hands and embraced, and
hate each other more than ever.'  Lord Derby has offered a seat
in the Cabinet to Sir James Graham, who has refused, saying he
is too old and broken in health to accept, and that his sympathies
were always with Lord John.

*May 18th.*—The debate last night in the Commons was much
in our favour.  Whiteside's speech was very powerful.

Lord Harry Vane proposed to suspend legislation on the
Indian Government Bill until next session ; a motion which was
negatived by a majority of 390.  This was the more satisfactory
as it was considered in the light of a vote of want of confidence.

Lord Derby had a meeting at the Treasury yesterday, which was very enthusiastic.

*May* 19*th.*—The Opposition had another uncomfortable night yesterday in the Commons. Mr. Vernon Smith, ex-Minister for India, was dreadfully badgered. Disraeli said that the letters received by Lord Ellenborough from Lord Canning allude to occurrences which appear to have been explained in former letters, which have never been seen by this Government. Lord Palmerston would not allow Mr. Smith to answer, but got up himself and said that if there were other letters they must have been lost, as he had never seen them. Lord Canning's despatches have been received, and are to be laid on the table of the House of Commons to-morrow, before the division takes place. The whole world has gone to the Derby. It is now believed that the Proclamation was sent to Lord Canning from England by the last Government, but I can't credit it. Lady Malmesbury informed me there was a report that Mr. Cardwell would withdraw his motion of censure ; but I hope that Disraeli will insist upon dividing, and Lord Derby is also of that opinion, seeming sure that Disraeli will not give way. I had great misgivings, and too truly, for at seven P.M. Mr. Bidwell arrived in great glee, and told us that the resolutions were withdrawn, without any objection from Disraeli, and that we should have had a majority of thirty if he divided. I regret it, as a motion of censure is like an attack on a man's honour, that ought to be met and defeated, not evaded. Disraeli defends the course he has taken, of allowing the motion to be withdrawn, by saying the feeling of the House was decidedly in favour of it, and that none but the immediate partisans of Lord Palmerston wished to go on with it ; the debate having from the first day taken a much larger view of the question than the motion indicated, and turned entirely upon the policy of the Proclamation and of the Government's disapprobation of the policy it enunciated. In this temper of the House the publication of Sir James Outram's remonstrances, even though coupled with Lord Canning's defence, had a great effect, and they felt they could not do otherwise than approve of our policy. Our people also wished to avoid a dissolution.

*May* 27*th, Heron Court.*—We came down here for the holidays ;

Lady Jersey, Lady Clementina Villiers, the Baillie-Cochranes are with us, and also Lord and Lady Raglan. Ossulston and Mr. Bidwell arrived. The last brought a telegram announcing the arrival of the 'Monarch' at St. Helen's, with my brother and his family on board, returning from Chili.

*May 29th.*—Beautiful weather. I drove the party to Avon Cottage, a very pretty fishing lodge on the river, five miles from Heron Court.

*June 5th.*—Lord Bath, who took the Garter to the Queen of Portugal, has received a Portuguese Order of the first class in diamonds, and has got permission to wear it.

*June 8th.*—Mr. Gladstone's amendment to the India Bill for postponing legislation to next session was negatived by a majority of 149.

*June 9th.*—Bill for the Abolition of Church Rates passed the Commons, and Mr. Berkeley's motion for ballot was rejected by 97.

*June 11th.*—I got a telegram this morning from Mr. Lyons, announcing that the King of Naples grants the compensation of 3,000*l.* asked for the English engineers, which is to be paid immediately to the Foreign Office, and that he gives up the 'Cagliari' and crew to the English Government. I kept this a secret from everybody, as I wished to have the satisfaction of announcing it myself in the House of Lords this evening.

*June 12th.*—Disraeli's announcement of the termination of our dispute with Naples by the grant of 3,000*l.* to the engineers and giving up the 'Cagliari' to England was received with enthusiastic cheers. The ex-Ministers and their adherents were completely taken by surprise, and would not even pretend to be pleased that a quarrel which at one moment threatened a general war should have terminated in a manner so satisfactory. This news had evidently a great effect upon the House, for the Government passed a resolution on the India Bill, relating to the number of the Council, by a large majority.

*Lord Clarendon to Lord M.*

Grosvenor Crescent: June 13, 1858.

My dear Malmesbury,—I was glad to find that you took the same view I do of the neutral Senate which the French want to impose on the Principalities, and which is nothing else than a plan for establishing and perpetuating anarchy by means of an oligarchical Republic. The plan is of Imperial, and not Walewskian, origin, which is the reason why I suggest to you that it might be easier to render the proposed arrangement harmless than to have it altogether withdrawn. My notion is that the Central Senate ought not to be a deliberating and law-passing assembly, but should be simply a Committee consisting of a small body of members, appointed, not by the provincial assemblies, but by the Hospodars; and that this Committee should meet solely for the purpose of framing and suggesting measures to be submitted for the consideration of the two Governments, who, if they approved of them, might propose those measures to their respective provincial assemblies. Modified in this way, the French project would be comparatively harmless. If Walewski tries to wriggle out of the agreement come to at Osborne last year, pray do not hesitate to call me as a witness.       CLARENDON.

*June 21st.*—The heat of this last month has been quite exceptional, the thermometer constantly rising to 84°. Went to the Palace to present to the Queen my brother, who kissed hands on his appointment as Minister at Berne.

*June 23rd.*—The pestilential smell from the Thames is become intolerable, and there has been a question of changing the locality of Parliament. Nothing can be done during this heat. Great dinner at the Mansion House. The person most cheered was Sir Archdale Wilson, who took Delhi. The Lord Mayor, by mistake, mentioned him as Sir *Alexander* Wilson, the *defender* of Delhi. There was a general laugh, which greatly surprised him. Pélissier made a very good speech, which was loudly cheered, to his evident delight. I hear he prides himself upon his public speaking.

*June 26th.*—Our Government had large majorities last night on the India Bill in the Commons. Lord Palmerston moved an amendment fixing the number of the Council at not more than twelve, which was rejected by a majority of 62. He then moved that all the members of the Council should be appointed by the Queen. This was opposed by Disraeli, and negatived by 93.

*June 27th.*—I dined at the Palace. The Queen expressed a wish that I should attend her to Germany, but was quite aware of the difficulty of my absenting myself from London whilst the

Paris Conferences were going on.   Her Majesty will probably take me to Cherbourg, where she has decided to go, and also Sir John Pakington.

We have ordered large quantities of lime to be thrown into the Thames, for no works can be begun until the hot weather is over.   The stench is perfectly intolerable ; although Madame Ristori, coming back one night from a dinner at Greenwich given by Lord Hardwicke, sniffed the air with delight, saying it reminded her of her ' dear Venice.'

*July 1st.*—Lord Lucan's bill for admitting the Jews to Parliament passed the House of Lords by a majority of 46.   Almost all our party voted against it, many Peers actually holding office having done so.   An amendment to a clause in the India Bill by Mr. Vernon Smith was negatived by 146 to 71.   The same fate attended two by Sir James Graham and Mr. Gladstone.   The clause disqualifying members of the Council of India from sitting in Parliament was discussed at great length and carried.   I expect that the bill will pass the Commons, and be brought to the House of Lords without opposition.

*July 2nd.*—Dined at the Palace.   The King of the Belgians and Duke and Duchess of Brabant were present.   A few people were asked in the evening, which made enough for one large quadrille.   The Queen danced every quadrille, and seemed to enjoy herself thoroughly.   The Church Rates Bill was thrown out by a majority of 151.

*July 4th.*—I have settled to accompany the Queen to Coblentz.   She wishes me to go, and so does the Government.

*July 12th.*—The Queen has written to me to say that I must go to Cherbourg with her on board the royal yacht.   Pélissier and Sir John Pakington go in one of the ships of the squadron. Sir John is not at all pleased at having Pélissier put under his charge, as he meant to take Lady Pakington and a large party of friends and relations on board the ship, meaning to turn a great national ceremony into a Worcestershire picnic.   Pélissier's presence will interfere with this arrangement.

### From Lord M. to Lord Cowley.

Foreign Office: July 13, 1858.

My dear Cowley,—The flag of the Principalities is entirely in your hands. I am sorry you have had such a trial of patience and temper. Stratford is going to Stamboul to take leave of the Sultan. His visit is strictly complimentary, and his written orders are not to interfere with Bulwer in any way. He will take the opportunity, if he finds one, to urge on the Sultan the observance of the Hatti, but his mission is strictly confined to one of compliment. He goes in August. Pray inform Fuad of this, and the French Government. There is a *nasty* article in the 'Times' to-day about Cherbourg. I depend upon seeing you there on the 4th, and I hope Walewski.

Yours sincerely,

MALMESBURY.

*July 15th.*—Lady Louisa Hamilton had a bad accident riding in the Park, her horse running away, leaping the iron rails and falling with her on the other side. She was picked up senseless, but is not seriously hurt. Lord Ellenborough made a violent speech against the India Bill. There was no division. The unusual heat of the weather continues.

*July 24th.*—The Ministerial fish-dinner took place to-day at Greenwich. I went down with Lord Hardwicke. Lord Derby having to propose 'Sir John Pakington and the Navy,' alluding to Sir John having received the 'wooden spoon' which is given to the Minister in the House of Commons who has been in the fewest divisions, proposed 'Sir John Pakington and the Wooden Spoons of Old England.' This created much laughter from all but Pakington himself. Sir John Pakington is, however, no shirker of work, and has always been ready to direct the most important departments, such as the Colonies and the Admiralty. He is a very young man of his age, both in activity and appearance. A slight figure, he is generally to be seen on horseback, and always with spurs and dapperly dressed. I remember once his keeping us all waiting at a Cabinet Council. When at last he appeared, Lord Derby said, 'We have been waiting for you, Sir John.' 'I am sorry, my Lord, but I was at Spithead.' 'Then,' said Lord Derby, 'I'll be bound there never was such a *swell* there before.'

*July* 30*th.*—I returned from Osborne. The Queen much pleased at the Lords' amendment to the India Bill relating to competitive examination having passed the Commons by a large majority, as it trenched on her prerogative.

### Lord M. to Lord Cowley.

Heron Court: July 30, 1858.

My dear Cowley,—I send you back the *projet de convention* for the Principalities, and wish you joy of having ended this work. I have made some observations where I did not think the meaning clear in the text, and I send an elaborate review by Hammond Bergne, our clever little treaty clerk, who seems satisfied with the *rédaction* on the whole. Pray make one more attempt before we go to Cherbourg to persuade Walewski not to publish the fact that the Conference was divided as to Union. It is only holding up discontent for the future and proclaiming that France was beaten, *à quoi bon ?* The questions we must treat at Cherbourg are :—1st. This, if not agreed to before. 2nd. Naples. 3rd. Plan for settling mode of verifying flags. If I cannot get through my political conversations by Friday, the Queen has given me leave to stay after she is gone. I go from here to Osborne to-morrow for a Council.           Yours sincerely,
                                                    MALMESBURY.

*August* 1*st.*—On the 30th Disraeli stated in the House of Commons the nature of the Lords' amendment to the India Bill, and it was agreed to by 98 to 53.

*August* 4*th.*—I went to see Mr. Rarey's establishment. We had 'Cruiser,' the untameable stallion, and a zebra shown us as being quite tame. The former certainly appeared to be so completely ; he followed Mr. Rarey wherever he went, without being led, and gave him his foot like a dog. Mr. Rarey then put his cap into his mouth ; 'Cruiser' took it, but let it drop immediately, when Mr. Rarey took it up and offered it again, upon which 'Cruiser' gave a shriek of rage, but took up the cap. The zebra is less tame, but walked, led by Mr. Rarey, who, however, did not dare let him loose. We afterwards saw two horses thrown, and it is curious how convinced they are that they cannot get up without Mr. Rarey's help. Went to Osborne. Sailed for Cherbourg.

*August 5th.*—It blew hard in the night, but subsided towards morning. The Queen not ill. The approach to Cherbourg very fine. Arrived there at seven P.M. At eight the Emperor and Empress came on board the Royal yacht without any suite. Nobody was admitted. Marshal Pélissier, who went in without invitation, was immediately turned out by the Emperor. Next morning, the Queen, Prince Albert, Prince of Wales, Duke of Cambridge, Sir John Pakington, and myself, breakfasted at the Prefecture. After which, the Royal personages drove over the town. I took a walk with Mr. Hamond, the consul. Returned to the Royal yacht, and accompanied the Queen to dinner on board the 'Bretagne.' Among the officers at dinner was General MacMahon.[1] Next morning, the Emperor came to take leave of the Queen. When the Emperor left the Queen's yacht the previous evening, all our ships illuminated in the most brilliant manner with blue lights. The yacht had red, white, and blue, and the electric light was thrown on the Emperor's barge, following it the whole way to the harbour. The effect was beautiful: the light shining only on the barge, whilst all around remained in darkness. Nothing could be finer than the whole display; and the Emperor was friendly in his manner; but both he and the Empress could not digest some articles in the 'Times' which had been offensive, especially against her, and it was in vain that I tried to make them understand what freedom the Press had in England, and how independent it was of all private and most public men.

An absurd occurrence took place when Sir John Pakington, as first Lord of the Admiralty, landed Lord Hardwicke and Admiral Dundas in his barge. As he steered her, he kept time with the men as he would if he had been rowing on the Thames, bending his body backwards and forwards, and as he approached the pier, not having given the order of 'Way enough,' the boat with her whole force struck the mole, and the two Admirals and the whole crew fell sprawling on their backs. The rage of the two former after recovering themselves was vented with uncontrolled expressions on the unfortunate First Lord, amidst the laughter of the spectators who were standing on the pier.

[1] Afterwards Duke of Magenta and President of the French Republic.

*From Lord M. to Count Walewski.*

Londres : ce 8 août, 1858.

Mon cher Walewski,—Avant de partir pour l'Allemagne, je ne puis me refuser le plaisir de vous exprimer la vive satisfaction avec laquelle la Reine a vu sa noble et amicale réception à Cherbourg. Tous les nôtres en ont été enchantés, et rien ne peut être meilleur que l'esprit public de ce côté de la Manche. J'ai beaucoup regretté de ne pas vous avoir revu Vendredi matin à bord du yacht. J'ai dit quelques mots à l'Empereur au sujet des Protocoles des Conférences. Je vous avoue que je trouve leur publication très-inutile, si ce n'est pour démontrer et établir à tout jamais les différences d'opinion entre les Puissances, et pour qu'un jour nous puissions avoir le triste privilège de nous faire mutuellement des reproches inutiles. Ceci est surtout important à l'endroit des Principalités. Passons en Chine : les dernières nouvelles promettent bien, et il est possible que les Chinois admettent des Ambassadeurs européens à Pékin. Il me semble pourtant que ce serait mieux de les établir à quelque autre ville du Nord plus près de la côte. Ils seraient dans une souricière à Pékin si les Chinois voulaient nous jouer un tour. Je vous prie de ne pas oublier notre conversation sur les Consuls de l'Orient et de leur faire comprendre qu'ils ne doivent pas se regarder en antagonistes, et surtout qu'ils sont assujettis aux ordres des Ambassadeurs à Constantinople. Finalement, ne prenons jamais de grandes mesures sans nous entendre et nous mettre autant que possible d'accord. Voilà ma politique. MALMESBURY.

*August* 10*th.*—I went down to Basingstoke to meet the Queen and Prince and their suite, and to embark at Gravesend for Antwerp on our way to Berlin. The suite consisted of Sir Charles Phipps, Lady Macdonald, and Miss Cavendish. I brought with me my two secretaries, Bidwell and Dashwood. The weather was tremendously hot.

---

I was relegated with Lord Bloomfield, our Ambassador at Berlin, the two ladies and Phipps in the second carriage ; the Prince and Queen travelling alone. After going through Düsseldorf, Hanover, and Brunswick, we of the suite arrived at Potsdam on August 14, too late for the supper which had been prepared.

The Queen came the next morning, which obliged me to attend a great luncheon at the Palace. My two secretaries have been invited to everything given here (Potsdam). I have dined every day at Babelsberg, a beautiful palace a few miles out of Potsdam, with the Queen and the Prussian Court. Babelsberg is four miles from Potsdam. I used to drive there with Lord Bloomfield, our Ambassador, and the Court ladies. Three of these were handsome, especially the Countess Hohenthal, a Maid of Honour, a beautiful girl, and clever.[1] Two others were Countess Lynar and Countess Oriola, a Portuguese, and a very attractive woman.

One day there was a great review of the Prussian Guard. I was very well mounted on a quiet charger, and also on another occasion I rode a perfect mare with the ladies Hohenthal and Oriola; but we were reproved by Count Perponcher, the Master of the Horse, for riding too fast, as he would have kept us at a walk.

Lord Bloomfield, who was very amiable to me and my secretaries, received, at my request, the G.C.B. from her Majesty. He was a great disciplinarian as to our dress, and much moved at my not having a blue dress coat with brass buttons to go to church in. He is much and deservedly liked at Berlin.

I had very little political work here, but heard a great deal about the Schleswig treaty, which Palmerston drew up, and which I signed in 1852. It is evident that on the first opportunity Prussia will seize and annex it either by force or by some transaction, which will be a high-handed and unjustifiable act, inasmuch as the Schleswigers hate the Prussians, and they do not speak the same tongue. One day I had the opportunity of a private conversation with the Neapolitan Minister, and I took the occasion to make a strong intercession in favour of Poerio, the famous political prisoner, of whose treatment such horrors were related, and I obtained a promise that he (the Minister) would do all he could to obtain his liberty, on the ground that he gave his Government more trouble in prison than he would out of it, which fact I had pressed upon him. He afterwards redeemed his promise, and Poerio was released, and sailed on condition that he should go to America, and not to Europe; but he and his fellow-prisoners bribed the captain to bring them to England, where I saw him in the House of Lords, a very sleek

[1] Afterwards Lady Paget, and now Ambassadress at Vienna.

and healthy-looking man, just like his statue now in the Via
Toledo at Naples.

Poerio's treatment had been for some years the subject of
angry dispute between the English Liberal Governments and that
of Naples; but Palmerston and Gladstone made the mistake of
arguing with a despotic Government the right of the case, as if
an absolute *régime* had not the same privilege as a Republic, or
ourselves, of self-defence against those who would overturn it.
The police at Naples was corrupt and tyrannical; but the worst
feature of all in their system was the delay of justice, as we found
in all cases where Englishmen were concerned. The accused party
was often imprisoned for years before he was tried, and this was
the fate of Poerio; but the physical torture to which he was said
to be subjected, I believe to be apocryphal. No man who had
suffered such could so far have recovered in three months and be
so fat and sleek as he was when Lord Shaftesbury introduced him
to me in the House of Lords. I took him, as he stood at the
throne, for one of the new Peers, come up rejoicing from a
salubrious county. Some years after these events, the Marquis
d'Azeglio told me that a subscription had been raised among the
principal Whigs to procure Poerio's evasion through Garibaldi,
who was to have a ship ready to carry him off, but his release
anticipated their plan. Rightly or wrongly, Bomba had such a
bad name that all things were looked upon as fair against him;
but *minus* this feeling, it was a strong measure on the part of a
neutral country and its leading statesmen. The days of Queen
Elizabeth had returned in Italy, which felt justified in using the
sword and the intelligence of the great buccaneer Garibaldi
against her enemies, as England did those of Drake and Raleigh,
whom the Spaniards not unfairly called pirates. The French
have coined a new word for such unorthodox politics—namely,
'Opportunism.'

---

*August 28th.*—Arrived at Deutz on our way home. The
weather throughout our journey has been tropical. Fahrenheit
83° at night for a week. The Queen graciously allowed me to
leave here and to go to Achnacarry. Phipps came to me before

I left, much annoyed at having given one of the best snuff-boxes to ——, which was not intended for him. He went to —— to explain this, but found that the box was already converted into cash and irrecoverable.

*September 3rd.*—Joined Lady Malmesbury at Achnacarry, after a very bad passage across the Channel, the sea breaking heavily over the boat. So ill, I could not have walked to the hotel without the help of the popular Captain Smithett.

The time passed at Achnacarry as usual, in fishing, shooting, and receiving a great deal of company, among whom were Lord Durham, Mr. and Lady Hermione Graham, George Barrington, the Delameres, the Wiltons, Mr. and Mrs. Rose, Mr. Bruce (Lord Elgin's brother), who was just returned from China with a treaty, Lord and Lady Abercorn, the Duke and beautiful Duchess of Manchester, who is Mistress of the Robes.

*From Lord M. to Lord Cowley.*

Achnacarry : September 4, 1858.

My dear Cowley,— . . . . . There never was such a hash as between Bulwer and Stratford about their palaces. Stratford has taken out *six gentlemen* as attachés, but not one do I know by name, and not one has had his appointment signed, so they will have no *status* at all! Lady S. has ordered the house at Therapia to be prepared for her, and Lord S. the one at Pera, so that Bulwer will have to go to the Inn. It is his fault, for in the overflowing joy of his nomination he wrote in May to offer him either palace, *a la disposicion de Vd.* !

Yours sincerely,

MALMESBURY.

*From the same to the same.*

Achnacarry : September 7, 1858.

My dear Cowley,—Pray show Palmerston the Principalities Reform Bill, and tell him I hope ours next year will be better. All the good in it is yours—*mais, que voulez-vous* when a Frenchman who has trampled down the constitution of his own country begins to make one for others ? You may also show him my despatches on our Turkish policy and on Montenegro. I have only followed in his wake.

Yours sincerely,

MALMESBURY.

*September 16th.*—The largest comet I ever saw became visib
with a very broad tail spread perpendicularly over the sky, t
weather being very hot.   Everyone now believes in war.

*September 25th.*—Mr. Bruce took his first lesson in de
stalking, and came back in a very bad humour.   He says th
the forester wanted him to go *up a waterfall*, which created mu
laughter.   The Persignys arrived after midnight.   They had post
from Inverness in dogcarts and various vehicles.

*September 26th.*—Madame de Persigny has been horribly c
of humour all day.   She never spoke a word at dinner, and w
not answer when spoken to.   She is said to be always so whe
ever there is a woman in the house handsomer than herself, whi
in this case is the Duchess of Manchester.

*September 28th.*—Madame de P. came down in a dreadf
humour to breakfast, and would speak to no one.   Persigny tc
her to sit by me, when she said, stamping her foot, 'Je ne ve
pas,' loud enough for everyone to hear.   Poor Persigny look
much annoyed, saying to her, 'Je vous ordonné de parler,' whi
order was not obeyed.   Her temper relapsed again at lunchec
and afterwards she had a severe shock when Colonel Scarle
having called, she saw his fly drive up, and—Heaven knows w
—fancied that Persigny, who had gone to the forest, had m
with an accident.   She burst into tears.   No one could unde
stand what connection there could be between 'Mon petit Victc
and a fly, and how she could imagine, if an accident had ha
pened, that two men in a carriage, with a pair of post-horse
could be sent down from the highest hill in the forest to announ
it.   Mr. Bidwell said she evidently thought there was a cab-stai
on the top of Corry Dhu.   When she came down to dinner, s
appeared with her eyes very red, and before the fish was tak
away rushed out of the room in a flood of tears.   Persigny fo
lowed, and neither returned until the end of the first cour
when they resumed their places, she looking like a sulky chil
and he the picture of misery.   These scenes are repeated daily.

*From Lord M. to Lord Cowley.*

Achnacarry : September 28, 1858

My dear Cowley,—Pélissier has written to ask me my opinion as
the danger to Mexico of American annexation.   I have answered hi

that I look upon it as probable, and not at all dangerous to European interests. Trade would be improved, and the Union certainly broken up. The Yankees know this fact so well that they hesitate to touch it. Otway says Mexico is ready to give herself up to be governed by us or France. The latter would not suit us in the rear of our West India Islands and commanding the Gulf; as little would it be to our interest to meddle with such a hornets' nest. We had better leave it to its fate, taking care of our subjects. What is of great importance is that France should join in securing a passage for herself over Nicaragua, and thus act in unison with us on this critical point.

Yours sincerely,<br>MALMESBURY.

*September* 30*th*.—The Persignys started for Glasgow. Such a relief to everybody in the house to hear the carriage drive off.

*October* 3*rd*.—Hearing that Sir James Hudson, our Minister at Turin, was at Fort William, we sent a gillie to invite him. He was in bed when the messenger arrived, but in such a bad one that he was too glad to get up again, and arrived at Achnacarry at eleven o'clock.

*From Lord M. to Lord Cowley.*

Achnacarry : October 3, 1858.

My dear Cowley,—Pray ascertain the views of the French Government on the state of the Danish question. Elliot is much alarmed. The violent German party have taken advantage of my presence at Berlin to circulate false reports of conversations which I had with Platen at Hanover, and the Prince of Prussia and Manteuffel, to the effect that we should not interfere if the question were extended to Schleswig. Now, what I said to one and all of these persons was that her Majesty's Government considered the Holstein question as purely German, and amenable to the Diet, the King being Duke of Holstein, and that our only feeling was an apprehension that an occupation of Holstein by German troops would break up European peace. As to Schleswig, that if that point was ever unfortunately mooted, we and the other Powers who contracted the treaty must settle it, as the Diet had no business with Schleswig. Her Majesty's Government think that this last proposal of the Danes deserves every consideration, and ought to lead to negotiation. Pray state this to the French Government, and ask them what their policy is under the contingencies referred to. Elliot thinks Prussia is joining Hanover in pushing the

G G

Diet to extremities. Paget says, if so, it is in direct contradiction of
Manteuffel's language.              Yours sincerely,

                      MALMESBURY.

*October 4th.*—Beautiful bright morning. The whole party
went up Loch Arkaig for a deer-drive in the Forest of Gerraran.
By the time we got there, about ten miles off, the weather changed,
and it blew a hurricane with torrents of rain, so we were obliged
to return in the boat with a favourable wind. This, however,
increased to such violence that the surface of the loch was torn
up by waterspouts and very heavy seas. The wind suddenly
changing, we had to keep her head to it. The Highlanders were
panic-stricken, and stopped pulling, when Sir James Hudson
seized an oar and encouraged the men to renew their efforts. For
some time it was impossible to make way against the storm,
and all we could do was to keep her head to the sea. By desperate efforts we got into a small bay in shelter. The ladies behaved
beautifully, and did not say a word; but the position was very
critical, as, if the gentlemen and crew had failed, we must have
been swamped. Bidwell, I conclude, was rather frightened, for
at the worst moment he began to sing, which displeased the
Highlanders, who are very superstitious. If we had gone down,
there would have been considerable patronage for Lord Derby—
namely, Duchess of Manchester, Mistress of the Robes; myself,
Foreign Secretary, with two private secretaries, Bidwell and Dashwood; Sir James Hudson, Minister at Turin; and Mr. Hamond,
Consul at Cherbourg. I never saw anything more striking than
the columns of water which, driven up by the wind, crossed the
lake in all directions, and which, if striking the boat, would have
filled her at once.

*October 7th.*—The Duke and Duchess of Manchester left. She
was very amiable, and is at the climax of her beauty, and we all
regret her much. The mountains are covered with snow.

*October 14th.*—We left Achnacarry, and got as far as the
King's House in Glencoe.

         *From Lord M. to Lord Cowley.*

                Achnacarry: October 14, 1858.

My dear Cowley,—What passed at Berlin with Massone, the Neapolitan, was this: Manteuffel and Paget told me he wished to be

introduced and speak on our quarrel with Naples. I agreed to do so in a private character, and met him at Bloomfield's. He said his Government was anxious to renew. I stated that we could not act without France, and that I thought that, if Naples would give her the *forms* she wished, and us the *substance*, which we must insist upon, it might be done. Q. What was the substance ? A. The basis of the proposal made eighteen months ago to Clarendon, which he would have taken, but the implacable Palmerston refused—namely, that the prisoners should be provided for and sent to Buenos Ayres or Monte Video. I said that if these people were delivered in some analogous manner, without exacting any confession or pledge, provided for temporarily, and exiled, we might come to some understanding. Massone jumped at the notion, and I suppose this will again be the basis on which they will start the negotiation of which Paget speaks. Now just look at the incongruous position of England at this moment and of its Government, upon this question. England rose as one man last February because France was supposed, notwithstanding her assurances to the contrary, to interfere with *our internal jurisdiction,* and here she is quarrelling with Naples because Naples won't alter her laws at the beck of our Government !  Yours sincerely,

MALMESBURY.

*October 15th.*—Went on, and arrived at Glasgow. Our party had killed 30 stags, of which I got but few, as I was obliged to attend to my official business. Sir James Hudson shot several, being a first-rate rifle-shot and sportsman.

From Lord M. to Lord Cowley.

Knowsley : October 22, 1858.

My dear Cowley,—Massone deceived Paget.[1] Bernstorff arrived yesterday, and stated that he was instructed to say that the King of Naples would not re-open the negotiations, which Clarendon unfortunately refused, for the release of the prisoners; that he would have no interference with his affairs; and that all he would do would be to send a Minister to London and Paris, if we would reciprocate. I of course said that, this being the case, I preferred the *status quo.* Bernstorff added that the King was in reality delighted at there being nobody at Naples to bother him, as the French and English Ministers always did.  Yours sincerely,

MALMESBURY.

[1] On the contrary, he kept his word.

*October 23rd.*—I went to Knowsley, and found there such a heap of Foreign Office boxes that I was obliged to stay at home two days to work instead of shooting. Lord Derby in great force.

*October 24th.*—The Duke of Hamilton told me that when he was at Paris a few days ago the Empress observed that she thought she had made a mess of the Malakoff marriage, and that when she saw his white head and her black one at the altar she feared it would not turn out well. The Duc de Malakoff called upon me to-day, and did not look happy. Sidney Herbert is very ill, and so is Lady Clementina Villiers, with intermittent fever. She is reduced to great weakness.

*October 25th.*—We have received an invitation to Windsor, where Lady Malmesbury is to present the Duchesse de Malakoff.

*October 26th.*—Duc and Duchesse de Malakoff called. She is a Spaniard, pretty, with a very fine figure, and extremely graceful, with pleasing manners. Looks about twenty-six.

### From Lord M. to Lord Cowley.

London : October 26, 1858.

My dear Cowley,—I send you the report of Saunders to show what a *canard* Walewski and the Emperor swallowed in believing that Bernard advocated openly the murder of the Empress and her child. It is bad enough without that, but I see there is a party, and its name is Legion (for it is composed of every party and some Governments) striving to drive England and France into a war. This Portuguese business [1] proves to me that the Emperor has lost all his sense of right and prudence, and is acting on passion. I am not sure even that the transaction was not meant to lower *us* on the sore point of the Slave Trade. If Lisbon is like Lavradio, it will scream loud enough to raise a storm from the Tagus to the Neva. A complete plan for the invasion of England by Admiral de la Gravière, made in 1857, is in my possession. It is satisfactory to know that they only meant to stay a week, and to be nearly sure that not a man would have returned. The Emperor *does not wish for a reconciliation* with Naples, and is glad to annoy Austria by this Italian distress. Stratford has upset everything at Stamboul, but I think that may be set right. Our Consul McLeod has, I hear, come

---

[1] The capture of the 'Charles et Georges.'

home open-mouthed from Mozambique, glorying in having, by his
own suggestion, effected the capture of the ' Charles et Georges,'
which, but for him, he says, never would have been touched. He
then ran away home from the row he had raised.

Yours truly,

MALMESBURY.

*October 27th.*—Went to Windsor with the Malakoffs, who
came to our room soon after we had arrived, and remained till
six o'clock, the hour fixed for the Duchesse to be presented.
The ladies waited in the gallery whilst I had an audience ;
after which, I came to fetch the Duke, who had a book to present to the Queen from the Emperor. Then Lady Malmesbury
went in to present the Duchesse, and left her with the Queen.

*October 28th.*—Had a long conversation with the Prince,
who came to my room. Prince Arthur [1] performed on the drum
for the edification of Pélissier, who exhibited his own talents
in that line so well that he must have begun his career as a
drummer. He certainly rose from the ranks. His Christian
name is, as he says himself, most inappropriate—' Aimable.'
He is a short, fat man, of rough manners, but good-hearted
withal. He related to me, and I believe also to the Queen,
the following anecdote. After Waterloo, a great part of the
French army was disbanded, Pélissier among them. He went
home on foot, somewhere in the South of France, at a time
when the whole country was flooded and crossed by narrow
plank bridges. In approaching one of these, he saw he must
meet a Prussian soldier, and both got on the bridge, neither
giving way, when Pélissier pushed him into the river, and as
the man rose, hit him on the head with his stick, saying, with
a descriptive gesture, ' Je l'ai frappé comme ça, et il n'a plus
reparu.' As a contrast to this brutal act, he formed such a
romantic affection for his fellow-soldier, Lord Raglan, that,
after the death of the latter, he used, when Ambassador in
London, to go constantly to see Lord Raglan's little grandson,
and play with him. He once struck one of his soldiers for
some offence, which is not permitted in the French army, upon

---

[1] Afterwards Duke of Connaught.

which the man aimed at him, but his musket missed fire.
'Maintenant,' said Pélissier, perfectly unmoved, 'je vous donne
dix jours de salle pour des armes mal-tenues.'

*October 29th.*—The Malakoffs, who had intended returning
to London, put off their departure to go with us. I went out
shooting with the Prince at 9.30, and returned at half-past
twelve, as I had several presentations to the Queen to make at
one. We returned to London after luncheon.

*November 3rd.*—First Cabinet Council took place to-day.
All the Ministers attended. Lord Derby in great spirits; but
I think we shall have a stormy session, and probably be turned
out about May. Intrigues go on apace.

### To Lord Cowley.

London : November 3, 1858.

My dear Cowley,—Lavradio is holding insane language here,
saying to me, and afterwards to Hammond[1] during my absence, that
we had deserted Portugal. I have telegraphed to Howard to ask the
Portuguese Government if their Minister is instructed to talk in this
way. I hope you will urge on Walewski the expediency of dropping
the demand for indemnity, because, whether pirate or orthodox, the
'Charles et Georges' did break the municipal law of Mozambique.
Pray tell the Empress that we like the Duchesse de Malakoff extremely. Lady Malmesbury and she have made great friends, and
really she is to be pitied, looking so lonely in that uncomfortable
house, gutted as it is of all ornament.        Yours truly,

MALMESBURY.

*November 12th.*—Lord De la Warr called. He was at Blair
with the Persignys, and says she behaved very strangely, crying
and making scenes. She asked to see a deer-drive, and when
she was posted with the Duke of Athole, and the deer were
coming towards them, she was suddenly seized with a terror
of the guns, burst into tears, exclaiming, 'Je serai tuée ! O mes
pauvres enfants !' and insisted upon going home. The Duke
at first thought she was joking ; but seeing her get pale and cry
bitterly, he promised not to fire. Fortunately, the deer went
another way, but she did not recover, and remained quite sulky
the rest of the day. Such is the grand-daughter of Marshal

---

[1] Under Secretary at the Foreign Office, and now Lord Hammond.

Ney!—sent here as an Ambassadress. I went to Windsor to present Lord Bloomfield and Sir James Hudson.

*November* 13*th*.—Returned from Windsor with the Prince of Wales, who invited me into his carriage, after a long audience with the Queen. He was very agreeable.

*November* 14*th*.—Went to Kimbolton. The Malakoffs there. They joined in a paper-chase with great spirit.

*November* 19*th*.—Lord Derby has sent Mr. Gladstone to the Ionian Islands as Commissioner, to report upon the state of the islands.

*November* 20*th*.—I hear that Lords Palmerston and Clarendon now think they have done a foolish thing by going to Compiègne, and that their doing so is generally disapproved in England.

*November* 21*st*.—Lord Clarendon lunched with us, and stayed an hour and a half with me talking about the Emperor. He only returned from Compiègne this morning, and told us that the whole party went out hunting on a very wet day, all being muffled up in waterproofs, except Palmerston, who wore a red coat and nothing over it. The Emperor observed that he would get wet, when he replied, ' Rien ne perce un habit rouge.' Lady Mary Craven was immensely admired. The Empress and Madame Walewska were loud in their admiration of her, but towards the end of the week they had very much cooled. Lord Clarendon said they prevented the Duchess of Manchester from being asked. He also told me there is an intrigue going on to get rid of Walewski, the principal conspirators being Prince Napoleon and Persigny.

*November* 22*nd*.—I got a dreadful account of Lady Clementina Villiers from Lady Jersey. She is much worse, and I now despair of her recovery. I fear she is sinking fast. I am very unhappy, as she is my greatest friend, and I always spent two or three evenings every week at Lady Jersey's, and found everybody there whom I know and like.

*November* 24*th*.—Lady Clementina continues very ill; the fever has lasted three months, and she cannot have strength to resist it much longer. Poor Lady Jersey is nearly distracted. Lord Ranelagh called, and seems much alarmed at the state of

the defences at Portsmouth.  But they are being strengthened
at a vast expense.

*December 2nd.*—Went to Middleton yesterday.  Lady Jersey
proposed that I should see Lady Clementina, but, having heard
that she was painfully changed, I would not do so, and only
talked to her through her door.  She wished me good-bye.  She
is constantly fainting, and kept up by champagne.

*December 3rd.*—Cabinet Councils almost every day on the
subject of the Reform Bill, but I have little expectation of the
Government producing a measure that will satisfy either themselves or the public.  To-day Lord Derby was beaten on one
point which he considered most important, Lord John Manners
and I being the only Cabinet Ministers who stood by him.
Disraeli, Stanley, Pakington, Lords Salisbury and Lytton [1]
voted for the most liberal of the three propositions submitted ;
the Chancellor (Chelmsford), Walpole, Henley, Hardwicke,
and General Peel for the most Conservative, so nothing was
done.

*December 6th.*—Lady Clementina died yesterday.  She
gradually sank, and died so calmly that her mother, who held
her hand, was not aware she was dead until she felt it grow
cold.

*Lord M. to Lord Cowley.*

Foreign Office : December 13, 1858.

My dear Cowley,—We have been to see the infernal machine,
which is openly shown at the shop, not as an 'infernal machine,'
but as a twenty-barrelled gun upon wheels—the most harmless and
useless thing you ever saw.  The best of the story is that, as the
showman is *Palmerston's bootmaker,* he has been one of the first to
examine it.  It would do for firing into a flock of duck—provided the
ducks, the machine, and the shooter were all *d'accord.*  What fools
the French police here must be !

*Lord M. to Lord Cowley.*

Foreign Office : December 13, 1858.

My dear Cowley,—Apponyi came to me this morning to read a
despatch from Buol to Hübner about Italy.  It began by finding fault

---

[1] The late Lords Salisbury and Lytton.

with the French press and lamenting its effects as between Austria and France, and it stated that the treaties of 1815 were as sacred as those of 1856; that in 1815 the *Italian* question was settled and could not be reopened; that in 1856 the Turkish was settled; that Austria would insist on both being respected, and that no exchange, no cession, and no negotiation would be granted by her for any part of her Italian dominions. This led to a conversation, in which I repeated exactly the same views as those given to you in my private letter on the subject. Apponyi agreed with me, but thought France would never act fairly, but looked to convulsions by which Piedmont would get Lombardy, France Savoy, and Murat Naples.

*December 15th.*—I received a grateful letter from Augustus Paget, whom I have appointed Minister at Dresden.

*December 31st.*—I left this morning for Windsor, from Heron Court. Mrs. Anson is dead, from taking by mistake an overdose of laudanum. They kept her walking about for several hours, but in vain. One of the handsomest women of her day.

# 1859

*January 1st.*—Yesterday we danced at Windsor, and when the clock struck twelve all the Royalties embraced. I had the honour of dancing a country dance with her Majesty.

*January 2nd.*—Returned to Heron Court.

### Lord M. to Lord Cowley.

Heron Court: January 7, 1859.

My dear Cowley,—I will send you a very important paper in a few days (the Queen must approve of my reply first), which I have got from Bloomfield, asking me on the part of the Prussian Government what we mean to do if Austria and France go to war. I have answered, neutrality at all events, and as long as possible. We are ready, if Austria and France choose to join, to improve the Legations, to give our moral support, and even to consider a reconstruction of the *Central* territory if we see hopes of improving the condition of the people without weakening the spiritual authority of the Pope; but we will not consent beyond this to any alterations in the territorial arrangements of 1815, which have ensured the longest peace on record.

*Lord M. to Lord Cowley.*

Foreign Office : January 11, 1859.

My dear Cowley,—You will see that we have taken a line, and I leave you to carry it out with your usual straightforward exactness. If the Emperor cares for the public opinion of this country, he must be made to understand that it will be against the aggressor, whoever he may be, who is the first cause of a European war. That it will cost him his life or his crown I have not the least doubt. Eventually, as it spreads, Germany is sure to be found united against the Latin nations, therefore it is as a friend I wish to warn him before he decides at his age and in his position on such a *coup de dés.* Persigny went back yesterday to intrigue against Walewski and her Majesty's present Government. I conclude the Buol escapade is over. Pélissier, as usual, approved of my conduct, and is disgusted at being kept in the dark as to everything that is going on at Paris. The Russians are trying to get ports in Spain, Sicily, and Egypt, like Villafranca—that is, military ports. You should ask Walewski quietly how that suits France? It is very well known Russia is with her, but does she wish to have her a maritime Power in the Mediterranean? The Russians boast that we have overreached ourselves because she was blocked up at both ends before for nine months, and at one end all the year, while now she can keep a fleet all the year round in the Mediterranean. When the Emperor pretended to Clarendon that he did not know where Villafranca was, it was clearly a *comédie.* Of course you will see the Emperor himself, and give all the solemnity you can to the advice, leaving all the consequences and calamities of a European war on his head if he begins, or *allows Sardinia to begin.*

*January 12th.*— The King of Sardinia has made a speech which can only mean war. Things look bad all over Europe, and it will be very difficult to avert a general war if Louis Napoleon wants one. Great panic in Paris, and war very unpopular. The Emperor is getting alarmed at the feeling in France and the extraordinary fall in the funds; also at the unpopularity of the marriage arranged between Prince Napoleon and the King of Sardinia's daughter. Lord Cowley writes that he was much depressed at his ball; but I believe it is his fear of assassination, which haunts him perpetually, and has robbed him of all his former courage and coolness. It is driving him on to war, thinking that by supporting the cause of Italian nationality he will disarm those men who, in his earlier days, were his confederates in Carbonarism, and to whom he is pledged by former promises, and perhaps oaths. Cavour, knowing these facts, works upon them to induce him to take part openly with Sardinia. Austria is behaving with a folly which is perfectly inconceivable considering her position surrounded by enemies on all the frontiers. But what can one expect from Buol? I care for neither Austria nor France, but Lord Derby and I are determined to use every effort to prevent war, which would cost 100,000 lives and desolate the fairest parts of Europe. My whole mind is occupied by that object.

*Lord M. to Lord Cowley.*

Foreign Office: January 15, 1859.

My dear Cowley,—We are extremely obliged to you for keeping us so well *au fait* of everything at this critical moment. I hope and believe that Walewski knows he is not the man for a War Minister, and this will keep him in his pacific path. I am very glad you liked my *great* despatch, and I hope you will approve of the one I wrote Hudson, which was as strong as I thought it prudent to write at first. Your offer to submit your views to Palmerston is a patriotic one, and, if he receives it as I do, it will be to thank you. The great duty of every honest man must be to prevent the scourge which two or three unprincipled men would inflict on mankind for their personal profit; though, as to that, I believe a war would sweep them from their high places. Laffitte was with me on Thursday. He is here to borrow 2,000,000*l.* for Cavour, and cannot get 2,000*l.*, ditto Austria. Laffitte speaks of Cavour as a desperate adventurer, who has ruined his country by his expenses. He says he is ready to go anywhere for a sum to cover his financial bungling, and that if he does not have a war he will be turned out on his Budget. He works the Orsini gang by saying, 'Don't be such fools as to kill the only man who can help Italy, but frighten him into it.' Hence the continual terror agitated around the Emperor, about which Bernard's publication respecting the great *canardière* at Palmerston's bootmaker's, and his rhodomontade speech, is a specimen. Tell Walewski this: It is an abominable *trame*. We are really forming no Anti-French League beyond begging the Germans to remain united and independent of external politics until obliged to take a part.

Yours truly,

MALMESBURY.

*January* 16*th.*—I fear war cannot be avoided. The Emperor of the French seems determined, though his country is strongly against it; but I hope he will be induced to pause, especially as he finds he cannot draw England into taking his part. Lord Cowley says the Emperor avoided talking to him at the last ball. The Queen and Prince are very anxious, and the latter has written to me. The Emperor threatens Belgium if she does not go with France. The Prince de Chimay is evidently for the French alliance.

*January* 18*th.*—Pélissier called and told me that fears of war were at an end, as France was against it. It is, however, quite clear the Emperor has done all he could to stir it up, notwithstanding his former declaration, 'L'Empire c'est la paix!'

*January* 19*th.*—Went to Windsor, and returned to-day with Disraeli.

*January* 23*rd.*—Lord Cowley telegraphs that Persigny is to come here directly as Ambassador. This was arranged at Compiègne whilst Lord Palmerston was there, and is a most hostile move on the part of the Emperor, as he knows perfectly well the terms Persigny and I are upon, and the inexcusable behaviour of Madame de Persigny to Lady M. Sending him back again when Parliament is going to meet must be done with a view of intriguing against our Government as he did before.

*January* 25*th.*—Lord Cowley writes that he has seen Persigny, who says that the Emperor wishes him to return to England as Ambassador. The next day, Lord Cowley saw Walewski, who told him that Persigny was urging the Emperor to appoint him against his wishes, and he is unable to ascertain which of these accounts is true. The preparations for war continue on all sides. The French Emperor is very hostile to our Administration, and anxious to upset it.

*January* 26*th.*—There was a cordial Cabinet to-day on the principal clause of the Reform Bill. Lord Derby much pleased, as he feared dissensions, and even resignations. The 'Morning Post' has received orders from the French Emperor to attack me on every possible occasion. Mr. Borthwick, the editor, saw him at Paris, and got his orders from himself. This paper is also Lord Palmerston's, so the connection between them is clear.

The case of the 'Charles et Georges,' which is a French ship, is that the Portuguese seized her, according to our treaties, for being fitted as a slaver, and took her into the Tagus. The French Government screamed very loudly at this, and, on the other hand, the Portuguese claimed our assistance, as bound by treaties, to resist the French threats. After a great deal of noise on both sides, we arranged the dispute, which, although the Opposition made capital of it, was never more than a storm in a tea-pot.

*Lord M. to Lord Cowley.*

Foreign Office: January 26, 1859.

My dear Cowley,—I must thank you for the manner in which you have met without any instructions from me the idea on the part of the French Government of sending Persigny here again. I will tell you frankly that when Persigny assured you he only saw Palmerston *once* after he left office, it is entirely untrue. When violently insisting on the necessity and ease of passing the Conspiracy Bill he came out with this: 'J'ai répété à Palmerston plus d'une fois tous vos raisonnements, et il me dit qu'il n'y a pas un mot de vrai dans tout cela.' It was then I told him that I must do all business at Paris through *you*, if he saw our opponents and repeated our conversations to them. Before he left Paris, where he was when Palmerston was turned out, he said to several people that in a week he would put him again in his place by forcing us to pass the same bill. I could add half-a-dozen witnesses to this. For three weeks after he returned I heard of nothing but his violent language against Lord Derby and me in every *salon*, and it was the talk and astonishment of the whole Corps Diplomatique to see a French Ambassador holding forth like an electioneering agent. The fact is that, as his master has always been and always will be a conspirator, so he has always been and will always be a partisan of somebody. These are their idiosyncrasies. Be that as it may, confidence is not an act of volition, and if Persigny came, I should carry on the whole business with *you*. In doing this I should be still more justified by what I know now of the Emperor's sentiments towards our Government. Borthwick, after dinner, told —— that when the other day in Paris the Emperor sent for him, and he never saw a man so irritated as he is against Lord Malmesbury. He said: 'You must write him down; he has leagued Germany against me, and is entirely opposed to my policy. "I have proof of it by his own hand, in which he says that Austria has the same right to Lombardy as England has to Ireland and India."' This quotation leaves no doubt as to Borthwick's veracity, for it is the

very phrase which I used in my letter to you of December 7, as you
will see. Did you give him a copy of it or read it to him? Since the
above orders, the 'Morning Post' attacks me every other day. I have
therefore no doubt, and I may say I *know*, that Persigny is meant to
restore our ex-Premier; but this country is not Spain, and a Government is not to be upset by a foreign ambassador. . . . . Buol has
received our counsels of prudence with nearly equal sulkiness, and I
think the best attitude for us now is to fold our arms like men who
have advised madmen in vain to refrain from mutual follies, look on as
if they thought them mad, and leave them with sorrow to their fate.

Yours truly,

MALMESBURY.

*January* 27*th.*—There is a violent and mischievous article in
the 'Morning Post,' accusing me of forming a German league
against France, showing the Emperor's anger at our opposing his
warlike proclivities. The Princess of Prussia was confined this
afternoon of a son. The news reached Windsor by telegraph in
six minutes.

*January* 28*th.*—I went to Windsor to present Lord Lyons
and Mr. Paget. Had a long audience. Walpole and Henley
have resigned on the Reform Bill; the former because we go too
far, the latter because we don't go far enough. Walpole is a con-
scientious man, and a Tory. Henley very shrewd and clever, but
crotchety and easily offended; he is much looked up to in the
House of Commons.

*Lord M. to Lord Cowley.*

Foreign Office : January 28, 1859.

My dear Cowley,—I cannot but think that your apprehensions will
be realised; Hudson thinks so too. Malaret says the public feeling in
France against a war is tremendous and most openly expressed. Dare
the Emperor face this? I think you had better not tell the Emperor
that I know of his conversation with Borthwick. A man never forgives
being *found out* in such a treacherous action. It appears he *showed
him the extract you gave him of my letter.* Yours truly;

MALMESBURY.

*January* 31*st.*—Mr. Henry Greville called and was very
friendly, expressing great interest in our success in keeping off

war. He appeared very favourable to our Government ; if so, it is an extraordinary change. His brother Charles,[1] who is Clerk of the Council, has never attended since Lord Derby has been in office, and did not conceal his omitting to do so on purpose. When Lord Derby's attention was called to this fact, he said 'he had not observed his absence, as he never knew whether it was John or Thomas who answered the bell.'

*February 1st.*—Lady Ely told me that the Malakoffs expected to be recalled. Pélissier is not in the confidence of his Court, and knows nothing, not even what concerns himself personally. He is certainly not fond of the Emperor, of whom he never says any good. He told me that the French army was not in a state for a campaign.

*February 3rd.*—The Queen in person opened Parliament to-day. Crowds larger than usual, the weather being beautiful, and her reception very enthusiastic. Lords Winchilsea and Ravensworth were the mover and seconder. Lord Granville was followed by Lord Derby, who was nervous, and forgot to mention India till I reminded him of it ; but when he began on foreign politics, which was evidently the subject uppermost in his mind, nothing could be more dignified or more eloquent. He declared for upholding all the treaties of 1815, spoke very openly against war, and on the responsibility that would be incurred by any sovereign who disturbed the peace of Europe for purposes of aggrandisement or ambition, and announced the firm determination of the English Government to observe perfect neutrality, declaring that we had neither engagements, obligations, treaties, nor understandings which bound us or prevented our following the course we considered best for the honour and interest of England. He was received with great cheering on all sides. It was amusing to watch the faces of Count Corti and Baron Chotek,[2] who were present during Lord Derby's speech, the former looking discomfited and miserable, whilst the latter had an expression of the greatest delight.

*February 6th.*—I went to Windsor. The Queen has written a letter to Lord Derby insisting upon the Indian army being

---

[1] Author of the well-known memoirs published after his death.

[2] Italian and Austrian Secretaries.

under the Horse Guards ; but as he cannot, or thinks he cannot, get the House of Commons to repeal that part of the India Bill, he has written to say that if she makes it a *sine quâ non* he must resign.

*February 7th.*—Returned from Windsor. The Queen and Prince both very gracious and friendly, but much alarmed at the clause in the India Bill relating to the army.

*February 8th.*—Lord Derby has settled not to *disfranchise*, and Mr. Walpole objects. It is impossible to please him. This last is opposed by Lord Stanley, which makes it the more strange that it should also be opposed by the other. Napoleon's speech is not so pacific as Lord Cowley informed us it would be. Not a word is said about treaties, but a good deal about the interests and honour of France. I have no confidence in peace being preserved. The French Ministers had a hard fight with him to make as moderate a speech as the one he delivered at the opening of the Chambers. Funds are gone down.

### Lord M. to Lord Cowley.

Foreign Office : February 8, 1859.

My dear Cowley,—The speech has not been taken so ill here as in Paris, and we all feel, I think, that the Emperor must have had great difficulty in backing out handsomely. That he *should* back out is the great point. 'The treaties '—i.e. of 1815—are the sentence of condemnation of his uncle, and no wonder the words are hot potatoes in his mouth. It is a good thing that he does believe Europe is arrayed against his ambitious dreams. Have you seen the map of Europe for 1860 ? Here they believe it to be issued by his *permission*. Pray assure Walewski how much her Majesty's Government appreciate his wise and friendly conduct during the past crisis (if past it is). If we can get a good agreement about the Coolies and the Slave Trade Treaty, of which you gave us hopes, it would do very great good. Your language throughout these difficulties has been most judicious and useful. The Emperor sent me a message by the Duke of Hamilton, expressing his regret for having *shown Borthwick my letter* to you. The Duke says he told him plainly his mind on the subject. The Emperor also reiterated to him assurances of the value he placed on our firm alliance. Buol promises everything we wish as to the Danube.          Yours truly,
                                                        MALMESBURY.

*February 9th.*—Cabinet this afternoon. Lord Derby announced the resignation of Walpole and Henley. He has been obliged to have moderate disfranchisement and redistribution. But this does not satisfy Lord Stanley, who talks of resigning if the measure is not more liberal. Lord Hardwicke and General Peel are dissatisfied because it goes too far already. It may possibly end in Lord Derby's resigning. Disraeli has behaved beautifully throughout, trying to smooth all difficulties and faithful on all points to Lord Derby. So have the others.

### *Lord M. to Lord Cowley.*

Foreign Office : February 13, 1859.

My dear Cowley,—Since telegraphing to you, I have seen Lord Derby, who says with truth that you are the only man who can carry out our views with respect to France, Austria, and the Italian question. If, therefore, you have no decided reasons against it, I would urge you, having first come to an understanding with the Emperor, to go on a special mission to Vienna, and even to Turin afterwards, if necessary. The obstacle that rose to my mind was the Congress on the Principalities,[1] but it cannot meet before the 27th, as Musurus would scarcely be ready sooner. The next question is whether you think it desirable to come over here first, and see Lord Derby and me. He seems to think you should; but you have the whole business so completely at your fingers' ends, that, unless you prefer it yourself, I would not press it. The great object is to effect such a reconciliation between France and Austria that they would agree to withdraw their armies from the Papal States partly or altogether, and come to an agreement to try an amelioration of the Papal Government; to obtain positive declarations with respect to peaceful intentions, and a partial disarmament founded upon them ; to induce, if possible, Austria to amend the treaties *obliging* her to enter the Italian Duchies—this I doubt. You could at the same time at Vienna sound Buol as to our admitting the double election of Couza, provided we fortified the *suzeraineté* of the Porte and the divisions of the provinces by stringent declarations, stating our admissions to be favours, and contrary to the original convention. Your full powers might be sent over to you as soon as I

---

1 This Congress was to meet to decide whether there should be a union of the two Principalities under one Hospodar or under two. The Porte and England were for the latter, France and the other Powers for the former.

hear from you by telegraph as to substance, and by special messenger as to detail. Yours truly,
MALMESBURY.

*February 16th.*—The Queen sent me a letter she had just received from Louis Napoleon. It professes friendship for England, respect for treaties, and evidently reserves for himself the interpretation he chooses to make as to how the honour and interests of France are concerned in their observance ; and as he says plainly that those are his first objects, it is quite clear that he keeps himself free to act as he himself may judge. The truth is that he is determined to go to war with Austria to propitiate the Italians and to save his own life from assassination, since the *attentat* of January, 1858. Cavour worked upon this at their interview at Plombières last autumn, and persuaded him that taking up the cause of Italy will save his life, forfeited according to the laws of the Carbonari. If this is so, there must be war, for a personal motive is generally stronger than a public one, and everybody agrees that his terror of assassination is very great. No wonder, as he knows what a set of villains Carbonari are. I have reason to know he is making immense preparations for war, though he denies it in his letter to the Queen.

*February 23rd.*—We dined at the Palace. The Queen was very amiable, and spoke a great deal to Lady Malmesbury ; and the Princess Alice, who is very charming, talked to me about music, on which subject she must have found me sadly ignorant.

*February 24th.*—I have sent Lord Cowley to Vienna to try and settle matters. Count Buol is much pleased. Lady Tankerville says that Lady Palmerston told her that the attack upon the foreign policy of our Government, for which her husband has given notice to-morrow, was made in compliance with the Emperor's wish !

*March 1st.*—Two hundred and eleven members of the House of Commons were present at Lord Derby's meeting this morning, and expressed themselves perfectly satisfied with the Reform Bill, and determined to support the Government.

*March 3rd.*—Lord Henry Lennox has resigned. His elder

brother, Lord March, accepts office, and addresses his constituents, expressing thorough confidence in Lord Derby. Bidwell told Lord Henry that he, Walpole, and Henley were like the three men who deserted their ship at Calais the other day, thinking she was going down ; they were drowned, but the ship was saved. The Radicals are furious with us for bringing in such a moderate measure, and are holding meetings to get up an agitation against it.

*March 4th.*—The new Ministers, Mr. Sotheron Estcourt as Home Secretary, and Lord Donoughmore as President of the Board of Trade, with Lord Lovaine as Vice-President, were sworn in by the Queen at a Privy Council.

*March 6th.*—Louis Napoleon means to command his army in person in the event of war. He has an idea that he is a military genius, and used to send plans of operations to the army in the Crimea ; but Pélissier on one occasion made some remarks to me rather derogatory of his master's generalship.

I went to the Palace at six and had an audience of the Queen, which lasted an hour.

Lord John Russell means to propose resolutions against the disfranchisement of the forty-shilling freeholders, which are sure to pass, and if we dissolve we shall have them all against us, probably getting a worse Parliament than we have at present. My idea is that the best move would be to resign at once, before the second reading. The Queen would then send for Palmerston, and the 'old lot' would come in, to the disgust of the Radicals.

The case of the 'Charles et Georges,' to which I have before alluded, came on this afternoon in both Houses. Lord Wodehouse made a violent speech against me, and I replied, showing that I had done all that could be done without going to war with France ; and as the Portuguese never considered it was a *casus belli*, and M. de Loulé admitted they had never asked for anything but our good offices (which we gave), the case was a perfectly clear and simple one. The Opposition are now using every endeavour to damage us before a general election. After a great clatter, Lord Wodehouse withdrew his motion, but the newspapers continue writing everything that is most false on the subject. I wish I could settle the affairs of Italy as satisfactorily.

*March 9th.*—I dined at the Palace and came home very tired. I should be glad to resign, as I am worn out. The only people at the Queen's dinner were the Duke of Montrose, Lord Derby, and myself. Lord Raglan [1] is still at Berlin, where he was sent by the Queen to represent her at the baptism of the young Prince. To the great joy of his beautiful wife he returns on the 12th.

The Conservative members of the House of Commons have objected *en masse* to the proposed disfranchisement of the forty-shilling freeholders, and Disraeli announced a modification of the clause. I fear, however, that nothing will give us a majority at the second reading. There is no doubt that the defection of Walpole and Henley has done great harm to our Government.

*March 13th.*—Lord Cowley crossed yesterday in the storm (which amounted to a hurricane), and called this evening. We went together to Lord Derby, who does not appear sanguine as to the success of Lord Cowley's mission to Vienna, though the Austrians have agreed to all we asked, but he fears Louis Napoleon wants war, and if so he will not be satisfied with any concession. It is said that the Italians have again threatened his life if he draws back. If so, which I believe is the case, such an existence must be misery ; and no wonder he tries to escape from it. The chances of death on the field of battle would be nothing compared to the hourly expectation of the dagger of an assassin. I hear that one of Rossi's murderers formed part of the deputation sent to the Emperor in Paris, and he is constantly going to him with accounts of plots against his life.

Lady Londonderry called. She dined several times at the Tuileries, and gave us very much the same account of the Emperor, who was in low spirits. She saw Madame de Persigny, who complained of being so poor that she could not afford herself a new gown. This was accompanied with tears ; so she is just as childish and silly as ever.

A Committee has been formed, with Lord Shaftesbury at its head, to collect subscriptions for Poerio and other refugees who have landed at Cork, into which port they had forced the American captain to enter, and are now coming to London, *en route* for Turin, having broken their parole to the Neapolitan Govern-

---

[1] Lord Raglan died in 1884.

ment. Pélissier called this morning ; he is annoyed at the papers having announced that he was at Paris, and considered it as a sort of joke in allusion to his retired life. So I told him he had better give a dinner, and send the list to the ' Morning Post.'

I went at three o'clock to accompany Count Lavradio, who had an audience of the Queen, but he forgot all about it, and had to apologize to her Majesty, who took it most good-humouredly.

Big Ben, M.P. for Norfolk, headed a rebellion against the second reading of the Reform Bill. About forty members met, and agreed that Lord Derby ought either to withdraw the bill, or, if beaten, resign without dissolving. They probably mean to effect the last alternative by adding themselves to the majority.

*March 18th.*—The Duchesse de Malakoff called on Lady Malmesbury. Very amiable, but always in the same low spirits. She makes no effort to amuse herself. Pélissier now never stirs from home.

To-morrow will be decided whether, in case Lord John Russell's resolution on the Reform Bill passes, we shall withdraw the bill and dissolve Parliament, or wait a fortnight and then dissolve it on our general policy. Lord Cowley telegraphs that the Emperor, in a conversation, suggests a Congress of the five Powers to settle the affairs of Italy, excluding Sardinia. He says that would show the Italians that he had done all he could for them, and that they could not expect him to oppose the will of the rest of Europe. It is evident from this that it is the Italians whom he fears.

*Lord M. to Lord Cowley.*

Foreign Office : March 19, 1859.

My dear Cowley, We have just had a Cabinet upon your despatch and the proposal it contains for a Congress—a proposal which was made to me formally by Pélissier yesterday. Also upon your various telegrams relating to details, and the one from Loftus announcing the adhesion of Austria and her conditions. We think Rome *too far*, and also that to hold a Conference on Italian affairs anywhere in Italy is to be avoided. I cannot see how either France or Austria, after what they have said, can refuse our proposal as to Sardinia disarming ; but Austria should make a declaration besides, and in the most public way, that she will not attack her. Our guarantee of Sardinia with France ought to please the Emperor, and it will take off the edge of leaving her out of the Conference. The further answer to the Liberals, who are sure to find fault with that exclusion, is, that her admission must involve that of Naples, Rome, Tuscany, Modena, and Parma, and thus five votes at the Conference. You must make the Emperor understand that we can only address ourselves to the four points—viz. evacuation, reform, security for Sardinia, and substitute for treaties of 1847. If we go farther we shall be at sea. . . . .

Yours truly,      MALMESBURY.

*March 21st.*—The second reading of the Reform Bill comes on to-day, and Lord John Russell's amendment is to move that the forty-shilling freehold franchise, as hitherto exercised in the counties, shall not be abolished. Russia declares that she prefers a Congress to a Conference on the affairs of Italy, to be attended by the Secretaries of State, which will oblige me to go, and Lord Derby told me to-day I was to do so, also that I should have the G.C.B.

*March 22nd.*—The Marriage Bill was thrown out in the Lords, by a majority of ten. Lord Derby is annoyed at my having to go to the Conference. The Italian Minister complains that he is so rude to him that he does not dare to speak to him for fear of a quarrel. The fact is, as he himself confessed to me, that he is much too honest and *brusque* to make a good diplomatist, and go through the necessary humbug of the profession.

*March 24th.*—Azeglio is going to Paris to meet Cavour, and professes to be quite satisfied with my proposal to admit envoys from the Italian States, to be heard at the Congress, though not to sit at the Council. It is Austria that makes difficulties, and has not as yet agreed to the basis. The Emperor Louis Napoleon goes on with his preparations for war. I suspect he agrees to the Congress merely to gain time, as he is not ready. If this is the case, it would almost be better to let things take their course. Austria could not crush Sardinia before France could come to the rescue, and it would then be a fair fight between the two Great Powers ; but I feel that it is an imperative duty in me to prevent so awful a calamity as such a bloody war would be.

*March 25th.*—The arrangements for the Congress do not get on well. Louis Napoleon is now making difficulties and temporising. Cavour is making mischief, and says that he has letters from the Emperor and minutes of his conversation with him at Plombières, 'et qu'il le tient.' I fear this is the case.

The Queen has written a very gracious letter to Lord Derby, giving him leave to dissolve Parliament and to make four Peers. Lady Derby called on Lady Malmesbury, and said that after the Queen's letter it was Lord Derby's duty to stay in as long as he could.

Austria has agreed to all my propositions, but will not hear of Sardinia being represented at the Congress in any way. I had proposed that the small States of Italy, including Naples, should send representatives to the Congress, though only with a consultative title without a vote, and if Austria refuses to consent to this there is an end of the Congress, and war must ensue, as none of the other Powers would allow such an act of injustice. Count Apponyi called, in low spirits, and says that Austria refuses to consent to our proposals, and that there will be no Congress. The position of affairs in England complicates matters and adds to my difficulties, as none of the Great Powers, except Russia, who agrees to everything, would move an inch till it is decided whether Lord Derby's Government can hold on or not. If we were secure, Austria might make the concession we require, which she would not if Lord Palmerston and Lord John were in office ; and Louis Napoleon, seeing a chance of his friends being in power, and of following a policy in accordance with his wishes, throws, of course, every kind of delay in the way of settling the case by negotiation. This is the consequence of the unpatriotic and factious conduct of the Opposition, who appear perfectly unconcerned at the slaughter their policy will occasion. The 'Morning Post,' which is the organ of the Emperor, Palmerston, and Azeglio, is more violent every day against our *peaceful* foreign policy.

*Lord M. to Lord Cowley.*

Foreign Office : March 25, 1859.

My dear Cowley,—Your letter of yesterday is very alarming, showing, as it does, that the Emperor is no longer the same strong man in mind and nerve that he was formerly. Five years ago he would have put his cousin and Cavour in their proper places in five minutes, but

now he seems to be their victim. Firmness on our part may yet save
Europe from a war, by giving him courage to do what is right, and even
what is best for himself. It is now quite clear to me that we could not,
with all your ability and energy, have obtained an immediate disarmament. The sulky slowness of Austria herself was as great an obstacle
as Cavour's frantic struggles, and, as she is playing just as false as the
rest (Prussia excepted), no dependence could be placed on her assertions
to us. Austria would like to stay the war, see Sardinia *made safe*, and
then have the *status quo* in Italy. My object, therefore, has been to
remove all pretexts of excuse, both on the part of France and of Austria,
for preventing a Conference. Sardinia was their mutual pretext, and
my proposal that all the Italian States should be *invited* to attend *at*
but not *in* the Conference, as Belgium and Holland did at that of London, is unanswerable in equity, and supported by a precedent of the
greatest importance, inasmuch as the question there involved the
creation of two new kingdoms. Russia without hesitation, nay, with
eagerness, accepted all we proposed—viz. the condition restricting the
subjects to our four points, and also the above-mentioned invitation to
and admission of the Italian States. Prussia has done the same, and
is urging the whole scheme at Vienna. If, therefore, the Conferences
are to be stopped, it must be there or at Paris. We cannot agree to
admit the six Italian States into the body of the Congress, for they
would make it a Babel, and Scarlett has ascertained that Parma and
Modena have no wish to be so admitted. But if they and Rome are
not parties to it, no more can Sardinia (with whose internal relations
we do not intend to interfere) have a right to sit there. I think it desirable that you should know step by step what course we have followed
in this important crisis, as the rapid succession of telegrams crossing
one another from every part of Europe is very trying to the memory.

On Saturday, the 19th, Pélissier brought me a despatch from his
Government, informing me that Prussia had suggested a Congress, and
asking the opinion of her Majesty's Government. A Cabinet met at
three o'clock, and that evening I wrote a note to the French Ambassador
telling him we should consent on condition that the subjects discussed
should be confined to four—namely, evacuation, reform, security against
war between Austria and Sardinia, substitute for Austro-Italian treaties.
The next day I sent for Brünnow and informed him of the answer
which I had sent to Pélissier, and giving him the four points in writing,
begged him to inform his Government that such would be our conditions if the proposal was made by it to us. He did so by telegraph, and
on the 22nd I received a telegram from Crampton [1] to say that all our

_____
[1] Our Ambassador at St. Petersburg,

points were accepted. On the same day Brünnow called to confirm this, and gave me a memorandum to that effect, but he did not give me the official proposal for a Congress until the following day, the 23rd. Subsequently the Russian and Prussian Governments have accepted our four points, including a distinct declaration that no territorial re-arrangement was to be discussed, and that the treaties of 1815 were to be left intact. Immediately after my note of the 19th to Pélissier, I submitted our conditions to Austria, who, in reply, insisted on the admission of all the Italian States, except Sardinia, to the Congress; a proposal perfectly inadmissible, which I rejected, but upon which, up to this moment, Austria is apparently not prepared to alter her intentions. The Russian and Prussian Governments have also entirely adhered to my suggestion that the States of Italy should be present at the Congress only *en titre consultatif*. The only point, therefore, to be settled is *this last one*, and I hope you will be able to show the French Government, as Loftus, I trust, will be able to convince the Austrian Government, that it was the only alternative desirable. With regard to the question of Conference or Congress, we agree with you, and have recommended the former, but as we are not the proposers of either we cannot urge it very strongly. If the adoption of the latter name involves a general representation by Cabinet Ministers, I *must go*, because the Queen must be placed on the same footing as the other sovereigns, and, such being the case, I do not see how Walewski can avoid being present—*ergo, you* also.                            Yours truly,

MALMESBURY.


*April 1st.*—The division took place in the House of Commons on Lord John Russell's resolution, and we were beaten by 39. A Cabinet Council took place to-day, and immediately afterwards Lord Derby went to the Queen, but the result of his interview is to be secret till Monday, when he and Disraeli are to acquaint the Houses of Parliament with our decision. Lord Derby will not resign, but dissolve Parliament.

Lord Waterford was killed out hunting, near Curraghmore, a few days ago. His horse stumbled over a small fence, and, falling on his head, Lord Waterford dislocated his neck—a singular death for a man who had had so many escapes. Lady Stuart de Rothesay started immediately to go to her daughter, who is said to be quite composed, but is probably stunned by the shock.

*April 4th.*—Lord Derby made his explanation this afternoon

in the House of Lords. Disraeli spoke in the other House, and was best, as his speech was shorter.

*April 9th.*—Bad news from Paris. Lord Cowley had a long conversation with the Emperor yesterday, and it is quite clear that he is determined upon war. He will not induce Sardinia to disarm, and says he thinks war inevitable, as the Congress will only patch up matters and retard it. This agrees in every point with a report which I received from Turin, saying that the Sardinians were determined to go to war, and were sure of the Emperor's support; that they would be satisfied with nothing but the expulsion of Austria from Italy and the annexation of Lombardy; and that France is to get Savoy and Nice in return for her assistance. This is very annoying after having done all we could to prevent hostilities.

Lord M. to Lord Cowley.

Foreign Office: April 9, 1859.

My dear Cowley,—Your very interesting and important letter has just been read to the Cabinet, and they all agreed that you did not say a word too much to the man who broke his word to you, and who, it is evident to me, has from the first meant an Italian war, but has wanted both to gain time and, if possible, to put Austria in the wrong. It appears now that Austria is reverting to her first obstinate language about Sardinian disarmament, or that Loftus misunderstood Buol in thinking that he included her in the scheme of general disarmament. I have telegraphed to say that I will let the point stand as you put it to the Emperor, who, if he refuses (which apparently he will do), will place himself in the wrong. I send you a copy of Buol's telegram to Apponyi, received this morning. If you will write a private letter to Buol to show him how well he will stand if the negotiations break off by France refusing an offer of general disarmament as a principle, the detail to be carried out in Congress, and the free corps specified as part of the troops to be disbanded, I think you will do good. We are not prepared to give any guarantee as against France or upon eventualities; but the unanimous sentiment of the Cabinet was, that you might let it be felt by your *manner* and by *mezze parole*, that if France adopts a course of violence after the language held to you both before and after your Vienna mission, and after encouraging Russia to humbug us into these negotiations for a Congress, we shall look upon the whole proceeding as an affront as well as an unwarranted act of political profligacy. A reserved and cool demeanour is proper at this juncture.

and I believe it will be the best and most useful line to take. I can only add, therefore, that I wish you to adopt it towards France on the subject of the Congress and Italy, and at once to write to Count Buol, saying that his proposal, as we understood it, and as you made it at Paris, is the only one we can support among those he now suggests. We will not ask Sardinia to disarm without being able to offer her a guarantee, and that France, by refusing to join, prevents. I have been so harassed to-day between the Court and the Cabinet, that I must have written very confusedly.

P.S.—You will not entertain at present any other proposal but the one you submitted to the Emperor.      Yours truly,

MALMESBURY.

*April 10th.*—I hear that Massimo d'Azeglio is coming to England on a special mission, which gives hopes that some arrangement may be made. He is a very distinguished and prudent man, and has been Prime Minister at Turin. Lord Palmerston announces that his Government is ready. It is the 'old lot,' Sir Charles Wood, Vernon Smith, Lord Granville, &c. This Cabinet would not have the Radicals.

*April 11th.*—Sir James Hudson arrived this morning from Turin, having travelled day and night. He breakfasted with us, and talks confidently of the possibility of preventing war. I gave him all the Italian papers to read. He came in a state of great alarm, fearing he might not be allowed to return to Turin as Minister, and took leave of Cavour, saying it was doubtful whether he would see him again. The fact is that he is more Italian than the Italians themselves, and he lives almost entirely with the ultras of that cause. I had reason to complain of his silence, and quite understand how disagreeable to him it must have been to aid, however indirectly, in preventing a war which he thought would bring about his favourite object—namely, the unification of Italy. France having agreed to a general disarmament, it remains to be seen what Austria will say; but I fear her obstinacy will throw some obstacle in the way of peace.

Lord M. to Lord Cowley.

Foreign Office : April 11, 1859.

My dear Cowley,—I am quite determined to withdraw from this fool's paradise about a Congress if we cannot settle the matter on the

present basis of a general disarmament. I will agree, of course, to
the detail being before or after the Congress as the armed Powers may
please to arrange, but I cannot think we should risk the public *fiasco*
of being refused by Cavour *en plein Congrès*. I send you my proposal
as dictated to Pélissier on Monday last, which Walewski has, of course,
received, and in which you will see that Sardinia is specifically mentioned. I have also telegraphed to West [1] this day, and send you a
copy of it. It will be followed, should he refuse, by a *note raisonnée*,
which I shall send him alone, should the other Powers decline addressing him in the same sense. England cannot go on running from
one to the other like an old aunt trying to make up family squabbles,
and when I wind up, it will be to put the saddle on the right horse.
The papers will show that you and I have done our best to prevent a
war, and to obtain a Congress which nobody but Prussia and ourselves
ever intended should take place. Brünnow writes me a long paper to
prove that no disarmament should take place before the Congress. My
impression is that France, Russia, and Sardinia want to gain time,
because every day costs Austria 50,000*l.* for her army, and France will
pay Sardinia.

6 P.M.—I am glad to add that Azeglio has just been here, and has
written a most urgent telegram to Cavour to induce him to agree to
general disarmament. The debate coming on Friday has done this.

6.30 P.M.—Your telegram has arrived, and only confirms me in my
determination not to go to a Congress without a positive agreement
among all parties to disarm.                    Yours truly,
                                        MALMESBURY.

*April 12th.*—The Emperor Louis Napoleon refuses to ask
Sardinia to *disarm*, which, of course, makes his offer for France
to disarm perfectly useless. Lord Cowley writes that he has
good information that Louis Napoleon told Cavour he must wait
till July, and not mind in the meantime what he says or does.
If this is true, it is clear that he is playing a deep game towards
England and Austria, as well as to Italy, by waiting to see if
Palmerston comes in.

*April 14th.*—We went to the Drawing Room, and were introduced to the new Lady Eglinton, Lord Essex's daughter.

*April 15th.*—The Emperor will not consent to the *disarmament*
of Sardinia, but makes a ridiculous counter-proposition—namely,

---

[1] Lord De la Warr's son, Chargé d'Affaires at Turin.

that ' Austria should disarm under a guarantee from France and England that she will not be attacked by Sardinia.' It is clear that all he wants is to gain time. Lord Clarendon quite approves of my Italian policy. He told me so himself to-day in the House of Lords, adding that he had tried to prevent Lord Palmerston and Lord John from making their intended inflammatory speeches on behalf of Italy next Monday, in which Mr. Gladstone intends also to join. This will do immense harm at this moment, for it will encourage Louis Napoleon.

Lord M. to Lord Cowley.

Foreign Office : April 15, 1859.

My dear Cowley,—If you wish for more proofs than those you have personally received, in broken promises, of the falseness of the Emperor, you will have them in the paper I send you, written by the surest informer I ever employed. His knowledge of what *we* have been doing is of itself corroborative security for the truth of the rest. Now, we cannot stand before England and Europe on a better base than the last Austrian proposal, which is good in common sense and common equity. It is better than ours, because simpler and safer. I would of course go into Congress upon *ours*; but if Austria insists on *hers*, I cannot oppose her by insisting on mine *against* hers. I wish you distinctly to let this be understood by Walewski and the Emperor, and that if Sardinia refuses to agree to disarm with Austria and France, we shall withdraw from any further negotiations, as we do not mean to be dragged into being accessories before the war, whatever we may be obliged to become afterwards. You may depend upon it that to the common sense of Englishmen, of whatever party they may be, the fairness of the Austrian proposal will be convincing. I expect the French will try to ride off upon our proposal of a *previous agreement* to disarm and a post-Congress execution because Austria has declared she will not consent. It is necessary, therefore, that you should state at once we will not insist on ours as against Austria's plan if she persists in it. If Sardinia refuses disarmament now, and Austria makes it a *casus belli*, accompanying it with a note showing her cruel position in being made to wait and bleed to death, or till her enemies are ready, I believe public opinion will be with her. I shall not mention the Emperor personally at all on Monday.

Yours truly,<br>MALMESBURY.

(Paper referred to in foregoing.)

Londres, 15 avril 1859.

L'une des raisons principales (peut-être la cause essentielle) qui forceront le gouvernement français à admettre le Congrès, c'est qu'en dépit de tout ce que ses journaux semi-officiels déclarent, il n'est pas encore préparé pour la guerre. Je tiens du ——, que la nouvelle artillerie ne répond pas à l'attente qu'on en avait conçue, que les projectiles fabriqués pour les canons rayés n'offrent pas assez de résistance et éclatent bien avant de toucher au but, que tous ceux déjà forés ont dû être repesés; que les nouveaux, pour être prêts et efficaces, demandent des essais et des délais de fabrication qui exigeront deux mois au moins. Deux ouvriers employés dans le temps à Newcastle par Sir William Armstrong sont en effet employés à Vincennes; aujourd'hui l'insuccès des nouveaux projectiles—on les appelle 'bolt' à Vincennes —fait dire que ces hommes ont été induits en erreur. D'un autre côté, le désarmement général proposé par l'Autriche et appuyé, m'a-t-on assuré, par Votre Seigneurie, embarrasse singulièrement le gouvernement français : ou il doit conseiller au Piémont de désarmer, et alors il humilie mortellement le Comte Cavour; ou il prouve au monde que ses protestations pour la paix étaient mensongères. Le Général Ulloa, réfugié vénitien, et intermédiaire du Prince Napoléon, se retranche derrière 'l'indépendance du Piémont' pour laisser ce pays libre de désarmer ou non. Des renseignements reçus de diverses sources, toutes dignes de foi, m'imposent le devoir d'apprendre à Votre Seigneurie qu'à Vienne on ne fait pas mystère d'accepter des négociations qui font perdre un temps précieux, et compromettent, en temporisant, l'excellente position militaire de l'Autriche aux instances du gouvernement britannique. S'il n'y avait pas de Congrès, ou si le Congrès n'allait pas aboutir, il est à craindre que, dans le cas où les hostilités seraient funestes à l'Autriche, celle-ci ne reprochât alors à son gouvernement d'avoir trop écouté l'Angleterre.

*April 16th.*—Madame Bernstorff [1] called. She told us that great laughter was created at the Drawing Room by Mr. Under-Sheriff Thomas Jones passing the Queen with his wife's cloak on his arm. I had an audience at the Palace afterwards. The Queen did me the honour to say she was pleased at Lord John Russell praising me in his speech yesterday in the City. So

---

[1] Wife of the Prussian Minister.

friendly an interest on the part of her Majesty is a great satisfaction to me in the midst of my labours and anxiety.

*April* 18*th*.—Went to the House of Lords to make my statement. Nervous at not having any good news to announce, and
the subject being one of such extreme delicacy, that it was
necessary to weigh every word. But I am satisfied with my
speech, which was much cheered. Lord Derby made a very
fine impromptu one, which had a great effect, and the debate
was altogether in our favour. Lord Clarendon made a friendly
speech. The French, not being ready, are in a state of alarm,
and willing to do almost anything we choose, having received
news that the Austrians have marched on the Ticino, and are
going to send a summons to Sardinia to disarm instantly, or
they will attack them without further delay. They have applied
for aid to France, which has sent two divisions to the foot of
the Alps, but can render no further assistance, being still so
unprepared for war that General Renaud has refused to take
the command of the army in its present state. Walewski has
telegraphed to Malakoff and to me imploring me to consent to
admit Sardinia at the Congress, and he will urge her to disarm
under a guarantee. I refused, and sent the following proposition,
which, if not accepted by France and Austria, is the last I will
make—namely, ' *A general and simultaneous disarmament previous to the Congress, under the superintendence of a military
commission to ensure its being efficiently carried out*. Sardinia
to be invited to attend the Congress with the other Italian
States, after the precedent of the Congress of Laybach in 1821 ;
but, in accordance with the agreement entered into by France
and Austria, Sardinia is not to sit in the Congress as one of
the Great Powers.' If these propositions are rejected, I will
give up all further negotiation ; and if Austria is aware of her
position, she will probably attack Sardinia at once, and crush her
before France or Russia can come to her assistance.

*April* 19*th*.—Sardinia accepts the *general disarmament* on
the condition proposed by me, that she and the other Italian
States shall be admitted into the Congress on the same footing
as at Laybach. It remains to be seen whether Austria consents.
If she does, all the difficulties preparatory to the Congress are

overcome. If she refuses, our Government will withdraw from the office of mediator, and leave the three disputants to settle their affairs as they like. I went to Windsor with Massimo d'Azeglio. We dined and slept there.

*April 20th.*—Austria has returned no answer yet to my last proposal. If she refuses the case becomes very complicated, and it is impossible to say what will happen.

Lady Cowley called on Lady Malmesbury, and spoke in high terms of the agreeable footing established between her husband and myself in our official capacities. She expressed herself much pleased also at Lord Clarendon's taking the same view of Italian politics as I do.

*April 21st.*—The French, to whom the Sardinians have applied for advice and assistance, recommend them to disarm, as they cannot send any troops to help them in sufficient force under ten days, when they could land a hundred thousand men at Genoa; but before that the Sardinians would be crushed, and Turin taken. This information comes from Pélissier.

The Staffords, Shaftesburys, the Sardinian Minister, his uncle Massimo d'Azeglio, and Sir James Hudson, dined with us. The warlike news cast a gloom over the whole party, and the only laugh created was by my telling them that when a circular was sent to the foreign Courts announcing the confirmation of the Princess Alice, which took place to-day, it was discovered that in the Foreign Office cypher the same figures stood for *confirmation* and *confinement*.

*April 25th.*—The Austrian summons to Sardinia to disarm was given at Turin on the 23rd. The Queen was very anxious about the war when we went down to Windsor for a Council.

*April 26th.*—Duc de Malakoff is recalled from London, and is to command the Army of Observation on the Rhine. Persigny is said to be appointed Ambassador here in his place. If true, it is a hostile demonstration on the part of the Emperor towards our Administration, for he well knows how Persigny and his wife behaved when last in England, and how disagreeable it will be for us to have them here, and for me to transact business with him almost daily. He will go and repeat everything I say to Lord Palmerston. Lord Cowley has begged me not to object to him, and M. de Malaret told me that the Emperor objected to the Duc de Gramont, about whom there was a question, coming here as Ambassador, because he married Miss Mackinnon, an Englishwoman. Several thousand French troops have landed at Genoa, whilst another division is crossing the Alps.

*April 29th.*—All Italy is now up ; some of the Tuscan superior officers required the Grand Duke either to abdicate or declare himself for Sardinia. He refused to do either, and left Florence. Victor Emanuel has been proclaimed Dictator. The French have experienced great difficulties in crossing the Mont Cenis, on account of the snow. Four thousand workmen were employed in clearing the way.

*April 30th.*—The elections are going on badly for our Government. Count Kielmansegge, the Hanoverian Minister, says openly that Germany ought to declare war with France at once, and tells me that the Germans are very anxious to do so. This summons of the Austrians to Sardinia is a great disadvantage to us at the elections, but we must try to localise the war outside the bounds of the Confederation. If the French enter the Tyrol the German Confederation would be bound to assist the Austrians, which Prussia is very anxious to do. It is for this reason, and to minimize the war as much as possible, that our Government has urged Prussia [1] to remain tranquil, and I have written a strong despatch on the subject. The French Emperor would naturally be glad to manœuvre on his left flank, but would find himself in a hornets' nest, and all Europe would be in a blaze. The Duke of Saxe-Coburg, whom I saw at Windsor, is very eager to command the Prussian army. I went to Windsor this morning to meet him, but by some mistake he came up to London to see me.

---

[1] This despatch to Prussia, which is in my Blue Book, was (unknown at the time to me) never shown to the Emperor, and when, three years later, I saw him and he stated that I had encouraged Germany to act against him, I proved to him the contrary by sending him a copy of it through the Duke of Hamilton. I conclude that Lord Cowley, to whom I sent it, at the time showed it to Walewski, and that the latter purposely suppressed it. The reader will find it given at full length further on.

*Lord M. to Lord Cowley.*

Foreign Office : May 2, 1859.

My dear Cowley,—Before the Emperor leaves Paris, make a great effort to keep us out of the war, by obtaining his consent, with that of Russia and ourselves, to neutralise the Adriatic and Baltic. Ask for both, and if he consents, get both. Ask for the east shore of the Adriatic up to Trieste and the Baltic ; and if you cannot get that, the Baltic alone. To *us* the former signifies less, although attacks on Austrian territory in the north-east corner of the Adriatic might bring Turkey into play, and so have us into it. But the neutrality of the Baltic would be a great security for our remaining neutral, and I think the Emperor must see it. If Germany goes to war with France, the blockade of her ports by France or Russia must eventually drag us into the war, as our trade would be ruined, and this is the only question besides the Turkish one that would do so. Urge it, therefore, in your best style. I telegraph to Crampton to moot it at St. Petersburg.

Now for yourself. I am told that if the Emperor goes to Italy you ought to be with him—I mean *near* him, because an Ambassador is accredited to the sovereign himself. The Queen thinks it would look too French, but I do not agree. What I am convinced would be valuable, would be your advice and *coup d'œil* at critical moments, when a gleam of light might break in to give a chance for pacific counsels and mediation. I have seen the Duke of Coburg, who is red hot. He says Prussia cannot resist the pressure of public opinion, and has therefore armed, and his aide-de-camp goes so far as to hope that the Austrians will be beaten this week, because then all Germany will rise as one man and invade France. I told his Royal Highness that if they did, and France attacked them in the Baltic, not one atom of help would they get from us. He then stated that as long as the fighting was confined to Piedmont, Germany would look on, but if the Austrians were repulsed and the French followed over the Ticino, they would at once say, ' So far, but no farther, or it is a German war.' If this is true, you see how useful it would be in such an eventuality to have a man like you by Louis Napoleon to stop him, and the war too, at the Rubicon. If you come over with your daughters, I shall see you, which would be, at all events, desirable, but do not start till you have done your best for the maritime neutralities.

Yours truly,<br>
MALMESBURY.

*May 5th.*—I had visits from the two Counts Hallwyl, both gentlemen-like young men. They are Swiss and of a great family, being descended from the elder branch of the Hapsburgs, in consequence of which the late Emperor of Austria at his Court is said to have given them precedence over the Archdukes. I went to the Palace at three, to present the Duc de Malakoff, who had an audience to deliver his letters of recall. He very nearly cried when he left the room, and when he got to the top of the staircase he embraced me, and went downstairs crying like a child. He is miserable at leaving England. The Queen was quite touched, and when I returned to her Majesty she desired me to write in her name to the Duchess to say how much she regretted her departure. Disraeli says that 315 members are pledged to him to support the Government, and is in great spirits.

The Austrians have crossed the Po at Cambio, advancing upon Sala, and are entrenching themselves, nobody knows why, as they are said to have 90,000 infantry, 13,000 cavalry, and 200 guns; against 70,000 infantry, 4,000 cavalry, and 80 guns. They will, however, lose all by their slowness; when the snow is melted on the Cenis the French artillery will be able to cross and their opportunity will be lost.

*May 6th.*—The Duchesse de Malakoff, accompanied by Lady Ely, paid us a parting visit. She looked ill and very low, and cried so much at taking leave of Lady Malmesbury that Lady Ely said she would bring her back again to-morrow to wish her good-bye. Lord Cowley told me this morning that he had remonstrated with Walewski against M. de Persigny being named as Pélissier's successor, and had received a promise that he would not send him. If he does I shall transact business only through Lord Cowley and the French Foreign Minister at Paris—namely, Walewski.

*May 8th.*—Lady Palmerston is quite sure of turning us out, and of her husband being sent for, and will not hear of Lord John Russell being a more likely man. She says that Lord Palmerston had already formed his Government, and was quite ready to accept office. Lady Mary Craven, who is just returned from Paris, told me that all the English were rushing home from Italy and France, and that six hundred English left Paris the day before she did, as there is a strong feeling that Paris will not be safe after the departure of the Emperor.

The Emperor has been obliged to leave many more troops than he at first intended, owing to the excitement and dissatisfaction known to exist at Paris. All his best friends have warned him against the course he is pursuing, but he has been obstinately bent upon war. If he is beaten he will lose his crown, for his defeat and that of a legitimate sovereign would not have the same consequences, the relative positions not being equal.

Sir John Lawrence dined with us. He is, in appearance as well as intellect, just the man to govern a rebellious India. He has the most determined expression of countenance I ever saw, and no one who met him this evening felt a doubt that he would hesitate for a single moment in doing what he thought necessary for the safety of the country he governed, however arbitrary the measures required might be.

*May 10th.*—M. de Malaret called at the Foreign Office, much disturbed because I had not yet returned any answer to the announcement of Persigny's appointment ; and he was not satisfied with my message, which was simply that ' the Queen would receive anyone that was sent by the Emperor of the French.' M. de Malaret observed that the answer was ' very *short* ; ' but I replied that ' it would be the more easy for him to telegraph.' M. de Malaret then, without my having made a single remark, began a vindication of Persigny's conduct last year, which I received very coldly, so they must be perfectly aware at the French Embassy how disagreeable the appointment is to us.

*May 12th.*—Lord Clarendon called upon me this morning, and stayed for an hour talking politics.

*May 14th.*—Persigny called upon me at the Foreign Office, and I received him in a friendly manner, as he appears anxious to be on good terms with our Government. He spoke very frankly, and gave the same account as Lord Cowley of his nomination— namely, that the Emperor had given him the Foreign Office in the place of Walewski, when, at the last moment, Madame Walewska went to the Emperor, threw herself at his feet, and persuaded him to reinstate her husband. The Emperor then desired Walewski to send Persigny to London as Ambassador, ' et sans raisonnements.' His credentials are not signed, and must be sent to Italy for the Emperor's signature, so in the meantime he returns to Paris. *Quære*, whether this was not done to prepare an honourable retreat for him if the Queen had objected to his appointment ?

*May* 16*th*.—Prince and Princess Obrenovitch called on us. He is son of Prince Milosch, Prince of Servia. She is a Hungarian, and has a great reputation for beauty. They are very anxious to have children, and have come to consult the English doctors.

Lord M. to Lord Cowley.

Foreign Office : May 17, 1859.

My dear Cowley,—

.   .   .   .   .   .   .   .

Persigny gave Lord Derby and me three hours of assurances respecting himself and the entire innocence of the Emperor of all previous intention to go to war against Austria before the 15th of last month ! ! We received him very civilly, but he said with some confusion that his letters would have to go all the way to Italy to be signed. I suspect that he and his master are waiting to see what the 7th June may bring about, and perhaps it is as well it should be so. He told me the Emperor could win a *couple* of victories, and, having driven the Austrians into their *tanière*, leave a Marshal to enjoy the marshes of Mantua, and return to Paris.      Yours truly,

MALMESBURY.

*May* 18*th*.—Persigny has returned from Paris, and I presented him to-day to the Queen to deliver his credentials. Her Majesty received him civilly, but coldly, and he made no speech. He did not appear satisfied with his reception, and did not speak for five minutes after he left her Majesty. He is very anxious at the menacing attitude of Germany and Prussia, and with reason ; but the *casus belli* depends on the Emperor and his ally not crossing the bounds of the German Confederation. We are doing all we can to localise the war in the Lombard provinces.

I dined at the Palace ; as did the Duchess of Manchester.

*May* 19*th*.—We went to the Drawing Room, which was very full. Mrs. Dallas presented a Mrs. Morgan, wife of the United

States Minister at Lisbon. Her appearance was peculiar, her dress consisting of a green silk train, and a white petticoat, without a bit of tulle or ribbon—nothing but a plain hem at the bottom, and, I should think, nothing but a chemise under. She looked as if she had forgotten her gown and petticoat altogether, and had come in her slip.

I gave my diplomatic dinner this evening. Persigny looked very melancholy, so I went up to him in a friendly manner, at which he seemed quite pleased.

Count Vitzthum, the Saxon Minister, called in the most excited state about the war, and says that, if the Austrians are defeated, nothing will prevent Germany from rising, and if the allies gain a battle, 400,000 men will at once march upon Paris. The French have no army to oppose them on the Rhine, and Pélissier would be crushed. Azeglio has sent a telegram to the Duke of Cambridge announcing a victory gained by the Sardinians and French at Montebello. The French admit a loss of 500 killed and wounded.

*May 22nd.*—A telegram from Sir J. Hudson confirming the above gives some additional details. The first troops engaged were the Sardinian cavalry, under General Sonnaz, who charged six times, and kept the Austrians in check until the arrival of Forey's division, which took the town of Montebello, house by house, at the point of the bayonet. The Austrians then retreated, leaving 200 prisoners. This happened on the 20th, and the next day Cialdini is said to have forced the passage of the Sesia. The Austrian version, which I received this afternoon, was, that General Gyulai sent Count Stadion to make a forced reconnaissance of the French position. He fell in with a superior force, and retired according to orders. He makes no mention of Cialdini's victory. General Count de Flahault, who was with me, seemed to think it an affair of outposts. He is much pleased with me for having accepted him when it was proposed to send him here as Ambassador, and told me that I had done more for him than his friends the Whigs ever had, Lord Palmerston having once positively refused to have him. Lord John Russell is said to be ready to serve under Lord Palmerston.

*May 23rd.*—The King of Naples, *alias* Bomba, is dead. I hear the Austrians boast of having resisted, with 15,000 men, 40,000 of the Allies, for four hours, and only retreating before over-whelming masses without losing a gun ; but the natural question is, Where was the rest of their army ? and why was it not present ?

Lord Normanby, who is at Florence, says that Sardinia now pays taxes to the amount of 55 per cent. for the support of the army. At this moment the poor peasants are in a lamentable state, the mulberry trees cut down, which feed the silkworms —their great article of trade.

*May 24th.*—The French papers give an account of the battle of Montebello, making out they were only 4,000, and the Austrians 18,000. Lord Cowley told Walewski he wondered he was not ashamed of putting such statements in the ' Moniteur,' to which he returned no answer. The account from Turin, dated May 21, says that the Piedmontese cavalry were driven out of Casteggio by the Austrians, and followed by them to Montebello. The French, under Forey, arrived to their support, but after a severe contest of two hours the Allies were driven out of Montebello. They were then reinforced, and recaptured the village after much fighting and slaughter, the Austrians suffering severely during the retreat. At Casteggio they rallied and waited for the French, who were repulsed, and retired in disorder to Montebello, both parties entering the village pell-mell with fearful slaughter. The French admit having had between six and seven hundred men *hors de combat*. It is said that General Baraguay d'Hilliers sent to wake Louis Napoleon in the middle of the night of the 19th and 20th, telling him he expected to be attacked before daybreak. The Emperor replied, ' Est-ce là tout ? Ce n'était vraiment pas la peine de nous déranger ! ' and went the next morning to visit the battle-field of Marengo.

*May 27th.*—The Queen returned to London yesterday, and we are invited to dinner to-morrow.

Hudson telegraphs that Garibaldi has beaten the Austrians at Varese.

The Dowager Duchess of Hamilton died last night. She had been one of the handsomest women of her time, and was the daughter of Mr. Beckford, well known for his love of art and his collections.

It is said the Emperor is at Alessandria, and following the dangerous precedent of Marc Antony in Egypt.

*May 29th.*—The Queen and Prince feel very strongly the defeat of the Austrians, and are anxious to take their part, but I told her Majesty that was quite impossible ; this country would not go to war even in support of Italian independence, and there would not be ten men in the House of Commons who would do so on behalf of Austria.   Her Majesty and his Royal Highness are quite aware of this.

Garibaldi is reported to have gained three victories.

The number of French killed at Montebello is now officially announced as being 1,163.

Very little joy is shown at Paris at the French victory.   It seems well ascertained that the Emperor went off sight-seeing at Marengo instead of joining his troops or sending reinforcements to the front !   The Piedmontese say they have crossed the Sesia and defeated the Austrians at Palestro, and that Garibaldi is at Como.   At these last battles the King of Sardinia showed great intrepidity.   He headed his troops and was in the thick of the *mêlée.*

*June 1st.*—I hear there is to be no vote of censure on our Government, but no doubt Lords Palmerston and John Russell, with those who expect to form part of their Government, are most factious, and determined to turn us out if they possibly can.

Madame de Persigny was at the Queen's concert last night, dressed like a little girl, in white, with pink ribbons, without jewels or flowers.

*June 3rd.*—The newspapers are beginning to make remarks on the difference between Victor Emanuel and Louis Napoleon —the former fighting for three consecutive days at the head of his soldiers, and bivouacking with them on the field of battle, whilst the latter picnics with Madame C——.   However untrue this may be, there is no doubt that the French are giving the Sardinians the roughest portion of the business to perform.

*June 4th.*—Lords Palmerston and John Russell and Sidney Herbert have issued a paper signed by them, to call a meeting at Willis's Rooms, and to agree upon an amendment to the Address,

*June 6th.*—I received this morning from Lord Cowley a telegram announcing a great victory gained by the French at Magenta. The Emperor's message to the Empress admits 3,000 French killed and wounded, and 15,000 Austrians *hors de combat.* After the battle of Palestro, in which the French took no part, the King asked for a French division to assist him and enable him to get a little rest, as his forces were exhausted after twelve hours' fighting. The French, though they had 50,000 men near or in the town, refused, and the King had to entrench himself, and his men slept with their muskets piled before them. The Austrians attacked them the next day, and drove them back. A French division came up, but remained some distance behind, and when the King sent to General Trochu to beg him to advance, he refused to engage in the action without orders from the Emperor, who was not there. The Sardinians would have been completely crushed if the Colonel of the 3rd Regiment of Zouaves had not rushed to their rescue without orders, crying, ' Mais, ces malheureux vont être abîmés ! ' and then made the famous charge which resulted in taking the Austrian battery and saving the Piedmontese army.

*June 7th.*—The Queen opened Parliament. I acted, as Lord Willoughby's substitute, as Lord Great Chamberlain.

There are no details of the battle of Magenta, but the French loss is so great that they do not dare announce it in Paris. Two generals, Espinasse and Claire, are killed. At Castelnovello, near Mortara, wounded Austrians were murdered by the peasants.

*June 8th.*—Telegram from Lord Augustus Loftus from Vienna, saying the fighting continued all Sunday, the bridge of Magenta being taken and re-taken six times, and the slaughter great on both sides. The Austrians had not retreated or the French gained an inch.

*June 9th.*—I received a telegram from Paris, announcing the entry into Milan of the Emperor and King. I cannot understand why the French were so long entering Milan, as the battle of Magenta was fought on June 4, and it was not till the morning of the 8th that the two sovereigns made their entry. The distance is only twelve miles. General Baraguay d'Hilliers and Marshal Vaillant have been superseded by Marshal Randon and General

Forey.  The former is accused of allowing himself to be surprised at Montebello, and the latter is too heavy to ride, and is obliged to go about in a carriage.  The retirement of Baraguay d'Hilliers throws great doubt on whether Montebello was a victory to the French.  If it was, this is the first instance of a general in command of a victorious army being superseded.

Lady Palmerston told Lady Tankerville that we should be beaten by twelve on the Address.  I am also of that opinion, and, as far as I am personally concerned, shall be glad, as I am ill and tired.

*June* 10*th.*—I had an audience of the Queen to-day.  Both her Majesty and the Prince appeared to be anxious about the position of the Government, and the events of the war in Italy, which must affect all Germany.  They know Lord Palmerston's sympathies with France and Sardinia against Austria.

*June* 11*th.*—Lord Derby's Government was beaten this morning by a majority of 13—323 for the amendment to the Address, 310 against.  The division took place at half-past two, and the result was received with tremendous cheers by the Opposition. Azeglio and some other foreigners were waiting in the lobby outside, and when Lord Palmerston appeared redoubled their vociferations.  Azeglio is said to have thrown his hat in the air, and himself in the arms of Jaucourt, the French Attaché, which probably no Ambassador, or even Italian, ever did before in so public a place.  We held a Cabinet Council at eleven A.M., and at twelve Lord Derby went to the Queen to tender his resignation and that of his colleagues.  The Queen wrote him a very kind letter this morning, saying that she was much grieved at his Government being defeated, but would not part from him a second time without a mark of her favour, and gave him the Garter, making him an extra knight, which is hardly ever done, except for Royalties, and at the same time she told him she would give Sir John Pakington and me the Grand Cross of the Bath, on which I was congratulated in the kindest manner by all my colleagues.  It is much better for our credit to resign now, than to struggle through another session with a majority against us, hampering every measure brought forward, and obliging us to make humiliating concessions derogatory to the character of the party. We have now been turned out by a mere trial of strength. Nothing serious has been brought forward against us, only vague and general accusations of having mismanaged Reform and *not preventing war* ; but, as the Italian papers have not yet been given to Parliament, they have condemned us without evidence on the latter point.

*June 12th.*—It is said that Lord Clarendon refuses positively to join Lord Palmerston. The same authority declares there is no doubt that Persigny came with orders not to spare money in getting votes against us at the election ; that one gentleman received 480*l.*, the cost of his late election, is well known.

---

Thus fell the second Administration of Lord Derby. With a dead majority against him, it is evident that he could not, for long have maintained his ground, but it is equally certain that he would not have been defeated on the Address if Disraeli had previously laid on the table the Blue-Book containing the Italian and French correspondence with the Foreign Office. Why he chose not to do so I never knew, nor did he ever explain it to me ; but I presented it to the House of Lords at the last moment when I found he would not give it to the House of Commons, and at least twelve or fourteen members of Parliament who voted against us in the fatal division came out of their way at different times and places to assure me that, had they read that correspondence before the debate, they never would have voted for an amendment which, as far as our conduct respecting the War was concerned, was thoroughly undeserved, we having done everything that was possible to maintain peace. Mr. Cobden was one of these, and expressed himself most strongly to me on the subject. It may be asked why Lord Derby did not himself order this Blue-Book to be produced ; but the fact was that he wished to resign, worn out by repeated attacks of gout and the toil of his office, and was indifferent to continuing the struggle. When, a few days after, the Blue-Book was read I received as many congratulations upon its contents as during the past year I had suffered attacks from the Opposition and from the 'Press,' and many members repeated over and over again that, had they read it, they would not have supported the amendment.

*June* 14*th.*—Everybody is at Ascot, The Queen is gone to Windsor, but returns to hold a Council, when the new Ministers will be sworn in if their Government is formed. At present only Lord John Russell is appointed as Foreign Secretary. Lord Palmerston wished for Lord Clarendon, but the former insisted on having it himself. Our party are very much displeased with Disraeli for not laying the French and Italian correspondence on the table of the House of Commons in time, as all agree now that we should have had a majority if that had been done.

*Lord M. to Lord Cowley.*

Foreign Office : June 14, 1859.

My dear Cowley,—It only remains for me to thank you for all the able and cheerful assistance you have given me. You have been my right-hand man, and I hope the future Government will continue to avail themselves of your services. . . . . .

They are squabbling about the Chancellor at this moment, as to whether he should be Cranworth, Bethell, Cockburn, or Romilly. I conclude Hudson is dancing about with joy at the development of his lucubrations. Azeglio was waiting at the House of Commons door, and when the division was announced, cheered and drummed on his hat, to the indignation of our defeated M.P.s. Fancy you, the English Ambassador, playing such antics at the gates of the Tuileries ! What mountebanks Italians are ! He and Jaucourt embraced and halloed in the most frantic way when Palmerston walked out of the House. Persigny has not been near me for above a week. Dizzy would not let me lay the Italian papers the first night, and Clarendon says this lost us the division ! If I had not insisted on Friday, they could not have appeared at all. Adieu. Yours truly,

MALMESBURY.

*June* 16*th.*—Lord Derby made a short statement about his resignation of office, and attacked Lord Granville for having repeated what had passed between the Queen and him. The substance of their conversation appeared in the ' Times' next morning, and must have been either sent by him or repeated to some one who sent it, the only people present being the Queen,

Prince, and Lord Granville. I hear her Majesty was very much displeased when she read the article. Lord Granville confessed he had been indiscreet, and had repeated his conversation with her Majesty to his political friends, and as Mr. Delane dined with him on that day, there is little doubt how the statement got into the ' Times.'

*June 18th.*—We all went to Windsor to give up our seals of office. I had a long audience of the Queen, who was most kind and gracious, and went so far as to say she was sorry to lose my services. All my colleagues, as they were coming back in the railway carriage, praised the Blue-Book on Italy, except Disraeli, who never said a word.

The new Cabinet is as follows : Prime Minister, Lord Palmerston ; Chancellor of the Exchequer, Mr. Gladstone ; Foreign Secretary, Lord John Russell ; Home Secretary, Sir George Cornewall Lewis ; Colonial Secretary, Duke of Newcastle ; War Secretary, Mr. Sidney Herbert ; Indian Secretary, Sir Charles Wood ; Admiralty, Duke of Somerset ; Lord Chancellor, Lord Campbell ; President of the Council, Lord Granville ; Privy Seal, Duke of Argyll ; Postmaster-General, Lord Elgin ; President of the Board of Trade, Mr. Cobden ; Poor Law Board, Mr. Milner Gibson ; Secretary for Ireland, Mr. Cardwell ; Chancellor of the Duchy of Lancaster, Sir George Grey.

Lord John Russell came to see me at seven o'clock this afternoon, as is customary for the new Secretary to do, in order to get a *résumé* of the state of foreign affairs. He expressed himself anxious to keep up the navy and defences of the country, and observe strict neutrality, although we know that Lord Palmerston wishes the war to proceed at any cost for the emancipation of Italy. Gladstone announces his intention of cutting down our expenditure, and has refused to take our estimates. I foresee in all this the seeds of future discord ; and the amount of talent in the Cabinet, instead of facilitating legislation, will impede it.

*Lord M. to Lord Cowley.*

Foreign Office : June 18, 1859.

My dear Cowley,—I am just come from Windsor, where the last act was consummated, and I am about to have a long hour's conversa-

tion with Lord John. The Cabinet is remarkable for its *personn*
of talent, and for having *three* Dukes in it. The successes of th
French army give serious cause of reflection. Here is a man profes
ing to be *unprepared*, who has in six weeks sent an army of 150,00
men and 400 guns, with pontoons, &c., from France to the Minci
driving the finest army possible before him like sheep. To believe he wi
stop or be stopped is what I cannot do. The next year will be one
triumph and debauchery. Then will come the Rhine quarrel, but I
will fight shy if he can of England. It is a superstition with him
do that. You still seem to believe in Walewski and Louis Napoleor
I cannot do so. Now our Blue-Book is together, it is evident that I
never meant a Congress. The proofs are the Russian proposal, whic
floored you, and his refusal to make Sardinia disarm on our guarante
Our Blue-Book—for it is yours and mine—has had the most wonderft
success, and completely turned the tide which the newspapers ha
driven against us; but Disraeli would not let me lay it the first da
Clarendon, and all the Whigs, and our men say that it would hav
saved us if it had come out. If I had not laid it myself on the Friday,
would never have appeared at all ! His real reason for this strange lir
was that he *had not read it*, and could not have fought it in debat
The absence of the document enabled both Palmerston and J. Russe
to make the most unfounded assertions that we 'had threatene
France,' &c. I suppose all this will end in a Congress at last.

Yours truly,

MALMESBURY.

### Mr. J. T. Delane to Lord M.

16 Serjeants' Inn : June 20, 1859.

Dear Lord Malmesbury,—Allow me to suggest in reply to your phra
'posthumous praise,' that it was not my fault that the praise came tc
late. I sincerely believe that if you had published your despatches
fortnight earlier they would have had a very important influence o
the division, and I think it has been sufficiently proved that I shoul
have done you justice irrespective of party interests.

Faithfully yours,

JOHN T. DELANE.[1]

[1] I wrote to thank Mr. Delane for his posthumous praise of my Italian cori
spondence in the Blue-Book. Mr. Delane was the celebrated editor of the *Tim*
and a man of great intelligence, much appreciated in society by both politic
parties.

This was an answer to a note which I wrote to Mr. Delane, the editor of the 'Times,' for praising my Blue-Book on the Italian war, after a long course of abuse.

_June 21st._—Ferdinand St. Maur, the Duke of Somerset's son, called to thank me for the letter of introduction which Count Apponyi has given him at my request to Count Rechberg, the Austrian Prime Minister. Ferdinand wishes to join the Austrian army and see the campaign.

_June 22nd._—Mr. Burrell called. He came from Hamburg, and travelled in the train with a French colonel, who was going to join the army in Italy, and who said they were sadly in want of officers, an immense number having been killed. They were picked off by the Tyrolese riflemen.

_June 23rd._—An order has been given by Lord John Russell that everything _without exception_ is to be sent to Lord Palmerston and the Queen without his marking it. I suppose this is to make a contrast with Lord Palmerston's conduct when Foreign Secretary under _him_, and when he turned him out for not sending the _famous_ despatch to the Queen and himself.

_June 25th._—My father-in-law, Lord Tankerville, died last night. He was above eighty. He walked to his bed without any assistance, and his valet found him dead in the morning. He had always been most kind and friendly to me.

_June 26th._—The French gained another great victory [1] on the 24th, owing, it is said, to the folly of the Emperor of Austria, who, contrary to every rule of strategy, crossed the Mincio to offer battle to the Allies, with the river in his rear. The battle lasted twelve hours. The right wing of the Austrians, under Benedek, had defeated the Piedmontese, but their centre being broken, they were forced to retire, which they seem to have done in good order, not having lost any of their field artillery. The French claim three flags and 7,000 prisoners, but say nothing of their own losses, which must have been great, as they were unable to pursue the Austrians ; and it is remarkable that in both the last combats, after desperate fighting, the Allies have never been able to follow up the beaten army. They are, therefore, very much of the nature of drawn battles.

[1] On the plain of Solferino.

At Magenta it was quite so, for on the second day they were held in check, and the greater part of their army retired across the Ticino to reorganise, which they did not effect till three days after the battle, when they entered Milan, only twelve miles off. The Austrians had the best of the battle till one o'clock, when MacMahon came up and saved the day.

*June 29th.*—The French losses must be very heavy, as they have been three days inactive since the battle of Solferino, and, according to the telegrams, are only just crossing the Mincio. The Sardinian cavalry have been nearly annihilated.

*June 30th.*—Colonel Claremont, our Commissioner with the French army, writes that it has lost 15,000 killed and wounded, among whom are two generals, Dieu and L'Admirault. He says that the wounded suffered horribly from the intense heat and want of water ; the drought in the country where the French are encamped being so great that many children belonging to the peasantry in the villages have died of thirst. Colonel Claremont says also that the Austrians retreated in perfect order, and at that moment a tremendous storm came on ; the sky was perfectly black, and the constant flash of the lightning, the hurricane, and deluge of rain and hail, all mingled with the roar of cannon, made the most awful scene that can be imagined. When the sun again shone forth, the Austrian columns were just visible in the distance. The French, though victorious, had suffered so much that they could not pursue. The feeling at Vienna is very bad. They accuse the Emperor of having sacrificed the army by his own and Gyulai's mismanagement. This is supposed to be the reason of his return to Vienna.

I went at three o'clock to the Palace to attend the chapter of the Bath and to receive the Cross from her Majesty's hands.

*July 1st.*—Ossulston, Lord Wrottesley, and I attended Lord Tankerville's funeral, which took place at Harlington, in the churchyard of which stands, I believe, the largest yew tree in England. I never saw one so enormous, excepting perhaps that at Broomfield, in Somersetshire.

*July 2nd.*—The losses of the French and Austrians are beginning to ooze out. They are apparently terrible, judging by what they admit. The 'Moniteur' confesses to the French loss being

720 officers *hors de combat*, 120 of whom are killed, and 12,000 privates killed and wounded ; but private accounts state the numbers to be three times as great.   The French Chasseurs d'Afrique, who were sent in pursuit of the Austrians on the 24th, were completely ridden over by the Uhlans.   The Sardinians own to having lost 5,000 killed and wounded.   The Emperor Louis Napoleon announced in a despatch to the Empress, dated July 1, that the arrival of Prince Napoleon at Villaggio with 35,000 men has enabled him to approach Verona ; that he has left the *corps d'armée* at Goito to watch Mantua, and is about to assemble another at Brescia to watch the passes of the Tyrol.   The Austrians own to having lost 2,000 killed and 8,000 wounded.

*July 4th.*—The King of the Belgians sent for me to-day, but had nothing particular to say, so it was evidently only a compliment.   He sent for Lord Derby in the same way yesterday.   He told me, however, that Lord John Russell had sent a very sneering despatch to Prussia, but he did not think Prussia would go to war, and that he meant to fortify Antwerp.

The heat is becoming fearful, and the smell from the Thames so bad in Whitehall Gardens, where we live, that we cannot open the windows.

Lord John Russell has cancelled Sir Arthur Magenis' appointment to Naples, and recalled Lord Chelsea, who is Secretary of Embassy at Paris.   Lord John's brother-in-law, Elliot, is to have Naples, and a Grey gets Lord Chelsea's place in Paris, so the old favourites of fortune are sitting on the sunny side of the hedge.

Prince Esterhazy called upon me, and admitted the mistakes of the Austrian generals, but said that the troops fought heroically.   The Emperor Francis crossed the Mincio, contrary to Marshal Hesse's advice.   His army marched fifteen miles, fought for fourteen hours, and then marched back fifteen miles without tasting food, and under a burning sun.   Many who were unwounded left the battle-field, lay down, and died from pure exhaustion.

*July 8th.*—This great heat is increasing.   Fahrenheit stands at 90° in the shade by day, and 80° at night.   The French and Austrians have agreed upon an armistice, in consequence of which

Lords Stratford and Elcho will withdraw their resolutions tending to force the Government to keep peace. So it is saved. The demand for the armistice came from the French Emperor. I believe our Ministers telegraphed to tell him the danger they were in, should these motions be carried, as the effect would be, even if they were not turned out, to tie their hands and prevent their being of use to him during the recess. A very bad fever has broken out in the French army, and this, combined with his losses at Solferino, has obliged the Emperor to ask for an armistice. The request came from himself; it is to last till August 15. Another report is that the two Emperors are to settle everything between them without the interference of any other Power.

'Bear Ellice' is just returned from Paris, where he dined with M. Fould, and he says the French Ministers, now they have read my Blue-Book, do me justice, and profess to be satisfied that I behaved impartially and fairly towards them.

*July 10th.*—I hear that the Emperor Napoleon and Cavour are quarrelling. The latter wants to annex everything to Sardinia, and the former will not agree, and is alarmed at the state of Romagna. The Pope threatens to excommunicate Victor Emanuel; the French clergy take the Pope's part, and it was with great difficulty that the Archbishop of Paris was persuaded to officiate at the *Te Deum* in honour of the battle of Solferino.

Madame Apponyi called. She said, respecting the armistice, that though it was Louis Napoleon who asked for it, there were some things which made it advisable to grant it; but that no unreasonable concessions would be made, and quite scouted the line of the Adige, saying the Austrians would not give up the Quadrilateral. She spoke bitterly of the present Government, saying, when I mentioned that they promised neutrality, 'Elle est jolie, leur neutralité.'

*July 11th.*—Hotter than ever. Persigny called on me, and told me he thought there was a good chance of peace. The two Emperors were to have a conference this morning at nine. Louis Napoleon goes directly to Paris. He has issued an address to his army announcing his departure, and that Marshal Vaillant is to have the command in his absence. At the first shot he will return to them.

The thermometer is 97° Fahrenheit in the shade, and the French are devoured by flies and other insects.

*July* 12*th.*—I got a letter from Persigny announcing that peace was signed between the two Emperors, and the conditions, saying that the Emperor of Austria gives up Lombardy, to the line of the Mincio, to Louis Napoleon, who gives it to the King of Sardinia. This is a repetition of the 'Cagliari' story, and is humiliating to Sardinia, for in both cases the concession has not been made to her but to her protectors. In the 'Cagliari' case, the ship was given to England and made over by her to Sardinia. In this one, Lombardy has been conquered by France, who has assumed the whole glory of the campaign.

Parma, Modena, and Tuscany are restored to their former possessors, and the Pope is to be the head of an Italian Confederation, but this never can be carried out. Venice and its territories still belong to Austria, but are in some way to be independent. This part I do not understand, and the whole arrangement must be very unsatisfactory to the Italians, who have every reason to think themselves sold; the more so that the French get Nice and Savoy, which are the most ancient of Victor Emanuel's family possessions.

*July* 13*th.*—A fresh breeze, which makes the heat more endurable, though 90° in the shade and 84° in the house. Everybody is laughing at the peace, particularly at the Pope's title of 'honorary president,' which is certainly absurd. The whole arrangement is astounding, as pretending to be a solution of the Italian question, and as giving independence to Italy. Lombardy, up to the Mincio, is annexed to Sardinia—not made a free State, as the Lombards wished, for they hate the Piedmontese. Modena, Parma, and Tuscany are forced to return to their allegiance and rejected sovereigns; and the Pope, whose territories are worse governed and more miserable than any part of Italy, is made honorary president over the whole confederation. And it is for this miserable humbug that a hundred thousand lives have been sacrificed.

Count Cavour has resigned in a rage at the way in which the Italians and his master have been sold, as he intended to have annexed the whole of Italy to Sardinia. He is especially furious

at Louis Napoleon annexing Savoy.[1] It is said a very angry
scene took place between them, and that Cavour was so violent
and insolent in his language, that the Emperor threatened to have
him arrested, when he replied, ' Arrêtez-moi, et vous serez forcé
de retourner en France par le Tyrol.'

*July* 16*th.*—We went to the banquet given to the late Ministers
at Merchant Taylors' Hall ; very splendid. Lord Derby made a
fine speech. Disraeli followed ; after which my health was proposed.

*July* 20*th.*—The papers give an account of Louis Napoleon's
reception at Turin, which was a very cold one, he and the King
entering the town together in an open carriage. The latter was
cheered, but there was not a single cry of ' Viva l'Imperatore ! '
or ' Viva la Francia ! ' Cavour, who was alone in the next carriage, was received with showers of nosegays. The Emperor left
the following morning at 6 o'clock, arriving at St. Cloud at
8.30 P.M. next day.

*July* 21*st.*—Persigny came to give me the account of how the
peace was brought about. M. de Persigny, after the armistice,
by the Emperor's order, went to Lord Palmerston and said that
the time was come for mediation, and suggested conditions—
namely, Venice and its territories to be taken from Austria, not
annexed to Sardinia, but made into a separate and independent
State. There were other conditions, but this was the principal
one. That Lord Palmerston agreed to this, and rode down to
Richmond to tell Lord John Russell, who was equally delighted ;
and that the proposal was adopted by them and sent to the
Queen, who was at Aldershot, which occasioned some delay. That
her Majesty refused her consent, saying the time was not come
yet to make these proposals, as the fortresses were not taken.
That, however, in the meantime, Persigny had telegraphed the
consent of the English Government to his master, who immediately
asked for an interview with the Emperor of Austria, showed
him Persigny's despatch, saying, ' Here are the conditions pro-

---

[1] This fury of Cavour at the cession of Savoy was the consummation of his
histrionic powers. He had promised it to Louis Napoleon ever since their
meeting at Plombières two years before, and it was in fact the condition of the
Emperor's assistance.

posed by England and agreed to also by Prussia. Now listen to mine, which though those of an enemy, are much more favourable. So let us settle everything together, without reference to the neutral Powers, whose conditions are not nearly so advantageous to you as those I am ready to grant.'

The Emperor of Austria, not suspecting any reservation, and not knowing that the Queen had refused her consent to these proposals, which, though agreed to by her Government, were suggested by Persigny evidently to give his master the opportunity of outbidding us, and making Francis Joseph think that he was thrown over by England and Prussia, accepted the offer, and peace was instantly concluded.

Louis Napoleon in his speech to the Senate and Chamber, who waited upon him at St. Cloud, acknowledged fairly that he could not have taken the fortresses, if at all, without too great a sacrifice of life, and also that it would have entailed a general war and revolution all over Europe.

I think it right in this place to interrupt my diary, and passing over two years for a time, to relate a conversation which I had with Napoleon III., on the subject of my tenure of the Foreign Office, previous to and after the war in Italy.

The Emperor entertained throughout Lord Derby's Administration of 1858-9 a real or pretended conviction, encouraged by Walewski and the English ex-Ministers, that we were irreconcilably hostile to the liberation of Italy, and to the French Government, which had determined to effect it, as far as concerned the Northern part. It was therefore that, being on a tour through France in 1861, I wrote to Persigny from Tours to say that I should be soon at Paris, and wished to have an audience of the Emperor. To this his Majesty consented. I had not seen him since Cherbourg, where I attended the Queen in August 1858, and when I found him still resenting our coming into office upon the question which arose from Orsini's attempt on his life. The House of Commons had refused to pass Lord Palmerston's bill to alter the law under which Dr. Bernard was to be tried as an accomplice, and Lord Palmerston had resigned in consequence.

Since then, being at the head of the Foreign Office, I received various hints from the Emperor's Ambassadors that he considered our party hostile to himself, and all my attempts to check his interference with Lombardy had confirmed his dislike. Palmerston and his then slave, Persigny, with all their following, male and female, both in London and Paris, aggravated the Emperor's prejudices to such an absurd degree as to make him believe that I was getting up a *German coalition* against him. These impressions, I knew, remained; and my object was to remove them for the sake of the two countries, should the Conservatives again return to power.

He received me on April 6, at two P.M., in a room on the ground floor, opening out of the central pavilion of the Tuileries. I told him why I wished for an interview, and he said it was quite true that my party had behaved to him in the most hostile manner, but that he did not wish to go over the past. I insisted on doing so, and told him that, on Bernard's affair, when we first came into office, Persigny was so excited with the defeat of Lord Palmerston and his quarrels with Walewski, that I never could have a moment's reasonable conversation with him, or get any notion of his Majesty's ideas ; that when Pélissier came we all liked him, but that never once could I have an open and argumentative discussion with him on any points of policy, as he apparently had no information or orders from Paris, so that, in fact, for the fifteen months I was Foreign Secretary, I never had a chance of personally holding frank communication with *any* French Ambassador. As to planning a *German* coalition against him, I said my despatches were printed and extant, to prove that it was our Government who had prevented the Prussians and other German States from joining Austria when he and his allies crossed the Ticino. He was very much struck with this statement, and said :

It is always so, when one hears from one's Ministers at the small Courts, as I did this from the Court at Saxe-Weimar.'

The Emperor then held forth on the hatred of the aristocracy in England and of the Press against himself, though he believed that the people had no such feeling. He abused our suspicious fears and useless preparations. I replied that no man could astonish the world as he had done lately by his performances in

Italy, without frightening it also, and that all we did was for defensive purposes.

His Majesty was as abusive and evidently as ignorant of the nature and power of the English Press as I had always found him, exaggerating both its vices and its influence. He was much out of humour with Lord Palmerston's Government, which suspected all he did, and was always complaining of his building ships, and he ridiculed it as childish. 'Let each build what he considers the right number ; you ought to have twice as many as I, as they are your principal protection.'

He confessed he did not know what to do with the Pope, who, though defended and protected by him, harboured his enemies under his own flag, meaning the French Royalists.

He then plunged into the history and results of the Lombard war.

'When I determined to support the Piedmontese in the event of Austria crossing the Ticino, and saw Cavour in 1858, it was agreed between us that France should expel the Austrians from the *whole* North of Italy, and that the Piedmontese should pay the cost. At the battle of Solferino the French victory left my army very short of ammunition, with a loss of 17,000 of its prime troops, 150 miles from my base of operations, and with fever, still more fatal than the battle, raging in its ranks. I could not advance, and my retreat must have been through a *hostile* country, as the Italian peasants east of Milan were strongly for the Austrians. Fortunately for myself and the shattered Italian army, I obtained the Peace of Villafranca ; but Cavour, who is no soldier, and either did not or would not comprehend the situation, was furious, and declared that the Piedmontese Government, as I had not fulfilled my covenant by conquering Venetia, was not bound to pay the expenses of the war. It was impossible for me to return to Paris with a loss of 50,000 of my soldiers, and ask the French to pay 30,000,000*l.* without any equivalent. There would have been one in the glory and political and national influence of my victories if Piedmont paid the cost ; but as that was refused, I was obliged to take the material compensation of annexing Savoy, which might be considered by France to be worth the price of her men and money.'

Such was the Emperor's account to me of this great trans-action ; and no doubt the Piedmontese Government found it easier to pay in territory than in cash, and were in reality better pleased with the bargain, for, besides this, they eventually annexed Modena and Tuscany to Turin.

The following is the circular addressed in a despatch to her Majesty's representatives at the German Courts, a copy of which was sent to Paris but *which the Emperor never saw*, and which I therefore subsequently gave to the Duke of Hamilton, who showed it him to prove that our Government had done all they could to localise the Italian war and prevent a general one.

Foreign Office : May 2, 1859.

Sir,—I have to acquaint you that her Majesty's Government witness with great anxiety the disposition shown by the States of Germany to enter at once into a contest with France.  Her Majesty's Government cannot perceive that at the present moment Germany has any grounds for declaring war against that Power, and still less would the Confederation, in their opinion, be justified in prematurely adopting any course which would bring on a European war.

It is desirable, however, that the Governments of Germany should entertain no doubt as to the course which in such a case her Majesty's Government would pursue, and therefore you will explicitly state to the Government to which you are accredited that if Germany should at present, and without a *casus foederis*, be so ill-advised as to provoke a war with France, and should, without any sufficient cause, make general a war which on every account ought, if possible, to be localised, her Majesty's Government determine to maintain a strict neutrality, can give to Germany no assistance, nor contribute by the interposition of the naval forces of this country to protect her coast from hostile attack.

The elections now proceeding afford an undeniable test of public feeling on this point, and it may be said to be the only one in which the English people appear to be at the present moment absorbed. That Germany should arm and prepare for eventualities is natural and right, but in the opinion of her Majesty's Government no act has as yet been committed by France against Germany, and no treaty obligation subsists which justifies her to provoke an attack on her own territory or an invasion of France.          I am, &c.,

MALMESBURY.

Both Count Walewski and I had received intelligence that the whole of the Prussian army was to be mobilised in consequence of the strong feeling in Germany against France.

---

*July 23rd.*—Louis Napoleon is evidently alarmed at the results which the peace may have for him, as he loses no occasion for giving explanations ; but all he says appears to me to make the matter worse. In his speech to the Diplomatic Body he said Europe was so unjust to him that he was compelled to conclude the peace to show his moderation and his wish not to engage Europe in a general war. The tone of this speech was considered so unsatisfactory that the Funds fell directly.

*August 5th.*—Sir John Burgoyne, who had paid us a visit at Heron Court to survey the site of Hengistbury Head for military defences, left. He stated that if there were an accessible harbour at Christchurch there must be a fortress to defend it, but that at present it was not required.

*August 11th.*—Left London for Achnacarry. We travelled all the way by land.

*September 1st.*—I went to the Forest of Gusach, killing three good stags. I was obliged to help to carry them down the hill, so that I did not get home till ten o'clock.

*September 5th.*—The Tuscans have offered the sovereignty of Tuscany to Victor Emanuel, who declines giving a positive answer, saying that he would willingly accept their offer, but must first consult European Powers, and hints at a Congress.

*September 16th.*—Accounts from China very sad, and, if true, Mr. Bruce is to blame. It is reported in a private letter published by the 'Times' that the Chinese authorities sent word that the Peiho was blocked up, and no ships of war would be allowed to go up to Pekin ; but that if they went by another road farther north, they would be received. Mr. Bruce determined to force the passage in spite of this warning, and a disastrous defeat has been the result. Admiral Hope never sent any reconnaissance, so that he was ignorant of the erection of the batteries, which were carefully masked. He then landed the crews of the gunboats without knowing the nature of the ground. The men floundered through a deep morass, their ammunition got wet, they were

unable to take scaling-ladders, and after a hard struggle, under a
heavy fire, found themselves close to the walls of the battery
without the means of defence or attack ; but not a man thought
of retreating until orders were sent from the rear, when they
retired with great reluctance, carrying off all their wounded,
among whom was Admiral Hope himself.

*September* 19*th.*—Duke of Manchester's servants arrived,
bringing the news that the Duke and Duchess had reached
Tomadown, and, being unable to procure ponies, had started on
foot across the mountains. They had no guide and no gillies, so
we could not help fearing that they had either lost their way or
that the Duchess had knocked up and been unable to proceed, for
they started at eleven and ought to have arrived by five. I immediately sent off ponies, and Mr. Bidwell went with them ; but returned saying he had gone three miles along Glen Keich to a point
where he could see five miles along the road to Glengarry, and
with the exception of a stag, which he put up, there was not a
living creature visible. Upon this I despatched John Macdonald
the stalker, though one might as well look for a boat in the
Atlantic as search for anybody in these wild hills. We therefore
remained very anxious until nine o'clock, when we heard the door-
bell ring. We all rushed into the hall, and the Duke and Duchess
were gladly welcomed by the whole party. They had walked the
whole way from Tomadown, mistook the path, and found themselves
overlooking Loch Lochy, eight miles from Achnacarry. They
descended Clunes with great difficulty and some danger, and came
along the shore of the lake, where there is a safe road. It was a
most imprudent expedition.

*September* 30*th.*—Lady Chesterfield and Lady Evelyn Stanhope
arrived. The former caught several *salmo ferox* in Loch Arkaig.

*October* 6*th.*—Sir James Hudson arrived yesterday, and to-day
went out and killed an enormous stag in Gerraran, not getting
home until eleven at night. The wind was contrary, and so strong
that the men could not pull down the lake against it, and were
obliged to beach the boat in a sheltered place, and walk eight
miles along the shore. News of Lord Jersey's death, on the 3rd,
at above eighty.

*October* 10*th.*—Sir James Hudson went to Glen Kamachray,

intending to sleep at the shepherd's hut in order to be on his ground early the following day.

*October 11th.*—Sir James returned for dinner, having killed nothing, and gave a very amusing account of his night at the bothy. He said there were seven men, five dogs, three women, and a cat in two small rooms, more like hencoops than rooms, and only three beds for the whole party. The maid-of-all-work asked him with whom he would like to sleep, and he answered that if he couldn't sleep with her he would prefer Macoll, the stalker. The latter, however, replied, 'Methinks you had better sleep alone' So Sir James had a bed to himself, as far as I know.

*October 15th.*—Mr. Ogle, the photographer, arrived, and made some excellent photographs of the beautiful scenery here and of our party. The cold is intense, and we are buried in snow.

*October 20th.*—A heavy snowstorm came on, lasting all day. The mountains in all directions are covered with snow. The newspapers announce that a treaty of peace has been signed between France and Austria at Zürich, but there is to be a Congress, in which the five Great Powers join.

*October 21st.*—News of Lord Westmoreland's death arrived. I went to the Pine Forest and had it driven. The twelve-pointer, *alias* 'the enchanted stag,' came out, and stood staring at the beaters several minutes at not more than ten paces, but I did not get a shot. The Highlanders are more than ever convinced that the life of this enormous beast is charmed. Saw a flock of wild swans going south—a broad hint to me to do the same.

*October 25th.*—I beat the woods of Auchnasoul, and killed six woodcocks, twelve blackcocks, also the stag whose leg I broke two days ago. This good day's sport and luck has closed my connection with Achnacarry, which has lasted for fifteen years of the prime of my life. I rowed home from Moich with a heavy heart. Loch Arkaig was motionless, and of the colour of obsidian. The sun, after a bright day, had set behind a heavy mass of clouds, against which the mountains of Scaurnahat and Murligan looked ghastly in their garments of snow, whilst the northern slopes and corries of the Pine Forest retained every flake that had fallen. The stags, as is usual in a hard frost, were roaring with redoubled passion in the wilds of Gusach and Gerraran. The herons were

screaming as I disturbed them from their shelter in the islands ;
and then again the roaring of the harts re-echoed through the
forest.   As I landed at the pier, a freezing mist fell over the
whole scene, and thus we parted.   *Vale !*

*November 4th, Chillingham.*—Lord Wemyss told me to-day
that Lord Elcho had seen a letter from Louis Napoleon to M.
de Flahault, saying that he still was attached to the English
alliance more than to any other, but that the feeling in France was
getting too strong for him to resist it.

*November 11th.*—The dinner at the Mansion House on the 9th
was a very flat affair.   Lord Palmerston and Lord John Russell
were both absent—the former at Windsor, the latter ill.   Sir G.
C. Lewis made some sort of speech on foreign affairs, the only
important point being that England had received no invitation to
the Congress.   None of the foreign Ministers were present, except
the Turkish Ambassador, which probably Lord Palmerston knew
would be the case, and paid them in the same coin.

*November 16th.*—My ex-private secretary, Bidwell, is gone to
Australia for his health.

We went to Windsor, where we were invited.   The party at
the Castle consists of Prince and Princess Frederick William of
Prussia, Prince Hohenzollern, Mr. and Mrs. Sidney Herbert,
Countess Blücher, the Duchess of Athole, Count Perponcher, &c.
Prince Albert told me that Balmoral was the driest place in
Great Britain.   Only sixteen inches of rain fell during the year,
whilst in Glasgow they have an average of sixty-two, and in
London twenty-five.

*November 18th.*—Returned to London.

*November 26th.*—Lord Cowley called on me, and told me that
he distrusted the Emperor, and has urged the Government not to
relax in their preparations.   Louis Napoleon is in very bad
health, and though he has lost his energy he has become restless,
and it is impossible to know what he will do next.

*November 27th.*—I hear that neither Lord John Russell nor
Lord Clarendon will go to the Congress.   It will be held in Paris,
and may last six months.   The former could not well go if he
wished it.

*December 2nd.*—I returned from Buckenham, Mr. Baring's

place in Norfolk. Mrs. Baring is French, a daughter of the Duc de Bassano. Jem Macdonald[1] was there in great spirits, and, as usual, the soul of the party.

The reported bombardment of Tetuan is untrue. What happened is this : a French line-of-battle ship approached too near a small mud fort at the entrance of the river, and was fired at by the fort, but it is doubtful whether the guns were shotted. The captain did not return the fire, but joined the French squadron for orders, and, returning the next day with four ships of war, destroyed the fort—an outrage.

*December 4th.*—The Duke of Somerset called and told me that Lord Palmerston was not going to the Congress, and they had great difficulty in finding a proper person.

*December 8th.*—Lord Derby says he will not support Lord Grey's amendment to the Address, but will vote for the loan for the national defences, and for a 10*l.* franchise for the counties, and 8*l.* for boroughs.

# 1860

*January 1st.*—The principal news is that Lord Palmerston has agreed to a 6*l.* franchise, and has determined to dissolve Parliament if beaten. It remains to be seen whether the Queen will consent to this.

Persigny is in Paris, intriguing to get rid of Walewski, and to try to prevent our party coming to office. He is completely managed by Lord Palmerston, and the two together do all they can to persuade the Emperor that the Tories are opposed to him. The person who gave me this information said that if we came in again the Emperor means to ask for me as Ambassador at Paris. I told him honestly I should refuse.

*Lord Derby to Lord M.*

Knowsley : January 15, 1860.

My dear Malmesbury,—I return the well-known handwriting enclosed in your letter of the 13th. The information there given tallies

---

[1] General the Honourable J. Macdonald, A.D.C. to H.R.H. the Duke of Cambridge, died 1882.

with what I have received from other quarters, among others from Madame de Flahault, whom I met at Bretby. The offer of a commercial treaty was, however, coupled, though she did not tell me so, with the proposal of an alliance, *offensive* and *defensive*, with France, and a joint guarantee of the independence of Central Italy! Cowley came here specially to urge the adoption of these two measures; but my latest intelligence is that they were debated in the Cabinet on Tuesday last, strenuously urged by Palmerston and J. Russell, who had confidently assured the Emperor of their success, acquiesced in by Gladstone by the double inducement of his Italomania and his Free Trade policy, but, on discussion, rejected by a majority of the Cabinet![1] This, if true, and I am assured it is, is very damaging to Palmerston, and will be both embarrassing and irritating to the Emperor. It is added, and not improbably, that the Court has had a good deal to do with the Cabinet decision.

Ever yours sincerely,

DERBY.

*January 22nd.*—Captain Harrison, of the 'Great Eastern,' was drowned yesterday morning at the entrance of the Southampton Docks in crossing from Hythe in a gig with a lug-sail. It was blowing a hurricane. The 'Great Eastern' is a most unlucky ship, and I remember saying, when I heard the ridiculous way in which people boasted that such a ship had never been built before, that we had at last overcome the power of the waves, and no one would be sea-sick, that such language was a defiance of fate. The event has proved it. The first mishap was in launching her, when she stuck fast and it took six weeks to get her to move, and an additional expenditure of 70,000*l.* The disappointment and excitement killed Brunel, the celebrated engineer. When she started on her trial trip, she nearly went ashore at Greenwich. On arriving at the Nore one of her boilers burst, killing several men, and people became so distrustful about her that she could get no passengers, and was laid up for the winter at Southampton. Now she has reached the climax of misfortune by the death of Captain Harrison, a very clever seaman and gentlemanlike man.

---

[1] This monstrous policy is confirmed in Mr. Ashley's *Life of Palmerston.* If this is a true account, the *Court* showed its wisdom. What would have been our position in 1870 if we had had an offensive and defensive alliance with France?

*January* 24*th*.—Lord Grey means to propose an amendment to the Address about the Chinese war. We shall not vote with him, but intend to express our opinion of Mr. Bruce's conduct in that country. Disraeli is against the loan for the national defences. If he opposes it in Parliament he is done for, both with his party and the country. There is a very strong feeling in favour of it. There is a hitch in the commercial treaty, and the 'Times' is writing against it.

*January* 25*th*.—The Queen opened Parliament yesterday—the longest Speech ever known, and abominably written. Debate dull and flat. Lord Derby praised the volunteers, Lord Canning, Admiral Hope, and the seamen who fought so gallantly in the unfortunate attack on the Peiho; but he reserved his opinion upon Mr. Bruce and upon other subjects mentioned in the Speech, one of which was the commercial treaty.

*February* 3*rd, Heron Court*.—Lord and Lady Somerton, Mr. and Lady Rose Lovell, and Lord Seymour arrived; also Mr. A. Lane and Major Nevill. The latter is the second son of Lady Georgina Nevill, Lord Lucan's sister. He is in the Austrian army, and was aide-de-camp to the Commander-in-Chief in the late war, Gyulai. He said that nothing could be worse than the Austrian generals, and that Gyulai himself had been named to the command by the influence of the Jesuits, whom he toadied. Hesse very old and worn out; Benedek good, but in a subordinate position. We passed a very merry evening.

### Lord M. to Lord Derby.

Heron Court : February 6, 1860.

My dear Derby,—I am much obliged to you for your note, and I will come up on Tuesday. I was going to London on Wednesday for a meeting which Colville has called on the subject of our party press. My impression was that we would take no part in what is going on abroad, and that any connection with Normanby and his moves would rather bring down odium (not to say ridicule) on our party. All he does is in a strong *Codino* spirit, in which neither you nor I have any sympathy, and our traducers wish for nothing more than to identify us with that bigoted and unpopular set. As to our coming into office, I confess I have the strongest repugnance to do so upon our *former* basis, twice tried, and twice with the same result—namely, ten or twelve months of sufferance, then a beating, then a dissolution, and then an ejection.  Personally, none of us can desire to play so disagreeable a *rôle* once more with the same play and the same parts, and still less can we wish it for the good of the country.  It is, therefore, with great satisfaction I hear you say that we must help to keep these cripples on their legs.

Ever yours sincerely,<br>
MALMESBURY.

*February 7th.*—Lord Derby has written to me to come to London for Lord Normanby's motion about Savoy and Nice.

*February 8th.*—The debate was good, Lord Derby speaking beautifully.  Lord Normanby withdrew his motion, but it gave the House an opportunity to show their feeling on the question of the annexation of Savoy and Nice to France, and it was evident that the great majority, if not the whole House, was against France.  There is a great outcry against the treaty, which, I believe, was signed by France and Sardinia for the cession of Savoy on January 18, 1859, and that Marshal Niel signed it for France.

*Lord Clarendon to Lord M.*

Grosvenor Crescent : February 8, 1860.

My dear Malmesbury,—I think you ought to see the enclosed, which I received this morning.  The commercial treaty is, in my opinion, thoroughly unsound, and a great mistake ; but I am sure that rejecting it, making an enemy of the Emperor by delighting his foes and displeasing his friends in France, would be a far greater mistake for all concerned in it.  Pray return the letter.

Ever yours sincerely,<br>
CLARENDON.

*February 9th.*—Persigny is furious at the debate on Savoy in the House of Lords, and I suppose he will be more so if he knows that the petition from Chambéry, addressed to the English people against the annexation, was sent to the newspapers by Lord Derby, to whom it had been addressed by the petitioners.

*February 15th.*—I went down with Lord Derby to Heron

Court after the Levée. We hastened home and caught the three o'clock train after changing our dress—quick work ! Lord Derby was in great spirits about his last meeting, which was fully attended, and he seems ready to come in again.

### Lord John Russell to Lord M.

Chesham Place : February 15, 1860.

My dear Lord,—I see in the 'Times' and 'Daily News' of this morning that you are represented to have said that I had stated in the House of Commons that Mr. Bruce, in forcing the passage of the Peiho, had acted exactly according to his instructions. It is always dangerous to rely on reports of what passes in another House of Parliament, and perhaps you never made the remarks I have mentioned. With regard to myself, however, it is due to you to state what I did say.

I said that Mr. Bruce by his instructions was ordered to go to the mouth of the Peiho with a sufficient force, and I read to the House of Commons the words of your instructions. But I said the case of resistance by force to his proceeding up the river in a friendly manner was not contemplated by those instructions, though I did not blame you for the omission. I said that consequently Mr. Bruce found himself with a considerable naval force at the mouth of the Peiho, in face of probable resistance, without instructions.

That no case could be more embarrassing, for, if he returned, he would be blamed for retreating before a force which in the past year had been easily overcome, and if he advanced he ran the risk of the defeat and repulse he had actually experienced.

That no situation could be more embarrassing, nor could anyone pretend to say what Mr. Bruce should have done, having *no instructions* for such a case.

I think I did justice both to your Lordship and to Mr. Bruce. I am sure I meant to do so.—Yours, &c.        J. RUSSELL.

*February 16th.*—Gloomy day, with a high gale. We went out and shot over the rivers, killing sixty head of wild-fowl. Sidney Herbert seems determined to abolish the place of Commander-in-Chief, and to put the army under the House of Commons. If so, the Queen has every right to be indignant at this interference with the rights of the Crown. Nothing will dissuade him from the plan.

*February* 21*st.*—The Government had a majority of 63 on Mr. Disraeli's amendment to discuss the treaty before the Budget. Lord Palmerston lost his temper and made a most angry speech.

*February* 29*th.*—The Government will carry their Budget. Lord John has declared what we all along suspected, though Lord Palmerston never would give a straightforward answer— namely, that though Parliament may alter any article of the Budget or treaty, yet that any alteration may cancel the whole, as the Emperor, of course, will not be bound by them. It is cleverly managed, but in a very underhand way.

*March* 4*th.*—It is now certain that the Emperor means to annex Savoy and Nice without the sanction of the other Great Powers. He now says that he merely meant that he would explain to them his reasons for doing so, but he evidently intends to listen to no objections. The subject was alluded to in the House of Commons, and Sir Robert Peel spoke against the annexation, upon which Bright got up and made the most un-English speech ever heard in Parliament. He was answered in an eloquent and spirited one by Lord John Manners. Mr. Kinglake has given notice that he will move an address to the Queen, condemning the annexation.

### Lord Derby to Lord M.

St. James's Square : March 5, 1860.

My dear Malmesbury,—I have received your précis books, which with the other volumes I will keep safely till I have an opportunity of returning them to you here. I do not think we shall do any good by moving for the papers of 1852, but we shall be quite justified in stating, if necessary, the positive assurances which we had from Louis Napoleon previous to our recognition, not of the Empire but of the numeral. He does not, however, deny these assurances, but rests his demand of Savoy on the readjustment which is taking place of the territorial limits of Northern Italy. The plea is futile enough ; but it relieves him from the necessity of denying his former engagements, while it leaves him free, in his own mind, to dispense with them. There is likely to be a very interesting discussion in the Commons to-night on the Address; and from what I hear I think it is likely that Savoy may again be brought on the *tapis* by Sir Robert Peel, and possibly a motion made by some outsider, if not by him, for the addition of words condemnatory of the proposed annexation. There may, however, be a preliminary discussion as to the effect which the adoption or rejection of the Address would have on the treaty, of which a word by-and-by. Meanwhile Palmerston is unwell, threatened with an attack of gout ; John Russell very much out of humour, and on very bad terms with the Emperor, who complains that he has not been properly defended by the Government, the truth being, as I believe, that J. Russell and Palmerston are on different tacks—the first opposed to the projects of France, and fancying that he is supporting the cause of Liberal Sardinia; the second hampered by private engagements contracted with the Emperor before his accession to office, which he is afraid either to repudiate or avow.

I saw Lord Chelmsford yesterday, and had a long conversation with him on the subject of Grey's suggestions. I agree with you that we ought not to attempt by a vote of the House of Lords to set aside the French treaty, objectionable as I think it; and our course will require careful consideration, after the elucidation which we shall receive from to-night's debate in the Commons. Lord Chelmsford remains firm in the opinion, which is shared by Cairns and Kelly, that although the passing of the Customs Acts by Parliament may be held to be such an assent as the treaty requires to the commercial articles, the eleventh article, that on coal, cannot be sanctioned but by an Act of Parliament. The Queen, under an Act of Parliament, has the power of prohibiting the export of certain articles, or rather of articles which she may deem to come under certain conditions ; and she has no power to divest herself of that which Parliament has given her for the security of the country by any contract with a foreign Power, except under the same authority of an Act of Parliament. If this be so, the Address is an unmeaning form, unnecessary for the commercial object, valueless for the political ; and it may be adopted or rejected without in the least degree affecting the treaty. If the Government contend successfully that the Address is such a signification of the Parliamentary assent as is required by the treaty, and is necessary as a supplement to commercial legislation, I should pause before I took the responsibility of attempting to reject it; and in that case I would wish to carry my opposition no farther than would enable me to record a protest, if the forms of the House will allow me, against the Address, that is, against the terms of the treaty. But my final decision must be influenced by what may take place to-night in the Commons. In any case, we ought to have one good debate in our House, embracing the treaty, the Budget, and Savoy. They ought not to be frittered away in separate

discussions. This may come on, if the Commons pass the Address to-
night, as early as Thursday or Friday. I am not disposed to fight for
delay, as I do not want a division.        Yours sincerely,

DERBY.

*March 8th.*—The papers give Cavour's answers to the Emperor's proposals, which were to annex Parma and Modena to
Sardinia, to govern Romagna under the Pope, and to leave Tuscany
an independent State : and in case of a refusal of these propositions, he threatens to withdraw his army, and leave the King of
Sardinia and the Italians to fight their own battles as well as
they can. Cavour has refused—a bold, not to say a most rash
and imprudent step ; but with him it is *tout ou rien—per fas aut
nefas.*

### Mr. Kinglake to Lord M.

12 St. James's Place : March 9, 1860.

Dear Lord Malmesbury,—I never made any communication to your
Lordship personally, but I conveyed the intelligence privately to
Mr. Seymour Fitzgerald, who then represented the Foreign Office in
the House of Commons.

What passed was as follows : About this time last year I received a
communication from Turin disclosing the scheme for the annexation to
France of Savoy and Nice, and it came to me from such a quarter that
I could not doubt its truth. In the then state of Europe I did not
think it prudent to state the intelligence publicly in the House, but I
thought the knowledge of it might be useful to Her Majesty's Government. Lord Palmerston agreed with me that it would be right to
communicate it to the Government, but he suggested that the best way
to do this would be by speaking to Seymour Fitzgerald. I accordingly
told Seymour Fitzgerald that I wished to speak to him, and after in-
dicating the grounds on which I believed my information to be accurate,
I read to him twice over the words of which the enclosed paper is a
copy. He seemed to be impressed and much interested. I begged him
to remember that the paper signed by the Emperor was a 'pacte de
famille,' and *not* a 'treaty.' This took place in the month of March
of last year as well as I can recollect.

I trust that this statement will convey to your Lordship, with
sufficient clearness, the information you desired to receive.

Yours, &c.        A. W. KINGLAKE.

[ENCLOSURE.—' On the evening before the marriage with the Princess Clothilde, a paper was signed by the Emperor of the French which was called a " Pacte de famille " (not a treaty or convention), promising aid, offensive and defensive, to Sardinia, the King on his side promising Savoy and Nice in return for whatever possessions he may gain in Lombardy. The paper was signed by Walewski.']

*March 16th.*—Went to the House of Lords for the debate on the Address for the treaty. The debate was a very fine one. The Address was seconded by Lord Cork. Lord Grey then made a fine speech, objecting to it. Lord Wodehouse answered him, and then I was followed by Lord Grey.[1] Lord Overstone spoke against the treaty. Lord Grey persisted in dividing the House, though Lord Derby asked him to abstain from doing so. The division took place, and the Government had a majority of 30.

*March 17th.*—Naples is in a dreadful state. The tyranny of the present King far exceeds that of his father, and the exasperation is so great that a revolution may take place at any moment. But events in the North of Italy have much to say to these feelings, and naturally encourage the Neapolitans to imitate them.

Lord John last night in the House of Commons announced that he had read a very important despatch written by M. de Thouvenel to Persigny relating to Savoy, that he had not yet laid it before the Cabinet, but when he had done so, and was in a position to answer it, he would lose no time in laying the despatch on the table of the House. This statement produced an extraordinary sensation amongst the occupants of the Treasury Bench, for it is contrary to all rule that the Foreign Minister should announce to either House the receipt of a despatch before his colleagues have seen it.

*March 19th.*—The Municipality of Nice has protested against the annexation, and sent a deputation to Turin to lay their petition before the King, asking to form an independent State if it should be necessary to separate them from Sardinia.

*March 23rd.*—Lady Derby and Lady Edward Thynne called, and both said that there has been a secret correspondence between the Emperor and Lord Palmerston, and it was said in the House

---

[1] Now Marquis of Ripon, and late Viceroy of India.

of Commons the night that Lord John Russell mentioned M. de
Thouvenel's despatch, adding that he had not yet shown it to his
colleagues, that he had discovered Lord Palmerston's correspondence, and was so angry that he did this out of revenge.  The
Emperor seems to have betrayed Palmerston's confidence, for all
Paris is talking of these letters, and expressing their astonishment
at such a transaction.  Louis Napoleon has evidently done this to
revenge himself for the Government's not being as subservient
about the Savoy business as he expected ; and it is easy to understand now why the Ministers were so eager to please him about
the treaty, in hopes, probably, that he would overlook their remonstrances on the annexation of Savoy, which the tone of the
Houses of Parliament obliged them to make.  It is evident from
their desperate attempts to silence all discussion that they were
very anxious not to interfere with the Emperor's projects.  The
annexation of Savoy, together with the neutral States of Chablais
and Faucigny, which is now a *fait accompli*, has shaken the confidence of the people in the Government.  There is a *bon mot* of
the Princess Clothilde on this subject which is worth recording.
Alluding to the transfer of Savoy to France and her own unwel-
come marriage, she said : 'Quand on a vendu l'enfant, on peut
bien vendre le berceau.'

*March 26th.*—Lord John Russell made a violent speech against
Louis Napoleon last night in the House of Commons, and said
that England must not sacrifice the alliances of the rest of Europe
for the sake of France.  I hear that Persigny was in the House
and was in a dreadful state, exclaiming : 'Quel langage !  Faut-
il entendre de pareilles choses contre mon maître !  C'est à ne pas
y tenir !'  Lady Palmerston told Lady Tankerville that they are
dreadfully afraid of Louis Napoleon—that she believed he had
promised to allow Russia to take Constantinople, had promised
Saxony to Prussia, and meant to take Belgium for himself ; but
this is not credible.

*Hon. E. A. J. Harris to Lord M. (on the annexation of Savoy).*

Berne : March 26, 1860.

Dear Malmesbury,—  .  .  .  I wrote to you on October 15, 1858,
officially the first intimation of this business which I received from the

Swiss President, sending it under flying seal to Lord Cowley, and calling his attention to it in a separate despatch. The rumour was not believed at the time. I again wrote to you officially on the subject May 7, 1859. Neither of these has been comprised in the published despatches.

I do not believe in the *signed* 'Pacte de famille.' I think there was a verbal understanding between Louis Napoleon and Cavour in the autumn of 1858 at Biarritz. This verbal understanding was re-peated between Cavour and Walewski in January 1859, but they kept clear of written agreements in order to be able to say, 'There has been no treaty, agreement, &c., to cede, &c., &c.' But it was a compact between the giant and the dwarf in the fable from which the results followed which might have been anticipated.

> *   *   *   *   *   *   *   *
>
> Ever your affectionate brother,
>
> E. A. J. HARRIS.

*March 30th.*—I dined at the Palace yesterday. The Prince told me that Louis Napoleon had given them hopes that he would not annex Chablais and Faucigny, but that the Queen had received the news that the Emperor had sent for Lord Cowley, and had told him that he regretted very much being unable to keep his promise, but that Benedetti had made a mistake in drawing up the treaty, and it could not now be altered. I observed that it was of course easy to judge of events after they had occurred, but I could not understand why, when the Government became aware of the Emperor's intention to annex Savoy, they did not imme-diately apply to the Great Powers to join in a protest with England against the annexation. His Royal Highness answered, 'Of course they ought to have done so.'

*March 31st.*—Lord Grey brought on the question of China, and I was obliged to speak, as Lord Derby is at Knowsley.

*April 2nd.*—At the Duchess of Somerset's party Lord Palmer-ston came up to me when I was talking to Lord Wodehouse, and shook hands in a very friendly manner, saying : 'Are you two settling the affairs of Europe?' and continued talking. Whilst the conversation was going on, Persigny passed and hardly bowed to Lord Palmerston. He afterwards came to me and abused the Government and Lord John for his speech on the 26th ; adding, what was perfectly true, that his threat of making other alliances was most imprudent, and, of course, would oblige the Emperor to do the same. He concluded, 'Et c'est déjà fait.'

There is a report that the Persignys are to return to Paris. He had a serious quarrel with Lady Palmerston at Countess Apponyi's a few days ago, lost his temper and all control, abusing her and Lord Palmerston in an audible voice. He was obliged afterwards to make an apology, but after such a scene he will probably be replaced.

M. de la Rive has arrived from Switzerland. He says that they are in a state of great alarm for their independence, as Louis Napoleon is now intriguing with the Catholic party at Geneva to get them to ask to be annexed to France, and if half a dozen rascals can be found to do it, he will call that the 'voice of the people,' and seize Geneva at once. The part of the Channel fleet which was at Lisbon was telegraphed for after Lord John Russell's speech.

*April 14th.* — It rained, snowed, and hailed at intervals all through the day, with north-east wind and fog. This sort of weather has now lasted six months.

*April 16th.* — It is said that the Emperor has offered Mr. Whitworth 10,000*l.* a year for life if he will come to France and manufacture his newly-invented cannon for him exclusively, and Mr. Whitworth has had the patriotism to refuse.

*April 19th.* — A debate in the House of Lords on the Reform Bill, on Lord Grey's motion for a Committee.

Madam Bernstorff told me that Persigny said to her before he went to Paris, 'Je vous jure, par tout ce qu'il y a de plus sacré, par la tête de mes enfants (et vous savez comme j'aime mes enfants), que l'Empereur n'a pas de vues ambitieuses. Il ne désire et ne veut rien, et il ne prendrait rien si on le lui offrait.' M. d'Azeglio told Lady Malmesbury that he believed the report of the Emperor being in bad health. D'Azeglio also said Persigny had made him a terrible scene, accusing him 'de faire la propagande' in England against the annexation of Savoy. He added that it was an unjust accusation, as he had known for a long time that Cavour intended to give up Savoy to France. This last assertion is certainly true, as he always held it out as a bait to Louis

Napoleon, though he pretended to be furious when the event happened.

*May 3rd.*—At the fancy ball at the Hôtel d'Albe, the Princess Mathilde was, I hear, dressed as an Indian, and had had her skin dyed brown. Her dress was of the scantiest, very *décolletée*, her arms bare up to the shoulders, with a narrow band by way of sleeve, fastened with a brooch. The body was slit under the arm to the waist, showing the skin. The drapery behind was transparent, which she was probably not aware of, as she had not dyed her skin in that particular place, and the effect was awful.

*May 7th.*—The Government are on very bad terms with France. The Emperor told Lord Cowley that he could no longer curb his people if England did not change her line of policy. This accounts for the gloomy looks of the Government in the House of Lords, and their request to postpone the discussion on Savoy, which was to have taken place to-day.

*May 9th.*—Concert at the Palace, where the heat was so great that several ladies fainted, as did Mr. Dallas, the American Minister. Sidney Herbert was very cordial to me, which I am glad of.

*May 13th.*—I hear that all sorts of stories are going about in consequence of my having been seen talking to Lady Palmerston at her party yesterday—' a coalition, &c.' But no one knows the real truth, which is, that I was deputed by Lord Derby and Disraeli to tell her that we meant to throw out the Duty on Paper Bill (for which she thanked us), and, further, to say that if Mackinnon's motion for postponing the Reform Bill until after the census of 1861 passed, and if Lord John and other members of the Government (meaning Gladstone and Milner Gibson) went out in consequence, and joined the Radicals against the Government, we would engage ourselves to support Lord Palmerston against them for this session. Lady Palmerston expressed herself as being very grateful for the offer, but said she did not think Lord John would go out if beaten.

*May 15th.*—Garibaldi has landed in Sicily, and it is said that some English ships prevented the Neapolitan ships from firing upon him.

*May 21st.*—I went to the debate in the House of Lords on

the Paper Duty. I never saw any place so crowded as the Peers' benches, the ladies' gallery and the steps of the throne, while the bar and the strangers' gallery were crammed.

Lord Lyndhurst opened the debate, showing a clearness of intellect and a memory which seemed hardly possible at his age ; his language forcible and eloquent, great information, no repetitions, altogether a most miraculous effort for a man of eighty-eight. It was his birthday, and he left a party of his children and grandchildren (who had assembled at his house to celebrate the occasion) in order to come and render this service, perhaps the last, to his country. Lord Monteagle then proposed his amendment, which was the rejection of the bill, and Lord Derby closed the debate by a splendid speech. The bill was thrown out by a majority of 89.

*June 1st.*—Garibaldi has stormed Palermo, so Sicily is now free, and, it is thought, will pronounce for annexation to Sardinia.

The Government are in convulsions. Lord John threatens to resign if the Reform Bill is not proceeded with, and Gladstone makes the same threat unless the Government propose a resolution to censure the House of Lords for rejecting their bill to repeal the paper duty, and that resolution is sanctioned by the Commons. In this critical state of public affairs, Lord Derby had desired me to go to Lady Palmerston and assure her of the support of our whole party against the Radicals, and to give a positive promise that we will not coalesce with them in or out of office. Disraeli is equally determined on this point.

*June 2nd.*—I had a satisfactory interview with Lord and Lady Palmerston yesterday. They are as anxious as we are to get rid of the Reform Bill, but do not exactly see their way. It is evident he does not wish to lose Lord John, though he would be very glad if Gladstone resigned.

Rumours of Lord John's and Gladstone's resignation continue. Some of the Whigs signed the round-robin blaming the former for his foreign policy, and asking him to resign. His only remark was ' Blackguards ! '

*June 8th.*—The adjourned debate upon Mr. Mackinnon's amendment to postpone the Reform Bill until after the census of 1861 came on yesterday. Sir James Fergusson rose to move that it be adjourned until the Scotch and Irish bills were introduced, but he was beaten by a majority of 21. The Government, except Lord John and Mr. Gladstone, are as much against the measure as we are.

*June 12th.*—The Emperor Napoleon went to Baden-Baden, to have a conference with the Prince Regent of Prussia, probably in the hope of making some arrangement about the Rhenish provinces, by promising some aggrandisement in another direction—perhaps Saxony; or to get him on his side, and by this means destroy the German League, which may interfere with his ambitious projects. But the Prince was on his guard, and invited all the German sovereigns and reigning princes to Baden to meet the Emperor. They all came, even the blind King of Hanover; no doubt to the disappointment of Louis Napoleon, who hoped to have a *tête-à-tête* with the Prince of Prussia.[1] He, however, seems to have put a good face on the matter and stayed from the 15th to the 17th, when he returned to Paris. All diplomatists consider it a *coup manqué*.

Garibaldi has taken Palermo by assault. The King's troops were, however, allowed to return to Naples. It is said that the King, by the advice of Louis Napoleon, means to give a constitution to his subjects, but they place no dependence upon him, and it will not save him.

*June 19th.*—The Bill for the Abolition of Church Rates is rejected by the House of Lords by a majority of 97 on the second reading.

*June 23rd.*—The Queen reviewed the Volunteers in Hyde Park. I went to Disraeli's house at Grosvenor Gate to see the sight, which was very fine. The enthusiasm of the men and spectators exceeded all description. There were 20,000 Volunteers, all active young men between eighteen and thirty. They went through their evolutions with the greatest steadiness and precision, and at the final advance in line, when they halted within a short distance of the Queen, and the band had ceased playing 'God save the Queen,' they raised a cheer which might have been heard for miles. This was taken up by the spectators, and the scene was so exciting that the Queen was quite overcome, and I saw

[1] Now Emperor of Germany, 1884.

many people the same.  It was enough to make an Englishman
proud of his country to see this wonderful demonstration of
patriotism and loyalty, and, as Lord Derby truly said in his speech
the same evening at Merchant Taylors' Hall : 'If the bare possibility of an insult to England could in six months raise a force
of 130,000 Volunteers, there is no doubt that, were the danger
imminent, we should have three times that number.'

*July 6th.*—Lord Palmerston has made a very good speech on
the resolution he proposes with respect to the Lords' rejection of the
Paper Bill.  Lord Derby said 'it was the best tight-rope dancing
he ever saw.'  It was, anyhow, a judicious act to prevent a collision between the two Houses.

*July 8th.*—Gladstone has not resigned, to the surprise of
everybody, for it was generally thought that he must do so after
his violent speech against Lord Palmerston.

*July 22nd.*—Lord Elphinstone is dead.  He returned very ill
from India, having had the Bombay fever.  He acted with great
courage and ability during the mutiny.  I was at Eton with him,
and he afterwards entered the Life Guards.

*July 24th.*—Lord Palmerston made a very plucky speech last
night in bringing in a bill to provide for the defences of the
country.  The French will be furious, for he said openly that
France was the only nation against which we had to defend ourselves.  And he did not conceal the fact that all our preparations were against the French.  Many consider his speech
imprudent, but that kind of imprudence is often the best policy.

Gladstone, who was always fond of music, is now quite enthusiastic about negro melodies, singing them with the greatest spirit
and enjoyment, never leaving out a verse, and evidently preferring
such as 'Camp Down Races.'

*August 1st.*—Lord Clanwilliam came to breakfast.  The
'Times' publishes a letter from Louis Napoleon to Persigny,
professing great friendship for England, and a desire for peace
with the whole world.  I attribute this letter to his fear of the
Volunteer movement, and his wish to stop our fortification, ship-
building, &c.

*August 3rd.*—Lord Palmerston's resolutions respecting the
loan to be raised for fortifying the dockyards were discussed in

Committee.   Mr. Lindsay proposed an amendment, ' That, as the main defence of Great Britain against aggression depends on an efficient navy, it is not now expedient to enter into a large expenditure on permanent fortifications.' This, after a long debate, was negatived by 268 to 39, and the resolution passed.

*August 7th.*—The Government had a majority of 33 on the Paper Duty Bill last night.

*August 8th.*—We got a letter from Lady Derby, announcing her daughter's marriage with Colonel Talbot.

*August 21st, Heron Court.*—Went to Christchurch to see my Volunteers reviewed by Colonel Luard, who appeared satisfied with them.

*Lord Derby to Lord M.*

Taymouth Castle : August 29, 1860.

My dear Malmesbury,—The Liverpool Conservatives have got up an address to me, which I understand is most numerously signed, expressive of entire approval of the course of our Government, and of their ' increased confidence,' &c., and they are very desirous that the presentation of the Address should be followed by a dinner (or, as they call it, a banquet), to celebrate at the same time the Conservative triumph in South Lancashire.   They are particularly anxious for your presence and Disraeli's, and if you could manage it I think it would both please them and do good.   I have told them that you are in Scotland, and that I thought you would not return until the latter end of October.   They wish me to fix a day, with your concurrence, between Saturday, the 13th, and Thursday, the 25th, and before I write to them or to D. I should be glad to know whether this will suit you. The later you can come, within these limits, the better probably it would suit your Scotch plans.

Ever yours sincerely,

DERBY.

*September 6th.*—Lady Adela Ibbotson died last Tuesday. Lady Jersey has now lost all her children.   Lady Adela was her last daughter, and though for many years they saw very little of her, as they did not forgive her marriage, yet since Lady Clementina's death Lady Jersey seems to have become fond of her, and the blow will therefore be much heavier now than if it had fallen a few years ago. I went to see her, and she expresses herself resigned to the will of God.

*September 7th.*—I went to Weymouth, where my yacht is to meet me.

Garibaldi entered Naples, accompanied only by his staff; the town is perfectly quiet, as all parties unite on the same side, and therefore there is no inducement to make a disturbance. All the forts have surrendered. Garibaldi and the English Admiral have exchanged visits. The former has given up the Neapolitan fleet to the Sardinian Admiral. The Sardinian troops have disembarked by order of the Dictator, as he is called. The whole army will arrive in Naples, and comprises 80,000 men, including the insurgent bands. The Sardinians have invaded the Papal States without any declaration of war. They have taken Pesaro, where they have made 1,200 Germans prisoners, also Fano and Urbino. General Lamoricière has concentrated his troops, amounting to 8,000 men, in Ancona, in defence of the Pope, and where it is said he will be attacked by 45,000 Sardinians.

*September 15th.*—In consequence of this violent act of invading Romagna, Louis Napoleon has recalled his Minister from Turin, leaving a *chargé d'affaires.* Is this a sham, intended to make the Courts of Europe believe that he disapproves of the invasion of the Roman States? There can be little doubt of it, as he had an interview with Cavour at Chambéry, and with General Cialdini at Nice, and that the whole of this violent proceeding was arranged with him, for the invasion took place directly after. This is too transparent to take anyone in, and will only confirm the distrust which of late years everything he says and does inspires.

*September 18th.*—I went out shooting, and could only kill three brace of partridges with great difficulty; they are so rare this year all over England that they fetch twelve shillings a brace in London.

*September 21st.*—The newspapers announce that a battle has been fought between Cialdini and Lamoricière,[1] in which the latter was completely defeated, as Lamoricière's whole army capitulated, and he, accompanied by a few horsemen, escaped through the

[1] Lamoricière was one of the best Algerian generals.

mountains and threw himself into Ancona. Great agitation reigns at Turin. Some suspicion is beginning to be felt respecting Garibaldi's intentions. His naming Saffi, an ultra-Radical, to be pro-Dictator of Sicily, and the arrival of Mazzini at Naples, coupled with Garibaldi's declaration that he will only proclaim the annexation of Naples to Sardinia from the top of the Quirinal, rather looks as if he would prefer being the head of an independent Republic to abdicating his authority in favour of Victor Emanuel.

*September 24th.*—News from Italy bad. Everything seems to be in confusion. Complete anarchy in Sicily. Great discord at Naples ; the roads infested with banditti, and no security for life. The King remains at Gaeta, and has a large army still faithful to him. The Sardinians have laid siege to Ancona by sea and land.

*September 28th.*—I have decided on buying Lord Wemyss's house in Stratford Place.

Garibaldi has been defeated at Capua by the King's troops. He has appointed Dumas, the novelist, Keeper of the Museum at Naples, and this has given immense dissatisfaction.

*September 29th.*—News from Italy is unfavourable for Garibaldi, for it now would appear that his successes did not proceed from his generalship, but from his meeting with no opposition ; as at Capua, when he and his best generals attacked the King of Naples' army, they were out-manœuvred and ran away. Whole regiments ran without firing a shot, but from the bare report that cavalry was coming to attack them, not even waiting to see if it were the case. It was a regular panic.

*October 1st.*—Letters from Ancona give a different account of the battle of Castel Fidardo from that published at Turin. It began at ten A.M. on September 18 ; the Papal troops had made a forced march of sixty leagues in six days ; the Sardinian army blocked the road to Ancona, and occupied with artillery the heights commanding it. Lamoricière's army fought gallantly against overwhelming odds ; 8,000 against 35,000. Numbers were cut down by grape-shot, and the Piedmontese thought they could easily capture the remainder, when Lamoricière commanded a charge with the bayonet, and succeeded in cutting through the compact mass of the Sardinian army, entering Ancona with, it is said, 1,500 men. The Papal army capitulated, with General Fanti, on September 29, and Lamoricière and his whole garrison are prisoners.

*October 21st.*—Victor Emanuel has entered the Neapolitan States, though the King of Naples is still at Gaeta..

*October 24th.*—The sovereigns of Russia and Austria, the Prince Regent of Prussia, and some minor German princes, met at Warsaw on the 20th. The reconciliation between the two Emperors is said to be complete. Louis Napoleon wanted very much to attend the conference, but could not get an invitation.

*November 1st.*—We were invited to Windsor; the party consists of Lord and Lady de Grey, Sir George and Lady Theresa Lewis. I sat by the Queen, and Lady M. by the Prince, at dinner. They are anxious that the Austrians should not go to war with Piedmont. Her Majesty was very anxious about Lord Derby, and made many inquiries about his health. The Holsteins dined at the Castle. After dinner the Prince, came up to Lady de Grey and Lady Malmesbury, and amused them immensely by giving an account of some ridiculous incidents that occurred at Levées. On one occasion a clergyman was to be presented. He, as the Prince said, 'overshot his mark,' and passed the Queen without the slightest notice. Lord De la Warr was very much put out, and began making signs to him to return. He stopped and stared at Lord De la Warr, imitating his gestures as exactly as he could, but nothing could induce him to return. Everybody was convulsed with laughter, for no etiquette could prevail against such a ridiculous scene.

*November 5th.*—I hear from the best authority that Lord John Russell wrote his last despatch to Mr. Hudson, dated October 27, 1860, without showing it to any of his colleagues, and that they are all indignant about it. The despatch in question is an unjustifiable one, approving of Victor Emanuel's invasion of the Roman States and Naples.[1] Lord John's first despatch, which was published, it is supposed, by order of Cavour,

---

[1] Sir J. Hudson told me that Lord John verbally encouraged the King to invade Naples, by asking his A.D.C. at Richmond whether he, the King, was not *afraid*. This was quite enough to send Victor Emanuel *anywhere*.

lost him his popularity with the Radicals, who were furious at his admitting the right of the Austrians to Venetia. He then wrote this, which is a direct recantation of the former one. The 'Times' of this morning attacks him violently for both despatches. Madame de Flahault told me that she heard it was Lord Palmerston who wrote the last despatch to Hudson, but I don't believe it, especially as she said she saw Lady John a short time ago, and she was much annoyed at the abuse in the 'Times' of Lord John's first despatch. She possibly made him write the last to try and set himself right with the public ; but all he has got is a still more severe article in the 'Times.'

Capua was bombarded on November 1, and capitulated on the 2nd.

*November 10th.*—When Brünnow read Lord John Russell's despatch of the 27th to Hudson, he observed, ' Ce n'est pas de la diplomatie, c'est de la polissonnerie.' It did not produce this effect upon Cavour, who, when Hudson read it to him, nearly fainted from joy. On the 8th, Garibaldi, accompanied by the Ministry, formally presented to the King the result of the *plébiscite* in the Throne-room. The Minister, Signor Conforto, spoke as follows : ' Sire, the Neapolitan people assembled in their Electoral Comitia have proclaimed you King by an immense majority ; 9,000,000 Italians are uniting themselves to the other provinces, which your Majesty governs with so much wisdom, verifying your solemn promise that Italy should belong to the Italians.'

The King said a few words, which are not recorded. The deed of annexation was then drawn up. The Dictatorship ceased, and the Ministry resigned. The following day, November 9, Garibaldi left Naples to return to his residence in the island of Caprera, having apparently accepted neither honours nor money.

The speeches at the Lord Mayor's dinner yesterday were uninteresting, and no declaration of policy on the part of the Government. Palmerston praised the glorious successes of our troops in China, and the Volunteers. Several of our party were present to do honour to the Lord Mayor, who is a Tory. None of the foreign Ministers were there, except Persigny and d'Azeglio ; the former spoke very well in French.

*November* 13*th.*—A leading article of the ' Times ' to-day is a panegyric upon Hudson and a great abuse of Lord John Russell, but more damaging to the former than to the latter, as it praises Hudson for having disobeyed the instructions of two successive Governments, and acted according to the wishes of the people of England.

*November* 14*th.*—Lord Dundonald's funeral took place this morning in Westminster Abbey. He died on October 31, having lived just long enough to complete his memoirs, of which he sent a copy to the Prince Consort. Admiral Sir Charles Napier only survived him a few days.

The Prince of Wales, who has been to Canada, arrived this morning at Plymouth. His ship, the ' Hero,' was so slow, that he was detained long enough to cause considerable anxiety.

*November* 16*th.*—The Empress of the French arrived in London, and drove with her suite to Claridge's Hotel in hack cabs. The following morning she went out shopping on foot, and to the Crystal Palace in the afternoon. The object of her journey is not known. Some say she is in bad health, and is going to Hamilton Palace for change of air ; another report is that she is unhappy at her sister's death.

The King of Italy seems to have treated his new subjects with very little consideration. His entry into Naples was a failure, as he fixed three different days ; and when he did at last arrive it was an hour too soon, and none of the preparations were completed. He must feel humiliated, for it is Garibaldi who has conquered the kingdom for him. He gives it him, refusing all rewards, resisting all entreaties to remain ; and, after giving up the Dictatorship and saluting Victor Emanuel as King of Italy, embarks the next morning, the 8th, before daylight, for his home in Caprera, paying Admiral Mundy a farewell visit on his way. Something must have occurred to disgust him with the King. It is said that at a great banquet on the day of the King's arrival in Naples, the officers of the Piedmontese army drank the health of Victor Emanuel but not Garibaldi's, whose name was never even mentioned.

*November* 19*th.*—I went to Buckenham.

*November* 25*th.*—The Empress Eugénie is going to Osborne on December 5.

*November* 26*th*.—M. de Flahault is named Ambassador in place of M. de Persigny, who was recalled in consequence of a quarrel he had with Lord Palmerston. Calling on *her*, I found her much pleased, but anxious for her husband's health, which is not strong.

The relations between England and France are not satisfactory. Lord Palmerston, who only sees through the eyes of d'Azeglio, is angry with the Emperor for his uncertain policy in Italy, which favours the Reactionists; and certainly things are going on badly for Victor Emanuel at Naples, Mr. Elliot, our Minister, having written to Lord John, saying that, bad as the late Government was, this one is much worse.

*November* 28*th*.—Lady Tankerville called and told me she went to see Lady Palmerston this morning. Whilst she was there Lord Palmerston came in in a furious passion with the Emperor of the French for preventing the bombardment of Gaeta, and saying the atrocities committed by Francis II. were dreadful; that he had ordered people's eyes to be put out, their noses cut off, &c., and that it was necessary to put an end to this state of things. Lady Tankerville expressed her disbelief of this story; at which Lord Palmerston got more angry and said it was official and therefore must be true.

*December* 1*st*.—Saw de Persigny, who abused Palmerston, saying he is not at all the man he used to be; that he was completely led by d'Azeglio, and believed everything he told him. He said the Emperor never would have annexed Savoy or Nice if it had not been for the English Government, who would not abide by the Treaty of Villafranca. He told them from the beginning that if Sardinia annexed Tuscany he must then have Savoy, as he could not sacrifice 50,000 Frenchmen merely to aggrandise Sardinia without some compensation to France. The dispute at present between our two Governments is about Gaeta, the French forbidding the bombardment, and Lord Palmerston, pushed on by Azeglio, being for it. They had a violent quarrel, and Lord Palmerston applied for Persigny's recall.

*Lord Derby to Lord M.*

Knowsley : December 4, 1860.

My dear Malmesbury,—I have been lazily intending to write to you for the last two or three days, when, ' to fire my flagging zeal,' I received this morning your letter of yesterday, and for which, and the political gossip it contains, many thanks. You disappoint me, however, by saying you must make this an exceptional year to your shooting visits, as I had hoped to catch you for the week after Bath's party, by which time I may hope to be about again, though I hardly expect to have a gun in hand this season. I am only afraid, if we have a hard frost at Christmas, that it may drive our woodcocks—at present it looks like the best year I have ever known. We have tried no coverts, but the park has been full. About the 14th of last month Freddy and Pat Talbot killed twelve : on the 24th Talbot alone killed twenty-two of twenty-four which he saw ; and yesterday the two went again into the park to see if any more were come, and killed sixteen, and they say ought to have killed four or five more. Fifty in three days over the same ground. Of yesterday's sixteen, my Lady has sent you up four with a hare. We have yet no pheasants, and I hardly know how I shall get through my shooting, even with the aid of two sons and a son-in-law, when they are here. I shall be very glad to see you at any time for a political chat, and if you will give me forty-eight, or even thirty-six hours, bring your gun also, and I will give you a nice little day over ground which I believe you have never been on ! Don't come, however, for a fortnight, as my Lady and I shall be absolutely *tête-à-tête*, except next Saturday and Sunday. I had a message yesterday from Taylor, who is on a visit at Gerard's, to know if I would see him to-day or to-morrow, to which of course I said yes, but am not surprised that he did not come over such a day as to-day has been. I shall hear from him all the little party details ; but I apprehend that our policy this year as well as last must be the ' masterly inactivity ' which was found so successful. Italy is a grand *imbroglio*, in which, however, France has the game in her hand so far as Rome is concerned, with the full power, of which she seems to mean to avail herself, of thwarting the Sardinian and united policy. Her conduct at Gaeta has been incomprehensible, except on the supposition that she wishes to keep the pot boiling, in hopes, in some way or another, of profiting by its boiling over. John Russell must not be let off his last despatch when Parliament meets, which I hear, as I supposed, is to be on Tuesday, February 5. Flahault's appointment is, I think, a good one, in spite of his age, but'I hear the ladies of his family say it will be too much for him. I am amused at Persigny, at last, having to confide his woes and grievances to your friendly bosom ! Madame is of course *tout éplorée.*

Ever yours sincerely,<br>DERBY.

*December 10th.*—The English and French in China hate each other. The latter are allowed to plunder, whilst our men are flogged if they take the smallest trifle without payment for it. Parkes and Loch are returned safe to the camp,[1] but it is feared that Captain Brabazon has been taken by the Chinese and murdered. Two others are missing, one of whom is the 'Times' correspondent.

The French Empress has been to Windsor, and the Queen and Prince, with Princess Alice, returned the visit.

*December 19th, Heron Court.*—Colonel Charteris, Mr. Barrington, and Lochiel had a good day up the Moor's river, killing seventy-two head of wild-fowl. Twelve degrees of frost. Matilda Butler's marriage with Lord Otho Fitzgerald is just announced, but it is not to take place until she is better, and may likely never do so at all, as she is in a dangerous state of health from an affection of the lungs, and the doctors will not allow her to be married at present.[2]

*December 24th.*—Sixteen degrees of frost last night. I went to London.

*Lord Derby to Lord M.*

Knowsley : December 26, 1860.

My dear Malmesbury,—I am obliged to you for a sight of Disraeli's letter, which I return. He had not written to me on the subject ; and I hope has not taken offence at my telling him in my last letter that I

---

[1] This refers to the surrender of Mr. (now Sir Harry) Parkes and Mr. (now Sir Henry) Loch by the Chinese, after their confinement for a month or more in a temple at Pekin, under hourly apprehension, and indeed threats, that at any moment they might be taken into the courtyard and executed.

[2] She died soon after, and Lord Otho married Lady Londesborough ; both the last dying in 1884.

thought he had gone rather too far in his declaration of 'no compromise' on the subject of Church-rates. In principle he is right; but it was our moderation and the refusal of the other side to listen to any terms which mainly caused the dwindling of the House of Commons majority and thus made *our* work the easier. I am afraid that Disraeli's outspoken declaration will lose us this advantage, which will not be counterbalanced by the increased support of the thoroughgoing Churchmen; and though the House of Lords will no doubt stand to their colours, yet an increased House of Commons majority, which I apprehend, will add to our difficulties. Observe that I am entirely against our originating any measure; but I doubt the policy of shutting the door beforehand against any overtures of our opponents. As to the main question of Disraeli's letter to you, I am very glad to find that he takes the view he does of our policy; and I shall be pleased to hear of the renewal of your confidential communications with *the Palmerstons*, for I suppose my Lady counts—*pour quelque chose*. I should not be afraid of entering on these *quasi* negotiations too soon. I believe Disraeli is quite accurate in his estimate of the relations between the Government and the Bright and Cobden party.

I think that in your communications with Palmerston you cannot be too explicit. He is a gentleman, and will know that you and I are dealing with him *de bonne foi*, and will not suspect a 'dodge,' if we make any exception to our promise of support. I should, however, be quite ready to assure him that, though we might, in debate, object to some of the 'sayings and doings' of the Foreign Office (and chiefly the *sayings*, or rather *writings*), we would not countenance any movement on the subject of foreign policy calculated to defeat the Government, unless it were on the impossible supposition that they should desire us to take an active part in an attack by Sardinia and France on Venetia. I cannot believe that the Government will be so mad as to sanction such a policy; but an exception made in such a case from our promise of support will rather serve to strengthen than to shake a belief in the sincerity of our general profession.

You seem to have had good sport with the wild-fowl. I am afraid my shooting will be quite spoilt by the intense severity of the weather, compared to which yours is a summer climate. You talk of the thermometer at eighteen: we had it at five the night before last, and last night one degree above zero, and at Windham Hornby's house, which lies lower and damper than this, it is said to have been, the night before last, at five below zero; what it was last night I do not know. Except that it keeps me from going out of the house, I do not find that this severe cold retards my recovery, which goes on, though slowly. I hobble about the house, though I am still obliged to be carried *down* stairs.

.    .    .    .    .    .    .    .

Ever yours sincerely,

DERBY.

*December 28th.*—Intense cold. Peace with China was signed at Pekin on October 24 by Lord Elgin and Prince Kung, brother of the Emperor. The Summer Palace of the Emperor has been plundered and burnt by order of Lord Elgin, in revenge for the cruelties committed upon the English and French prisoners whom they took treacherously on September 10. They were taken to the Summer Palace and tortured with the Emperor's sanction, so it was considered by our diplomatists and generals that the most just punishment was to destroy his property and not to burn the town, which would only have punished his subjects.

After the two armies had carried off everything they could, they destroyed property, it is said, amounting to at least two millions sterling. The town of Pekin disappointed everybody; it has been very magnificent, but is now in a state of complete decay, and so ruinous that it was with the greatest difficulty they could find a house to lodge Lord Elgin. It is feared that Captain Brabazon has been beheaded with the French Abbé Huc. They were taken to a Chinese general who had just been wounded by the English, and who in his rage ordered their execution.

*From Mr. Bidwell to Lord M.*

Foreign Office : December 28, 1860.

My dear Lord,—  .  .  .  .  I wanted much to see you, as I have learnt much of many things while I have been away, and from two distinguished people I heard you spoken of to my immense pleasure.

I went away, as I intended, right away to the south, and I spent five agreeable days at Algiers, basking in sunshine or shading myself under palm-trees, eating green peas and fresh strawberries, and I have come back to this! I went over to Algiers and lived there with Cobden! When we started I thought of Jonah, and was almost tempted to suggest a similar fate, for it came on to blow awfully, and we were knocked about off Minorca in great style.

However, Cobden and I became immense friends, for he gained my heart by the way he spoke of you. He said he had never been so struck or so surprised as on reading the Italian Blue-Book, and he should certainly have voted with the Government, and wondered why it had not been laid on the table before the want of confidence vote. We got on famously together, for I puzzled him with an apt quotation from Horace in one of our first conversations, and he frankly confessed that he had forgotten his classics—so ever afterwards, whenever he got the better of me on subjects of political economy, I brought up Numidia, Jugurtha, and Masinissa, and so we discussed Algiers and his treaty. . . . . I also had a long talk with Lord Cowley at Paris. He does not hit it off with Lord J., and once when I happened to mention you, he burst out: 'I wish to God he was back at the Foreign Office again!'

Ever yours faithfully,<br>BIDWELL.

## 1861

*January 1st, Heron Court.*—After three weeks of very hard weather, the wind veered to the south-west, with heavy rains, which flooded the river.

*January 8th.*—Thermometer again down to sixteen degrees.

*January 12th.*—My old servant, John Brenton, who has been with me five-and-twenty years, suddenly went out of his mind, and is, I am afraid, hopelessly insane. He has been a most faithful follower, and I feel for him as if he were a friend and relation. I have sent him to a private asylum at Salisbury, but with very little hope of his recovery.

*January 21st.*—I heard to-day a good story of the present Duke of Wellington. He and the Duchess were invited to Windsor. She was in London, and went; but the Duke, having a party at Strathfieldsaye, which he did not like to put off, sent an excuse, and when he was told of the offence he had given, he replied, 'Her Majesty has no right to be angry; I obeyed the back of the card, and the Duchess obeyed the front.' The invitation cards have printed directions on the back, desiring that the card should be returned should the ladies and gentlemen invited be away from London.

*January 23rd.*—I received a bad account of my servant from

the asylum.  They have been obliged to put him under chloroform, and give him medicine and nourishment by means of a stomach-pump.  He has a room to himself, well fitted up, and two men to take care of him.

*January* 31*st.*—A flock of wild swans pitched in Parley Heath.  I posted the gentlemen, and the swans were driven to them.  Mr. Mills and I killed three.

Lord Bath arrived.

*February* 5*th, London.*—No amendment to the Address was proposed in the House of Lords, but Lord Derby made one of his slashing speeches on the foreign policy of the Government.  In the Commons, Mr. White moved an amendment in favour of Reform, which was negatived.

*February* 10*th.*—Mr. H. Vernon, Lady Selina's husband, died a few days ago of rheumatic fever at Tottenham.

*February* 16*th.*—Gaeta surrendered on the 13th, and the King, Queen, and royal family embarked on board a French vessel.

*Mr. Disraeli to Lord M.*

House of Lords : February 22, 1861.

My dear Malmesbury,—I fear Fitzgerald is shaky about the great battle on Wednesday—Church-rates !  Pray write to him *decidedly*; it will never do to have our own men run riot.

The fact is, in internal politics there is only one question now, the maintenance of the Church.  There can be no refraining or false Liberalism on such a subject.  They are both out of fashion, too.

Your House of Lords' pens and ink must be my excuse for this miserable scrawl.        Yours ever,        D.

*March* 9*th.*—The affair of Mirès, the banker, is making a great noise in Paris.  Some time ago he had a great quarrel with one of his ex-partners, and the latter accused him of frauds in connection with a speculation called Roman Railways.  A prosecution was instituted against him, but he went to the Emperor, who stopped the course of justice.  It is supposed that he would have made revelations implicating high personages about the Court.  As the distress consequent on the stoppage of Mirès' bank is very great, and falls principally on the lower classes, it must make the Court very unpopular.  M. Jules Favre declared that he would, on the approaching discussion on the Address, denounce the extraction of a wealthy man from the fangs of the law, when a poor man who offends from want is relentlessly prosecuted. The threat caused alarm in high quarters. A Cabinet Council was held ; most of the Ministers were of opinion that Mirès ought to be protected from prosecution for the reason that many persons, some of them *pillars of the State*, might turn out to be implicated in his acts. Count de Persigny, however, insisted that he should be treated like everybody else. The Emperor took the same view, and Mirès has been sent to prison, where he is to be kept in solitary confinement. One of the council of surveillance of his bank, Vicomte de Richemont, has committed suicide, and another, Count Simeon, has left France. Storms seem to be collecting round the Emperor on all sides. The bishops and clergy are denouncing him from the pulpit and in pastoral letters as the enemy of the Pope and the Catholic religion.

*March* 13*th.*—Lord Palmerston yesterday moved two resolutions for the appointment of a select committee to consider the system of promotion and retirement in the Royal Navy, and that it be an instruction to the select committee to inquire into the Board of Admiralty. The first resolution was agreed to without a division, and the second was carried on a division by 96 to 33.

*March* 14*th.*—The House of Commons threw out Mr. Locke-King's bill for reducing the county franchise to 10*l.*, by a majority of 28. We had agreed with the Government that if they helped us to throw out this bill we would help them to pass Lord Palmerston's resolution, reversing their former vote on the payment of the Navy.

*March* 23*rd.*—I crossed to Paris, and thence proceeded by the Western Railway to Brittany. I am much struck with the appearance of the country. Laval is a most interesting town ; the inn not at all a bad one, and a good dinner at the *table d'hôte*. The waiter had a face and figure which nobody can forget, and boasted to me that he could fold a napkin in twenty-four different ways. The bridge at Laval once divided the English from the French portions of France. The Castle is an old donjon, with the most frightful *oubliettes*.

*March 28th.*—I took a carriage and post-horses to Vitré, stopping on my road to see a very curious Druidical circle, in the middle of an oak-wood, and composed of immense stones supported by others of equal size, called 'La Grotte des Fées.' At Vitré there is a very fine mediæval gateway with two round towers.

*March 29th.*—Went on to Rennes. Very good inn and curiosity shop, in which I bought a box which the archbishop wished to sell. It was of old enamel inlaid on gold, which the prelate had used for holding the holy wafer, and with that view had the sacred monogram engraved inside. It had been given by Louis XII. to his Minister, Cardinal Amboise, whose arms, with the *fleur de lys*, are on it, with a burning mountain as a rebus on the name of his place of residence—*Chaumont.*

*March 31st.*—From Rennes I went to the Baie des Trépassés, the wildest sea-view it is possible to imagine, where there is a picturesque rock called the Torch of Penmarch, on which a chapel has been erected, and round which the sea is continually breaking. There is a current here which washes those who perish in the Bay of Biscay up on this shore, and it is seldom that the rocks on this stormy coast are without a dead body, which circumstance gives its sinister name to this fatal place. From thence I went to Quimper, with its beautiful spires and churches, and thence made expeditions to the dolmens of Carnac[1] and to St. Auray. Here, in a vault some hundred feet deep, looking very like a large well, lie, in full view, the bones of the Royalists who were taken and murdered by the Republican soldiers during the great French Revolution after our fatal expedition at Quibéron. A very old man, evidently one of that terrible epoch, was looking down with his eyes full of tears.

*April 16th, London.*—I had an audience of the Emperor before leaving Paris, and found him very much prejudiced against the whole Tory party, having been told an enormous quantity of lies, which he apparently believed. I spoke very openly to him,

---

[1] Here I met a very intelligent priest, who went round with me to show me this mile of Druidical stones, and the great barrow of St. Michel. He had studied the origin of these mysterious remains, and proved, I think satisfactorily, that they were sepulchres.

and think I succeeded in undeceiving him on some points,
but one never can be sure, as he carries dissimulation to the
greatest pitch. I think the party he would like to see governing
England are the Radicals. He fears our aristocracy, whom he
knows to be thoroughly English, and the most energetic of all
the classes ; and he would like a Government who would diminish
our army and navy, and so weaken our influence abroad. He
entered into the whole question of Italy, and confessed that he
was now much perplexed what to do about Rome. He evidently
would like to throw over the Pope, but fears the Church party.
He abused Palmerston. Madame Walewska was very friendly.
She is in greater favour with the Emperor than ever. I also
saw the Persignys, and was well received by both. Madame de
Persigny regrets England, and perhaps hopes, as they were
recalled in consequence of a quarrel with Lord Palmerston, that
the return of Tories to office might enable them to go back.

*April 18th.*—Our party last night threw out in the House of
Commons Mr. Monckton Milnes' bill for legalising marriage with
a deceased wife's sister by a majority of 5, and the Trustees
of Charities Bill by 29 ; the latter being a question of Church
*versus* Dissenters.

*May 1st.*—Dined at the Mansion House, where there was
a great dinner to Lord Derby.

*May 3rd.*—Mr. Horsfall's amendment to reduce the tea duty to
a shilling was rejected in the House of Commons by 18.

*May 5th.*—The state of affairs in America is getting worse
every day, and civil war has actually begun. The first shot was
fired by the Secessionists on April 12 against Fort Sumter,
in Charleston Harbour, and after a bombardment of forty hours
Major Anderson surrendered. The fort was completely destroyed, but not a single man killed on either side. The last news
mentions the destruction of Norfolk Dockyard, with eleven ships
of war, to prevent their falling into the hands of the insurgents.

*May 13th.*—There are dreadful accounts from the country,
which makes one fear a worse harvest than the last. Captain
McClintock, who has just returned from the Polar regions,
has reported to the Admiralty that there is an accumulation
of three years' ice.

*May* 14*th.*—The Duc de Richelieu told me that the only thing which could prevent a war with France was Lord Derby's return to office. His late speech, in which he advocated two kingdoms of Italy divided by the Papal States, was admirable, and his policy the only one to follow to ensure a sincere friendship between England and France.

*May* 31*st.*—The adjourned debate upon the Paper Duty came on, and the Government had a majority of 15.

*June* 2*nd.*—Lord Ossulston attributes the bad division on the Paper Duty to the stupid dislike of our party to Disraeli and their wish not to turn out the Government to put him in office; but I think it more probable that they feared a dissolution.

*June* 5*th.*—I received a letter this morning from my agent, with the melancholy news that my poor old servant, John Brenton, had cut his throat yesterday. On a *post-mortem* examination they found a drop of blood on the brain, which no doubt was the cause of his insanity; and this resulted from a fall he had from his pony, when he was stunned, but not apparently injured, and took no notice of it. He was the last man likely to go mad, as he was shrewd and practical to a degree, and remarkable for his common-sense and good nerve. He had served my grandfather, father, and myself for forty years, and was of that class of servant, now long extinct, born on the place and brought up in the family, who treated him as one of themselves, and on the same footing by my friends and acquaintances, who were much amused at his dry wit and intelligence.[1]

*June* 6*th.*—I dined with the Duke of Cambridge, and there heard of the death of Count Cavour, which took place this morning. It is too soon to judge of his character, although he was certainly a great statesman and deep intriguer.

*June* 7*th.*—We had a dinner for the Duchess of Cambridge and Princess Mary. Tankervilles, Lady Chesterfield, Carnarvons,

---

[1] I remember a specimen of the former which amused me much at the time. I was fishing in Loch Arkaig, which is fifteen miles long, and having great sport, I exclaimed to John Brenton in my excitement, ' I wish I had this lake at Heron Court!' 'I don't,' cried John, 'as it would drown your miserable estate and half the county besides.'

Lord Dunkellin, Lord Loughborough, Lord Hardwicke, Lord Stanhope, Mr. Barrington, &c.   Afterwards to Madame Apponyi's ball.

*June 13th.*—Sir John and Lady Crampton called. She was Miss Balfe, and sang for one or two seasons at Covent Garden ; Sir John then married her and took her to St. Petersburg, where he was Minister, and they are now just going to Madrid. She is very pretty and ladylike.

*June 14th.*—Dined with the Buccleuchs, and went to Lady Craven's ball. The marriage of her second daughter with Lord Ernest Bruce's eldest son is arranged.

*June 18th.*—Called on the Duchess of Marlborough, where Count Brandenburg told me that Louis Napoleon is going to send an Ambassador to Turin ; so Azeglio will be Ambassador in England. All the Corps Diplomatique have heard of my sending him an invitation as Sardinian *Minister*, and seem greatly delighted ; but nothing I can say will persuade them that I did so by mistake.

I went to Lady Molesworth's theatricals. The first piece, 'Un Caprice,' beautifully acted by Mesdemoiselles Duverger and Colas and Mr. Fechter ; the latter piece is *mauvais ton.*

*June 19th.*—Went to the fullest Drawing Room I ever saw, and in the evening to Lady Derby's—a small and pleasant party. Count Vitzthum was going about in a state of great excitement because the Neapolitans (as he said) had roasted alive four Piedmontese, and the latter had shot twenty Neapolitans.

Sir J. Trelawny's bill for abolishing Church-rates was rejected on the 17th on the third reading, House of Commons. The division was equal, 274 on both sides. The Speaker then gave his casting-vote against the bill.

*June 21st.*—Lord Lansdowne called on me ; he is grown very deaf, but his intellect remains clear.

A tremendous fire broke out in some warehouses on the banks of the Thames. I went in a Hansom cab to see it. It was awful beyond description. An explosion took place which threw down a wall close to Mr. Braidwood, and four or five of his brigade of firemen were crushed in a moment. At one time London Bridge station and a church near it were threatened with fire, as also the

Custom House, though on the opposite side of the river. There was fortunately no wind, or the whole of Southwark must have been destroyed.

The Lord Chancellor (Campbell) died suddenly last night. He had given a dinner, and was apparently in good health, but the next morning was found dead in his armchair.

*June 26th.*—Sir Richard Bethell is the new Lord Chancellor, and received to-day the Great Seal from the Queen. The Sultan is dead.

*June 27th.*—We dined with Lady Truro, where we met the Duc d'Aumale, a very gentlemanly and agreeable man.

*June 28th.*—Concert at Buckingham Palace. Whilst we were waiting for our carriage to go away Lord Derby joined us, and immediately after Lord John Russell came up. Lord Derby exclaimed, ' How do you do, Lord John ? You have got into very bad company.' He looked round at us all with a grim smile and said, ' I see I have ; ' when Lord Derby, looking at him attentively, observed that he was incorrectly dressed, having his Levée uniform instead of the full dress which he ought to have worn. Lord John said, ' I know I am wrong, and the porter wanted to turn me out.' ' Oh, did he ? ' exclaimed Lord Derby. ' Thou canst not say *I* did it.' Of course all those round laughed at this apt quotation from Shakespeare, and no one more than Lord John himself.

*July 6th.*—We went to the Duchess of Cambridge's breakfast at Kew—a small but very good party. Madame de Persigny had a pork-pie hat of blue velvet and a white veil which only came to the tip of her nose, her hair in a net, and a sash tied behind. I did not know her when she came up to speak, but recognised her by her lisping voice. She was most friendly, so I suppose she is looking forward to returning here as Ambassadress.

Dr. Bence Jones told me that Lord Herbert's case is hopeless. He might have lived many years, and Bence Jones did not say positively that he might not have got well had he given up office and led a quiet life. He told this to Lady Herbert, but she would not believe him. He is now so ill at Wilton that he cannot be moved to London, and she has written to the Duke of Cambridge to ask him to take his place at the dinner given on the Queen's birthday.

The news from Naples is very bad in an Italian sense. Complete anarchy prevails. The 'Reactionist brigands,' as the Piedmontese call them, increase every day, and no one's life is safe out of the town. The army is to be increased by 60,000 men, and to be commanded by Cialdini. It is said that Ricasoli, Cavour's successor, refuses to name Azeglio Ambassador. He is taking a very high tone, and made a very spirited speech in the Chambers, declaring that he would not give up another inch of Italian territory ; that the 'King's Government saw a territory to defend and a territory to recover ; it saw Rome, it saw Venice '—a pretty plain declaration of war to Austria.

*July* 13*th*.—All London is talking of a supposed attempt of Baron Vidal to murder his son yesterday week. The story is that they went to Claremont, where they remained about an hour. They had gone by rail to Twickenham, where they had hired horses to ride to Claremont, but the Baron diverged from the road under the pretence of calling on the Duc d'Aumale, and, on arriving in a secluded lane, made an attack upon his son, hitting him on the head with a stick or riding-whip, and cutting his forehead open. The young man galloped away, his father pursuing him, until he met a man and woman coming along the lane, when he rushed to them, imploring protection. They, of course, granted it, and a surgeon, who was sent for, sent his assistant with him to London, as he expressed the greatest terror of going alone with his father. The next morning he went to his uncle's house and told the story. The police were sent to arrest the Baron, but he had escaped to France.

*August* 3*rd, Heron Court.*—Mr. Mills called and told us of Lord Herbert's death, which took place at Wilton. He will be a great loss as a public man, being one of those who was looked upon as likely to be a future Prime Minister, but a still greater to his family and friends, who knew all the excellence of his disposition and generous character. Among the latter I must include myself.

*August* 6*th.*—News has arrived of a great battle having been fought at Manassas Gap, in Virginia, between the Federals and Secessionists, in which the former were totally routed.[1]

---

[1] This battle was afterwards known as Bull's Run.

Parliament was prorogued yesterday. Lord Herbert's death has obliged Lord Palmerston to rearrange his Cabinet. Sir George Lewis is War Secretary ; Sir George Grey, Home Secretary ; Sir Robert Peel, Secretary for Ireland ; Lord Ripon, Under Secretary for War ; Mr. Layard, Under Secretary for Foreign Affairs in the place of Lord Wodehouse, who resigned when Lord John became Earl Russell, as he would not submit to be second where, on all questions relating to foreign affairs, he had been first. It is supposed that he will have an Embassy, and the Whigs want Lords Cowley and Bloomfield and Sir Henry Bulwer to make room.

*August 11th.*—Went to church at Christchurch for afternoon service, and to my horror I found that seven babies were to be christened. Afterwards to Highcliffe, to see the Princess Edward, who was much amused when I related this to her, and said ' the clergyman ought to have used a watering-pot to sprinkle them.'

*August 21st.*—All the party from Highcliffe arrived. Some of us fished, and some walked to the top of Ramsdown. Lady Salisbury and Lord Odo Russell [1] also called, and he sang—a very fine tenor voice.

I went to meet my yacht at Weymouth.

*August 25th.*—There has been a great battle fought at Springfield, in which the Federals were defeated, and lost their best general, Lyons.

*August 30th.*—A most lovely day for our *fête* given to the Volunteers, the parade being in the park.

Lady Salisbury and the Russells came over from Bournemouth. I had to make a speech and present a rifle to the sergeant-major. We had a good band from Poole, to which the party danced till seven o'clock. I opened the ball with the Princess Edward of Saxe-Weimar. Croquet on the lawn and Aunt Sally in the more retired parts. Bowls and cricket in the park. An enormous quantity of eating and drinking in the courtyard—altogether the most animated scene, everyone appearing amused. About 2,000 people.

[1] This able and amiable man died as Ambassador at Berlin in August, 1884 : a great loss to the public service. In 1852 I sent him as our diplomatic agent to the Pope. He was created Lord Ampthill in 1881,

*September* 6*th*.—Poured all the morning, so we were obliged
to go in the brougham to Mr. Grantley Berkeley's cottage, where
we found Princess Edward, Lady Conyngham, and the Binghams
already arrived and looking extremely disgusted at the rain,
which was coming down in torrents. It is altogether a pretty,
wild place, and a few hundred pounds, which poor Berkeley has
*not* to spend, laid out upon it would make it quite lovely. The
sun came out, and we had a beautiful afternoon, which revived
the spirits of the party. We all amused ourselves after luncheon
by pulling up a number of lines which Berkeley had laid along
the banks of the river, and caught several fine eels. Mr. and
Mrs. Brett and Lord Ranelagh arrived in the evening.

*September* 12*th*.—The Bretts and Ranelagh left. The Princess,
Lady Conyngham, and Lord George Lennox came about one, and
we proceeded to draw up the lines which I had placed in the
Stour. The Princess pulled them up, and got three pike of
twelve or fourteen pounds, one large tench, and seven eels. The
latter and the large pike had been put on previously, but we all,
including the keeper, looked so innocent, that no one suspected
the trick.

*September* 14*th*.—News from America describes the Federals
as beaten in every engagement. Mr. Russell evidently got into
disgrace by his account of Bull's Run, and now writes more
cautiously ; being afraid, I suppose, of being tarred and feathered
—a common punishment in the Union. We had a great function
at Bournemouth on opening the new pier.

*September* 21*st*.—Returned to London.

*September* 23*rd*.—Left for Gedling, Lord Chesterfield's place.
Nobody here except Lord Granville, Colonel Forester, and Lord
Stanhope.

*September* 24*th*.—We killed 300 partridges and an immense
quantity of hares. The rents of this estate have not been raised
for more than fifty years, and consequently the farmers do not
complain of them, although they swarm.

*September* 27*th*.—I went to London and on to Paris ; Lady
Malmesbury to Knowsley.

From Paris I made a tour to see all the castles on the Loire. First to Blois, which is very interesting, as being the scene of the crimes of the later Valois. The apartment is shown in which Henri III. had the Duc de Guise assassinated. From thence to Amboise, where there is a round tower so spacious and so well built, that a carriage and four horses can drive up from the bottom to the battlements and terrace at the top. Abd-el-Kader had been imprisoned in this castle, and was released by Louis Napoleon. From there I proceeded to Loches, one of the donjons of Louis XI. Thence to Chenonceaux, the castle bower of Diane de Poictiers, built astride upon the Loire, now belonging to a dentist! I went to see Azy-le-Rideau, a beautiful castle belonging to M. de Briancourt, and in perfect order. On my way to Tours, I happened to find in 'Galignani' an account of the death of my dear friend, Lord Eglinton, who had been seized with apoplexy at Mr. Whyte-Melville's house, where he had gone to attend a golf meeting. He is a sad loss to our political party and to me personally. He used to complain to me that he constantly saw a figure retreating before his eyes, disappear and appear again—an evident proof that his brain suffered under some kind of pressure.

---

*November 9th.*—The Federals at Leesburg have lost six or seven hundred men. They crossed the Potomac, taking only two small boats, intending probably to surprise the Confederates. Having got across without opposition, they formed their whole force, about eighteen hundred men, in a field of twelve acres, with the river at their backs, the three other sides of the field being enclosed by a thick wood filled with their enemies, who immediately fired upon them from behind the trees. The Federals then attempted to re-cross the river, but having no boats except the two mentioned, a regular rout and dreadful loss of life ensued. The disgrace of it rests at present between Generals Macmillan and Scott. It is a fearfully cruel war.

I am alarmed at the state of America, and if the war continues they will, of course, gain experience, and the Northern provinces will be left with a fine army, which they may use in attempting the conquest of Canada, a country difficult to defend.

·*November 28th.*—Important news has just arrived by the ' Plata.' Messrs. Slidell and Mason, the Confederate Commissioners to England and France, with their secretaries, were forcibly taken out of the Royal Mail steamer ' Trent,' whilst on her passage from Havannah to St. Thomas, by the American war-ship 'San Jacinto.' The steamer ' Theodore,' with the Commissioners on board, ran the blockade at Charleston on October 18 ; they were accompanied by their families.   They left Havannah, on board the ' Trent,' on the 7th.   At noon on the 8th, as the ' Trent ' was approaching the narrow passage between the reefs, a large war-vessel was observed waiting ahead, and showing no colours.   On coming nearer, the 'Trent' hoisted her ensign, and met with no response from the man-of-war, which when within the eighth of a mile fired a round-shot across the 'Trent's' bows.   Captain Moir, of the 'Trent,' thereupon hailed the captain of the other ship, asking what he meant by stopping him.   He replied that he wished to send a boat on board, and at the same time one was lowered containing two officers and twenty men.   The officers came on board and demanded the 'Trent's' list of passengers, which was refused.   Lieutenant Fairfax, the officer in command of the party from the war-steamer (which proved to be the 'San Jacinto') then said that Captain Wilkes, his captain, had received reliable information that Messrs. Slidell, Eustace, Mason, and Farland were on board the ' Trent,' and demanded that they should be given up.   This was peremptorily refused, both by Captain Moir and Commander Williams, R.N., the naval agent in charge of the mails.   The lieutenant then said he would take charge of the steamer.   Commander Williams thereupon made a protest to the effect that he accused the Americans of piracy and of the violation of international law ; an act which, had he the means of defence, they would not have dared to attempt.   The Americans stated that they were short of provisions, and asked for a supply to maintain the prisoners.   Captain Moir furnished them with supplies, stating distinctly that they were for the exclusive use of the four gentlemen.   The American lieutenant then said that his orders were to take Captain Moir and his papers on board the

'San Jacinto,' and that the 'Trent' was to be moored near her, Captain Moir replied, 'You will find me on the quarter-deck.' The lieutenant, however, called his men together and went over the side, returned to the 'San Jacinto,' and the 'Trent' proceeded on her voyage. The despatches of the Commissioners did not fall into the hands of the Americans, as Mrs. Slidell is said to have concealed them inside her 'cage.'

As soon as this event was known at Liverpool an indignation meeting was held, and a resolution passed, insisting upon the Government demanding instant reparation for the insult offered to our flag.

*December 1st.*—Lord Lyndhurst declares that if the Government show the least wavering about this American outrage they must be turned out when Parliament meets.

*December 5th.*—A telegram has just been received announcing the death of Lady Canning on November 14. Lord Palmerston telegraphed immediately to Lady Stuart, who is at Highcliffe with Lady Waterford. The blow will be the more cruel as she expected the Cannings home next March.

*December 6th.*—Dined at Lady Tankerville's, where we met the Saxe-Weimars, Lord Granville, Ben Stanley, Count Brandenburg, and Miss Gorges. The Princess was low. She dreads the Prince being ordered to Canada. At present the two first battalions are under orders, and are to start at forty-eight hours' notice. Lord Granville told me that the Government would not be satisfied with anything except the restoration of Slidell and Mason. They have allowed the American Government seven days to come to a decision, and if they refuse Lord Lyons was to leave Washington directly.[1]

*December 8th.*—Lady Canning's death was broken to Lady Stuart de Rothesay by General Stuart. The shock was terrible, and she has not been able to leave her bed since. Mrs. Stuart had received a letter from Lady Canning on the 27th, only two days before the arrival of the telegram announcing her death, in which she said, 'Home now seems so near.'

*December 9th.*—Left London for Longleat, where we met a family party. Lord Bath, as usual, uncertain in his politics.

---

[1] The Emperor Louis Napoleon supported us manfully on this occasion.

Prince Albert is ill, and there is a sort of bulletin in the 'Times' which does not seem comfortable.  His illness is said to be gastric fever.

*December 12th.*—Very wet and stormy.  We went out shooting, though it blew a regular gale.  I got a letter to-day from Lady Ely, who says the Prince's illness is gastric fever and inflammation of the mucous membrane of the stomach, and that he is anxious about himself.  Lady Somerton and Mr. Fountaine, on the violin, played duets.  He plays with great taste, and brings out great tone in the slow passages.  Lady Louisa Fielding's voice is charming.  Big Ben's[1] conversation consisted of violent abuse of Disraeli and Lord Derby.

*December 13th.*—Left Longleat after a very pleasant visit. The bulletin about the Prince is not satisfactory ; no change in the symptoms.  Lady Munster has seen Dr. Jenner, who told her that the Prince's fever was of a typhoid character.  The Queen has sat up with him for two nights, and never leaves his room— quite in despair.

*December 15th, Heron Court.*—We got a letter from Lady Ely, saying that the Prince is as ill as possible.  I telegraphed to Princess Edward, and at half-past six received the sad news that the Prince died last night at eleven.  The greatest anxiety is felt on the Queen's account, for it is feared that this affliction may be too much for her health or mind to bear.  She has lost everything that could make life valuable to her, as all her happiness was centred in her husband, who was not only most devoted and affectionate to her, but her best friend ; advising her in all her difficulties, consoling her in all her annoyances, and saving her, as much as possible, trouble and anxiety of every kind.

*December 17th.*—Lady Ely writes that the Prince's fever was the same as that which the King of Portugal died of, and that he had from the beginning a presentiment that he would not recover.

*December 18th.*—I got a letter from Princess Edward, giving a good account of the poor Queen, who bears her affliction most nobly.

*December 20th.*—We continue to receive good accounts of the

[1] Member for Norfolk, Tory, but a general *frondeur.*

Queen. The Princess says she has signed some papers, and seen Lord Granville.

*December 28th.*—I hear that Ministers have signed a memorial to the Queen, refusing to transact business with her through Sir Charles Phipps. This, though right, is certainly cruel under present circumstances. No news can be received from America as to the reception of our demands until the 30th, but our Government are preparing for war. Lord Palmerston has been dangerously ill, but is better. His death at this moment would be a national misfortune, when we consider who the men are who are likely to succeed him among the Whig party.

## 1862 •

*January 11th.*—The town of Southampton is rather excited by the arrival of an American frigate, the 'Tuscarora,' evidently come to look after the 'Nashville'; the captain of the latter is supposed to have sent for the 'Sumter,' which is at Cadiz, and the two together will be a match for the frigate. They cannot fight in our waters.

*January 16th.*—Messrs. Slidell and Mason embarked on board the 'Rinaldo,' either for England or Halifax. Lord Lyons has written a very dry despatch in answer to Mr. Seward's, not replying to any of his arguments as to the legality or otherwise of the seizure on board the 'Trent.'

*January 17th.*—There is a report to-day that the 'Parana' steamer is lost in the Gulf of St. Lawrence. She sailed with the 'Adriatic' in December. The 'Parana' carries the 1st Battalion Fusilier Guards with their officers, amongst whom are Lord Dunmore, Colonel Charteris, and many others of my acquaintance.

*January 19th.*—Lady Margaret Charteris gave me the pleasing intelligence that the 'Parana,' on board which was her husband, Colonel Charteris, is safe in the St. Lawrence.

*January 26th.*—Saw Lord Derby, and talked over his future Government. He insists on my again taking the Foreign Office, which I do not think my health will allow. Lord Palmerston is in a very weak state, so it must be doubtful whether he will be able to carry on the Government.

*January* 30*th*.—Messrs. Slidell and Mason arrived at Southampton yesterday. A crowd collected to see them land, but not a single person cheered. Mr. Mason remained at Southampton until the evening, and received a visit from the officers af the 'Nashville.'

One of our finest line-of-battle ships, the 'Conqueror,' 100 guns, has been stranded on a reef near the Bahama Islands ; the crew are saved, and the guns will be recovered, but the ship is a complete wreck.

*February* 1*st*.—Lord Russell has addressed a letter to the Admiralty declaring it to be the Queen's pleasure that the ships and privateers belonging to the Federals and Confederates should not enter any English ports, except in cases of bad weather and want of provisions.

*February* 4*th, Heron Court*.—Lady Ely arrived. She seemed very low, and the account of her life at Osborne for the last five weeks quite accounts for the depression of her spirits. She gives a sad report of the poor Queen, who talks continually about the Prince, and seems to feel comfort in doing so. She takes great pleasure in the universal feeling of sympathy for her and sorrow for him shown by all classes.

*February* 6*th, London*.—Parliament met to-day. The Queen, of course, did not come. Lord Derby made a speech on the Address ; the part relating to the Prince Consort's death was beautiful. There was no amendment.

*February* 9*th*.—I hear Mr. Mason says that it will be impossible for the Confederates to continue the war much longer, as they will have no more money with which to pay their troops ; their army and navy together costing half a million per day.

*February* 19*th*.—Lord Clarendon in the House of Lords attempted to explain the part he had taken with reference to Italy at the Congress of Paris in 1856. Some private letters of Cavour's have just been published by Jeffs, from which extracts have appeared in the 'Times,' showing that Lord Clarendon encouraged Cavour to go to war. His defence was most feeble, and fell perfectly flat on the House. The solemn silence which followed Lord Clarendon's speech must have been very galling. He admitted that he saw Cavour daily, and conversed with him a great deal on the affairs of Italy, but kept no notes of his conversations, as he did not consider them of sufficient importance for him to report them to his Government. This is quite incredible to those who know his *cacoëthes scribendi*.

*February 28th.*—Lord Derby brought forward yesterday the question of which he had given notice respecting a most infamous proclamation issued by the military commandant of Lucera, near Naples, ordering every human being to withdraw in three days from a certain district or to be shot as brigands, and the woods houses, and cattle to be destroyed. Lord Russell and the Duke of Argyll denied its authenticity, saying that it was only an old proclamation of Murat's republished, but that they would write to Sir James Hudson on the subject.

*March 4th.*—I was detained at the House by a debate upon the Revised Code. Lord Derby spoke against the measure, upon which he feels strongly.

*March 20th.*—Dined with the Salisburys. My speech on Italian affairs seems to have pleased my party. We have won the North Riding, Mr. Morritt beating Mr. Milbanke by 473.

A letter from Italy states that the proclamation of Lucera, issued by Fantoni, who, according to Lord Russell, was alone responsible for it, was really issued by General Della Rovere when Minister of War, and that three colonels were dismissed summarily for not carrying out their orders with sufficient severity. Fantoni's conduct was in pursuance of direct orders from Generals Govone and Chiabrera, commanding in the Neapolitan provinces, who have since been decorated as Grand Officers of St. Maurice.[1]

*March 25th.*—Polish debate came on this afternoon, so I took Madame Zamoiska to hear it. Lord Carnarvon spoke well. Lord Russell said that the Government could not offer advice to the Emperor of Russia with respect to his mode of governing his own subjects.

Mr. George Russell has had a dreadful accident in the Park.

[1] The cruelties of the Piedmontese armies to the Neapolitan Royalists taken prisoners were unsurpassed in any civil war or by any tyrant.

His horse ran away with him in Rotten Row, and crushed him against the iron rails ; he is in a precarious state.

*April 2nd.*—The Government were beaten last night by a majority of 11 on Mr. Sheridan's motion to reduce the duty on fire insurances. Both Lord Palmerston and Gladstone spoke against it.

There has been a naval engagement between two iron-clad ships in America. The Confederate ship 'Merrimac' destroyed two frigates, the 'Cumberland' and the 'Congress'; a third steam frigate was saved by the appearance of the 'Monitor,' which, after a fierce battle, compelled the 'Merrimac' to retire. They fought at close quarters, but without any effect, as the balls glanced off the sides. The 'Monitor' being very low in the water, poured its shots into the lower part of the 'Merrimac,' which was not defended by iron plates.

*April 10th.*—Great exertions are being made to organise a society for raising a subscription to erect a memorial to the Prince Consort. Resolutions were passed unanimously at the Lord Mayor's, and a committee was formed consisting of Lord Salisbury, Lord Derby, myself, &c.

*April 18th.*—Good Friday. I left for Paris.

---

After two or three days I proceeded to Dijon, and thought I would try a new hotel close to the station. It was kept by a young man who had just entered business, named David, and his wife was a super-excellent cook. He gave me some very fine trout for dinner, which led to a conversation upon fishing, and I found that my landlord was a great admirer of the art, and was constantly going to Dôle to fish in the river Louve. He informed me that I could reach it in two hours by rail to Dôle ; and by enquiring at a fisherman's at Parex he would put me in the way of having good sport. I therefore diverged from the course of my journey to Dôle, and, putting up at a very bad inn, proceeded to the small village of Parex. Here I found the fisherman, quite ready to accompany me. He lived close by the river, which is a very fine and rapid stream descending from the Jura. We started

in his boat, and for two hours tried in vain with a rod. Tired of
this, he then produced a long trammel-net, which he laid outside
the bushes on the banks of the river. In a short time we pulled
out a trout of seven pounds, and several smaller ones. I went
back to Dôle in the evening, carrying my spoil with me, and sent
the trout as a present to Lord Cowley at Paris. This fisherman
rented about two miles of the river Louve for ten pounds a year,
and must have made it a profitable business.

Returning to Dijon, I went on to Lyons, where a new park
has just been made, but too far from the town for general use. On
climbing up to the church of Notre Dame de Fourvières, which is
supposed to be a cure for the lame, I found the most magnificent
panorama that can be seen—the Rhône and the Saône dividing
the town at one's feet, and the white Alps in the far distance
bounding a splendid open country. In the church of Notre Dame
there were thousands of votive offerings, with a representation in
painting of every illness, accident, and misfortune to which human
nature is liable, and from which we must suppose the donors were
saved or recovered. Remains of the Roman masonry were
everywhere to be seen.

On leaving Lyons I stopped at Nîmes ; and I think the Pont
du Gard, a few miles from the town, is, after the Coliseum, the
grandest remains of the Roman Empire. It is in the greatest
perfection, and still spans the river unharmed. Spring was everywhere breaking out, and the scent of the wild thyme was delicious.
I could not resist the temptation of bathing in the blue pool
below the bridge. I stayed some days at Nîmes enjoying the most
splendid weather, and visiting the Maison Carrée, an old Roman
temple turned into a museum, in which is the famous picture by
Delaroche of Oliver Cromwell standing over the body of Charles
I. I was so struck with it that I sent Mr. Middleton to Nîmes
to copy it, which he did with great success. The Easter holidays
being over, I returned to London on May 14. I stopped in Paris
for a ball at the Tuileries, and was very well received by the
Emperor. During my absence the Federals and Confederates had
had several engagements, with various success on both sides.

*May* 17*th.*—Dined at Lady Ailesbury's, and went afterwards to Lady Palmerston's party and Lady Carrington's ball.

*May* 19*th.*—We went to the Exhibition ; it was the first half-crown day, which accounts for the increased number of visitors. We dined with Lady Tankerville, and met there Vladimir Davidoff, whose wife, a Georgian, left him for Prince Bariatinski, who was his commanding officer and general in the Caucasus.  He never could get any redress from the Emperor or the Russian laws, if there are any.

*May* 20*th.*—I took Vladimir Davidoff to the Royal Academy. There are some beautiful landscapes by Stanfield, Lee, Creswick, and Cooper, and some pretty *tableaux de genre* by Millais, finished like miniatures ; some portraits by Grant, none good, and that of Lady Mary Craven atrocious.

*May* 22*nd.*—I went with Vladimir to the Zoological, which seemed to amuse him ; but he is very low, not only about his wife, but from the destruction of all his prospects in life.  At the time the *esclandre* took place he was on the point of being made a general ; and if he had chosen to connive at his own dishonour, his career might have been a brilliant one so far as satisfying his ambition. Now, all hopes of advancement are at an end, and he has left the army ; his having challenged Bariatinski, who was his commander-in-chief, and has been a great hero, makes all chance of promotion impossible.

*May* 23*rd.*—There is a rumour that the Confederates have been defeated and Beauregard taken prisoner, which everybody regrets. The feeling for the South is very strong in society.

*June* 2*nd.*—A meeting took place to-day at the Duke of Marlborough's to agree about the amendment to Mr. Stansfeld's resolution respecting the national expenses and the necessity for retrenchment ; 186 attended.  Lord Derby addressed them, and was much cheered.

*June* 3*rd.*—Dined with the Marlboroughs ; a small party. Mr. Damer came from the House of Commons, and told us the excitement there was intense.  Lord Palmerston made a very dictatorial speech, declaring that Mr. Walpole's amendment to Mr. Stansfeld's resolution was in effect a vote of want of confidence. Mr. Walpole said that the House had been placed, by what Lord

Palmerston had said, in a position of great difficulty. The object was to determine whether the House would come to any resolution as to the mode and direction in which reduction and expenditure should be made. Mr. Stansfeld then proposed his resolution, after which Disraeli made a clever speech ; and after two others from Mr. Horsman and Cobden, Mr. Walpole got up and withdrew his amendment. Disraeli rose and made the most violent diatribe against Mr. Walpole, to the disgust of almost all the Conservative party, who feared to disturb the Government and risk a dissolution, which Lord Palmerston threatened. The division took place upon the original resolution, and it was negatived by 367 to 65.

It is reported that General Butler governs New Orleans with the utmost severity, and has issued an order that all ladies or women who show dislike or contempt for the Federals by word, look, or gesture, are to be treated as women of the town. Meanwhile, the French expedition to Mexico bears the fruit that might have been expected. They have sustained a reverse at Puebla, and their communications with Vera Cruz are cut off ; if so, they will make a great outcry against us for deserting them, as they will call it, of course saying nothing of our reasons, which were that they broke the treaty which they had made jointly with England and Spain, in consequence of which the English and Spanish troops left them to carry on their operations alone.

*June 17th.*—No details are yet published, beyond those that the French attacked the heights of Guadalupe, were repulsed, and retreated upon Vera Cruz. ` The Emperor has ordered the immediate despatch of a brigade of 5,000 men ; but the whole expedition is a great mistake, as there is no feeling in Mexico for the French and against Juarez ; it has been got up by the priest party in France, strongly supported by the Empress.

Lord Canning died this morning. Poor fellow ! he has had little enjoyment of his hard-won honours. Supported by his admirable wife, he was put in one of the most trying situations a man could endure, and when the rebellion was quenched, and his anxieties at an end, he came home only to die. We were very intimate friends.

*June 25th.*—The Duchess of Cambridge and Princess Mary

dined with us, also the Carnarvons, Baths, Lady Cowley and daughter, Count Apponyi, Count Vitzthum, Count Wimpffen.

*July 2nd.*—The Duke of Athole has a beautiful cow exhibited at the Battersea Agricultural Show. The dairymaid who has the care of the cow appears in a sort of costume, very becoming, and is of course much admired by gentlemen. The Duke attended upon her and the cow, bringing hay and water for the latter. One day he and the dairymaid sat together on a bundle of straw, eating sandwiches, and she and the cow were the admiration of society.

The civil war in America continues without any positive advantage on either side.

*July 14th.*—We went to Stafford House, where there was a breakfast for the Viceroy of Egypt and about forty people.

Mr. Mason, the Confederate, called upon me this morning and told me that the battle before Richmond had lasted six days. He has four sons in the Confederate army.

*July 31st.*—Lord Palmerston stated in the House that the manufacturers had sold the cotton which they ought to have kept to work their mills, utterly unmindful of the starving people round them. Mr. Cobden was furious, and said that 'the assertion was but another instance of that habitual recklessness and incorrectness for which the Premier was remarkable.'

*August 11th.*—I left London for Lowther Castle. News from Italy is bad ; Garibaldi is apparently in open rebellion against Victor Emanuel, and is raising an army in Sicily to march upon Rome. There is little doubt that the King is playing a deceitful game, and secretly encouraging Garibaldi.

*August 24th.*—Garibaldi is in Sicily, and has taken Catania, where he has seized the Treasury, and is levying forced contributions. The general feeling seems to be in favour of the King, who, at last, has issued a proclamation against him, and is going to send a large force under Cialdini to Sicily.

*August 27th.*—Garibaldi has landed in Calabria, and is advancing on Reggio, whilst Cialdini is sent to Sicily, thereby humbugging the Government of Victor Emanuel.

*Lord Ranelagh to Lord M.*

London : August 30, 1862.

Dear Malmesbury,—I have just returned from the Camp of Châlons, and am for many reasons very glad I went there ; the military portion of what I saw will keep until we meet. The Emperor was very civil and kind to me. After dinner I made a point of talking about you, and told him what an old and real friend you were of his, and regretted that those Whigs had done all they could to make mischief between you, &c. &c. He seemed to think that you had been in Paris very often without calling upon him ; which I explained by the difficulty you had in calling upon him without its making a good deal of jealousy over here. However, I said it would be all right next year, as you would be Foreign Secretary.

I was very much struck by a conversation about America, for in the most open manner after dinner he said he was quite ready to recognise the *South*, but Palmerston would not do so, and he could not unless Palmerston did. The result of this (pretended ?) frankness is that Slidell in Paris tells everyone that England is the cause of the South not being recognised. He abuses England and says we are their enemy ; in fact, we are in the happy position of being hated by both North and South. I think you may look out for some curious results in Italy. I can only mention one little fact. Young Murat, when I was at Châlons, told a French lady friend of mine that he had an idea that he may be wanted before long at Naples ! He said it was a great bore, but still it was his duty to go if wanted.

.      .      .      .      .      .      .      .

Yours truly,

RANELAGH.

*September 1st.*—The news of Garibaldi's capture is confirmed. He was attacked on August 29 at Aspromonte, ten miles from Reggio, by Colonel Pallavicini. He is said to have had 2,000 men, and had intrenched himself in a strong position. This was carried by the King's troops after an obstinate defence, and Garibaldi wounded and taken prisoner.

*September 3rd.*—The account given in to-day's papers of Garibaldi's capture increases my suspicion that the whole affair is a cross, the object being to prove to Europe that Italy never can be quiet until she gets Rome. The Piedmontese Press already begins urging the withdrawal of the French troops on this plea.

*September 13th.*—The Federals and Confederates continue to gain victories by turns, and I see no daylight as yet to show the result of this bloody war. Rattazzi has sent sixteen surgeons and physicians to Garibaldi, and his English sympathisers have sent a surgeon of the name of Partridge to him.

*September 15th.*—General Lee has gained a victory. Both armies were in great numbers, but the Federals were obliged to retreat, leaving all their wounded on the field.

*September 19th, Heron Court.*—Mr. and Mrs. Augustus Paget and Lord Ranelagh arrived. Mr. Paget is the first person who suggested the Princess Alexandra for the Prince of Wales, and negotiations were commenced a year ago. Mrs. Paget says she is beautiful—lovely eyes and good teeth. She is tall and graceful, with a good figure.

Our whole party went to play at croquet at Hinton. Grantley Berkeley and his son appeared in costume : Garibaldi shirts, knickerbockers and coloured stockings, hats with feathers. They looked very ridiculous.

*October 1st.*—The Confederates have been reinforced by Stonewall Jackson, who, after his capture of the fort of Harper's Ferry, where he took 8,000 prisoners, stores and guns, crossed the Potomac to assist General Lee, who was hard pressed by McClellan. The battle that ensued on the 17th must have been the bloodiest of the war. The Federals own to a loss of 10,000 men. General Mansfield was killed, and twelve other generals wounded. The Federals claim the victory, though their enemies did not retire till the evening of the 18th.

*October 5th.*—Lady M. went to Knowsley. I started to-day for Paris.

---

After staying a week at Paris, I left it for Nevers and Moulins, wishing to see the centre of France. It is infinitely preferable in every way to the old route by which most Englishmen travel to Lyons. When once you reach Auvergne nothing can be more picturesque than the country. Moulins and Nevers have all the character of old French towns, and when you arrive at Clermont you are *en pleine Auvergne*. There are many ruined old castles perched upon inaccessible places, and which, at times, belonged to great feudal families, and at others to robbers, who had taken possession of them during the absence of their masters in the wars of the Middle Ages.[1]  Clermont is a large town without ornament or natural beauty, but very interesting from its historical associations.  Within a few miles is the hill on which stood the camp of Vercingetorix, who gave Cæsar more trouble than any of his enemies.  On the mountains stood the great city of the Gauls, which he took after repeated repulses.  A large number of men are now excavating and laying bare its remains by orders of the Emperor, who is at this time writing a life of Julius Cæsar, and very much wrapped up in the subject.  I drove here from Clermont, and, curiously enough, a large eagle was soaring over the hill during the whole time of my stay.  From Clermont I took a carriage to Mont d'Or, a distance of forty or fifty miles through the wildest possible country.  I had visited the Puy-de-Dôme, the highest of the volcanoes, which were exhausted, probably, before the existence of man, for there is no history, or even tradition, of their being active since his creation.  On arriving at a sort of station-house at the foot of the mountain, where the horses were to rest, I heard a roar like that of a wild beast, and suddenly a large donkey, which was feeding in the meadow, rushed at full gallop at one of my horses, and fixed his teeth in his neck.  It required several men to drive off this savage brute, which had upset all the ideas I had formed of his race as seen in England.

From this station-house I took a strong two-wheeled cart, drawn by two powerful cart-horses, harnessed tandem, up to the observatory at the top of the mountain.  The path was rough, narrow, zig-zag, and almost perpendicular, with nothing between me and eternity if the horses chanced to slip or the harness gave way.  Whenever we came to a turn in the road, the guide gave a flick to the horse in the shafts to prevent his turning too short, the effect of which was that the outside wheel was constantly almost over a precipice of thousands of feet.  At the observatory they keep a magnificent breed of mastiffs, and received me hospitably with a cup of coffee, which I was glad enough to get.  The wind is so violent at that height that it nearly carries even those

[1] *Vide* Froissart.

accustomed to it off their feet and over the precipice. From there
I had a magnificent panorama of the entire country, showing its
volcanic formation, and on descending the other side of the mountain had an experience of the force of the wind, which blew me and
the guide flat on our faces by a sudden gust, just on the edge of
an extinct crater, called the Nid de Poule, from its perfect shape,
covered with fine turf and extremely deep.

The country about Mont d'Or is very picturesque and wooded,
with a beautiful trout stream flowing under the town. The
inns, which are more like *pensions* than hotels, are comfortable,
with plenty of horses, both for carriages and riding, at the
service of visitors. I returned to Clermont, and from there went
to Lyons, and back to Paris by Geneva.

On my return to Paris I went on a visit to Chamarande,
a *château* given by the Emperor to Persigny, who has furnished it
with great taste and luxury. It is of Louis XIII.'s time, and a
very fine house, on the main road from Paris to Lyons, near
Étampes. The Emperor and Empress arrived there at one o'clock
on the 27th, and returned late the same night to St. Cloud. The
time was passed in discussing a substantial luncheon and dinner—
served after the English fashion—and in driving about the park,
which is large and picturesque, all rock and heather, like Fontainebleau. I found the Emperor strong for the American
Confederates, and anxious to propose, together with England and
Russia, an armistice of six months to the combatants, during
which time the blockade should be raised. He thought that if
they could be muzzled for that time they would not begin again.
The position of the two armies is that of mutual observation on
the Potomac after the drawn battle of Antietam. The Emperor
did not enter upon politics with me except on this question, but
seemed much absorbed in the internal improvements of France,
asking me many questions on the state of the provinces I had seen,
and seeming to think that his trade and commerce were capable of
enormous development. He was also much occupied with the life
of Julius Cæsar, which he is writing, and told me that in one of
Cæsar's camps in Auvergne a splendid silver vase had been found,
which could only have belonged to himself. Persigny and others
look upon this and discoveries of the same sort as apocryphal, and

say that his Majesty is perpetually victimised by those who know his hobby for Cæsarian relics, to the extent that one officer got three promotions for successive trovers of the kind. He has, however, great knowledge of this period of history, and his excavations in the camp of Gergovia, which I saw, have laid bare the foundations of a large Gaulish city still perfect. After dinner, the Emperor, Morny, Persigny, Pietri, and I smoked together. The conversation fell upon painters and pictures, about which the Emperor professed complete ignorance, and, indeed, showed it by confusing, in his usual unaffected and natural manner, the names of the most famous. In the same way he spoke of the great French national vice of vanity, which would admit of no merit equal to their own in all things, and the general mediocrity in every art, excepting mechanics, physics, and chemistry. We then got upon Home and spiritualism, which I saw he half believed in ; and as he had been speaking of the many doubtful pictures in the Louvre, I suggested that it was desirable that Mr. Home should call up Titian's spirit and ask him whether he really painted the portrait of Francis I. which is in that gallery. Morny and Pietri took advantage of this to laugh at his belief, upon which he looked displeased, saying that if we could explain all we believed our religion would be a very easy task.

I returned to Paris in the Royal carriage—a large omnibus—the party being M. and Madame de Morny, M. and Madame Walewski, and the two ladies in waiting, one of whom, Madame de Pierre, an American, *née* Thorne, and the Duchess de Morny, a Russian, just married, smoked all the way in the Empress's face, notwithstanding her plain hints against the proceeding. She is much too good-natured to her *entourage*, but enhances her singular beauty by the most natural gaiety and fascination of manner. The *genre* of the women about her, with the exception of Madame Walewska, is vile. Their hair is dragged off their faces so tightly that they can hardly shut their eyes, and their scarlet accoutrements, jackets, cloaks, &c., as they happen to be very fair, made an *ensemble* indescribably unbecoming.

I had a conversation of above an hour with the Empress on politics, chiefly on the Roman question. Thouvenel had just been dismissed as being too anti-Papal, and as leaning to the abandonment of his Holiness, and Drouyn de l'Huys has replaced him. The Empress did not, as I expected, treat the subject as a *dévote*, though she said that no scandal could be greater than an exiled Pope with no foot of earth belonging independently to himself, and that the honour of France was engaged to protect him from being driven out of Rome ; that, if he were, the Austrians would come to his rescue, and France have no right to prevent it, as, by the treaty of Zürich with Austria, the Pope was to be maintained ; that the Italians should be satisfied, for the time, with what they had got, and not attempt impossibilities, but organise what they possessed ; that there was no such thing in Italy as an organising mind or a man of business.[1] She came to the charge about the English Press and its abuse of the Emperor. This is a *parti pris*, and, I believe, only meant to elicit a denial of our hostility. I had an easy reply to her assertion that such a feeling existed, by reminding her of her own reception in England and Scotland two years ago, when she was obliged to escape from the ovation she met with. To this she succumbed, as she was evidently delighted with her journey to England. I went over with her the old ground of my policy previous to the Italian war, as I had done with the Emperor last year, and told her of my having sent him a copy of my despatch to Prussia, preventing that Government from joining Austria, and thus localising the war. Neither Cowley nor Walewski had ever told the Emperor this important fact, and last year I sent the Emperor the copy privately by the Duke of Hamilton.

On arriving at Paris, Bacciocchi drove me home in his carriage. Whilst at Chamarande I observed that Persigny had got a complete record of the *château* and its antecedents, going back for three centuries, and taken from the archives of the small town adjoining. It is very remarkable how the local history of these places has been preserved in France, whilst in our minor towns no such records have been kept to which the historian could refer. This may be explained by the fact that there was no Protestant

---

[1] The Emperor came from the war much disgusted with the Italians and Cavour, who, with Prince Napoleon and other *intrigants*, were encouraging Mazzini and the other Republicans to extend the theatre to Tuscany and Rome, the Emperor never intending to create an independent kingdom on the side of France.

Reformation in France, as in England, where the libraries and journals of the monks were savagely destroyed by the Reformers.

*Lord Derby to Lord M.*

Knowsley: October 31, 1862.

My dear Malmesbury,—I have delayed answering or thanking you for your very interesting letter from Geneva until the time when you would·probably be back in England; and though I have not heard of your arrival, I know that Lady Malmesbury expected you about this time. In the first place I am sorry to say that our attempt at a party for the 25th has been so much interfered with by the rival attractions of Longleat and Wilton for the same week, that we have reluctantly been obliged to put it off altogether; and though you know that we should be glad to see you at any time, yet I hope that it will not be inconvenient to˜you to revert to your original intention, and to come to us the following week, the first in December, instead. It would be an additional pleasure to us to see Lady Malmesbury with you; but I am afraid she will hardly venture at that time of year.

I think John Russell is getting us into all sorts of complications; and that the state of Europe becomes more and more critical every day. What on earth does he mean by turning round on Denmark, and taking up all at once the Prussian views about the Duchies? And how will Palmerston stand it, the original author of the Protocol which was the basis of the treaty of 1852? I cannot help connecting with this affair, and perhaps with a renewed misunderstanding arising out of it with his old *friend* and colleague, the sudden and mysterious postponement of the Cabinet which was to have been held a week ago; and which seems to have been put off *sine die*, so absolutely at the last moment, that the Ministers had all come up to town for it, includ· ing the Duke of Argyll all the way from Scotland! It is evident, too, that we are on the point of a quarrel with Russia, whose intrigues, I have no doubt, have led to the revolution which has broken out in Greece; though I should be sorry to swear that our ubiquitous friend Louis Napoleon has not thought that a little *imbroglio* in the East might serve to distract attention from the difficulties and embarrass- ments of the Italian question. The Greek affair, I am afraid, may be most formidable, and altogether, with Prussia in a state of quasi- revolution, and with the Italian, Greek, Montenegrin, Danish, and Polish questions all in a ferment at once, I can hardly imagine a more unpleasant state of foreign affairs. The American war, too, appears to be as far from a solution as ever. In the meantime the distress here is rapidly and fearfully augmenting, and we fully expect that by Christmas there will be over 250,000 paupers in twenty-four unions! They are already 186,000 against 43,000 last year. The prospects for the winter, especially if it should be a severe one, are fearful; and, admirably as the people have behaved hitherto, it is impossible to say what continued and aggravated suffering may lead them to.[1]

Ever yours sincerely,     DERBY.

*November 2nd.*—Arrived in London. During my absence abroad the American Civil War had been raging continually with various success. Some Englishmen made considerable fortunes by running the blockade, many others lost all they possessed by being captured. But this species of smuggling induced many to invest money on the chance ; men who did not appear on the surface employed adventurers to do the work.

*November 14th.*—Drouyn de l'Huys has written to Lord Russell to propose a joint mediation to induce the Americans to consent to a truce for six months. It is said there was a stormy discussion in the Cabinet in consequence ; the result, a refusal to interfere at present, as the Americans would decline the proposal.

*November 18th.*—Baron Gros is appointed Ambassador in the place of M. de Flahault. I suspect he is only a stop-gap, and we shall have the Persignys later. The 'Times' of to-day has a strong article against Lord Russell's despatch of September 24 relating to Denmark. It is a most extraordinary and offensive one, giving advice upon subjects of internal administration, in which we have no business to meddle, and, in fact, re-opening the whole question of Schleswig and Holstein, saying Holstein and Lauenburg should have everything the German Confederation asks for them. This restless and impotent meddling is peculiarly ill-timed on the eve of the marriage of the Prince of Wales with a Danish Princess.

*November 20th.*—Lord Russell wrote his despatch to Mr.

---

[1] This period of Lord Derby's life will redound for ever, to his honour. He devoted all his business-like qualities, his valuable time and great fortune, to the relief of his suffering countrymen ; and it must also be added that his noble and successful exertions were fully appreciated in all parts of England.

Paget[1] some days before he left Gotha. Mr. Meade, who remained behind, telegraphed to the Foreign Office to announce Lord Russell's departure in these words : ' Earl Russell has skedaddled.' As the message was in cypher, and such a word as ' skedaddle ' was unknown, they were obliged to telegraph back to know what he meant. These jokes might be extremely inconvenient.

*November 22nd.*—News is arrived that General McClellan is dismissed from the chief command of the Federal army. He submitted quietly, professing respect for the constitution, and retired to his own home.

*November 24th.*—Sir Henry Wolff has had a long conversation with Lord Palmerston about the affairs of Greece. He is anxious that Prince Alfred should accept the crown, and that England should give up the Ionian Islands, the Turks giving up Albania. I conclude that Wolff would get compensation for losing his lucrative place there ; Disraeli has promised him a place if he would devote himself and his pen to our party. He is fond of writing, and writes well.

### Lord Derby to Lord M.

Knowsley : November 25, 1862.

My dear Malmesbury,—I quite agree in your view of the proposal, which I conclude will be made, and I fear will be accepted, of placing Prince Alfred on the throne of Greece. It appears to me the greatest possible blunder, whether we look at it in its immediate effects upon our relations with France and Russia, or at the interests of the Prince himself, or at the complications which our connection with such a throne and such a people must infallibly produce. I wonder that the Queen should have given her consent; I am certain that the Prince never would have done so. If this step be finally taken, I suppose it must be mentioned in the Queen's Speech; and if it be, it will be difficult to avoid an amendment, and impossible to join in an expression of congratulation.

I did not answer your former letter, partly because I thought you would find some answer to your inquiries in a letter of mine to Mr. Kingscote, which he published about the day you wrote; and partly because my time is so fully occupied in answers to similar letters, and in other correspondence, and in attendance at Manchester.

[1] Then her Majesty's Minister at Copenhagen.

shall be glad to talk over the subject with you next week; but with espect to the breakdown of the Poor Law, I will say, first, that hough no *one* rate of a high figure has been levied, there have been wo or three in the course of the year in some towns, which have mounted in the whole to 7s. 10d. and 11d. on the solvent property, every new rate finding fewer people able to pay it; and next, that the pressure of a poor-rate which is levied on the occupiers is not to be neasured by the actual amount, but by the sudden increase on the normal figure. The former is taken into account in settling rent, and alls on real property; the latter falls exclusively on the occupiers, who in this case are themselves on the verge of pauperism. You are quite right, however, when you say that the pressure would have been comparatively light had the law of Elizabeth remained unaltered, and personal as well as real property been liable; as it is, no increase of rates will reach the vast amount of realised wealth, except that very small fraction of it which is invested in buildings and machinery. I must say, however, that some of the mill-owners have behaved nobly under great difficulties, some of them quite the reverse; but, as a class, they have done far more than the wealthy bankers, merchants, brokers, and other speculators, some of whom have made enormous sums in cotton, and whose contributions are very much below what they ought to be. I hope our county meeting will catch some of them.

Ever yours,

DERBY.

*November* 30th.—I hear that Lord Russell has recanted his Danish despatch, which confirms the suspicion that it was written without the knowledge of Lord Palmerston.

*December* 7th.—Count Sabouroff, a young Russian, called and told us that his valet was walking in Bond Street at one o'clock this afternoon, when the streets were full of people coming out of church, and he saw two men attack a gentleman, rob him of his watch, and run away. They were pursued, and one was caught.

*December* 8th.—We spent three days at Savernake, and went thence to Highclere, where we were very kindly received. Lord Carnarvon and I talked about necromancy and spiritualism. He told me that he had read a great number of books upon the Black Art, and in some found *formulæ* of so horrible a nature that they quite haunted him.

*December* 12th.—We drove over the park, which is fourteen

miles in circumference, and the most beautiful I think I ever saw
—miles of green drives through, rhododendrons, enormous beeches,
and cedars in every direction.  I never was more delighted with
any drive in England.

*December* 13*th*.—Sir Henry Wolff told me that he knew from
a good source the Government had decided to give up the Ionian
Islands to Greece if the Powers who signed the Treaty of Vienna
in 1815 consented.

### Lord Derby to Lord M.

(Dictated by Lord Derby.)

December 28, 1862.

The cession of the Ionian Islands is decided upon.  I learn this
positively this morning by a letter from Stanley, on the authority of
Cornewall Lewis, whom he met at Chevening.  There is to be a Congress to decide what is to be done with them.  The cession includes
Corfù.  I think the measure at any time one of very doubtful policy,
but the present moment appears to me singularly ill-chosen.  The
islands were entrusted to our keeping as a maritime Power which
could, and would, keep down the system of piracy by which those
coasts have been so long infested, and the occupation gave us a naval
position highly important in case of a European war, as influencing
our hold upon the Adriatic and the Levant; and these are considerations
which ought not to have been lightly overlooked.  At the same time it
is not to be denied that the occupation was accompanied by considerable
expense and some inconvenience, that the Constitution was absolutely
unworkable, and that the Government was only carried on by a continual violation of its spirit, even when there was adherence to its
letter.  Taking all this into consideration, there might have been much
to say in favour of the cession, could they have been handed over to a
Government willing to accept the responsibility, firmly established,
politically and financially, and with sufficient power and self-control to
keep an excitable people from insane schemes of aggression upon their
neighbours.  But it strikes me as the height of folly to make a gratui-
tous offer of cession, and to throw the islands at the head of a nation in
the very throes of Revolution, the form of whose government is yet undecided—much more so, the person of the sovereign, if they are to have
a sovereign—whose finances are bankrupt, whose naval power is insig-
nificant, and the first of whose political aspirations is accession of
territory at the expense of a war with its most powerful neighbour.  I

cannot conceive greater improvidence than making the offer of the cession under such circumstances. If accepted, while it will diminish our prestige in the East, it cannot but lead to future and embarrassing complications; and if from any circumstances the cession should not be accepted, the offer will not have added to our facilities for governing the islands. You will see that generally I agree in the view which our papers have taken, though I think they have been too sweeping in their condemnation of the idea of cession at any time and under any circumstances.                                        Yours truly,
                                                                    DERBY.

## 1863

*January 30th.*—The Federals have been repulsed with great loss at Vicksburg; the army of the Potomac is thoroughly demoralised, disgusted with their generals, in whom they have no confidence, and mortified at their defeats.

*February 9th.*—The insurrection in Poland is increasing every day, and in many places the Russians have been defeated. The King of Prussia has sent a strong body of troops to his frontier. The feud between him and his Parliament grows more bitter every day, and neither side will give way. It is a struggle between freedom and despotism, the King attacking the Constitution by insisting that the Parliament should have no control over the expenditure of the army. Looking at the safety of the country, no doubt he is right, and time will prove it.

My youngest brother is made Archdeacon of Wilts by the Bishop of Salisbury, who has also given him the living of Bremhill, the two together worth about 700*l.* a year; but it is a large parish, and he must keep two curates.

### *Mr. Charles Lever*[1] *to Lord M.*

                                        Hôtel d'Odessa, Spezia : February 16, 1863.

My dear Lord,—I am sincerely obliged by your Lordship's note in acknowledgment of Barrington.

I am sure you are right in your estimate of Kinglake's book.[2]

---

[1] The novelist and Consul at Spezia.

[2] Alluding to his abuse of Louis Napoleon and charging him with personal cowardice. No man could be less exposed to such an accusation. I saw him jump

Such diatribes are no more history than the Balaclava charge was war. It was, however, his brief to make out the Crimean war a French intrigue, and he obeyed the old legal maxim in a different case—'Abuse the plaintiff's attorney.'

Italy is something farther from union than a year ago. In dealing with the brigandage Piedmont has contrived to insult the feelings and outrage the prejudices of the South by wholesale invectives against all things Neapolitan. French intrigues unquestionably help to keep up the uncertainty which all Italians feel as to the future, and the inadequacy of the men in power here contributes to the same end. Indeed, what Kinglake says of the English generals—questioning how the Great Duke would have dealt with the matter before them—might be applied to Italian statesmen as regards Cavour. They have not a shadow of a policy, save in their guesses as to how *he* would have treated any question before them. To get 'steerage way' on the nation, Cavour had to launch her into a revolution; but if these people try the same experiment they are like to be shipwrecked.

It would be both a pride and a pleasure to me to send your Lordship tidings occasionally of events here if you cared for it. Meanwhile I am, with sincere respect, most faithfully yours,

CHARLES LEVER.

*February* 18*th.*—The Confederates have gained a naval victory at Charleston. They sank two gun-boats and drove off the rest.

*February* 20*th, London.*—We went to the Lyceum to see 'The Duke's Motto,' translated from 'Le Bossu.' Fechter acts the part of Lagardère beautifully; Miss Leclercq is too fat and fair for the gipsy; Miss Terry did Blanche de Nevers very nicely, and like a lady.

*February* 27*th.*—Met Count Kielmansegge. He has to attend the Prince of Wales's marriage. The invitations are limited to the Garters and their wives, who must be asked, the Corps Diplomatique, the Foreign Princes and their suites, with the entire household of the Queen and of the late Prince. The procession on the 7th is to pass through London at a trot, which will disappoint the public, who will hardly be able to see the Princess; the Lord Mayor is not to go, as his equipage and attendants are

off the bridge over the Rhône at Geneva when a youth, and all men can feel what must have been his agonies when riding all day at the Battle of Sedan with his deadly malady upon him.

obliged to walk, and had he headed the procession all the carriages
must have gone at a foot's pace. The Corporation met in great
indignation at this interference with their rights ; so he is to be
permitted to head the procession as far as Temple Bar.

*February 28th.*—There was a Drawing Room held by the
Princess of Prussia.

*March 6th.*—The French are very sore at the refusal of
the American Government to accept their mediation, and at
the peremptory contradiction by Mr. Seward of M. Mercier's
despatch.

The insurrection in Poland is gaining strength, and the French
Emperor has written to the Czar advising him to make concessions,
' and to give to Poland large and serious guarantees in conformity
with treaties and with the principles of civilisation.' But it is
not likely that France will assist Poland by arms, as that would
interfere with their policy with respect to Turkey, which is founded
on an *entente cordiale* with Russia.

*March 7th.*—We went to Lord Willoughby's house at a quarter
before one to see the entry of the Princess. The houses along
Piccadilly were decorated, with few exceptions, but I saw nothing
really pretty except Lord Willoughby's and Lord Cadogan's.
There were a good many people in the drawing-room. It was the
coldest day we have had for a long time ; no sun, with occasional
showers, and we were half frozen standing on the balconies. The
Duke of Cambridge rode by two or three times with his staff, and
was greatly cheered. Lord Ranelagh passed at the head of his
brigade of Volunteers. Then appeared the royal carriages ; and
I was never more surprised and disappointed. The first five contained the suite and brothers and sisters of the Princess Alexandra ;
the carriages looked old and shabby, and the horses very poor,
with no trappings, not even rosettes, and no outriders. In short,
the shabbiness of the whole *cortège* was beyond anything one
could imagine, everybody asking ' Who is the Master of the
Horse ? ' The Princess kept bowing right and left very grace-
fully. The moment the procession had passed, the crowd dispersed, but there were universal remarks and compliments on the
Princess's beauty.

*March 8th.*—I saw Lord Derby to-day ; he is still confined to his bed, and looks very ill. He says that the Queen has invited the Disraelis to the wedding. I hear that on the arrival of the Prince and Princess at Slough the horses of the first carriage jibbed, and the leaders of the second turned right round upon the wheelers, the harness got entangled, and the confusion was very great. Altogether, everything done by the Court authorities was bad, and the management of the City no less so. All offers of assistance were refused ; both the Duke of Cambridge's of cavalry and Sir Richard Mayne's of police to keep the line in the City were declined, and the result was that the streets were quite blocked up, and if it had not been for the good temper of the people some terrible catastrophe must have occurred. As it was, there was great danger opposite the Mansion House, and the Danes were very much frightened ; the Prince of Wales, on his side, showing great coolness. To make up for these deficiencies, those who were present say that nothing could exceed the splendour of the scene in St. George's Chapel. The foreigners were all much struck with it ; it was so grand as to be quite overpowering. Mr. Paget confirmed all I had heard of the confusion on the departure of the special train for London. Lady Westminster, who had on half a million's worth of diamonds, could only find place in a third-class carriage, and Lady Palmerston was equally unfortunate. Count Lavradio had his diamond star torn off and stolen by the roughs.

*March* 13*th.*—Second reading of Mr. Adderley's Security from Violence Bill passed by a majority of 131 to 68, in spite of the opposition of Sir George Grey, who objected to garotters being flogged, saying that some were too delicate to undergo the punishment, to which some one replied that if a man was strong enough to rush out like a tiger and strangle another man, he was strong enough to bear a flogging.

*March* 20*th.*—We went to a party at St. James's Palace, and arrived in time to see the entry of the Prince and Princess of Wales, but it struck me as very melancholy, when one considered the cause of the Queen's absence.

*March* 22*nd.*—News from Poland is bad for the Poles. A battle has taken place. The insurgents under the Dictator, Langiewicz, were defeated after a desperate fight, and gave them-

selves up to the Austrian hussars, who conducted them to
Turnau.

*March 25th.*—I went to Windsor Castle and returned next day.
The Queen was quite calm and even cheerful, and looks well, but
she complains of not feeling strong and being unable to stand much.

The Prince of Wales asked me to smoke with him, Lord
Sydney, and two other men, and we sat up till nearly two in the
morning.

---

I went through Paris to Bordeaux on March 28, and was
charmed with the appearance of the town, which gives one a
perfect idea of a combination of business and pleasure. The
quays remind one much of Holland—a great activity of commerce
and a perpetual noise of voices in every language; but, away
from the shipping, the streets are ornamental and the shops handsome and luxurious. The dwellings of the great wine merchants
seem to lie in a district of their own, and are not distinguishable
by any advertisements or ostentatious names. The hotels are all
so good that one can hardly choose between them, and the best
claret is to be had in them without putting any pressure on the
waiters. There is a magnificent equestrian statue of the Emperor in the principal square, and it was here that he proclaimed
his dictum, ' L'Empire, c'est la paix,' which reassured Europe for
a time, but was before long proved to be a convenient phrase only.

In an old tower which stands by itself there is one of the most
horrible sights I ever beheld. Descending into a dungeon, you
find a collection, not of skeletons, but of shrivelled mummies, for
the skin and flesh are still on their bones, and they *stand* in a
ring with every diabolical contortion of pain and rage in their
faces. There are two stories respecting these dreadful remains—
one is, that they were a whole family poisoned by mushrooms,
whose death agonies were so terrible that they stiffened into the
contortions I have described, and that, being afterwards buried
without coffins in a peat soil, they were preserved in this horrible
state ; the second story is that they had been left to perish in the
dungeon. I heard that the Emperor had given positive orders for
them to be removed and buried, being much disgusted at the
ghastly spectacle.

From Bordeaux I went to Bayonne and Biarritz, crossed the
Bidassoa, and went as far as St. Sebastian.  This country is full
f associations, especially to an Englishman, for here the most
esperate fighting took place between us and the French in 1813,
nd between the river and Fuentarrabia the Paladins of Charle-
nagne fought and fell to a man.  Returning on my steps, I went
o Tarbes, and on my way visited the feudal castle of the Gramonts,
Bidache, or rather its ruins.  In the days of the famous Corisande
t had as many windows as there are days in the year, but with
he exception of a stable newly built on a large scale, and appa-
ently useless, there is little to be seen.  An old church in the
illage contains some of their family monuments.  Tarbes has a
ood inn, and is famous for its horses.

From Tarbes I proceeded leisurely to Toulouse.  I never saw
o vile a pavement as in this great city, composed as it is of sharp
lints.  A cicerone showed me over the field of battle, on which
ur Duke and Marshal Soult were engaged, and where the
Spaniards suffered so terribly.  Proceeding by the railway, I
stopped a day at Carcassonne, an ancient city, so famous for the
lesperate fighting of the Albigeois and the deeds of Simon de
Montfort.  The Emperor has had the city and fortifications restored exactly to the state they were in at that time ; the streets
ire just wide enough for a cart to pass, and the towers and battle-
nents are what they were in the thirteenth century.  In every
part of France he is making archæological restorations, and his
ictive mind seems as much interested in this pursuit as it is in
politics ; but, as far as I can observe, the French do not appreciate
his efforts as they deserve.  From Carcassonne I went to Montpellier,
which, to our ancestors, was what Cannes is now to us—namely,
an asylum from the English climate.  Whilst I was there, the
weather was anything but genial, and I returned to London on
May 10.

*May 27th.*—News has arrived from America of the death of
Stonewall Jackson.  He was wounded in the battle of May 2 ;
one ball striking him in the left arm near the shoulder, and
another in the right hand.  The arm was amputated, but he died
on the 9th.  The most melancholy part of it is that his death was
the result of accident, his own men, who would have died for him,

having shot him in a wood by mistake. This event will, I think, have a fatal effect on the prospects of the Confederates, for he was idolized by the whole army, who would have followed him anywhere, in full confidence that he was leading them to victory. He was only thirty-eight years of age.

*June 4th.*—Mr. Soames' bill to shut up public-houses on Sundays was rejected by 278 to 103.

*June 7th.*—All the elections in Paris have gone against the Government, showing strong feeling either against the Emperor or Persigny. The Opposition now number from twenty-five to thirty instead of five, and are almost all Red Republicans.

*June 19th.*—I spoke on the Brazilian question and on the conduct of Mr. Christie.[1] Lord Russell replied, but less well than usual, and the Government, seeing they were getting the worst of the debate after Lord Chelmsford's speech, and fearing that Lord Derby would get up, gave orders to their men not to answer Lord Chelmsford, and the debate was adjourned.

*June 20th.*—The French have taken Puebla, and are advancing upon Mexico.

*June 22nd.*—I went to the Duchess of Buccleuch's ball, where the Princess of Wales was asked, and had dined.

*June 23rd.*—Went to Mrs. Rose's concert. Mario sang at the Opera, and did not come till late. I asked him what he thought of Titiens' ' Marguerite,' and he said : ' Elle chante bien, mais elle est trop grosse ; elle ferait trois Marguerites.' He also said that the pitch at the Opera in England is three-quarters of a tone higher than abroad. The French pitch has been lowered, but Costa [2] will not change his, as it is more brilliant for the instruments ; but it is very hard upon the singers, the more so as the modern operas are written extremely high, and if they have to sing three-quarters of a tone higher than the composer intended, it must be a terrible strain upon their voices.

*July 1st.*—We went to the Mansion House, where we were

---

[1] Mr. Christie, who had been a Liberal M.P., was made by Lord Palmerston Minister at Brazil, where his acts and language were very high-handed.

[2] Sir Michael Costa died in 1884. I was at Naples when he left it in 1829 for England, with nothing but his talent for music to trust to. He became a general favourite in society as well as at the Opera, which he led for many years.

invited to a great dinner to meet Lord Derby. Almost all the principal members of the Conservative party were present, and it was a brilliant scene, though very long. Lord Derby's speech was extremely good, statesmanlike, and moderate, but giving no hope of his soon being in office.

*July 5th.*—Several people called, who told me that the scene in the House of Commons when the division took place on the vote for the purchase of the Exhibition building was extraordinary. Sir Stafford Northcote's speech was the signal for a storm, and he was forced to sit down. Disraeli had canvassed his supporters, telling them that he had a letter in his pocket from the Queen. This had a disastrous effect, and when he got up the hooting was so terrific that he could not be heard. Gladstone's speech had already excited great indignation, for it showed how completely the Government had deceived the House when Lord Palmerston had induced them to vote for the purchase of the land, leaving them under the delusion that the contractors for the Exhibition were bound to remove the building if it was not sold within a certain time. Gladstone had told them that there was no engagement of the sort, and that he believed they were not obliged to remove it at all. This, whether true or not, was taken as a menace to force them to buy the building, and infuriated the House of Commons the more, as Lord Elcho proved that the purchase would be a most disadvantageous one, entailing an enormous expense. So the House rose *en masse*, and after a scene of the utmost confusion and excitement, defeated the Government by more than two to one ; Gladstone and Disraeli looking equally angry.

*July 13th.*—We are deeply grieved to hear that our old friend, the Duke of Hamilton, has had a most serious accident. He left London last Friday, and dined that evening at a *café* in Paris with Mr. Henry Howard. On coming out at one o'clock in the morning he fell down the stairs, and was picked up senseless. I fear it will prove fatal.

*July 15th.*—We dined with the Chesterfields, where we heard of the Duke of Hamilton's death. It appears that he never rallied, except for a few minutes after the arteries of the temples had been opened, and he relapsed into a state of insensibility until his death. The Empress Eugénie was very kind, and remained with him until the arrival of the Duchess, who was at Baden.

We went to the Duchess of Wellington's concert.

A drawn battle has been fought between the armies of Lee and Meade. It began on July 1 and continued till the 3rd.

*July 17th.*—The Duchess of Hamilton and her daughter are gone to St. Cloud for the present. The sons remain in Paris, and accompany the body to Glasgow, where it is to be transported in a French man-of-war.

*July 21st.*—At Greenwich at the dinner which Lord Redesdale gives every year to the House of Lords.

*July 26th.*—News from America states that Vicksburg surrendered on July 4 unconditionally ; the garrison, amounting to 31,000 men, having been paroled. Lee has retreated safely across the Potomac with all his artillery and the booty he took in Maryland. He has certainly lost prestige by the ill-success of his expedition.

---

*August* 1, *Heron Court.*—I went to London on my way to Dover, where Lord Willoughby d'Eresby's yacht was lying. He has been so kind as to lend her to me for the season. She is a very large lugger, built by himself. I went over to Boulogne in her with Lord Ranelagh and Colonel Knox, and, on my return to Calais, sent her to meet me at Cowes ; but when I arrived there I found she had lost her foremast, being commanded by a very incompetent man. Lord Willoughby used her principally for fishing in Torbay, but she was a very bad sailer, being unable either to tack or to wear. I took her down Channel to the westward, to Torquay. To manage her sails properly she would require thirty men, and I had only sixteen. Her mainsail had a thousand yards of canvas, and altogether I consider her a very unsafe vessel, though perfectly fit for fishing.

*August* 11th.—I returned to London and went to Lowther Castle, where there was an agreeable party. We went to Horswater, a most beautiful lake enclosed in hills ; we netted it and caught a number of char.

*Mr. Disraeli to Lord M.*

Hughenden Manor : August 22, 1863.

My dear Malmesbury,—The Carlton and the Conservative Clubs are overflowing, and years must elapse before some men can enter them. They are also very exclusive. The Carlton rarely admits professional persons, and the Conservative only an insufficient percentage.

Taylor impresses on me the absolute necessity of a Junior Conservative, which shall be a central point for those country attorneys and land agents, &c., who are winning, and are to win, our elections. He thinks that it will powerfully organise and encourage our friends.

But there must be no mistake about the politics, and he wants, for trustees, Lord Derby, Lord Malmesbury, Mr. Disraeli, Lord Colville, Col. Taylor.

I have, at his suggestion, communicated with Lord Derby, who is favourable to the suggestion, if no liability is incurred by the trustees. This of course must be a *sine quâ non.*

What do you say to it ?                 Yours sincerely,                 D.

*September* 10*th, Heron Court.*—The Duc de Gramont arrived from Folkestone in time for dinner. He is obliged to be at Vienna in six days. He had not seen Lady Tankerville, his aunt, for eleven years, and was anxious to do so. He told me it was very probable he might some day come as ambassador to England, but not whilst Lord Palmerston is Minister ; for, besides that he could not get on with a Whig Government, he and d'Azeglio are not friends, and as long as Palmerston is Premier d'Azeglio is all-powerful.

*September* 14*th.*—We went to Longleat, where I was laid up for two days with gout.

*October* 5*th.*—The news from America is that the Confederates under General Bragg, who had been reinforced by Generals Lee, Johnstone, and Beauregard, defeated General Rosenkranz after two days' severe fighting. The Confederates took above 2,000 prisoners and twenty guns.

On October 5 I left for Paris and thence started on a journey to Tours and down the Loire, After again visiting Chenonceaux and some other castles on the river, I stopped at Saumur, a town

that is *à cheval* on this glorious stream. I went to see the old
feudal tower of Monsereau, which was seized during the Revolution of 1789 by the populace and has been held by them ever
since ; there must be at least a dozen families inhabiting its
ancient halls. I proceeded thence to the famous Abbey of Fontevrault, which is now a prison, but used to be a convent for ladies
of the highest rank in France. In visiting the vaults I found
the recumbent effigies, dressed in their royal robes, of our Henry II.
and his wife, Eleanor of Guienne ; their son, Richard Cœur-de-
Lion ; and Isabel d'Angoulême, widow of King John. The
Republicans of the last century, who wished to destroy them, were
prevented by some priests, who hid them away. They are very
fine specimens of the work of that time. Henry and his son
Richard are both of gigantic proportions, the latter being six feet
six. It struck me as so sad a thing to see these statues of the
great Plantagenets cast away in the cellars of a French prison
that I wrote to Persigny to entreat him to urge the Emperor from
me to give them up to England, that they might be placed in
Westminster Abbey. His answer to me for some reason miscarried, but when I did receive it, it regretted that at the present
time the English and French Governments were not on a footing
of cordiality, and that it was not a favourable moment for an interchange of compliments ; but that if our Party came in again
the Emperor would remember my request and would accede to it.[1]
At this time Lord John Russell had expressed his disagreement
with the Emperor on the subject of the Danish war and his wishes
to have a European Conference in so rough a style that his despatches had created considerable animosity. I do not blame his
disagreements, but the language in which he expressed them. The
consequence was that I failed in my attempt to rescue these
statues.

I went on from Saumur to Nantes, which is a fine and rich
town, and famous, or rather infamous, for the ' Republican Mar-

[1] In 1866, when Lord Derby was Premier for the third time, he was informed by
the Emperor that he would keep his promise if Lord Derby insisted upon it, but
that when he signified his intention of doing so and ordered the removal of the
effigies, the people of the district, although they had never taken any interest in
them, showed so violent an opposition that he hoped Lord Derby would release him,
which was done.

riages ' and other horrors committed by the notorious Carrier. I then went on to St. Nazaire, a new town at the mouth of the Loire. On entering the public room of the inn I found about a dozen French officers at supper, bound for Mexico, in high spirits at going there. After returning to Nantes I went to see the famous Château de Clisson, where the Vendeans in 1793 gained a great victory over the Republican troops, and were afterwards defeated, the prisoners taken alive being thrown down a well, on the site of which a fine spruce fir is now growing. It reminded me of Cawnpore, with its sinister associations.

---

*From Lord Malmesbury to Count Persigny.*

Saumur : le 12 octobre 1863.

Mon cher Persigny,—Vous savez que durant mon venvage politique je me plais souvent à parcourir la France. Cela vous expliquera pourquoi je vous écris d'une ville que personne ne visite que des commis-voyageurs, et qui cependant le mérite excessivement. Je m'adresse à vous pour vous faire une demande qui peut-être ne serait guère justifiée si nous n'étions de si anciens amis, et que je ne fusse certain que vous en apprécieriez le motif. Maintenant au fait. J'ai été voir Fontevrault, cette ancienne abbaye si célèbre, et qui aujourd'hui (comme vous le savez), au lieu de contenir de belles et nobles nonnes, renferme un millier de scélérats de toutes les couleurs. Là, dans le coin obscur d'un caveau en ruines, sont réléguées—*proh pudor !*—les statues de Henri II. et de son fils Richard Cœur-de-Lion, avec celles de leurs reines. C'est tout ce qui reste de ces grands rois d'Angleterre, dont les barbares de 1789 ont brisé et violé les tombes et dispersé les cendres. Ainsi, négligées, exploitées par un gardien de détenus, vues de presque personne dans leur position actuelle, ces effigies me semblent intéresser peu la France et être malheureusement inconnues et perdues pour l'Angleterre.

Croyez-vous que, si l'Empereur était informé de ces circonstances, il agirait avec sa générosité habituelle, et rendrait ces derniers souvenirs de la grande race des Plantagenets à Westminster Abbey où gisent leurs aïeux et leur postérité ? Mais, si toutefois S.M. pensait autrement, ne donnerait-il pas au rival et au compagnon d'armes de Phillipe-Auguste un coin plus digne de cette large France dont jadis le ' Cœur de Lion ' possédait le quart ? Si, mon cher Persigny, ma réclamation vous paraît inconvenante ou mal imaginée, je me fie à votre amitié de ne pas en parler à Sa Majesté, et de regarder cette lettre comme non-avenue.　Je ne l'aurais écrite à personne qu'à vous.　Mille amitiés,

MALMESBURY.

*November 1st.*—The monster balloon at Paris has come to grief, and M. and Mme. Nadard are much hurt.　The anchors would not hold, and the balloon dragged along the ground for several leagues, knocking over trees and doing much damage.　It was finally stopped near Neuburg, and the passengers taken to Hanover.

The accounts from Prussia are very bad for the King.　The elections are going on unfortunately for his Government, being more Liberal even than the last, and he has not the resource of another dissolution of the Chambers, as this is the third within the year ; but he is apparently determined to have an army formed according to his own ideas.

The papers mention that the large ironclad steamer, the ' Prince Consort,' which was sent to Liverpool to prevent the two rams built by Mr. Laird from leaving for America, encountered the gale of last Friday in the Irish Channel, and put into Kingstown almost in a sinking state.　She sprang a leak and had seven feet of water in her hold.　Nothing but the most arduous exertions on the part of her officers and crew could keep her from going down.

*November 4th.*—I met Lord Palmerston in the train at Bishopstoke, where he was waiting for the Portsmouth train.　He was much annoyed at the loss of his trees at Broadlands in the late storms.　I lost many of mine, some elms as old as the time of Henry VIII.

*November 7th.*—The English papers consider the Emperor Napoleon's speech very pacific, but I cannot view it in that light, for though he declares he has no intention of going to war in support of the Poles at present, he calls upon the sovereigns of Europe to appoint a Congress for the discussion of the Polish question and the settlement of others affecting the nationalities ; adding *that the treaties of* 1815 *are at an end,* and that if the Great Powers refuse the Congress, there must eventually be war. The Paris papers look upon this speech as threatening, and the Funds went down in consequence.

*November* 12*th*.—The Duke of Somerset, who dined with us, said that the ironclad steamer 'Prince Consort,' which was in such danger in the late storm in the Irish Channel, did not spring a leak as was supposed, but was nearly sunk by her own crew, who pumped the water *in* instead of pumping it *out*.

The Emperor Napoleon has written a circular to all the sovereigns of Europe inviting them to a Congress at Paris to settle the affairs of Europe.  As he says in his speech in opening Parliament that the treaties of 1815 have ceased to exist, and he talks of sacrifices to be made for the public good, I suspect there will be great disinclination to respond to the summons, which he has also sent in an offensive and dictatorial manner. Victor Emanuel telegraphed his acceptance at once, showing that he expects to gain by the new distribution of Europe. Probably England would be required to give up Gibraltar.

*November* 16*th*.—The King of Denmark is dead, and Prince Christian succeeds him.

*November* 24*th*.—We went to Blenheim, which well deserves to be called a palace.  It has been fitted up almost entirely by the Duke and Duchess, and does great credit to their taste ; in fact, it has all the magnificence of a palace and all the comforts of a small house.  We dined in the Saloon, a very handsome room, and after dinner the tapestry rooms were opened and we sat there, as they join the library, where the ball was to take place.  The ball-room is 180 feet long and very high.  The pleasure grounds, which are very beautiful, slope down to the edge of the lake on one side, and on the opposite shore a hill, covered with wood, rises from the water.  It must be a perfect Paradise in summer.

*November* 29*th*, *Heron Court*.—Mr. Seymour Fitzgerald arrived from Paris, where he says the refusal of our Government to attend the Congress proposed by Napoleon, and especially the rude tone of Lord Russell's despatch, has created great irritation.  The correspondence between the English and French Governments respecting the Congress is published in to-day's papers.  Lord Russell's despatch is published in the 'Gazette,' and I am not surprised that the French are angry, for not only is it very rude,

but it was sent without the least delay, and published in the
'Times' before it was delivered to Drouyn de l'Huys !

*December 5th.*—I returned from Windsor. The Queen sent
for me before dinner and spoke of the Danish question ; though
she is annoyed about it, she told me that it was not my fault,
that I could not do otherwise than sign the treaty of 1852, which
had been drawn up by Palmerston.

*December 7th.*—Sir Augustus Paget has written to say he
cannot leave Copenhagen in the present state of affairs. Austria
and Prussia threaten a Federal execution, and the King of Den-
mark has withdrawn the patent giving a joint Constitution to
Holstein, which was the great cause of offence, as it incorporated
Holstein with Denmark. Schleswig has offered 35,000 men to
Denmark if the Federal troops cross the Eider and if they enter
Schleswig.

*December 8th.*—Lord Henry Lennox and the Marchese Fortu-
nato called, with the news that the Confederates had been totally
routed by General Grant at Look-out Mountain, General Braggs
having been defeated with the loss of sixty cannon.

*December 31st.*—The Federal troops have entered Holstein
and been received with acclamation.


# 1864

*January 9th.*—The Princess of Wales has been safely confined :
a prince. The event was not expected till March, and as it was
intended to take place at Marlborough House, no preparations
had been made at Frogmore. There was no nurse, no baby linen,
and no doctor, except Mr. Brown, the Windsor physician, who
attended her, and brought the child into the world, for which, it
is said, he will be made a knight and receive 500*l.* Lady
Macclesfield was fortunately in waiting, and as she has had a
great many children, she was probably of use. Lord Granville
was the only Minister in attendance, having come to dine with
the Prince, and there was not time to summon the others, as the
Princess was not ill more than three hours. She had been to see

the skating, and did not return to Frogmore till four o'clock, soon after which she was taken ill.

I saw Disraeli, who called to-day, and wanted to talk to me upon political arrangements to be made, should our party come in. He quite scouted the idea of being Foreign Minister himself, as he has no intention of giving up the leadership of the House of Commons ; he said it would be quite impossible to do the work of both,[1] and that Lord Palmerston, when he was Foreign Secretary, hardly ever appeared in the House of Commons.

*Lord Derby to Lord M.*

Knowsley : January 10, 1864.

My dear Malmesbury,—I need not tell you how sincerely sorry I am to hear your report of yourself, and how anxiously I hope that Bence Jones may be able to set you right, even in a shorter time than you seem to anticipate. Private and public feelings are in this case in entire accordance ; for I do not know what I should do in the House of Lords, and still less if there were to be a change of Government, if you were not in a condition to give me your assistance. We have too few good men capable of holding office, and especially connected with foreign affairs, to be able to spare one. Stanley has a contempt for the arts of diplomacy, and an intense dislike to be involved in any foreign affairs. . . . In short, if we are *doomed* to come in, I *must* have *you* again. So get well as fast as you can. Vitzthum has sent me, confidentially, his and Beust's correspondence with John Russell ; the latter, as usual, effusive in tone, but, as I have not concealed from Vitzthum, having the best of the argument. I have given him my opinion very plainly, and expressed an anxious hope, in the interests of Germany, that war may yet be avoided. But I fear that with the Germans just now passion is too strong for reason ; and Austria and Prussia are so mutually afraid of each other gaining the ascendency in that pestilent body, the Diet, that they will both be driven to be the slaves of the minor States. Austria, however, can hardly engage in a crusade for 'Nationalities,' nor Prussia for 'Constitutional Rights.' I quite agree with you that if we had taken a firm tone at once, there would have been no invasion of Schleswig ; and everything else was capable of adjustment. Now, if there be such an invasion, war is declared,

---

[1] This is quite true, and I found what Lord Palmerston told me was correct— namely, that the average work of the Foreign Office took him ten hours of the twenty-four.

and we shall have placed Denmark in a very disadvantageous position, having abandoned Holstein at our suggestion.

.　　.　　.　　.　　.　　.　　.

Ever yours sincerely,　　　　　DERBY.

P.S.—Do you know, or can you find out, whether the Emperor gave our Government any hint as to his intention to propose a Congress, before he made his public announcement? If he did not, it does not look like very cordial feelings, and, I must add, he laid himself open to the rebuff he met with. That, however, is no sufficient vindication of our *brusquerie*.　　　　　D.

### From Count Persigny to Lord M.

Paris : le 12 janvier 1864.

Mon cher Malmesbury,—La poste me renvoie aujourd'hui une lettre que je vous écrivis il y a deux mois. Un singulier accident paraît avoir causé cette mésaventure. Soit que l'encre fût mauvaise ou qu'un acide tombé sur l'enveloppe en ait altéré la qualité, il a été impossible de lire l'adresse : elle était presque complètement effacée.

Il n'y avait rien de bien important dans cette lettre. Je vous disais que j'avais soumis à l'Empereur la question archéologique que vous soumettez au sujet du tombeau de Richard Cœur-de-Lion et de son père, et du désir que vous exprimez. L'Empereur en principe était favorable à l'idée de donner ce monument à l'Angleterre ; mais à cause des contretemps diplomatiques qui embrouillaient un peu nos relations, il désirait ajourner cette petite affaire. Je reste, quant à moi, chargé de votre commission, et dès que je verrai le moment favorable de renouveler la démarche, je le ferai avec le grand désir, et, du reste, la presque certitude de réussir.

Mille amitiés dévouées,　　　　　PERSIGNY.

*January* 19th.—The Austrians and Prussians have decided upon entering Schleswig should the King of Denmark not revoke the Constitution of November 18. Their envoys presented a note to that effect on the 16th, and, on the refusal of the King, left Copenhagen on the 18th.

### George B. Mathew,[1] Esq., C.B., to Lord M.

San José, Costa Rica : January 20, 1864.

Dear Lord Malmesbury,—I took the liberty of sending to your address one of the famed 'quezals,' whose plumage under the Aztec

H.M. Chargé d'Affaires at Costa Rica, and a very able man.

Emperor was reserved for Imperial wear; but I have been so unlucky in my attempts to send any sort of parcel to England, that I delayed to write until I heard of their safe arrival there. Guatemala can boast of no other curiosities, and indeed of nothing else save cochineal; but I trust you will deem the birds deserving a place on your hall table, from their former fame.

My stay in these wretched Republics is drawing to a close, as our objects are, *tant bien que mal*, carried out, and though I have, inevitably, incurred animosities in some quarters, I venture to hope that I have done some good, and have further established, by an impartial course, and by a frank avowal of my opinions, the *prestige* that should attend an English Minister in these half-civilised countries. Lord Russell has been good enough to give me the C.B., and though some of my friends think I might have expected it on my return from Mexico, and the higher grade now, I feel that any mark of approval from a Minister who may not view with partiality my political opinions and antecedents is very acceptable and gratifying.

For the last two years Mexican affairs have had a leading influence in some of these Republics, and a dream of a French Protectorate, or, at least, of annexation to an Ultra-Catholic Empire in Mexico (nurtured by the unwise and indecent partizanship of the French Chargé d'Affaires), induced Guatemala and her paid ally, Nicaragua, to enter upon the late sanguinary war with Salvador and Honduras. The clerical party, who hold despotic sway in Guatemala, through the hands of a debauched Indian savage, have succeeded in overthrowing in the two neighbouring States administrations that had alarmed them by their union and constitutional tendencies, and had offended them by so-termed 'impious' acts of placing the clergy on a level with others before the ordinary tribunals. Some of the members have been murdered in cold blood, and others, including Barrios, the late President of Salvador, have saved their lives by escaping from the country. Assuredly, the rule of France or of any other Power would therefore be a blessing to humanity, and a great boon to civilisation and commerce; but M. de Cabarras, in following the precise footsteps of M. Dubois de Saligny, takes the least effectual and the least creditable way of popularising the idea. To describe the utmost excesses of arbitrary despotism, murder, plunder, and an utter absence of justice, as the rule of religion, law, and order, and to accuse those who do not concur in this conclusion of being imbued with revolutionary ideas, is *un peu fort*, and is not, I think, likely to achieve the object in view.

I am really glad to gather from the papers that the Emperor has found out at last the real value of M. Dubois' statements. They have cost France dear; but even now, if the laws of France as to religious as well as civil matters are declared in force, and if such men as Miramon, Marquez, and others, who, when *bought* by the clergy, were wholly without any party in the nation, and disgraced their cause by their atrocities, are sent for a time out of the country, an agreement with the National Party in Mexico would be facile. Indeed I feel sure, from my influence with the honest, kind-hearted, but obstinate and ill-informed Juarez, that on such terms I could ensure his submission, which, once declared, would be permanent. But I suffered so much from the rarefied atmosphere—being, indeed, threatened with an attack of the same nature as that which has just carried off one of my earliest and best friends, poor Elgin, that I should be very loth to return to Mexico save for a brief visit. All Europe may be interested in the occupation of Mexico by France, whether as an empire or as a protectorate, for it may serve better than Algiers as an outlet for hot blood; but if peace be long delayed we shall see the unscrupulous Government of Washington pouring into the North their disbanded and homeless soldiers.

The horizon seems as much clouded in Europe as on this side of the Atlantic. It struck me long ago that it would be wise to tempt the Duke of Augustenburg with Greece!

No man can read the horrors perpetrated in Poland without indignation. I know no kindlier man than the Emperor Alexander, with whom I was once on very friendly terms at Rome; but there is much irritable weakness in his character, and he needs the influence of good men to counteract the bad about him. The savage hatred felt towards all Poles by the older men in the Russian nobility is as unaccountable as it is deep. At all events, Russia can no longer quote treaties in Greece or in the East: 'Quis tulerit Gracchos de seditione querentes?'

Very faithfully yours,            GEORGE B. MATHEW.

*January 24th.*—I have been very ill for the last month, and living upon opiates. Lord Derby came to see me to-day, and gave me an outline of his intended speech at the meeting of Parliament, which is, of course, an attack upon Lord Russell's foreign policy. He and Lady Derby are going to Osborne next Thursday. He is decidedly Danish.

*January 25th.*—Mr. Bentinck called to tell me that the Austrians and Prussians have refused the request of the Danish Government for delay to enable their Parliament to meet and deliberate upon the withdrawal of the Constitution for Schleswig, and intend to invade the province directly.

*January 27th.*—The 'Standard' of this morning contains an article, which was sent by Brünnow, saying that at the Cabinet held last Monday Ministers arrived at a very grave decision respecting the Dano-German conflict—that that decision had been submitted by Lord Russell to her Majesty, and that despatches had been sent off to the Ambassadors at the Courts of Prussia and Austria, notifying the hostile attitude that the Government of Great Britain would be compelled to assume in the event of the Prussian and Austrian troops invading Schleswig. The French Government is, it is said, upon this point at union with the British, and it is hoped that with the prospect of this opposition the great German Powers will not persist in provoking a war.

*January 29th.*—The 'Standard' has an article this morning announcing Lord Russell's resignation on account of his disagreement with his colleagues, as he takes the German side. This is not true. The Prussians and Austrians are advancing towards the Eider with the intention of entering Schleswig ; the Danes are preparing to resist, but can have little chance unless England or France come to their assistance, which the latter, it is said, is ready to do, but the Queen will not hear of going to war with Germany. No doubt this country would like to fight for the Danes, and, from what is said, I infer that the Government is inclined to support them also, but finds great difficulties in the opposition of the Queen.[1]

*January 31st.*—A dreadful catastrophe occurred at Santiago on December 8, at a religious ceremony at the Jesuits' Church. A transparency on the altar caught fire, and the flames were communicated so rapidly to the muslin and gauze dressing that was hung all over the church that very few made their escape. The men, who were in a separate part of the church, divided by a grating, got away, but 2,000 women, comprising the greatest part of the ladies of Santiago, most of them young girls with their

---

[1] It is perhaps well that we did not enter into this contest, as our army was not armed at that time, like the Prussians, with the breechloader, and we should probably have suffered in consequence the same disaster as the Austrians did two years later.

mothers, were burnt to death. The lamps were filled with paraffin
oil, which fell upon the poor women in streams of liquid fire, and
the work of destruction was so rapid that but a quarter of an
hour elapsed from the beginning to the end. The bigotry of the
people in Santiago can hardly be believed if we did not know as
a fact that there is a public post-office for the Virgin, who corre-
sponds personally with her votaries.

*February 2nd.*—The Prussians have entered Schleswig. The
Danes withdrew. Count de Flahault has been made Chancellor
of the Legion of Honour—a great place, which gives him a large
salary and a fine house in Paris.

*February 6th.*—News from Rendsburg says that in the attack
upon Jagel on the 3rd, the Austrians, who were repulsed, lost 600
men and many officers, since which there has been more fighting,
and the Danes were defeated, although the Austrians lost seventeen officers and 500 men. The Prussian Press now declares that
Schleswig-Holstein is irreparably separated from Denmark, and
that war puts an end to treaties.

*February 9th.*—Severe fighting at Flensburg. Barricades
were erected in the street, and the Austrians lost 1,100 men.
Most of the Danish troops have escaped to Alsen Island, but,
the channel being only 1,000 yards broad, they will not be secure
from the cannon. News from Vienna of yesterday says that a
Council of Ministers was held, under the presidency of the
Emperor, on the 7th, at which highly important resolutions were
passed, the purport of which was that the London treaty of 1852
can no longer be considered by Austria as a basis of negotiation.
I made a speech yesterday in the House of Lords, explaining the
share I took in that treaty ; and Lord Russell, though he confessed, in reply to my questions, that the Government had received
no guarantee that Austria and Prussia would evacuate Schleswig
when the King of Denmark had fulfilled his engagements, yet
said they were bound by that treaty to respect the integrity of
the Danish monarchy. Lord Palmerston made the same declaration in the House of Commons. If it is true that Austria has
committed such a breach of faith, I hope she will lose Venetia.

*February 11th.*—The Duke of Augustenburg is proclaimed
everywhere in Holstein and Schleswig in the presence of the

Austrians and Prussians, who make no objection, thereby making it very evident that they do not intend restoring the Duchies to Denmark.

*February* 13*th.*—The Austrians are said to show symptoms of backing out of the war, probably frightened for Venetia, as the Italians are evidently preparing themselves.

*February* 16*th.*—The Danes are in the island of Alsen and at Düppel, a fortified place in the mainland. General Meza's retreat has saved the Danish army, for it was too weak to hold the Dannewerke, and would have been cut off had he delayed.

*February* 21*st.*—I hear that Lord Russell has sent for M. Bille,[1] the Danish Minister, and told him his Government must not depend upon any material support from England, as we would not go to war for Denmark. M. Bille asked if an invasion of Jutland would make us alter our minds, and Lord Russell replied that, even if the Germans went to Copenhagen, it would make no difference. The Prussians occupied Jutland for two days, but have retired in consequence of orders from Berlin.

*February* 23*rd.*—The Prussians made an attack on the village of Düppel yesterday, but were repulsed, leaving many dead and wounded on the field. The Danes lost 200 men ; the battle lasted four hours.

*February* 24*th.*—The Government had a majority of 25 last night on Mr. Fitzgerald's motion for copies of the correspondence between the Government and Messrs. Laird relating to the steam-ram. House divided : 178 to 153.

On a motion for the Schleswig-Holstein papers they had a still larger majority. Lord Palmerston was ill in bed with cold and gout, but was sent for, his colleagues being much alarmed, and came tottering in after the division had taken place. Austria and Prussia have accepted our proposal for a conference to be held in London, but the war is to go on just the same.

*March* 1*st.*—I dined at Marlborough House. The Princess of Wales told me that her father and mother's health had suffered much from the constant anxiety they had gone through.

*March* 6*th.*—I passed the morning writing copies of my letters to the Prince of Schleswig, the latter having begun a correspon-

[1] Danish Minister in London.

dence on the subject of Schleswig-Holstein by asking me to
retract a statement I had made in the House of Lords, which I
refused to do.

*March 9th.*—Lord Derby called, and seems *préoccupé*. I
believe he is much puzzled what to do on the Danish question.
All his party are for the Danes, and he also sympathises with
them ; but the Court is against them. As Lord Bath was there
and is very German, of course Lord Derby did not feel himself on
safe ground.

Everybody is talking of Count Bernstorff's having refused to
drink the King of Denmark's health at the banquet at Buckingham
Palace yesterday, after the christening of the young prince, the
child of the Prince and Princess of Wales. He, however, denies
the whole thing, and gave an official denial to Lord Russell.

### From the Comtesse de Flahault (on the death of the Duc de Morny).

Paris : March 11, 1864.

Alas ! dear Lord Malmesbury, all was over at eight o'clock yesterday morning, and I have only to thank you for your kind sympathy,
which we feel deeply. We are overwhelmed with grief at this most
unlooked-for misfortune, but M. de Flahault has gone through these
trying scenes with courage and composure, and will, I hope, now be
able to take some rest. It has been a comfort having Emily with us,
and Shelburne arrived last night. You, who knew Auguste well, will
understand how well he merited all our love, and what a loss he is to
his family. In Paris the consternation is general, and there is every
demonstration of its being felt as a public calamity. The Emperor is
deeply affected, and on the evening of his death was for two hours at
his bedside, where we were assembled.

Adieu, dear Lord Malmesbury, again . . . Believe me truly yours,
M. M. DE FLAHAULT, K.N.

I ought not to omit that the Empress was there also, and very kind.

*March 12th.*—I was introduced to the new French Ambassador, the Prince de la Tour d'Auvergne. He is very pompous,
and much out of humour with this country, declaring that
England is more bound than any other to support the Danes,
because the treaty of 1852 was signed in London. The sympathies

of our party are entirely with the Danes, and the Emperor Napoleon would be ready to declare war against the Germans if we would join him ; but, in my opinion, neither his army nor ours would have been equal to such a policy, for neither of us have the needle-gun, with which the Prussians are armed.

*March* 18*th.*—Sir Henry Stracey moved a vote of censure on Mr. Stansfeld, for allowing himself to be the medium of communi‑ cation between Mazzini and his friends. The subject was mooted ten days ago, and Mr. Stansfeld's explanation was unsatisfactory, as he confined himself to praising Mazzini, and evaded answering the question whether the name of Fiori or Flower was an *alias* of Mazzini's or not. The subject being resumed to-day, he at last confessed very reluctantly that he had allowed Mazzini to have his letters addressed to his (Mr. Stansfeld's) house under that name. A division took place, and Sir Henry Stracey's motion was only negatived by ten : 171 to 161. The Government defended him vigorously, and the utmost efforts were made to get a good majority. Considering that Mazzini's policy was perfectly well known to be founded on assassination, and that they must have known it, they can hardly have been proud of this victory. Lord Palmerston, however, seems not to think so, as, when Mr. Stansfeld offered to resign his place under Government, he refused, and said he would take the responsibility upon himself.[1]

*April* 12*th.*—Garibaldi has arrived in London, and went to Stafford House. His reception was enthusiastic.

*April* 13*th.*—We dined at Stafford House to meet Garibaldi. The party consisted of the Palmerstons, Russells, Gladstones, Argylls, Shaftesburys, Dufferins, &c., and other Whigs, the Derbys and ourselves being the only Conservatives ; so I greatly fear we have made a mistake, and that our party will be dis‑ gusted at our going. Lady Shaftesbury told me after dinner, in a *méchante* manner, that we had fallen into a trap, to which I answered that I was very much obliged to those who laid it, as I should be very sorry not to have seen Garibaldi. The Dowager Duchess of Sutherland walked off with him to her boudoir, where he smoked. This created great astonishment and amusement, as

---

[1] On any question concerning Italy or an Italian Lord Palmerston had no scruples.

this boudoir, which is fitted up most magnificently with hangings
of velvet and everything that is most costly, has been considered
such a sacred spot that few favoured mortals have ever been
admitted into its precincts ; and to allow anyone to smoke in it
is most astonishing to all who know the Duchess.

The Government were defeated last night, on the motion of
Lord Robert Cecil,[1] on the reports of the inspectors of schools, by
101 to 93.

*April 15th.*—Our party are furious with us and Lord Derby
for dining with the Sutherlands last Wednesday, and Lord Bath
has written to Lord Colville to resign his office of Whip, and says
he will not spend a farthing upon elections.   Lord Derby has
written him a very temperate letter.

*April 18th.*—I dined with the Clanricardes to meet Garibaldi,
and smoked a cigar with him after dinner.   He spoke very sensibly,
and, far from seeming proud of the fuss that was made with him,
he said he feared it might become ridiculous.   Sir Robert Peel,
talking of Rome, said that he did not think it possible to get rid
of the Papacy ; that Garibaldi might drive the Pope out of Rome,
but another would be elected, as long as the Roman Catholic
religion existed.   Garibaldi replied, ' Vous l'avez bien fait, cependant.'   Again, some one said that the career of the present Emperor Napoleon was a more successful one than that of the first.
Garibaldi answered, ' *Il faut attendre la fin.*'

Düppel has fallen, and the Danes have lost many officers and
men.

*April 20th.*—Garibaldi leaves England on Friday.   Lord
Clarendon, who has just returned from Paris, has informed the
Government that the Emperor has made *that* the condition of his
joining with us in the conference ; and certainly there must be
some intrigue, as Mr. Ferguson, the surgeon, writes a letter to the
Duke of Sutherland—which is published—saying it would be
dangerous for Garibaldi's health if he exposed himself to the
fatigue of an expedition to Manchester, &c.   On the other hand,
Dr. Basile, Garibaldi's own doctor, says he is perfectly well and
able to undergo all the fatigue of a journey to the manufacturing

---

[1] Now Marquis of Salisbury, 1884.

towns. The publication of this letter in contradiction to Mr. Ferguson's must have been done with Garibaldi's consent ; it shows he is angry, and does not leave England willingly.

*April 22nd.*—Garibaldi goes to-day to Cliefden, where he remains with the Dowager-Duchess of Sutherland until the 25th, when he leaves for Plymouth.

The Duchess of Cambridge and Princess Mary attacked me for going to Stafford House to meet him, saying that they admired my devotion to Lord Derby, which induced me to accept the invitation.

*April 28th.*—We had a dinner for the Duke of Cambridge, the Princess Edward, the Tankervilles, Lady Ely, Sir A. and Lady Paget, Colonel and Mrs. Macdonald, the Cadores, Lord Clanwilliam, Lord E. St. Maur, and Count Apponyi. Lord Bath complained of Sir Augustus Clifford's having turned on the gas in the House of Lords when Garibaldi entered ; and said he had told Sir Augustus that he meant to bring his conduct before the House, but that Sir Augustus expressed his regret and begged to be let off on account of his old friendship with Lord Bath's father. So Lord Bath forgave him. This story was received with a good deal of laughter, which Lord Bath took very well.

———————

On May 6 I crossed to Paris, and, after two or three days, taking the road to Lyons, went down the Rhône to Arles, a very interesting old town, evidently peopled in former times by a colony from Central Italy, so very remarkable is the physique of the inhabitants. The women are proverbially handsome, but entirely of the Etruscan type, with magnificent dark hair and eyes, good teeth, and fair complexions. They have beautiful round throats, set on fine shoulders and busts, but their legs are much too short for their general build. I had a good opportunity of seeing the population, as it was a *jour de fête,* and there were games in the square, such as climbing a greased pole for a leg of mutton placed at the top, which no one succeeded in winning. The women were all in costume, with black veils worn like the mantilla. I noticed that the men were remarkably plain, sallow, undersized, and narrow-chested—in every way a striking contrast to the women.

The old Roman Amphitheatre here is very perfect, with towers added in the Middle Ages. Having heard of an old feudal castle called Les Baux, some twelve or fourteen miles from Arles, I took a carriage to visit it. We passed through an arid country till we reached a village with an ancient tower and other buildings, at the foot of which was a hermit's cell very curiously contrived in the rock, where there was a secret way of escaping and hiding in the deeper recesses in case of danger. Here was the hermit's bed of stone ; he is supposed to have been the first to introduce Christianity in that country. His name, which I forget, is held in high reverence, and a church there is dedicated to his memory.

Proceeding on my road, the mountains loom in the distance with the colour of yellow sandstone, and, on their summit, the castle and town of Les Baux. They appear perfectly bare and scorched by the burning sun of Provence. At the foot of the mountain there were some beautiful pomegranates and fine cypresses, but no other vegetation. The ascent to the town is winding and very steep. At the top there are the remains of a street of what must have been formerly very handsome houses, the ruins of which show the remains of the Renaissance carvings on the door-posts. A solitary priest came out of a small church, kept in tolerable order, and lamented the fate that forced him to live in so desolate a region. Higher up you reach a plateau with the castle and an enormous *pigeonnier*—sign of feudal privilege.

From quite a short distance the whole town is invisible, as it is not built of stone, but hewn out of the solid rock. It is altogether the most curious place I ever visited, and hardly ever seen by English travellers, although it is worth any trouble. From the summit the view is splendid, with a mirage which makes the plain below look like the sea. It was on these plains that Charles Martel gained a final victory over the Saracens.

After this I retraced my steps to Grenoble, close to which Casimir Périer has a very fine château ; and, after seeing the Great St. Bernard, I proceeded through Geneva to Berne to pay a visit to my brother, who is Minister there. I returned to Paris by the Basle Railway.

On passing through Paris I had a satisfactory conversation with Drouyn de l'Huys, and there I also heard of the death of the Duc de Malakoff, partly caused by his annoyance at the insurrection which has broken out in Algeria.

*June 1st.*—I returned from Paris, and we dined with the Derbys. Fred Stanley was married yesterday to Lady Constance Villiers.

*June 8th.*—Left London for Heron Court to see the famous rhododendrons, which are all in flower.

*June 11th.*—Returned to London.

*June 16th.*—Went to a party at the Duchess of Buccleuch's, where Count Sabouroff told me that, at the last meeting of the Conference, the Germans proposed to submit the disputed territory in Schleswig to arbitration, that this was supported by the neutral Powers, and the Danish plenipotentiaries had asked for delay to refer to their Court. He could, or would, not tell me who is to be arbitrator, but everybody supposes it will be the French Emperor.

*June 17th.*—There was a debate in the House of Commons on the Ashanti question. Lord Palmerston made an angry speech, accusing and misrepresenting Lord Derby's Government for having established a protectorate of the Fanti tribes, which has got us into the present difficulty. This was denied by Disraeli, who asserted that it began in 1826, and Lord Palmerston had not a word to say in reply. The House divided, and Government had a majority of seven.

Both sides cheered when the numbers were read, ours being pleased at the smallness of the majority and glad not to turn out the Government on a comparatively unimportant question.

*June 20th.*—The papers to-day give an account of a naval engagement off Cherbourg between the celebrated Confederate blockade-runner the 'Alabama' and the Federal ship 'Kearsage.' After about an hour's fighting, a shot struck the 'Alabama' just above the water line, and she sank. The crew jumped overboard, and a great many were saved by an English steam-yacht, the 'Deerhound,' which picked up Captain Semmes, thirteen officers, many

men, and immediately steamed off with them to Southampton, the
Americans saving a good many more.

*June 27th.*—The armistice having expired between the Germans and Danes, hostilities have recommenced by the Prussian
batteries opening fire upon Alsen.

I went to the House of Lords, which was immensely full, the
anxiety being very great to hear the explanation of the Government with respect to the war.  Lord Russell got up and spoke for
nearly two hours ; for the first half-hour he was almost inaudible,
but after that I heard enough to know that the Government were
for peace at any price, and meant to desert the Danes.  Lord
Derby, who was in his place, though suffering from gout, answered
him, and after deprecating any discussion, begged his party to say
nothing that evening.

*June 29th.*—I went to the ball at Buckingham Palace.  There
was a great crowd and some ridiculous-looking women in high
dresses.  The royal party came in by a door close to the daïs, so
they did not pass up the room, and sat down without taking notice
of anybody.

Everybody is talking of the absurd ending of Lord Palmerston's speech last Monday, in which he said that ' if the Government had reason to expect to see at Copenhagen the horrors of a
town taken by assault, the destruction of property, the sacrifice
of the lives, not only of its defenders, but of its peaceful inhabitants, the confiscations which would ensue, and the capture of
the sovereign as a prisoner of war,' he (Lord Palmerston) ' did not
mean to say that if any of those events were likely to happen, the
position of this country might not be subject to reconsideration.'

*July 3rd.*—Lord Derby is so ill with the gout that he cannot
bring on the question of the correspondence between Denmark and
Germany next Friday, and he has deputed me to do it in his place,
and Lords Salisbury,[1] Donoughmore, Colville, Hardwicke,[2] Carnarvon, and Chelmsford came this afternoon at one o'clock to
consult with me respecting the motion to be made in the House
of Lords.

Lord Derby is nervous in consequence of some objections made

---

[1] The late Lord Salisbury.        [2] The late Lord Hardwicke.

by the Duke of Buccleuch [1] and Lord Stanhope, who talk of a collision between the two Houses, and he fears the party will not be unanimous. I am, however, for going on with it, and so were the rest. We adjourned at two o'clock to Lord Salisbury's, where a large meeting took place, I being in the chair. The two above-named peers, with Lords Winchester and Bath, made some difficulties, but ended by giving way, and it was settled unanimously that the same resolution which Disraeli makes to-day in the Commons is to be moved on Friday in the Lords. I went yesterday to Disraeli to settle about this, he merely pointing to a chair. I did not sit down, but gave him the message Lord Derby had sent, and went away. After the meeting at Lord Salisbury's I went to Lord Derby's to report what had occurred. He was pleased to hear that the motion was not given up, but he was in such dreadful pain that I did not stay.

*July 8th.*—I went to the House of Lords to bring forward my resolution against the foreign policy of the Government. The Duke of Argyll replied, and then Lord Brougham got up, being followed by Lords Chelmsford and Carnarvon. The division took place at half-past two A.M., and we had a majority of nine—177 to 168. In the House of Commons the Government had a majority of eighteen—313 to 295.

*July 11th.*—A horrible murder was committed last Saturday evening in a first-class carriage on the North London Railway. The victim was Mr. Briggs, a clerk in Robartes's bank, who was attacked, robbed, and thrown from the carriage.

After giving a dinner for the Duchess of Cambridge and Princess Mary, we went to Lady Rokeby's, who had tableaux, which were beautifully got up, and would have been better still if the singing behind the scenes had been in tune.

*July 13th.*—Mr. Briggs's chain has been identified. It was pawned by a man who had the appearance of a foreigner.

*July 24th.*—The murderer of Mr. Briggs is suspected to be a German tailor, called Franz Müller. Müller had bought a hat of a certain Matthews, who identified it as being the one found in the railway carriage after the murder.

---

[1] The Duke of Buccleuch died 1884.

*August 2nd.*—I went to Lowther Castle and Lady Malmesbury to Chillingham.

*August 17th, Heron Court.*—This place is completely burnt up; the lawn is like a stubble field, there are no vegetables in the kitchen garden, the farmers are obliged to feed their cattle on hay, and all the small birds are starving as if in a hard frost.

*August 21st.*—Rain has come at last and penetrated about an inch into the ground, so it will do some good.

*September 7th.*—News has arrived of the capture of Müller at New York with Mr. Briggs's hat and chain upon him, and it is thought that he will arrive in England about the 15th.

I leave London for Paris on the 27th.

*October 2nd, Aix-les-Bains.*—I went down to Lyons and Avignon, where I found the cold so intense that I proceeded to Aix-les-Bains, but without any improvement. The weather here is bitter, and I am writing, shivering close to a blazing fire. I shall go back to Paris.

*October 18th.*—Reached Paris, which is much warmer than the South of France.

*October 19th.*—Returned to London.

*October 30th.*—The murderer Müller has been convicted and sentenced to death.

*November 3rd.*—We left London by the Paddington Railway and reached Hughenden by three o'clock. Mrs. Disraeli was at home, and after luncheon we took a walk in the woods. She says she has laid them out herself, and certainly she deserves great credit, as I never saw any prettier. They are very extensive, on two sides of a narrow valley, with walks in all directions. We returned about four, just as the rest of the party came back from Cliefden. It was composed of the Duke and Duchess of Wellington, Lord and Lady Raglan, Lord Orford, and Mr. Courtenay. The dinner was very gay; Disraeli exerted himself to the utmost to be agreeable. The evening was very short, Mrs. Disraeli sending us all to bed at half-past ten.

*November 4th.*—Beautiful day. We all went out driving through Hampden Park, where there are some fine beeches and a long grass drive, down which Hampden rode at the head of his men (not soldiers) to present the Bill of Rights to Charles I. We then crossed the Chiltern Hills, and on reaching a plateau, from whence there is a beautiful view, we got out of the carriage and walked down the hill to a lovely spot at Chequers Court, called Velvet Lawn, where we had luncheon, after which we returned to the carriage and drove through Lady Frankland Russell's park home.

*November 7th.*—Left London for Broke Hall, in Norfolk, which is hired by the Charteris' for the shooting. The owner is the grandson of the celebrated Sir Philip Broke, who captured the American frigate 'Chesapeake' by boarding her. The figure-head of the 'Shannon,' which he commanded, stands at the entrance to the house.

*November 14th, London.*—Müller was hanged this morning. He refused to confess until the last moment, till the rope was round his neck, when he said to the clergyman : 'Ich hab' es gethan!'

*November 15th.*—We heard of the death of my cousin, Lord Manners.

*November 16th.*—We went to Leiston Old Abbey, Mr. William Rose's place in Suffolk, where we met the Carletons[1] and Colonel Tower, and had very good partridge-shooting.

*November 17th.*—We left London for Longleat. Nobody there but Lady Louisa Fielding and Lord Canterbury.

*November 18th.*—A fall of snow in the night and hard frost. Had service in the chapel belonging to the house.

*November 19th.*—Left Longleat for Heron Court. Whilst in Salisbury, on my way home, went to see my old family house in the Close, a most curious and gloomy abode. There are fifty-one rooms in it and a great many passages and staircases—altogether a most ghostly place. The snow was so deep that we were obliged to put four horses to the fly from Fording Bridge to Ringwood, whence it took us an hour and a half to get to Heron Court, only seven miles.

*November 23rd.*—Was shot badly in the face, and was laid up for four days.

*November 30th.*—Accounts from America all tend against the Confederates.

[1] Now Lord and Lady Dorchester.

Mr. Bidwell, of the Foreign Office, told me that the Emperor of the French had offered us a defensive alliance in case we engaged in war against Germany, meaning, I suppose, in case of England being invaded.

*Lord Derby to Lord Malmesbury.*

Knowsley : December 9, 1864.

My dear Malmesbury,—I am glad you are pleased with the Homer. I never was more astonished in my life than on reading the puff of it in the 'Times'!—by whom written I have not the least idea, and Murray professes himself as much at a loss as I am. However it may be, it threw out a bait to the ingenuous British public, the result of which has been that the first edition of 1,000 copies has been disposed of in a week, and that a second, of double that number, is in the press, and will be out in a fortnight. I was sorry you could not come to us this week; but, as it happens, I should not have seen much of you if you had, for I have again been confined to my bed with a renewed attack, and have not yet left my room, though I hope I am on the way to recovery.

The Baillie-Cochranes came here on Saturday and stayed till Wednesday, but I was not able to see them. I have not, however, given up the hope of seeing you yet—if not this year, at least this season, for I am going to write to Dizzy and some of our political friends, to ask them if they can come here for a few days on the 9th of next month, and I shall still have a good beat or two untouched, so as to mix a little shooting with our politics. If we should make up such a party, could you join it? You would find companions, whether you shot or not; but I hope you will find yourself equal to it at Wimpole, if not to one of Bath's tremendous days.          Every yours sincerely,

DERBY.

The Earl of Malmesbury, G.C.B.

# 1865

*January 3rd.*—Lord and Lady Bath, Mr. Fane, and Col. and Lady Margaret Charteris arrived at Heron Court. A very agreeable party.

*January 12th.*—Sir A. Paget, Lochiel, Mrs. Brett, Sir William Jolliffe and his two daughters came. We shot the park, and the

Miss Jolliffes accompanied us.    In the evening we all went to the ball at Christchurch.

We left the ball with Mr. and Mrs. Brett, and found a storm raging outside the ball-room—rain coming down in torrents, and the wind so high that the horses could hardly get on.    I thought several times that the omnibus would have been blown over.    We were obliged to go a roundabout way, as some cottages were on fire in the street, the flames preventing any passage, and adding to the horrors of the hurricane.

*January 14th.*—We left Heron Court suddenly with our guests, Lady Malmesbury having heard that her mother, Lady Tankerville, has had a stroke of paralysis.

*January 18th, London.*—Lady Tankerville lingered three days, when the Abbé Tourzel thought her so ill that he would not put off any longer administering extreme unction.    She bore the ceremony very well, and was quite aware of all that was going on, every time he made the sign of the cross.

She was a remarkable woman, and we all very much lament her.    Ossulston passes the whole day with my wife, which is a great comfort to me, as he is always so kind and sympathetic.

*January 26th.*—Lady Willoughby d'Eresby died to-day.    She was one of Lady Tankerville's most intimate friends, and, as they entered the world together, they left it together within a few days. She was one of the four or five ladies who, for forty years, had been ' the glass of fashion.'

*Lady Palmerston to Lord M. on the death of Lady Tankerville.*[1]

Brocket : January 29, 1864.

My dear Lord Malmesbury,—I cannot say how thankful I felt for your very kind letter, and for the considerate feeling that induced you to write to me at a moment when I was so deeply afflicted, and when your assurance gave me a double satisfaction, as it strongly verified the hope that I had already felt as a consolation, that her end was a most happy one, and that she suffered no pain or anxiety.    She is a great loss to me, after an intimacy of so many years; but I do feel it a great comfort that she had such a blessed death and expired in the arms of

---

[1] Lady Palmerston and Lady Tankerville had been intimate friends for more than fifty years.

her children, to whom she was so devotedly attached. I hope dear
Emma has not suffered in her health from the sad scene she had to go
through for so many days, and believe me, dear Lord Malmesbury,
yours ever very sincerely,                    E. PALMERSTON.

Palmerston was, like me, very thankful for your letter, and he regrets
almost as much as I do the loss of such an attached and excellent friend
—so attractive and so good.

*February 1st.*—Another blow has fallen upon my family. The
wife of my younger brother, Charles, has died of scarlet fever. I
got a letter from him a few days ago, condoling with me upon my
mother-in-law's death.

*February 7th.*—Parliament meets to-day, but is not opened by
the Queen.

*February 9th.*—Lord Derby spoke very well at the opening,
and with great fluency, but he looks very ill. His last attack of
gout was very serious, and for some hours he was in great danger.

*February 15th.*—Ossulston and I had great sport at the wild-
fowl on the Moor's River. He had a good story about the examination at a boys' school. The master asked why Moses left Egypt.
The boy answered: 'You know, sir; that little affair with Poti-
phar's wife.'

*March 1st.*—I hear that Lord Willoughby, when dying, would
not see his daughter at the last. She passed the whole day in the
house, hoping to see him, but he never sent for her. I know this
was not from want of affection, as he was extremely fond of her;
but both he and Lady Willoughby have all their lives had a
horror of anything painful, and have carefully shunned anything
that could agitate them, so I have no doubt that he dreaded
her emotion, for he was in perfect possession of his faculties. I
believe it was the same with Lady Willoughby, who was very
religious. I suppose they wished to avoid taking leave of those
they loved, and to pass their last hours undisturbed by any dis-
tressing scenes.

*March 4th.*—News from America says that Charleston was
evacuated by the Confederates on February 17, and 200 pieces of
cannon taken. It is said that the French have been defeated in
Mexico by Juarez. The Duc de Gramont called.

All London is talking of the way in which the Corps Diplomatique has been invited to the Queen's reception. It was, as far as I could understand, in these terms : 'That the Queen would graciously receive them, *male and female*, at a Court to be held at Buckingham Palace.'

All those concerned are trying to shift the responsibility upon one another. The diplomatists have sent their cards of invitation to their respective Courts; and therefore it has produced a great sensation all over the world, as the term *mâle et femelle* is never used in French, except in speaking of animals.

*March 13th.*—I attended the Queen's reception at Buckingham Palace. Her Majesty inquired very kindly after Lady Malmesbury, who has been very ill.

*March 22nd.*—The Government were beaten last night on the Fire Insurance Duty by a majority of 72, the resolution for a reduction of the duty being carried in spite of Gladstone's opposition.

*March 27th.*—The Duchess of Marlborough called with her daughter, Lady Cornelia.[1] Such a pretty, graceful girl; very distinguished in her appearance, amiable and intelligent, and with a beautiful complexion.

*March 29th.*—I dined at Marlborough House; very pleasant evening. Parry sang some amusing comic songs, and the party did not break up till half-past twelve.

*April 1st.*—Lord Desart died this morning. He had been ill some years with a creeping palsy.

A dissolution is expected on July 15, and Colonel Taylor, our Whip, says we shall gain twenty-five seats.

*April 5th.*—It is said that the Russian plague is approaching England, but Brünnow told me that there is always a fever at Petersburg at this time of the year, as the lower classes feed chiefly on frozen fish.

*April 15th.*—News from America of April 4 would appear to show that it is all over with the Confederates. After three days' severe fighting, Grant and Sheridan succeeded in turning Lee's right wing, and driving him into Pittsburg. Lee has been defeated again since that, with great loss of prisoners and guns.

---

[1] Lady Cornelia Churchill afterwards married Lord Wimborne.

*April 25th.*—The Czarewitch died yesterday. The Princess Dagmar, whom he had expressed a wish to see, and who was betrothed to him, arrived with her mother the day before his death.[1]

*April 26th.*—Miss Constance Kent has confessed to having murdered her half-brother on June 29, 1860, and came to London yesterday to surrender herself. She was accompanied by the Rev. Mr. Wagner, of St. Paul's, Brighton, to whom she had revealed her guilt. She behaved with great composure, and I hope it will be proved she was mad, as her mother and grand-mother were so.

The report of President Lincoln's assassination is true. He was shot through the head at Ford's Theatre, at Washington. The assassin procured admission to his private box on pretence of bearing despatches from General Grant, and shot him with a double-barrelled pistol. He then jumped upon the stage, flourish-ing a dagger, and exclaimed, ' Sic semper tyrannis ! ' and made his escape through the back entrance to the theatre. He is an actor of the name of Wilkes Booth, and has been arrested. About the same time an attempt was made to assassinate Mr. Seward.

*April 30th.*—Dr. Pusey has sent a letter to the ' Churchman,' praising Gladstone and urging the High Church party to support Lord Palmerston, also giving his opinion that universal suffrage would strengthen the Church.

*May 1st.*—The Emperor of the French left Paris on the 29th for Algiers, against the reclamations of all his Ministers. He is in bad health, and goes to drink some waters celebrated for renovating the constitution. It is said that Lincoln's assassina-tion has produced a very painful impression on him, as he had hitherto disbelieved in the pistol for the purpose, and only feared the dagger.

The Government was beaten in the Lords on the Oaths Bill.

*May 5th.*—Miss Constance Kent was examined by the magis-trates at Trowbridge, and committed for the murder of her brother. She is sent to Salisbury gaol. Mr. Wagner refused to answer any questions that touched upon her confession, and was hissed by the audience.

[1] She afterwards married his brother, the present Emperor.

*May* 10*th.*—Wilkes Booth has been shot by a sergeant, and his companion taken.

*May* 12*th.*—Started for Paris to see the Great Exhibition. Paris is now at the apogee of its magnificence, and is the wonder of the world.

News from Mexico is very alarming for the French, and produces great consternation in Paris, where the Emperor's return from Algiers is anxiously looked for. The rebels under Juarez have gained some advantage over the French, and now that the war in America is over a great number of adventurers, who form the principal part of the Federal army, are disbanded, and are going to join Juarez, who will thus be more than a match for Maximilian with his French and Belgian allies.[1]

*May* 29*th.*—The Confederate party in America has been completely overcome in spite of an heroic resistance. It is expected that Jeff Davis will be executed by the Federal Government or lynched by the mob.

*June* 10*th.*—The general impression is that Lord Palmerston is in a very bad state of health, and will not meet the new Parliament as Minister. He now seldom attends the House of Commons, and, when he does, only comes for a short time and says a few words, evidently that his name may appear in the newspapers.

*June* 20*th.*—Lord Palmerston's illness has been very severe. His colleagues are therefore anxious to get the elections over as soon as possible.

*June* 22*nd.*—A telegram arrived to-day in London, announcing the death of Mrs. Arbuthnot, who was killed by lightning in Switzerland. She was a daughter of Lord Rivers; was married two months ago, and they were on their wedding tour. She had remained sitting on a rock, being tired, whilst her husband and the guide had gone on; a sudden storm came on and she was struck by a flash of lightning, which left a black mark all across her body. Decomposition set in instantly where the electric fluid had passed.

*July* 8*th.*—Dined with Lord Redesdale at the annual dinner which he gives to the Peers at Greenwich.

[1] The brave and amiable Archduke Maximilian had been induced to accept the crown of Mexico, under French protection.

*July* 11*th.*—We dined with the Duke and Duchess of Wellington to meet the Queen of the Netherlands, who talked a great deal to me about politics, as she does to everybody. Parry sang some of his comic songs.

The elections are going badly for us. Sir A. Malet came up to me after dinner, and said how much he rejoiced at the turn they were taking, although he supposed it was not a matter of rejoicing to me. I replied that of course he (Sir Alexander) ought to be glad, as otherwise he would not occupy his present post. We have already lost six seats and shall lose at least as many more, instead of gaining from fifteen to thirty, as we expected. Our agents must be very stupid to have miscalculated to such an extent, and the party are much disheartened. We have lost some of our best men : Seymour Fitzgerald, Sir John Elphinstone, and Sir John Hay. We have, however, got a Tory into Tiverton, as a colleague for Lord Palmerston. The election returns show we have lost fifteen seats, so there is no chance of our party coming into office; but the Whigs have not gained. The increase is in the Radicals.

*July* 28*th.*—The trial of Constance Kent is over, but the Queen has commuted the sentence of death to penal servitude.

*August* 20*th.*—The 'Great Eastern,' about which there has been much anxiety, in consequence of making no signals for a fortnight, has returned to Valentia, the cable having broken in the middle of the Atlantic, where the sea is two miles deep. They let down a grapnel, and fancied they hooked it; but the rope broke, and they have returned to get more.

*October* 1*st.*—Left Heron Court for London on my way to Paris, and made a tour of three weeks in Brittany over the same ground I have before described.

*October* 12*th.*—I arrived at Brest. Went yesterday to Plougastel, but the abbey described in books is a fiction of romance. There is only an old church. The inns at Brest are abominable.

I hear the cholera has broken out in many parts of England. In a house at Epping everybody died, the master having it twice.

*October* 18*th.*—I hear from England that Lord Palmerston is very ill at Brocket, and a bulletin was issued, very unfavourable. I fear there is little chance of his recovery.

*October* 19*th, Nantes.*—A telegram announcing the death of Lord Palmerston, which took place yesterday at eleven. He sank gradually, and died without pain. Lady Shaftesbury, Lady Jocelyn, and William Cowper [1] were at Brocket. I shall always recollect him as one of the kindest men to me in private life, which I attribute mainly to his affection for my grandfather, the first Lord Malmesbury, who was his guardian. As a Minister, although I often differed from him, I looked upon him as one of our greatest, especially in his knowledge of foreigners and their character. He was clear headed, always knew what he wanted, and was determined to carry it out, with great moral and physical courage. We shall be long ere we see his like again. He was *English* to the backbone.

*October* 23*rd.*—Arrived in London. Found Lord Russell Prime Minister. Lord Palmerston is to be buried in Westminster Abbey, and, by the wish of the Queen, to have a public funeral.

*October* 27*th.*—Lord Palmerston was buried to-day in Westminster Abbey, near Lord Canning.

*November* 2*nd.* — Called on Lady Jersey, where I found General Peel. Parliament will meet on the 23rd, but only to elect a Speaker and swear in the members.

*From Lord Derby to Lord Malmesbury.*

Knowsley : November 6, 1865.

My dear Malmesbury,—I have been wishing for some time to write to you, but I need not say that I had not a moment to myself last week, and the close of it left me with an arrear which I have not yet succeeded in writing off. I am happy to say, however, that our Royal party went off as well as possible, and without the slightest hitch. The weather, with the exception of one day, was magnificent, and it was impossible to exceed the enthusiasm of their reception at Liverpool. It was admirably managed, and though nearer half than a quarter of a million of people were assembled, there was not a single accident. Both the Prince and Princess of Wales made themselves exceedingly agreeable, discarding all approach to form, and setting everybody at their ease. They were in excellent spirits, and

---

[1] The Hon. William Cowper was afterwards made Lord Mount Temple, and Lord Palmerston made him his heir.

professed themselves, as indeed they seemed, delighted with their v
Though rather too early in the year, I managed to give H.R.H.
very good days' shooting; the first on the Stockbridge beat (ending
the Liverpool Lodge), on which, with five guns, they killed 717 h
of which 280 were pheasants. The second day, our only bad on
rained incessantly, but nothing would satisfy the Prince but shoot
through it all, and on Massborough they bagged 967 head, of wl
440 were pheasants—six guns. . . . And now a word or two u
political matters. I return the two documents enclosed in your le
of the 26th ult. There can be no doubt as to the correctness of y
statement to the ' France,' as indeed that paper acknowledges,
several of the English papers made precisely the same mistake, c
founding the recognition of the Empire in 1852 with the *coup d'*
in 1851. Some are of opinion that the ultimate solution is to be fo
in a fusion. I do not greatly differ from them in this : but how i
to be effected is not so clear. If my retirement will facilitate
operation, and make way for a *substantially* Conservative Governm
I shall put no obstacle in the way.

From what I hear, they mean to bring in a Reform Bill, but
of a very mild character, which we may find ourselves able to supp
but this will be a breach with Baines, Bright, & Co., unless t
announce that they mean it only as an instalment, in which case
could hardly support it, and they would fall between two stools.

Our policy must be regulated by that of the Government, and u
that is decided we cannot pretend to have ours cut and dry.

Believe me ever yours sincerely,

DERB

The Earl of Malmesbury, G.C.B.

*November* 16th.—Lady Ely called, and announced the marri
of Princess Helena to the second son of the Duke of August
burg, and the Queen lends them Frogmore, so they will reside
England. The Duke of Wellington has made his wife resign
place as Mistress of the Robes, as he says he supposes L
Russell will act consistently with his Whig principles, but I h
since heard that she will remain for the present.

*November* 17th.—An insurrection has broken out in Jam
at Morant's Bay, in the parish of St. Thomas. As far as car
at present known the object of the rioters was to make a gen
massacre of all the white population, but the arrest of one of
principal leaders occasioned a premature outbreak, which has b

suppressed in consequence of the vigorous measures taken by the authorities. Generals O'Connor and Nelson have done very well, and shown great determination. The chief ringleader, Gordon, has been hanged. These men were not driven to these atrocious acts by ill-usage, but in order to get possession of the property of the English population, to murder all the men, and share the women amongst them.

*November 27th.*—I went to Knowsley.

*December 5th.*—The Queen has officially announced her intention of opening Parliament, but some slight alteration in the ceremony will be made. It is said that she will not read the Speech herself, and does not mean to wear her robes.

The King of the Belgians is dying, which may prevent her going there at all.

*December 6th.*—Went to see the Sphinx in the Egyptian Hall. It is certainly a wonderful illusion. The smile is the most extraordinary part, for it is so human, and such a merry one, quite lighting up the face. The movement of the lips was also perfectly natural ; the only part which looked like mechanism is the stiff way in which the head bent forward. It was placed in a box on a small table, quite in front of the stage, under which one could see perfectly.

I hear that Sir Augustus Paget is to be sent to Mexico, which I sincerely hope, for his sake and my own, is not true.

*December 10th.*—The negro sympathisers have sent a deputation to Mr. Cardwell to ask for Governor Eyre's recall from Jamaica, which was saved by his courage ; much to his credit, he has refused to do so. No man has been so unjustly maligned or deserves greater reward ; but humbug is the rule of the day.

King Leopold died yesterday at Laeken. The last years of his life were spent in perpetual terror of Louis Napoleon, and he was constantly alarming our Ministers and everybody on the subject.

*December 14th.*—The Government have given way to the clamour of the anti-slavery faction and of Exeter Hall, and have issued a proclamation suspending Mr. Eyre from his functions until after the investigations—a pretty reward for doing one's duty to one's country.

*December* 29*th*.—We have received the news by telegraph from India of the death of Lord Edward St. Maur, who, being out shooting, was attacked by a grizzly bear.  Lord Edward defended himself with his knife, and they rolled down a hill together, the animal lacerating his knee.  In the wild country in which he was, he could receive no medical assistance for two days, when his leg was amputated and he died under the operation.  He was handsome, clever, and amiable, and being his mother's favourite child, I can hardly understand how she will be able to bear his loss.


# 1866


*January* 1*st, Heron Court*.—I arrived here from London, and brought down the Bretts, the Baillie-Cochranes, A. and Lady Paget, and the Charteris', but the rivers are too flooded for any wild-fowl shooting, and the gentlemen are restricted to killing pheasants—comparatively very tame sport.

*January* 10*th and* 11*th*.—It snowed for two days and nights, with a gale from N.E., which has blown down many of my trees.

A *pronunciamiento*, under General Prim, has taken place in Spain.  He is one of the Queen's best generals.  General Zabala has been sent in pursuit, and martial law is proclaimed in Catalonia and Arragon.  The clubs and theatres are shut up at Madrid.

*January* 14*th*.—The flood of the Stour is higher than it has been since 1809, judging from the water-gauges which have been kept.

*January* 16*th*.—I went to a meeting at Christchurch, to defend the ancient rood screen at the Priory Church.  The vicar, Mr. Nash, who wanted to remove it, has at last given in, finding the committee was against its demolition.  I consider such an act would be barbarous and most silly as well, for 600*l.* were spent in the renovation of its carvings only twenty-five years ago ; besides which, there is no doubt that it is one of the main supports of the church itself.  The last century was passed by our church-wardens and parsons in whitewashing our ancient churches ; the rage now is to alter and restore them according to the temporary rule of these authorities.

*February 1st.*—Parliament met to-day, Mr. Denison was chosen Speaker without opposition. Lord Russell wants to have Bright in the Cabinet, but the other Ministers refuse to admit him. Ossulston arrived for dinner.

*February 6th.*—The Queen opened Parliament to-day. She came in a state coach with her eight cream-coloured horses, but entered by the Peers' entrance. She was well received, but did not wear her robes, which were placed on the Throne, and did not read the Speech, which was read by the Lord Chancellor. I did not attend the opening, being lame with gout, but reserved myself for the debate on the Address. The Government were severely attacked for their negligence with respect to the cattle plague. I am sorry to see that Lord Russell looks very old and feeble.

*February 9th.*—Returned to Heron Court. Sir Henry Wolff and Mr. Philip Rose arrived. The latter is Disraeli's legal adviser, and has been very useful to him, by his devotion and undoubted ability and knowledge of the world.

*February 11th.*—A violent gale, or rather hurricane, came on in the night, and continued till five or six in the afternoon. From two to four it was quite awful, and we thought every large tree in the place must be blown down. Seven gigantic elms fell in front of the drawing-room windows whilst Wolff and I were looking out, and the people in the cottages, wherever there were trees near, forsook them in terror and rushed to the house for shelter. The roads were so completely blocked up by fallen timber that Sir Henry Wolff, who meant to leave for Bournemouth, could not proceed half a mile, and had to come back.

*February 12th.*—We went out before breakfast and walked round the park. It was a sad sight to see those splendid elms lying prostrate, and the wide gaps they have left, which can never be filled up in the life of a man. Some were certainly three centuries old. I hear the storm was marked at Portsmouth at the figure 12, which is the highest known, and this is illustrated by the supposition that if the keeper of an observatory saw the whole building on the point of being swept away, and kept his head cool, he would write down 12 and perish. The ' Times ' adds that the force of the wind was forty pounds to the square foot, which is a regular East India cyclone.

*February* 16*th*.—Government in both Houses have announced the suspension of the Habeas Corpus in Ireland, such is the alarming aspect of the Fenian conspiracy.

*February* 17*th*.—The bill for suspending the Habeas Corpus in Ireland has passed by 364 to 6. It was passed in the House of Lords before five and sent to Osborne immediately for the Queen's signature ; it was returned to the House of Lords, who summoned the Commons and passed the bill by commission at a quarter before one o'clock in the morning.

*February* 18*th*.—There is an attempt just now among a small and unimportant knot of individuals in the Conservative ranks to get rid of Lord Derby and put Disraeli or Lord Stanley in his place. I do not believe that either of them was privy to the scheme. I was sounded on the subject by one of the conspirators, but I met his very first observations, when I saw his drift, with the ridicule which it deserved, and asked him, ' Where is the rank and file ? ' to which he gave no answer, and I turned my back on him.

*February* 19*th*.—I was told by a lady just returned from Paris that, at a party at the Tuileries, Madame Korsakoff appeared in a dress cut almost down to her waist, looped up at the knee, and with a very long train. A gentleman happening to tread upon it, she turned round very angrily, saying, ' Fichu maladroit ! ' to which he replied, ' Madame, le fichu serait mieux sur vos épaules que dans votre bouche.'

*March* 8*th*.—Second reading Church Rates Abolition Bill passed the Commons by 285 against 252.

*March* 11*th*.—Had a conversation with Lord Bath, and learnt from him that he wished for a coalition under a Whig Premier, but, although Gladstone is not called a Whig, I believe he was the man meant.

*March* 12*th*.—Gladstone introduced the Reform Bill this afternoon, and Barrington called soon after ten, and told me it was very ill received by the House. It is what is called a single-barrelled bill—*i.e.* only treats the question of the franchise and not the redistribution of seats, and is very unfair for the county constituencies, as it gives great preponderating power to the towns. The general impression is that it cannot pass.

*March 15th.*—I have had a very severe attack of gout in both knees and feet. I find our party are desponding about the Reform Bill; but Mr. Lowe, who opposes it, and who is Lord Lansdowne's member for Calne, says he can influence from thirty to thirty-five votes, and if so we are safe. The 'Times,' too, is beginning to write against it.

*March 20th.*—Lord Grosvenor [1] has given notice of an amendment to the second reading of the Reform Bill, to the effect 'that, in the opinion of the House, it is inexpedient to discuss a bill for the reduction of the franchise in England and Wales until the House has before it the entire scheme contemplated by the Government.'[2] This was received by the Opposition with loud cheers, and Ministers looked furious as much at its being brought on by the son of a great Whig Peer as at the resolution itself. This is the first symptom of desertion from them, and it will probably not be the last.

*March 22nd.*—Lady Derby has been at the point of death, having had congestion of the lungs. She had mistaken her doctor's order, and continued to lower herself, and had taken no nourishment for thirty-six hours; and when the doctor, who lives in the house, went to see her, she was sinking so fast, that he sent Fred Stanley to Lord Derby to say that she had not ten minutes to live; but he, being confined to his bed by a severe attack of gout, could not go to her, and sent her a farewell message by Lady Constance, who fortunately consulted the doctor before giving it; as he prevented her doing so, saying, 'A mouse running across the room might kill her.' Happily her life has been spared.

I hear the Dukes of Cleveland and Sutherland, Lord Lichfield, and other Whig Peers are against Gladstone's Reform Bill, but I am afraid the Government have got back some of Mr. Lowe's friends. The Queen of the French died yesterday at Claremont, aged eighty-two; she survived her husband sixteen years.

---

[1] Now Duke of Westminster.
[2] History repeats itself, e.g. 1884, but not the Duke of Westminster.

*March 30th.*—There are rumours of war between Austria and Prussia, on the subject of Holstein, which Prussia intends to annex. Thus the two spoilers are following the usual course under such circumstances.

*April 13th.*—The debate last night in the House of Commons was interesting, Gladstone not explaining anything, but personal and abusive of Mr. Lowe, who made a spirited reply. Lord Grosvenor made a gentlemanlike speech in proposing his resolution, and Lord Stanley a magnificent one in seconding it, which is the finest and most statesmanlike speech Stanley has ever made.

*April 14th.*—We went to the private view of the portrait gallery at South Kensington. The light is perfect, and the pictures are well arranged. There are several of Mary Queen of Scots, but almost all different. None give one the idea of the great beauty she is supposed to have possessed. It was probably the prestige of her manner and of her great misfortunes that gained her this reputation.

*April 18th.*—Sir Fitzroy Kelly moved the rejection of the malt tax in the Commons, and was beaten by 235 to 150.

*From Lord Derby to Lord Malmesbury.*

St. James's Square : April 22, 1866.

My dear Malmesbury,—Whatever may be my regret at the decision which you have come to, as announced in your letter of Friday, I cannot say that it has taken me by surprise, or that I think your objections, with your frequent attacks of ill-health, to take an office involving such incessant and anxious labour as the F. O. are unanswerable. Your withdrawal will no doubt increase the difficulties of my position if I should be called on again to attempt the task of forming a Government; and though I should still hope to have the advantage of your services in some less hard-worked department, I confess that I do not, in the present state of parties, see my way to acceptance of office. I know that the disappointment of our friends, should I be called on and decline, will be very great; but I cannot, especially in the present unsettled state of affairs both at home and abroad, again undertake the duty without at least a reasonable prospect of an assured majority. And even if we should succeed in carrying Lord Grosvenor's amendment, of which there is a fair prospect, the men who would vote with us on that question are so diametrically opposed to us on others of no less importance that, even if they had leaders with whom it would be more easy to confer than with those apparently at their head, I do not see how we could come to such an understanding as would enable us to carry on a Government together; and of the ordinary supporters of the present Administration, who will reluctantly go with them on this occasion, I cannot look to any who would have the courage to break off from their party to support a Government of which Disraeli and I should be the leaders. The prospect, however, of my being *sent for*, with whatever result, is sufficiently near to make it necessary to consider all possible courses, and I should be very glad to have an opportunity of talking the matter over with you, if you could call here at almost any hour to-morrow or Tuesday. On that day I am going over to Accrington for three nights, but I shall not go down till after the House of Lords on that evening, when I must say a word or two on the Qualification for Offices Bill.             Yours sincerely,       DERBY.

The Earl of Malmesbury, G.C.B.

*April 23rd.*—Every day increases the probability that the Government will be turned out on the second reading of the Reform Bill. I have told Lord Derby that my health will not allow me to take the Foreign Office again, and he was very kind about it, though he said it would add to his difficulties. He will, I hope, give the place to Lord Stanley, if he accepts office, which is doubtful, as the majority against us in the Commons is greater than in 1852 or 1858, and there is little chance of a coalition strengthening us sufficiently or permanently.

*April 28th.*—The second reading of the Reform Bill has passed by a majority of five only. At twelve o'clock I went to Disraeli and Lord Derby to tell them that I had seen Lord Granville, who said that Sir George Grey had gone down to Windsor, so it is evident that Ministers have resigned.

*May 1st.*—Everything looks warlike, and I am afraid Austria will be crushed. Prussia and Italy are evidently in league together, and Count Apponyi suspects Louis Napoleon will join them for the purpose of getting the Rhine Provinces as the price of his assistance. Young Lord Lansdowne [1] called, and is giving our party all his aid.

[1] This was the young Lord Lansdowne who died in 1866. His father, the eminent statesman, died in 1863.

*May 3rd.*—Lady Augustus Loftus [1] called, and said that when she left Berlin a few days ago the prospects of peace were improved ; that Bismarck is the only person in the whole kingdom that wants war.

*May 4th.*—M. Rouher has declared that France will be strictly neutral between Prussia and Austria, and, if Italy attacks the latter, she must take the consequences. Lady A. Loftus told me that Victor Emanuel asked whether Prussia really meant to fight this time, and, on being answered in the affirmative, replied that this would be his opportunity. Italy has certainly been arming for the last month, which has of course occasioned a corresponding demonstration on the part of Austria ; and the Prussians have coolly objected to their increasing their army in Venetia. The French might as well object to our sending troops to Ireland.

*May 8th.*—Gladstone brought forward his bill for the redistribution of seats. By grouping boroughs in Schedule A, and taking one member from boroughs in Schedule B, he gains forty-nine seats. He proposes giving twenty-six to the counties, sixteen to boroughs, and seven to Scotland.

The prospect of peace diminishes every day, and the Emperor Napoleon's speech at Auxerre will encourage the war party. He says : ' This department was the first to give me its suffrages in 1848, because it knew, with the majority of the French people, that its interests were my interest, and that I detested equally with them those treaties of 1815 which it is now sought to make the sole basis of our foreign policy.' This speech has produced great consternation at Paris. No one now doubts that an understanding exists between M. de Bismarck, France, and Italy, as against Austria. It is also rumoured that the Emperor never mentioned the treaties of 1815 in his speech, but sent the paragraph to the 'Moniteur' on his return to Paris with that addition. This makes it rather worse.

*May 16th.*—General Peel, whom I met to-day, is confident that the House of Commons will throw out the Reform Bill ;

Lord Augustus Loftus was our Ambassador at Vienna.

but Mr. Lowe says that he has no material to work with, as people are so full of crotchets.

*June 1st.*—Lord Chesterfield died of a paralytic stroke. A very amiable man, and who had led the fashion in his day.

*June 3rd.*—Sir Henry Wolff called. Says the Conference is given up, and war will break out directly ; also that the Government have promised the Adullamites to withdraw the Reform Bill altogether if they will steadily support them on all other occasions. The compromise is a disgrace to both parties. That is their affair, and we are, of course, too glad to get rid of this foolish bill.[1]

*June 5th.*—The scene in the House of Commons yesterday was extraordinary when Captain Hayter's amendment was introduced. Lord Grosvenor declared he would vote against it, though he thought the Government bill a very bad one, but he has such confidence in Lord Clarendon that he was afraid of a change of Government, which would deprive the country of his services. Disraeli made a good speech in reply to prove that Lord Clarendon had failed in everything he undertook, and Captain Hayter withdrew his resolution.

*June 12th.*—Princess Mary's marriage with Prince Teck took place this morning. Count Karolyi, the Austrian Ambassador, has received orders from his Government to leave Berlin directly in consequence of the interference of Prussia in Holstein, which is a direct infringement of the treaty of Gastein and a *casus belli.* M. Rouher read a letter from the Emperor Napoleon to M. Drouyn de l'Huys in the Corps Législatif, in which he says, ' That, had the Conference assembled, his Government would have declared that France repudiated all idea of territorial aggrandisement so long as the European equilibrium remained undisturbed ; that France would only think of an extension of her frontier in the event of the map of Europe being altered to the profit of a Great Power. France would, therefore, continue to observe an attentive neutrality.'

---

[1] The Adullamites obtained that name when Lord Grosvenor divided the House on the second reading of the Reform Bill, and rallied round him a variety of politicians, who were compared to those who took refuge in the Cave of Adullam.

*June 16th.*—News has been received that the Prussians have invaded Hanover and Saxony, so the war has begun.

*June 18th.*—I found the poor Grand Duchess of Mecklenburg very unhappy. They are obliged to return directly on account of the war, fearing that Prussia will seize their territory.

*June 19th.*—The Government were beaten last night by a majority of eleven on Lord Dunkellin's amendment to substitute rating for rental. The numbers were 304—315.

*June 20th.*—Gladstone announced yesterday that, in consequence of the vote of the previous night, the Government had communicated with the Queen at Balmoral, and Parliament would be adjourned until next Monday. Lord Russell made the same declaration in the Lords.

*June 22nd.*—We dined at the Tankervilles', and met Sir Robert and Lady Emily Peel, Mr. and Mrs. Lowe, Lord Abercorn, and Lord Dunkellin. Mrs. Lowe told me what I had heard from Lord Cranborne, that the Adullamites would not join Lord Derby, as they looked upon that as ratting, but were ready to coalesce with our party under Lord Stanley. This plot is therefore ripening, but it remains to be seen whether it can be put in execution. There is to be a debate upon foreign affairs to-morrow, and an attack upon Lord Clarendon, which, if successful, will be a vindication of my policy in 1859. Kinglake brings it on, and Sir Robert Peel supports him. The object is to show the injustice of accusing the Tory party of incapacity because they did not prevent the war of 1859 between Austria and Sardinia, whilst the Whigs have made precisely the same failure this year.

*June 25th.*—A battle has been fought by the Italians, under the King, and the Austrians, commanded by Archduke Albert, near Verona. It lasted all day, and ended by the defeat of the Italians, who recrossed the Mincio. The Archduke has named it the ' Battle of Custozza.'

*June 26th.*—By her invitation, Lady Malmesbury went to see Lady Palmerston, who was much affected at seeing her, and talked a great deal about Lord Palmerston, regretting he had not given up office, as she thought if he had he might be alive now. Lady Malmesbury told her she felt sure it would have

made no difference, only that he would have lost his interest
in and enjoyment of the last months of his existence ; for, having
spent almost all his life in office, he would have missed the
occupation dreadfully. Lady Palmerston was pleased to say
that she regretted my intention of giving up the Foreign Office
hereafter, and said she did so the more that her husband considered me the fittest man for it in our party. In further
conversation she added that he had very serious apprehensions
respecting Gladstone's future career, and considered him a very
dangerous and reckless politician.

*June 27th.*—Lord Russell and Gladstone both announced
that the Government had resigned, and the Queen accepted
their resignation. I had an interview with Lord Derby this
morning, and advised him, if sent for, to tell the Queen what
was said about Lord Stanley being supported by a section of
the Moderates. Forty Adullamites would join him, whilst only
twelve would join Lord Derby.

After Lord Palmerston's death, which followed the dissolution
of Parliament, the Liberal Government met the session with a
nominal majority of seventy, believing them to be staunch
supporters of Lord Russell, whereas many of them were
Palmerstonians, and, as such, against Reform bills. The
Government brought one in, but it was introduced in a piece-
meal form and at once disgusted the House. Gladstone's want
of temper rendered the measure still more unpopular, and its
fate was settled by Lord Dunkellin, who beat Ministers by
eleven. They threatened a dissolution, but found they would
lose by it. The Queen being on a visit to Osborne for ten days,
refused to shorten her stay, and the country remained for a
month with Government in abeyance. At last her Majesty
returned, and appointed Lord Derby Prime Minister. He
tried to form a coalition with some Whigs, and invited Lord
Clarendon and the Duke of Somerset to join him. They refused.
He then did the same by the Adullamites, most of whom also
declined. Young Lord Lansdowne, who, at their head, had
promised to support him, died suddenly, and this accident
increased his difficulties. Encouraged by a meeting of twenty-
three leading Conservatives, held at his house, Lord Derby

formed the following Cabinet :—Lord Chancellor, Lord Chelms-
ford ; President of the Council, Duke of Buckingham ; Privy
Seal, Lord Malmesbury ; Secretary for Home, Walpole ; Secretary
for Foreign Affairs, Lord Stanley ; Secretary for War, General
Peel ; Secretary for Colonies, Lord Carnarvon ; Secretary for
India, Lord Cranborne ; Poor Law Board, Mr. Hardy ; Board
of Trade, Sir S. Northcote ; Chancellor of the Exchequer, Mr.
Disraeli ; Secretary for Ireland, Lord Naas ; Board of Works,
Lord John Manners ; Admiralty, Sir John Pakington.

*June 28th.*—The Prussians are said to have been defeated in
a great battle near Josefstadt.

*July 1st.*—The Duc de Richelieu and Lord Bath called, the
latter very angry at Lord Derby's not giving up the formation of
a Government when the Adullamites and Whigs refused to join
him.  The news from Germany is very unsatisfactory, but so
confused that one may hope it is not so bad as it appears.  Count
Apponyi told me there was no reason to be discouraged at anything that has taken place, as Benedek declares himself quite
satisfied ; but a great battle is imminent.  The Duc de Richelieu
says that the feeling in Paris in every class is for the Austrians,
and when the news arrived of their victory at Custozza, the
French soldiers wanted to illuminate their barracks.  This may
prevent the Emperor interfering.  Madame Apponyi told Lord
Stanley there were two things he required to fit him to be
Foreign Minister—namely, a wife and a house.  He replied that
a wife was easily got in London, but a house was much more
difficult.

*July 2nd.*—We had a dinner for the Duchess of Cambridge.
Hardwickes, Wiltons, Barringtons, Tankervilles, Dalkeith, Colville, Sir Hugh Rose, Mr. Corry, and Lord Cadogan.  The
Duchess of Cambridge is very low, bad news having been received
of the Austrian army, which seems to have had the worst of it
in several engagements.  The needle-gun gives the Prussians an
immense superiority, as it is a breechloader, and fires at least five
shots to one of the common muskets.

*July 4th.*—There are reports of a great battle, in which the
Austrians have been defeated, near Königgrätz.

*July 5th.*—The news of the battle between the Austrians and

Prussians near Königgrätz is confirmed. It lasted thirteen hours. The Austrians fought gallantly, but were overpowered by numbers, and the Prussians have taken 1,400 prisoners and 116 guns. Field-Marshal von Gablenz is stated to have gone to the Prussian head-quarters with a flag of truce. Prince Lichtenstein and Count Windischgrätz are taken prisoners. Three Archdukes are wounded. The handsome Count Festetics, who was the great dandy at Milan, has lost a leg. The Austrians have given up Venetia to the Emperor of the French, so that the consequence of this defeat is terrible.

*July 7th.*—Received the account of the death of young Lord Lansdowne, which took place yesterday. Whilst playing at cards at his club he was seized with paralysis, and became insensible till he died. I went to Windsor to-day with all my colleagues to receive the seals of office. A violent thunderstorm came on whilst we were there. The extraordinary success of the Prussians has alarmed all nations, who must lose no time in adopting the breechloading gun, the main cause of their success. The muzzle-loading musket must be consigned to the company of bows and arrows.

*July 9th.*—The Prussians and Italians have agreed to an armistice of six weeks. The Italians ask to occupy two of the fortresses of the Quadrilateral at once ; not a very modest request, considering that they have been lately defeated on every occasion. The House of Lords was quite full of peers and ladies to-day. Lord Derby entered soon after five, looking very pale and nervous when he rose to address the House. His speech was good, and some parts very eloquent ; but he was evidently enfeebled by illness. He was cautious in what he said about Reform, declaring that he would not commit himself. He was followed by Lords Russell and Brougham, both looking very old and broken.

*July 12th.*—The accounts of the battle of Königgrätz (now called the battle of Sadowa) are most disastrous ; the Austrian defeat has been complete, and, coming at the moment when they thought themselves victorious, the disappointment is harder to bear. Benedek had unaccountably left the key of his position unguarded, and the Prussians forced their way through his rear,

He also had posted himself with a river in his rear, and without
any bridges to facilitate retreat, so that many Austrians were
drowned.   The Austrians, having given up Venetia to the French,
have withdrawn their troops, so the Italians may take possession
without resistance, if the French allow them to do so.   The
Italians, on their part, refused to receive Venetia from the
French, and Cialdini has crossed the Po.

*July* 15*th.*—Nothing can be worse than the news from abroad
since Sadowa.   There have been various engagements, in all of
which the Prussians have been victorious, and they are in possession of Olmütz.   The Emperor Joseph has, however, refused the
conditions of the armistice, and will go on with the war.   Benedek is superseded by the Archduke Albert, who beat the Italians
at Custozza.   The Austrians have retired from Venetia to join
the main army at Vienna, only leaving garrisons in the fortresses.
Louis Napoleon's mediation has come to nothing.

*July* 21*st.*—Disraeli made a speech on economy.   Pakington
showed the navy to be in a very low state, and wished to build
six turret-ships.   The late First Lord, the Duke of Somerset, had
spent much time and money in experiments, and there are not
ships enough for our reliefs.   The navy of France is superior in
ironclads to ours, and that of Italy and Russia combined equal to
ours.   Disraeli would not believe this, and refused even 50,000*l.*
to begin the turret-ships.   General Peel has ordered breechloaders
for our army.

*July* 22*nd.*—Notices were posted to say Mr. Beales's meeting
of the Reform League would not be permitted in Hyde Park to-
morrow, and that the gates would be closed.

*July* 23*rd.*—The Reform League, after a notice to that effect,
accompanied by an army of roughs, demanded an entrance into
Hyde Park.   This was refused ; and their processions, headed by
Mr. Beales and Colonel Dickson, of notorious memory, proceeded
to Trafalgar Square ; but the mob, to the amount of some 20,000,
invaded the Park, tore down the iron railings, and were not driven
out till after a desperate battle with the police, with the assistance
of the Life Guards.

*July* 24*th.*—Walpole, Home Secretary, determined to guard
the Park with police and troops.   Another affray took place

between seven and ten, when the cavalry cleared the park ; the roughs had passed the day in pelting carriages and people in the park.

*July* 27*th.*—These outrages have continued till to-day, when the Duke of Cambridge has decided that three more regiments of cavalry should be brought up if these demonstrations do not cease.

*July* 28*th.*—Quiet is restored in London. The preliminaries of peace between Austria and Prussia were signed at Nicholsburg. A naval engagement took place at Lissa between the Italian fleet, commanded by Admiral Persano (the man who betrayed the King of Naples), and Admiral Tegethoff, commanding the Austrian fleet, in which the Italian flagship, an ironclad, was run down and sunk by Tegethoff's flagship.

*August* 11*th.*—Parliament was prorogued.

*September* 1*st, Heron Court.*—The ratification of peace between Austria and Prussia was exchanged yesterday at Prague.

*September* 14*th.*—I got a letter from Lord Stanley, saying he fears the Americans intend to renew their claims for compensation for the mischief done by the 'Alabama.'

*September* 23*rd.*—The Italians are making preparations for celebrating the expulsion of the Austrians whilst they are still in Venice ; their doing so with impunity speaks well for the good-nature of the Austrians. The Emperor Napoleon has gone to Biarritz. He returned very ill from Vichy.

*November* 1*st, London.*—Lady Paget and Sir Augustus came to-day to luncheon.

There is a horrible account in to-day's 'Times' of the atrocities committed at Palermo, encouraged by the monks and nuns, who themselves took part in them. The monks actually roasted one poor man alive, and another was condemned to be bitten to death, which was done by the women.· I saw some despatches to-day confirming this account.

Dined with the Derbys, and met Sir Augustus and Lady Paget, Lord Carnarvon, Lord John Manners, Sir Stafford Northcote, and Lord Stanley. The Pagets start for Lisbon to-morrow, where he is appointed Minister.

*November* 9*th.*—Went at six o'clock to Guildhall to attend the Lord Mayor's annual dinner.   Lord Derby made a very good speech and was greatly cheered.   So was Disraeli.   The dinner was over about eleven o'clock, which is earlier than usual.

*November 16th.*—I called upon Princess Edward, and found Lady Mary Craven there, both in the greatest alarm at hearing a report that the Prince of Wales has been killed in Russia.   My arrival comforted them, for, as I knew nothing of it, it was evident that nothing had happened, or a telegram would have been received at the Foreign Office, and communicated to the Ministers.   The two ladies were studying Zadkiel's almanack, and appeared to place implicit confidence in it, there being a prediction that some accident is to happen to the Prince in 1867.

*November 17th.*—I forgot to mention that on the night of the 13th, from twelve to four in the morning, a wonderful fall of aerolites took place.   It had been foretold by the astronomers, but the newspapers made so little of it that we did not sit up, and missed a sight that will never occur again in our lifetime.   On this occasion there were above a thousand of these meteors.

Mr. Barrington says he likes his place of private secretary to Lord Derby very much, and Lord Derby praises him.

*December 1st.*—I am invited by her Majesty to Windsor, and have sent an excuse to the Charteris', to whom I was engaged.

*December 6th.*—I returned from Windsor after two days.   The Queen was very gracious, and complimented me upon the way I had conducted the Foreign Office when I was secretary for that department.

## 1867

*January 3rd, Heron Court.*—Lord Bath and Mr. Bentinck arrived.   The thermometer has been down to 9°, and never rose above 17° all day.   We killed fifty head of wild-fowl.

*January 22nd.*—Went to London to attend a Cabinet.

---

Cabinets every day to the end of the month; some at Lord Derby's, who was ill with the gout.

Parliament was opened by the Queen on February 5.

---

*February* 11*th.*—Disraeli laid our Reform Resolutions on the table. He dissatisfied the House by too long and ambiguous a speech.

*February* 16*th.*—New plan on Reform proposed by Disraeli. Four franchises, namely—5*l.* rated house; 50*l.* in savings bank; an educational franchise; and direct taxation, supposed, in its result, to give 680,000 voters to property and 360,000 to democracy. General Peel positively objects. The Press, in a body, abuse our resolution.

*February* 19*th.*—Cabinet on Reform. General Peel gives way, as he is the only dissentient.

*February* 20*th.*—Am summoned to Heron Court by Lady Malmesbury's dangerous illness.

---

She was unable to leave her bed till March 23. For three weeks she was given over, without hope of recovery, with congestion of the lungs. She was out of danger on the 20th, and her recovery regarded as miraculous. Meanwhile, after a Cabinet held on Saturday, Feb. 22, at which no difficulty occurred, and after Lord Derby's having gone down to Windsor to announce unanimity of the Cabinet, on Sunday night Lord Cranborne informed Lord Carnarvon that he could not agree to the Reform Bill as it stood, and must resign. Lord Carnarvon did the same, and at 8.30 on Feb. 25 they wrote to Lord Derby to call a Cabinet at twelve for Lord Cranborne to explain his objections. The confusion may be conceived, as at two P.M. Lord Derby had summoned his party to hear the new Bill, and Disraeli was to explain it at five in the House of Commons. It was a paralysis. The dissentients were now joined by General Peel, who refused to remain (he had dissented from the first), and in half-an-hour, at Stanley's suggestion, they agreed to meet the M.P.s with a bill founded on the 6*l.* and 20*l.* rating, to which the trio agreed. This crude action exposed us to great condemnation and ridicule.[1] No doubt the best thing in such a position would have been to accept the resignation of these three able and honourable men (however

---

[1] It was nicknamed the 'Six Hours' Reform Bill.' The seceders refused to adopt household suffrage and duality. It was also called the 'Ten Minutes' Bill.'

serious the loss), and to tell the truth to Parliament, deferring the
bill for a week.   I wrote a strong letter to Lord Derby from
Heron Court begging him to do this.   The following Saturday it
was done, and the Dukes of Richmond and Marlborough, and Mr.
Corry, took the vacant seats in the Cabinet—the first as Board of
Trade, the second as Colonial, Secretary ; the third as First Lord
of the Admiralty ; Northcote, India ; and Pakington, War Office.
The statement made by Lords Cranborne and Carnarvon was that
Disraeli and Baxter had completely mistaken their figures, and
that the results would not be what we intended and would be perfectly fatal.

### From Lord John Manners to Lord Malmesbury.

10 Downing St. : Feb. 26, 1867.

My dear Malmesbury,—I am truly sorry to hear of the cause of
your absence from our distracted councils, and hope you will soon be
able to bring a better account of Lady Malmesbury.   I really hardly
know where we are, but yesterday we were suddenly brought together
to hear that Cranborne and Carnarvon withdrew unless we gave up
household suffrage and duality, upon which announcement Peel said
that, although he had given up his opposition when he stood alone,
now he must be added to the remonstrant Ministers.   Stanley then
proposed that to keep us together the 6l. and 20l. rating should be
adopted, which, after much discussion, was agreed to.   We have
decided to abandon the Resolutions altogether, and to issue the
Boundary Commission ourselves.   We are in a very broken and
disorganised condition.                     Ever yours truly,
                                            JOHN MANNERS.

### From the same to the same.

10 Downing St. . Feb. 28, 1867.

My dear Malmesbury,—I cannot tell you how sorry I was to read
the sad opening sentence of your letter this morning.   But I will
obey your wish and send you a few words on the political situation.
A meeting of Conservative M.P.s was held at the Carlton to-day, Sir
M. W. Ridley in the chair ; between 120 and 150 present.   Much
difference of opinion, no resolutions passed, but a general disposition
evinced in favour of rated residential household suffrage v. 6l. rating
and an equal division of new seats between the counties and boroughs.

An anxious desire expressed that we should fix upon the franchise we thought best and then stick to it, declining to carry our opponents' measures. They (our opponents) are, I believe, in equal difficulties, and are quite unable to take office at present. On the whole, though the situation is dangerous, I don't think it desperate.

Ever yours truly,

JOHN MANNERS.

*March 19th, London.*—To-day, all danger being now over, and having been allowed, by Lord Derby's kindness, to remain with my wife and attend her, I came up to town and heard that during my absence my dear old friend, Lady Jersey, had died, suddenly and without suffering, at the age of eighty. She was a most remarkable woman, and almost a European *personage*, for no crowned head or representative of royalty ever landed in England without immediately calling upon her and being found in her *salon* during his stay. Being, herself, the head of Child's bank, she had a very large fortune, and her husband might be said to be in manners and appearance *le plus grand seigneur* of his day. After a prosperous and exceptionally remarkable life she died, having lost, before its close, within a short time of each other, her husband and all her children, who had grown up to maturity, still showing, to the last, the courage and coolness for which she was famous.

*March 23rd.*—On Reform Bill. Dual vote given up.

*March 25th.*—Second reading of Reform Bill carried without a division, after a masterly speech of Disraeli's.

*March 30th to April 6th.*—Continual Cabinets on Reform Bill, Lord Derby being absent from gout.

*April 13th.*—Continued arguments in the Cabinets respecting the Reform Bill. Lord Derby still ill. Prussia has agreed to a conference respecting the garrison of Luxemburg. If she does not evacuate the place, Napoleon says he is resolved to make war. During the past week Gladstone resigned his leadership of the Opposition.

*From Lord Stanley to Lord Malmesbury.*

Foreign Office : April 23, 1867.

Dear Malmesbury,—Peace or war depends on whether Bismarck consents to withdraw the Prussian garrison from Luxemburg. If he consents, France will raise no difficulties as to the disposal of the territory. If he refuses, the Emperor must fight. He (Bismarck) is gone off into the country, evidently with the idea of escaping from inquiry and discussion till he can make up his mind. This is all we know, but any day or hour may bring decisive news.

We are asked to use our good offices, and are advising Prussia to give way, as the concession is slight, the justice of the claim unquestionable, and no other course holds out a hope of preserving peace.

I am not sanguine of averting a war, but in three or four days we shall probably know more.

Ever yours,        STANLEY.

*May.*—Cabinets all May on Reform Bill. The *laissez-aller* system followed by the Government, trying to make the best they could of it, but constantly yielding something. The Conservative members seem disposed to adopt anything, and to think that it is ' in for a penny, in for a pound.' Seventy-two of them voted against their leaders upon Mr. Baines's motion to take one member from every borough whose population was below 10,000. Government was beaten by 127, thus abolishing fifteen members returned by the agricultural interest, which will lose immensely by this bill.

The Sultan is coming to London. The Queen will not invite any of the other sovereigns who are at Paris. She appeared in state to lay the first stone of the Hall of Arts,[1] and then went off to Balmoral on May 22.

*From the Queen of Holland to Lord Malmesbury.*

Hague : May 4, 1867.

Dear Lord Malmesbury,—The bearer of these lines, Baron Fagel, heir to one of the best historical names of Holland, wishes to be introduced to you, and I cannot refuse him a few lines, as I well remember all your kindness when I had the happiness of being in London, two years ago.

Baron Fagel inherited all the papers of his uncle, Ambassador Fagel, who was the intimate friend of your grandfather. He possesses numerous letters of Lord M., several of which (those of the year 1813) I have read and found most interesting and curious, showing the elevated mind, the clear judgment of this eminent statesmen. If they were published, they would throw light on the events and transactions of the beginning of the century, and I have advised Baron Fagel to undertake it.

I am of opinion—and I hope you will share it—that, when a certain time has elapsed, those documents belong to history, which is often better explained by the familiar letters of a political man than by official documents, where only part of the truth can appear.

May I beg you to remember me to Lady Malmesbury, whose health has caused us very serious uneasiness ?

Believe me, dear Lord Malmesbury, very sincerely yours,

SOPHIA.[1]

*June.*—Several Cabinets during this month on the Reform Bill, which each time became more Radical. The treaty of London on Luxemburg was signed the 11th of last month, preventing the war between France and Prussia, both sovereigns being glad of a way out of their dilemma.

The Emperor of Russia and the King of Prussia visited Paris, and the former was shot at.

After many vicissitudes, the Reform Bill came up to the House of Lords, and Lord Derby moved the second reading without a division, saying it was ' a leap in the dark.' Peers on our side were averse to it, but, at a meeting of them, Lord Derby said he would resign if it was rejected.

*July 10th.*—There is a very touching account in to-day's papers of the Emperor Maximilian's execution. He died like a Christian and a soldier. His poor wife has become quite insane. The French expedition to Mexico and its tragical end are a sad blot on Louis Napoleon's career.

---

[1] The Queen was a very clever woman, and knew all the affairs of Europe better than most Ministers. In 1871, after the sacking of the Tuileries and the flight of the Empress from Paris, many public papers were stolen and published, and among them several letters from the Queen of Holland, giving the Emperor the best possible warning and advice as to the hostile intentions of Prussia and its military force ; but they were laid aside and unheeded, like those of Stoffel, the military French Attaché at Berlin.

*Mr. Disraeli to Lord Malmesbury (on Proxies).*

July 10, 1867.

My dear Malmesbury,—The Constitution of this country is a Monarchy, modified in its action by the co-ordinate authority of Estates of the Realm. An Estate is a political order invested with privilege for a public purpose.

There are three Estates—the Lords Spiritual, the Lords Temporal, and the Commons.

The Estates of the Lords Spiritual and Temporal being very limited in number, their members can easily meet in their own chamber.

The Estate of the Commons being, on the contrary, very numerous, choose, for convenience, representatives instead of holding general meetings, like the Polish Diets.

The House of Commons is not an Estate of the Realm; its members are only the proxies of an Estate.

The Lords, in using proxies, possess and exercise the same privilege as the Commons, no more; and if it is not convenient for them to attend the meetings of their orders, they have the right to choose their representatives.

.     .     .     .     .     .     .     .

Yours sincerely,          B. DISRAELI.[1]

*July 12th.*—We went to the Horse Guards to see the Sultan's entry into London. Two regiments of Life Guards lined the street, and the Foot Guards occupied St. James's Park. The Sultan has rather a melancholy, but noble, expression of countenance. The Prince of Wales was in the carriage by his side, and his ambassador, Musurus, opposite him.

*July 16th.*—Very stormy. Great fear entertained that the naval review to-morrow cannot take place, as a telegram arrived for the Admiralty saying that the ships at Spithead were pitching bows under at their anchors.

*July 18th.*—The Sultan went to Portsmouth, and was received on board the Queen's yacht off Osborne. He was invested by her

---

[1] This letter from Lord Beaconsfield was elicited, at my request, by the motion of the late Lord Stanhope in the House of Lords, abolishing the use of Proxies. It never was debated on really constitutional grounds, but merely on that of convenience, and the Peers appeared to have no idea of their origin, and that the custom was not a peculiar privilege or anomaly in the Constitution

with the Order of the Garter. Lord Derby had written to ask
her Majesty to give him the Star of India. Fortunately, Fuad
Pasha told Ossulston, who was Lord Steward, that the Sultan
would accept nothing but the Garter. The Sultan has the Bath,
and he considers the Star of India less than the Bath, and would
be much offended if it was offered him. I wrote to Lord Derby
at once ; and it was given him in grand style by the Queen herself on the quarter-deck of the yacht, in the midst of the howling
of the storm and the roaring of the cannon. As it was done in
a hurry, there was no ribbon ready, so the Queen took the Prince
of Hesse's ribbon, intending that it should be changed for a new
one afterwards, but the Sultan refused to give it up, saying that
the one he had was given him by the Queen, and that he would
wear no other.

*July* 19*th*.—A splendid ball was given at the India Office to
the Sultan. It was quite a fairy scene ; but a melancholy event
occurred, which will throw a gloom over the rest of the Sultan's
visit. Madame Musurus, the wife of the Turkish Ambassador,
was taken ill whilst leading her company to supper, and suddenly
dropped down dead. As I was walking with Lady Manners
through the ball-room, her dead body was carried out close to us.

*July* 29*th*.—Lord Derby is still confined to his bed, and I
have to conduct the Reform Bill through Committee in the House
of Lords. This is no easy work, especially with many of our men
against me. Lord Cairns,[1] for one, carried an amendment against
me by a large majority.

*August* 6*th*.—Lord Derby came down to the House, and gave
up the 10*l*. for 15*l*. The third reading passed.

*September* 27*th*.—Garibaldi has been arrested, just as he was
going to invade the Papal States. A few demonstrations have
taken place in his favour, but all were easily dispersed by the
troops, and Italy is quite quiet.

*October* 14*th*.—I went to London, on my way to Manchester,
to attend a Cabinet and a dinner given by Lord Derby. The
attendance was very large, and Lord Derby's reception enthusiastic.

*October* 27*th*.—Garibaldi has escaped from Caprera, and has

---

[1] The amendment was to raise the lodger franchise from 10*l*. to 15*l*.

joined the insurgents near the Roman frontier. The Papal
Zouaves have behaved gallantly and defeated the insurgents on
every occasion. An attempt at insurrection has been made in
Rome, but has failed ; the population have no wish to join it.
There is no doubt that the Italian Government have been favour-
ing the movement, and that Louis Napoleon's firmness, and the
demonstration he has made at Toulon, has frightened them.

*November 1st.*—The French army have landed at Civita
Vecchia, and the Italian troops have crossed the frontier. Gari-
baldi is within three miles and a half of Rome. It will be very
difficult now to prevent a collision between the French and
Italians, and if, in that case, the Prussians interfere on behalf of
Italy, there may be a general war.

*November 4th.*—Dr. Gull called and said that Lady Malmesbury must go to Pau, and that it would be very unsafe and dangerous for her to stay in England during the winter.

*November 18th.*—A Radical mob, calling themselves a deputation, forced themselves into the Home Office. Mr. Hardy refused
to see them and sent for the police, but Sir R. Mayne could
not be found, which created a delay, and in the meantime Mr.
Finlen, an obscure man, made a most incendiary speech, threatening that for every Fenian judicially murdered the life of some
eminent man would be taken.

*November 19th.*—Very cold. Parliament was opened by Commission.

*November 20th.*—The Duke of Cambridge dined with us, also
the Tankervilles, Saxe-Weimars, Stanhopes, John Manners, Mac-
donalds, Derbys, Wharncliffes, and Sir Edwin Landseer.

*November 22nd.*—There was a meeting yesterday at Clerkenwell, to petition the Queen to pardon the Fenians, but it was a
failure. Two thousand working men at Manchester have offered
to act as special constables, and have been sworn in. News from
Italy says that the King is bent upon going to Rome, even at the
risk of war with France.

*November 23rd.*—The three Fenian murderers were executed
this morning at Manchester.

*November 24th.*—A procession to sympathise with the men
who were hanged took place this afternoon in Hyde Park

*December 2nd.*—Lord Derby having given me leave to attend
Lady Malmesbury to Pau, we started, embarked at Folkestone,
and proceeded to Paris. The cold is dreadful, the whole country
covered with snow. We have a good apartment, but a very cold
one, at the Hôtel Meurice.

*December 5th.*—We could not get the temperature of our room
above 50°. Lord Edward Thynne called and paid us a long visit,
and, wanting to show us how to light a good fire by some dodge of
lighting the wood at the back, he set the chimney on fire. The
smoke came down in clouds, both in the drawing-room and bedroom, and we were driven into the dining-room, where we had to
remain the rest of the day, the other rooms being full of *Pom-
piers*, and uninhabitable from the soot.

*December 6th.*—Left Paris for Bordeaux. At the station a
porter let a heavy foot-warmer of iron fall on Lady Malmesbury's
foot, causing the most dreadful pain, which she bore without complaining until we got to Bordeaux. I had no idea of the mischief
done ; but on arriving there we found the foot perfectly black and
dreadfully inflamed.

*December 9th.*—After the appliance of some common remedies,
we left for and slept at Dax. Meanwhile, Lady M.'s foot got much
worse, and when we arrived at Pau the surgeon pronounced it a
very serious injury. We found an excellent house, well furnished,
with a beautiful view of the Pyrenees, taken for us by Baillie of
Dochfour ; but the cold was so fearful that we could not get the
thermometer above 50°, generally ranging from 42° to 47° in the
drawing-room. I put on my duck-shooting costume, and sat
shivering by the fire, unable to get warm.

*December 10th.*—Mr. Bagnall, the surgeon, arrived, and looked
very grave over Lady M.'s foot, saying the bone was splintered.

*December 15th.*—Heard from England that an attempt has
been made to blow up Clerkenwell prison, and rescue the Fenians,
Burke and Casey.

*December 16th.*—Got an official telegram saying that the report
is true. The prison wall had been blown up, and several houses
opposite destroyed ; three people killed, and forty wounded.

Miss Dashwood and I went to a play at Madame Paturle's, the
widow of a rich merchant who was made a peer by Louis Philippe.

The performance was an *opéra comique*, beautifully sung and acted.

*December 17th.*—It seems that some information of the intended attempt to rescue Burke and Casey had reached the Home Office. No one had any idea of the means that would be employed ; but orders were given to take the prisoners out for exercise at ten o'clock instead of three, so they were not in the yard at the time the explosion took place. What seems very strange is that the police, some members of which specially patrolled the prison, although without any detective, never saw the barrel of gunpowder which was placed close to the wall.

*December 21st.*—We have not seen the sun for four days. This place has a very heavy, depressing atmosphere, and it is a fact that one day, when I went into the club, I found seven or eight of its members fast asleep, of which they all complain, saying they cannot help it.

*December 26th.*—I left Lady Malmesbury and Miss Dashwood to return to London, with a very unfavourable impression of the climate of Pau, which however is a very gay place, owing principally to the Russian society.


# 1868

*January.*—Several Cabinets met during the month without Lord Derby, whose illness kept him at Knowsley.

*February* and *March.*—On February 13 Parliament met, Lord Derby still unable to come up ; and on the sixteenth there came very alarming accounts of him. Lord Stanley sent for. Lord Derby rallied two days afterwards, but resigned on Monday, 24th. Next day, Disraeli, who was made Premier, sent for me, and asked me to remain to lead the House of Lords as Privy Seal. Previously, and foreseeing this event, the Dukes of Richmond and Marlborough and I agreed to stand together and support the Government of Disraeli or Stanley, should the Queen appoint either of them to be Premier. I afterwards found that Disraeli had offered the leadership of the House of Lords to the Duke of Marlborough, who very generously refused, saying that I had a prior claim, and had filled the place to the satisfaction of the Peers.

Disraeli told me, on my going to see him, that he should part with Lord Chancellor Chelmsford, and appoint Lord Cairns, a very efficient addition to our strength in the Lords, where our bench is comparatively weak in debate.

Lord Chelmsford (as Lord Derby told me, when in 1866 he formed his Government) was re-taken, only *pro tem.*, and it was settled that he should make way some day for Sir H. Cairns. The health of the latter failed, and he took the Chief Justiceship for Appeals, but refused a Peerage. In 1867, the House of Lords required more strength for Appeals, and then Lord Cairns consented to be called up. This being the case, Lord Chelmsford had no right to be angry at Disraeli's arrangement, but he was so, and appealed to Lord Derby, who confirmed the decision, as being consistent with his original agreement. The fact is that Disraeli should have written a letter to Lord Chelmsford under the circumstances, which I believe he eventually did. Disraeli's first Cabinet met on Monday, March 2, Mr. Ward Hunt being added to it, as Chancellor of the Exchequer, besides Cairns. He is a giant in body, being six feet four, and weighing twenty stone. When he knelt to kiss hands, he was even in that position taller than the Queen. I led the House of Lords till the recess. No time was given them to discuss or alter anything in the Reform Bill. A violent altercation took place on the subject of the Lords altering the boundaries as fixed by the Commons, in opposition to the scheme of the Royal Commission. Walpole and Sir Stirling Maxwell have completely thrown us over on the Commission, and the Government was helpless, as they had not divided once.

*From Mr. Disraeli to Lord Malmesbury.*

March 2, 1868.

My Lord,—The lamented illness of Lord Derby having compelled his retirement from the head of affairs, I have been entrusted by her Majesty with the formation of a new Administration.

In making this announcement to your Lordship, permit me to

express an earnest hope that you will continue to the present Government the same measure of support which you extended to the last.

I should hardly presume to make such a request, had I not the consolation of feeling that I am supported by the confidence of Lord Derby.

I have the honour to remain, my Lord, your faithful servant,

B. DISRAELI.

*April 5th.*—Government has been beaten on Lord Stanley's amendment. We shall not resign, but dissolve, and meet a new Parliament.

*April 22nd.*—A gale has been blowing for the last three days, and the French boats have not been able to cross till to-day, when Lady Malmesbury arrived in London from Pau.

*April 24th.*—The Duke of Buckingham called on me to say that a telegram had just been received from Australia, saying the Duke of Edinburgh had been attacked at a public breakfast. The telegram in cypher was so unintelligible, that it was impossible to make out whether he was killed or wounded. The Duke wrote to Sir Charles Grey, leaving it to his discretion to tell the Queen.

*April 25th.*—Another telegram has been received. The Prince was shot at by a Fenian of the name of O'Farrell, and was wounded in the back. The ball struck a rib near the spine, and ran round his body, but without touching any vital organ.

*April 26th.*—News has been received announcing the fall of Magdala, and the Abyssinian king, Theodore, killed. The battle took place on the plain before Magdala, on Good Friday, and the Abyssinian army was totally defeated by General Napier.[1] Theodore sent all the prisoners to the camp—men, women, and children : but Napier insisted on his surrendering himself a prisoner. This he refused, and shut himself up in Magdala, a strong fortress, with those troops that remained faithful. The fortress was stormed and taken ; Theodore being found dead, though it is not known whether he was killed or committed suicide.

The Duke of Edinburgh is going on well. The Duke of Buckingham saw the Queen last Saturday at Osborne. She cried

---

[1] He was raised to the peerage with the title ' of *Magdala*,'

at first, but soon recovered her calmness, and thanked the Duke for coming down to Osborne.

*May 2nd.*—The Ministers are very angry with Disraeli for going to the Queen without calling a Cabinet, and the Duke of Marlborough wants to resign, but I have done all I could to dissuade him from this course.

*May 4th.*—Disraeli, in the Commons, and I, in the House of Lords, announced that the Queen had refused to accept the resignation of her Ministers, and consented to dissolve Parliament if necessary.

*May 6th.*—Gladstone made a bitter attack on the Government, saying that the above-mentioned speeches required further explanation as to what passed between Disraeli and the Queen. Disraeli said the permission her Majesty gave him to dissolve only applied to the Irish Church question, and, if other difficulties arose, he must of course again refer to her. Nothing can exceed the anger of Gladstone at Disraeli's elevation. He wanted to stop the supplies on Monday, the 4th, but found his party would not go with him.

*May 8th.*—Second and third resolutions on the Irish Church Bill came on first, and were passed without division, but under protest from Disraeli; after which a very angry discussion ensued. Disraeli said the Irish Church question had introduced the elements of confusion, and its partisans were already quarrelling over the plunder. Bright got up, and attacked Disraeli in his most violent hustings style, calling him pompous and servile, accusing him of deceiving the Queen, &c. Disraeli replied in the most gentlemanlike manner, and was cheered by both sides of the House.

*May 18th.*—We dined with the Hardwickes, and met Lord Clarendon, who told some amusing stories of the sayings of the Americans at Rome. One lady, who lived in the Via Babuino, near a Jesuit propaganda college, said, ' I live in Baboon Street, opposite one of the Pope's propagating houses.' An American gentleman, being asked what he thought of the Venus de' Medici, said, ' I never allow myself to be sat upon by those stone girls.'

*May 19th.*—Government were beaten last night in two divisions on the Scotch Reform Bill by twenty-one and twenty-two.

*May 21st.*—Disraeli asked the Commons to reconsider their vote on the rating clause of the Scotch Reform Bill.

*May 23rd.*—I dined with Disraeli, who gave a great dinner to the Peers for the Queen's birthday. The Duke of Cambridge was present. We went afterwards to Apsley House, where there was a smart, very small party, all beautifully dressed. The Duke of Wellington has just been made Lord-Lieutenant of Middlesex.

*May 25th.*—Went to St. James's Church for Lady Cornelia Churchill's marriage. She looked lovely, and I never saw anything more perfect than her manner.

*May 29th.*—I had to speak in the House of Lords in answer to Lord Russell's attack on the Government, and when I sat down no one supported him. Lord Derby seemed pleased and satisfied.

*June 14th.*—The Prince of Servia has been murdered, as he was walking in his park. His cousin, Princess Anka, and her daughter, who were walking with him, were also shot by the three assassins, who were armed with revolvers. The Prince was killed on the spot, Madame Anka died in a few hours, the Princess was only slightly wounded.

*June 22nd.*—The Queen gave a breakfast in the garden of Buckingham Palace, and 600 were asked. She walked from the Palace, attended by the Lord Chamberlain and the Duchesses of Wellington and Roxburgh, and received her company very graciously. She was looking remarkably well, and everybody said she seemed to enjoy her party.

*June 24th.*—The heat is extraordinary ; the papers state that the maximum in the shade from the 12th to the 21st has ranged from 78° to 95° Fahrenheit.

*July 9th.*—In the middle of the debate in the Lords, Hardy and Hunt came to me to say that the Commons had passed an important amendment to the Scotch Reform Bill on its being brought back from the House of Lords. The Government, not expecting such a breach of faith, were not prepared to oppose it, and it was carried, but they were most anxious that the House of Lords should be firm and throw it out *coûte que coûte.* Cairns was half inclined to let it pass, but I took the responsibility upon myself and appealed to Lord Russell, who promised to assist me in rejecting this amendment, which he owned was a breach of faith.

*July* 13*th.*—The heat is quite extraordinary, and no such summer has been known in England for many years.

*July* 27*th.*—A sad accident occurred at Portsmouth, by which Herbert Meade [1] lost his life. He was sealing a cap of a shell with gutta-percha, when it exploded and killed him, with his attendant. Lord Clanwilliam was at Homburg. The Queen is going to Switzerland on the 5th.

*August* 21*st.*—A fearful accident happened yesterday to the Irish Limited Mail, which ran into some trucks laden with petroleum near Abergele. The concussion was not very severe, but the oil exploded and set fire to the carriages next to the engine, consuming four with everybody in them. The Duchess of Abercorn, with several of her children, were in the train, but, being at the other end, escaped unhurt. The smoke produced by the petroleum was so thick that those who got out of the carriages were not aware that the front of the train was on fire, and only thought of saving the mail-bags. The unfortunate passengers must have been suffocated at once, for not one attempted to escape, and not a cry was heard. Upwards of twenty are supposed to have perished, amongst whom were Lord and Lady Farnham, Judge Berwick, and Miss Berwick.

*August* 31*st, Heron Court.*—Sir Augustus and Lady Paget, Sir Henry Wolff, the Duke and Duchess of Marlborough, and Lord Edward Thynne, arrived.

*September* 10*th.*—I rode to Canford. Lady Cornelia looks very happy and pleased with her house and everything belonging to her.

*September* 23*rd.*—I left for London, intending to embark to-morrow for France.

----

On leaving Paris I went to Nancy, which is an interesting town, and thence down the valley of the Meurthe to Remiremont, which is a most beautiful drive. The whole scenery of the Vosges is equal to anything I know. On arriving at Remiremont, I strolled out from the inn and met a man fishing in a beautifully clear river. For a five-franc piece he lent me his rod, and in half

----

[1] Lord Clanwilliam's son.

an hour I had caught some very fine trout of two or three pounds each.   The inn is not very good, and I left Remiremont the next day, and reached Gérardmer, a sort of watering-place in the mountains.   The scenery here is perfection ; lakes and thick pine forests, with large openings made in them where inns and villas have been built.   The country is full of bright streams, in which it is said there is excellent trout-fishing, and this must be the case.   The pines are of vast size, and numbers of walks and paths have been cut through the woods.   The hotel was very comfortable, but it is new, and the place not yet frequented ; when developed and better known it cannot fail to be a favourite resort for a holiday.

From Gérardmer I went on to Plombières, where Louis Napoleon and Cavour met in 1858 and settled the fate of Italy and Savoy. It is a clean, but very dismal, town, with nothing to distinguish it but the compact between these two men.

I returned to Nancy, and on reaching Strasburg and entering the hotel I was told to my horror that Count Walewski was just dead there.   He was seized with apoplexy soon after he had arrived with Madame Walewska.   She is in bad health, and he had helped to carry her upstairs, seated her on a chair, and went into the next room.   He immediately called out to his daughter, 'Give me a glass of water, quick ! and a doctor ! ' They rushed in and found him on the floor quite dead.   He had a complaint of the heart, and carrying Madame Walewska upstairs probably brought on the attack.   I have had a great deal of official business and social relations with him, and always found him agreeable and a perfect gentleman.

From Strasburg, I returned straight to London, vià Rheims and Amiens, the shortest route to England.

------

*October* 28*th*.—The Dowager Duchess of Sutherland died yesterday.   We returned from Benacre, in Norfolk, which had been hired by Colonel Charteris, where we had some very good partridge-driving.

*November* 12*th*.—I went yesterday with the Duke of Marlborough to Windsor for the Privy Council.   Disraeli looked put out. I think her Majesty wanted the Bishop of London to be made Archbishop, but he objected.

*November* 18*th.*—Sir Henry Wolff has been beaten at Christchurch by a majority of forty-two. Everything proves what a Radical bill Lord Derby and Disraeli have brought in, for Sir Henry was supported by every gentleman in the neighbourhood.

The elections are going on as badly as possible all over the country, so our fate is decided.

*November* 21*st.*—Blenheim, where I am having some excellent shooting. A large party here : Mr. and Mrs. Holford, Lord and Lady Mount Charles, Mr.[1] and Mrs. Hardy, Lord and Lady Feversham, Lord and Lady Alan Churchill. Mrs. Holford sings beautifully.

*November* 26*th.*—Seeing we were in a dead minority, Mr. Gathorne Hardy told me that he was for resigning at once, without waiting to be turned out by a vote of the Commons.

*November* 28*th.*—We held a Cabinet, and determined to resign at once.[2] Disraeli is going to Windsor immediately. The counties have behaved splendidly, and the ' Times,' of course, says that they must be reformed, grudging us our miserable minority of 272. Mrs. Disraeli has been made Viscountess Beaconsfield.

*December* 2*nd.*—Cabinet Council to-day, at which Disraeli read the manifesto which he addresses, on going out, to his party in both Houses. The Government are unanimous for resignation.

*December* 5*th.*—I went to Hatfield. The ' Times ' says that Gladstone has nearly completed his Cabinet, and gives a list of its supposed members, which are certainly as Radical as possible. Big Ben called, and said he had heard that Disraeli wanted to throw over the Irish Church, but, finding his colleagues would not go with him, was forced to resign. I told him this was not true, and that I believed he invented the story himself. The majority of my people and labourers at Heron Court voted against Wolff, my bailiff telling them, 'You must vote for Wolff, but you are voting against yourselves.'

*December* 10*th.*—Parliament met to-day, but the Queen's

---

[1] Afterwards Viscount Cranbrook.

[2] In 1874 our successor, Mr. Gladstone, saw himself in exactly the same predicament, and resigned without facing Parliament.

Speech will not be before Tuesday. The new Administration is
composed as follows :—Premier, Mr. Gladstone ; Foreign Secretary,
Lord Clarendon ; Home Secretary, Mr. Bruce ; Colonies, Lord
Granville ; War, Mr. Cardwell ; India, Duke of Argyll ; Admi-
ralty, Mr. Childers ; Lord Chancellor, Lord Justice Wood ;
Chancellor of the Exchequer, Mr. Lowe ; Board of Trade, Mr.
Bright ; Lord President, Lord de Grey ; Privy Seal, Lord
Kimberley ; Postmaster-General, Lord Hartington ; Poor Law
Board, Mr. Goschen ; Secretary for Ireland,[1] Mr. Chichester For-
tescue ; Lord-Lieutenant of Ireland, Lord Spencer ; Attorney-
General, Sir Robert Collier ; Solicitor-General, Mr. Coleridge ;
Lord Steward, Lord Bessborough ; Lord Chamberlain, Lord Sydney.

A Council is held at Windsor to-day, for the Household to give
up their badges of office.

*December 15th.*—The two Houses will probably adjourn till
February, when the Queen's Speech will be delivered. Lord
Derby is still ill, and obliged to be carried up and down stairs.

*December 19th.*—It is now settled that Lord Cairns is to lead
the Conservative party in the House of Lords, as I have given up
the leadership. Lord Cairns sounded Lord Salisbury as to whether
he would lead the Opposition, but he refused to do so at present,
although he seemed pleased, but promised his support, and is now
cordially with us.

*From Lord Derby to Lord M.*

Knowsley : December 20, 1868.

My dear Malmesbury,—Your ideas about the 'latter half' of a
month appear to be of the vaguest, as you were unable to come here
either on the 11th or from the 18th to the 23rd—however, come when
you will, you will always be sure of a welcome. I had hoped to get Lord
and Lady Cairns down here on the 11th, but they are making a flying
visit to Rome, and will not, I imagine, be back till just before the meeting of Parliament, which, by the way, the new Government have put off
quite as long as was decent for men who were in such breathless haste to
carry out their policy. I should have liked to have had an opportunity
of talking over the subject of the 'lead' with you and Cairns, but on the
whole I think the proposed arrangement, subject to Disraeli's concur-

---

[1] Now Lord Carlingford, President of the Council, 1884.

rence, which of course should be had, is satisfactory.  I am not sure
that it would not be more so, considering how new Cairns is to the
bulk of the party, if you were to hold on till Easter, before which,
especially as it falls early, our House will not have much to do.

Yours sincerely,

DERBY.

## 1869

*January 1st.*—Left London for Heron Court.

*January 5th.*—Lord and Lady Bath, Lady Ailesbury, and
Colonel and Lady Margaret Charteris arrived, but the rivers were
too high for any wild-fowl shooting.

*January 19th.*—I went to Knowsley, where Lord Derby is laid
up with gout.

*January 26th.*—Lord Derby approves of my having given up
the leadership of the House of Lords.   He also acknowledges that
he was wrong in his disapproval of Government going out before
Parliament met.   He thought at the time that our party would
blame us for doing so, but now he sees that, far from that, they
applaud what they all consider a dignified and honest course.   The
little Prince Royal of Belgium is dead, after a long illness.   He
was the only child, and his loss is much regretted by his country.

*February 6th.*—A terrible accide nthas occurred out hunting
near Newby.   Sir Charles Slingsby, master of the hounds, Sir
George Wombwell, two Mr. Vyners, some other gentlemen, and
eleven horses, attempted to cross a ferry.   The river was flooded
and rapid, and the horses became restive, upsetting the boat.   Sir
Charles Slingsby got clear, and nearly reached the shore, when he
threw up his arms, and immediately sank.   Sir George Wombwell
was saved by Mr. Vyner, who pulled him out of the boat, which
was floating bottom upwards.   Five persons and eight horses were
drowned.

*February 15th.*—I gave the Parliamentary dinner to-day to
twenty-three Peers.   I addressed them, and informed them of my resignation of the leadership of the Opposition in the House of Lords,
and proposed as my successor Lord Cairns, who was unanimously
chosen.

*February 16th.*—Parliament was formally opened to-day but

the Queen was not present. The Address was carried without opposition. Lord Derby is better, and went to the House.

Everybody is talking of Mr. Bright's speech at the Fishmongers' dinner, in which he said that the advice he gave his colleagues was seldom followed, and his whole tone was so offensive that it is supposed he intends to resign office whenever he can do so. He is said to be perfectly inefficient as a man of business, and so indolent, that he hardly ever goes to his office.

*February* 18*th*.—I called on Lady Palmerston to inquire after her daughter, Lady Jocelyn, who has been thrown out of a cab and much hurt. I hear that 8,000 people attended Sir C. Slingsby's funeral. His horse and the hounds, immediately after the accident, returned to look for him, and remained by the body.

*March* 2*nd*.—Gladstone introduced his Irish Church Bill yesterday in a speech of three hours. It disendows as well as disestablishes the Irish Church, and abolishes the right of the Bishops to sit in the House of Lords after January 1871. The property of the Church amounts to sixteen millions, all of which falls into the hands of the State. It is a complete act of spoliation, and far beyond what was expected.

We went to Miss Pennefather's wedding-breakfast at Lady Emily Hankey's. She marries Lord Stanhope. Disraeli was there. He told me the Queen had sent him her last book.

*March* 3*rd*.—A very hard frost, which has killed all the blossoms.

*March* 8*th*.—I left London for Italy, on a visit to the Pagets. Sir Augustus is Minister at Florence. I crossed in a snowstorm, and the cold was so great at Calais that I could not sleep undressed.

*March* 10*th*, *Paris*.—I started at 7.15 this evening for Nice, from whence I posted by the Corniche to Genoa, and then by railway to Florence.[1]

*March* 25*th*.—We heard that the Irish Church Bill was carried in the Commons by a majority of 118. The weather at Florence was very bad ; it rained all day.

[1] I found the Pagets in the Orlandini Palace. They received me with the greatest kindness and hospitality, and I enjoyed myself for three weeks in this beautiful town, which is much improved, and made the capital of Italy. There are an immense number of new buildings, and large sums have been invested in new streets.

*March 26th.*—I sent a telegram to Lady Malmesbury asking her to ascertain whether our party meant to oppose the Life Peerages Bill, which I should resist to the utmost if I were present, and I would go back on purpose to do so.

The state of Italy is most wretched, and it is on the eve of bankruptcy ; they are paying dearly for their dream of liberty. They have got conscription, ten per cent. income tax, all other taxes trebled, and money is so scarce that they have paper notes down to $2\frac{1}{2}d$. They still cry out to have Rome as a capital. If that is ever accomplished, the people who are laying out money to enlarge Florence will be half ruined.

*March 30th.*—I heard with great grief of the death of my popular old friend, Matt Burrell. He was thrown from his horse on the 24th, in a remote part of his parish of Chatton, in Northumberland, and lay in the road, quietly waiting for the labourers to come home from their work, as he could not move, having broken both bones of his leg. He was taken home, and at first was thought to be doing well ; but his heart suddenly stopped, and he died on the 29th. He was a most popular man and an excellent clergyman.

*April 16th.*—Returned from Italy on the 13th. The Irish Church Bill was resumed last night, and Mr. Newdegate's motion, 'That the bill be committed that day six months,' was rejected by a majority of 126.

*April 20th.*—Called on Lord Derby, who was very feeble, and suffering to-day from the exertion of going to the House of Lords yesterday.

*April 27th.*—In the House of Lords the Life Peerages Bill came on. Lord Derby and Lord Cairns supported the second reading, which passed without a division. I shall divide the House upon it at a future stage.

*Lord Malmesbury's Speech on the Life Peerages Bill,*
*April 27, 1869.*

My Lords,—It is not my intention to oppose the second reading of this bill, although I confess that if I had been present when it was first introduced into your Lordships' House I should have been an exception to the unanimity with which it seems to have been received. Let your Lordships consider what you are about to do in agreeing to the principle of this measure. From what I have heard and read of the last debate, I think that the importance of this measure has hardly been realised by your Lordships, and that, in assenting to it, you may perhaps be doing more than you are aware of. The noble earl who has introduced the bill (Earl Russell) is no doubt one of our greatest reformers. He has also written upon the Constitution—a subject which no man is supposed to understand better than himself. But in all his reforms, important as they have been—in his reform of the House of Commons in 1832 ; in his proposed reform of the House of Commons afterwards, which he did not carry into effect ; and in the reforms of the House of Commons which he assisted the late Government to carry—the noble earl has always kept strictly within the lines of the Constitution. In altering the House of Commons, he proposed nothing that could be called innovation ; he extended the lines of the Constitution, but kept strictly within them. Now, in the present measure, the noble earl has proposed a great innovation—he has gone altogether beyond the lines of the Constitution, and is not only proposing to alter the principles upon which the House of Lords has always existed, but he is altering the Constitution at the same time. I am very much mistaken if it is not one of the first principles of the Constitution that a peerage should be hereditary ; that, indeed, is the very essence of a peerage. Now, the bill at once sweeps away that principle.

The term 'Life Peer' is a singular blunder, as it appears to me, for the life peers contemplated by the bill would not really be peers, because they will not be the *pares* of those who will be their colleagues in this House. The meaning of that word, as we have always understood it, is, that here all are equal in social position, in political rights, and in that great privilege of handing down our names and titles to our posterity. Now, the life peers will not be equal to ourselves in respect of this most important privilege ; they will be unable to transmit to their sons the titles and dignities given them by the Crown. Nor, again, if we look upon ourselves as the nobility of the country, will they be noble, because the very essence of nobility is the transmission of that distinction to the son of the recipient. A peerage, as it exists in this country, is a very modern institution as compared with that of nobility. Nobility is one of the oldest institutions in the world. In the Roman Empire, from the earliest ages, there were patrician families, showing that the nobility was handed down from generation to generation. In the feudal ages, also, nobility was always considered hereditary ; and to such an extent was this carried, that though the Crown could create, it could not withdraw a title, except by reason of felony, treason to the Crown, or cowardice in the field, proved against a person in the ranks of the nobility. No doubt the monarchs of those days were often reckless of all principles whatever ; but they adhered still, for form's sake, to the one I have mentioned, when they wished to get rid of certain nobles—organised conspiracies against them, and got up sham accusations and sham trials ; but they were always obliged to prove acts of felony before they could deprive these nobles of the titles which the Crown had conferred upon them.

Your Lordships are therefore, I think, about to go a step further than you really intend, because you will, by the creation of these life peerages, be making a very great innovation, not only among your own nobility, which has the privilege of being also an Estate of Parliament, but infringing on the first principles of nobility, as it has existed for fourteen centuries before the establishment of English peerages. I am, moreover, afraid that some members of your Lordships' House, who have spoken on this question, have made rather too light of the apprehension that those peers, who, being created only for life, will be unable to hand down their titles and honours to their descendants, will be regarded as not being equal to those whose peerage is placed upon a different footing. If I know something of human nature, I cannot help being of opinion that there will be a feeling, so far as they are concerned, not certainly of the slightest disrespect, bu that they are of a grade not quite on a level with the rest of your Lordships. I may add I have always observed that the greatest pleasure a man derives from having the honour of the peerage conferred upon him by the Crown arises from the fact that he is enabled to transmit it to his son and his successors. I have even

known instances of men who, being childless, declined the honour
of a peerage, saying it was of no value to them, but that, if they
had sons, they should be glad to accept it. Now, that is the
feeling ; it appears to me to be a noble sentiment, and one which
ought to be respected, and I should be very sorry that the
nobility of this country should not look upon it as the highest
privilege they could possess to be able to transmit their title and
distinctions to their posterity.

I very much doubt whether many persons will be found to
seek for the honour of a life peerage, for it seems to me it would
amount—I will not say to an insult, but to a very humiliating
slight, to offer a gentleman a peerage, and at the same time to tell
him that the title and dignity conferred upon him shall not
descend to his son, supposing him to have one. To a man who
happens to have no son, indeed, it may be of less consequence
whether his peerage is for life or not ; but then no good reason
can be urged against making a man in that position a peer after
the old fashion, if it is deemed desirable that the peerage should
be conferred upon him at all. You object to giving a man a
peerage which shall be hereditary because he does not possess the
means you deem to be necessary to support the honour of the next
generation ; but how do you know that his son, if he had one,
might not, by marriage, or some other honourable means, acquire
a fortune sufficient for the support of the dignity ? But, my
Lords, I, for one, protest against the justice of the statement that
it is necessary a peer should be rich in order to maintain in this
country the respect which belongs to his position. It might have
been very well to use such an argument as that seventy or eighty
years ago, when public opinion obliged every peer to live ostentatiously ; when he could not drive out without having four horses
to his carriage, and being attended by outriders, and when he
wore his stars and ribands morning and night. There is, however,
no sort of resemblance between the state of things which existed
in those days and that which exists at present. A peer now comes
up to town by railway, in the company of every person who
chooses to travel in that way ; he moves about as unostentatiously
as any other class of persons. There are, in fact, no such distinctions in many respects as formerly prevailed between a peer

and other members of the community, and there is, therefore, I contend, no necessity whatever why they should require to have large fortunes to maintain what is called their dignity in this country. They are respected, not according to their riches, but their usefulness as members of the legislature and in their several localities.

It seems to me, then, that the arguments founded on poverty, when urged in favour of the institution of life peers, fall altogether to the ground. And let me suppose that poverty furnishes a good reason why we should resort to the creation of life peers. Would not such a state of things be calculated to throw a dangerous power into the hands of the Minister of the Crown who is to decide upon the persons who are to receive such peerages? Would not peers so made be very much under the command of the Minister by whom they happened to be created? Again, a life peer falls into bad health, and the Minister will have twenty applications to supply his place. Now, that being so, I should like to know from the noble earl who has brought this bill forward, and who has said it will not have any effect on the state of parties, how he arrives at that conclusion. Let your Lordships consider the probabilities of the future by the experience of the past. The noble earl is aware that his party has been in office twenty-nine out of the last forty years, and, if that be true, is it not fair to calculate that they would have had the appointment of at least three-fourths of those twenty-eight life peers in that time, enough to decide, in the course of seven years, the result of a division in your Lordships' House, for, when I divided the House on a question relating to the Danish War, the party majority in a full House, was, I believe, only nine?

These, my Lords, are some of the objections which I entertain to this proposal. It would, however, seem that you are about to give a second reading to the bill; and I would simply observe, in conclusion, that I cannot help thinking you may hereafter have cause to repent what you will have done, if you assent to the creation of life peerages, when, on the occasion of great divisions, much discontent will be expressed; and it will be said by the public, 'Such and such a bill was only carried by the votes of life peers.'

*May 1st.*—Debate last night in both Houses on the state of Ireland, which is worse than it has been for some time. Two murders have been committed within the last week, and a great number of threatening letters have been received, which always precede the murders. It is evident that the Church Confiscation Bill has increased the agitation rather than diminished it, as the lower orders think they will now get all they want by violence. What they really want is the land.

*May 6th.*—The state of Ireland gets worse, and the Government have decided to pass a bill to deprive the Mayor of Cork of his office of mayor, and to prevent his exercising the duties of magistrate. One morning he got up, went to the court two hours before the other magistrates, and discharged all the prisoners, without hearing any evidence.

*May 12th.*—My uncle, Admiral Dashwood, died at Geneva. He had been all through the great war, at the battle of Copenhagen with Nelson, and lost his arm in the celebrated frigate action when Sir James Gordon, in the ' Active,' took the ' Pomone.' Subsequently he was at the battle of Algiers, &c.[1]

*May 17th.*—A most curious discovery has been made at Madrid. Just at the time when the question of religious liberty was being discussed in the Cortes, Serrano had ordered a piece of ground to be levelled, in order to build on it, and the workmen came upon large quantities of human bones, skulls, lumps of blackening flesh, pieces of chains, and braids of hair. It was then recollected that the *auto da fé* used to take place on that spot in former days. Crowds of people rushed to the place, and the investigation was continued. They found layer upon layer of human remains, showing that hundreds had been inhumanly sacrificed. The excitement and indignation this produced among the people was tremendous, and, the party for religious freedom

---

[1] He was sent there in H.M.S. ' Prometheus,' a month before the battle, to get the English Consul and his family off, which, as the Dey was very suspicious of our intentions, was difficult. The Consul refused to leave, but his wife, in disguise and her baby in a basket, went down to Captain Dashwood's gig. Just as they passed through the gate of the town the child cried and betrayed them ; the guard turned out, and it was only by rushing down to the boat that the crew and the whole party narrowly escaped being taken prisoners, and reached the ' Prometheus ' in safety.

taking advantage of it, a bill on the subject was passed by an enormous majority.

*May 18th.*—We went down to Heron Court for the Whitsun-tide holidays. Thorns, laburnums, and rhododendrons in a blaze of colour, but I was kept at home by the gout.

*May 29th.*—There was a meeting of a few Peers at Chester-field House to receive some deputations from the religious bodies in Ireland. One deputation from the Presbyterians stated that they had made up their differences with the Established Church, seeing that they had been deceived as to the Catholics, having been made to believe that they would not benefit by the plunder, but they now saw their mistake and would stand by us. A great meeting is to be held at Glasgow directly ; it looks as if a reaction had set in. Dined at the Wiltons—a large party.

*June 1st.*—A meeting of the principal Conservative peers took place this morning at the Carlton Club, to consider what course they will take on the Irish Church Bill. Opinions were divided, but the majority were for throwing it out. If our party were united we might do so, but no doubt some will either vote for the Government or stay away—amongst them the two archbishops—so there is no chance of the bill being rejected on the second reading.

*June 3rd.*—The Life Peerages Bill passed the second reading, on the understanding that only two were to be created every year, and the number limited to twenty-eight. This is the most absurd arrangement that could possibly be conceived, and I shall try to throw it out on the third reading.

*June 11th.*—Lady Carrington called to announce the marriage of her daughter with Lord Petersham. Lord Derby intends to speak on Thursday on the Irish Church Bill.

*June 14th.*—The discussion on the Irish Church Bill came on to-day in the House of Lords, and I could not dine at the Done-gals in consequence. Great ball at the Brünnows.

*June 17th.*—A great many went to the House of Lords to hear Lord Derby speak on the Irish Church Bill. All the good places in the gallery were taken early, but several ladies were there who had no right, and some Peeresses were excluded in consequence. Lord Derby's speech was a very good one, and the peroration very eloquent and touching ; but his voice was feeble, he looked pale and ill, and his manner had lost its energy. It was altogether very painful for those who love him to see such evident symptoms of failing strength. The mind, however, is as clear and fresh as ever. I came home at half-past three A.M. with the news that the second reading of the Irish Church Bill had passed by thirty-three—179 to 146. Fifty or sixty of our party voted with the Government.

*June 28th.*—I went to the Queen's breakfast to the Viceroy of Egypt, which was very brilliant ; but the wind was so cold from the N.E. that it spoiled all enjoyment. Dined afterwards at Stafford House, where there was a banquet to the Viceroy.

*July 1st.*—The Irish Church Bill has been in committee all this week, and several amendments have been passed.

*July 3rd.*—Lord Salisbury's amendment respecting the glebe-houses and land was carried by a majority of 144—213 to 69—many Liberal peers voting with the majority. The Duke of Cleveland's amendment to grant equivalent gifts to the Roman Catholics and Dissenters out of the surplus was rejected by a majority of 33.

*July 6th.*—The debate on the Irish Church Bill was resumed last night in the House of Lords, and the Archbishop of Canterbury proposed three amendments. He withdrew the first two, but the last, ' to vest grants, royal as well as private, in the new Church body,' was carried by a majority of 50. Lord Cairns's amendment on the sixty-eighth clause, reserving the surplus for future Parliamentary distribution, was carried by a majority of 70, and the bill passed through committee.

*Lord Malmesbury's Speech on the Third Reading of the Life Peerages Bill, July 8th, 1869.*

My Lords,—I have given notice, even at this late period of the session, that I shall feel it my duty to oppose the bill of the noble earl (Earl Russell), and to move that it be read this day three months a third time. It is now exactly three months since the noble earl introduced it, and it is for him to explain why he has allowed it to remain so long under your Lordships' consideration ; but I believe the more you have seen of it the less you have liked it. The object of the noble earl in bringing forward the bill is, no doubt, a very worthy one. It is, as I understand, to strengthen the practical powers of the House, to increase its prestige, and enable eminent men, who do not possess a large fortune, to sit in the House, without transmitting to their descendants the expenses, or supposed expenses, of an hereditary peerage. Now, I venture to think that this House requires very little increase of practical power and prestige. I am aware that many persons, both in their speeches and writings, have represented that this House is not on a level with the opinions of the times, and that it cannot, therefore, march *pari passu* with the House of Commons ; but that does not appear to me to be the case.

What, let us consider, is the composition of this House, as the oldest legislative body in Europe, and as the highest in character and general respect ? Some persons have said that it is a House of mere landowners—that is, men of a sort of upper-class farmers—and being so, that they are not as fitted as they might be for the consideration of the general questions which agitate the world. But is that the fact ? Of course many of us are land-owners, and are not, I think, as such, incapacitated from con-sidering general questions ; but it is not true that we are only landowners. Property of every kind belongs to members of this House. We are not only owners of land, but owners and even lessees of mines and other industrial property. Among us there are also bankers, railway directors, and men most eminent for their knowledge of commercial affairs, such as the Marquis of Salisbury and other peers. There are others who are eminent officers in the army and navy, who are ready to enter upon discussions of interest to your Lordships relative to those profes-sions. There are more than fifty peers who have been eminent and distinguished members of the House of Commons. There are eminent diplomatists like Lord Stratford de Redcliffe and Lord Cowley. There are historians, among whom I may name my noble friend behind me[1] (Earl Stanhope), who, if ever your Lord-ships were mistaken on any point of history, would set you right. There are writers, both of prose and poetry, including my noble

---

[1] The late Lord Stanhope.

friend opposite (Lord Houghton), and another noble lord (Lord
Lytton), than whom no English writer can be more distinguished.
There are twelve or fifteen peers who possess immense leasehold
property in this metropolis, and who can assist us in discussions
on property, and who are conversant with the wants of the middle
and lower classes. There are eminent lawyers, and a great number of magistrates, accustomed to judicial decisions, many of them
being chairmen of quarter sessions. Now, if your Lordships consider this catalogue of peers with various qualifications, is it
possible to suppose that a legislative assembly can be more complete in its construction than the House of Lords is ?

This assembly, as I understand it, has existed for about four
centuries, and I am not aware that at any period it has done anything to derogate from its character and dignity. It is not for a
member of the House to say much on the subject ; but during the
last few days or weeks your Lordships—according to the opinions
of the public Press, and of public opinion everywhere expressed—
have most creditably, in the eyes of the country, maintained your
powers of debate and your general capacity in considering important subjects. Well, that being the case, I ask your Lordships whether you think there is any necessity for altering one of
the fundamental rules of our Constitution—namely, that peerages
should be hereditary ? I venture to think there is not. When I
consider the opinion of the noble earl himself, that such a
measure as he has proposed is necessary in order to popularise
this assembly, I feel compelled to differ from him altogether.
We have had what may be considered the test of the opinion of
the people transmitted to us recently by a gentleman supposed to
represent the most popular opinions of the day, and one, at the
same time, representing her Majesty's Government. That right
hon. gentleman has publicly declared that this bill is but a
childish tinkering of legislation. It is no less a person than Mr.
Bright, a distinguished member of her Majesty's Government,
who has expressed himself thus. Now, I want to know whether
her Majesty's Government generally agree with Mr. Bright on this
point. At all events, so far as the argument of the noble earl
goes, as to the necessity of such a bill in order to make this
assembly more popular, I think the evidence of the right hon.

gentleman in question is worthy of consideration, for he is sup posed to know pretty well what the popular opinion is, and it would be hardly fair to make this an exception and assert that he cannot answer for popular opinion on this subject.

The noble earl's second reason for introducing this bill was, that it would give an opportunity to men of eminence and ability, but without fortune, to enter this House. Now, he has not given any names to prove that any eminent men who would have done good service in this assembly would have refused peerages on account of their being hereditary. It would be hardly be- coming to mention the names of living persons ; but I may mention two very eminent men who declined entering this House because they had no children. And I have always thought it one of the noblest feelings of human nature that a man should not be ambitious of a seat in your Lordships' House from any selfish vanity, but in order that he might transmit the honour to his descendants. Your Lordships will probably recollect the very touching letter written by Mr. Burke to Mr. Pitt, when, being offered a peerage, he said that ambition and life had lost all interest in his heart since the death of his only son. On that ground he refused a peerage ; and Lord Kingsdown, whose death has been so great a loss to this House, to my knowledge, more than once refused to accept a peerage—although he was so eminent in his profession and was so calculated to confer honour on the House —because he had no family. It is true that, ultimately, he felt it his duty to accept it. It is supposed that there are men who would accept life peerages ; but I very much doubt whether any such men as your Lordships would wish to enter this House would do so. Of course, there are men who would accept anything that is offered them ; but these are not the persons whose admission the noble earl contemplates. It appears to me that they would stand in such a false position that no men with the usual amount of pride and self-respect would accept these peerages. They would not be your Lordships' peers, according to the true sense of the expression, because they would not be your equals in respect of privileges. They would not transmit the title to their descend- ants ; and they would, therefore, be on a different and lower footing from the rest of the House. They would not be nobles,

because the very essence of nobility is in the succession of the
title to posterity.  They would thus be in a false position, to say
nothing of the equivocal position of their families, both sons and
daughters.

I do not think, therefore, the noble earl would really get such
recruits as he wishes, and such as your Lordships would like to
see added to this assembly.  If, however, such recruits could be
got, observe the political power which would be given to a Prime
Minister.  I have seen in the public prints a suggestion that a
man with such a philosophic mind as the late member for Westminster (Mr. Mill) might very properly be made a life peer if
such a measure as the present were passed.  Now I do not
think that that was a good illustration of the advantage supposed
to be derived from this measure ; for supposing the noble earl
had been Prime Minister, and had created Mr. Mill a life peer under
this bill, he would certainly not have popularised this House by
admitting a man who had just failed in an attempt to get a seat
in the House of Commons by popular election.  Life peerages
would present a temptation to a Minister, much more than is the
case with hereditary peerages, to create peers in order to gain
political strength ; and if they were courted, the result would be
that every year the Minister would have before him a list of
candidates for that distinction.  Thus, if the noble earl's expectations be correct, there would be great objection from a political
point of view.  Mr. Bright has spoken of the bill in terms of the
utmost contempt ; and whether or not he is right in thinking
this bill would give no satisfaction to the middle and lower classes,
it is my belief that persons who accepted these peerages would
find themselves attended with such inconveniences that they would
regret having done so.  At all events, I think that it has not been
proved that this change in our ancient Constitution is necessary
or expedient, and, in the absence of such proof, I protest against
a change in our Constitution, which has been successful in operation for more than four centuries.  For these reasons it is that I
move that the bill be read a third time this day three months.

---

*July 9th.*—Third reading of the Life Peerages Bill came on
last night in the House of Lords, which I was determined to

oppose, although it had been supported by Lord Derby, Lord Cairns, and a number of my party. I therefore made a deliberate speech against it, and to my great satisfaction succeeded in throwing it out by a majority of twenty-nine—106 to 77—converting to my views both my leaders and many others who had supported the bill. I had returned from Italy on purpose to effect this, and to have done so at the last stage was an unexpected and very agreeable success.

*July* 12*th.*—Wilberforce, Bishop of Oxford, voted with the Government on the Irish Church Bill. Someone observing him going out with them in the division said : ' The Bishop of Oxford is going the wrong way.' ' No,' observed Lord Chelmsford, 'it is the road to Winchester.' [1] Lord Devon moved the omission of the reservation in Clause 13 of the right of present Irish Bishops to retain their seats, and carried it by 182. He had never given Lord Cairns the slightest intimation of his motion, and had been canvassing, with the assistance of Lord Bath. Lord Stanhope then moved his amendment to provide residences for the Roman Catholic priests and Presbyterian ministers, and carried it by 121 to 114. A great many Whigs voted against the Government, and a number of our side with them. The bill then passed, and the House adjourned at twelve o'clock.

*July* 16*th.*—Dined at the Bradfords. The House of Commons threw out the Lords' amendment last night in the preamble, postponing the appropriation of the surplus, by 222. The Concurrent Endowment clause was rejected by a majority of 89, and all the other amendments, except immaterial ones, met with the same fate, Gladstone showing the greatest hostility and bitterness. He proposes to give 500,000*l.*, in lieu of grants, to the Church, which, of course, is a much smaller sum than it is entitled to.

*July* 21*st.*—The Irish Church Bill was brought back to the Lords, and Lord Cairns moved ' that the Lords do insist on the amendment made in the preamble to which the Commons have disagreed.' The motion was carried by 78. Lord Granville then adjourned the House, saying he could not go on with the bill without consulting his colleagues.

[1] He was afterwards made Bishop of Winchester.

*July 22nd.*—The House of Lords has agreed to a compromise. Lord Cairns settled it with Lord Granville, taking the whole responsibility upon himself, for he never consulted any of his party, and a great many are much displeased. Lord Derby was so angry that he left the House. Gladstone wanted to throw up the bill after the debate of last Tuesday, when the words of the preamble were re-inserted, but he was out voted in his Cabinet, and it is said that Lord Granville told him that if he gave up the bill he must find somebody else to lead the Lords. He must have intended to provoke a collision between the two Houses, and the feeling he showed on this occasion proves, and not for the first time, what his sentiments are against that institution.

*Lithographed Circular from Lord Cairns to the House of Lords.*

July 24, 1869.

My Lord,—I am unwilling to rest upon my public statement the explanation of the course adopted by me on Thursday in reference to the Irish Church Bill; a course which was, and to those Peers who have honoured me with their confidence must have appeared to be, a wide departure from the limits of duty under which such confidence is usually reposed.

It was only at mid-day on Thursday that I satisfied myself that there was a willingness on the part of the Government to make such concessions as it might be possible to accept, and it was not until a few minutes before five o'clock that the precise details of these concessions were completely specified.

It would have been an inexpressible relief to me had I then been able to consult with all, or even some, of those with whom I was acting; not only because I should thus have avoided a serious responsibility, but also because I could have pointed out in private, what I could not do publicly, the material advantages which appeared to me to flow from these concessions, as compared with a prolonged contest.

To consult, however, or even to delay, was obviously impossible, and I had to choose between the alternatives of declining an arrangement which could not have been renewed after the debate had commenced, or of accepting terms which, while they secured more for the Church than I believe would ever again have been obtained, enabled us to put an end to what was a violent, and was rapidly becoming a dangerous, strain upon the constitutional relations of the two Houses.

I could not but choose, at any risk, the latter alternative, and the only circumstance which could make me regret my choice would be if any member of the party should suppose that I had wantonly, or even willingly, taken such a step without that full communication and con-sultation which is always desirable.—I have the honour to be, my Lord, your faithful servant,                                    CAIRNS.

*August 12th.*—I arrived at Chillingham from Lowther Castle. Found Sir Edwin Landseer staying here, with his friend Mr. Hill, who is taking care of him, as his mind is affected, and has been so, more or less, ever since he had a severe accident on the railway ; yet he painted two beautiful life-size pictures of red deer for Lord Tankerville.

*August 13th.*—The papers to-day announce the death of Lady Palmerston,[1] which took place at Brocket, after a week's illness. She was the last of the four friends—Lady Jersey, Lady Willough-by, and Lady Tankerville. They began life together, married at the same time, were firm friends all their lives, and died at the same age.

*August 18th.*—We went to Longleat, where we found a family party and Sir A. Paget.

*August 23rd.*—Returned to Heron Court.

*October 3rd.*—I was grieved to-day to hear that Ferdinand St. Maur died last Thursday. It must have been sudden, for when I saw Lady Ulrica, his sister, at Longleat, she never mentioned that her brother was ill. What dreadful sorrow has fallen on the Duke and Duchess of Somerset, losing their two sons within so short a time !

*October 14th.*—The accounts of Lord Derby are bad, and I am very unhappy. I got a sad letter from Freddy Stanley, but he does not seem to have quite given up all hope.

*October 16th.*—Left Heron Court for London. I called to inquire for Lord Derby—the account was very bad. I saw Colonel Talbot, his son-in-law, who says there is no hope.

*October 17th.*—The news of Lord Derby is much the same. He is gradually sinking.

---

[1] Lady Palmerston had been the widow of Earl Cowper, and was sister of Lord Melbourne. Her younger son inherited Broadlands, Lord Palmerston's property in Hampshire,

*October 18th.*—Lady Malmesbury got a very pretty letter from Lord Stanley, full of affection for his father and mother, and kindness to us, but he gives very little hope. There is a report that the Liverpool doctor, not calculating on his weakness, gave him a dose of opium equal to what he was accustomed to prescribe for him when in comparative health, and that it produced a state of collapse from which he has never rallied.

*October 21st.*—Lord Derby still lives, but gets weaker every day ; he is quite unconscious, and has taken no nourishment for several days.

*October 23rd.*—Lord Derby died this morning at seven o'clock. In him I lose my greatest friend, and the country a most brilliant and accomplished statesman.

---

The public acts which will be most closely associated with his name are the emancipation of our slaves in the West Indies, which he accomplished when Colonial Secretary ; in the ready recognition of the Second French Empire under Louis Napoleon, in spite of the grudging hesitations and objections of the Great Powers to follow suit ; and thirdly, the passing of his Reform Bill in 1867, under which law we are now living and have lived for seventeen years. When Prime Minister, which he was three times, he was always in a dead minority in the House of Commons, and therefore hampered in all his policy. He thus never had a fair chance of developing his wishes, and died before the wheel of fortune turned, in 1874, in favour of the Conservatives, which enabled Disraeli to display unfettered that genius which will render his administration one of the great landmarks of English history.

With regard to Lord Derby's power of speech, I never heard but one opinion—namely, that he was the most popular orator of his time. This seemed proved by the fact that whenever he was expected to address the House of Lords on any great question the place could hardly hold the audience which flocked to hear him from every part of the building—the galleries being always crowded with peeresses. I never saw this impression made by any other speaker there excepting Lord Lyndhurst. There was a

peculiar charm in Lord Derby's voice—which was a pure tenor—
and in the brilliancy and English character of his diction. If
he has been called the Rupert of Debate, it must be from the
vigour of his charge alone, for he had none of the rashness of his
prototype, but, on the contrary, much reflection and calmness
before action, and was very nervous before making a prepared
speech.

The death of Lord Derby was followed, in 1870, by that of
Lord Clarendon, the able English Foreign Secretary, by the
Franco-German war, and by the collapse of Louis Napoleon's
Empire. I have had so many relations with the latter which I
have noticed, that I do not think it out of place, before I conclude
my memoirs, to relate some episodes of his remaining life.

On April 18 I left London for Florence, on a visit to Sir A.
and Lady Paget,[1] who held the British Legation, and after a
fortnight most agreeably passed there, returned to Paris. The
*plébiscite* had just been repeated, to confirm the Liberalised Constitution under the Olivier Ministry, and resulted in an approval
of the Emperor and his Government by above 7,000,000 votes.
The Duc de Gramont was just made Minister of Foreign Affairs,
and on May 19 the Emperor gave a dinner, said to be in honour
of the Duke's installation, to which he invited me.

I found him much altered in appearance, and looking very ill,
it being three years since I had seen him. He received me with
his usual kindness, and made me sit by the Empress at dinner,
where I had the advantage of admiring her beautiful shoulders.
On her right sat the Duc de Gramont, the rest of the company
consisting of Sir John and Lady Stanley (*née* Talleyrand) and ·
some French guests. The Empress and Gramont both abused the
Press, which always was her *bête noire*. Increased liberty had
been given to it, or rather to newspapers, and both my neighbours
seemed to think it dangerous, although the *plébiscite* had been so
favourable to their wishes. After dinner the Emperor invited the

---

[1] When the monarchy of Italy was unified, Sir A. Paget was appointed
Ambassador at Rome. The Embassy residence near Porta Pia was a very bad one,
but is now the best and handsomest in the Diplomatic Service, having been nearly
rebuilt, principally under the direction of Lady Paget, who has all the instincts of
art in practice as well as theory.

men to the smoking-room, where he took me aside, and I had a
remarkable conversation with him. I naturally began by congratulating him on his *plébiscite*, which was just counted up, but
I found that he was not satisfied, as some 50,000 of the army had
voted '*Non.*' He, however, explained that this had taken place
in certain special barracks where the officers were unpopular and
the recruits numerous, and that 300,000 soldiers had voted
for him. This immediately struck me as strange, for I imagined
his army was in numbers 600,000, and I made the remark, to
which he gave no reply, but looked suddenly very grave and absent. He observed later that Europe appeared to be tranquil, and
it was evident to me that at that moment he had no idea of the
coming hurricane, which suddenly broke out the first week of the
following July.

His tone was altogether more sedate and quiet than I found
him formerly employing. No speculative and hypothetical cases
were discussed by him, and I feel sure that not a thought of the
impending idea of a Hohenzollern being a candidate for the
Spanish throne had crossed his mind. Count Bismarck had kept
it a profound secret, and that very deep secrecy and sudden surprise is the strongest proof of his intention to force a quarrel
upon France. The Emperor did not conceal, in his conversation
with me, his disappointment in regard to Italy, which had become
free, and then was under one sovereign ; and he recognised that
a great number of his own subjects considered that he had committed a terrible political error in being the cause of creating a
strong and growing kingdom on the very frontier of France and
·in the Mediterranean. 'What would Italy do to show her
gratitude ?' he asked. The events of the following two months
answered his question : 'Nothing.'

My impression as to his having given a Constitutional Government to France was that it was more the result of bodily suffering and exhaustion from a deadly disease than from any moral
conviction ; and that he felt, as he must have done, that the life
left him was short, and that his son would have a better chance
of quietly inheriting his throne under a parliamentary and irre-
sponsible *régime*. Perhaps he was right, if he had found able
Ministers ; but that was not the case, and their mismanagement

at the provocations of Prussia under Bismarck must always be cited as the most incapable diplomacy on record.

The result of my visit and conversation with the Emperor was one of extreme pain, for I saw that he was no longer the same man of sanguine energy and self-reliance, and had grown prematurely old and broken. The Duc de Gramont was an agreeable and polished man in society, but vain and impetuous, and had more liberty of action than was given by the Emperor during his former *régime* to his Foreign Ministers. The Duke himself gave me the following account of the last scene on July 14, before the declaration of war :—

The Hohenzollern candidateship to the throne of Spain was abandoned, and the Emperor was decidedly disposed to accept this renouncement and to patch up the quarrel, and turn this result into a diplomatic success ; but his Ministers had avoided no opportunity of publishing the insult to all France, and the Press stirred the anger and vanity of the public to a pitch of madness. None had yet taken advantage of this characteristic temper of the Emperor. Before the final resolve to declare war the Emperor, Empress, and Ministers went to St. Cloud. After some discussion Gramont told me that the Empress, a high-spirited and impressionable woman, made a strong and most excited address, declaring that 'war was inevitable if the honour of France was to be sustained.' She was immediately followed by Marshal Le Bœuf, who, in the most violent tone, threw down his portfolio and swore that if war was not declared he would give it up and renounce his military rank. The Emperor gave way, and Gramont went straight to the Chamber to announce the fatal news.

Such was his account to me of the most momentous transaction which has occurred in Europe since 1815. In it I do not see in the Emperor the same man who, with so much caution and preparation, bided his time before he attacked Austria in Italy in 1859, and who with such rare perseverance after years of failure and prison raised himself to what appeared to the world an impossible throne. I attribute this change in the Emperor, first, to his broken health and acute sufferings, and to a mind which had been weakened since he renounced his personal rule for the advice of responsible Ministers. From the moment he did this in 1860

and 1869 his old enemies attacked and undermined him with
increased power, and were joined by those who had formerly upset,
by their incapacity, the Bourbon and Orleans dynasties,[1] all being
bent on abusing the new freedom he had granted.

On March 20, 1871, Louis Napoleon landed at Dover after
his captivity at Wilhelmshöhe, and on the 21st I went down to
Chislehurst to see him. The Empress and his son met him at
Dover, and his hearty reception by the crowd must have shown
him the generosity and also the gratitude which the English
people felt at the steadfast policy[2] of friendship which he had for
twenty years displayed for their country. After a few minutes
he came into the room alone, and with that remarkable smile
which could light up his dark countenance he shook me heartily
by the hand. I confess that I never was more moved. His quiet
and calm dignity and absence of all nervousness and irritability
were the grandest examples of human moral courage that the
severest Stoic could have imagined.

I felt overpowered by the position. All the past rushed to
my memory : our youth together at Rome in 1829, his dreams of
power at that time, his subsequent desperate attempts to obtain
it ; his prison, where I found him still sanguine and unchanged ;
his wonderful escape from Ham, and his residence in London,
where, in the riots of 1848, he acted the special constable like
any Englishman. His election as President by millions in France
in 1850 ; his further one by millions to the Imperial Crown ; the
part I had myself acted as an English Minister in that event,
which had realised all his early dreams ; the glory of his reign of
twenty years over France, which he had enriched beyond belief,[3]
and adorned beyond all other countries and capitals ; his libera-

---

[1] Thiers, Guizot, &c.

[2] Englishmen remembered the Crimean war and his sympathetic action when
*proprio motu*, he took their part against the seizure of the American delegates who
were coming over in the British packet. Still more when, in the crisis of our
Indian Mutiny, our safety depended on rapid action, the Emperor offered to allow
our troops a passage through France. His reception of the English at Paris during
his reign was exceptionally friendly, and must have been felt and contrasted with
that which they used to meet with under previous Governments.

[3] This was proved by the facility with which France paid her enormous forfeit
to Prussia for the War.

tion of Italy—all these memories crowded upon me as the man
stood before me whose race had been so successful and romantic,
now without a crown, without an army, without a country or an
inch of ground which he could call his own, except the house he
hired in an English village.

I must have shown, for I could not conceal, what I felt, as,
again shaking my hand, he said : ' A la guerre, comme à la guerre.
C'est bien bon de venir me voir.' In a quiet, natural way he
then praised the kindness of the Germans at Wilhelmshöhe ; nor
did a single complaint escape him during our conversation. He
said he had been *trompé* as to the force and preparation of his
army, but without mentioning names ; nor did he abuse any one,
until I mentioned General Trochu, who deserted the Empress,
whom he had sworn to defend, and gave Paris up to the mob,
when the Emperor remarked, ' Ah! voilà un drôle.' During half
an hour he conversed with me as calmly as in the best days of his
life, with a dignity and resignation which might be that of a
fatalist, but could hardly be obtained from any other creed ; and
when I left him that was, not for the first time, my impression.

When I saw him again in 1872 I found him much more
depressed at the destruction of Paris, and at the anarchy prevail-
ing over France, than he was at his own misfortunes ; and that
the Communists should have committed such horrors in the presence of their enemies, the Prussian armies, appeared to him the
very acme of humiliation and of national infamy.

On January 9, 1873, he died in the presence of the Empress,
who never left him, released from the storms of a fitful existence,
from intense physical suffering, and saved from knowing the loss
of his only son, whose fate she was soon destined to deplore alone.

# INDEX.

www.ingramcontent.com/pod-product-compliance
Ingram Content Group UK Ltd.
Pitfield, Milton Keynes, MK11 3LW, UK
UKHW031438191224
3776UKWH00040B/375

9 789353 978594